POLITICO'S GUIDE TO PARLIAMENT

Politico's Guide To Parliament

By

Susan Child

First published in Great Britain 1999
by Politico's Publishing
8 Artillery Row, London, SW1P 1RZ, England

Tel. 0171 931 0090
Email politicos@artillery-row.demon.co.uk
Website http://www.politicos.co.uk

A catalogue record for this book is available from the British Library.

ISBN 1902301234

Printed and bound in Great Britain by St Edmundsbury Press.
Cover design by Ad Vantage.

Other books in the series of Politico's Guides to Politics

Politico's Guide to Electoral Reform
Politico's Guide to Political Lobbying
Politico's Guide to Politics on the Internet
Politico's Guide to Who's Who in British Politics
Politico's Guide to Electioneering
Politico's Directory of Think Tank Publications
Politico's Directory of Political Lobbying

SIDNEY	Hello, they're holding a by-election round here. I didn't know that.
TONY	Yes. The last one applied for the Chiltern Hundreds.
SIDNEY	Oh I see. Well if he gets it, I think the others ought to get a raise as well.
TONY	So do I, after all fair's fair.
BILL	No, no, that's not it, that's not it at all. The Chiltern Hundreds is a position created by the Government, which MPs have to apply for when they want to give up their seat, on account of … they're not allowed to just resign …
TONY	What do you know about it?
SIDNEY	Yeah, why don't you mind your own business?
TONY	You buffoon, you come over here, you don't know what you're talking about, trying to tell us how our parliamentary system works. The Chiltern Hundreds is an ancient custom. They apply for it when they want promotion. They get a hundred pounds, a new suit and a badge allowing them to use the House of Lords canteen without being accompanied by Black Rod. I think you'll find that's right.

Hancock's Half Hour: The Election Candidate
Script by Alan Simpson and Ray Galton
Broadcast 25 January, 1959

CONTENTS

INTRODUCTION

If, like Tony Hancock you have long been under the impression that taking the Chiltern Hundreds involves an increase in parliamentary salary accompanied by extra rights of entry to the House of Lords canteen, I hope this book may be of assistance. If you thought the 'Five O'clock Shuffle' was a dance, or the Table Office a storeroom for disused Commons' furniture, help may be at hand. Those who work inside Parliament have become so inured to peculiar procedures and arcane practices that they often treat the incomprehension of those outside with a mixture of amusement and contempt. Yet for most people, the world of Westminster is a closed book, full of strange characters with exotic names and bizarre titles – the Chairman of Ways and Means, the Serjeant at Arms, the Gentleman Usher of the Black Rod. Like any community, Parliament has its own language, its own terminology. We complain about the techno-speak of the information technology age, but is the language of the gigabyte or the website really any more impenetrable than that of the scrutiny reserve or the negative statutory instrument?

Anyone who needs to understand the complexities of parliamentary procedure, perhaps for professional reasons, faces an uphill struggle. They are not alone; the new MP, the new researcher or secretary, faces a similarly daunting task. It can often seem that bills, orders, regulations and the like are deliberately designed to confuse the uninitiated. Obfuscation is the order of the day. In this book, every attempt has been made to explain all parliamentary terms as fully as possible. Sometimes, shorthand terms have been used to avoid the text becoming unduly cumbersome. For example, where the phrase, 'the House agrees' has been used, it denotes the House of Commons - as in Members of the House of Commons - agreeing or voting as such, in the Chamber of the House of Commons. The term 'forthwith' means without debate or amendment and appears frequently throughout the book.

Those who are familiar with the workings of Parliament may feel that such explanations are unnecessary or that terms such as 'the Bill was committed', 'the motion was taken forthwith' or 'with leave of the House' are self-explanatory. I have to disillusion them; they are not. Imagine you were attempting to explain the process of legislation to a lobby correspondent from the Martian Times, on his first day in the press gallery; would he readily understand what you meant if you informed him that 'the Standing Committee was sitting'? Whilst I would not go so far as to say that I have written this book with an extraterrestrial audience in mind, I hope the explanations provided in it will reassure those who feel that Parliamentary events are so incomprehensible they might as well be taking place on another planet.

So, if you are perplexed by Parliament, confused by committees or bewildered by bills, I hope this book will go some way to explain and elucidate.

NOTES

Readers may notice some inconsistencies in the spellings of some names, terms, etc. This is because Hansard extracts have been reproduced exactly. Where Hansard uses only a lower case for 'hon. Members', this has been left unaltered. In the main text of the book, however, the 'hon' of 'Hon. Members' has been capitalised. The following abbreviations have been used:

Conservative: Con
Labour: Lab
Liberal Democrat: LibDem
OUUP: Official Ulster Unionist Party
DUP: Democratic Unionist Party
SDLP: Social Democratic and Labour Party
SNP: Scottish National Party
PC: Plaid Cymru

Column numbers (Col:) refer to the column numbers in either the House of Commons or House of Lords Hansard; e.g., HC Col:23 or HL Col:29. The letters 'HC' after a publication denote a 'House of Commons Paper'; for example, a Select Committee report. The letters 'HL' denote a publication from the House of Lords and 'Cm' denotes a Command Paper – a Government publication; for example, a White Paper or consultation document. The terms 'peer' and 'Lord' have been used interchangeably as have the terms 'Private Members' and 'Backbenchers'.

Both the House of Commons and House of Lords have two sets of Standing Orders; one for public and one for private business. In the text, SO denotes the Standing Orders relating to Public Business of the House of Commons – the House of Lords Standing Orders of Public Business have been denoted by the addition of (HL). Standing Orders govern some of the proceedings of both Houses, although there are certain procedures and practices which are governed by precedence, and in the House of Commons, by the rulings of previous Speakers. Where procedures are based on Standing Orders, this is indicated in the text. Standing Orders for public business in both Commons and Lords are available on the Parliament website and Standing Orders for private business in both Houses can be obtained from either the Parliamentary Bookshop or The Stationery Office.

References to 'Erskine May' are to Erskine May's Parliamentary Practice - 22nd Edition (1997), published by Butterworths. Erskine May, or Rt Hon Sir Thomas Erskine May KCB (and later Lord Farnborough) to give him his full title, was the Parliamentary Clerk who in 1844 compiled what was to become the bible of parliamentary procedure. He went on to become Clerk of the House in 1871. Erskine May is really the final written authority on parliamentary procedure. Anyone who needs to follow events in Parliament on a regular basis may be well advised to acquire a copy.

ACKNOWLEDGEMENTS

I would particularly like to thank Ruth Best, Jenny Darnley and Emma Wegoda for their help and support during the writing of this book. Thanks are also due to Suzy Awford, Lord Clement-Jones, Susannah Collier, Iain Dale, Jennifer Ewing, Emma Francis, Maureen Newman, Janet Rivers, Renah Valeh and Heather Wood. I would also like to thank the staff of both Houses of Parliament who create and maintain the Parliament website, without which the writing of this book would have been almost impossible.

Susan Child - May 1999

CHAPTER ONE - THE PALACE OF WESTMINSTER

The British public can turn up, pay an entrance fee and visit Westminster Abbey or the Tower of London, but they cannot do the same at the Mother of Parliaments. At the time of writing, anyone wishing to take the official tour of the 'Great Palace' needs to make a prior arrangement with their own MP to take them on what is known as the 'Line of Route' – a task usually delegated by the Member concerned to his or her researcher or secretary. Parliament has recently been debating whether to allow members of the public to turn up unannounced and pay £6.50 for a tour along the Line of Route in the Summer Recess. A parliamentary question from Paul Tyler MP (Liberal Democrat – Cornwall North) on 11 June 1998 elicited an admission from the then Leader of the House of Commons, Rt Hon[1] Ann Taylor MP, that a consultant's report had been commissioned into possible charges for Line of Route visitors (HC Col: 1218). On 3 February 1999, Archy Kirkwood MP (a Liberal Democrat and one of the few non-Government Members to answer questions in the House) replied, in his capacity as a member of the House of Commons Commission (the body charged with overseeing the staff, accommodation and general management of the House of Commons) to some written questions on opening up the 'Line of Route' in the summer (HC Col: 625, 3 February 1999).

Line of Route (Summer Opening)

Mrs. Gordon: To ask the hon. Member for Roxburgh and Berwickshire (Mr. Kirkwood), representing the House of Commons Commission, if he will make a statement on opening the Line of Route during the summer adjournment. [69171]

Mr. Mitchell: To ask the hon. Member for Roxburgh and Berwickshire, representing the House of Commons Commission, if he will make a statement on proposals to open the Palace of Westminster to visitors on Saturdays, Sundays and during periodic adjournments; and what plans there are to charge such visitors. [68598]

Mr. Kirkwood: The Commission has approved in principle the re-opening of the Line of Route during the Summer Recess. The need to comply with EU procedures in letting contracts makes it impossible, however, to achieve the re-opening earlier than the summer of 2000.

On the advice of the Administration Committee, the Finance and Services Committee will look at the viability of a project prepared by a firm of outside consultants on how the Line of Route re-opening is to be managed. It will report its conclusions to the House of Commons Commission.

---

[1] Rt Hon is the title accorded to members of the Privy Council – traditionally advisers to the Crown. All members of the Cabinet are appointed Privy Counsellors. By convention, the title is also given to the Leaders of the main Opposition Parties. Not all Privy Counsellors are, or have been members of the Cabinet. In this book, the title 'Rt Hon' has often been omitted from individuals' titles, to avoid the text becoming unduly cumbersome. For example, Rt Hon Dr Gordon Brown MP is referred to simply as Gordon Brown or the Chancellor of the Exchequer. Anyone needing to find out the full title an MP or Peer should consult either the House of Commons or House of Lords Information Office or a copy of a reference work such as DOD's Parliamentary Companion or the PMS Parliamentary Companion. Do check before writing to an MP or Peer – they will not thank you if you miss out a vital 'JP' or 'OBE'.

In respect of the specific matter of charging visitors who wish to use the Line of Route, the Commission has taken the view that this is a matter which the House itself should decide. A motion will be put before the House in due course.

The House of Commons did indeed debate the matter, on 26 May 1999 and sadly, in the view of the author at least, decided against the proposal. So tourists will continue to be denied the delights of the Royal Gallery or the Prince's Chamber. No one was arguing that the public should be charged for access to the Strangers' Gallery, or that an entrance fee should be levied when the House was sitting. The plan would have raised much needed cash to help with the upkeep of the Palace and would have given a great deal of pleasure to overseas visitors in particular. The House can be a pretty reactionary place when it wants to be. All the talk of 'charging for democracy' was pure humbug.

There are other parts of the Palace of Westminster, apart from the Line of Route, which are open to the public; not least of which are the Strangers Gallery, from where members of the public can watch the debates 'on the floor' of the House of Commons and the equivalent gallery in the House of Lords, from where their Lordships can be viewed in their natural habitat. The majority of the public are probably less aware that they may also watch the numerous Select and Standing Committees at work. So, if sewage disposal is your passion, you could have indulged it to the full in the last Session of Parliament (1997/98) by attending the meetings of the environment sub-committee of the House of Commons Select Committee on the Environment, Transport and Regional Affairs. Alternatively, if you prefer something more sedate, a little light-hearted entertainment may often be had at a sitting of the Public Accounts Committee or the First Standing Committee on Delegated Legislation. There is something in the Committee Corridor to suit everyone.

Westminster Hall

Those wishing to attend a Select Committee should enter the House of Commons at the main St Stephen's entrance. To the left of the security gates is one of the oldest parts of the Palace of Westminster. Westminster Hall was originally built in the reign of William Rufus, between 1097 and 1099. The walls of the current Westminster Hall contain part of William Rufus' original Hall, which he called 'New Hall' to distinguish it from the Great Hall which Edward the Confessor had built to the South. Hence, the courtyard at the end of Westminster Hall is known as New Palace Yard. The Westminster Hall we see today was built in the reign of Richard II, between 1394 and 1399 by Henry Yevele. The hammerbeam roof was built by Hugh Herland. The roof was repaired between 1914 and 1923 and the story goes that some tennis balls were found, thought to date from Henry VIII's reign – perhaps the monarch himself enjoyed the occasional game here between executing wives. Portions of the roof were damaged both during the Second World War and subsequently, when a bomb exploded in 1974 in an annexe to the North West of the Hall.

The first mention of the site of 'Westminster' is found in the Anglo-Saxon Chronicles which refer to it as the 'Isle of Thorns' or 'Thorney Island'. It is also described as 'in loco terribili', which roughly translated means 'a terrible place' A Benedictine monastery was founded here in 960 but the first King to establish a royal palace was King Canute. An early control-freak, he is said to have sat on the banks of the Thames and commanded the waves to obey him. Westminster remained a royal palace until the reign of Henry VIII when it was destroyed by fire and the King moved to Whitehall.

Westminster Hall has formed the backdrop for many important historical events. It was the Great Hall of the royal palace and the King's Council used to meet here. Parliament originated in the King's Council, known by the Norman and Angevin Kings as the 'Great Council' and the Anglo Saxons as the 'Witenagemot', and consisted of archbishops, bishops, abbots, earls, barons, royal ministers, etc. By 1236, some of the meetings of the Council were being called 'Parliaments' and by the end of the 14th Century the House of Commons sat separately from the Lords. Gradually, the Parliaments began to hear petitions from the King's subjects. One of the greatest spurs to the development of Parliament was the need for taxation. In the 12th century the monarch had been able to wage military campaigns without the need for general taxation, but by the 13th century he was no longer able to do this. Normandy had been lost to France in 1204 and as a result, royal revenues had decreased substantially leaving Henry III's coffers severely depleted. It was a problem which continued to trouble the monarchy and King John was no exception. The Magna Carta signed at Runnymede in 1215 stated that 'extraordinary taxation' could only be levied by 'Common Counsel' of the Realm, i.e. parliamentary consent.

Disagreements between the Crown and the leading magnates of the realm continued under John's son, Henry III, and came to a head in 1264 when Simon de Montfort, Earl of Leicester (married to the King's sister) and a former royal ally, defeated him at the Battle of Lewes. He took control of the Government and in 1265 he assembled the first parliament here, in Westminster Hall. However, he met a somewhat grisly end at the Battle of Evesham where he was decapitated by forces led by the King's son Edward. By the end of the 13th century the attendance of representatives from the counties and towns was a normal occurrence at Westminster. Each sheriff sent two knights from his county and two burgesses from the towns. In the 14th century the right to a summons to Parliament became the hereditary title of roughly 70 families. They were to become the parliamentary peerage.

Westminster Hall was also the setting for many a legal battle. The King's court, consisting of Exchequer, Commons Pleas, King's Bench and Chancery all met in Westminster Hall until 1882 when the Royal Courts of Justice were opened in the Strand. The Court of Requests sat to the south of Westminster Hall in a building known as the White Hall. The House of Commons was evacuated there after the great Fire of 1834, while their own Chamber was being rebuilt. Meanwhile, their Lordships, who had been using the Court of Requests, moved to the Painted Chamber. Both were destroyed when the Palace was rebuilt. A number of great show-piece state trials took place in Westminster Hall: Thomas More, Guy Fawkes, Charles I, to name but a few. Gladstone lay in state here, as did Churchill (they are commemorated by plaques in the floor).

Westminster Hall was spared in 1834, when fire spread through the Palace of Westminster. The fire began when some notched 'tally sticks' being burned in a stove, set fire to some nearby wood panelling. Even in 1834, wooden sticks were still used as receipts of sums of money paid into the Exchequer. They were notched to indicate the amount paid and were then split in half, with the debtor retaining one half as a receipt and the Exchequer the other. In 1834, the decision was taken to move to a more technologically sophisticated system – pen and ink, with disastrous results. All the tally sticks were to be burned. Remarkably, no one was injured in the ensuing fire and many important papers were saved and stored in St Margaret's Church, although, according to Christopher Jones in his fascinating book, 'The Great House', some apparently ended up as wrapping paper in Walworth Road.

A committee was established to decide how the Palace of Westminster should be rebuilt. They hit upon the idea of holding a competition for the best Tudor or Gothic design. The winner was Sir Charles Barry The foundation stone was laid in 1840 and the Commons first sat in their new Chamber in 1850. Much of the interior was designed by Augustus Welby Northmore Pugin, who was only 22 at the time of the fire, but already in the vanguard of the Gothic Revival in Victorian architecture and design. No detail escaped his attention and their Lordships have reason to be thankful to him every time they step on an encaustic floor tile, sit on one of the many chairs he designed or use one of his ornate stationery holders.

St Stephen's Hall

St Stephen's Hall is named after King Stephen who originally built a royal chapel on this site. It was later rebuilt by Edward I (who reigned from 1272 to 1307), but, along with the other free chapels, was suppressed by a Statute of Edward VI in 1547 and was handed over to the Commons. They sat here until 1834. Brass studs in the floor indicate the position of the Speaker's Chair and the Table of the House. The two brass tablets in the side walls mark the position of the wall which separated the lobby from the Chamber. The Hall is the site of the assassination of Prime Minister Spencer Perceval, shot here in 1812 by John Bellingham on the grounds that the Government's economic policies were responsible for the failure of his own business. The statues are of famous debaters. Lord Falkland's spur is broken, as a result of some direct action by a suffragette, who chained herself to it in 1908. At the East and West ends of the Chapel are two large mosaic panels by R. Anning Bell, relating to the founding of the earliest chapel by King Stephen. The Hall, which was damaged in the Second World War and only finally rebuilt in 1960, is where you will be asked to wait if you have come to watch a debate from the Strangers Gallery in the House of Commons. Wednesdays are particularly busy, as the House now sits in the morning and Prime Minister's Question Time now takes place once a week on a Wednesday, starting at 3.00pm and lasting for half an hour.

The Central Lobby

The Central Lobby is really a meeting place where constituents can come and lobby their MP. They can fill in a 'Green Card' which is then sent into the Chamber to the relevant Member. The Central Lobby is the centrepiece of Barry's design and the ceiling is 75ft high.

The brass chandelier weighing three tons was made by Jon Hardman of Birmingham and is raised and lowered by an electric motor in the roof above the Lobby. The mosaics above the doors depict the patron saints of the UK. Above the North Door is St David and opposite, St George - both designed by Sir Edward Poynter and made in Venice by

Salviati. Over the east door is St Andrew and over the west door, St Patrick, both designed by Anning Bell.

The four marble statues are:

- First Earl Russell, Prime Minister from 1846 to 1852 and again from 1865 to 1866, who was responsible for drafting the Great Reform Act of 1832 and whose great grandson, Professor the Earl Russell, a notable historian and author of 'The Crisis of Parliaments', currently sits in the House of Lords on the Liberal Democrat benches;
- Sir Stafford Northcote, later Earl of Iddesleigh, Chancellor under Disraeli and Foreign Secretary under Salisbury;
- Lord Granville, a Liberal politician who served under Gladstone;
- Gladstone - the Grand Old Man himself - minus a finger, which he lost when indulging in one of his favourite pastimes - chopping wood.

The Latin inscription on the floor is from the Vulgate and reads: 'Except the Lord build the House they labour in vain that build it'. Barry had originally wanted a much higher ceiling, but he was prevented from building one by Dr David Reid, who was selected to build a ventilation system in the House after the fire of 1834. This was a disastrous mistake for two reasons; he and Barry were unable to work together and the system that Reid put in place simply did not work. Some form of ventilation was badly needed. Members had complained for decades about the smell from the Thames; it was known as 'the great stink'. Business in the House was frequently adjourned as a result of the foul smell from the river. This was hardly surprising, as roughly 400 sewers emptied into the Thames from Blackwall to Putney. Unfortunately, Dr Reid's system made the Palace a fire hazard. Air was drawn in from the top of the Clock Tower and the Victoria Tower and was then circulated through the Palace by means of fires which were supposed to be kept burning constantly. It was then expelled through the spire which Barry had been forced to build over the Central Lobby. The scheme proved to be totally impractical. MPs in the Chamber could smell cooking from the Speaker's kitchens and some of them very nearly passed out. Eventually a suitable system was found which was used until the Chamber was destroyed in the Second World War.

Just off the Central Lobby and on the way to the Strangers' Gallery (anyone who is not a Member of Parliament, Officer or Official of the House is a 'stranger') is the Admission Order Office, which deals with requests for Gallery tickets and which will issue you with a ticket for Prime Minister's Questions, if you have the patience to queue up for what may be several hours on a Wednesday. Strangers Gallery tickets for Prime Minister's Questions are allocated to Members on the basis of a rota (according to surname) and constituents are always keen to obtain them. Until 1845, 'strangers' were excluded from all parts of the House; however, since that time, strangers have been admitted to those parts of the House which are not exclusively for Members. The public gallery, from where you can watch the proceedings of the House of Commons is known as the Strangers Gallery.

The Upper Waiting Hall and Committee Corridor

If you have come to watch a Select or Standing Committee at work you should head through the East Corridor from the Central Lobby (i.e. straight ahead) where you will see six frescoes depicting scenes from the Tudor period. At the end of this short corridor you will be in the Lower Waiting Hall. If you bear right up the stairs you will find yourself in the Upper Waiting Hall. You will usually find a temporary exhibition of some sort or another on display and these can provide an interesting way of passing the time before attending a Select Committee meeting. MPs who wish to apply to set up an exhibition in the Upper Waiting Hall, usually on behalf of a worthy cause, must take part in a ballot. The Serjeant at Arms puts a notice of the successful bookings in the All Party Notices, along with the name of the sponsoring Member. MPs should also take advice from the relevant Government Department on whether or not the exhibition would be a suitable one. This information is then given to the House of Commons Administration Committee. At the end of the Upper Waiting Hall is the Committee Corridor and it is here, in one of the rooms off the corridor, that the Committee you wish to attend will be found. Some of the Committees sit in the Upper Committee Corridor and this can be accessed by the stairs directly off the Upper Waiting Hall. Provided you have arrived in good time, you will usually have to wait before going into the Committee Room; often Select Committees sit in private for 10 or 15 minutes before members of the public are allowed in. The Committee Clerk will usually come out into the corridor and call in the witnesses who are giving evidence to the Committee (if it is a Select Committee) before allowing members of the press and public into the room. Briefing Papers prepared by the witnesses are often left on a table near the door and these are often extremely useful.

[A word of advice from the author: it is often impossible to hear what the witnesses are actually saying during a Committee hearing, as they sit facing the Committee, with their backs to the public; so it is advisable to get as near to the front as you possibly can. Do not, however, place yourself directly behind the witnesses, as this is where their advisers usually sit. If you do, do not be surprised if a key witness turns to ask for your views on the import of genetically modified maize or the current figures for domestic water leakage in the Thames Region.]

Following the Line of Route

If you are being taken on the official Line of Route through the Palace of Westminster, you will begin your journey, not outside St Stephen's entrance but at the entrance to the Norman Porch. Before entering, take a look across the road where you will see the Jewel Tower, built in 1365 by Henry Yevele to house the King's treasure. It was later to house Acts of Parliament until 1864 when they were transferred to the Victoria Tower.

The Norman Porch

This part of the Palace of Westminster dates from the great fire of 1834. It was originally intended to place statues of the Norman Kings here - hence the name 'Norman Porch'. The portraits are of King William IV and the Duke of Wellington and the busts are of 18th and 19th century Prime Ministers including the elder Pitt, Palmerston and Disraeli.

The Queen's Robing Room

This room was only completed in 1866. It is where the Queen puts on the Imperial State Crown and robes at the opening of Parliament. The frescoes are by William Dyce and depict the knightly virtues of generosity, courtesy, mercy, hospitality. Unfortunately, Dyce died before he could reach fidelity and courage. The ceiling is by Frederick Crace and the metalwork by Hardman. Both the floor and the chimney piece, depicting St George and the Dragon, are by Edward Barry, son of Charles Barry who died in 1860 before all the rebuilding work on the Palace of Westminster was completed. The former took over much of the design work still remaining. The carved panels are by H Armstead and again depict scenes from the Arthurian legends. The portraits of Queen Victoria and Albert are by Winterhalter. The Chair of State is carved with the rose of England, the thistle of Scotland and the shamrock of Ireland and Queen Victoria's monogram. In 1941 the Chamber of the House of Commons was badly damaged during a bombing raid and the Commons moved into the House of Lords' Chamber. The House of Lords moved into the Robing Room until 1951.

The Royal Gallery

The Royal Gallery is 110ft long, 45ft wide and 45ft high. Both the floor and the ceiling are by Pugin. The two frescoes by Daniel Maclise, both 45ft long, depict the death of Nelson at Trafalgar in 1805 and the meeting between Wellington and Blucher after the Battle of Waterloo. Together, they took seven years to complete. The Royal Gallery is basically a processional hall although it has been the scene of some notable parliamentary events. Lord Russell was tried here by his peers for bigamy in 1901 and sent to prison for three months (the right to be tried by one's peers was abolished in 1948). Visiting Heads of State have addressed both Houses of Parliament here and a banquet was given in 1972 for the Queen's Silver Jubilee.

The Prince's Chamber

There is no real significance in the name of the Prince's Chamber, other than to remind people that there was a Prince's Chamber next to the House of Lords in the old Palace of Westminster. The two octagonal tables are by Pugin and the Tudor portraits are by students of the Royal School of Art, South Kensington and date from the 1850s. The statue of Queen Victoria is by John Gibson. The stained glass windows are by Carl Edwards and the bronze reliefs by William Theed.

The Bishop's Corridor

From here, their Lordships can gain access either to the House of Lords Library or the Chamber itself. The statue of William Pitt is by Francis Derwent Wood and the bust of the Fourth Marquess of Salisbury is by Benno Elkan.

The Chamber of the House of Lords

All the design work in the Chamber was carried out by Pugin, whose tour-de-force was the throne itself. The Royal Coat of Arms is directly behind the throne. At the State

Opening of Parliament the brass rail is removed and the two thrones are installed under the canopy, one for the Queen and one for HRH The Duke of Edinburgh. HRH The Prince of Wales sits to the right and HRH The Princess Royal to the left. During debates, Privy Councillors and the eldest sons of peers may sit on the steps to the throne. Behind the Throne, is the Cloth of Estate, which is not made of cloth at all, but of carved wood. It is extremely ornate and covered in gold leaf and, along with the Throne itself, symbolises the authority of the monarch. New peers bow to the Cloth of Estate during the ceremony of introduction. The Mace, a symbol of royal authority, is placed behind the Woolsack when the House is sitting. It accompanies the Lord Chancellor whenever the Sovereign is not present. There are two Maces in use in the House: one dates from the reign of Charles I and the other from the reign of William III.

When the Lord Chancellor is in the Chamber, he sits on the Woolsack - literally a sack stuffed with wool. The tradition dates from the reign of Edward III when the Woolsack served as a reminder that Britain's prosperity depended on the wool trade. Today, the stuffing is still of wool - from England, Wales, Scotland, Northern Ireland and the Commonwealth. In front of the Lord Chancellor's Woolsack is another subsidiary Woolsack, used by Appeal and High Court Judges at the State Opening of Parliament.

The House of Lords has two functions: legislative and judicial. It is the highest court in the land and the Lords of Appeal in Ordinary (the 'Law Lords') form the final court of appeal. The Lord Chancellor is head of the judiciary as well as the House of Lords' equivalent of the Speaker of the House of Commons. He is also a political figure with a seat in the Cabinet. He has recently won an important victory and in a concession to modernisation below the waist, has been allowed to swop his traditional breeches for trousers.

To the right of the Lord Chancellor sit the bishops (known as the Lords Spiritual). There are 26 bishops who sit by right, including the Archbishops of Canterbury and York, the Bishops of London, Durham and Winchester and 21 others in order of seniority. Theoretically, a bishop could be appointed a Government Minister, but the last time this happened was in 1711. The Government Front Bench Spokesmen also sit on the 'spiritual side' whilst the Opposition peers sit on the other 'temporal' side of the Chamber. The Lords Temporal are, as you might imagine, peers who are not bishops. They can be divided into hereditary and life peers. The Crossbenchers sit, as the name implies, on those benches between the spiritual and temporal sides of the House. These peers, who do not have an allegiance to any political party actually form a distinct group within the House of Lords, with their own Leader, currently Rt Hon Lord Weatherill. There are some peers who view even the Cross Benches with suspicion and sit as 'Independents'.

At the other end of the Chamber from the Throne, are bronze statues of the 18 barons who forced King John to sign the Magna Carta. The frescoes behind the throne represent: Edward III conferring the Order of the Garter on the Black Prince by C W Cope, the Baptism of St Ethelbert by William Dyce and Prince Henry acknowledging the authority of Judge Gascoigne by C W Cope. The frescoes behind the Strangers Gallery depict: the Spirit of Justice by Daniel Maclise, the Spirit of Religion by J C Horsley and the Spirit of Chivalry by Daniel Maclise. The ceiling is divided into 18 compartments showing many ancient emblems including the White Hart of Richard II. The Lords'

Chamber was restored in 1980, after part of the ceiling began to collapse onto the peers beneath, just missing Lord Shinwell by inches. The cause turned out to be gas lamps which had been used for a period of about 40 years and had literally turned parts of the ceiling to dust. More recently, a similar fate befell the Chamber of the House of Commons, when part of the ceiling fell onto the Government benches. Fortunately, no one was hurt.

The Peers' Lobby

This is the House of Lords' version of the Members' lobby in the House of Commons. The solid brass door is by Hardman and Son of Birmingham. Above each arch are the arms of the Royal lines of England: Saxon, Norman, Plantagenet, Tudor, Stuart and Hanoverian.

The Peers' Corridor

The Peers' Corridor is lined with paintings depicting scenes from the Stuart period by C W Cope. The most important depicts Speaker Lenthall asserting the privilege of the House of Commons when Charles I came to arrest five of its members on 4 January 1642. He had accused them of treason and had come to the House to confront them, accompanied by troops. It was the first and last time that a monarch crossed the Bar of the House of Commons. He called out the names of the five members and approached the Speaker's Chair, demanding to know where they were. They had been warned of his arrival and had sailed up the Thames. Speaker Lenthall refused to inform the King of their whereabouts and it was this act which established the independence of the Commons and the parliamentary privilege of MPs; i.e. freedom from arrest (this does not apply to criminal charges) and freedom of speech.

The Commons' Corridor

The Commons' Corridor leads into the Central Lobby and from here the Line of Route leads into the Members' Lobby of the House of Commons. The frescoes are by E M ward and depict various scenes from the Stuart period, that of Charles II landing at Dover in 1660 is somewhat inaccurate including as it does, the Union Jack, which did not exist prior to the Act of Union. It is here that the change from the plush red, sumptuous splendour of the House of Lords to the rather more utilitarian House of Commons green becomes noticeable. The adoption of green as the Commons' favoured colour dates from the mid 17th century, but the reason for the choice is unclear.

The Members' Lobby

This is where MPs can meet before going into the Chamber. Once the House is sitting, no member of the public is allowed into the Members' Lobby. Members of the press with lobby passes may enter when the House is sitting – hence the term lobby-journalist – and attempt to inveigle an unsuspecting Member into revealing something he shouldn't. The various Party Whips' offices are to be found off the Lobby. The Members' Lobby was badly damaged during the Second World War and on Churchill's insistence the arch into

the Chamber was not repaired - to serve as a reminder of the damage and devastation which had taken place. It is now known as the Churchill Arch.
The statue of Churchill is by Oscar Newton and it is supposed to be lucky to rub the statesman's left foot before entering the Chamber and making a speech. A snuff box is kept to the right of the doorkeeper's chair, it being the inalienable right of any MP to demand a pinch of snuff before entering the Chamber. How many Members now avail themselves of this opportunity is unclear. The principal doorkeeper also operates the Division bell, which is concealed in the right hand arm of the doorkeeper's chair. The door to the Chamber itself is famous for being shut in the face of Black Rod at the State Opening of Parliament. He is then required to knock three times to gain admittance and to summon the Commons to hear the Queen's Speech in the House of Lords. Since Charles I's unfortunate appearance in the House of Commons, no monarch has been allowed to set foot in the Chamber and as a result, the Queen's Speech is heard in the Chamber of the House of Lords.

The 'No' Lobby

When a Division takes place, the Division bell sounds throughout the Palace and members have a total of eight minutes to get into the appropriate lobby before the doors are locked. There are Division bells in all rooms in the House and in nearby pubs and restaurants and in Members' homes, if they are within the 'Division bell area'. Members also have 'annunciators' in their offices - monitors which display the name of the speaker, the time at which they began speaking and the current time. In most cases these now carry live coverage of the debates themselves.

There are copies of Hansard in the Division lobbies. This is the official report of proceedings in the House of Commons and takes its name from Luke Hansard, printer to the House of Commons, whose son Thomas Curson began 'Hansard's Parliamentary Debates' in 1829. It was eventually taken over by the Government in 1890 and debates in the Lords were printed separately from 1909. In that year it became known as the Official Report, but in 1943 the word 'Hansard' was added in brackets. There had been some reporting of parliamentary affairs before this date, but theoretically it was a breach of privilege of the House. However, the Commons soon realised that they could not prevent reports of their deliberations from being published and from 1771 reporting was openly tolerated. In 1803 the press obtained a reserved portion of the gallery, to be used by reporters. Select Committee proceedings are recorded by a firm established by Joseph Gurney. His son was the first to be appointed official shorthand writer to Parliament in 1806. Gurney's continue to provide shorthand writers and stenographers to Parliament today.

When MPs actually vote they give their names to the clerks sitting at the desks who tick their names off the roll. MPs must bow to the tellers at the doors. There is one teller from the 'ayes' and one from the 'noes' at each door. They count the numbers of those voting. At the end of a Division, the tellers, having given their figures to the Clerk of the House, line up in front of the Table and bow to the Speaker, with the winning pair standing on the right.

The Commons was badly damaged in the War. The new Chamber was designed by Sir Giles Gilbert Scott. The green felt bag behind the Speaker's Chair is where petitions are placed (the expression 'it's in the bag' is derived from this practice). They have to be handwritten in a special form and are presented by MPs at the end of the day's business or at the beginning on a sitting Friday. The most famous petition was the Chartists petition of 1839 containing nearly half a million signatures.

The Chamber of the House of Commons

The entrance to the Commons' Chamber is in the Members' Lobby. In the Chamber itself, the red stripes along the floor are two sword lengths apart; this dates from a time when warring factions on opposing sides of the Chamber were apt to be physically as well as verbally violent. Members are not supposed to step over these lines when addressing the House. In the Members' cloakroom each MP still has a loop of pink tape on which to hang his or her sword.

The Despatch Boxes are used by Government Cabinet Ministers and Shadow Cabinet Members to rest important looking papers on, lending even the most pedestrian speaker an air of authority. Inside are kept the authorised and Douai Versions of the Bible and the oath which MPs must swear before taking their seats. They must swear an oath or affirm allegiance to the Crown and in addition, sign the 'Test Roll', signifying their acceptance of the monarch as head of the Church in England. The Despatch Boxes were gifts from New Zealand, the Speaker's Chair came from Australia, the Table from Canada, the three Clerks' Chairs from South Africa and the bar of the House from Jamaica. In front of the Speaker sits the Clerk of the Commons with two deputies to the left. The Mace in the Commons dates from around 1660 and must always be present when the House is sitting. It is carried in the daily Speaker's procession by the Serjeant-at-Arms. This takes place just before 2.30pm, on Mondays and Tuesdays, 9.30am on Wednesdays and Fridays and 11.30am on Thursdays (for the 1998/99 Session at least). When the House is in full session the Mace is on the Table and when in Committee, under the Table. Placing the Mace under the Table dates from the days when the House went into Committee to discuss private matters which it did not wish others to hear. The Chairman of Ways and Means or one of the Deputy Chairmen takes the Chair for a Committee Stage of a Bill and the former always chairs the Budget debate. The House of Lords has two Maces and the House of Commons only one. If this seems a little unfair, it is because the Lord Chancellor is both head of the judiciary and the Speaker of the House of Lords (although he does not call the speakers in a debate as the Speaker does in the House of Commons).

There have been various 'incidents' with the Mace and on one famous occasion Michael Heseltine actually brandished it during a debate. The incident took place during a debate on the Aircraft and Shipbuilding Industries Bill in 1976 when the Conservative Opposition lost a division by one vote (because a Government Whip had voted at the last minute even though paired. Incensed, Michael Heseltine picked up the Mace and began advancing towards the enemy. According to Michael Crick in his biography of Michael Heseltine, Jim Prior grabbed it from him allowing his colleague to make a speedy exit.

The 19 MPs who died in the First World War are commemorated by the shields beneath the South Gallery. Similar shields beneath the North Gallery commemorate those 23 MPs who died in the Second World War. The Chamber is too small to accommodate all 659 MPs and this is deliberate. After the Second World War, Churchill wanted to retain the intimacy of the pre-War Chamber and as a result the Chamber was rebuilt to seat around half this number. This was probably a wise decision, as, although the Chamber is usually full to the brim for big set piece occasions, such as the Debate on the Address or the Chancellor's Budget Speech, it is rarely so during the rest of the Session. Now that the Commons is televised, a curious phenomenon has developed, designed to cunningly conceal the absence of Members. The practice is one called 'doughnuting' and involves MPs huddling together, not for warmth, but to give the viewer the impression that their colleague is addressing, not a half-empty Chamber, but a full House. For the more popular occasions, MPs can claim seats by using 'Prayer Cards', which they may place in slots at the back of the benches at the beginning of the day's sitting.

At the entrance to the Chamber from the Member's Lobby is the Bar of the House. This is not a reference to one of the many watering holes within the Palace of Westminster, but to what is in effect the point of no return, both in the House of Commons and the House of Lords. The Bar of the House is, quite literally, a bar to the entry of outsiders. In the House of Commons, no 'stranger' (member of the public) or member of the House of Lords may go beyond the Bar of the House into the Chamber, although a peer called to give an account of him or herself would do so from 'within the Bar'. The Bar is denoted by a white line on the floor and if needs be, two brass railings can be pulled out to physically prevent riotous strangers from proceeding any further. Some officials are, for obvious reasons, allowed beyond this point; for example, Black Rod at the State Opening of Parliament and on certain other occasions, the Serjeant at Arms and of course, the Clerks who sit at the Table of the House. Strangers may be called to the Bar of the House to explain themselves; for example, a witness who had refused to give evidence to a Select Committee. The last person to undergo this unfortunate experience was John Junor who, in 1957, had written an article in the Sunday Express to which several Members took exception.

In the House of Lords, MPs are not allowed beyond the Bar of the House, and they assemble at the Bar to hear the Queen's Speech at the State Opening of Parliament. There are some seats in the House of Lords, known as seats 'below the Bar' and this means that they are on the same level as the Chamber, rather than up above in the public galleries. In the House of Commons, the equivalent seats are known as 'under the gallery' seats and are used by officials (at the Speaker's end of the Chamber) and by advisers to the Opposition at the other end of the Chamber. If you happen to be watching a debate from one of these seats, do not get carried away and imagine that because you are sitting on benches which appear very like those occupied by Members, that you can somehow intervene in the debate. If you do attempt to intervene from a sedentary position or rise to your feet with a cry of 'shame' or 'what utter drivel', you will be hastily removed from the Chamber. This course of action is not recommended. If as a result of your outburst you were to be hauled before the Bar of the House to recant, the proceedings would be reported not by Hansard but by Gurney's - the official shorthand writers in the House. If you had committed a really grievous offence and been taken into custody by the Serjeant at Arms, he would accompany you to the Bar and stand beside you along with the Mace (the symbol of royal authority). In cases of minor misdemeanours, the Mace remains firmly on the Table.

Underneath the House

Everyone is familiar with the story of Guy Fawkes concealing himself in the cellars underneath the Houses of Parliament on 5 November 1605 (ready to blow the entire edifice sky high) but few people are aware that during the Second World War, underneath the ruined Chamber of the House of Commons, a secret submarine factory was established. In their book, *'The Making of Modern London 1939-1945: London at War'*, Joanna Mack and Steve Humphries refer to a comment from Vera Michel-Downes, the factory's welfare officer, who said, 'we had a fantastic atmosphere in the factory ... we had staff from all walks of life'. It would be nice to think that a few submersibles were actually launched from under their Lordships House into the Thames, but I fear this is a mere flight of fancy. Unfortunately, the cellars are not included on the official Line of Route – a pity really.

FURTHER READING

Inside the House of Lords, Clive Aslet & Derry Moore (Harper Collins, 1998)

The Pimlico Companion to Parliament – a Literary Anthology, Christopher Silvester (Sinclair-Stevenson, 1996 and Pimlico, 1997)

Inside Westminster, John Biffen (Andre Deutsch, 1996 – *first published as Inside the House of Commons, 1989 – Grafton)*

The Great Palace, Christopher Jones (BBC, 1983)

The Making of Modern London 1939-1945: London at War, Joanna Mack and Steve Humphries (Sidgwick & Jackson/LWT, 1985)

CHAPTER TWO - SELECTIONS & ELECTIONS

THE POLITICAL PARTIES AND THE SELECTION OF CANDIDATES

At first glance, the procedures employed by the political parties for selecting Prospective Parliamentary Candidates might seem arcane and irrelevant; however, these are the candidates who may come to represent us in the House of Commons, so ensuring their selection by democratic means is of the utmost importance.

The Labour Party

The bedrock of the Labour Party is the Constituency Labour Party (CLP). Individual members of the Party are members of a CLP, even if they joined the Party nationally. Each CLP is further subdivided into ward parties, corresponding to local government wards. Ward parties elect members of the CLP's General Committee. Societies, such as the Fabian Society, the Co-operative Society and trade union branches can affiliate to the CLP and are therefore eligible to send delegates to the General Committee. The General Committee elects the members of the Executive Committee, which deals with some of the day to day functions of running the local party.

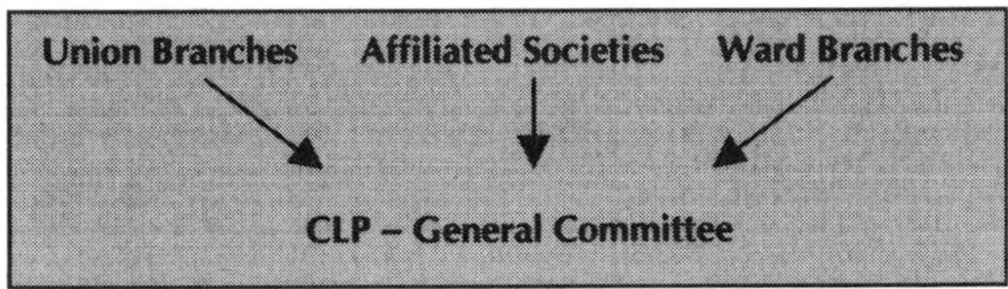

How are candidates selected?

Candidates are nominated by an affiliated branch of the local party; i.e. a union, an affiliated society such as the Fabians, or a ward branch. Each is entitled to one nomination, as is the CLP Executive Committee. The General Committee shortlists at least four candidates (five, if there is a sitting MP). The shortlist must include those with one quarter of all nominations (this must include at least one nomination from a ward or union branch) and any candidate with 50% or more of all nominations from affiliated organisations. At least one member of the shortlist must be a nominated woman and where a sitting MP is up for reselection, he or she must be included on the shortlist. Where a sitting MP has two thirds of all nominations he or she is automatically reselected and even if he or she has only one nomination, the CLP may automatically decide to reselect. In practice, a so-called 'trigger mechanism' operates, whereby sitting MPs are automatically reselected if, by the 'freeze date' agreed by the NEC, a majority of ward branches, affiliated groups, etc., decide not to seek further nominations.

The National Executive Committee (NEC) sets a 'freeze date' by which time all members and affiliated bodies must be registered (those not registered 12 months before the freeze date cannot participate in the ballot). The national approved list of candidates is sent to the nominating bodies who then make their nominations. There is no compulsion to nominate candidates on the approved list, although there are now proposals to encourage the use of such a panel.[1] However, only those who have been members of the Party for a year and who have agreed to accept the Standing Orders of the Parliamentary Labour Party (PLP) are eligible for nomination.

After the General Committee has completed the shortlist (determined by an election using the Single Transferable Vote) a selection meeting is called. Members of 12 months standing may attend. Postal votes are available to those unable to attend. The ballot itself is a 'one member, one vote' eliminating ballot using preferences (where each vote always has the value of 'one' and where a candidate has to gain 50% of the votes in order to win). The 'One Member, One Vote' (OMOV) system was introduced after a heated debate at the 1993 Labour Party Annual Conference.

The late John Smith had staked his leadership on Conference passing the OMOV motion, but only a barnstorming speech from John Prescott and a last minute decision by the Manufacturing, Science and Finance Union (MSF) to abstain, swung the vote the leadership's way. Under Rule 4A.7 of the Labour Party Rule Book 1998, 'The Selection of a parliamentary candidate shall not be regarded as completed until the name of the member selected has been placed before a meeting of the NEC and her or his selection has been endorsed.' The NEC also has the power to rescind an endorsement of a candidate. This power was nearly exercised in Exeter prior to the 1997 General Election. However, the Party's candidate, John Lloyd, resigned before such a course of action became necessary and was later replaced as candidate by Ben Bradshaw. The irony was that Mr Lloyd had been the Party's candidate in 1992, but it was only in 1996 that his past returned to haunt him. Six of his former colleagues from the African Resistance Movement, an anti-apartheid group, wrote to the NEC urging them not to endorse his candidature. In the 1960s, the group, of which Mr Lloyd was then a member, had planted a bomb in Johannesburg station, killing one person. At the trial, John Lloyd had become a witness for the State and given evidence against fellow member, John Harris, who was later hanged for the offence.

When a by-election is called, an NEC by-election panel, not the local CLP, shortlists candidates. Members of the CLP are then balloted. This procedure was introduced after a number of left-wing candidates were selected by CLPs in the 1980s, resulting in several spectacular by-election defeats for the party.

The Labour Party was criticised in the media for the way in which candidates for the Scottish Parliament, the Welsh Assembly and the European Parliamentary Elections were selected. The failure of party stalwarts such as Dennis Canavan MP to gain a place on the shortlist of candidates for the Scottish Parliament, led many to feel that only the most 'on-message' Blairites stood any chance of success. This was a little unfair. The 1997 Annual Labour Party Conference agreed to some basic procedures to be followed in the selection of candidates for Scotland and Wales. Details were then drawn up by

[1] The draft document, 'Labour's Future: keeping a strong voice in Parliament', which was debated and passed by the 1998 Annual Conference, established a National Approved List of candidates for Westminster elections. Members of the panel will be chosen from those candidates taking part in 'training and assessment weekends organised on a regional, national and specialist (e.g women, black and asian, young labour) basis' (para 3.1).

the Scottish and Welsh Conferences. Labour Party members of a year's standing could 'self-nominate'; i.e. apply to be a candidate. A selection board consisting of representatives from either the Scottish or Welsh Executive and the NEC, along with some Independent members, then selected a panel of candidates. Constituencies were then 'twinned' so that each CLP could then shortlist two men and two women from the panel with the final decision being taken by an OMOV ballot of CLP members. As far as the list section was concerned, lists of candidates taken from the shortlisted candidates were drawn up by a committee of four members of the Scottish or Welsh Executive, two members of the National Executive and the Secretary of the Scottish (or Welsh) Party and were then put to regional electoral conferences attended by three representatives from each of the CLPs within the relevant list region. They could reject the list and refer it back to the selection committee.

The process of selecting candidates for the European Parliament was initiated by an OMOV 'trigger' ballot of all European Constituency Labour Party members asking whether they wished to reselect their local sitting MEP. MEPs passing this hurdle were guaranteed a place on the relevant regional list. Each ECLP could then nominate an additional man and woman to be on the list. The final decision was taken by regional selection boards comprising representatives from the regions, the NEC and the Trade Union Liaison Committee. This had to be endorsed both by the NEC and finally approved by Conference. There were some concerns about the way in which candidates were selected for the new European regional lists and particularly the way in which candidates were ranked (an explanation of the electoral system to be used for the 1999 European Elections can be found later in this chapter). In London, for example, Carole Tongue, a popular and successful sitting MEP, was ranked five on a list of 10, leading many to suspect that there were serious flaws in the system.

Quotas for Women

One of the most contentious issues facing the Labour Party in the run-up to the 1997 General Election was that of all-women shortlists. The 1993 Annual Conference had agreed to introduce quotas for women and women-only shortlists were introduced in 50% of all marginals which could be won on a 6% swing and in 50% of vacant Labour-held seats. These were to be identified by meetings between local and national officials with the NEC intervening if no agreement could be reached. Problems surfaced immediately as some local parties resented what they saw as the imposition of women-only shortlists from the centre.

The matter came to a head when two male candidates, Peter Jepson and Roger Dyas Elliott, who had put themselves forward for selection as candidates in women-only seats, took the matter to an industrial tribunal on the basis that quotas were in breach of the Sex Discrimination Act 1975 as well as the 1976 EU Directive on Equal Treatment. They won the case and all-women shortlists were declared illegal. The Labour Leadership decided not to contest the decision. By this time, 38 women had been selected from women-only shortlists and 34 were in winnable seats. In 15 other seats, CLPs went on to select women even though the court ruling had meant the suspension of women-only selections. The Election was a success for Labour's women candidates and women now form approximately one quarter of the Parliamentary Labour Party (PLP).

The Future of the General Committee

The CLP General Committee (GC) is an institution whose days may well be numbered. A 'Healthy Party' task force has been set up under the Chairmanship of Ian McCartney MP, Minister of State at the Department of Trade and Industry (DTI), to consider proposals to abolish the GC. This would require amendments to the Rule Book at the Annual Conference. However, some CLPs have more or less dispensed with the GC and have moved towards greater use of all-member meetings. There are some in the Party who feel that the General Committee is a quintessentially 'Old Labour' institution, whose procedures baffle and alienate ordinary members, particularly the new members which the Party is so anxious to keep. GCs are sometimes dominated by those activists who enjoy discussing obscure procedural points and rule changes and are perhaps too large to be effective decision-making bodies.

One possible solution would be to retain an executive committee but to replace GC meetings with 'open meetings', to which all CLP members would be invited. The Party leadership may well be correct in assuming that one of the reasons for the fall in the Party membership since its General Election peak of 400,000, is the sheer tedium of some GC meetings. However, the proposals have already come in for criticism, particularly from Lord Hattersley, who has expressed his concern that they may be an attempt to suppress legitimate criticism of the leadership.

The Election of a Labour Leader

Before 1980, the Leader and Deputy Leader of the Labour Party were elected by members of the Parliamentary Labour Party alone. The left wanted to broaden the franchise, but in the form of an electoral college rather than by moving to a system of 'One Member, One Vote' (OMOV). The future Social Democrats (still Labour MPs at this time) profoundly disagreed with such a move. At the special conference held at Wembley in 1981, David Owen (now Lord Owen) opposed the electoral college formula and proposed in its place, OMOV. This was defeated and the Conference voted to set up an electoral college with affiliated societies having 40% of the votes (i.e. the trade unions), CLPs, 30% and MPs, 30%. If no candidate gained 50% of the votes in the first ballot, a second would be held in which second preferences of the last placed candidate would be redistributed. The system remained in place until the 1993 Annual Conference voted to alter the electoral percentages to give each section of the college one third of the votes. The 'block vote', as it was known, was also abolished. This meant that affiliated organisations could not cast all their votes in favour of one candidate, but had to ballot individual levy-payers. Tony Blair was the first Labour Party Leader to be elected using the new system in 1994.

In order to stand as a candidate for the leadership, a challenger needs the backing of 20% of the PLP, except when a vacancy occurs, when this is reduced to 12.5%. A challenge to a Labour Prime Minister requires a two-thirds majority at the Annual Conference.

The Role of the Annual Conference

The Labour Party Annual Conference itself has changed. The trade unions used to control 90% of the votes and both they and the CLPs cast their votes as a block. The 1993 Conference agreed to reduce the union block vote to 70% and this was reduced again to 50% at the 1995 Conference. Delegations may now split their votes to reflect minority views or may allow delegates to vote individually. Rather than introduce a pure system of OMOV at Conference, the Leadership seems to have opted for altering and redefining the role of Conference in addition to strengthening the role of the National Policy Forum. This was established after the 1990 Conference and is elected from all sections of the Party. The 'Partnership in Power' document, passed by the 1997 Conference, set up a new Joint Policy Committee, chaired by the Party Leader, with members from both the NEC and the Front Bench. The document also envisaged a new-look Conference and the 1998 Annual Conference was the first to be run on new lines. Gone are the pre-Conference Saturdays of 'compositing' - basically a process whereby a lot of small resolutions were cobbled together to form one big resolution, which was then debated and amended by Conference. In its place, Conference began on a Sunday and the debates were centred around policy documents from the National Policy Forum.

A new innovation was the introduction of 200-Member Policy Seminars, from which observers and other extraneous persons were excluded and where delegates could question Ministers about various aspects of party policy. The old composited resolutions were replaced by Emergency and Contemporary Resolutions. The latter had to be submitted by 18 September and affiliated organisations and CLPs could submit one such resolution; Emergency Resolutions had to be submitted by 25 September and their subject matter was limited to events which had happened in the last week before Conference. The resolutions to be debated were determined by delegates in a 'priorities ballot' on the Monday of Conference.

Policy-Making

Policy-making in the Labour Party is now run on a two-yearly cycle (see Table One). The advent of 'local policy forums' has meant that for the first time, ordinary members, other than elected representatives, have been able to involve themselves in policy making. The exercise seems to have been a great success with roughly 45 such forums being held, mainly over the summer months in 1998. These were organised on a regional basis and any member who wished to, could attend. Policy was debated in groups of around 30 and most of the forums were addressed by Ministers, who answered questions from Members. Whilst some of the 'old guard' in the party appear to resent the demise of the resolution and the composite, many others feel it has given them an opportunity to participate, which they did not have before. The views expressed at the local forums were fed into the deliberations of the policy commissions, of which there are eight. These are co-ordinated by the Joint Policy Committee, chaired by the Prime Minister and comprise members of the Cabinet, NEC and National Policy Forum (for more details see the Labour Party Annual Report 1998). Feedback from the various forums was seen as being extremely important in the development of policy-making.

Table One – POLICY MAKING IN THE LABOUR PARTY

Ballot for 54 CLP members of 175 member National Policy Forum (NPF) (*there are 7 other sections of the NPF – see Table One(a)*	**November 1997**
Joint Policy Committee (JPC) recommended Health, Crime and Justice, Welfare Reform and Europe for the first wave of policy making programme. Eight policy commissions established: Economy; Health; Crime and Justice; Education and Employment; Environment, Transport and the Regions; Industry, Culture and Agriculture; Democracy and Citizenship; and, Britain in the World.	**January 1998**
Policy Commissions met and reports went to the JPC for approval	**February 1998**
NPF discussed and amended documents	**May 1998**
CLPs, branches, affiliates and local policy forums discussed documents and submitted comments to the Policy Commissions	**June to December 1998**
NPF report published	**July 1998**
Annual Conference debated policies and results of debates sent to Policy Commissions (except in the case of Europe, where the policy was agreed at Conference in time for the 1999 European Parliamentary elections; CLP representatives to NPF elected	**October 1998**
Results of above consultations sent to NPF and new documents published on areas not covered in first year	**January 1999**
Final documents on health, welfare, crime and justice sent to NPF	**July 1999**
Final documents debated at Annual Conference	**October 1999**

Table One(a) – MEMBERS OF THE NATIONAL POLICY FORUM

Division	Members
I	54 CLP members
II	30 members elected by affiliate trade unions (15 must be women)
III	18 representatives from Scottish, Welsh and English regional conferences or regional policy forums
IV	9 local government representatives
V	3 members from the socialist societies
VI	4 representatives of the Black Socialists Society (two must be women)
VII	9 MPs (4 must be women)
VIII	6 MEPs (3 must be women)

The NEC

The ruling body of the Labour Party is the National Executive Committee, which is comprised of the following Divisions.

I. Trade Unions – 12 trade unionists elected at the Annual Conference (6 of whom must be women)

II. Socialist Societies – one member elected by the Annual Conference

III. CLPs – six CLP members elected at the Annual Conference, three of whom must be women

IV. Local Government – two members of the Association of Labour Councillors elected, one of whom must be a woman

V. PLP/EPLP (Parliamentary Labour Party/European Parliamentary Labour Party) - three members elected, one of whom must be a woman

VI. Government – three members of the Government, one of whom must be a woman, nominated by the Cabinet (or the Parliamentary Committee when in Opposition)

In addition to the Divisions, the Treasurer is elected by Conference to sit on the NEC, along with a Youth Representative (elected by the Labour Youth Conference) and the following ex-officio members: Leader and Deputy Leader of the Labour Party, the General Secretary and the Leader of the EPLP.

The Labour Party Annual Conference in 1998 was the first to elect the new-look NEC. The changes were prefigured in the 'Partnership in Power' document endorsed by the Conference the year before. Rather than members of the PLP standing for election to the NEC in the CLP section, leaving little room for ordinary CLP members, three members of the Government (or Parliamentary Committee when in Opposition) are now nominated to sit on the NEC. As the ruling body of the Party, the NEC has an important role to play in any disciplinary proceedings. For example, after the 1997 General Election, Mohammed Sarwar, MP for Govan, was suspended from the Party, pending judicial proceedings relating to allegations of illegal practices under the Representation of the People Act 1983. Although he was suspended from the Party and therefore could not sit on any of the Parliamentary Party's Departmental Committees, he still continued to take the Party Whip in the House of Commons (i.e. he was able to sit and vote as a Labour MP). In March 1999, the High Court in Edinburgh found Mohammed Sarwar not guilty of two charges of attempting to pervert the course of justice; charges of electoral fraud and understating election expenses were dropped during the course of the trial. [2]

---

[2] A candidate found guilty of election fraud can face up to two years' imprisonment or a fine (section 168, Representation of the People Act 1983 as amended by schedule 3, paragraph 8 of the Representation of the People Act 1985) as well as being precluded from standing as a candidate in the constituency in question for 10 years and in another constituency for five years (section 159, Representation of the People Act 1983). Under section 160 of the Act, such a candidate would be unable to vote in the constituency concerned for five years.

In fact, it is the National Constitutional Committee (NCC) rather than the NEC itself which has the responsibility for enquiries into disciplinary matters referred to it by the NEC. The NCC is elected yearly at Conference in four Divisions.

I. Five trade union representatives (two must be women) elected by trade union delegations on a card vote

II. One member elected by the affiliated societies (e.g. Fabians) on a card vote

III. Three members elected by CLPs (one must be a woman) by an OMOV postal ballot

IV. Two women nominated by an affiliated organisation and elected by those delegations at Conference and also by an OMOV postal ballot of CLP members (nominees must have been Party members for at least five years)

In the case of Tommy Graham, MP for Renfrewshire West, suggestions in a suicide note left by the former Member for Paisley South, Gordon McMaster, that Mr Graham might have been involved in attempts to smear him led to an investigation by the Party's National Constitutional Committee (NCC). In August 1997 he was suspended from the Parliamentary Labour Party (PLP) pending a full enquiry by the NCC. The then Chief Whip, Rt Hon Nick Brown MP, cleared him of any involvement in Gordon McMaster's death, but added that he had not lived up to the 'high standards expected of Labour MPs'. This effectively meant that he could not sit on any PLP Departmental Committees, but the Labour Whip was not withdrawn (i.e. he could still sit and vote as a Labour MP in the House of Commons).

The Labour Party in Renfrewshire had been dogged by infighting for some time - there had even been an internal inquiry into the Party two years previously, but no action had been taken against Mr Graham. Irene Adams, Labour MP for Paisley North and a friend and colleague of Gordon McMaster had repeatedly made known her concerns about a Paisley security firm - FCB, one of whose directors, Harry Revie, was a local councillor and Mr Graham's election agent. Those concerns may have been justified in view of the £320,000 which the liquidator reported missing from the company's books.

The NCC announced its decision to expel Mr Graham from the Labour Party on 10 September 1998. The grounds were that his behaviour had 'brought the Labour Party into disrepute'. He now sits as a Scottish Labour MP in the House of Commons and does not take the Labour Party Whip.

The Parliamentary Labour Party

The Parliamentary Labour Party (PLP) is, as one might imagine, the Labour Party in Parliament. It consists of all Labour MPs and peers. Its executive committee is the Parliamentary Committee which consists of four ex-officio members: the Prime Minister and Leader of the Labour Party, the Deputy Leader, the Chief Whip and the Chairman of the PLP (who is elected). Four Ministers are appointed by the Prime Minister (members of the Shadow Cabinet when in Opposition), six backbenchers are elected from the House of Commons and one from the House of Lords. The Labour Chief Whip in the House of Lords and the Labour Party General Secretary may also attend. The Secretary to the Committee, a Party official, who along with eight others, effectively runs the PLP in the House, servicing the departmental committees (each Labour MP can be a member of three) and the regional committees to which all Labour MPs belong. Both the Parliamentary Committee and the PLP meet once a week when the House is sitting. The PLP can take disciplinary action against its Members, without similar action being taken by the NEC. In the case of Robert Wareing, the then Chief Whip, Nick Brown, acted after receiving evidence that Mr Wareing had failed to register an agreement with a Serbian owned business to provide consultancy services in the Register of Members' Interests. He was suspended from the Parliamentary Party but continued to take the Labour Party Whip.

The Conservative Party

Selecting Candidates

It is only recently that the Conservative Party has become a national party, in the sense of having a national, centrally held membership list. Until the leadership of William Hague, the party had no single national organisation and was really an amalgamation of three different organisations; the Parliamentary Party (MPs), the voluntary Party (the National Union, comprised of local associations) and the professional Party (Conservative Central Office). Local parties are called 'Associations' and were, until the recent reforms, merely part of a national umbrella organisation – the National Union of Conservative and Unionist Associations.

Under the new constitution of the Conservative Party, the local associations have a governing body known as the Executive Council, elected by members at the Annual General Meeting. There will be one Deputy Chairman with specific responsibility for policy development (this provision is mirrored both at the new Area and at the Regional level). The Executive Council will be responsible for establishing a Candidate Selection Committee which will itself be responsible for selecting three candidates from the Party's 'Approved List'.

Anyone wishing to be a candidate, must be on the Approved List. Would-be candidates are interviewed by a panel of three and is then by one of the Party's Deputy Chairmen. If successful, he or she is asked to attend a weekend parliamentary selection board. If the hopeful applicant passes this hurdle, their name is added to the approved list. The only task remaining is to find a constituency looking for a candidate. The local Association's Candidate Selection Committee shortlists three candidates who are then interviewed by the Executive Committee. They recommend at least two candidates to a general meeting of the Association at which the final selection is made. Conservative Associations can and do deselect sitting MPs, as David Ashby in Leicestershire North West, George Gardiner in Reigate and Sir Nicholas Scott in Kensington and Chelsea, discovered before the 1997 General Election.

The Party's European Parliamentary candidates were shortlisted by a regional selection board consisting of Chairmen of the constituencies within the region and regional representatives. Party members then selected candidates at regional selection meetings.

The candidates for the Welsh Assembly were selected in a similar way, but all list candidates had to stand for a constituency seat as well, except for those on the last four places in each regional list, as there were only 40 constituency MPs to be elected and 20 additional list members. In Scotland, only candidates who had been chosen to contest the 73 constituency seats could be selected for the regional list. The list candidates were selected by a central committee assisted by the chairmen of the local associations for the relevant regions.

Electing the Leader

Before 1965, Conservative Leaders 'emerged' after discussions amongst Conservative MPs - what Iain MacLeod described as 'the Magic Circle'. The failure of the system to work effectively in 1963, after the resignation of the Prime Minister, Harold Macmillan led the Parliamentary Party to bring in a new procedure, which was used for the first time when Sir Alec Douglas Home resigned in 1965. Edward Heath was the first Conservative Leader to be elected under the new system. However, the rules made no provision for a challenge to an incumbent Leader and, as a result, were altered by the 1922 Committee in 1974. The consequence was a challenge to Heath in 1975. In 1990, Margaret Thatcher (now Baroness Thatcher) won the first ballot. New entrants were then allowed to enter the contest in time for the second ballot.

Table Two – CONSERVATIVE LEADERSHIP CONTEST - 1990

First Ballot	*Winner needed overall majority of the votes of those eligible to vote, but also needed to have 15% more votes than any other candidate – in 1990, this meant that Rt Hon Margaret Thatcher needed to gain 187 out of 372 votes and have 56 votes more than closest rival, Rt Hon Michael Heseltine MP – she failed by four votes to gain outright victory.* *Thatcher 204 Heseltine 152*
Second Ballot	*At this point Thatcher dropped out and Rt Hon John Major MP and Rt Hon Douglas Hurd (now Lord Hurd) entered the contest – the winner needed an overall majority – Major failed to do this by two votes, but Heseltine and Hurd withdrew, leaving Major the victor.* *Major 185 Heseltine 131 Hurd 56*
Third Ballot	*Candidates ranked in order of preference (not necessary in 1990)*

The rules for electing a Leader were altered in 1991, so that a challenger to an incumbent Leader would require the support of 10% of Conservative MPs. If there were a vacancy, only the backing of two MPs would be necessary. In 1995, John Major resigned, thus precipitating a leadership contest, but as there was no vacancy, his rival John Redwood required only the backing of two MPs. In 1990, there had been no provision for candidates to withdraw after the second ballot. The rules were changed so that a third ballot would consist of only two contestants and provisions were made for a fourth ballot if the third was tied. In the event, Major gained 218 votes and Redwood, 89 (a majority of 129).

In the 1997 leadership contest, in the first ballot, Michael Howard received 23 votes, Peter Lilley,24, John Redwood, 27, William Hague, 41 and Kenneth Clarke, 49. Michael Howard and Peter Lilley then withdrew from the contest, leaving Redwood, Clarke and Hague, who received 38, 64 and 62 votes respectively. Redwood then withdrew after the second ballot, leaving Clarke and Hague to battle it out in the third round. In the third ballot, Hague won with 92 votes to Clarke's 70.

An interesting study of Conservative Leadership elections can be found in 'The Selection of the Party Leader', by Vernon Bogdanor in 'Conservative Century' and in Alan Watkins' 'The Road to Number 10' (see further reading).

The new procedures for electing the Party Leader were proposed by William Hague in the 'Fresh Future' White Paper, published in February 1998. These formed part of a general reform package, designed to overhaul the Conservative Party, which was endorsed by Party members in a ballot in March 1998. The 1922 Committee had also voted in favour of a new procedure for electing the Leader – basically a 'One Member, One Vote' ballot of all Party members.

Table Three – THE NEW SYSTEM OF ELECTING THE LEADER OF THE CONSERVATIVE PARTY

Leader resigns, or no-confidence vote takes place	15% of MPs must write to the Chairman of the 1922 Committee requesting a vote – if the Leader wins a majority (of the parliamentary Party) no further challenge can be made for one year – if the Leader loses he must stand down and cannot take part in the ensuing ballot
	Nominations are then invited by the Chairman of the 1922 Committee
	Votes continue to be held by the parliamentary Party in order to reduce the number of candidates to two
	OMOV ballot of all members

The new Constitution of the Conservative Party sets out the membership and functions of the new Governing Board, headed by the Chairman of the Conservative Party and consisting of two Deputy Chairmen, four members elected by the National Conservative Convention, the Leader in the House of Lords, the Chairman of the 1922 Committee representatives for Scotland and Wales, the Chairman of the Conservative Councillors Association, the Treasurer, a senior member of staff and two others proposed by the Leader and Board respectively.

The Board, which will meet six times a year, will have three sub-committees: candidate recruitment (the Committee on Candidates); conference management, and membership. Schedule 6 (12) of the Constitution states that the Committee on Candidates, on behalf of the Board, can produce mandatory rules concerning the selection of candidates which are to be followed by local Associations. The Constitution also contains new rules for the running of local associations and sets out the new 'Area Structure'. There will be 42 new Areas, each with an Area Council, consisting of association chairmen and other local association representatives, who will be responsible for electing the Area Executive Committee. In addition, there will be nine regions, to deal with such matters as boundary reviews, which need to be considered on a regional basis.

The National Conservative Convention will meet twice a year and will include the Chairman of all local Associations, Area Management Executives, Regional Chairmen and Deputy Chairmen, representatives from Conservative Future (the new youth wing) and the Conservative Women's National Committee. The Convention will elect three representatives to the Board, in additional to a Chairman, who will be a Deputy Chairman of the Board and a President who will chair the Annual Conference.

The Conservative Political Centre (CPC) has been re-launched as the Conservative Policy Forum (CPF) and will be linked to local policy forums, the aim being to involve ordinary association members to a greater extent in policy-making. Each Association will have a Deputy Chairman with specific responsibility for policy development as will each Area Council. The Area Deputy Chairmen responsible for policy development will elect three representatives to the CPF Council, which will be chaired by a Cabinet or Shadow Cabinet member. There will be regional policy conferences, to which local associations will send representatives. All motions for Conference will be sent to the Director of the CPF. Traditionally, the Conservative Party Conference has been more of a rally than a serious debating body, but new procedures were introduced in 1998, which included, for example, question and answer sessions with Shadow Ministers.

An Ethics and Integrity Committee, chaired by a QC (currently Elizabeth Appleby QC) and consisting of the Chairman of the National Conservative Convention and the Chairman of the 1922 Committee has also been established to consider complaints against Party Members deemed to be bringing the Party into 'disrepute'. Instances of misconduct are referred to the Committee either by the Party Leader or by the Board. The Board will appoint a Compliance Officer, whose responsibility it will be to ensure that Party Members adhere to the provisions of the Constitution. The Compliance Officer will be responsible for informing the Board of any breaches of the Constitution. Disagreement with Party policy will not be considered evidence of having brought the Party into disrepute.

It will be possible for the Party to suspend an individual's Party membership whilst a case is being considered. A proper appeals procedure will also be established. Measures to reform the Party, similar to those in England, have been taken in Scotland, effectively merging the old voluntary and professional wings of the Scottish Conservative and Unionist Party.

The Liberal Democrats

The Liberal Democrats are a federal party and the parties in England, Wales and Scotland have a fair degree of autonomy. In many ways the Party has a model constitution, with the merits of being both democratic and relatively easy to understand. The Liberal Democrats have been using OMOV for much longer than the other Parties and their Prospective Parliamentary Candidates are elected by an OMOV ballot of all Party members in the relevant Local Party. They also elect their Leader by this means and there are no electoral colleges to complicate matters. Candidates for the Leadership must be proposed and seconded by an MP and have the support of at least 200 Party members in 20 Local Parties, the basic organisational unit of the Party. The President of the Party is elected by all Party members for a two year period.

All candidate selection is overseen by a Joint States Candidates Committee which is responsible for maintaining the approved list of candidates (Article 11 of the Liberal Democrats' Constitution). Article 11 specifies that shortlisting be carried out by the Local Party Executive or a sub-committee and that a shortlist include at least one man and one woman (two in the case of shortlists of five or more).

Names of shortlisted candidates are sent to all members of the Local Party in advance of a hustings meeting, and those attending the meeting are given ballot papers (those who cannot attend can apply for a postal vote). In some cases ballot papers are simply sent out to all members. A sitting MP can be reselected by a majority of those voting in a secret ballot of all Local Party members in attendance at such a meeting. If he or she is not reselected, a ballot of all Local Party Members is called to make the final decision. Candidates for the European Parliamentary Elections were selected by ballots of party members in each of the new regions. The Single Transferable Vote was used and members could vote for individual candidates and their ranking on the list. In Wales, the Liberal Democrats used an approved list from which parties could shortlist constituency and regional candidates. Final selections were made using OMOV ballots. In Scotland the Liberal Democrats selected their candidates for the 56 additional list seats using OMOV ballots in individual constituencies within the list regions.

The Party has three main Federal Committees: the Federal Executive, the Federal Policy Committee and the Federal Conference Committee. Local Parties elect Conference Representatives by means of a ballot of all members and the Federal Conference meets twice a year (one of these coincides with the Annual Assembly, which all members can attend, although only elected representatives can vote). The Party in England has 12 Regional Parties which appoint representatives to the Council, which in turn elects the English Council Executive. The Conference is the final arbiter of policy, but there are extensive discussions beforehand, overseen by the Federal Policy Committee. The policy-making process has been streamlined recently and final policy papers are preceded by brief consultation papers.

The Scottish National Party, Plaid Cymru, and Ulster Unionists

The SNP is comprised of Constituency Associations and they are responsible for the selection of candidates both for Westminster and for the new Scottish Parliament. The Party's eight 'list' candidates for the European Elections in 1999 were ranked and selected at the 1998 Annual Conference. Each delegate listed his or her selection in order of preference. Candidates for the Scottish Parliament were selected from an approved list by individual constituency meetings and by regional conferences, which decided how the regional lists should be ordered. The Annual Conference is where the National Executive Committee and the National Convenor (Leader) of the Party is elected.

Plaid Cymru selected its candidates for the Welsh Assembly by using a national approved list, from which constituency parties could select candidates. A selection conference was then held in each electoral region to select the list candidates. This was done by using the Single Transferable Vote (STV) with members voting for male and female candidates separately. The Party's President is elected for a two-year term at the Party's national Conference, which is attended by delegates from the various official Branches.

The Ulster Unionists select their candidates for Westminster Constituencies at general meetings of the various Constituency Associations. The Associations are autonomous bodies and the composition of the general meeting therefore varies between associations. Given the autonomy of the associations, there is no national 'approved list' of candidates. As far as Northern Ireland Assembly members are concerned, each association elects six members using the Single Transferable Vote (STV). However, an association may take the decision to field only three, rather than the full six candidates. As far as the European Elections are concerned, the selecting body is the Ulster Unionist Council; however, as the sitting Ulster Unionist member, Jim Nicholson, was reselected to contest the 1999 elections, there was no actual contest. The Ulster Unionist Party is governed by the Ulster Unionist Council, comprising 900 party members representing the 18 constituency associations and certain affiliated bodies; e.g., the Ulster Women's Unionist Council and the Ulster Young Unionist Council. The Council's Annual General Meeting is where the Leader of the Party is elected by means of a secret ballot.

TIMING OF ELECTIONS

It is a common misconception that a General Election must be held every five years. In fact, it is Parliament itself which may not sit for longer than five years. As a result, a General Election must be called within that period. Under the Septennial Act 1715, as amended by Section 7 of the Parliament Act 1911, a Parliament automatically terminates exactly five years after the date of its first meeting. Parliament has to be dissolved and a date set for a General Election before this date. Neither House actually has to be sitting for a dissolution to take place.

There is no statutory period of time which must be served between the calling of a General Election and the dissolution of Parliament; however; there is usually a period of at least a few days, to allow for any pending parliamentary and legislative business to be completed.

In the case of the last General Election in 1997, the period between the prorogation of Parliament and its dissolution was slightly longer than usual (see the timetable below). The interval between the dissolution of Parliament and polling day is set out in statute – in Schedule 1 of the Representation of the People Act 1983 and amounts to 17 working days (Saturdays, Sundays, Christmas Eve, Christmas Day, Boxing Day, Maundy Thursday,

Good Friday, Easter Monday and all other Bank Holidays are excluded from any calculations).

A General Election is announced by a press notice from No. 10 Downing Street. This notice also sets out the dates of the dissolution of Parliament, the General Election (by convention this is held on a Thursday), the date of the first meeting of the new Parliament and the State Opening. Formally, it is the Queen who dissolves Parliament. This prerogative power is not derived from any statute, it is a common law right which has never been codified.

There is no exact date on which a new Parliament must meet following a General Election, except that it must meet within three years, as set out in the Meeting of Parliament Act 1694. The date for the meeting of a new Parliament is decided by the Prime Minister and is set out in the Royal Proclamation which calls the General Election. There is no constitutional requirement for the Prime Minister to obtain the approval of either the Cabinet or Parliament before calling an Election, although as Alan Watkins points out in 'The Road to Number 10', the question may be considered by the Cabinet, 'but the form in which it is presented varies'. Some Prime Ministers have consulted Cabinet colleagues more than others. In the House of Commons, under SO 13 of the Standing Orders of the House of Commons, the Leader of the House simply makes a statement rearranging the parliamentary timetable before the dissolution.

The Royal Proclamation which dissolves Parliament requires writs to be sent out from the Lord Chancellor's office to returning officers in all 659 Parliamentary Constituencies. The Returning Officers must ensure that before 4pm on the second day after the day on which the Election writ is received, a notice of the election, including the invitations for nominations of Parliamentary Candidates, is published in the Constituency. An electoral timetable is shown in Table Four. By convention, General Elections are held on a Thursday with polling stations being open from 7.00am to 10.00pm (8.00am to 9.00pm in the case of local elections). In their Fourth Report of the 1997/98 Session, the House of Commons Select Committee on Home Affairs recommended that there should be some opportunity for 'early voting', particularly to help those with disabilities, who might find attending a particular polling station on a particular day difficult. They suggested that early voting stations should open on the Monday before polling day. There are problems with such a suggestion, not least the necessity to ban any exit polling, which could influence the result of the Election itself.

Early voting would also mean that for some voters, the Election campaign itself would have been foreshortened – early voters would not be able to respond to any momentous events which might occur between the last Monday of the campaign and Thursday, polling day itself.

General Election Timetable - 1992

Monday 16 March 1992 - Prorogation and Dissolution of Parliament
Thursday 9 April 1992 - General Election
Monday 27 April - House of Commons returns to elect Speaker and swear in new Members
Wednesday 6 May 1992 - State Opening of Parliament
(the Session then continued until 5 November 1993, when Parliament was prorogued)

General Election Timetable 1997

Friday 21 March 1997 - Parliament Prorogued
Tuesday 8 April - Dissolution of Parliament
Thursday 1 May - General Election
Wednesday 7 May - House of Commons returns to elect Speaker and swear in new Members
Wednesday 14 May - State Opening of Parliament
(the Session then continued until 19 November 1998, when Parliament was prorogued)

Table Four - GENERAL ELECTION TIMETABLE

Day	Procedure	Timing
0	Issue of writs by Clerk of the Crown in Chancery (Lord Chancellor's Office)	Usually on the same day as, but if not, as soon as possible after, the issue of the Royal Proclamation dissolving Parliament
1	Receipt of writs by returning officers	The day after the writs are issued
3	Notice of the Election	No later than 4pm on second day after writs are received
6	Applications for Postal or Proxy votes must be received	No later than 11th day before date of poll
6	Delivery of candidates' nomination papers (including appointment of Election Agent)	Between 10am and 4pm on any day after date of publication of notice of election, but no later than 6th day after day of Proclamation summoning new Parliament
	Making of objections to nomination papers	During hours allowed for delivery of nomination papers on last day for their delivery, plus one hour following
	Publication of statement of persons nominated	At close of time for making objections to nomination papers
11	Receipt of Applications for Postal or Proxy voting by those who are ill	No later than noon on sixth day before date of poll
17	Polling Day	Between 7am and 10pm on the tenth day after last day for delivery of nomination papers[3]

WHO CAN VOTE?

Anyone who is over 18 (Representation of the People Act 1969) on the date of the General Election, who is resident in a Constituency and whose name is on an electoral register; i.e. they were living in the Constituency on the qualifying date of 10 October (15 September in Northern Ireland), preceding the General Election, as set out in the Representation of the People Act 1983 and who is a British, Commonwealth or Irish Citizen may vote. Expatriates, who have lived abroad for up to 20 years can also vote

[3] For local elections, polling stations are open between 8.00am and 9.00pm.

(Representation of the People Act 1989). In Northern Ireland, to satisfy the residence criteria a voter must have lived in the constituency for the previous three months.

An electoral register is compiled from returns sent to all households. The qualifying date for appearing on the register is 10 October. The register comes into effect on 16 February, the following year and is operative for the next 12 months. One of the problems with the current register is that, inevitably, it includes some people who have died between compilation and its coming into force. This was one of the questions addressed by the House of Commons Select Committee on Home Affairs in its Fourth Report of the last Session, 1997/98 – 'Electoral Law and Administration' (HC 768 - 1 October 1998). A possible solution to the problem would be the use of a 'rolling register'. In fact, this has been recommended by the Home Office Working Party on Electoral Procedures, set up by the Government in January 1998 and chaired by Home Office Minister, George Howarth MP. Such a register would be continually updated and amended and would mean that polling cards could be sent out to all electors on the day a local or General Election was called. However, the Select Committee was unhappy with the thought that someone might be able to actually register, rather than simply amend an existing entry, after an Election had been called. They were concerned that in some constituencies, people might establish a temporary residence in order to try and influence the result.

Under the Representation of the People Act 1985, there are five categories of voters who may apply for a postal or proxy vote for an indefinite period:

- members of the armed forces, who are serving away from home;
- individuals no longer resident at their qualifying address, i.e., long-term patients in hospital;
- anyone with a 'physical incapacity' which prevents them travelling to a polling station;
- anyone whose occupation means that they cannot reach a polling station;
- expatriates living abroad, who were last resident in the UK within the last 20 years as set out in section 2 of the Representation of the People Act 1989 (as ballot papers may only be sent to UK addresses, they must vote by proxy).

If an elector cannot vote at a polling station for one of the above reasons, he or she can appoint a proxy to vote on his or her behalf. The proxy voter can either go to the polling station on their behalf, or apply for a postal vote (section 9(7), Representation of the People Act 1985).

To appoint a proxy indefinitely a voter needs their own doctor[4], registered nurse, employer or other relevant person to 'attest' that they, the voter, cannot get to the polling station (Representation of the People Regulations 1986 (No. 1081), paragraphs

[4] Representation of the People (Amendment) Regulations 1997 (SO No. 880, 1997) paragraph 4 states that the doctor concerned must be the patient's own GP.

64, 65 and 66). Voters who will be on holiday, or working abroad on polling day, or those with certain medical problems, can apply for a postal or proxy vote for one Election. As ballot papers cannot be sent abroad, anyone who knows they will be working overseas, or who will be on holiday on polling day, must apply for a proxy vote. Applications for proxy and postal votes must be received by the electoral registration officer no later than noon on the 11th day before the poll (as set out in the Representation of the People Regulations 1986, No. 1081, as amended by the Representation of the People Regulations 1997, No. 880). Late applications due to ill health must be received by noon on the 6th day before the poll. There is no specific time set out for the despatch of postal ballot papers. In their report, the Home Affairs Select Committee suggested that the deadlines for applications for postal and proxy votes should be reduced further, giving electors more time to apply and that the current grounds for entitlement be abolished, allowing applications for absent votes on demand.

WHO CANNOT VOTE?

The following may not vote:

- Peers, except for Irish peers (Peerage Act 1963) may not vote. There is some controversy over whether the Lords Spiritual may vote - Robert Runcie, then Archbishop of Canterbury, voted in the General Election of 1983. The proscription on peers voting is not laid down in statute, but is reconfirmed by the House of Commons at the beginning of each Session of Parliament in the Sessional Orders, which simply state that 'no Peer of the Realm, except a Peer of Ireland, hath any right to give his vote in the Election of any Member to serve in Parliament' (e.g., Sessional Orders, 1998/99 Session, 24 November 1998, HC Col:2). Peers may vote in local elections, European elections, elections to the Northern Ireland Assembly and in elections to the Scottish Parliament and Welsh Assembly.

- Those serving a prison sentence may not vote (Representation of the People Act 1983, section 3, as amended by the Representation of the People Act 1985, Schedule 54).

- Those who have committed a corrupt or illegal electoral practice are disqualified for five years and may not vote (Representation of the People Act 1983, section 160).

- 'Idiots' cannot vote and 'lunatics' only in their lucid moments. The Representation of the People Act 1983 states that a psychiatric hospital cannot be treated as a place of residence, so if a person is a long-term, compulsorily-detained patient, they are effectively prevented from voting. Under section 7 of the Representation of the People Act 1983 a 'voluntary mental patient' may vote if they sign a declaration under section 7(4)(d)(iv) specifying an address where they would be resident if they were not a voluntary mental patient.

In the aforementioned report, the Home Affairs Select Committee recommended removing restrictions on using psychiatric hospitals as residences for the purposes of electoral registration. Instead, they suggested that if there were psychiatric conditions which rendered voting inappropriate, then any bar on voting should be based on the condition itself and not on the fact of residency in a psychiatric unit.

Table Five – UK ELECTORATES

Election	Electorate
UK Parliament	Anyone resident in a Constituency whose name is on an electoral register; i.e., living in the Constituency on the qualifying date of 10 October (15 September in Northern Ireland), preceding the General Election, as set out in the Representation of the People Act 1983 and who is a British, Commonwealth or Irish Citizen may vote. Expatriates, who have lived abroad for up to 20 years can also vote (Representation of the People Act 1989). In Northern Ireland, to satisfy the residence criteria a voter must have lived in the constituency for the previous three months. Peers may not vote. Other exclusions as set out above.
Local Government	Same as UK Parliament but excluding overseas voters and including peers and EU nationals fulfilling residency criteria
European Parliament	Same as UK Parliament (overseas voters included) as well as peers and EU nationals fulfilling residency criteria
Scottish Parliament	Same as local government franchise (overseas voters excluded) plus peers and EU nationals fulfilling residency criteria
Welsh Assembly	Same as local government franchise (overseas voters excluded) plus peers and EU nationals fulfilling residency criteria
Northern Ireland Assembly	Same as local government franchise (overseas voters excluded) plus peers and EU nationals fulfilling residency criteria

WHO CAN BE A CANDIDATE?

There is no one Statute which defines eligibility to stand as a Parliamentary Candidate. In most cases, the holding of particular offices prevents certain individuals from membership of the House of Commons - theoretically, it does not prevent them from standing for election. Returning officers are not obliged to check whether or not a candidate holds an office which would debar him from being a member of the House of Commons, their function is only to ensure that the correct procedures for nominating candidates have been complied with. If a disqualified person is elected, an Election Court can rule that if the electors were unaware of the candidate's ineligibility, a by-election should be called. If on the other hand, it is clear that the electorate were aware of the reasons for disqualification, then the runner-up is declared the duly elected Member. For example; in 1960, Tony Benn, MP, succeeded to his father's title of Viscount Stansgate and his Bristol seat was duly declared vacant (he could not sit in both the House of Lords and House of Commons at the same time). A by-election in Bristol South-East was called, at which he stood. He won the election, but the Election Court declared the Conservative runner-up to be the elected Member[5]. This resulted in the passing of the Peerage Act 1963 which allowed a person who had succeeded to a hereditary title to relinquish it, rendering them eligible for membership of the House of Commons.

It is a curious feature of our electoral system that nothing actually prevents a candidate from standing in as many constituencies as possible. In 1880 Charles Stuart Parnell was elected in three Irish constituencies at the same time.

The question of what to do when a Member is elected to two constituencies simultaneously is not resolved in Statute, but is covered by the so-called 'Sessional Orders' which are passed by the House of Commons at the beginning of each Session of Parliament (see HC, Col: 2, 24 November 1998). Where a Member is elected for more than one constituency and no one petitions against his election, he or she must decide within one week,[6] 'after it shall appear that there is no question upon the Return for that place' which constituency to represent, but where someone does petition against him or her, he or she must await the decision of the Election Court.

Since 1888, election petitions of this nature, as well as those relating to corrupt, irregular or illegal electoral practices, have been heard, in England, by the Election Court - basically a Divisional Court of the Queen's Bench Division of the High Court (consisting of two judges), by the High Court of Justice in Northern Ireland and the Court of Session in Scotland.

The Election Court has the power to order a recount, disqualify a candidate from membership of the House of Commons and declare the runner-up the winner, declare the election void or declare that there have been 'corrupt or illegal practices'. For example, the result in Winchester at the 1997 General Election was challenged after the Liberal Democrat candidate, Mark Oaten won the contest by two votes after two recounts. The Conservative Candidate and sitting MP, Gerry Malone, petitioned the Election Court after some ballot papers were discounted as not having the official mark on them (the perforation which should be made in the ballot paper at the polling station). Without the mark, ballot papers are invalid.

The Liberal Democrats argued that had Richard Huggett not stood as the 'Liberal Democrat Top Choice for Parliament' candidate, receiving 640 votes, the Liberal Democrats would have had a clear victory. They had been forced to call themselves 'Liberal Democrat – Leader Paddy Ashdown', in an attempt to distinguish themselves from Mr Huggett, who had already caused problems for them in the European Elections. After an informal agreement was reached a by-election was called, at which Mr Oaten emerged the victor increasing his majority from 2 to 21,556.

---

[5] Re Parliamentary Election for Bristol South East (1964) 2QB 257

[6] Election Petitions must be submitted to the Election Court within one month after the disputed election – so this effectively means one week after that date

Any decision of the Election Court is then conveyed to the Speaker of the House of Commons and entered in the Journal of the House of Commons. Under Section 144(7) of the Representation of the People Act 1983, the House of Commons must then decide whether to confirm the result, or issue a writ for a new election. Where the Election Court has determined that the runner-up should have been elected, the Clerk of the Crown must substitute the new name on the return[7]. Under section 82(6) of the Representation of the People Act 1983 if a candidate or election agent knowingly makes a false declaration of election expenses, this is considered a corrupt practice. Where corrupt practices are alleged, the Director of Public Prosecutions can, under section 171 of the Representation of the People Act 1983 rule that the prosecution be heard in a Crown Court. A person charged with a corrupt practice can choose to be tried by jury rather than summarily before an Election Court.

A candidate found guilty of election fraud can face up to two years imprisonment or a fine (section 168, Representation of the People Act 1983 as amended by schedule 3, paragraph 8 of the Representation of the People Act 1985). A candidate found guilty of a corrupt practice may not stand as a candidate in the constituency in question for 10 years and in another constituency for five years (sections 159, 160 Representation of the People Act 1983) and may not vote in any constituency for five years.

An MP found guilty of corrupt practices must immediately vacate his or her seat and this is what happened in the case of Fiona Jones MP, the former MP for Newark who was found guilty of making a false declaration of expenses in the 1997 General Election. The Conservative Opposition moved the writ for a by-election in Newark in the House of Commons on 29 March 1999, but this was defeated by the Government who were keen to avoid a by-election before the case was heard by the Court of Appeal on 13 April 1999. The Representation of the People Act 1983 is unclear about the exact status of an MP found guilty by an Election Court but cleared by the Court of Appeal. It depends on the Court's interpretation of Sections 160(4) of the Representation of the People Act 1983, which states that an MP found 'guilty of a corrupt[8] practice shall for five years from the date of the report be incapable – (a) of being registered as an elector or voting at any parliamentary election in the UK or at any election in Great Britain to any public office, and (b) of being elected to and sitting in the House of Commons, and (c) of holding any public or judicial office and, if already elected to the House of Commons or holding such office, shall from that date vacate the seat or office.' This could be interpreted in two ways: firstly, an MP is disqualified from sitting in the House of Commons from the moment of the decision of the Election Court, but if cleared by the Court of Appeal, is therefore eligible to fight a subsequent by-election; secondly, he or she is reinstated as an MP if he or she wins her case in the Court of Appeal, thereby dispensing with the need for a by-election. In the case of Fiona Jones, the Court of Appeal overturned the original decision of the Crown Court and the matter was then

[7] a 'return' is basically an entry in the 'Return Book' listing the names of those Members 'returned' to serve in Parliament after the General Election – hence the title 'Returning Officer' – the local council official whose task it is to ensure that candidates nominations are valid and whose moment of fame comes on election night when he or she is called to read out the relevant constituency's election results.

[8] Section 164(5) of the Representation of the People Act 1983 states that where a person is found guilty of an 'illegal' as opposed to a 'corrupt' practice, they may not vote in the Constituency where the offence was committed, for the next five years.

handed back to the Speaker. The Court of Appeal made it clear that they did not have the power to reinstate Ms Jones or declare that there was no longer a vacancy in Newark. Unfortunately, nor does the Speaker, as was apparent from her statement to the House of Commons on 19 April 1999 (HC Col: 571). She informed the House that, 'It is for the courts, not for the House, to interpret the law'. The High Court was therefore, 'invited to make a declaration that .. Fiona Jones is entitled to resume her seat' and this they duly did, allowing her to retake her seat in the House.

Under part III of the Representation of the People Act 1983, election petitions must be presented within 21 days of the relevant Election. Such petitions may only be presented by an elector registered in that constituency or a candidate for that Election.

WHO CANNOT BE A CANDIDATE?

The following are not eligible to be candidates.

- Aliens; i.e., anyone who is not a British citizen, or a citizen of the Irish Republic or Commonwealth (British Nationality Act 1981).

- Those under 21 years of age (Parliamentary Elections Act 1695, Union with Scotland Act 1706, Parliamentary Elections (Ireland) Act 1823).

- Peers (Peerage Act 1963).

- Ministers of religion - this includes priests or deacons of the Church of England and Church of Ireland, Roman Catholic priests but not non-conformists or clergy of the Church of Wales or ministers of the Church of Scotland (House of Commons (Clergy Disqualification) Act 1801 and the Roman Catholic Relief Act 1829). Non-Christian faiths are not disqualified. In their Fourth Report of the previous Session (1997/98) the Home Affairs Select Committee recommended that all Ministers, of whatever religion, except for serving Bishops of the Church of England, be allowed to stand as parliamentary candidates. The restriction on bishops would clearly have to remain, as some of them sit in the House of Lords.

- Those suffering from a severe mental illness - under the Mental Health Act 1983, if an MP is compulsorily detained in a psychiatric hospital, his or her seat is vacated after six months and a by-election held.

- Those declared bankrupt by a court are disqualified from election to Parliament until their bankruptcy is discharged (Insolvency Act 1986).

- Those reported by the Election Court to have committed corrupt electoral practices as set out in the Representation of the People Act 1983 - this includes such practices as undue influence, impersonation of another voter, or bribery. Where a candidate is found to have committed such practices, the election is declared void and the candidate disqualified from standing again in that constituency for 10 years and in another constituency for five. He or she may not vote for another five years (sections 159 and 160, Representation of the People Act 1983). Candidates are held responsible for the electoral misdemeanours of their election agents and if an agent is found to have committed corrupt electoral practices, the candidate himself will debarred from standing again in that particular constituency for the next seven years.

- Under the Representation of the People Act 1981, anyone sentenced to more than one year's imprisonment is disqualified from being elected during the period of imprisonment.

- Those found guilty of treason under the Forfeiture Act 1870 (as amended by the Criminal Law Act 1967) (for as long as the sentence is in force or until a pardon has been granted)

- Those disqualified under the House of Commons (Disqualification) Act 1975 - there are six classes of office holders who are disqualified: -

- certain judicial office holders including High Court Judges and Judges of the Court of Appeal

- civil servants

- members of the armed forces

- police officers

- Members of legislatures outside the Commonwealth

- any holders of other offices listed in Schedule 1 of the House of Commons (Disqualification) Act 1975 are also disqualified. Additions can be made to the list of disqualifying offices by means of their inclusion in an Order in Council supported by a resolution of the House of Commons[9]. Schedule I of the Act is divided into four parts. Part I lists those judicial offices which debar holders from membership of the House of Commons; Part II lists those organisations, all of whose members are disqualified from membership; Part III lists those bodies, some of whose members may not be MPs and Part IV lists offices which disqualify holders from being MPs for particular constituencies. There are some curious inclusions in the list; for example, it is difficult to see why membership of the Sea Fish Industry Authority or the Crofters Commission should render anyone ineligible for membership of the House of

[9] Additions to and deletions from the 1975 Act are given effect by means of a draft Order in Council. A Treasury Minister (usually the Paymaster General) places a motion on the Order Paper of the House of Commons, to the effect that 'Schedule 1 to the House of Commons (Disqualification) Act 1975 be amended as follows ...'. Amendments may be tabled to this motion. If passed by the House, the 'resolution' as it is called, is embodied in an Order in Council which amends Schedule 1 of the 1975 Act. The former Member for Newham South, Nigel Spearing (Lab) tabled one such amendment when a Government Motion to amend Schedule 1 was debated on 13 February 1997. His amendment would have disqualified Recorders and Assistant Recorders from being Members of the House on the grounds that it was anomalous that temporary judges in Scotland and lay members of Industrial Tribunals should be barred from sitting as MPs, when part-time judges (Recorders) were not (at the time, three MPs were Recorders).

Commons (although it is hard to imagine why it would render them eligible either). An example of an officer included in Part IV of the Schedule is a Lord Lieutenant or High Sheriff of any county in England and Wales, who may not sit as an MP for any constituency within that county. He or she could stand for election in a constituency in another county. Whilst the Chairman of the Red Deer Commission apparently has duties too onerous to permit him or her to undertake the work of a Member of Parliament, a councillor and/or a Member of the European Parliament may sit in the House of Commons. The Reverend Ian Paisley is both an MEP and the MP for Antrim North. It is possible to be a councillor, MP and MEP simultaneously, but woe betide the member of the Covent Garden Market Authority or the Oil and Pipelines Agency who fails to resign his office on becoming an MP.

In addition, holding the offices of Bailiff or Steward of the Chiltern Hundreds of Stoke, Desborough and Burnham, or the Manor of Northstead disqualifies an MP from retaining his seat in the House. These are two fictional offices for which MPs technically apply if they wish to resign; there is no other way an MP can resign his seat (section 4, House of Commons (Disqualification) Act 1975).

There is no precise time at which the above disqualifying factors apply. For example; there is no clear statement set out in Statute to determine exactly when a candidate has to be 21 - is it, for example, at receipt of nominations or on polling day itself? Similarly, there is nothing in any Act of Parliament to indicate the legal position of a person who holds a disqualifying office when their nomination is submitted but who ceases to hold that office on the day of the Election. Under section 6(1) of the 1975 Act, if a person is elected to the House of Commons whilst disqualified under the aforementioned Act, the election is void[10]. This can only be determined on an election petition. Under section 6(2) of the Act, if it appears to the House of Commons that the grounds for disqualification no longer exist, it can order that those grounds be disregarded (for example, if the MP had resigned the offending office). This cannot, however, affect the proceedings on an election petition. If, once elected as an MP, a former candidate continues to hold a disqualifying office, he or she is deemed to have vacated his or her seat and a by-election is called.

The rules relating to disqualification grew out of the disputes between the House of Commons and the Crown and the concern of the Commons to control its own membership. As a result, anyone taking 'an office of profit under the Crown' could not at the same time be a Member of the House of Commons. The Commons was concerned that the Crown would attempt to seek influence over it by the use of patronage and by offering lucrative offices to its Members. The Succession to the Crown Act 1707 specified that no Member of the House of Commons could also hold 'an office or place of profit under the Crown'; however, Ministers were allowed to retain their seats, subject to the proviso that they seek re-election after appointment. Two of these offices, the Office of Bailiff or Steward of Her Majesty's Three Chiltern Hundreds of Stoke, Desborough and Burnham or that of the Steward of the Manor of Northstead are retained today for use by those MPs wishing to resign - hence the term, 'taking the Chiltern

[10] Under schedule 1, Part II, paragraph 8 of the Representation of the People Act 1983 (known as Rule 8) a candidate must sign a 'consent to nomination', stating that, 'to be best of his knowledge and belief he is not disqualified for membership of the House of Commons'.

Hundreds'. The practice is to appoint to the two offices alternately, so that two Members may, if necessary, resign at once. If the last Member to resign took the Chiltern Hundreds, the next would take the Manor of Northstead.

The House of Commons (Disqualification) Act 1975 consolidated the legislation in this area and also imposed an upper limit on the number of Ministers who could sit in the House of Commons – 95 in fact (this includes Ministers of State and Parliamentary Secretaries of State). This is why some Government Ministers are peers, who sit in the House of Lords. Parliamentary Private Secretaries (PPSs) are not included in the above calculation, but can be counted upon to support the Government in the House, thus increasing the 'payroll vote'. It is only convention which dictates that all Government Ministers must sit in either of the two Houses of Parliament - legally, the Prime Minister could appoint non-Parliamentarians as Government Ministers.[11]

Until the Re-election of Ministers Act 1926, any MP had to resign on appointment as a Minister and fight a by-election. This was taken as an endorsement of their appointment as a Minister. To avoid a series of by-elections after a General Election, Ministers would be appointed before an Election. The Election itself was taken to be an endorsement of both their candidacy and their appointment as a Minister. The electorate does not elect the Prime Minister, or indeed, any other Minister; the Prime Minister only holds that office by virtue of having been elected Leader of his or her Party and Ministers hold office merely by appointment.

Schedule 1 of the Ministerial and Other Salaries Act 1975 limits the number of ministerial salaries payable at any one time. As a result, there may only be 21 Secretaries of State and 50 Ministers of State. There can be a total of 83 Secretaries of State, Ministers and Parliamentary Secretaries, excluding the Parliamentary Secretary to the Treasury, also known as the Chief Whip. There may only be four Law Officers, five Junior Lords of the Treasury (Government Whips), seven Assistant Whips and five Lords in Waiting (Government Whips in the House of Lords). There may only be one Captain of the Honourable Corps of Gentlemen-at-Arms (Government Chief Whip in the House of Lords), one Captain of the Queen's Bodyguard of the Yeoman of the Guard (Deputy Chief Whip in the House of Lords), one Treasurer of Her Majesty's Household (Deputy Chief Whip in the House of Commons), one Comptroller of Her Majesty's Household (No. 3 Whip in the House of Commons) and Vice-Chamberlain of Her Majesty's Household (No. 4 Whip in the House of Commons). This makes a grand total of 110 paid officers. There are, in addition, numerous PPSs, who whilst considered part of the 'payroll vote' are not paid members of the Government. These restrictions were the reason why, on his appointment to Parliamentary Under-Secretary of State at the DTI, in December 1998, Michael Wills MP had to accept the position on an unsalaried basis.

The Judicial Committee of the Privy Council also has jurisdiction in the case of disqualifications under the 1975 Act. Anyone can apply to the Committee for a declaration of disqualification, but the Committee cannot oblige if the matter is awaiting the decision of the Election Court.

---

[11] The last non-parliamentarian to be a member of the Government was Jan Smuts, the South African Leader, who was a member of Lloyd George's wartime Cabinet.

A SECRET BALLOT?

Under the Representation of the People Act 1983, the General Election ballot is supposedly secret - in fact it is not. At the polling station, the elector is given a ballot paper on which is printed a serial number (also printed on the counterfoil retained by the electoral official). The elector will have previously given his or her name and address and preferably handed over his or her registration card. The electoral official then ticks off the person's name on the electoral register, gives him or her a ballot paper and then writes his or her electoral registration number on the counterfoil of the ballot paper. It is therefore possible, although illegal under the Representation of the People Act 1983, to trace the way in which an individual elector voted. The aim of the current system is to prevent voter impersonation and fraud by allowing votes to be traced. The Home Affairs Committee recommended abolition of the current system in their Fourth Report (as mentioned previously).

They also recommended that the official mark (a perforation made in each ballot paper as it is handed to the voter) which each ballot paper must carry and which is designed to prevent the use of counterfeit ballot papers, be updated. At present, the mark is sometimes forgotten, effectively depriving the voter of a valid vote. However, a mark made previously on a ballot paper might be rather easier to forge than a perforation made at the polling station in front of the voter.

THE DEPOSIT

When a candidate in an election registers his or her nomination with the returning officer, he or she must also submit a deposit of £500 (this is also the amount for both individual constituency candidates standing for election to both the Scottish Parliament and Welsh Assembly and for each party list). Elections to the Northern Ireland Assembly require a deposit of £150 per candidate. For European Parliamentary candidates the amount is £5,000 for each list or individual candidate. This is only returned if the candidate receives 5% of the total votes cast in that constituency (2.5% in the case of elections to the European Parliament). Lost deposits are paid to the Treasury. The candidate must also find 10 'assentors', who must be on the electoral roll for that constituency, to sign his or her nomination paper.

The Home Affairs Committee recommended in the aforementioned report that the deposit for parliamentary elections be increased to £700 for the next General Election and should be indexed for all subsequent Elections. It also recommended increasing the number of assentors to 50.

THE SPEAKER

The Speaker's constituency, currently West Bromwich West, the seat of Rt Hon Betty Boothroyd MP, is the one constituency which is not usually contested by the main parties at a General Election. This is a convention rather than an electoral rule and some argue it is an undemocratic one, effectively denying the voters of West Bromwich West the opportunity to vote Conservative or Liberal Democrat. This was certainly the view of the former SDP/Liberal Alliance, which always contested Croydon North East, the constituency of the then Speaker, Rt Hon Bernard Weatherill (now Lord Weatherill). The somewhat unconvincing argument in favour of the current practice is that the Speaker's role in the House of Commons is a non-political one. An alternative would be for the Speaker, on his or her appointment as such, to be dubbed the 'Member for the Palace of Westminster' and resign his or her seat, thereby allowing a by-election to be fought.

At the last General Election in 1997, the main parties contested all other seats, except for Tatton, where both the Labour and Liberal Democrat candidates stood down in favour of Martin Bell, who became the House of Commons' only Independent MP.

ELECTION EXPENSES

The campaign expenditure of Prospective Parliamentary Candidates is controlled in a number of ways. Candidates may not spend more than a specified maximum amount in their constituency and no expenditure may be incurred by anyone other than the candidate or his or her agent. Certain expenditure is prohibited altogether; for example, a candidate may not pay someone to canvass on his or her behalf. Canvassing may only be carried out by volunteers. No one may be paid to display posters or other election notices unless they are professional advertising agents.

No school premises may be hired for use as the candidate's election headquarters (called a 'Committee Room'). Under Section 101 of the Representation of the People Act 1983, candidates and their agents may not pay to take voters to polling stations. Transport may be provided but not on a commercial basis. Section 76 of the Representation of the People Act 1983 sets a legal maximum on the total amount which a candidate may spend on his or her campaign. This limit is set out the Representation of the People (Variation of Limits of Candidates' Election Expenses) Order 1997 No. 879. The Order distinguishes between by-elections and General Elections and between urban and rural constituencies. The current maximum amount which can be spent at a General Election in a borough (urban) constituency is £4,965 with an additional 4.2p per registered elector. In a county constituency the figures are £4,965 and 5.6p per elector. The same figures for a by-election in an urban constituency are £19,863 and 16.9p and in a County constituency, £19,863 and 22.2p respectively.

Under Section 75 of the Representation of the People Act 1983, no money may be spent by anyone other than the candidate or his/her election agent, unless the written permission of the agent is obtained. This then forms part of the candidate's overall expenses. There are no controls on the expenditure of political parties nationally, only on expenditure which relates to particular constituencies. The prohibition on expenditure by any person other than the candidate or his/her agent only applies to expenditure specifically related to a particular constituency. An individual may incur expenditure on election material provided it does not refer to a particular constituency or candidate.

For example, Company A could decide to fund production of a leaflet exhorting electors to vote Conservative to be distributed only within a certain constitutency and such a leaflet would be within the law, provided it did not urge voters to support a particular candidate.

PARTY FUNDING

Concern about the financing of political parties is nothing new. Traditionally, the Conservative Party was supported by the business community whilst Labour was funded by the trade unions. The Liberal Democrats and other parties rely solely on individual donations. However, whilst these sources of funding have not dried-up, they have become less reliable, for a number of reasons. The ability of individual trade unionists to contract out of the political levy (there is no comparable right for shareholders to contract out of company donations to the Conservative Party), a general decrease in trade union membership and moves towards individual membership of the Labour Party has meant that Labour has increasingly needed to look to individual donors to give large one-off donations to the Party. Individual membership of the Party peaked during the 1997 General Election at roughly 400,000 members, but has fallen off slightly since then. The Conservatives too have seen a decline in membership and funds, particularly since the 1997 General Election.

Unfortunately, this period of declining party funds coincides with an era of modern campaigning which seems to require ever-increasing levels of funding. The previous Conservative Government sought to deal with this shortage of funding by approaching foreign donors such as Greek shipping magnate, John Latsis and Hong Kong banker, Li Ka Shing. Their choices were often rather unfortunate.

There was also a shortage of funding for the parties inside Parliament. Trade union sponsorship of Labour MPs was discontinued in 1995 in an attempt to break the direct link between unions and MPs – in its place, came 'constituency plan agreements', whereby trade unions gave financial support in return for representation on CLP General Committees.

The question of how to finance political parties has been considered before; in 1976 by the Houghton Committee (Cm 6601) and more recently by the House of Commons Home Affairs Select Committee ('The Funding of Political Parties', 2nd Report, 1993/94 Session, HC 301). However, the composition of the latter at the time of the report was such that when it came to voting on the contents of the final report, the Committee split along party lines with the Chairman using his casting vote to support recommendations against disclosure of donations, against shareholder approval of company donations and in favour of foreign donations to parties.

The Conservative Government had also prevented the Committee on Standards in Public Life (at that time known as the 'Nolan Committee' after its first Chairman, Lord Nolan) from considering the subject of party financing. It was against this background that the Labour Party pledged in its 1997 General Election manifesto to, 'oblige parties to declare the source of all donations above a minimum figure', adding that: 'foreign funding will be banned'. After the 1997 General Election, the new Labour Government asked the Committee on Standards in Public Life, now chaired by Sir Patrick Neill QC (Lord Neill of Blaydon) to consider questions relating to Party funding.

Both Labour and Conservative Parties have had to deal with controversies concerning their Party finances in recent times. William Hague had just announced that the

Conservative Party would no longer accept foreign donations when allegations surfaced relating to a £1m donation from the son of an alleged fugitive drug trafficker in 1994.

The son of Ma Sik-chun alleged that the money had been given in return for all charges against his father being dropped. This sort of allegation is almost impossible to prove or refute in the absence of written evidence and demonstrates the difficulties inherent in accepting individual donations of any sort.

William Hague announced on 17 December 1997 that the Party would disclose the total sum of foreign donations received in the run-up to the 1997 General Elections, but not the individual amounts and sources of donations, on the grounds that past donors to the Party had made donations on the basis of anonymity; it would therefore be wrong to change the rules retrospectively.

The Labour Party has not been exempt from scandal. In November 1997, it was revealed that Bernie Ecclestone, Vice President of the Formula One Association had given a £1m donation to the Party. Unfortunately, these revelations surfaced soon after Labour had decided to exempt the sport from a general tobacco advertising ban. The donation was promptly returned. All three major parties now publish the names of donors who give more than £5,000 during any one financial year.

The names of those donating more than £5,000 per annum to Labour can be found in the Annual Accounts of the Labour Party, which forms part of the Party's Annual Report. The list makes interesting reading, with Eddie Izzard sitting somewhat incongruously next to Ispat International (UK) Ltd.

The Committee on Standards in Public Life published its report, 'The Funding of Political Parties in the United Kingdom' (Cm 4057) on 13 October 1998. It recommended that donations of more than £5,000 made to a political party nationally and donations of more than £1,000 made to a party locally, should be disclosed. It also recommended an end to foreign donations; an end to anonymous donations of £50 or more (intimidation of anyone as a result of having made such a donation would become a criminal offence); the introduction of tax relief at the basic rate on donations to political parties with at least two MPs, or one MP and 150,000 votes; and, shareholder approval before the making of company donations to political parties. The report was debated in the House of Commons on 9 November 1998. Opening the debate for the Government, the Home Secretary, Jack Straw said that whilst the Government had originally intended to bring forward legislation in the first Session of Parliament to ban foreign donations and enforce disclosure of donations over £5,000, he had been persuaded by the Neill Committee to defer such proposals until the Committee had completed its deliberations.

The Government's aim is to have legislation in place before the next General Election. The Government accepted most of the Committee's recommendations on donations, with the exception of tax relief on donations (which the Conservative Party now supports) which it has said it will 'consider'.

The question of whether or not transparency in donations would actually prevent the improper influence of policy was raised during the debate on the Neill Committee Report, by Shadow Home Secretary, Rt Hon Sir Norman Fowler MP (Con, Sutton Coldfield), who made the point (Col. 65) that: 'Transparency does not avoid the dangers of contributions influencing policy'. Indeed, it is almost impossible to devise a failsafe method of ensuring that contributions, made either openly or anonymously, do not 'influence' their recipients in some way. 'Influence' works on a number of levels and it would be impossible, nor would it be desirable, to seal politicians hermetically in a vacuum, free from anyone or any organisation which might seek to 'influence' them.

William Ross (OUUP, Londonderry East) (Col. 92) accepted the concerns of the SDLP concerning anonymity – 'I well understand that desire. A brick, or worse, through the window, attacks on one's children, and threats and intimidation are not common on this side of the Irish Sea, but we have to live with them'. However, he qualified this by saying, 'I believe that anyone prepared to put forward a political point of view must be prepared to defend it in every forum and against every enemy'. He questioned the Committee's decision to allow citizens in the Irish Republic to make donations to Northern Ireland political parties, but not to extend this right to other political parties. He pointed out that this might well be challenged in the European Court of Human Rights.

Phil Woolas MP (Labour, Oldham East and Saddleworth) made the point (Col. 89) that 'one share, one vote' does not necessarily equal 'one shareholder, one vote' and that the former could lead to large institutional investors voting one way and smaller shareholders another.

On the subject of 'blind trusts', the Committee recommended their abolition and suggested that donations of £1,000 or more to individuals or groups within a party be made through an 'open trust', with disclosure of other donations on the same basis as donations to the party generally. The Committee also proposed a £20m cap on national General Election expenditure by political parties fielding more than 600 candidates (a lower limit, calculated on a proportional basis, would apply to parties with fewer candidates), a cap on parties election expenditure for the Scottish Parliament of £1.5m and £600,000 for Wales and £300,000 for Northern Ireland.

Schedule 2, paragraph 6 of the European Parliamentary Elections Act 1999 inserts a new clause after paragraph 2(3) of Schedule 1 of the European Parliamentary Elections Act 1978 to allow regulations to be made relating to the 'limitation of elections expenses'. Similar provisions have been included in the Scotland Act 1998 (section 12(2)(c)) and in the Government of Wales Act 1998 (section 11(2)(c). The Government has accepted the need for a cap on election spending, proposing a figure of £15m - not as generous as the £20m limit proposed by the Committee.

John MacGregor, a former Conservative Leader of the House of Commons was the only member of the Committee to dissent from this proposal on the grounds that it would be almost impossible to ensure compliance.

The Committee also recommended the establishment of an Election Commission, whose role it would be to ensure compliance with electoral rules and to take over the role of registering political parties, which under the new Registration of Political Parties Act 1998, has been given to the Registrar of Companies. There would also be similar commissions for Wales, Scotland and Northern Ireland. Prosecutions would be brought by the Director of Public Prosecutions, not by the Election Commission. Rt Hon Jack

Straw MP, said in the debate on 9 November 1998 (Col: 55) that the Commission should be established in a similar way to the National Audit Office – funded from the Consolidated Fund and overseen by a parliamentary committee similar to the Public Accounts Committee (see 'An Alphabetical Guide to Parliament' for more information on the Public Accounts Committee). The Independent Commission on the Voting System (the 'Jenkins' Committee) recommended that a new Election Commission should also take on the role currently assigned to the four Boundary Commissions, but the Neill Committee disagreed. The proposal for an Election Commission has received more or less universal approval. The Home Affairs Select Committee recommended the establishment of an Electoral Commission in their Fourth Report of the 1997/98 Session. In their evidence to the Committee, both Professor Robert Blackburn and the doyen of electoral politics, Professor David Butler, argued for such a Commission. In their view the Commission should be empowered to consider all aspects of the electoral process, ranging from the electoral system itself, to issues such as party funding, broadcasting rules and any issues currently the remit of the Boundary Commissions.

The Committee also made recommendations relating to the so-called 'Short Money'. The Short Funds were established by Rt Hon Ted Short, the then Leader of the House of Commons (now Lord Glenamara) in 1975 (HC, 20 March 1975) to support the activities of the opposition parties in Parliament. Short Money is allocated at a scale of £3,975.07 for each seat won by that Party at the previous General Election, plus £7.94 for every 200 votes cast for that Party. This is uprated yearly in line with inflation – a measure introduced in 1993 (HC Col: 593, 4 November 1993). To qualify, the party concerned must have gained two or more seats at the preceding General Election or gained one seat and 150,000 votes. The motion passed by the House on 4 November 1993 also created a travel fund (currently £115,471) for opposition parties, to be distributed in the same proportions as the Short Funds.

The Neill Committee recommended an increase in both the Short Money and the 'Cranborne Money Scheme' - a similar fund in the House of Lords. The Cranborne scheme was named after the then Leader of the House, Rt Hon Viscount Cranborne, who proposed its adoption. Their Lordships agreed, by a resolution of the House in November 1996 (HL, 27 November 1996, Col: 267) to make £100,000 available to the main Opposition Party in the House of Lords and £30,000 to the second largest party (to be uprated yearly in line with inflation). The current figures are £106,191 (Conservatives) and £31,857 (Liberal Democrats) for the year 1 April 1998 to 31 March 1999.

The Neill Committee recommended that in the House of Commons, the Official Opposition's allocation of Short Money should be fixed and not vary according to the previous General Election result and that a portion of that amount should be earmarked for running the office of the Leader of the Official Opposition. Before the 1997 Election, the Labour Party received £1,530,190.51 (for the financial year 1996/7, excluding the period between 1 April and the General Election), whereas the Conservative Party, post-Election, received £986,762.82 (for the year 1997/98). The Committee also recommended the establishment of similar schemes for the Scottish Parliament, the Welsh Assembly and the Northern Irish Assembly. A clause to this effect was added to the Scotland Bill, now section 97 of the Scotland Act 1998.

Table Six – ALLOCATION OF SHORT MONEY

PARTY	1996/97	1997/98 * *does not include period between 1 April and General Election*
Conservative	*NA*	986,762.82
Labour	1,530,190.51	*NA*
Liberal Democrat	316,480.64	371,997.98
SNP	36,782.68	46,167.90
Plaid Cymru	22,040.36	21,210.96
Official Ulster Unionist	46,357.18	47,580.34
Democratic Unionist	15,954.37	11,618.90
SDLP	23,134.12	18,553.51

(Source: House of Commons Hansard, 24 April 1998, Col: 725)

One of the most contentious issues raised by the Neill Committee was their recommendation that in a referendum campaign, the Government should remain neutral and that there should be equal, core funding for both sides in the campaign. Donations of £5,000 would need to be disclosed. This would preclude additional Government funding for one side of the campaign. During the debate in the House of Commons, both the Home Secretary and a number of other speakers made the point that it would be almost impossible to ensure Government neutrality during a campaign; Ministers would still be in office and would need advice from civil servants and whilst members of the Government might be on different sides of the debate, there would still be a Government view on the matter in question.

PARTY POLITICAL BROADCASTS

Sadly, these cult classics of British broadcasting are no more, their passing mourned by party activists and connoisseurs of comedy alike. They were the 'Carry Ons' of the political world. However, for hopeless addicts, there will still be Party Election Broadcasts (PEBs). The allocation of PEBs used to be decided by the Committee on Political Broadcasting, which consisted of members of the main political parties and the BBC and ITC. The Committee had no legal status and its deliberations were not made public. In practice, the television companies issued a proposed allocation of broadcasts to the Secretary to the Government Chief Whip, who then liaised with the other Party Whips. A maximum of five PEBs was allocated to a single party; the Party in Government and the chief Opposition Party received parity of allocation. Any party fielding more than 50 candidates was entitled to a 5 minute broadcast. On this basis, the Natural Law Party was entitled to a broadcast, featuring the delights of yogic flying.[12]

If the parties failed to agree an allocation with the broadcasters, the latter could impose an allocation upon them. However, the Party could in turn, pursue an action for judicial review in the High Court on the grounds that the broadcasters had not adhered to the concept of political impartiality. The Committee was replaced in June 1997 by the Broadcasters' Liaison group, which liaises directly with the political parties. A consultation paper on the reform of party political broadcasting was issued jointly by the BBC, ITC, Radio Authority and S4C on 21 January 1998, which, apart from spelling the demise of the PPB, suggested amongst other things, reapplying the electoral support test for PEBs, abolished for the minor parties in 1996. This would entitle only those parties who had candidates in one sixth of all seats to a PEB. In 1997, eight parties with no MPs were entitled to PEBs.

The consultation paper also suggested introducing election broadcasts for the Scottish Parliament and Welsh Assembly, ending Budget broadcasts and increasing the number of local election broadcasts. The consultation period ended on 31 March 1998 and on 18 September the broadcasters announced that PPBs already planned for the remainder of the year would be retained, but that a further review would be undertaken in June 1999. There were a series of PEBs for the Scottish and Welsh Assembly elections, for the European Elections in 1999 and for the Local Elections in May 1999. The BBC will continue with Budget broadcasts and these will be available to other broadcasters. Under the Registration of Political Parties Act 1998, only registered political parties will be eligible for broadcasts, although the mere fact of registration will not be a guarantee of a PEB.

FORMER MEMBERS DURING ELECTIONS

Whilst Government continues during the period of a General Election, Parliament does not. No Parliament, no Members. Former Members contesting their seats, may not use any parliamentary facilities, although an exception is made in the case of Party Leaders, who may use their offices throughout the campaign period. MPs who stand down or who are not re-elected are entitled to a resettlement grant (a percentage of annual salary) based on age and length of service. Government Ministers also receive severance payments if they lose office under the age of 65 provided they do not hold office again within three weeks. The payment is equal to one quarter of the annual amount of the person's ministerial salary, reduced by one quarter of the difference between the ministerial salary and an ordinary MP's salary. MPs also receive a pension as set out in the Parliamentary and Other Pensions Act 1987 and subsequent regulations and the Ministerial and Other Pensions and Salaries Act 1991. Members contribute at a rate of 6% of salary and the pension is based on final salary, accruing at a rate of one fiftieth for each year of service, pro rata for a part year.

[12] A video of Party Political Broadcasts became a surprise bestseller of Christmas 1998.

BY-ELECTIONS

By-elections are held in order to fill vacancies in the House of Commons arising from the death of a Member, an MP's retirement from the House (known as 'taking the Chiltern Hundreds'), a Member's elevation to the peerage or declaration of bankruptcy, or on the occasion of an MP being declared of unsound mind under the Mental Health Act 1983 (some readers may be asking themselves why, in this case, there have been so few by-elections).

Technically, any Member of the House of Commons can 'move the writ' for a by-election and on occasion this has been used as a delaying tactic by MPs attempting to prevent a particular item of business from being reached, but in practice, such writs are usually moved by the Chief Whip of the Party which held the now vacated seat. Technically, any such motion is an 'order of the House to the Speaker to make out his warrant for the issue of a writ for the election of a new member to fill a vacancy' (Erskine May: Parliamentary Practice, 22nd Edition, Page 286[13]). In 1973 a Speaker's Conference recommended a time limit of three months within which the writ for a by-election should be moved (Cm 5500). Technically, as the motion for a new writ is a matter of privilege, no notice has to be given by a Member of his or her intention to move the writ. Members may also move amendments to such a motion. On 21 Februrary 1990, the House agreed that if a writ was moved on a Friday when Private Members' business had precedence, and was opposed, the motion to move the writ would lapse enabling debate to proceed with Private Members' Bills.

If a seat becomes vacant during a parliamentary recess, the Speaker can issue a warrant for a writ under certain circumstances. Under the Recess Election Act 1975, if the seat is vacated either because of the death of the previous member or his or her elevation to the peerage, the writ can be moved during a recess, provided six days notice is given in the London Gazette. However, the warrant cannot be issued, if the House is scheduled to return within that time. Where an MP dies during a recess, a by-election can only be called if the former Member's 'Return' is taken to the office of the Clerk of the Crown, 15 days before the end of the previous sitting of the House. A by-election cannot take place during a recess in those cases where a Member has resigned or been detained under the Mental Health Act 1959. In the latter case, where an MP has been detained on the grounds of mental illness, a by-election can only take place if two psychiatrists declare, after visiting the MP on two occasions, six months apart, that the said MP is indeed suffering from some form of mental illness. Where an MP becomes bankrupt, he or she has six months grace, but if after than time a Certificate of Bankruptcy is issued to the Speaker by the Court, the seat will be declared vacant and a by-election called.

---

[13] Erskine May's Parliamentary Practice is the 'bible' of parliamentary procedure. In addition to the Standing Orders of the House of Commons, it is the definitive source of guidance on parliamentary practices and procedural devices. It is now in its 22nd edition, having first been published in 1844. Quite clearly, it is no longer edited by its originator, Thomas Erskine May, himself a Clerk in the House of Commons, but by Sir Donald Limon KCB, Clerk of the House of Commons and W R McKay CB, the Clerk Assistant. The latest edition, the 22nd was published in 1997 by Butterworths. The first edition was apparently described by the Times as 'a popular work ... a compact and compendious volume'. To describe it as popular today, might be something of an overstatement, but compendious it certainly is. It is a vital reference work for anyone seriously interested in following the minutiae of parliamentary life.

Table Seven – BY-ELECTION TIMETABLE

Day	Procedure	Timing
0	Issue of writs from Clerk of the Crown in Chancery	Usually on the same day as, but if not, as soon as possible after, the issue of the Royal Proclamation dissolving Parliament
1	Receipt of writs by returning officers	The day after the writs are issued
3	Notice of the Election	No later than 4pm on second day after writs are received
6	Applications for Postal or Proxy voting must be received	No later than 11th day before date of poll
6 - 8	Delivery of candidates' nomination papers (including appointment of Election Agent)	Between 10am and 4pm on any day after date of publication of notice of election, but no earlier than 3rd day after and not later than the 7th day after that on which writs were received.
	Making of objections to nomination papers	During hours allowed for delivery of nomination papers on last day for their delivery plus one hour following
	Publication of statement of persons nominated	At close of time for making objections to nomination papers
11	Receipt of Applications for Postal or Proxy voting by those who are ill	No later than noon on sixth day before date of poll
15-19	Polling Day	Between 7am and 10pm on a day set by the Returning Officer, no earlier than the eighth day, nor later than the 10th after the last day for delivery of nomination papers

THE BOUNDARY REVIEWS

The Parliamentary Constituencies Act 1986 states that the number of constituencies shall not be substantially greater or less than 613 for England, Wales and Scotland combined. There are minimum figures set out for Scotland and Wales (71 and 35 respectively). For Northern Ireland there cannot be fewer than 16 or more than 18 constituencies. This effectively means that Scotland, Wales and Northern Ireland are over-represented, in that order. The number of MPs has not steadily increased as one might imagine; for example, there were more MPs in the 1918-22 Parliament (707) than there are in today's (659).

There are four Boundary Commissions, for Scotland, Wales, England and Northern Ireland. Since their establishment in 1944 (House of Commons (Redistribution of Seats)

Act 1944), there have been four reviews, in 1955, 1974, 1983 and 1995. Their reports are presented to Parliament as draft Orders in Council which then require the approval of both Houses of Parliament. The Boundary Commission Act 1992 specified that there must be a review every eight to 12 years. As well as general reviews, the Boundary Commissions may undertake special reviews; i.e. Milton Keynes in 1990, where the electorate had increased to 101,839 and the seat was consequently divided into two.

The Speaker is the ex-officio Chairman of all four Commissions. The Deputy Chairman of the English and Welsh Commissions are High Court Judges. There are two other members of each Commission, usually a judge, barrister or solicitor (appointed by the Home Secretary and Secretary of State for the Environment). The Deputy Chairman is unpaid, the other two members receive some remuneration. Assistant Commissioners are appointed by the Home Secretary to chair local enquiries.

The Boundary Commissions attempt to ensure that there are similar numbers of electors within each constituency - that a vote in one Constituency should be of equal value to a vote in another - whilst attempting to respect local boundaries. The 'electoral quota' is obtained by dividing the electorate of the given area; e.g., England, by the number of constituencies. The Commissions then attempt to ensure that the electorate of any constituency is as near to the electoral quota as possible.

The number of electors on the register at the beginning of a review forms the basis of the Commissions' calculations; unfortunately, these numbers are frequently out of date by the time the Commissions' proposals actually take effect. The Boundary Commissions also attempt to ensure that English and Welsh Constituencies do not cross County or London borough boundaries, that Scottish Constituencies do not cross local authority boundaries and that Northern Ireland Constituencies are contained within ward boundaries. This is not always possible as the most recent boundary reviews demonstrate.

The Boundary Commissions must take into consideration any representations resulting from the publication of their proposals. They may hold local enquiries where they consider this would be appropriate and are obliged to hold an enquiry where more than 100 electors in a constituency object (or if a local authority in the relevant area objects) to the proposals. Once an enquiry has been held a report is produced. The Commission may or may not revise its original recommendations in the light of the representations made. If it does revise its proposals and produces a new report, objections may be made to the new proposals, but another enquiry need not be held.

In most cases, the conclusions of local enquiries are simply adopted by the three working Commissioners when they meet once a month. This can lead to divergent decisions being made in different parts of the country with similar problems being resolved in a wide variety of ways. This lack of consistency is one of the problems of the current procedure.

Only the Home Secretary has the power, under Parliamentary Constituencies Act 1986, to make amendments to the Boundary Commissions' reports. Draft Orders must be approved by both Houses, but cannot be amended, before being submitted to the Queen for signature. The Parliamentary Constituencies Act 1986 also contains a so-called 'ouster clause', which excludes the jurisdiction of the courts in relation to any Orders brought in under the Act. The Order has no effect until the dissolution of the Parliament which approved it (i.e., it has no effect until the next General Election).

The last boundary reviews did not bring good news for many sitting Conservative MPs and resulted in what was known as the 'chicken run'. A number of MPs whose majorities were threatened as a result of the reviews sought selection elsewhere. Some, however, failed to gain re-election despite finding a supposedly safer seat – Rt Hon Norman Lamont (now Lord Lamont) who moved from Kingston-Upon-Thames to Harrogate and John Watts who moved from Slough to Reading East. Some were more successful: Sir George Young Bt MP, who moved from Ealing Acton to Hampshire North West, Hon Nicholas Soames MP, who moved from Crawley to Mid Sussex, Nick Hawkins MP, who moved from Blackpool South to Surrey Heath and Peter Bottomley from Eltham to Worthing West.

The four Boundary Commissions began work on the last boundary reviews between February, 1991 and March, 1993. England gained five seats, Wales two and Northern Ireland one. The trend was for urban areas to lose seats and for the more rural parts of the country to gain them; Greater London lost 10 seats and some of the new seats cut across London Borough boundaries. England now has 529 seats, Wales, 40, Scotland 72 (no change) and Northern Ireland 18.

THE REGISTRATION OF POLITICAL PARTIES

The Registration of Political Parties Act 1998 was initiated by the Government in response to a number of situations where candidates had stood in elections under party labels deliberately designed to confuse the electorate; the best known examples being the use of the names 'Literal Democrats' or 'New Labour'. The Liberal Democrats problems with Richard Huggett and the name Literal Democrats stemmed from the fact that under Rule 6(2) as set out in Schedule 1 of the Representation of the People Act 1983, a nomination paper must state the candidate's full name and home address and in addition, a description, if desired, of no more than six words. In 1994, Richard Huggett stood as the Literal Democrat in the European Elections in 1994 in Devon and East Plymouth. The Liberal Democrats failed in their application for judicial review as Rule 12(5) of the 1983 Act states that a Returning Officer's decision as to the validity of nominations is final.

After the Election, Liberal Democrat candidate, Adrian Sanders, who had failed to take the seat, brought an election petition, but even this failed on the grounds that the Returning Officer could only rule a nomination invalid under Rule 12(2) a, b or c (basically on the grounds that the particulars of the candidate are not as they should be by law). Richard Huggett was entitled to stand as a Literal Democrat and thoroughly confuse the voters.

Under the provisions of the new Act, political parties will have to register their party's name with the Registrar at Companies House. The Party will only be able to register a name if it does not 'result in the party's being confused by voters with a party which is already registered.'. In each constituency, the Returning Officer would then have to decide whether or not a nomination paper conformed to this rule. Problems could arise where the Registrar and the Returning Officer arrive at different conclusions. Other rules will apply; for example, a party name must not be 'obscene or offensive' and must be written in Roman Script – so Russian equivalents of much loved four letter words will not be appropriate. Existing parties with one or more MP will get the first bite of the cherry and will be able to register first. Under the Act, the Speaker will appoint a Committee of MPs to help her advise the Registrar on the registration process. The Act states that a nomination paper may not include a six word description of a candidate which is 'likely to lead voters to associate the candidate with a registered political party unless the description is authorised by a certificate. For the first time, party emblems will be permitted on the ballot paper in addition to the party's name.

Whilst the Act deals with the problem of misleading party names, it does not deal with those cases where one candidate uses the same name as another in order to mislead. Returning Officers have not been given any additional powers to investigate the names of candidates. In these cases, injunctions have to be sought before the close of nominations; for example, at the 1997 General Election, Alice Mahon, the sitting MP and Labour Candidate in Halifax, was faced with a male candidate who had changed his name to Alice Mahon.

Table Eight – GENERAL ELECTIONS SINCE 1945

Year	Party	Seats	Votes	Majority
1945 (5th July)	Conservative	213	39.8%	
	Labour	393	48.3%	146 (640 seats)
	Liberal	12	9.1%	
	Others	22	2.8%	
1950 (23rd February)	Conservative	299	43.5%	
	Labour	315	46.1%	5 (625 seats)
	Liberal	9	9.1%	
	Others	21	1.3%	
1951 (25th October)	Conservative	321	48.0%	17 (625 seats)
	Labour	295	48.8%	
	Liberal	6	2.5%	
	Others	3	0.7%	
1955 (26th May)	Conservative	345	49.7%	60 (630 seats)
	Labour	277	46.4%	
	Liberal	6	2.7%	
	Other	2	1.2%	
1959 (8th October)	Conservative	365	49.4%	100 (630 seats)
	Labour	258	43.8%	
	Liberal	6	5.9%	
	Others	1	0.9%	
1964 (15th October)	Conservative	304	43.4%	
	Labour	317	44.1%	4 (630 seats)
	Liberal	9	11.2%	
	Others	0	1.3%	
1966 (31st March)	Conservative	253	41.9%	
	Labour	363	47.9%	96 (630 seats)
	Liberal	12	8.5%	
	Others	2	1.2%	

Year	Party	Seats	Votes	Majority
1970 (18th June)	Conservative	330	46.4%	30 (630 seats)
	Labour	287	43.0%	
	Liberal	6	7.5%	
	SNP	1	1.1%	
	Others	6	2.1%	
1974 (28th February)	Conservative	297	37.9%	
	Labour	301	37.1%	No overall majority - Labour minority Government
	Liberal	14	19.3%	
	Plaid Cymru	2	0.6%	
	SNP	7	2.0%	
	Others GB	2	0.8%	
	Others NI	12	2.3%	
1974 (10th October)	Conservative	277	35.8%	
	Labour	319	39.2%	3 (635 seats)
	Liberal	13	18.3%	
	Plaid Cymru	3	0.6%	
	SNP	11	2.9%	
	Others GB	0	0.8%	
	Others NI	12	2.4%	
1979 (3rd May)	Conservative	339	43.9%	43 (635 seats)
	Labour	269	36.9%	
	Liberal	11	13.8%	
	Plaid Cymru	2	0.4%	
	SNP	2	1.6%	
	Others GB	0	1.2%	
	Others NI	12	2.2%	
1983 (9th June)	Conservative	397	42.4%	144 (650 seats)
	Labour	209	27.6%	
	SDP/Liberal	23	25.4%	
	Alliance	2	0.4%	
	Plaid Cymru	2	1.1%	
	SNP	0	0.7%	
	Other GB	17	3.1%	
	Other NI			
1987 (11th June)	Conservative	376	42.3%	102 (650 seats)
	Labour	229	30.8%	
	SDP/Liberal Alliance	22	22.5%	
	Plaid Cymru	3	0.4%	
	SNP	3	1.3%	
	Other GB	0	0.5%	
	Other NI	17	2.2%	
1992 (9th April)	Conservative	336	41.9%	21 (651 seats)
	Labour	271	34.4%	
	Liberal Democrat	20	17.8%	
	Plaid Cymru	4	0.5%	
	SNP	3	1.9%	
	Other GB	0	1.4%	
	Other NI	17	2.1%	
1997 (1st May)	Conservative	165	31%	179 (659 seats)
	Labour	419	43%	
	Liberal Democrat	46	17%	
	Plaid Cymru	4	0.5%	
	SNP	6	2.0%	
	Other GB	1	4.0%	
	Other NI	18	2.5%	

ELECTORAL REFORM

Different electoral systems

Concerns about our current electoral system and calls for its reform are nothing new. However, the First Past the Post System (FPTP) has its supporters as well as detractors and there are strong arguments in favour of its retention. It usually ensures strong majority governments, it is easy to understand, it militates against the undue influence of smaller political parties and avoids the need for coalitions. However, there are equally strong arguments against: it can, and frequently does, result in the election of Members by a minority rather than a majority of their constituents; it disenfranchises vast numbers of people in certain parts of the country (e.g. Conservative supporters in Scotland) – what the Jenkins' Committee calls 'electoral deserts'; it leads to the under-representation of smaller parties in the House of Commons and it can mean the election of a Government with a larger number of seats but smaller percentage of votes than its main rival (the General Election of 1951 is the best example). Unfortunately, there is no perfect electoral system – there are systems which can ensure more or less perfect proportionality (a national list system, for example) but it is hard to see them being accepted in the UK.

Debate about FPTP has rumbled on for decades. In 1917, a Speaker's Conference on Electoral Reform (Cm 8463) recommended the adoption of a combination of the Single Transferable Vote (STV) and the Alternative Vote (AV). These proposals were rejected by the House of Commons, as were subsequent proposals. Following three General Election defeats in a row, 1979, 1983 and 1987, the Labour Party was minded to at least consider the options for electoral reform and as a result a working party under the Chairmanship of Professor Raymond Plant (now Lord Plant) was established in 1990. Two interim reports were published and a final report, 'Democracy, Representation and Elections: Report of the Working Party on Electoral Systems' appeared in 1993.

The Committee recommended the adoption of the Additional Member System (AMS) for the Scottish Assembly, the Supplementary Vote for elections to the House of Commons and a reformed list system for the European Parliamentary elections and for elections to a reformed House of Lords. John Smith, the then Leader of the Labour Party, committed the Party to a referendum on PR for Westminster and this was endorsed at both the 1993 and 1995 Conferences. Tony Blair reiterated Labour's commitment to holding a referendum on PR when he gave the first John Smith Memorial Lecture on 7 Februrary, 1996. However, he expressed his own scepticism about the merits of electoral reform, saying, 'I have never been persuaded that under proportional representation we can avoid a situation where small parties end up wielding disproportionate power'.

A joint Labour/Liberal Democrat Consultative Committee was established by the two parties and reported prior to the 1997 General Election (5 March 1997). This recommended a referendum in the first term of a new Parliament, preceded by the establishment of a Commission to consider various options and propose an alternative to FPTP. The Labour Party's 1997 General Election manifesto merely committed the party to the holding of a referendum and no timescale was indicated. The Independent Commission on the Voting System was set up in December 1997 under the

Chairmanship of the Lord Jenkins of Hillhead and the report (Cm 4090) was published on 29 October 1998.

It now looks increasingly unlikely that a referendum on PR will be held in the current Parliament. The Cabinet is divided on the issue, with such heavyweights as the Home Secretary, the Chancellor of the Exchequer and the Leader of the House of Commons all known to be opposed to PR. This, coupled with the innate scepticism of the Prime Minister himself, makes it unlikely that a referendum on PR will be a priority for the Government in this Parliament.

One of the main problems in holding a referendum on PR is the question of how the ballot paper should be worded. A referendum on just this issue was held in New Zealand on 19 September, 1992. The electorate was asked firstly if it wished to alter the current electoral system and secondly, if the answer to the first question was 'yes', which, out of five listed systems they would prefer. A majority supported change and two thirds of those supported a 'mixed member proportional system' similar to AMS. Alternatively, details could be set out first in legislation, with the proviso that provisions relating to PR would not come into effect unless ratified by a majority voting in their favour in a referendum. Electoral systems can be based on one of the following three principles: Plurality; Majority or Proportionality.

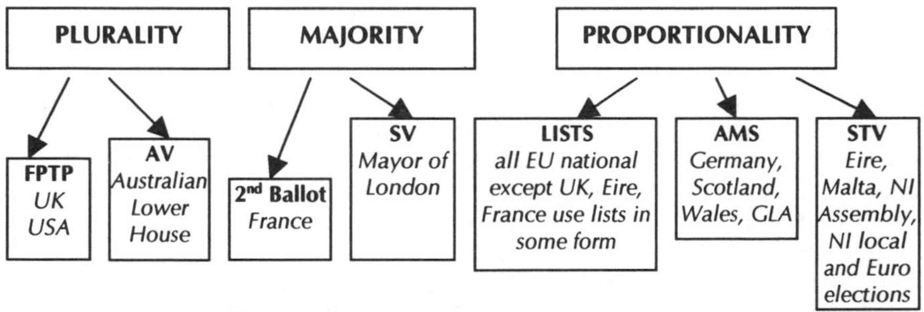

Plurality

Our own system of first-past-the-post elections is the best example of plurality; electors vote for one candidate and the candidate with the most votes wins. This is not the same as the candidate with an overall majority; for example the Report of the Independent Commission on the Voting System (Cm 4090) chaired by Lord Jenkins of Hillhead (the 'Jenkins Commission') made the point that of the present 659 MPs in the House of Commons, no fewer than 312 were elected with less than 50% of the vote – 49 of these were elected with less than 40% (Volume 1, Page 38, Paragraph 125).

Majority

There are three basic majoritarian systems: the Alternative Vote (AV), the Supplementary Vote (SV) and the Second Ballot system. These differ from FPTP in that, whilst they are not proportional, they do at least make some attempt to guarantee that MPs are elected by a majority, rather than just a plurality, of their electorate.

The Second Ballot

The Second Ballot system is used in France for legislative and presidential elections. In the first ballot, voters select their preferred candidate as they would under FPTP If any candidate receives an overall majority, he or she is elected. If not, candidates with a minimum of 12.5% of 'registered votes', as opposed to votes cast, proceed to the next round. If more than two candidates go forward there can be no guarantee that the winning candidate will have an overall majority. The Presidential elections differ in that only the two highest placed candidates can go through to the second ballot. In the French Presidential election in 1995, Lionel Jospin received the most votes in the first ballot, followed by Jacques Chirac and Edouard Balladur. Only Jospin and Chirac went through to the second ballot, where Balladur's votes switched to Chirac, giving him an overall majority.

The Alternative Vote

The Alternative Vote is used for elections to the Australian Lower House. Constituencies elect one candidate, but electors record preferences for the various candidates; e.g.

Twist, Oliver	Labour	1
Nickleby, Nicholas	Conservative	2
Copperfield, David	Liberal Democrat	3

If no candidate gains an absolute majority of the vote, the candidate with the fewest votes is eliminated and his second preferences are allocated to the remaining candidates. This process is continued until a winning candidate is secured. AV is the system recommended by the Jenkins Commission for the constituency section of its AV-Plus electoral system. This might be seen as rather contrary, as it specifically rules out using AV as a simple replacement for FPTP on the grounds that it would exacerbate what its Chairman, in typically florid language, describes as the 'cornucopia of luscious psephological fruit emptied over its (Labour's) head' at the last General Election. Simply put, this means that according to the models used by the Jenkins Commission, a re-run of the 1997 General Election using AV, would actually result in an even larger Labour majority and a smaller number of Conservative seats. This is set out below.

Table Nine – PROJECTED 1997 GENERAL ELECTION RESULT UNDER AV

Party	**FPTP - % of Votes**	**FPTP - % of Seats**	**FPTP – No. of Seats**	**AV – No. of Seats***
Conservative	30.7	25	**165**	**96**
Labour	43.2	63.6	**419**	**452**
Liberal Democrat	16.8	7	**46**	**82**

** based on work by Professor Patrick Dunleavy, Dr Helen Margetts and Stuart Weir in 'Making Votes Count' and 'Making Votes Count 2' (Democratic Audit, 1998) and cited in the Report of the Independent Commission on the Voting System (Page 25, Paragraph 82).*

The Supplementary Vote

This is really a variant of the Alternative Vote and was recommended by the 'Plant Committee' (Report of the Working Party on Electoral Systems - 1993) set up by the Labour Party after the 1992 Election. Its chief architect was Dale Campbell Savours, MP. Voters record only two preferences on a ballot paper, which would look something like the following:

Table 10 – EXAMPLE OF SUPPLEMENTARY VOTING BALLOT PAPER

	Mark X here for your first preference	*Mark X here for your second preference*
Twist, Oliver – Labour		
Nickleby, Nicholas – Conservative		
Copperfield, David – Liberal Democrat		

The returning officer would add up all the first preferences and if any candidate had gained over 50% of the votes he or she would be elected. If, however, there was no overall majority for one of the candidates, then all the candidates except the two with the highest number of second preferences would be eliminated. The second preferences on the ballot papers of the eliminated candidates would then be added to the totals of the top two candidates (second preferences of eliminated candidates for other eliminated candidates would be ignored). Whichever of the two remaining candidates received the most votes would be elected.

The Weighted Vote

Under this system MPs would be elected as now, but would be given a weight in the Division lobbies of the House of Commons. For example, if the Liberal Democrats had received a large percentage of the votes at the General Election, but won few seats, their votes would be weighted differently to those of their Labour or Conservative counterparts – so a Liberal Democrat vote would be worth more than a Labour vote. The Jenkins Commission rejected this system for obvious reasons.

When considering all the possible majoritarian systems, the Jenkins Commission took the view that none of them met the four criteria to which the Committee had been asked to ensure that any alternative to FPTP adhered, namely: broad proportionality, the need for stable government, extension of voter choice and maintenance of the link between MP and constituency.

Proportionality

Proportional voting systems fall into three main categories: lists, mixed member systems and the Single Transferable Vote.

Party List Systems

Open or Closed?

There are numerous different list systems, ranging from those which simply allow voters to express a preference for a party, to those which allow full preferential voting; i.e. the voter can list all the candidates in order of preference. Lists are said to be either 'open' or 'closed'. The former allows the electorate to vote for a candidate, the latter allows only a vote for a party. It is this distinction which caused the disagreements between the Government and the House of Lords in the last Session of Parliament (1997/98) (see chapter seven on Legislation for more details about the passage of the European Parliamentary Elections Bill). Interestingly, their Lordships did not seem so concerned that the same system will be used to elect the list members of the Scottish and Welsh Assemblies. Where a closed list is used the party simply draws up a list of its candidates (in the order it wants them elected) and the elector votes for a party, not for an individual. The number of seats which each party gains in the legislature is proportional to the number of votes received by the party and the most popular candidates from the list are elected.

Preferential or Non-Preferential?

In some party list systems the elector can alter the order of the candidates and in others, the elector has as many votes as there are candidates to be elected and can vote for candidates on different party lists. In Belgium, voters can choose either to vote for the party of their choice or for a candidate. In Luxembourg, voters have three choices – a vote for a party, two preference votes for one candidate (a procedure known as 'cumulation') or preferences for as many candidates as there are seats to be filled. In some countries, party lists are unordered and votes for the candidates on the list are the only determinants of who is elected. A vote for a particular party's candidate does not equal a vote for that party, purely a vote for that candidate. Voters can rank candidates preferentially from across the party's lists. Where party lists are ordered, preferential voting may result in reordering of the list, with a candidate lower down the list being elected before a candidate at the top of the party's list.

The most proportional list system is one in which the entire electorate forms one large constituency – this system is used in Israel and the Netherlands. If the 1997 General Election had been run on these lines the result would have been as set out below (excluding Northern Ireland). Even at the last General Election, Labour would not have gained an overall majority.

Table 11 – 1997 GENERAL ELECTION – PROPORTIONS OF TOTAL VOTES AS SEATS

Party	% of Votes	No. of Seats (total no. of seats excluding NI and seats held by minority parties =641)	Actual No. of Seats
Conservative	31.5	202	165
Labour	44.4	285	419
Liberal Democrat	17.2	110	46

Lists can also be regional or two-tier. There are several varieties of two-list systems. A two-tier system can be used to top-up candidates who may have been elected on a constituency basis, with those elected from a regional list. There are two ways of doing this: 'remainder transfer' or 'adjustment'. In the former, the proportion of additional seats is not fixed in advance (used with largest remainder systems), whereas under the adjustment method, a fixed proportion is set aside (this is usually used with the highest average systems). Some lists also allow preferential voting. Before the 1993 reforms, Italy elected its Chamber of Deputies by using the largest remainder Imperiali quota system, with preferential ranking of candidates (this was abolished in 1991), followed by a national top-up. The Senate was elected by using the highest average d'Hondt allocation formula. The system was replaced in 1993 by a system similar in some respects to the 'AV-Plus' system being recommended by the Jenkins Commission. Three quarters of both houses are elected in individual constituencies and one quarter are elected from PR lists (the Senate uses a single vote for the Party to calculate lists seats, whereas the Chamber of Deputies uses a two-vote system, with one vote for constituency candidates and one for a party list.

Quotas and Divisors

Pure list systems employ either a 'quota' or a 'divisor'. Systems which use quotas are called 'largest remainder' systems and those employing divisors are known as 'highest average' systems.

Largest remainder systems use either one of the three following quotas: Hare (named after Thomas Hare); Droop (after mathematician, H K Droop - also known as the Hagenbach-Bischoff system, after Eduard Hagenbach-Bischoff) or Imperiali. When such quotas are used, in the first round of the election, parties with votes over the quota are allocated seats; for example, using the Hare quota, if the number of total votes was 2000 and the number of seats five, the quota would be 400. Parties with over 400 votes are awarded seats and the remaining seats are awarded to parties in order, with the party with the largest number of votes gaining the first seat, and so on.

The Droop quota divides the total valid votes by the number of seats plus one (where the bracket is equal to the next whole number) i.e. votes divided by seats plus one, plus one (or part thereof). In the above example of 2000 votes with five seats, applying the Droop quota would result in the following: 2000 divided by six, plus one = 334. If there were, for example 54 votes and three seats the quota would be 54 ÷ 3 + 1 = 13.5 (plus one or part thereof) = 14.

$$\left[\frac{\text{Votes}}{\text{Seats} + 1}\right]$$

The Imperiali quota divides the total valid votes by the number of seats plus two and the Reinforced Imperiali quota by seats plus three. According to Professor David Butler in his evidence to the Jenkins Commission, 'these have no known mathematical justification ... they are not recommended' (Volume 3, page 24 of evidence – 'Report of group of academics chaired by Professor David Butler, Nuffield College, Oxford University). Using the above example again, the Imperiali quota would result in the following: 2000 divided by 7 = 286. Lower quotas favour larger political parties and vice versa.

There are three main forms of the highest average system: d'Hondt (after Victor d'Hondt) pure Sainte-Lague and modified Sainte-Lague. The d'Hondt system is the most widely used and involves the use of the divisors, 1, 2, 3, etc. The pure Sainte-Lague system uses the divisors 1,3,5,7, etc, whereas the modified Sainte-Lague system uses the divisors 1.4, 3,5,7, etc. The parties votes are divided by the divisor to produce an average vote and the party with the highest average vote after each stage of the process wins a seat, etc, etc.

Table 12 – ELECTORAL QUOTAS AND FORMULAS

Largest Remainder	Highest Average
quotas used include: ***Hare (valid votes divided by seats)*** ***Droop (valid votes divided by seats plus one), plus one*** ***Imperiali (valid votes divided by 2)*** ***Reinforced Imperiali (valid votes divided by 3)***	allocation formulas used include: ***d'Hondt (divisors 1,2,3, etc)*** ***pure Sainte-Lague (divisors 1,3,5,7)*** ***modified Sainte-Lague (divisors 1.4, 3,5,7, etc)***

Some examples using the various systems are set out below. These demonstrate the different results which occur using different quotas and different allocation formulas. The d'Hondt highest average allocation formula favours larger parties whilst the pure Sainte-Lague favours smaller parties; the Hare quota favours smaller parties whilst the Droop and Imperiali quotas favour larger parties.

The following tables are based on examples from David M Farrell's excellent book, 'Comparing Electoral Systems' (see Further Reading).

HARE – valid votes divided by no. of seats (2000 votes, five seats)

Party	*1st Round*	*Quota*	*Seats*	*2nd Round*	*Seats*	*Total Seats*
Con	720	400	1	720 - 400 = 320	1	2
Lab	620	400	1	620 - 400 = 220		1
Lib.Dem	300	400		300	1	1
SNP	240	400		240	1	1
Ind	120	400		120		

DROOP – valid votes divided by no. of seats plus one, plus one, or part thereof (2000 votes, five seats)

Party	*1st Round*	*Quota*	*Seats*	*2nd Round*	*Seats*	*Total Seats*
Con	720	334	2	720 - 334 = 386	1	3
Lab	620	334	1	620 - 334 = 286		1
Lib.Dem	300	334		300	1	1
SNP	240	334		240		
Ind	120	334		120		

IMPERIALI – valid votes divided by no. of seats plus two (2000 votes, five seats)

Party	*1st Round*	*Quota*	*Seats*	*2nd Round*	*Seats*	*Total Seats*
Con	720	286	2			2
Lab	620	286	2			2
Lib.Dem	300	286	1			1
SNP	240	286				
Ind	120	286				

d'HONDT – valid votes divided by aggregate of seats plus one

Party	*divide by 1*	*divide by 2*	*Total Seats*
Con	720 (1st elected)	360 (3rd elected)	2
Lab	620 (2nd elected)	310 (4th elected)	2
Lib.Dem	300 (5th elected)	150	1
SNP	240	120	
Ind	120	60	

MODIFIED SAINTE-LAGUE – valid votes divided by 1.4, 3, etc

Party	*divide by 1.4*	*divide by 3*	*Total Seats*
Con	720 ÷ 1.4 = 514 (1st elected)	240 (3rd elected)	2
Lab	620 ÷ 1.4 = 443 (2nd elected)	207 (5th elected)	2
Lib.Dem	300 ÷ 1.4 = 214 (4th elected)	100	1
SNP	240 ÷ 1.4 = 171	80	
Ind	120 ÷ 1.4 = 86	40	

PURE SAINTE-LAGUE – valid votes divided by 1, then 3, then 5, etc

Party	*divide by 1*	*divide by 3*	*divide by 5*	*Total Seats*
Con	720	240	144	2
Lab	620	207	124	1
Lib.Dem	300	100	60	1
SNP	240	80	48	1
Ind	120	40	24	

The Single Transferable Vote

STV is a preferential voting system used in constituencies returning more than one member. It is used in Eire , Malta, Australia (elections to the Senate) and for elections to the Northern Ireland Assembly. It is also used in Northern Ireland for local elections and European Parliamentary elections. Voters mark their ballot paper in order of preference; i.e., '1' against the name of their first choice candidate, '2' against their second preference, '3' against their third choice, etc., etc.

Table 13 – SAMPLE BALLOT PAPER FOR STV ELECTION

Mark Candidates in Order of Preference	
2	Twist, Oliver – Labour
1	Nickleby, Nicholas – Conservative
4	Copperfield, David – Liberal Democrat
3	Rudge, Barnaby – Residents' Association
5	Chuzzlewit, Martin - Independent

The expression of a preference means that if the elector's first choice candidate cannot use the vote either because he has a surplus and is therefore elected, or because he has too few votes and cannot possibly be elected, his vote can be transferred.

Firstly, a quota has to be calculated. This is the minimum number of votes needed to secure election. The quota is equal to the number of votes divided by the number of seats plus one, and plus one again (the Droop quota).

$$\frac{V}{(S+1)} + 1$$

In the example set out in the following table, taken from the results of the Sligo-Leitrim Constituency in the Irish General Election of 1969 [14] the calculation of the quota was:

$$\frac{29{,}974}{4} + 1 = 7{,}494$$

Any candidate who secured this number of votes was elected. In this example, no candidate reached the quota, therefore the candidate with the least number of votes was eliminated and his votes redistributed. Fallon, Higgins and Mooney were all eventually eliminated and McLoughlin finally reached the quota. His surplus votes were then transferred.

It is impossible to tell which votes are surplus, so the votes are given a value equal to the ratio of the surplus to the number of transferable votes cast for McLoughlin. McLoughlin's surplus votes (8,011, minus the quota) totalled 517. His transferable votes amounted to 8,011, minus the number of non-transferable votes (205) = 7,806. The surplus, 517 was then divided by the number of transferable votes (517 divided by 7,806) to give $^{33}/_{500}$. Therefore, each continuing candidate received that fraction of every ballot paper showing a next preference for him. Gilhawley received that fraction of every paper showing a next preference for him. He received 1,046 next available preferences out of 8.011 (1,046 x $^{33}/_{500}$ = 69). There were three candidates remaining, Gallagher, MacSharry and Gilhawley.

None had reached the quota, but as further transfers would have been pointless (because there were 1,158 votes which were non-transferable; i.e., no further preferences had been marked on the ballot papers and could therefore not be redistributed) MacSharry and Gallagher were elected. If some of those 1,158 votes had been transferred to Gilhawley he could have reached the quota and defeated Gallagher for the third seat.

[14] This example is taken from 'The People and the Party System', Vernon Bogdanor (Cambridge University Press, 1981)

Table 14 – RESULTS IN THE SLIGO-LEITRIM CONSTITUENCY IN THE IRISH GENERAL ELECTION OF 1969

Candidates by Party	Stage I	Stage II O'Rourkes votes	Stage III - Gallagher's votes	Stage IV - Fallon's votes	Stage V - Higgins' votes	Stage VI - Mooney's votes	Stage VII - McLoughlin's surplus	Result
Fianna Fail								
Gallagher J	6124	(11) 6135	(70) 6205	(135) 6340	(96) 6436	(645) 7081	(132) 7213	Third
MacSharry R	5616	(18) 5634	(198) 5823	(162) 5985	(424) 6409	(912) 7321	(111) 7432	Second
Mooney J M	2267	(203) 2470	(40) 2510	(11) 2521	(41) 2562	2562 (transferred votes)		Eliminated
	14007	14239	14538	14846	15407	14402	14645	
Fine Gael								
McLoughlin J	6053	(158) 6211	(100) 6311	(527) 6838	(455) 7293	(718) 8011	(517) 7494	First
Gilhawley E	5858	(8) 5866	(111) 5977	(373) 6350	(210) 6560	(48) 6608	(69) 6677	Runner Up
Fallon J	1332	(3) 1335	(44) 1379	1379 (transferred votes)				Lost Deposit
	13243	13412	13667	13188	13853	14619	14171	
Labour								
Higgins T J	1251	(29) 1280	(410) 1690	(122) 1812	1812 (transferred votes)			Lost Deposit
Gallagher J	967	(51) 1018	1018 (transferred votes)					Lost Deposit
O'Rourke P	506	506 (transferred votes)						Lost Deposit
	2724	2298	1690	1812				
Non-transferable votes		25	54 (25+ 54 = 79)	49 (49 + 79 = 128)	586 (128+586 = 714)	239 (239 + 714 = 953)	205 (205 + 953 = 1158)	
Total	29974	29974	29974	29974	29974	29974	29974	

One of the problems with using a quota is the problem of which papers to transfer; for example, if a candidate is 100 votes over a quota of 501 – 501 votes will be left in his pile, but 100 will have to be transferred; the question is which 100 votes. This is where an element of chance may creep into STV. For example, the 501 left in the pile might all have the Liberal Democrat as their second preference, but the 100 votes which are actually transferred might have the Labour candidate as their second preference. In Australia they deal with this problem by sorting the ballot papers according to the remaining preferences, then apportioning appropriate fractions to them. The Australian Senate elections give voters thc opportunity to either vote for a party or to rank candidates in order of preference.

Of all the proportional systems, STV seems to attract the most ardent supporters. Its followers are true believers. Equally, there are those who shudder at its very mention. The traditional arguments against STV are that it inevitably results in coalition government – Ireland is frequently cited. However, coalition government does not always equal unstable government and in fact on average, governments in the Irish Republic have lasted three to four years. Another argument against STV is that it produces what is known as 'alphabetical' or 'donkey' voting; all this means is that in some constituencies the list of candidates can be so long that voters have a tendency to rank candidates not in order of preference but in the order of names they recognise on the ballot paper. It has been suggested that the order of names on the ballot paper should be randomised, thereby reducing the tendency towards alphabetical voting.

The other main argument against STV, which the Plant Commission made much of, is its non-monotonicity; this is basically the paradox that some first preference votes can actually disadvantage a candidate (see the argument in 'Comparing Electoral Systems', by David M Farrell). The Jenkins Commission toyed with the idea of recommending STV for rural constituencies, coupled with AV in urban areas, but felt ultimately, that it would be unfair to have two contrasting systems for different parts of the country. It did not feel able to recommend STV for all constituencies on the grounds that it would be 'too big a leap' for an electorate used to a simple process of placing a cross on a ballot paper.

Mixed Member Systems.

Mixed member systems are known by a variety of different names: for example, Mixed Member Proportional in New Zealand and Additional Member System in Germany. Under the Additional Member System (AMS) used in Germany, half the Members of the Bundestag are elected by first-past-the-post, whilst the other half are elected from Party lists.

The elector has two votes, one for a constituency representative and one for a Party list (see overleaf an example of a ballot paper for an election using AMS). The list seats are distributed between the Parties so as to make their total representation in the Bundestag proportional to their respective second votes. No Party which fails to gain 5% of the votes or gain three constituencies can be elected. There are no by-elections and all vacancies are filled by co-opting the next candidate on the list. The majority of candidates stand for a constituency and are given a place on their Party's list. Under AMS, there are not, as is sometimes thought, two separate elections - one for constituency MPs and one for list members. The proportion of votes gained by a party in the list section is used to determine the number of additional (if any) constituency Members a party should have. In the German system, the number of constituency MPs gained is subtracted from the total votes received by the Party in the list section and any gap is then 'topped-up'. For example; if a party won 30% of the votes in the list section, but only 20% of the seats in the constituency section, it would be entitled to 10% more MPs; these would be allocated from the list section – in the case of the German system, using the Hare allocation formula.

Table 15 – SAMPLE OF VOTING PAPER FOR ELECTION USING AMS

Voting Slip for the Parliamentary Election in the Constituency of Upper Warlingham and Whyteleafe South on 2nd May, 2002

YOU HAVE 2 VOTES

1 vote here for the election of a constituency representative (first vote)	1 vote here for the election of a list (party) (second vote)

1	Twist, Oliver -Labour			Labour	1
2	Nickleby, Nicholas - Conservative			Conservative	2
3	Copperfield, David – Liberal Democrat			Liberal Democrat	3
4	Rudge, Barnaby – Residents' Association			Residents' Association	4
5	Chuzzlewit, Martin – Independent			Independent	5

Returning officers must first calculate the results of the constituency elections. If one Party has won fewer constituencies than its overall level of support, as measured by the results of the Party list elections would indicate, it is compensated by being allocated 'additional' seats from its Party list. For example; a Party wins 50 seats out of 500, although its support in the Party list elections indicates that its true level of support is 20% rather than 10%. It would therefore be entitled to 100 seats, so it would retain the 50 constituency seats it had won and be given an additional 50. If one Party exceeds its proportionality quota in the constituency elections, it is allowed to keep those 'extra' MPs and in the case of the Bundestag, this can lead to its temporary enlargement. The Scottish and Welsh Assemblies were elected and the proposed Greater London Assembly will be elected using AMS. The Jenkins Commission has proposed a variant of AMS – AV Plus for elections to the UK Parliament.

In 1979 the Hansard Society's Commission on Electoral Reform recommended a variant of AMS, whereby three quarters of MPs would be elected in single member constituencies, with one quarter being chosen from defeated candidates ('best losers') and allocated to each Party in proportion to its share of the vote in each region. A Party not securing 5% of the vote within the region would not be eligible for seats. One of the criticisms levelled against AMS is that in the case of the best known example – the system used in Germany – the Free Democrats (FDP) have served in every coalition Government since 1949, except between 1957 and 1960, despite its share of the vote rarely reaching double figures. Another criticism is the fact that the system leads to the election of two distinct types of MP – a constituency MP and a list MP (usually elected on a regional basis) who does not have the same concerns, or indeed the same responsibilities, as his or her fellow Members. AMS may also encourage what is known as 'split ticketing' or 'split voting', whereby smaller parties concentrate on the list elections on the basis that they cannot possibly gain any constituency seats, but can, if they gain enough votes overall, be allocated some of the 'top-up' members. AMS might also lead to more pre-election coalitions, as parties standing in the constituency section sought alliances with smaller parties who stood to do reasonably well in the list section.

There are other variants of AMS. In some systems, the two votes from the constituency and lists sections are not subtracted but added together, in others one vote is used twice; firstly to elect the constituency Member and secondly, as a vote for a party in the list section. It is also possible to vary the number of list members; for example, in Italy, the list comprises only 25% of the Members of the Chamber of Deputies and the Senate. The Jenkins Commission has recommended that the percentage of list Members should be somewhere between 15% and 20% of all Members.

The Independent Commission on the Voting System and AV-Plus

As previously mentioned, the Jenkins Commission has recommended that the current FPTP electoral system be replaced by a system of 'AV-Plus'. This is basically a form of mixed member system whereby between 80% and 85% of MPs are elected in single Member constituencies using the Alternative Vote and are then 'topped up' by the addition of Members from one of 80 'top-up' areas. In most mixed member systems, the constituency candidates are elected by FPTP, but the Jenkins Commission has curiously recommended AV – a system which it rules out as a general replacement for FPTP, earlier in its report.

Lord Alexander of Weedon was the one member of the Commission to dissent from the majority report on this issue. His criticisms of AV are worth noting. He asked in his 'Note of Reservation' (Volume 1, Page 53), 'why should the second preferences of those voters who favoured the two stronger candidates on the first ballot be totally ignored and only those who support the lower placed and less popular candidates get a second bite of the cherry? Why, too should the second preferences of these votes be given equal weight with the first preferences of supporters of the stronger candidates.' He makes a very valid point and one which could equally well be levied at the Single Transferable Vote.

Under AV-Plus, voters would have two votes: one for a constituency Member and another for a 'top-up' Member, elected from a regional list. The constituency Member would not be elected by FPTP but by the Alternative Vote – so voters would rank candidates in order of preference. There would be 80 top-up areas electing between 15% and 20% of the total number of Members (two in Northern Ireland, five in Wales, eight in Scotland and 65 in England). The top-up areas would be based on existing metropolitan areas and county boundaries. This would mean fewer constituency Members and consequently would entail the readjustment and enlargement of existing constituencies. Parties would not be eligible for top-up seats unless they had contested at least 50% of the constituencies in the top-up area. Votes for an individual party in a particular top-up area would be counted and then divided by the number of constituencies won by that party within the top-up area, plus one. The party with the highest average votes would be allocated a seat.

If a further top-up seat remained then the process would be repeated but the relevant divisor would be 2, not 1 (this is basically an application of the d'Hondt formula). Where vacancies occurred in constituencies, by-elections would continue to be held, but there would be none in the top-up areas, where the next placed candidate would simply be selected.

The Jenkins Commission estimates that if the 1997 General Election had taken place using AV-Plus, the results would have been as follows:

Table 16 – 1997 GENERAL ELECTION USING AV-PLUS

PARTY	FPTP	AV-PLUS (with top up Members comprising 15% of total of 659 MPs)	AV-PLUS (with top up Members comprising 20% of total of 659 MPs)
Conservative	165	160	175
Labour	419	378	360
Liberal Democrat	46	88	90
SNP/PC	10	14	15
Northern Ireland Parties	18	18	18
Other	1	1	1
DV Score*	21	14.8	12

* A DV score means the 'degree of deviation' between a party's share of the vote and its share of the seats; i.e. votes minus seats = DV. The overall DV score is arrived at by adding together all the party's DV scores (ignoring plus and minus signs) and then dividing by two. For 1997, the DV score was 21.

These projections are based on the work carried out by Professor Patrick Dunleavy of LSE, Dr Helen Margetts of Birkbeck College, London (who acted as advisors to the Commission) and on the work of Stuart Weir, Senior Research Fellow at the University of Essex and Director of Democratic Audit. All three collaborated on 'Making Votes Count' and 'Making Votes Count 2' (published by Democratic Audit) which looked at the likely outcomes of the 1992 and 1997 General Elections under various voting systems. Their work is set out in more detail in the excellent, 'Politico's Guide to Electoral Reform in Britain' (Politico's Publishing - November 1998), and is highly recommended for those readers interested in the methodology and remodelling used to obtain the above results.

THE SCOTTISH PARLIAMENT

The Scottish Parliament consists of 129 members, 73 of whom are directly elected on a constituency basis (using the same constituencies as those used for elections to the Westminster Parliament, but with the addition of an extra seat for Orkney and Shetland) and 56 of whom are additional members, elected from the eight European constituencies (as set out in the Parliamentary Constituencies (Scotland) Order 1996, SI: 1926) using a proportional list-based system.

Table 17 – THE EIGHT SCOTTISH ADDITIONAL MEMBER REGIONS

Region	Constituencies
Central Scotland	Airdire and Shotts Coatbridge and Chryston Cumbernauld and Kilsyth East Kilbride Falkirk East Falkirk West Hamilton North and Bellshill Hamilton South Kilmarnock and Loudon Motherwell and Wishaw
Glasgow	Glasgow Anniesland Glasgow Baillieston Glasgow Cathcart Glasgow Govan Glasgow Kelvin Glasgow Maryhill Glasgow Pollock Glasgow Rutherglen Glasgow Shettleston Glasgow Springburn
Highlands and Islands	Argyll and Bute Caithness, Sutherland and East Ross Inverness East, Nairn and Lochaber Moray Orkney and Shetland Ross, Syke and Inverness West Western Isles
Lothians	Edinburgh Central Edinburgh East and Musselburgh Edinburgh North and Leith Edinburgh Pentlands Edinburgh South Edinburgh West Linlithgow Livingston Midlothian

Mid Scotland and Fife	Central Fife Dunfermline East Dunfermline West Kirkcaldy North East Fife North Tayside Ochil Perth Stirling
North East Scotland	Aberdeen Central Aberdeen North Aberdeen South Angus Banff and Buchan Dundee East Dundee West Gordon West Aberdeenshire and Kincardine
South of Scotland	Ayr Carrick, Cumnock and Doon valley Clydesdale Cunninghame South Dumfries East Lothian Galloway and Upper Nithsdale Roxburgh and Berwickshire Tweeddale, Ettrick and Lauderdale
West of Scotland	Clydebank and Milngavie Cunninghame North Dumbarton Eastwood Greenock and Inverclyde Paisley North Paisley South Strathkelvin and Bearsden West Renfrewshire

The list is a closed list and electors vote for a party not an individual candidate, except in cases where candidates stand as Independents. The Parliament has a fixed four-year term, although dissolution before this time is possible with the agreement of at least two thirds of MSPs (Members of the Scottish Parliament) or if it is not possible to agree on the appointment of a First Minister. The first elections were on 6 May 1999. MPs, peers (but not Lords of Appeal in Ordinary) EU citizens and Ministers of Religion are eligible to stand for election to the Scottish Parliament. Those disqualified to stand are basically those disqualified from membership of the House of Commons under the provisions of the House of Commons (Disqualification) Act 1975.

The right to vote was based on residency and the franchise is the same as for local government elections. This means that peers resident in Scotland are able to vote as well as EU nationals. However, UK residents overseas, eligible to vote in UK Parliamentary Elections, are not eligible to vote in elections to the Scottish Parliament.

Table 18 - MEMBERS OF THE SCOTTISH PARLIAMENT

73 Constituency MSPs	56 Additional Members
73 MSPs will be elected using the current first-past-the-post system with one MSP being elected per Constituency	7 MSPs will be elected from each of the 8 regions (the old European Parliamentary Constituencies) giving a total of 56 Additional Members. Electors within each Constituency, within each region, have two votes, one for the Constituency Member and one regional vote for a party. Where a party gains, for example, 40% of the regional votes but has already gained 40% of the Constituency seats, it will not be entitled to any Additional Members (the reason for having a list is to 'top-up' parties who have gained votes, but not seats).
	Account is taken of the number of Constituency seats gained within the European Parliamentary Constituency area.
	The number of regional votes cast for each party within the European Constituency will be counted.
	The number of regional votes cast for each party will be divided by the number of Constituency MSPs gained in the Parliamentary Constituencies contained within the relevant region, plus one.
	The party with the highest total after these calculations have been made gains the first additional member.
	The remainder of the additional Members are allocated in the same way except that the additional Members themselves are included in the calculations for the Party for which they were elected.

The d'Hondt allocation formula was selected for use in the elections for the list element of the Scottish Parliament (a fictitious example is set out below). One argument against this system is that it favours larger parties at the expense of smaller ones. This can be rectified by using different divisors. The Sainte-Lague and the Modified Sainte-Lague Versions use larger divisors, making it more difficult for larger parties to win each additional seat. It should be remembered that the Party with the highest average *after* each round gains a seat, NOT the Party with the highest average *in* each round – so for example, after round 1, the Conservatives do not gain an Additional Member, but, after round 2, they win three seats. There would be no point in continuing with another round as no Party could achieve a higher average than has already been achieved and as a result, all the seats are allocated after only three rounds.

The Scotland Act allows the number of Scottish MPs at Westminster to be reduced, if necessary, following a review by the Boundary Commission for Scotland. This will allow the Boundary Commission for Scotland to apply the 'English' rather than the 'Scottish' quota, thereby reducing the number of Scottish Constituencies. However, the Boundary Commission could still take into account 'special geographical' features. This impacts on the Scottish Parliament as the Constituency MSPs are directly related to the number of Scottish MPs at Westminster.

Orkney and Shetland are guaranteed two separate MSPs, irrespective of any reduction in the number of Scottish MPs at Westminster. There is also provision in the Act for the number of Regional seats to be reduced if the number of Constituency seats were to be reduced, so that the proportion of 56:73 can be maintained if possible. So, if the number of Constituency seats fell to 60, the number of Regional List seats would fall to 46. As the number of European Regions has to be eight, some Regions would have six Regional List Member and some would have five. The Boundary Commission has to ensure that Regions elect the same number of Regional List members, but where they differ, this should only be by one. The next Boundary Commission Review must be between 2002 and 2006, so Scotland will still elect 72 MPs to the UK Parliament at the time of the next UK General Election.

By-elections for vacancies in constituency seats will only be held three months after a full Election to the Scottish Parliament. Where a vacancy occurs before this time, it will not be filled until three months after the Election. If a vacancy occurs amongst the MSPs elected from the Regional List, the next highest eligible candidate on the relevant Party list will take the seat. The candidate may decline to take the seat. If there is no eligible candidate left on the list the seat is left vacant until the next full Election. It is not clear from the Act what the legal position will be if the next eligible candidate on the Party list is no longer a member of the Party concerned.

Table 19 – APPLYING THE D'HONDT FORMULA IN SCOTLAND

Region with 9 Constituency Members and 7 Additional Members

(* = elected)

	Seats gained in const-ituency section	**Votes gained in Region**	**1st round (votes ÷ aggregate of 1 + seats gained) (= d'hondt divisor 1)**	**2nd round (votes ÷ aggregate of 1 + seats gained) (= d'hondt divisor 2)**	**3rd round (votes ÷ aggregate of 1 + seats gained) (= d'hondt divisor 3)**	**Region-al Seats gained**
Labour	7 *(as Labour has 36% of the regional vote and approximat-ely 80% of the seats – it is not entitled to any additional members)*	400,000	400,000 ÷ 7 + 1 = 50,000 (no seat gained in 1st round, so aggregate unchanged in next round)	400,000 ÷ 7 + 1= 50,000 (no seat gained in 2nd round, so aggregate unchanged in next round)	400,000 ÷ 7 + 1= 50,000	

Conservative	2	300,000	300,000 ÷ 2 + 1 = **100,000*** (no seat gained in 1st round, so aggregate unchanged in next round)	300,000 ÷ 2 + 1 = **100,000***	300,000 ÷ 2 + 2 = **75,000***	3
Liberal Democrat	0	200,000	200,000 ÷ 0 + 1 = **200,000*** (gains 1 seat – added to aggregate in next round)	200,000 ÷ 1 + 1 = **100,000***	200,000 ÷ 1 + 2 = 66,666	2
SNP	0	200,000	200,000 ÷ 0 + 1 = **200,000*** (gains 1 seat – added to aggregate in next round)	200,000 ÷ 1 + 1 = **100,000***	200,000 ÷ 1 + 2 = 66,666	2

THE WELSH ASSEMBLY

There are currently 40 Welsh MPs – 34 Labour MPs, four Plaid Cymru MPs and two Liberal Democrats. The new National Assembly consists of 60 members, 40 Constituency Members and 20 elected using the Additional Member System from the five existing European Parliamentary Constituencies (now renamed Assembly Electoral Regions) as set out in the European Parliamentary Constituencies (Wales) Order 1994, SI: 428. Each Assembly Electoral Region returns four Members (see Table 20 overleaf).

Table 20 – WELSH ADDITIONAL MEMBER REGIONS

Region	Constituencies
North Wales	Alyn and Deeside Caernarfon Clwyd North West Clwyd South West Conwy Delyn Wrexham Ynys Mon
Mid and West Wales	Brecknock and Radnorshire Carmarthen Ceredigion Gogledd Penfro Llanelli Meirionnydd Nant Conwy

	Montgomeryshire Pembroke
South Wales West	Aberavon Bridgend Gower Neath Ogmore Swansea East Swansea West
South Wales Central	Cardiff Central Cardiff North Cardiff South and Penarth Cardiff West Cynon Valley Pontypridd Rhondda Vale of Glamorgan
South Wales East	Blaenau Gwent Caerphilly Islwyn Merthyr Tydfil and Rhymney Monmouth Newport East Newport West Torfaen

Electors have two votes – one for a Constituency MP and one for a registered Party or Independent candidate (Part I, section 4, Government of Wales Act 1998, chapter 38). The elections are carried out in the same way as the elections to the Scottish Parliament and the d'Hondt allocation formula is used (see above for an example of this). The Electoral Region Members, as opposed to the Assembly Constituency Members are elected from a closed list. Those entitled to stand as Assembly candidates are basically those who may also stand as Parliamentary Candidates, and in addition, EU citizens, peers (but not Lords of Appeal in Ordinary), ministers of religion and MPs. All those entitled to vote in Parliamentary elections may vote, with the addition of peers and EU nationals but with the exception of overseas voters.

LONDON GOVERNMENT

In a referendum on 7 May 1998, 1,230,715 (72%) Londoners voted in favour of a new Greater London Authority and an elected Mayor, whilst only 478,413 (28%) voted against. The Greater London Authority Bill 1998, sets out the details of the various functions of the GLA. Elections for the Mayor and Assembly Members will be held in May 2000. The Mayor will be elected using the Supplementary Vote, although there will be no second ballot. Under this system, voters place a cross beside the name of their first preference and beside the name of their second preference (if they wish to do so). The first preferences are then counted and if one candidate gains over 50% of the votes, he or she is elected. If no candidate receives over 50%, all the candidates, except the two receiving the highest number of votes, are eliminated and their second preferences, where applicable, are allocated to the two remaining candidates.

Assembly Members will be elected using the Additional Member System (AMS) – there will be 25 elected members and the new authority will cover the area of the 32 London Boroughs and the City of London. 14 members will represent specific geographical areas, whilst the remaining 11 will be London-wide members. Electors will have two votes, one for an Area Member and one for a political party. The Area Members will be elected using FPTP, whilst the London-wide Members will be elected from the Party lists. The Local Government Commission has now recommended the boundaries for the 14 voting areas (please see below) and these will be implemented by secondary legislation after the passage of the Greater London Bill 1998/99 (under consideration in the House of Commons at the time of writing). The Mayor and Assembly will be elected at the same time for a four-year period. The Conservatives will select their candidate for Mayor by a ballot of all party members. Potential candidates will be interviewed by representatives from each Conservative Association in the Greater London area who will shortlist three or four candidates who will then go on to a hustings stage, where all members of the Conservative Party in London will be able to vote in person. The two highest placed candidates will then go on to a postal ballot of all party members in the London.

At the time of writing, the Labour Party had yet to finalise selection methods for its candidate for Mayor of London. As far as the selection of candidates for the Assembly is concerned, 93 candidates have been shortlisted and Regions will be twinned to ensure the selection of one man and one woman.

Table 21 – GREATER LONDON ASSEMBLY ELECTORAL REGIONS

ELECTORAL REGION	BOROUGHS
Barnet & Camden	Barnet, Camden
Bexley & Bromley	Bexley, Bromley
Brent & Harrow	Brent, Harrow
Croydon & Sutton	Croydon, Sutton
City & East London	Barking & Dagenham, City of London, Newham, Tower Hamlets
Ealing & Hillingdon	Ealing, Hillingdon
Enfield & Haringey	Enfield, Haringey
Greenwich & Lewisham	Greenwich, Lewisham
Havering & Redbridge	Havering, Redbridge
Lambeth & Southwark	Lambeth, Southwark
Merton & Wandsworth	Merton, Wandsworth
North East London	Hackney, Islington, Waltham Forest
South West	Hounslow, Kingston upon Thames, Richmond upon Thames
West Central London	Hammersmith & Fulham, Kensington & Chelsea, Westminster

THE EUROPEAN ELECTIONS

The Government first introduced the European Parliamentary Elections Bill on 29 October 1997. However, the House of Lords would not give way on its amendments to the bill and it eventually ran out of parliamentary time. It was therefore reintroduced in the 1998/99 Session, paving the way for the 1999 European Elections on 10 June 1999 to be held using a regional list system of PR. The total number of MEPs remains at 87 (71 from England, eight from Scotland, five from Wales and three from Northern Ireland. England is divided into nine regions based on the regions currently covered by the Government Offices of the Regions (except for the combination of Merseyside and the North West) and Scotland, Wales and Northern Ireland constitutes single regions. Northern Ireland retains its current electoral system – the Single Transferable Vote. The responsibility for any realignment of European boundaries or revision of the number of seats per region will pass from the Boundary Commissions to the Home Secretary, who will seek to ensure that the ratio of electors to MEPs is the same in all regions. MEPs are elected from a closed regional list. Voters may choose either a party or an Independent candidate. The order in which candidates are elected depends on the order in which their Party has placed them on its list. A candidate's placing on his or her party list is crucial. For example, in the last European Elections on 10 June 1999, London returned 10 MEPs. Labour received 399,466 votes; this meant that only the first four candidates on its list were returned. Carole Tongue, an existing Labour MEP, who was placed fifth on the list, was therefore not elected. The d'Hondt formula is used to allocate seats. The deposit is £5,000 for each list of candidates and a party needs more than 2.5% of the vote to avoid its forfeiture.

Anyone entitled to vote in parliamentary elections (this therefore includes British nationals overseas) may vote in the European Parliamentary elections with the addition of peers and other EU nationals who fulfill the residency criteria. Under Schedule 2 of the European Parliamentary Elections Act 1999, regulations will set out the detailed provisions governing by-elections to fill vacancies between elections; there is likely to be a by-election only when the previous Member was an Independent candidate, in other cases a vacancy will be filled by the next candidate on the relevant party's list. Those who may stand as candidates are those who may stand in parliamentary elections, with the addition of EU nationals, peers, ministers of religion and MPs.

Table 22 – EUROPEAN PARLIAMENTARY ELECTIONS – English Electoral Regions

Region	Local government areas included	No. of MEPs
EAST MIDLANDS	44 Parliamentary Constituencies in counties of Derbyshire, Leicestershire, Lincolnshire, Northamptonshire & Nottinghamshire & unitary authorities of Leicester, Nottingham, Derby & Rutland	6
EASTERN	56 Parliamentary Constituences in counties of Bedfordshire, Cambridgeshire, Essex, Hertfordshire, Norfolk & Suffolk & unitary authorities of Luton, Peterborough, Southend-on-Sea and Thurrock	8
LONDON	74 Parliamentary Constituencies in the London Boroughs & the City of London	10
NORTH EAST	30 parliamentary constituencies in counties of Durham, Northumberland, Tyne and Wear & unitary authorities of Darlington, Hartlepool, Middlesbrough, Redcar and Cleveland & Stockton-on-Tees	4
NORTH WEST	76 parliamentary constituencies in counties of Cheshire, Cumbria, Greater Manchester, Lancashire & Merseyside & unitary authoriites of Blackburn, Blackpool, Halton & Warrington	10
SOUTH EAST	83 parliamentary constituencies in counties of Buckinghamshire, East Sussex,Hampshire, Kent, Oxfordshire, Surrey & West Sussex & unitary authorites of Bracknell Forest, Brighton and Hove, Isle of Wight, Medway Towns, Milton Keynes, Portsmouth, Reading, Slough, Southampton, West Berkshire, Windsor and Maidenhead & Wokingham	11
SOUTH WEST	51 parliamentary constituencies in counties of Cornwall, Devon, Dorset, Gloucestershire, Somerset & Wiltshire & unitary authorities of Bath and North East Somerset, Bournemouth, Bristol, North Somerset, Plymouth, Poole, South Gloucestershire, Torbay and Swindon & Isles of Scilly,	7
WEST MIDLANDS	59 parliamentary constituencies in counties of Herefordshire, Shropshire, Staffordshire, Warwickshire, West Midlands, Worcestershire & unitary authorities of Stoke-on-Trent & The Wrekin	8

Region	Local government areas included	No. of MEPs
YORKSHIRE AND HUMBERSIDE	56 parliamentary constituencies in counties of North Yorkshire, South Yorkshire & West Yorkshire & unitary authorities of Kingston upon Hull, east Riding of Yorkshire, North East Lincolnshire & North Lincolnshire and York	7

Source: European Parliamentary Elections Bill, Schedule 1

THE NORTHERN IRELAND ASSEMBLY

The new Northern Ireland Assembly consists of 108 seats, with each existing UK parliamentary constituency electing six members. Eligibility to stand for election is the same as for Westminster elections, but in addition, EU citizens, peers and members of the Irish Seneadd can also stand. Detailed rules governing the elections were set out in the New Northern Ireland Assembly (Elections) Order 1998 (No. 1287). The franchise is basically the local government franchise, so overseas voters are excluded but peers and other EU nationals may vote. The first elections were on 25 June 1998 and will take place every four years thereafter, on the first Thursday in May.

FURTHER READING

The Power Brokers: the Tory Party and its Leaders, Robert Shepherd (Hutchinson, 1991)
Constitutional and Administrative Law, A W Bradley and K D Ewing (12th Edition, Addison Wesley Longman, 1997)
Constitutional and Administrative Law, Hilaire Barnett (2nd Edition, Cavendish Publishing, 1998)
British Political Parties Today, Robert Garner and Richard Kelly (2nd Edition, Manchester University Press, 1998)
Labour's Landslide, Andrew Geddes and Jonathan Tonge (editors) (Manchester University Press, 1997)
New Labour Triumphs: Britain at the Polls, Anthony King (editor) (Chatham House Publishers, 1998)
The British General Election of 1997, David Butler and Dennis Kavanagh (Macmillan Press Ltd, 1997)
The Politico's Guide to Electoral Reform in Britain, Patrick Dunleavy, Helen Margetts and Stuart Weir (Politico's Publishing, 1998)
A Short History of the Liberal Party 1900-1997, Chris Cook (Macmillan Press Ltd, 1998)
Comparing Electoral Systems, David M Farell (Prentice Hall/Harvester Wheatsheaf, 1997)
An Appetite for Power: A History of the Conservative Party Since 1830, John Ramsden (Harper Collins, 1998)
The Electoral System in Britain, Professor Robert Blackburn (Macmillan, 1995)
'The Funding of Political Parties in the United Kingdom' – Fifth Report of the Committee on Standards in Public Life (Cm 4057,13 October 1998)

Report of the Independent Commission on the Voting System (Cm 4090,
25 October
1998)
Conservative Century: The Conservative party Since 1900, ed. Anthony Seldon and Stuart Ball (Oxford University Press, 1994)
Electoral Systems and Party Systems: A Study of Twenty-Seven Democracies, 1945-1990, Arend Lijphart (Oxford University Press,1994)
The Price of Power: The Secret Funding of the Tory Party, Colin Challen (Vision,1998)
Why MMP Must Go:The case for ditching the electoral disaster of the century, Graeme Hunt (Waddington Press Ltd, 1998)
Making Votes Count: The Case for Electoral Reform, Martin Linton & Mary Southcott (Profile Books, 1998)
The Fall of Margaret Thatcher: A Conservative Coup (Duckworth, 1991)
Honest Opportunism, Peter Riddell (Indigo, 1996)
New Britain, New Elections: The Media Guide to the New Political Map of Britain, edited by Colin Rallings and Michael Thrasher (Vacher Dod Publishing, 1999)

CHAPTER THREE - PARLIAMENT AND THE CONSTITUTION

THE UK'S UNWRITTEN CONSTITUTION

It if often said that the UK's constitution is 'unwritten', having emerged gradually over the centuries. This is only partly correct. Our constitution is only unwritten in the sense that there is no one single document to which one can refer which sets out how the country is to be governed. Constitutional matters are contained in a number of disparate Acts of Parliament, which some 'laws' derive purely from custom. For example, the Cabinet does not derive its authority from law and its functions and composition are not set out in any statute. We have no 'supreme' constitutional court whose role it is to interpret the constitution, although the House of Lords seems to have taken on this role in a recent case.[1] Whilst the way in which Members are elected to the House of Commons is set out in a number of Acts of Parliament, the way in which Parliament passes such Acts is a matter for self-regulation based on precedents, rulings and the Standing Orders of both Houses. The main disadvantage of an unwritten constitution is its lack of certainty; for example, experts disagree about the extent to which the Queen would be justified in refusing a dissolution to a Prime Minister who requested one or whether she could, constitutionally, dissolve Parliament without the consent of the Prime Minister. However, an unwritten constitution does not equal a non-existent constitution. There are five statutes which, taken together, could claim to represent a partially written constitution: Magna Carta 1297, the Petition of Right 1627, the Bill of Rights 1689, the Act of Settlement 1700 and the Human Rights Act 1998. There are numerous other statutes which one might classify as being constitutional in nature; for example, the various Representation of the People Acts, which set out who may vote in elections to one Chamber (the House of Commons) of the supreme legislative body – Parliament. There are two doctrines central to the constitution: the rule of law and the sovereignty of Parliament.

THE CONCEPT OF PARLIAMENTARY SOVEREIGNTY

Our system of government in the UK is based on the concept of parliamentary sovereignty. Whereas at one time, the sovereign or supreme body was the monarch, this role is now accorded to Parliament. Until the passage of the Human Rights Act, UK citizens did not have 'rights' set out in statute, but were entitled to do what they liked provided it did not infringe any Act of Parliament or common law rule (including the royal prerogative). Authorities on the other hand, including Parliament, were prevented from doing anything which they were not authorised to do by statute or by common law rule (including the royal prerogative). This is still the case, except with the addition of the specific rights accorded to UK citizens under the Human Rights Act 1998 (see later). If

[1] In the case of R v Secretary of State for Employment, ex parte the Equal Opportunities Commission (1994) 2 WLR 409, the House of Lords decided a UK statute was incompatible with EU law and called it 'unconstitutional'. For an interesting discussion on this case, please see, 'The House of Lords as a Constitutional Court – The Implications of EX PARTE EOC', by Patricia Maxwell in 'The House of Lords, its Parliamentary and Judicial Roles', edited by Brice Dickson and Paul Carmichael (Hart Publishing, 1999).

the Government wished to legislate to prohibit the consumption of pineapples on a Sunday, it could do so, provided Parliament agreed to the legislation. In an extreme example, if a future Parliament wished to overturn the Scotland Act 1998, which established the Scottish Parliament, it could do so, despite the fact that its establishment was endorsed in a referendum. The results of referendums carry no special legislative authority and if Parliament wishes to ignore the results of a referendum it may do so. This is not to say that Parliament or Government is unaccountable; the courts are responsible both for the interpretation of statutes and for the judicial review of ministerial decisions.

A doctrine central to parliamentary sovereignty is the concept that no Parliament may bind any future Parliament. In any conflict between a new Act of Parliament and a previous Act, the more recent prevails. The Deregulation and Contracting Out Act 1994 gave Government the power to amend statutes (primary legislation) by order (secondary legislation), but only those Acts passed in that Session, or previous Sessions of Parliament. There are some exceptions to this rule; for example, where independence has been granted to a former colony, the practice is to state that no future Act of the UK Parliament shall be deemed to extend to that country.

The most obvious limitation to parliamentary sovereignty, is the superiority of EU law, which takes precedence over UK legislation. This resulted from the passage of the European Communities Act 1972. The most famous example of this superiority is the Factortame case.[2] In this case (five cases in all) it was decided that the Merchant Shipping Act 1988 which sought to restrict foreign nationals from registering fishing fleets in the UK in order to use part of the UK quota, was contrary to EU law and that the latter took precedence.

THE SOURCES OF LAW

There are two main sources of law in the UK: legislation and judicial precedent; i.e. decisions of the courts expounding the common law or interpreting legislation. There are some Acts of Parliament which have special constitutional significance; for example, Magna Carta, which was first signed in 1215 by King John at Runnymede and which listed Baronial grievances and protested against arbitrary taxation. Other examples include the Petition of Right of 1628 and more importantly, the Bill of Rights and the Claim of Right of 1689. The latter entrenched the concept of a 'constitutional monarchy' at the accession of William and Mary to the throne. Many of its articles are still in force today; for example, Article 9, which guarantees Members of Parliament freedom of speech. The Act of Settlement of 1700 added further provisions; for example, that no one holding an office of profit under the Crown should be a Member of Parliament. This is still the case today: when a Member wishes to resign he or she applies for what is known as the 'Chiltern Hundreds', an office which does not exist, but which used to be an

[2] *R v Secretary of State for Transport, ex parte Factortame Ltd and Others (1990) 2 AC 85*
R v Secretary of State for Transport, ex parte Factortame Ltd and Others (1991) 1 AC 603
R v Secretary of State for Transport, ex parte Factortame Ltd and Others (1992) QB 680
R v Secretary of State for Transport, ex parte Factortame Ltd and Others - Case C-48/93 (1996) 2 WLR 506
R v Secretary of State for Transport, ex parte Factortame Ltd and Others (1997)

office of profit under the Crown. Taking the Chiltern Hundreds therefore disqualifies the Member concerned from continuing as an MP.

The courts follow a number of important principles when interpreting statutes; for example, that legislation is not retrospective unless specifically stated, that a more recent Act supersedes an earlier one and that Acts cannot bind the Crown unless expressly stated. Before the Crown Proceedings Act 1947, the Crown could not be sued in tort. Crown immunity was abolished by the Act. Under the 1947 Act, the Crown can be sued for breach of statutory duty; however, nothing alters the fact that Acts cannot bind the Crown unless this is expressly stated in the Act itself. For example, Crown property is in law exempt from local tax, taxation generally and public health law. This immunity has begun to be removed piecemeal; for example, by Section 60 of the National Health Service and Community Care Act 1990.

THE SEPARATION OF POWERS

It is, of course, a myth that there is any real separation of powers between the executive (government), legislature (Parliament) and judiciary in the UK. The Lord Chancellor is a member of all three, being head of the judiciary, a member of the House of Lords and a senior member of the Cabinet (its highest paid, in fact). The Attorney General and Solicitor General are Members of the Government and of the House of Commons and may act as legal advisers both to to the Government and to Parliament as a whole. The Attorney General is head of the English Bar, represents the Crown in civil matters and prosecutes in important criminal cases. In the UK, the Prime Minister is only Prime Minister by virtue of the fact that he or she is Leader of the party which commands a majority in the House of Commons. The last Prime Minister to be a Member of the House of Lords was Lord Rosebery in 1894. However, it gradually became the practice for the Prime Minister to sit in the House of Commons and when Earl Home became Leader of the Conservative Party in 1963, he had to renounce his peerage in order to seek election to the House of Commons as plain Alec Douglas-Home.

Theoretically, the Sovereign appoints members of the Government (they are technically the 'Queen's Ministers') but in practice, they are chosen by and appointed on the advice of the Prime Minister. As Ministers are required to be accountable to Parliament, they are all required to be Members of either the House of Commons or the House of Lords.

PRIME MINISTER AND CABINET

The 'Curia Regis' was the group of counsellors to whom the Norman Kings turned for political advice. It developed in the 13th century into the Privy Council. Members of the Privy Council are known as Privy Counsellors and are denoted by the prefix 'Right Honourable', or 'Rt Hon' for short . All past and current members of the Cabinet are Privy Counsellors as are the past and present Leaders of the Official Opposition and Leaders of the Liberal Democrats. Other worthies are often given the title as are some ministers who are not members of the Cabinet. Originally, the Privy Council constituted a select group of royal advisers and their heyday was probably under the Tudor monarchs, but their pre-eminence was gradually challenged by the emerging Cabinet and today the title is for most Privy Counsellors, a nominal one. Members of the Royal

Family, Archbishops and Lord Justices of Appeal are all members. Leaders of the main opposition parties are made Privy Counsellors mainly so that they can have access to what is classified information affecting national security. On being made a Privy Counsellor, members are sworn to secrecy and must sign an oath to the effect that they will not reveal anything said 'in council'. The fact that some Privy Counsellors are also members of the Cabinet, has been taken to mean that details of Cabinet meetings should not be revealed to the public. However, since the publication of the Crossman Diaries, little credence has been given to it and a succession of Cabinet Ministers have published memoirs of one sort or another.

Orders in Council (see chapter nine on delegated legislation) are approved by the Queen at a meeting of the Council, but these proceedings are merely formal. The President of the Council is a senior member of the Government and the holder is usually also the Leader of the House of Commons.

The Privy Council Office comes under the auspices of the Cabinet Office and has seven sub-committees, the most important of which is the Judicial Committee. There are six others: the Universities Committee, the Scottish Universities Committee, the Committee for the Purposes of the Crown Office Act 1877, the Committee for the Affairs of Jersey and Guernsey, the Baronetage Committee and the Political Honours Scrutiny Committee. The Judicial Committee of the Privy Council was established in 1833 to hear appeals from what were then the colonies. It is still the final court of appeal today for some Commonwealth countries and for the Channel Islands and Isle of Man. The Judicial Committee usually consists of three or five Lords of Appeal in Ordinary. The Lord Chancellor, the Lord Justices of Appeal and other members of the Privy Council who have held, or currently hold, high judicial office in the UK, or who are or have been judges in the higher courts in the Commonwealth are included. In theory, the Committee advises the Government in question.

When this body became too large and unwieldy to give effective advice, a smaller body, the 'Cabinet' came into existence. In the Eighteenth Century George I decided not to attend Cabinet meetings and as a result the Cabinet became more independent and a Leader, the Prime Minister evolved. The origins of the modern Cabinet and today's prime ministerial government may be traced back to this period. Robert Walpole was the first to be called Prime Minister – he was First Lord of the Treasury from 1721 to 1742. In the Eighteenth Century, those holding high office could only maintain support in the House of Commons through methods such as the purchase of pocket boroughs, but after the Great Reform Act of 1832 it was no longer possible to govern by such means and it came to be accepted that Ministers should hold the same views as the majority in Parliament and that the executive should be responsible to the electorate. The result of the conflict between the House of Lords and the House of Commons in 1911 (see later) left the House of Commons in the dominant position.

THE CONSTITUTIONAL MONARCHY

The Bill of Rights of 1689 confirmed the powers of Parliament and the limitations of the Monarchy. The Bill of Rights stipulated that the Crown could not tax without the consent of Parliament nor could it suspend laws or dispense with statutes unless so authorised by Parliament.

The Royal Prerogative

The royal prerogative refers to the right which, in the past, monarchs claimed gave them the power to rule. That right now belongs to Parliament; however, there are vestiges of the royal prerogative which are still exercised by the Sovereign and some which are exercised by the Government on the Crown's behalf. For example, the Queen opens each Session of Parliament and must give her assent to legislation. All Bills must receive royal Assent before becoming Acts of Parliament. Ministers may answer parliamentary questions relating to the way in which they have exercised prerogative powers. Bradley and Ewing refer to the term royal prerogative as being 'properly applied to those legal attributes of the Crown which the common law recognises as differing significantly from those of private persons'.[3] There are some very strange vestiges of the royal prerogative indeed. In his fascinating work on the royal prerogative, 'Crown Powers, Subject and Citizens', Christopher Vincenzi alludes to several, including the right to royal fish. Whales and sturgeons which are thrown ashore or caught near the shore are the property of the Sovereign. Apparently 'estrays' (tame animals which may be valuable) which are found wandering or generally loitering about the local manor or lordship are in fact the property of the Sovereign. These are not aspects of the royal prerogative which generally give rise to either concern or debate amongst constitutional experts. Of more interest, is the role played by the Queen in choosing the Prime Minister.

Theoretically, the Queen chooses her Ministers and appoints the Prime Minister. In the latter case, she must appoint the person most likely to command majority support in the House of Commons. There are some who argue that even in this day and age, where a Prime Minister dies, resigns or loses a leadership contest, the Queen is not obliged to appoint as his or her successor the duly elected Leader of the political party concerned, but could, if she chose, appoint an alternative, provided they could command a majority in the House of Commons. It is hard to imagine that the current monarch, at least, would actually go to such lengths to assert the royal prerogative. As Alan Watkins points out in 'The Road to Number 10', with regard to the election of Rt Hon John Major MP as successor to Rt Hon Margaret Thatcher as Leader of the Conservative Party and Prime Minister in 1990, 'if Her Majesty had chosen aberrantly to disregard the wishes of the MPs of the ruling party, the politician whom she chose would have refused to accept her invitation or would have been unable to form a government.' In the days before party leaders were elected, the ruling monarch could exercise some discretion as to who to appoint, but could only do so today in the most extreme circumstances. As A W Bradley and K D Ewing point out in 'Constitutional and Administrative Law', this might be where there were 'serious internal dissensions' within the ruling party or where no one party had a majority in the House or where a coalition had broken down. Where a General Election produces a majority government, exercising the royal prerogative is not a problem, but where an Election produces a hung Parliament, the monarch's position becomes more controversial.

In the event of a hung Parliament where no one party has an overall majority (more than 330 seats), the monarch faces a potentially difficult decision. The Queen is obliged to summon the Leader of the largest Party in Parliament to ask him/her to form a Government. If they are unable to do this; i.e. they cannot gain sufficient support in the

[3] A W Bradley and K D Ewing, 'Constitutional and Administrative Law' (Longman, 12th Edition, 1997)

House of Commons and have just lost, or are likely to lose, a motion of no-confidence in the House, the Queen may either agree to a request for a dissolution of Parliament and hence a General Election, or send for the Leader of the second largest Party to form a Government.

There is some dispute as to what the Queen should do in this situation - accede to a request for an immediate dissolution and second General Election? Some argue that for the monarch to refuse a Prime Minister a request for a dissolution in such circumstances equals dismissal. If the Prime Minister had been in power for a matter of months rather than weeks, a dissolution would be more acceptable. For example, on 24 January 1924, the Prime Minister, Stanley Baldwin, was defeated on an amendment to the debate on the Address and Ramsay MacDonald, Leader of the Labour Party was invited to form a Government. Writing to the Times on 14 May, 1950, when the Labour Government had a narrow majority, the King's Private Secretary, Sir Alan Lascelles, using a pseudonym, argued that the monarch should refuse a request for a dissolution if it was apparent that an alternative Government would be able to gain an overall majority in the House of Commons.

However, many believe that the Queen is constitutionally obliged to grant a dissolution to a duly appointed Prime Minister, even if he/she had never had the endorsement of the House of Commons; for example, where he/she had been returned after an Election as the Leader of the largest Party but did not have an overall majority and was likely to be defeated on the Debate on the Address. Problems also arise where an Election results in no one Party having an overall majority and where the Prime Minister attempts to hold on to power and to form a Government with a minority party. This situation arose in March 1974, when, rather than resigning immediately after the Election on 28 February, Edward Heath attempted to reach an agreement, unsuccessfully as it turned out, with the Liberal Party. His failure to do so enabled Harold Wilson to form a Government and to request a dissolution in October of that year. As Alan Watkins points out in 'The Road to Number 10', a book which does the impossible and makes constitutional issues riveting and entertaining (readers are advised to purchase a copy as soon as possible), 'Edward Heath quite properly remained Prime Minister for a few days after the February 1974 election. If he had asked for a second dissolution, there is little doubt that the Queen would have been entitled to refuse. He would then have had the choice of either continuing as Prime Minister or of resigning. The latter is the course he took, without asking for a dissolution or meeting Parliament.' Constitional experts disagree amongst themselves about the extent of the royal prerogative as it relates to Parliament. As Hilaire Barnett states in 'Constitutional and Administrative Law', 'Doubt exists as to whether the Queen can refuse the royal assent, dissolve Parliament against the government's will, and dismiss the government[4]. No government has been dismissed by the Crown since 1783'. As the last occasion on which Parliament was dissolved against the will of the Prime Minister was in 1835 and the last monarch to refuse Royal Assent was Queen Anne, there are no modern precedents on which to draw.

Some have suggested that one way to avoid controversy would be to remove the power of dissolution from the monarch to another person; for example, the Speaker of the

[4] Hilaire Barnett, 'Constitutional and Administrative Law' (Cavendish Publishing Ltd, 2nd Edition, 1998)

House of Commons. However, this might give rise to as many problems as it solved; for example, the House of Commons' first task on assembling for the first time immediately after a General Election, is to appoint a Speaker. It would be difficult for a Speaker to decide on whether or not a Prime Minister should be granted an immediate dissolution and another General Election, if that Speaker had not yet been elected. Any Speaker faced with a controversial decision would inevitably be accused of bias and this could make his or her position in the Commons intolerable.

The Government exercises the royal prerogative on behalf of the Crown in a number of ways. In civil matters, the Attorney General represents the Crown and on the advice of the Home Secretary, the Crown may pardon offenders or remit or reduce sentences. The conduct of foreign affairs is carried out by the Government by means of the royal prerogative rather than by recourse to Parliament, although the latter would be necessary in order to finance any conflict. The Government may sign treaties without consulting Parliament but where the treaty concerned envisages changes in domestic law, Parliament could frustrate the treaty if it refused to pass any subsequent legislation necessary to ratify it. As Wade and Ewing point out, 'Although an Act of Parliament may abolish or curtail the prerogative, the prior authority of Parliament is not required for the exercise of a prerogative power. For example, the Crown may recognise a new foreign government or enter into a treaty without first informing Parliament'.[5]

In opposition, the Labour Party suggested that the royal prerogative to declare war and ratify treaties should be placed on a clear statutory footing. The document 'A New Agenda for Democracy', the NEC's Statement to the 1993 Annual Conference, stated that: 'Whilst accepting that in the case of national emergency the government may be forced to act without the immediate consent of the House, adequate safeguards should be put in place to ensure that if British servicemen and women are sent into battle, there will be adequate debate over the reasons for that decision. Formal ratification by Parliament of executive action in going to war is the absolute minimum that is acceptable in a democracy.'

Until the mid-1980s it was the commonly held view that the exercise of prerogative powers by ministers was not subject to judicial review. However, two cases changed this view. The House of Lords decided in the case of *Council of Civil Service Unions v Minister of State for Civil Service (1985) AC 374* (the banning of trade unions at GCHQ) that the courts could review the way in which 'discretionary powers' under the prerogative were exercised just as they could review the way in which discretionary powers were exercised under statute. It was made clear, however, that not all prerogative powers could be subject to review in this way. It would be impossible to allow judicial review in the courts of a decision to grant a dissolution of Parliament. In the case of *R v Home Secretary, ex parte fire Brigades Union (1995) 2 AC 513* the House of Lords took the view that the Home Secretary's action in replacing a statutory scheme with one brought in using prerogative powers was an abuse of those powers. Briefly, the Criminal Justice Act 1988 introduced a new criminal injuries compensation scheme to replace the old 'tariff' scheme which had been introduced in the 1960s using prerogative powers. However, before the Act came into force, the Home Secretary decided not to proceed and to introduce a new tariff scheme instead, using prerogative powers. The Act would then be

[5] A W Bradley and K D Ewing 'Constitutional and Administrative Law' (Longman, 12th Edition, 1997)

repealed. The House of Lords came to the conclusion that this was an abuse of prerogative powers as it attempted to override the decision of Parliament to introduce a statutory scheme.

The Liberal Democrats would abolish the royal prerogative, and a written constitution would regulate the operation of government. Any action by the executive, apart from very occasional and special circumstances, would have to be justified by reference to the constitution. The Prime Minister would be directly elected by the House of Commons and the Head of State would have no right to refuse a dissolution, provided the Prime Minister had lost a vote of no-confidence. The Liberal Democrats are critical of the current abundance of Ministers in the House of Commons, which they feel increases the chances of the Government being able to push through legislation through sheer weight of numbers. They feel that, 'by consuming so large a proportion of the Commons' membership and making ministerial office the be-all and end-all of parliamentary ambition, it undermines the very processes of scrutiny and accountability it was intended to sustain'. The Liberal Democrats would allow those who were not members of either House of Parliament to be appointed Ministers, up to a limit of one-third of Cabinet and other ministerial posts. All nominations to such positions would be subject to approval by the House of Commons and those who were not Members of either House would still be expected to answer questions and make statements, etc. The ministerial payroll would be restricted to no more than 10% of the House of Commons. The Liberal Democrats would also extend judicial review to prerogative powers.

THE HUMAN RIGHTS ACT

In 'A New Agenda for Democracy' (1993) Labour backed incorporation of the European Convention on Human Rights into UK law. The document stated that: 'Incorporation could be achieved fairly easily. Parliament should pass a Human Rights Act that incorporates the rules of the convention directly into UK law, and give citizens the right to enforce those rules in the courts. It is often argued that in technical terms a British Act of Parliament cannot be 'entrenched'. We propose to protect the Human Rights Act from being undermined by either Parliament or the courts by a clause that requires that any other Act that is intended to introduce law inconsistent with the convention must do so specifically and in express terms.' This cannot prevent a future Parliament from overturning a Bill of Rights as no Parliament can bind another.

The European Convention for the Protection of Human Rights and Fundamental Freedoms is not a European Union document but a Treaty of the Council of Europe – a body established at the end of the Second World War. The UK helped draft the Convention and indeed ratified it, in 1951. However, until the passage of the Human Rights Act 1998, it had never been enshrined in UK law. Prior to the passage of the Act, although a UK citizen could bring a case against the UK in the Court of Human Rights in Strasbourg, they first had to exhaust all legal remedies within the UK.

Once this had been done, the Commission sent a report to the European Council of Ministers who could then refer it to the European Court of Human Rights. Even if the latter found that there had been a violation of the Convention (it did so in 50 cases) it could not of itself bring about any necessary changes to UK law. However, such findings were an embarassment to the UK Government which had, like all other parties to the

Convention agreed to abide by the decisions of the court. It was therefore in the position of having to rectify any problems with its national law in order to bring it into line with the Convention. The advantage of enshrining the Convention in UK law is that aggrieved UK citizens will be able to seek redress here in the UK rather than having to wait, up to five years in some cases, for a hearing in Strasbourg.

The European Convention guarantees the following basic human rights (the Articles to which the UK is a party are now set out in Schedule 1 of the Act). Articles 1 and 13 oblige parties to the Convention to apply Convention rights to all those within their jurisdiction and to secure remedies for violations of those right. They were omitted from the Bill, because in the view of the Government they would be given effect by the very passage of the Bill into law.

2. The right to life (the following are exceptions: capital punishment*; killing in self defence; in attempting a lawful arrest or preventing an unlawful escape; or whilst quelling a 'riot or insurrection') **the Sixth Protocol, also part of this Schedule, abolishes the death penalty, except in time of war*

3. The prohibition of torture

4. The prohibition of slavery or forced labour (does not include labour as part of a prison sentence or national service)

5. The right to liberty (except in the case of lawful arrest and detention – this includes the detention of those with infectious diseases, those of 'unsound' mind, vagrants, drug addicts, alcoholics and illegal immigrants)

6. The right to a fair trial (including the right to be considered innocent until proven guilty and the right to a free defence when the interests of justice so require).

7. The right not to be convicted for a criminal offence which was not an offence at the time committed (does not include crimes against humanity)

8. The right to respect for 'private' and family life (no interference with this right by a 'public authority' is allowed unless 'in the interests of national security, public safety or the economic well-being of the country, for the prevention of disorder or crime, for the protection of health or morals, or for the protection of the rights and freedoms of others')

9. The right to freedom of thought, conscience and religion (this can be limited in the interests of public safety and order, health or morals)

10. The right to freedom of expression (this may be curtailed in the interests of national security, to prevent crime, to protect health or morals or the 'reputation and rights of others' or to maintain the 'authority and impartiality of the judiciary' or to prevent the 'disclosure of information received in confidence')*

11. The right to peaceful assembly and association with others, including the right to join a trade union (rights can be restricted in the interests of national security or public safety, to prevent crime, to protect health or morals or the rights and freedoms of others)*

12. The right to marry

14. The right not to face discrimination on the grounds of sex, race, colour, language, religion, political or other opinion, national or social origin, association with a national minority, property, birth 'or other status'*

*Article 16 states that nothing in these Articles prevents signatories from restricting the 'political activity of aliens'.

The First Protocol to the Convention guarantees the right to peaceful enjoyment of possessions (Article 1), the right to free elections (Article 3) and the right to education, with respect to the 'right of parents to ensure such education and teaching in conformity with their own religious and philosophical convictions' (Article 2 on education, is subject to the UK's 1952 Reservation which states that the principle of the Article is accepted 'only in so far as it is compatible with the provision of efficient instruction and training, and the avoidance of unreasonable public expenditure').[6]

Schedule 3 of the Act gives continuing effect to the UK's derogation from Article 5(3) of the Convention which allows detention for up to seven days under the Prevention of Terrorism (Temporary Provisions) Act 1984. There are certain protocols which the UK has never ratified; for example protocol 4 which prohibits the expulsion of aliens. If in future, the UK ratifies other protocols to the Convention this can be effected by both Houses' agreement to an affirmative SI (see chapter nine on Delegated Legislation for more information).

The Human Rights Bill received Royal Assent on 9 November 1998. In brief, under section 4 of the Act, if in future the House of Lords, the Judicial Committee of the Privy Council, the Courts-Martial Appeal Court, the High Court, the Court of Appeal or the High Court of Justiciary, find that a provision of an Act of Parliament or delegated legislation is incompatible with the Convention rights as set out in the Human Rights Act 1998, they may make a declaration of incompatibility. Under section 6 of the Act it will also be unlawful for a public authority to act in a way which is incompatible with the Convention rights; however, 'public authority' does not include Parliament. A public authority will not be deemed to have acted unlawfully, if as the result of primary legislation it could not have acted differently.

The courts will not have the right to strike down legislation and necessary amendments to existing legislation will be a matter for Parliament under section 10 of the Act. Under this section, a Minister will be able to amend the offending piece of primary legislation by order (see chapter nine for more information). Schedule 2 of the Act specifies that these orders will be draft orders, to be approved by both Houses after a period of 60 days.

[6] The Convention allows a signatory state to enter a 'reservation' when one of its laws is not in conformity with a Convention provision.

However, in urgent cases, an order can be made without being first laid in draft. Representations may be made for 60 days after that and if the Minister considers it necessary, a new remedial order may be laid, but will cease to have effect unless confirmed by both Houses within 60 days (120 days after the original order was made).

When introducing a Bill, a Government Minister now has to include a statement (alongside the Explanatory and Financial Memorandum) to the effect that it is, in his or her view, compatible with the Convention. Where the Government wishes to introduce legislation which although not compatible with the Convention, it believes to be essential, it will have to make this explicit to Parliament.

It is beyond the scope of this book to consider in detail the provisions of the Human Rights Act 1998 as they relate to privacy, the press or religious organisations. The House of Commons Library has produced a series of Research Papers on the Human Rights Bill[7] during its progress through the House and these can found on the Parliament website.

THE TWO CHAMBERS OF PARLIAMENT

The UK Parliament, as denoted by the title 'Houses of Parliament', consists of more than one Chamber. The new Scottish Parliament will be unicameral (one Chamber) but the UK Parliament is bicameral (two Chambers). The Upper Chamber, the House of Lords is sometimes referred to as the second Chamber or the Parliament Chamber or, by Members of the House of Commons, as the 'other place'. The House of Commons is the lower or first Chamber. Members of the House of Commons (all 659 of them) are elected, but Members of the House of Lords are unelected; they are either members by right (they have inherited a title which permits them to sit in the House of Lords), they are one of the 26 Archbishops or Bishops entitled to sit in the House, or they have been granted Life Peerages.

The House of Lords

Parliament originated in the King's Counsel, consisting of Archbishops, Bishops, Abbots, Earls, Barons, Royal Ministers, etc. By 1236, some of the meetings of the Counsel were being called 'Parliaments' and by the end of the 14th Century the House of Commons sat separately. From its earliest days the House of Lords has been composed of Lords Spiritual and Lords Temporal. The House of Lords is essentially a revising Chamber. It 'fine tunes' legislation. There is more cross-party co-operation and less party-political point-scoring. This is partly due to the presence in the Lords of the Crossbenchers. These are peers with no party allegiance who sit as 'Crossbenchers' in the House (the Crossbenches are physically in the middle of the Chamber between the Government and Opposition front benches). Crossbenchers are peers who are not aligned to any one particular party grouping in the House of Lords. The Crossbenchers often vote as a

[7] The Human Rights Bill (HL) Bill 119 of 1997-98: churches and Religious organisations (13 February 1998); The Human Rights Bill (HL), Bill 119 of 1997-98: privacy and the press (13 February 1998); The Human Rights Bill (HL) Bill 119 of 1997-98: Some constitutional and legislative aspects (13 February 1998) and The Human Rights Bill (HL), Bill 119 of 1997-98 (13 February 1998).

distinct group and have weekly meetings. Some peers prefer to call themselves 'independents' rather than Crossbenchers, but the majority of those who do not belong to a party grouping, sit on the Cross Benches. There are also places designated for Cross-benchers in the House of Commons, but as there is only one independent MP, the space is usually used as an overflow for other Members.

The following are disqualified from sitting in the House of Lords:

- aliens
- persons under 21
- bankrupts
- those convicted of treason

As of 1 March 1999, there were 1,294 Peers entitled to sit in the House of Lords. The House of Lords can be divided into two groups: Lords Spiritual and Lords Temporal.

Lords Spiritual

Two Archbishops and 24 bishops of the Church of England (those appointed after 1976 are subject to a retirement age of 70) are entitled to sit in the House of Lords. Those bishops entitled to sit in the House of Lords are the Bishops of London, Durham and Winchester and the 21 next most senior bishops.

Lords Temporal

Hereditary Peers

This includes 'peers by succession' who have inherited their titles and 'Hereditary Peers of the First Creation' - those peers who have had hereditary titles conferred on them; e.g. the Prince of Wales. It is not true to say that only male heirs inherit – some baronies originally created by a Writ of Summons, not Letters Patent can descend to female as well as male heirs, as can some Scottish peerages. Some peerages created by Letters Patent descend by something called 'Special Remainder', which means they can be inherited by a woman. Hereditary peeresses in their own right were permitted to take their seats in the House of Lords under the Peerage Act 1963. Lord Diamond's valiant attempt to allow peers to choose to whom their title should descend was defeated at Second Reading in the House of Lords in 1992 and again in 1994 (26 November 1992 and 7 March 1994). Until the passage of the Peerage Act 1963, hereditary peers were not able to renounce their titles. The succession of Tony Benn MP to the Viscountcy of Stansgate in 1960 meant that he could no longer sit as a Member of the House of Commons (you cannot be a member of both Houses at the same time). He wished to renounce his peerage in order to continue to sit in the House of Commons. As his Bristol South East seat had become vacant as a result of his succession to the title, a by-election was called, which he fought and won. The Election Court disbarred him from taking his seat and it was the runner-up, St Clair, who took his place in the Commons. Eventually, the leadership crisis in the Conservative Party lead to the passing of the Peerage Act 1963, allowing both Tony Benn and Earl Home to renounce their titles. Under the provisions of the Act, peers may renounce their titles for their lifetime.

Life Peers

Life Peers under the Appellate Jurisdiction Act 1876

These are the so-called 'Law Lords', who are appointed to sit in the House of Lords in order to hear appeals, although they may take part in all non-judicial business of the House as well.

Life Peers under the Life Peerages Act 1958

The 1958 Act empowered the Crown to create Life Peers who would be entitled to sit and vote in the House of Lords and whose peerages would expire on their death. Life Peerages are usually given to those who have given a lifetime's service in a particular field and/or to those who are to become 'working peers', those appointed by the Crown on the advice of the Government and Opposition Parties, to carry out the hard graft of day to day business in the House. Former Prime Ministers and most former Cabinet Ministers are given Life Peerages. The Life Peerages Act 1963, enabled someone to disclaim a peerage for their own lifetime. They could therefore stand and vote in parliamentary elections. Under the Act, Hereditary Peeresses in their own right were also admitted to the House as were all Scottish Peers.

Lords who have not received a Writ of Summons issued by the Lord Chancellor's office, cannot take their seat. These include peers under 21, those who have not established their right to succession or those who have not completed the formalities required on the death of a predecessor. Bankrupts and aliens are disqualified from receiving a writ of summons. At the beginning of a new Parliament, Lords present their writ of summons at the Table of the House and take the Oath (or Affirmation) of Allegiance to the Queen.

Composition of the House of Lords (1 March 1999)

Type of Peerage	*No*	*Women*	*Party (figures for Party do not include any peers who have not received a Writ of Summons or who are on leave of absence)*				
			Con	Lab	Lib. Dem	Cross Bench	Other
Archbishops	2						
Bishops	24						
Hereditary Peers (who have succeeded to their titles)	751	16	303	18	24	208	78
Hereditary Peers of the First Creation	8		3	1		4	
Life Peers under the Appellate Jurisdiction Act 1876 (Law Lords)*	29						
Life Peers under the Life Peerages Act 1958	480	87	171	157	44	124	6
TOTAL (including 67 Lords without Writs of Summons, three of whom are minors (under 21) and 60 peers on leave of absence from the House)						***1,294***	

* Law Lords sit as Crossbenchers

Source: House of Lords Information Office

Composition of the House of Lords by Rank (1 March 1999)

Princes ('of the Blood Royal') (the Prince of Wales)	1
Archbishops	2
Dukes	25
Dukes of the Blood Royal (Duke of Edinburgh, Duke of Gloucester, Duke of Kent and Duke of York)	3
Marquesses	34
Earls	169
Countesses	5
Viscounts	103
Bishops	24
Barons/Lords	830
Baronesses	95
Ladies	3
TOTAL	***1,294***

Source: House of Lords Information Office

Since coming to power in May 1997, Rt Hon Tony Blair MP has created half the number of life peerages created by Rt Hon Margaret Thatcher during her entire period of office (1979-1990). However, not all the recipients sit as Labour peers.

Many peers rarely or never attend the House of Lords – they are referred to as 'backwoodsmen'. They occasionally emerge from their country estates to vote on matters of great importance to the Government. Lord Williams of Mostyn referred to the backwoodsmen who had appeared in support of the Opposition on 18 November 1998, during the show-down between Commons and Lords on the issue of closed lists for the European Elections.

Lord Williams of Mostyn: 'My Lords, everyone here tonight knows the genuine regard that I have for this place, which grows - as for all of us - from year to year. I say "everyone here tonight" - even those noble Lords whom I have never seen before.
Noble Lords: Name them!
Lord Williams of Mostyn: My Lords, I cannot name them because I do not know their names. (18 November 1998 – HL Col: 1354)

The Role of the Lord Chancellor

The Lord Chancellor, currently Rt Hon Lord Irvine of Lairg QC, has three roles; he is head of the judiciary, a senior member of the Cabinet in charge of the Lord Chancellor's department and the House of Lords' equivalent to the Speaker of the House of Commons. His functions are executive, legislative and judicial. In fact, the Lord Chancellor outranks the Prime Minister and receives a higher salary in recognition of the fact. The position of Lord High Chancellor of Great Britain was originally one of adviser to and signer-of-letters for the King. All correspondence was signed with a seal – the Great Seal and, as a result, the Lord Chancellor became the official Keeper of the Great Seal. The Great Seal is basically a mould, from which individual seals can be made for use, for example, on the Letters Patent which all new peers receive (the seals themselves are plastic). There have been three saintly Lord Chancellors: Thomas More, Thomas a Becket and Thomas Cantilupe.

There is no Department of Justice in this country and legal functions and responsibilities are scattered throughout Whitehall, from the Attorney General and Solicitor General to the Home Office and the Treasury; however, the Lord Chancellor's Department is responsible for the administration of the courts, the Law Commission, Land Registry and Public Records Office, amongst other things. The Lord Chancellor advises the Crown on the appointment of High Court judges and circuit judges and is also responsible for the appointment of recorders, JPs and stipendiary magistrates. The Lord Chancellor is also the Chairman of the Judicial Committee of the Privy Council.

In the Lord Chancellor's absence the Woolsack is occupied by a Deputy Speaker or Deputy Chairman. Whilst the Speaker in the House of Commons has but three deputies, the Lord Chancellor has 28. He may take part in debates and may vote in all divisions, although he does not have a casting vote. He announces the motion to be debated or the amendment to be considered and the results of any divisions, but does not call speakers other than the movers of amendments. The Lord Chancellor does not rule on procedural matters as the Speaker would in the House of Commons; this is more likely to be done by the Leader of the House.

Control of accommodation and services in the House of Lords is vested in the Lord Chancellor but this control is exercised by the House of Lords Offices Committee and its Sub-Committee on Administration whose agent is the Gentleman Usher of the Black Rod.

The Chairman and Principal Deputy Chairman of Committees

The Chairman and Principal Deputy Chairman of Committees in the House of Lords are salaried positions and are appointed at the beginning of each Session of Parliament, on the afternoon of the Queen's Speech.

The Chairman of Committees takes the chair in all Committees of the Whole House. His role is similar to that of the Chairman of Ways and Means in the House of Commons. He supervises all Provisional Order Confirmation Bills, Private Bills and certain delegated legislation. He is also Principal Deputy Speaker and has a panel of Deputy Speakers and Deputy Chairmen to assist him in his roles as Deputy Speaker and chair of Committees of the Whole House, respectively. The Principal Deputy Chairman assists the Chairman in his duties and acts as Chairman of the European Communities' Select Committee. At the beginning of every Session a number of peers are, on the recommendation of the Committee of Selection, appointed Deputy Chairmen of Committees. They are able to take the Chair, in the absence of either the Chairman or Principal Chairman, during any Committee Stage on the floor of the House.

The other major function of the Chairman of Committees is his chairmanship of the House of Lords Offices Committee – the nearest the House of Lords has to the House of Commons Commission (although it does not appoint staff – this is the role of the Clerk of the Parliaments department and Black Rod's Office). The Clerk of the Parliaments sits on the Committee along with 29 Peers. There are five sub-committees: Finance and Staff, Library and Computers, Administration and Works, Refreshment and the Advisory Panel on Works of Art. Estimates of House of Lords' expenditure are presented to the House of Commons by the Treasury.

The Counsel to the Chairman of Committees performs a similar role to that performed by Speaker's Counsel in the House of Commons. He/she can provide legal advice to peers, particularly members of the Delegated Powers and Deregulation Committee.

Earl Marshall

The Earl Marshall is the Queen's representative in the House of Lords with responsibility for ceremony. In fact, this responsibility is delegated to Black Rod.

Garter King of Arms

The Garter King of Arms has responsibility for the introduction of peers and for making sure that their titles are correct; for example, you cannot choose as your title, 'The Duke of Crouch End' if some other unfortunate peer has already laid claim to it. Garter King of Arms heads up the College of Arms which is the home of the Heralds. If for any reason you want a coat of arms, these are the people to see.

Lord Great Chamberlain

The Lord Great Chamberlain is the Queen's representative at Westminster and officially has responsibility for the State Opening of Parliament, although Black Rod now undertakes this task. By a strange historical quirk, to be appointed Lord Great Chamberlain you have to be either the Marquess of Cholmondeley, the Earl of Lincoln or the Earl of Ancaster. The title of Lord Great Chamberlain was somehow inherited by two sisters in 1781 and their male descendants now swop it amongst them at the end of each reign.

Some Important Officers of the House of Lords

Black Rod

What the Serjeant at Arms is to the Speaker of the House of Commons, Black Rod (or the Gentleman Usher of the Black Rod and Serjeant at Arms, to give him his full title) is to the Lord Chancellor. The first such usher (Latin for doorkeeper) was employed by the Knights of the Order of the Garter, an order which had been established by Edward III. His symbol of office was a black rod. It was only later that he began to fulfil the same functions in the House of Lords.

Black Rod is responsible for the administration of the House of Lords; i.e. accommodation, security and the general services and running of the House. The Clerk of the Parliaments is responsible for the legislative functions of the House of Lords and his equivalent in the House of Commons is the Clerk of the House. Black Rod is usually an ex-serviceman (the position is now open to competition) as are the majority of the doorkeepers under his command. This elite battalion is responsible for maintaining law and order in and around the Chamber and for preventing unseemly behaviour and general disturbances in the public galleries. As Secretary to the Lord Great Chamberlain, Black Rod is responsible for ceremonial arrangements in the House.

Black Rod's deputy is the Yeoman Usher of the Black Rod and Deputy Serjeant at Arms and it is his duty, at the beginning of each day's sitting in the House of Lords, to precede the Lord Chancellor in the Lord Chancellor's procession, carrying the Mace. Black Rod brings up the rear. On two nights each week, Black Rod must accompany the Mace out of the Chamber at the end of the sitting.

It is, of course, for having a door slammed in his face that Black Rod is most famous. At the State Opening of Parliament, Black Rod is ordered to summon the Commons to hear the Queen's Speech in the House of Lords (see chapter five for more information on the State Opening). Black Rod always acts as the Messenger of the Sovereign whenever the attendance of the Commons is required. When he arrives, the Commons slams the door in his face as a symbol of their determination not to be bullied by the monarch and of their independence from the Crown. He has to knock three times before being admitted.

The Clerk of the Parliaments

The Clerk of the Parliaments is the head of the permanent staff of the House of Lords and is appointed by the Crown. He is responsible for producing the House of Lords

Minutes of Proceedings and in the Chamber has responsibility for calling each item of business as it is reached. He also gives advice to peers on procedural matters. It is the Clerk of the Parliaments who endorses bills before their return to the House of Commons. He is the corporate face of the House of Lords, having ultimate responsibility for the property and land of the House of Lords; however, the day-to-day running of the House is the responsibility of Black Rod.

He is responsible for the preparation of the texts of Acts of Parliament and has the task of reading out the Royal Assent to bills in Norman French. When the House sits to hear judicial business he acts as the Registrar of the Court. He is assisted by the Clerk Assistant and Reading Clerk, who sit to the right of him at the Table of the House. The former is responsible for keeping the Minutes of proceedings of the House and prepares the Order Paper and the latter records daily attendances and reads out the Letters Patent of new peers, as well as the Royal Commissions for prorogation and Royal Assent. They both have innumerable other duties.

There are a number of offices under the auspices of the Clerk of the Parliaments Department. These include:

The Accountant's Office

The Accountant's Office is responsible for the payment of Peers' daily expenses and staff salaries and, as the name would suggest, keeps all the accounts of the House.

The Committee Office

The Committee Office is responsible for the conduct of the committees of the House.

The Establishment Office

The Establishment Office is responsible for personnel management within the House; for example, recruitment, pay, conditions, etc.

The Journal and Information Office

The Journal and Information Office is responsible for the compilation and issue of the Journals of the House and for the provision of general information to the public.

The Judicial Office

The Judicial Office adminsters all the judicial business of the House of Lords. The Principal Clerk is also the Registrar of Peers' Interests.

The Printed Paper Office

The Printed Paper Office is the House of Lords' equivalent of the Vote Office and is the office where peers may obtain parliamentary papers of all kinds, including Bills, marshalled lists of amendments, Lords Minutes, House of Lords reports, etc.

The Private Bill Office

This office supervises the passage of Private Bills through the House of Lords.

The Public Bill Office

The Public Bill Office supervises the passage of public bills through the House of Lords and is responsible for the printing of bills and amendments.

Other offices include the Library, the Overseas Office, the Computer Office, the Refreshment Department and the Record Office. Having escaped the worst of the fire of 1834, the House of Lords, unlike the House of Commons, has records dating back to 1510, when a Journal of Proceedings was first begun. These records are now held in the Victoria Tower (the opposite end of the Palace from Big Ben). The Record Office contains 'master' copies of all Acts of Parliament from 1497. Other historical gems include the Bill of Rights of 1689 and the record relating to the trial of Mary Queen of Scots. A number of publications are available from the Record Office, including the 'Letters of the Second Earl of Tweeddale, 1672 to 1692' (£3.00), and 'Witnesses before Parliament: A Guide to the Database of Witnesses in Committees on Opposed Private Bills 1771-1917' (£3.00). You can also purchase a copy of Charles I's death warrant, a 'Short Guide to the Records of Parliament' and a guide to the works of art in the House of Lords. In short, the Record Office overseas a wealth of material relating to the history of the House of Lords and had it not been for the accursed tally sticks there would be an equal abundance of material about the House of Commons.

The Role of the Law Lords

In the early middle ages, the supreme law giver was the King and all petitions for justice were addressed to him. He sought advice from the 'Curia Regis' (King's Council) which later developed into the Mediaeval 'concilium regis ordinarium'. From the late 13th century it sat with the Lords spiritual and temporal to form the 'magnum concilium in parliamento' or 'curia parliamenti'. Hence, the House of Lords became the highest court in the land and the final court of appeal. The Lords of Appeal in Ordinary (Law Lords) are Life Peers created under the Appellate Jurisdiction Act 1876. The Act was a recognition of the need to appoint well-qualified people as Law Lords and provided the first life peerages. The term Law Lords covers both serving and retired Law Lords. They sit in the House just as other Members, taking part in all and not just judicial business. There can be up to 12 serving Law Lords at one time. Under the Judicial Pensions and Retirement Act 1993, Law Lords must retire at 70; however, they continue to sit in the House of Lords after they have retired as active Law Lords and make a considerable contribution to debates on judicial and criminal matters. The Lord Chancellor is the only Member of the House of Lords who may sit in a judicial capacity after the age of 75. The Appellate Committee usually consists of five Law Lords (occasionally this is seven). The final judgment of an appeal is always given in the Chamber itself, usually on a Thursday afternoon and a vote is taken on the report of the Appellate Committee which heard the appeal. This is a reminder of the fact that it is the Court of Parliament which hears and determines the appeals. It was only in 1948 that the practice of being tried by ones peers was abolished. The last time it had occurred was in 1935 in the case of

Lord de Clifford. Judicial business can be taken even on days when the House is prorogued or during a dissolution.

Leave to Appeal

If a lower court grants leave to appeal to the House of Lords, the appeal proceeds directly to one of the two Appellate Committees of the House of Lords, but if the lower court refuses leave to appeal this may be sought from the House itself, by presenting a petition for leave to appeal within one month (14 days for criminal cases). Leave to appeal is sought by petition and these petitions are referred to an Appeal Committee (there are two) consisting of three Lords of Appeal in Ordinary. The Committee decides whether or not leave to appeal should be granted. If leave is granted, the 'Respondents to the petition' (the opposing party in the case) may object within 14 days. If the Committee cannot reach a unanimous decision, there is a public hearing attended by both parties, where evidence is heard. Then the Committee makes its decision. The subsequent course of an appeal is governed by the House of Lords rules (Judicial Standing Orders) and the Practice Directions in Civil and Criminal Appeals.

When leave to appeal has been granted, a petition is presented to the House praying that the order may be 'reversed, varied or altered'. The appellant must deposit a substantial sum of money as security against costs which may be awarded against him. The case is then referred to an Appellate Committee (of which there are two) consisting of five (or occasionally seven) Law Lords. The Committee is addressed by Counsel. Judgments are given at 2.00pm on Thursdays in the Chamber of the House of Lords. Any peer can attend but only the Law Lords may take part in the proceedings. The Law Lords' opinions are printed just before the House sits and in the Chamber they simply read out the reasons for reaching those opinions. The House then votes on whether or not to accept the report of the Appellate Committee.

Decisions of the House of Lords need not necessarily be final, as the Pinochet case demonstrated. Briefly, Senator Pinochet came to England in October 1998 for medical treatment. Spain issued international warrants for his arrest and extradition to Spain. As a result he was arrested in London under the Extradition Act 1989. He then applied to the Queen's Bench Divisional Court to have the warrants quashed. The court quashed the warrants but stayed the case whilst an appeal was made to the House of Lords on a question of law, which was the extent to which a former Head of State enjoyed freedom from arrest and extradition in the UK in relation to crimes committed whilst Head of State. The appeal in the House of Lords was heard by Lord Slynn of Hadley, Lord Lloyd of Berwick, Lord Nicholls of Birkenhead, Lord Steyn and Lord Hoffmann in November 1998.[8]

Amnesty International was given leave to intervene in the case. By a majority of three to two (Lords Slynn and Lloyd disagreed) their Lordships reinstated the second of the warrants and held that Senator Pinochet was not entitled to immunity. It was therefore a

[8] *Regina v Bartle and the Commissioner of Police for the Metropolis and Others (Appellants) Ex Parte Pinochet (Respondent) (on Appeal from a Divisional Court of the Queen's Bench Division) and Regina v Evans and Another and the Commissioner of Police for the Metropolis and Others (Appellants) Ex Parte Pinochet (Respondent) (On Appeal from a Divisional Court of the Queen's Bench Division (25 November 1998))*

matter for the Home Secretary to decide whether to continue proceedings for Senator Pinochet's extradition under the Extradition Act 1989.

It was only after the decision that the links between one of the Law Lords, Lord Hoffmann and Amnesty International became clear. Lady Hoffmann worked for Amnesty and Lord Hoffmann was a Director of Amnesty International Charity Limited. As a result, Pinochet petitioned the House of Lords to have the previous decision set aside. In his conclusions,[9] Lord Browne-Wilkinson stated that, 'In principle it must be that your Lordships, as the ultimate court of appeal, have power to correct any injustice caused by an earlier order of this House. There is no relevant statutory limitation on the jurisdiction of the House in this regard and therefore its inherent jurisdiction remains unfettered'. He cited the case of *Cassell & Co Ltd v Broome (No. 2) (1972) AC 1136* in which the House of Lords varied an order for costs which it had made previously. It was for this reason that the previous decision of their Lordships was set aside. The case was reconsidered and their Lordships gave judgment on 24 March 1999. They ruled that Senator Pinochet was entitled to immunity for crimes committed whilst head of state, but that he was not entitled to immunity from prosecution for crimes of torture after 29 September 1988, the date on which section 134 of the Criminal Justice Act 1988, which implemented the Torture Convention of 1984 in the UK, came into force. Anyone who would like to read this and other judgments in full can find them on the Parliament website (www.parliament.uk).

Rights of Appeal to the House of Lords

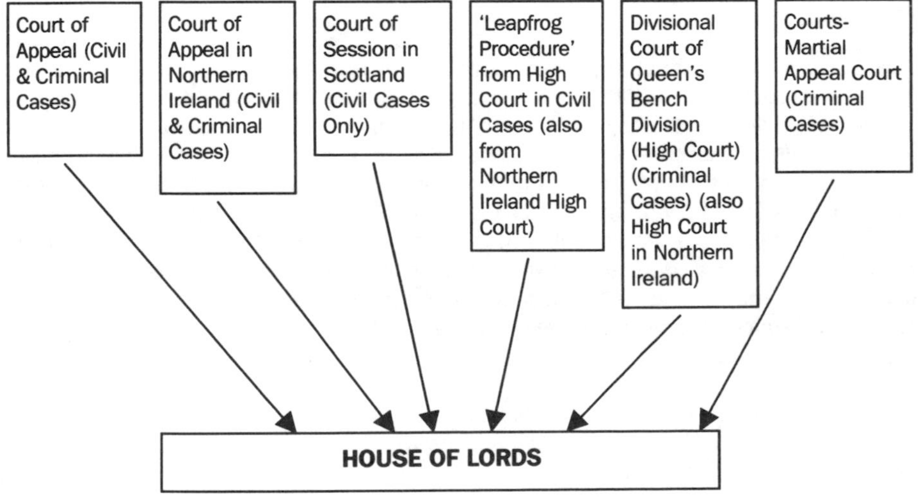

[9] *In Re Pinochet (Oral Judgment, 17 December 1998, Reasons, 15 January 1999)*

HOUSE OF LORDS REFORM

Previous Attempts at Reform

The most important 20th century reform of the House of Lords (to date) has been the implementation of the Parliament Act of 1911 and subsequently the Parliament Act 1949. The gradual practice of the House of Commons of embodying all taxation changes in a single Bill, the Finance Bill, meant that the House of Lords could reject the entire Bill and hence all the Government's revenue raising plans. The rejection by the House of Lords of the Liberal Government's so-called 'People's Budget' (the Finance Bill of 1909) persuaded Prime Minister, Herbert Asquith, to call a General Election in January 1910, which he won. Although the House of Lords then passed the Budget, the Government decided to curb their powers and introduced a Parliament Bill to abolish the House of Lords veto on legislation. In order to ensure the Bill's passage through the House of Lords, they threatened to create 1000 Liberal peers. The King refused to consent unless a General Election was called, which the Liberals subsequently won in December 1910. The prospect of 1000 Liberal peers was too horrible to contemplate and their Lordships reluctantly gave way and passed the Parliament Bill.

The Parliament Act was finally enacted in 1911. Its provisions mean that a Bill certified as a 'Money Bill' will be presented for Royal Assent, even if it has not been passed by the Lords without amendment within one month of being received from the House of Commons, provided it has been sent to the Lords one month before the end of the session.

The Act also provided that any other Public Bill, except one for extending the life of a Parliament, could become an Act of Parliament without the consent of the House of Lords if it had been passed by the House of Commons in three successive Sessions - two years having elapsed since its first Second Reading in the House of Commons and its final passing in that House, provided it had been sent up to the House of Lords at least one month before the end of each of the three Sessions. The Act also reduced the maximum duration of a Parliament from seven to five years. The Parliament Act 1949 reduced the number of sessions (which need not necessarily be two sessions of the same Parliament) in which a bill must be passed by the House of Commons from three to two and reduced the period between the first Second Reading and the final passing of the bill from two years to one.

The effect of the two Parliament Acts is therefore, that when a bill which originated in the House of Commons is passed in two successive Sessions, one year having elapsed between the first Second Reading and the final passing of the bill in the House of Commons, it will receive Royal Assent, even if disagreed to by the House of Lords, provided it was sent from the House of Commons to the House of Lords one month before the end of each Session.

The Parliament Acts do not apply to the following: bills originating in the House of Lords, bills to extend the life of a Parliament beyond five years, Provisional Order Confirmation Bills, Private Bills and delegated legislation. When a bill, other than a Money Bill, is presented to the Queen for Royal Assent, it must be endorsed with the signed certificate of the Speaker that the provisions of section 2 of the Parliament Act 1911 have been complied with.

An interesting feature of the Parliament Act 1911 is its Preamble, which states that, 'it is intended to substitute for the House of Lords as it at present exists a Second Chamber constituted on a popular instead of a hereditary basis'. Attempts to remove hereditary peers from the House of Lords are nothing new.

Other attempts at reforming the House of Lords have not met with much success. The Queen's Speech for 1967/68 pledged the Government to eliminating the hereditary basis of the House of Lords. All-party talks on Lords' reform took place between 8 November 1967 and 20 June 1968. When the Conservative Opposition in the House of Lords opposed the Southern Rhodesia (United Nations Sanctions) Order 1968, the Government broke off the talks, but decided to pursue reform of the Upper Chamber, publishing a White Paper in November 1968. The White Paper would have established a two-tier House of Lords, with 230 voting peers. Existing hereditary peers would not have been able to vote but would have been able to continue to sit in the House of Lords for the remainder of their lifetime. The time in which the Lords could delay legislation would have been reduced to six months. The Parliament (No 2) Bill 1968/69 embodied these reforms but received a majority of only 100 in the House of Commons on Second Reading. After the House had spent 11 days in Committee on the floor of the House, the Bill was abandoned in April 1969.

Party policy on reforming the House of Lords has changed over the years. After the failure of the 1968 Bill, Labour moved to a position of outright abolition of the Lords, whereas the Conservatives considered its replacement with a two-thirds elected, one-third appointed Chamber. By 1992, Labour was advocating reform not abolition and in 'A New Agenda for Democracy' (NEC Statement to Labour Party Conference, 1993) Labour stated that: 'We therefore propose replacing the House of Lords with an elected second chamber'. However, the 1997 manifesto committed the Party to a two-stage reform: firstly, the removal of hereditary peers from the Lords, followed by a review of its future membership and structure.

The House of Lords Bill

In accordance with this manifesto commitment, on 20 January 1999 the Labour Government published a bill to remove hereditary peers from the House of Lords (House of Lords Bill 1999/2000) and in addition a White Paper, 'Modernising Parliament, Reforming the House of Lords' (Cm 4183) setting out its proposals for the transitional House of Lords. A Royal Commission under the Chairmanship of Lord Wakeham was also established to consider the role and functions of any new second Chamber. The reforms can be broken down into two stages: Stage I – the removal of hereditary peers and the maintenance of a transitional House of Lords; Stage II – the implementation of the Royal Commission's proposals after consideration by a Joint Committee and the passage of any necessary legislation.

The Government's proposals were, in brief:

- to remove the right of all hereditary peers to sit and vote in the House of Lords
- to allow hereditary peers (after the passing of the House of Lords Bill) the right to vote and stand in parliamentary elections without the need to disclaim their peerages
- the Government might accept an amendment to the Bill in the House of Lords to allow some hereditary peers to remain, provided 'normal conventions relating to the Government's legislative programme are being observed' (HC Col: 909)[10]
- a new Appointments Commission to appoint new Cross Bench peers to the transitional second Chamber
- a Royal Commission to make proposals for a new Second Chamber (by the end of 1999)
- a Joint Committee of both Houses to consider the Commission's proposals

At the time of writing, the House of Lords Bill, having emerged unamended from the House of Commons, had just undergone a mammoth two-day Second Reading debate in the House of Lords and was in the midst of its Committee Stage. The Government accepted the amendment tabled by Lord Weatherill, Leader of the Crossbenchers, to retain 92 hereditary peers in the interim House of Lords. These 92 peers would comprise the Earl Marshall and the Lord Great Chamberlain, 75 peers elected by party grouping (42 Conservatives, 28 Crossbenchers, 3 Liberal Democrats, 2 Labour) and 14 deputy speakers.

The Transitional House of Lords

Once hereditary peers have been removed from the House of Lords, the composition of the House by party will be as follows (based on numbers of peers at 1 March 1999 and excluding Lords Spiritual and Lords of Appeal in Ordinary):

Con	Lab	LibDem	Xbench	Other
171	157	44	124	6

In the White Paper, 'Modernising Parliament, Reforming the House of Lords' the Government stated that it would seek only 'broad parity of numbers with the main Opposition party'. Before the publication of the White Paper a number of people had expressed some concern at the prospect of a second Chamber packed with 'Tony's cronies', and to deal with this criticism the Government has decided to establish a new Appointments Commission to oversee recommendations for new Crossbench peers. The White Paper makes clear that 'new members of the House of Lords will continue to be appointed in accordance with the Life Peerages Act 1958'. The new Commission will be an advisory non-departmental public body consisting of respresentatives of the three main political parties. However, the independent members of the Commission will be in the majority and one of their number will be its Chairman. It will invite nominations for

[10] It was this plan, proposed by Lord Weatherill (former Speaker and Leader of the Crossbenchers in the House of Lords) and the then Leader of the Conservative Opposition in the Lords, Lord Cranborne and agreed with the Government without the consent of the Leader of the Conservative Party, Rt Hon William Hague MP, which led to Lord Cranborne's dismissal.

new Crossbench peers from members of the public. The party Leaders will continue to put forward nominations for new life peers to represent them in the House of Lords, but the new Commission will be able to vet these nominations. The Prime Minister will not have a right of veto over nominations which the Appointment's Commission has accepted. The Political Honours Scrutiny Committee will continue to oversee nominations for other honours. Peerages will still be awarded by the Queen and the names of those recommended will continue to be submitted by the Prime Minister.

The Royal Commission

The Royal Commission[11] which has been established to consider longer term proposals for reform of the House of Lords has been charged with reporting before the end of 1999. Its proposals will then be considered by a Joint Committee of both Houses of Parliament. The terms of reference under which the Royal Commission has been established specifically state that it must 'have regard to the need to maintain the position of the House of Commons as the pre-eminent chamber of Parliament'. The Royal Commission is also precluded from considering the judicial functions of the House of Lords and will not therefore be able to consider whether those functions would be more appropriately dealt with by a Supreme Court, entirely separate from the House of Lords. This more or less rules out any serious consideration of an entirely elected second Chamber, unless, of course, the Law Lords are to be elected. The existence of the Lords Spiritual, the two Archbishops and 24 bishops, is also not to be questioned, despite the feeling of some that an established church with unelected representation in the second Chamber is even more of an anachronism than the presence of hereditary peers. Rather than making the House of Lords a secular Chamber the White Paper advocates just the opposite and states that the Government will be 'looking for ways of increasing the representation in the Lords of other religious traditions'.

The White Paper recognises the importance of the House of Lords in revising and scrutinising legislation – 'without which the burden on the House of Commons would be greater and the quality of government legislation diminished'. It suggests that, given the establishment of a Scottish Parliament and a Welsh Assembly, the reformed House of Lords might have a useful role to play as a representative of the regions.

The White Paper also suggests that consideration be given to extending the Parliament Acts to cover both Government Bills introduced in the House of Lords and delegated legislation and to reducing the period of time by which the Lords can delay legislation.

As far as the composition of a reformed House of Lords is concerned, the Government states in chapter eight of the White Paper that its 'own view is that the best solution is likely to be found among the more conventional options of nomination and election'. It sets out four main options for consideration by the Royal Commission: an entirely

[11] The Chairman of the Royal Commission is Rt Hon Lord Wakeham FCA. The other members of the Commission are: Rt Hon Gerald Kaufman, Lord Butler of Brockwell, Baroness Dean of Thornton-le-Fylde, Lord Hurd of Westwell, The Right Reverend Richard Harries, Bishop of Oxford, Sir Michael Wheeler-Booth, Professor Anthony King, Bill Morris, Professor Dawn Oliver, Ann Beynon and Sir Kenneth Munro.

nominated Chamber, an entirely directly elected Chamber, an indirectly elected Chamber and a mixed, partially elected, partially nominated Chamber. Each option has its advantages and disadvantages. Whilst nobody could doubt the legitimacy of an entirely elected second Chamber, it might constitute a threat to the supremacy of the House of Commons. It would also probably lead to the diminution, if not eradication, of the Crossbenchers, as the majority of those willing to stand for election to a second Chamber would probably be party representatives. An entirely nominated second Chamber would inevitably become known as the Patronage Chamber and whilst an attractive option in some ways would always be open to the suspicion that it was being packed with Government supporters. Yet this is the option which Labour proposed in its submission to the Royal Commission. Ironically, the Conservatives proposed either an entirely elected or partially elected Chamber. Indirect election would avoid the necessity for nationwide elections, and members could be elected by, for example, the new Greater London Assembly, the Scottish Parliament, the Welsh Assembly, etc, etc. This would avoid the problem of members of a reformed second Chamber having constituents and constituency responsibilities which might bring them into conflict with Members of the House of Commons. A mixed, partially elected, partially nominated Chamber might combine the best (some say the worst) of both worlds. There are a number of different ways in which such a Chamber could be constituted; for example, the ratio of elected to non-elected Members could vary from 50:50 to 25:75. The elected Members could be elected en-bloc at the same time as Members of the House of Commons, or on a rolling-basis of one third each year. The nominated Members could continue to be appointed much in the same way as they are at present. The most obvious problem with a mixed chamber of this sort would be the existence of two very distinct types of Member: one elected and one non-elected. Whilst there are two types of Member at present, at least neither hereditary or life peers have been elected. They have that in common. In a mixed Chamber of elected and non-elected Members, the elected Members might well feel that they had a moral if not an actual superiority over those who had merely been appointed. It would of course be possible to have a Chamber consisting of elected voting Members and appointed non-voting Members.

It is beyond the scope of this book to consider in detail all the possible permutations of membership in a reformed second Chamber. The role of the present House of Lords is worth a book all to itself and proposals for its reform worth several volumes at the very least. However, for those with a particular interest in this subject, the House of Commons Library once again comes to the rescue, with several invaluable Research Papers, which can be obtained either by accessing the Parliament website or by contacting the House of Commons Information Office. Of particular interest are:

- House of Lords reform: developments since the general election (19 August 1998)
- Lords Reform: the Legislative Role of the House of Lords (1 December 1998)
- Lords Reform: Recent Developments (7 December 1998)
- Lords Reform: Background statistics (15 December 1998)
- The House of Lords Bill: Lords reform and wider constitutional reform (28 January 1999)
- The House of Lords Bill: 'Stage One' Issues (28 January 1999)
- The House of Lords Bill: Options for 'Stage Two' (28 January 1999)

Also of interest are William Wyndham's book, 'Peers in Parliament Reformed' and 'The House of Lords – its Parliamentary and Judicial Roles', edited by Brice Dickson and Paul Carmichael (see Further Reading). 'Unfinished Business: Reforming the House of Lords', by Ivor Richard and Damien Welfare is a very useful guide to the current debate on the future of the House of Lords.

THE HOUSE OF COMMONS

The House of Commons is the elected Chamber and consists of 659 Members of Parliament. The methods of election to and the criteria for membership of, the House of Commons are set out in chapter two. The role of the political parties and whips' offices is set out in chapter four.

Composition of the House of Commons (1 March 1999)

Party	***No of Members***
Labour (including Speaker and one Deputy who do not vote)	418
Conservative (including two Deputy Speakers who do not vote)	164
Liberal Democrat	46
Official Ulster Unionist Party	10
Scottish National Party	6
Plaid Cymru	4
Social Democratic and Labour Party	3
Sinn Fein	2
Democratic Unionist Party	2
UK Unionist Party	1
Independent	1
Scottish Labour *(Tommy Graham MP was originally elected as a Labour MP)*	1
Vacancy	1
TOTAL = 659 (comprising: 527 English Members, 72 Scottish Members, 40 Welsh Members and 18 Northern Ireland Members)	

Constituencies

There is an unwritten rule in the House of Commons that Members do not intervene in matters relating to another Member's constituency. Members will always refer letters dealing specifically with another Member's constituency to the Member concerned. This does not mean that members of the public may not write to MPs other than their own on matters of general public policy; merely that, on specific constituency matters they must approach only their own MP. Anyone who is uncertain about which constituency they live in can use the constituency locator on the Parliament website. It helps to have the exact postcode to hand, as this is the most accurate way of finding out in which constituency a particular address is situated. By typing in the postcode, the locator can determine both the constituency and list the Member.

An MP who has accepted a speaking engagement in another's constituency, should inform the Member concerned and if a Member wishes to make an accusation about another MP in the Chamber he or she is supposed to inform them in advance.

The House of Commons Commission

The Commission is responsible for appointing all staff in the House, excluding the Clerk of the House, the Clerk Assistant, the Clerk of the Crown in Chancery and the Serjeant at Arms, all of whom are appointed by the Crown, and the Speaker's personal staff, all of whom are appointed by the Speaker. The Commission also determines the pay and conditions of all House of Commons' staff. The Commission comprises the Speaker, the Leader of the House, a Member nominated by the Leader of the Opposition and three Members (non-Ministers) nominated by the House.

The Commission is funded from Estimates presented to the House by the Speaker (the House being responsible for its own funding and administration). There are two Votes: one for administration and one for work. The Commission's Board of Management consists of the Heads of the six main departments of the House (Clerk of the House, Library, Serjeant at Arms, Official Report, Finance and Administration and Refreshment) with the Clerk of the House as its Chairman. As Accounting Officer of the Commission, the Clerk is responsible for the money which the House has voted to run its own affairs. The Commission is advised by the Finance and Services Committee which consists of 11 MPs. It prepares the Estimates and is advised by four domestic committees (the Chairs of which sit on the Finance and Services Committee) Accommodation and Works, Administration, Catering and Information. They have the same powers as Select Committees. There is also a Broadcasting Committee which oversees the televised coverage of Parliament.

The Clerk of the House

The Clerk of the House is the chief officer and senior official of the House of Commons (equivalent to a Permanent Secretary in a Government Department) and its corporate face to the world outside. His equivalent in the House of Lords is the Clerk of the Parliaments. The Clerk of the House is responsible for the legislative functions of the House (in an administrative capacity) and also oversees a large number of different departments within the House, from the Journal Office to the Public Bill Office. He or she also advises the Speaker and other Members on all procedural matters. The Clerk of the House sits at the Table of the House and has to ensure that all the decisions of the House are properly recorded. The Clerk Assistant, who sits to his left, takes responsibility for the actual preparation of the Order of Business, Order Book and the Votes and Proceedings of the House. On the Clerk Assistant's left at the Table, is the Principal Clerk of the Table Office. Other Principal clerks may take his or her place as and when necessary.

SPEAKER

Clerk of the House | Assistant Clerk | Principal Clerk

TABLE OF THE HOUSE

For anyone interested in the history of the position of Clerk of the House, the House of Commons Information Office publishes an interesting factsheet on this subject.

The Department of the Clerk of the House comprises the following offices, each headed by a Principal Clerk.

The Public Bill Office

The Public Bill Office is responsible for the procedure relating to Public Bills. It assists Members with drafting amendments to bills and ensures that all Private Members' Bills are in conformity with the rules and procedures of the House. Ten Minute Rule Bills are also submitted to the Public Bill Office. The Office also gives advice on financial business in the House and deals with delegated legislation. The Clerks to the various Standing Committees are also based in this office.

The Journal Office

The Journal Office is responsible for compiling both the daily Votes and Proceedings and the sessional Journals. Petitions are also dealt with by this office.

The Committee Office

The Clerks of all the Select Committees are based in this office. The Clerks play a vital role in the work of the Select Committees, who could not function without them or their assistants. This is the largest office in the Clerk's Department.

The Private Bill Office

The Private Bill Office assists in the conduct of Private Bill legislation and supplies the clerks for the Private Bill Committees.

The Table Office

The Table Office assists the Clerks at the Table in the preparation of the Order of Business, Notice Paper and Order Book. Members hand in parliamentary questions to the Table Office, which has the task of ensuring that they are in order.

Vote Office

The Vote Office has nothing to do with voting or divisions, but is the office responsible for the distribution within the House of all parliamentary papers. The Vote Office is where MPs collect 'the Vote' each day – the Order of Business, Notice Paper, Order Book, Votes and Proceedings, command papers, House of Commons papers, etc. Members and their secretaries and researchers can order any Stationery Office publication, however obscure, from the Vote Office, using a special green form. The Vote Office has a number of branches – in the Members' Lobby, in the bowels of the House of Commons, in the Norman Shaw North building, etc. Members of the public can obtain the same documents from the Parliamentary Bookshop, from another Stationery Office outlet or from the internet.

Overseas Office

The Overseas Office advises Parliaments in other countries on legislative and procedural matters and also provides staff for such organisations as the Western European Union, the Council of Europe, the Organisation for Security and Co-operation in Europe, the North Atlantic Assembly.

POST

POST is run by a Board comprising Members of both Houses of Parliament. Although independent, it is administratively part of the House of Commons. It began life as a charity in 1988 before being taken on by the House in April 1993. Its aim is to provide Members with research and information on recent developments in science and technology. It also carries out work for some of the Select Committees. You can access POST reports and notes via the Parliament website and recent briefing notes include Genetically Modified Organisms (Post Report Summary 115, May 1998), Nuclear Fusion (Postnote 40, November 1998) and Organophosphates (Postnote 122, December 1998) and what at the time of writing was the first in a new series of E-reports (reports published only on the internet). The first of these related to the Data Protection Act and was the result of a parliamentary online conference on the subject.

The Clerk of the Crown in Chancery

The Clerk of the Crown in Chancery is appointed by the Queen and both he and his deputy are officers of both Houses of Parliament. The Clerk of the Crown is based in the Crown Office in the Lord Chancellor's Department and is responsible for issuing writs for parliamentary elections and for issuing Writs of Summons to peers. At the beginning of each Parliament, the Clerk of the Crown must enter the names of all MPs into a 'Return Book' – hence the phrase 'the Member was returned for' and 'returning officer'.

The Library

Both the House of Lords and House of Commons have their own Library. In the House of Commons, the Department of the Library has two branches – the Members' Library in the House and the Derby Gate Library (next door to the Norman Shaw North building). The former is for Members only. The Library provides excellent research facilities for Members and the Research Papers, which it publishes, cover a wide range of subjects. These are now available on the Parliament website. Occasionally, you will hear at question time, that a particular paper has been 'deposited in the Library of the House'; this means that it is available to Members only from the Library. Members of the public can have access to such documents, but through the department which issued them rather than the House of Commons Library.

The Speaker

The importance of the Speaker in the life of the House of Commons cannot be overestimated. There is no real equivalent in the House of Lords, the nearest thing being the Lord Chancellor. The Speaker, or one of her three Deputies, acts as Chairman of the

House and has responsibility for calling Members to speak and for selecting any amendments for debate. The Speaker is also the representative of the House of Commons in relations with other outside bodies, with the Crown and with the House of Lords. The Speaker has responsibility for deciding whether or not to allow an application for an emergency debate under SO 24 or a Private Notice Question. The Speaker is also called upon to interpret previous rulings of the House and to apply the Standing Orders. Neither the Speaker nor her three Deputies take part in Divisions, nor indeed do they speak in debates.

Of the Speaker and three deputies, two are usually from the Conservative Party and two from the Labour Party. Whilst the Speaker continues to deal with enquiries, letters, etc., from constituents, she does not play a 'Party political' role in the House. The Speaker is not a member of the Cabinet or indeed a Minister of any sort. Former Speakers of the House of Commons also eschew Party politics and for this reason Lord Weatherill, the former Speaker, sits on and indeed convenes, the Cross Benches in the House of Lords. The Speaker is also the ex-officio Chairman of the House of Commons Commission, the House of Commons employer.

The first person to be accorded the title of Speaker was probably Sir Thomas Hungerford in 1377. There have been some illustrious holders of the office since, including Sir Thomas More and William Lenthall, who happened to be in the chair when Charles I came to arrest five Members of the House of Commons. The latter, perhaps unwittingly, established the independence of the Commons from the Crown as Charles I was the last ever monarch to set foot in the Chamber. Under the Ministerial and Other Salaries Act 1972 and the House of Commons (Administration) Act 1978, the Speaker continues as such after a dissolution until a new Speaker is chosen in the new Parliament. Former Speakers receive a pension under the Parliamentary and Other Pensions Act 1972. The Speaker may also be called upon, from time to time, to chair a Speaker's Conference on Electoral Law to examine certain aspects of electoral law and procedure.

The Speaker	*- Rt Hon Betty Boothroyd MP (Lab)*
The Chairman of Ways and Means	*- Sir Alan Haselhurst MP (Con)*
First Deputy Chairman of Ways and Means	*- Michael J Martin MP (Lab)*
Second Deputy Chairman of Ways and Means	*- Michael Lord MP (Con)*

Before every sitting of the House, the Speaker processes from her residence in the Palace of Westminster to the Chamber of the House of Commons, via the Library, Lower Waiting Hall, Central and Members' Lobby. She is preceded by the Serjeant at Arms with the Mace. If you happen to be in the Central Lobby when the Speaker's Procession arrives, you must be standing and not sitting, skulking, lying down or generally lounging about. If you happen to be reclining or snoozing on one of the green benches at the time, you will be told in no uncertain terms to get up. You will also hear the cry, 'hats off strangers'. When the Speaker's Procession leaves the Chamber at the end of the day, policemen in the Central Lobby shout, 'Who goes home?' If you happen to be there at the time, a reply is not expected. If, for some reason, the House of Commons sits after midnight, the aforementioned policemen must remove their helmets. There does not appear to be any good reason for this.

The Speaker's Counsel is the person appointed to give legal advice to the Speaker. He or she also assists the Chairman of Ways and Means with matters relating to Private Bills. He also advises the Joint Committee on Statutory Instruments and the Select Committee on Statutory Instruments. There are two Assistant Counsel who deal with any work relating to delegated legislation and one who advises the House on matters relating to EU law, particularly any Statutory Instruments which implement European directives, etc.

The Role of the Chairman of Ways and Means

The Chairman of Ways and Means is the Deputy Speaker and takes the Chair in the House of Commons when the House is in Committee or when the Speaker is absent. He or she also takes the Chair for the Budget Debate, as the financial measures contained in the Chancellor's Budget are brought in on Ways and Means Resolutions. The Chairman of Ways and Means also has responsibility for Private Bills (see chapter 12*)* in the House of Commons and for deciding on which days debates on Opposed Private Business should take place. There are two Deputy Chairmen of Ways and Means, who may take the Chair in the absence of the Chairman of Ways and Means and, who like the Chairman and the Speaker, do not take part in Divisions. They absent themselves from party political activity, but unlike the Speaker, their constituencies *are* contested at General Elections.

The Chairman's Panel

This panel is appointed at the beginning of each parliamentary Session and the members are nominated by the Speaker. There must be 10 or more members of the Panel, who act as temporary chairmen of committees as and when required. A Temporary Chairman may take the Chair for a Committee of the Whole House. The chairmen of Standing Committees are appointed from this Panel. The Chairman's Panel may also consider certain procedural matters and occasionally produce reports; for example, their response to the first report of the Select Committee on Modernisation of the House of Commons of the 1997/98 Session (HC 190) on reforming the legislative process. In the way that the Speaker has the power to select amendments, the Chairman of Ways and Means and his deputies can select amendments during a Committee of the Whole House.

The Serjeant at Arms

The first Serjeant at Arms was Nicholas Maudit, appointed in 1415. In the 13th Century a body of serjeants was formed to provide a bodyguard for the King. The Commons wanted their own equivalent and were eventually given their own Serjeant at Arms.

The Serjeant at Arms is essentially the 'housekeeper' of the House of Commons, being responsible for security, accommodation, and other related matters. He (and invariably it is 'he') is usually a retired officer from one of the armed forces and is appointed by the Crown. He is the second most senior officer of the House, the most senior being the Clerk of the House. The police and the doorkeepers in the Palace of Westminster are under his direction. The Serjeant at Arms Department is responsible for issuing photo-identity passes through the Pass Office and for regulating admission to the Press Gallery and Lobby. The Serjeant at Arms is also responsible for the admission of strangers to the galleries through the auspices of the Admission Order Office. The Serjeant at Arms carries the Mace in the Speaker's procession each day and has a seat near the Bar of the House, so that he can ensure that there are no riotous assemblies or disturbances in the lobbies. Should the House decide to commit a deviant Member or dissolute journalist to the Tower, the Serjeant at Arms would execute the warrant and could even take the person concerned into his own custody.

The Role of the Attorney General and Solicitor General

Together the Attorney General and Solicitor General are known as the Law Officers. They are members of the Government although not usually members of the Cabinet. The Attorney General is appointed by Letters Patent under the Great Seal and is usually a Member of the House of Commons. He represents the Crown in civil matters and prosecutes in important criminal cases. He is the head of the English Bar and also advises departments on legal matters. He can also instigate litigation on behalf of the public as a whole and may also take charge of legal proceedings on behalf of another, in what is known as a 'relator action'. The Solicitor General is subordinate to the Attorney General and in spite of his title, is a barrister. He does not necessarily sit in the House of Commons.

The Treasury Solicitor

The Treasury Solicitor is the head of the Government's Legal Service and his/her role is to provide legal advice to Government Departments. The post dates back at least to 1661. From 1885 until 1908, the Treasury Solicitor was also the Director of Public Prosecutions, but in that year the two functions were separated. The Scottish equivalent is the Solicitor to the Secretary of State for Scotland. Occasionally, the Treasury Solicitor will give advice to Parliament. The Treasury Solicitor is also the Chief Executive of the Treasury Solicitor's Department, which is an executive agency. The Agency has a number of different Divisions; for example, the Bona Vacantia Division, which deals with the administration of estates of those dying intestate.

The Role of the Ombudsman (Parliamentary Commissioner for Administration)

The Parliamentary Commissioner for Administration is more commonly known as the Ombudsman. He/she is appointed by the Crown and investigates complaints of maladministration against Government departments, made by individuals and referred to him/her by an MP. The Ombudsman cannot question matters of Government policy only questions of administration. He may not investigate relations with other countries or the actions of British officials abroad, nor may he investigate cases concerning nationalised industries, the Police or the Army. Whilst he has access to departmental papers he may be precluded from seeing Cabinet papers. His findings cannot be enforced.

The Ombudsman is also Health Service Commissioner and can deal with claims against the NHS, in this case brought to him directly from the public. His quarterly reports to Parliament are considered by the House of Commons Select Committee on Public

Administration. There is a separate Parliamentary Commissioner for Administration for Northern Ireland whose powers are more extensive than his British counterpart.

There are also Commissioners for Local Administration in England and Wales, appointed by the Secretary of State. Complaints about local authorities may be made directly to them by members of the public. In Northern Ireland, when the Ombudsman finds a local authority guilty of maladministration the complainant has the right to pursue the matter in Court, but this right does not exist in England and Wales.

SCOTLAND, WALES AND NORTHERN IRELAND

The various methods of election to and the composition of the Scottish Parliament, Welsh Assembly and Northern Ireland Assembly have been dealt with in chapter two. This section deals very briefly with the powers of the above and the impact this is likely to have on the UK Parliament at Westminster.

Scotland

The Scottish Government, or Scottish Executive as it will be known, is accountable to the Scottish Parliament and its 'Prime Minister' is known as the First Minister. The First Minister is elected by the Parliament and appointed by the Queen. Other Ministers also have to be approved by the Parliament. The Law Officers of the Scottish Executive are the Lord Advocate and the Solicitor General for Scotland (they need not be MSPs). They ceased to be members of the UK Government once the Parliament was established and a new law officer, the Advocate General for Scotland was appointed to advise the UK Government on Scottish Law. The Parliament will sit for a fixed term of four years (give or take a month) unless two-thirds of Members of the Scottish Parliament (MSPs) agree to a dissolution before that time, or if the Parliament cannot elect a First Minister.

The Scottish Parliament has an overall budget broadly comparable to the current budget of the Scottish Office (the 'Scottish Block'). As the Information Pack which the Scottish Office prepared for candidates (and which is available on the Scottish Office website – http://www.scottish-devolution.org.uk/) explains, 'Changes in the size of the block are currently determined by reference to planned changes in those English or English and Welsh programmes which are comparable with Scottish programmes. If planned spending on, for example, a comparable English programme goes up or down, an increase or decrease to the Block is calculated by reference to a population-based formula known as the "Barnett Formula", so named after Joel Barnett, the Chief Secretary to the Treasury in the 1970s. The sum of changes calculated by this means across all comparable programmes represents the change to the Block each year from previous plans'.[12] From 1 July 1999 the responsibility for allocating resources from within the Block will belong to the Scottish Parliament. In addition the Parliament will have tax varying powers allowing it to either lower or raise the basic rate of income tax set by the UK Parliament by 3p. Income from savings and dividends will not be affected. Schedule 5 of the Scotland Act lists those 'reserved matters' on which the Scottish Parliament will not have the power to legislate. The power to legislate in these areas will be reserved to the UK Parliament, or in the case of prerogative powers to the Crown in

[12] now assessed on a three-year cycle.

Parliament. These are set out in detail in Part II of the Schedule and include constitutional matters, foreign affairs and defence, the Civil Service, 'fiscal, economic and monetary policy' (this does not include the tax raising powers accorded to the Scottish Parliament and specifically excludes the council tax and non-domestic rates), control of drugs, data protection, elections, firearms, immigration and nationality issues, extradition, competition policy, a number of matters relating to health, including abortion, and vitally 'the computation of periods of time' and 'regulation of activities in outer space'. Unfortunately, the prospect of a Scottish Sputnik looks dim and a return to the Julian Calendar north of the border seems unlikely. The above is only a very brief list of some of the reserved matters listed in Schedule 5 and there are exceptions to most of them. Anyone requiring a comprehensive list of reserved and non-reserved matters must consult Schedule 5 of the Scotland Act 1998.

The Scotland Act 1998 restricts the power of the Scottish Parliament to modify the Scotland Act itself. It also stipulates that the Scottish Parliament may not pass any laws incompatible with either the Human Rights Act 1998 or with EU law, nor may it remove the Lord Advocate from his position as head of the system of criminal prosecution and investigations of deaths in Scotland. The list of reserved matters in Schedule 5 may be amended by an Order in Council in the UK Parliament, supported by an affirmative instrument in the Scottish Parliament (i.e. the approval of both Parliaments will be necessary). When a Bill is introduced in the Scottish Parliament, both the Presiding Officer (the Speaker) and the member of the Executive introducing the Bill, will have to certify that it is within the legislative competence of the Parliament. Prior to its final passing by the Scottish Parliament, there will be a four week delay before the Bill is passed for Royal Assent, to ensure that the UK government is satisfied that it is not 'ultra vires', (outside the powers granted to the Scottish Parliament). If there is any uncertainty the Bill will be referred to the Judicial Committee of the Privy Council. If they decide that the Bill is ultra vires then it cannot be introduced as it stands, but the Scottish Parliament will be able to reconsider it.

The Scottish Parliament can introduce legislation which affects 'reserved matters' where the legislation only relates to Scots private law or criminal law. However, the Secretary of State for Scotland will be able to intervene to prevent such legislation from receiving Royal Assent, where he or she feels that it touches upon reserved matters which are not related specifically to either.

The proceedings of the Scottish Parliament will be governed in its first few days by the rules which were drawn up by the Consultative Steering Group (CSG) - an all-party group set by the Government in January 1998, whose draft Standing Orders were set out in the The Scotland Act 1998 (Transitory and Transitional Provisions)(Standing Orders and Parliamentary Publications) Order 1999 (No. 1095). These will have to be confirmed by a majority of MSPs. In Wales a two-thirds majority will be required. The Standing Orders specify the following Committees:

- a Business Committee
- a Procedures Committee
- a Standards Committee
- an Audit Committee
- a Finance Committee

- a European Committee
- an Equal Opportunities Committee
- a Public Petitions Committee
- a Delegated Legislation Committee

'Plenary' (a full meeting of the Parliament) sessions of the Parliament take place on Wednesday afternoons, Thursdays, with some additional business on Mondays and Fridays if necessary. Committees sit on Monday afternoons, Tuesdays and Wednesday mornings with some additional business on Mondays and Fridays. The recommended hours of business are 9.30am to 5.30pm. The CSG recommended that the Parliament should sit for approximately 30-33 weeks each year, with an 8-10 week break in the summer (mid-June to end-August) and with 2-4 week breaks at Easter and Christmas with possible mid-term breaks in February and October. In debates, it is intended that Members will refer to each other by name rather than by constituency. MSPs will be paid a salary of £39,000, which will be reduced to a third if they are already MPs or MEPs. The First Minister will be paid £62,556 and the Presiding Officer £32,451 and members of the Executive, £32,451 (in addition to their salaries as MSPs). Anyone requiring more detailed information about the proposed procedures of the Scottish Parliament; for example, in the examination of bills or the role of the committees, can find the CSG's report on the Scottish Office website (http://www.scotland.parliament.uk). The Centre for Scottish Public Policy has also produced a very useful Guide to the Scottish Parliament, edited by Gerry Hassan and which is published by The Stationery Office.

Wales

The Welsh Assembly will take over the funding currently allocated to the Welsh Office and will take over the existing functions and responsibilities of the Secretary of State for Wales. For the time being at least, there will continue to be a Secretary of State for Wales in the Cabinet. The Assembly will be lead by a First Secretary, who will appoint an Executive Committee – a 'Cabinet' consisting of 'Secretaries' with responsibility for particular policy areas. The Speaker of the Assembly will be known as the 'Presiding Officer'. Members of the Welsh Assembly will be paid a salary of £33,500 (cut to a third if they are already MPs or MEPs). The First Minister will be paid £62,556 and the Presiding Officer £32,451 and members of the Executive, £32,451 (in addition to their salaries as Assembly Members).

There will be a committee structure consisting of the following (as set out in sections 54-61 of the Government of Wales Act 1998):

- Subject Committees (there will be as many of these as there are 'Secretaries')
- Regional Committees (the only such committee specified in the Government of Wales Act is a Regional Committee for North Wales)
- An Audit Committee (the functions of the Audit Committee will be similar to those of the Public Accounts Committee in the UK Parliament)
- A Subordinate Legislation Scrutiny Committee (this committee will have the responsibility for scrutinising all delegated legislation – some of its functions will be similar to the Joint Committee on Statutory Instruments in the UK Parliament)

The Assembly will have responsibility for those functions currently undertaken by the Welsh Office, but it will not be able to make primary legislation, only secondary legislation. The functions for which the new Assembly will have responsibility (as set out in Schedule 2 of the Government of Wales Act 1998) are:

- Agriculture, forestry, fisheries and food
- Ancient monuments and historic buildings
- Culture (including museums, galleries and libraries)
- Economic development
- Education and training
- The environment
- Health and health services
- Highways
- Housing
- Industry
- Local government
- Social services
- Sport and recreation
- Tourism
- Town and country planning
- Transport
- Water and flood defence
- The Welsh language

The actual Acts of Parliament under which delegated legislation in these areas will be made were listed in the National Assembly for Wales (Transfer of Functions) Order 1999. This Order transfers to the Welsh Assembly the power to make delegated legislation under the Acts listed. For a very thorough and interesting account of the role of delegated legislation in the Welsh Assembly please see the chapter by Paul Silk (The Assembly as a Legislature) in 'The National Assembly Agenda'.

The Government of Wales Act 1998 provided for the appointment of Commissioners to draw up the draft Standing Orders of the Assembly. A National Advisory Group was set up to assist in their preparation. Their recommendations were largely encompassed in the draft Standing Orders, which the Assembly will adopt when it first meets. It will be able to amend the Standing Orders only with the agreement of a two thirds majority. The Standing Orders are available on the following website -http://www.wales.gov.uk.

The National Assembly will not have any national tax-raising powers, but it will have responsibility for local taxation. The Development Board for Rural Wales and the Land Authority for Wales will be merged into a Welsh Development Agency.

Northern Ireland

The new Northern Ireland Assembly first met on 1 July 1998. There are 108 members and the Presiding Officer (the Speaker) is Lord Alderdice. Rt Hon David Trimble MP is the First Minister and Seamus Mallon MP the Deputy First Minister. Members of the Assembly receive a salary of £37,000 (cut to a third if they are already MPs or MEPs) and the First Minister is paid £62,556 and the Presiding Officer £32,451 and members of the Executive, £32,451 (in addition to their salaries as Assembly Members). Three main committees have been established: the Committee on Standing Orders, the Committee to Advise the Presiding Officer and an Ad Hoc Committee on the Procedural Consequences of Devolution. Under the Northern Ireland Act 1998, the Assembly will be able to legislate on 'transferred' matters, but not on 'excepted' and 'reserved' matters. Excepted matters are set out in Schedule 2 of the Northern Ireland Act 1998 and includeS, as one might imagine, major constitutional issues, economic policy, foreign affairs, defence, judicial appointments and certain other issues. Reserved matters are set out in Schedule 3 and include, the criminal law, civil aviation, data protection, firearms policy, consumer safety, competition policy and a number of other policy areas. Anything which is neither an excepted nor a reserved matter, is a transferred matter. Whilst it does not have tax-raising powers, the Northern Ireland Assembly will have the power to pass primary legislation. This will not affect the ability of the UK Parliament to make Orders in Council (see chapter nine for more information on Orders in Council and other delegated legislation). The 'Council of the Isles' was provided for in the Belfast Agreement to enable links between the Irish Government, the UK Government, the administrations in the Isle of Man and the Channel Islands and all the devolved assemblies. It will not have any legislative powers

Impact on the House of Commons

The House of Commons Select Committee on Procedure is currently conducting an enquiry into the procedural consequences of devolution. It published its interim report on 18 January 1999 (HC 148, 1998/99) and at the time of writing was taking evidence from interested parties including Members and academics. The Government has adopted a 'wait and see' approach and in her memorandum to the Committee (included in the interim report) the Leader of the House of Commons, Rt Hon Margaret Beckett MP stated that any changes to procedures at Westminster should be 'in the light of experience'. For example, the time given to Scottish and Welsh questions may well be reduced. It may be that in time, the work of at least the first two of these deparments can be dealt with by one 'Secretary of State for the Devolved Legislatures', overseen in the House of Commons by a Select Committee for Devolution, rather than two separate Select Committees. In addition, the need for both a Scottish and Welsh Grand Committee must surely diminish over time.

This book is essentially a guide to the workings of the UK Parliament and therefore the discussion of Parliament's role in the constitution has of necessity been brief. For those interested in the monarchy's relationship to Parliament and its role in the constitution, Vernon Bogdanor's book, 'The Monarchy and the Constitution' is essential reading. 'The Law and Parliament' contains a number of extremely interesting chapters on a wide range of legal and constitutional issues. These and other useful works have been listed below.

FURTHER READING

Constitutional and Administrative Law, Hilaire Barnett (Cavendish Publishing, 1998)
Constitutional and Administrative Law, A W Bradley and K D Ewing (Longman, 1997)
The House of Lords – its Parliamentary and Judicial Roles, edited by Brice Dickson and Paul Carmichael (Hart Publishing, 1999)
The Constitution After Scott – Government Unwrapped, Adam Tomkins (Oxford, 1998)
The Law and Parliament, edited by Dawn Oliver and Gavin Drewry (Butterworths, 1998)
The Road to Number 10: From Bonar Law to Tony Blair, Alan Watkins (Duckworth, 1998)
Prime Minister and Cabinet Today, Graham P Thomas (Manchester University Press, 1998)
Constitutional Futures: A History of the Next Ten Years, Edited by Robert Hazell (Oxford, 1999)
Ruling Britannia: The Failure and Future of British Democracy, Andrew Marr (Penguin, 1996)
This Time: our constitutional revolution, Anthony Barnett (Vintage, 1997)
The British Constitution Now, Ferdinand Mount (Mandarin, 1992)
The Hidden Wiring: Unearthing the British Constitution, Peter Hennessy (Indigo, 1996)
Crown Powers, Subjects and Citizens, Christopher Vincenzi (Pinter, 1998)
Cabinet, Peter Hennessy (Blackwell, 1986)
The Monarchy and the Constitution, Vernon Bogdanor (Oxford, 1997)
The British Prime Minister, Edited by Anthony King (Macmillan, 1986)
Peers in Parliament Reformed, William Wyndham (Quiller Press, 1998)
The Politics Today Companion to the British Constitution, Colin Pilkington (Manchester University Press, 1999)
Devolution in the United Kingdom, Vernon Bogdanor (Oxford University Press) 1999
Unfinished Business: Reforming the House of Lords, Ivor Richard and Damien Welfare (Vintage, 1999)
The Politics of the British Constitution, Michael Foley (Manchester University Press, 1999)
A Guide to the Scottish Parliament:The Shape of Things to Come, edited by Gerry Hassan (Centre for Scottish Public Policy, The Stationery Office, 1999)
The Scottish Parliament, Jean McFadden and Mark Lazarowicz (T&T Clark, 1999)

CHAPTER FOUR – PARTIES, PENSIONS & PAY

PARTY ORGANISATION IN PARLIAMENT

All Members of the House of Commons, except one, belong to a political party. Martin Bell MP is, at the time of writing, the only independent Member. In the House of Lords, the main party groupings exist, but with the addition of the Crossbenchers. These are peers who are not members of any political party, but who nevertheless sit together as a defined group. Some peers feel even this is too much and call themselves 'independents'.

In the Commons, whilst party loyalty is clearly important, Members represent all their constituents, not just those who voted for them. In some cases, they are elected as much for their individual qualities as for their party affiliation. Similarly, Members are elected simply as MPs, not as Ministers, Secretaries of State, Prime Minister, etc. When a Member is elevated to ministerial office, he or she is not endorsed by the House in any way. The House is not asked to ratify Prime Ministerial appointments to the Cabinet. The Prime Minister may appoint whomsoever he wishes to his Cabinet or to a junior ministerial position. In the new Scottish Parliament, members of the Government will have to be ratified by the Parliament itself. The demise of Rt Hon Margaret Thatcher as Prime Minister and Leader of the Conservative Party seemed unjust to many outside Parliament - she had never lost a General Election, having been endorsed on three occasions by the electorate; however, constitutionally, she was only elected as MP for Finchley, not as Prime Minister or Leader of the Conservative Party. A Prime Minister is only Prime Minister by virtue of being Leader of the Party which commands a majority in the House of Commons. He or she is not elected as such.

Members themselves - whilst, in most cases standing for election under a party banner – are elected as individual representatives, not as party ciphers (theoretically, at least). It is for this reason that when a Member 'crosses the floor of the House' – as many notable people have done, he or she is not obliged to give up his or her seat and fight a by-election. Peter Temple-Morris MP was elected as a Conservative MP, but crossed the floor of the House and now sits as a Member of the Labour Party. Alan Howarth MP was elected in 1992 as Conservative MP for Stratford-on-Avon, crossed the floor of the House to join the Labour benches and stood in the 1997 General Election as Labour Candidate for the constituency of Newport East. He is now a Minister in the Labour Government.

When the so-called Gang of Four left the Labour Party to establish the Social Democratic Party in 1981, they, and all but one of the other Labour MPs[1] who joined them, did not resign their seats to fight by-elections, they simply changed their party designation in the House of Commons. There were some in the fledgling party who felt that had they all

[1] Bruce Douglas-Mann, in Mitcham & Morden (June, 1982) was the only Labour MP who resigned and fought a by-election in order to join the Social Democrats. He lost the seat to the Conservatives in the shape of Angela Rumbold. As Ivor Crewe and Anthony King record in 'The Birth, Life and Death of the Social Democratic Party' (OUP, 1995), 'Other SDP MPs did not greatly appreciate the contrast that Douglas-Mann was implicitly drawing between the quality of his conscience and the quality of theirs' (page 163).

resigned and fought what would have amounted to a mini General Election, those who lost their seats in 1983 might well have hung on to them. However, we can all rewrite history with the benefit of hindsight.

The organisation of the political parties in the House of Commons differs according to whether or not the party concerned is in Government or in opposition. When in opposition, the Conservative Back Bench 1922 Committee consists of all Conservative MPs, but when the Conservative Party forms the Government, this Committee comprises only Back Benchers. As was mentioned in chapter two, this particular group has an important role to play in the election of the Leader of the Party. The Officers[2] and Executive of the 1922 Committee are elected each year.

The Parliamentary Labour Party (PLP) consists of all Labour MPs accepting the 'Party Whip' in the House of Commons. When in opposition, there are yearly elections to the 'Shadow Cabinet'. In the 1995/96 Session, the number of Shadow Cabinet members was increased from 18 to 19 on the basis that the Leader would appoint one of the elected members to the position of Chief Whip. Each MP must vote for four women candidates. The Party Leader allocates portfolios to successful candidates. He may also include in the Shadow Cabinet those who were unsuccessful in the ballot; for example, Martin O'Neill, MP, was for some years Shadow Defence Spokesman, despite his not having been elected to the Shadow Cabinet. Since 1980, Labour Party rules have dictated that the Leader of the Party must include in his first Cabinet all those holding Shadow Cabinet positions at the time of the General Election. However, there is nothing to prevent the removal of an incumbent after a decent interval and indeed this is exactly what happened in Rt Hon Tony Blair MP's first Cabinet reshuffle in 1998 when Rt Hon Harriet Harman MP was replaced as Secretary of State for Social Security by Rt Hon Alistair Darling MP.

The Chairman, Deputy Chairman and other officers of the PLP are elected annually after the Queen's Speech. The election is conducted on a 'first past the post' basis. The PLP's Officers meet with the Prime Minister after Prime Minister's Questions each week and the PLP itself meets regularly. There is also a representative of the Labour peers on the PLP.

The Liberal Democrats' Parliamentary Party consists of all those MPs in receipt of the Liberal Democrat Whip. There is a Parliamentary Committee in both the Commons and the Lords. They meet separately, but the Party Leader occasionally attends the meeting of the Peers' committee. The Chief Whip in the House of Commons is elected by fellow Liberal Democrat MPs and his/her counterpart in the House of Lords is appointed by the Leader of the Liberal Democrats in the Lords.

The Leader's Office and the Chief Whip's Office are the most important party offices in the House of Commons, with the latter assuming a particular prominence if a Government possesses only a small majority.

[2] Chairman, Vice Chairman, Treasurer, two Secretaries and 12 members

WHIPS, PAIRS AND BISQUES

The various party Whips Offices fulfil a vital function in the House; they are there to ensure that Members vote according to the Party line. They are not always successful, as the passage of the European Communities (Amendment) Bill in the 1993/4 Session of Parliament clearly demonstrated. When it comes to Europe, individual conscience takes precedence over party loyalty – and quite rightly so. Each Government Whip and Official Opposition Whip is usually responsible for a particular area of policy and a specific geographical area. The Whips Offices are often referred to as the 'usual channels' and along with the Office of the Leader of the House and the Speaker's Office, are responsible for the smooth running of Parliamentary business. They are also responsible for issuing the weekly 'Whip'. This is a statement of the business of the House for the following week, indicating when MPs, should or must be present.

If a Member's attendance for a particular debate is 'requested', this constitutes a 'one-line whip' and he or she can relax and have an early night. A 'two-line whip' is indicated by the words 'your attendance is necessary'. This means that Members really ought to be present to vote, but to be absent would not be considered a major misdemeanour. The words, 'your attendance is essential' constitute a 'three-line whip' and are underlined three times. This indicates that all Members must be present to vote. A 'three-line whip' is not advisory and Members have been rushed from hospital and carried into the precincts on stretchers where necessary. All officially recognised parties in the House are entitled to send out their party whips each Thursday evening in special envelopes, bearing the signature of the party's Chief Whip, which the Post Office guarantees to deliver the next morning (although they have been known to go astray). The provisional business for the following week in the House of Commons is usually circulated to the party Whips' Offices on a Wednesday, but the official business statement is not made until Thursday afternoon by the Leader of the House (in fact this is in response to a Private Notice Question), so whips are not sent out until Thursday evening.

The party groupings in the House of Lords issue a weekly Party Whip, much as their counterparts do in the House of Commons and these are also sent to peers as a special delivery. In addition in the House of Lords, peers receive a copy of the 'All Party Notices' – a sheet of A4 containing notification of future meetings of All Party Groups. These range from the sublime to the ridiculous; for example, on Thursday 4 July 1991, peers could have attended 'Beginners German' or a meeting of the Parliamentary Magic Group.

As party whips are 'private and confidential', the following is a fictitious example of what a typical whip might look like.

ON MONDAY	1 March the House will meet at 2.30pm
Questions:	Culture, Media & Sport, Millennium Experience, President of the Council, House of Commons Commission
Followed by:	Second Reading of the Cod and Whiting (Miscellaneous Provisions) Bill

A DIVISION WILL TAKE PLACE AND YOUR ATTENDANCE IS NECESSARY AT 9.30pm

ON TUESDAY	2 March the House will meet at 2.30pm
Questions:	Health
Followed by:	Remaining Stages of the Monarchy (Privatisation) Bill

DIVISIONS WILL TAKE PLACE AND YOUR ATTENDANCE IS ESSENTIAL FROM 4.30pm

ON WEDNESDAY	3 March the House will meet at 9.30am
	Wednesday Morning Adjournment Debates
Questions:	(2.30PM) Wales, Prime Minister
Followed by:	Consideration of any Lords Amendments which may be received to the Abolition of Lobbyists Bill

DIVISIONS WILL TAKE PLACE AND YOUR ATTENDANCE IS REQUESTED FROM 4.30pm

ON THURSDAY	4 March the House will meet at 11.30am
Questions:	Chancellor of the Exchequer
Followed by:	Debate on Disestablishment of the Church of England on a Motion for the Adjournment of the House

The House will not sit on Friday

Technically, an MP is not a member of a Parliamentary Party grouping unless he is in receipt of the party's Whip; therefore, to have the Whip withdrawn is a serious matter.

After failing to support the Government on the Second Reading of the European Communities (Finance) Bill in November 1994, eight Conservative 'rebels' had the whip withdrawn (Sir Richard Body, MP resigned the whip voluntarily) seriously reducing the Government's majority. The whip was not restored until April, 1995.

The Government Chief Whip is also known as the Parliamentary Secretary to the Treasury and sometimes as the Patronage Secretary. There are three Government Whips who are also members of Her Majesty's Household. The Deputy Chief Whip and Treasurer of Her Majesty's Household, the Controller of Her Majesty's Household the Vice Chamberlain of Her Majesty's Household. The Deputy Chief Whip and the Controller of Her Majesty's Household both travel in the Royal Procession at the State Opening. The Vice Chamberlain of Her Majesty's Household, has to remain at Buckingham Palace during the State Opening as a hostage for the Queen's safe return from Parliament. The Vice Chamberlain also acts as the Queen's messenger and if the need arises must convey any messages from the Palace to the House of Commons. He or she has a wooden wand of office which the Monarch used to break to signify that his or her message had been safety delivered. The wand which is now used can be conveniently unscrewed in the middle.

There are five Government whips in the House of Commons known as Lords Commissioners. These should not be confused with the Lords Commissioners in the House of Lords, who are also known as the Lords with White Staves.

In the House of Lords, the Government Chief Whip is known as the Captain of the Honourable Corps of the Gentlemen-at-Arms. The title relates to the ceremonial role he or she plays at the State Opening of Parliament. The Gentlemen-at-Arms are all ex-servicemen and line part of the route at the State Opening. The Government Deputy Chief Whip is known as the Captain of the Yeomen of the Guard and the title relates to the ceremonial role played by the aforementioned at the State Opening of Parliament, when the Yeomen of the Guard line part of the processional route through the Royal Gallery. The Yeomen of the Guard still ceremonially search the cellars beneath the House of Lords before each State Opening. The Government Whips in the House of Lords are all members of the Royal Household. Junior Government Whips in the House of Lords are either Lords-in-Waiting or Baronesses-in-Waiting.

'Pairing' is an arrangement whereby a Member of one Party agrees with a Member of an opposing Party that both should be absent for a particular vote, thereby cancelling out each other's votes. This enables both parties to the agreement to have a night off without in any way affecting the outcome of the Division. This is not an officially recognised practice and is arranged through the Parties' Whips' Offices. When pairing was in use, the practice was for it to be used only on less important votes and not in cases where a three-line whip had been imposed. At the end of 1992/93 Session, the then Labour opposition instituted a period of non-cooperation with the 'usual channels' as a result of the Government's decision to guillotine the Statutory Sick Pay and Social Security Contributions Bills. This meant that pairing was prohibited - resulting in Members from both sides of the House having to be present for all divisions. Members faced many more late-night sittings as a result. Pairing has really fallen into abeyance since the 1997 General Election, simply because of the Labour Government's huge majority, but as a result, 'Bisques' have come to the fore. This does not mean that all Members partake of a large bowl of lobster soup in the Member's Dining Room before voting, but that on certain days, a proportion of their number may be absent. Apparently the term is taken from the game of Croquet. A Bisque is usually arranged on a alphabetical basis, so that, for example, on a Monday, Labour Members whose surnames begin with the letters A to C may be absent, etc., etc.

The Payroll Vote

The 'payroll vote' simply refers to all those MPs who are deemed to be members of the Government; i.e. Ministers, junior Ministers, Parliamentary Private Secretaries (PPS), etc. They can usually be relied upon to vote with the Government on any issue.

The Leader of the House

Both the House of Commons and House of Lords have a Leader of the House. The Leader of the House of Lords is also usually the Lord Privy Seal and the Leader of the House of Commons is also usually the President of the Council. The President of the Council is head of the Privy Council Office, which comes under the auspices of the Cabinet Office. However, the Leader of the House of Lords may be Lord President and the Leader of the Commons, Privy Seal. Both are members of the Cabinet. They have important roles to play in ensuring that there is enough time for Government business, for steering any major procedural changes through the House and, in the Commons, for announcing the business of the House once a week and answering subsequent questions (see chapter six for more information on business questions). In the House of Commons, the Leader of the House chairs the new Select Committee on the Modernisation of the House of Commons. The Official Opposition appoints a Shadow Leader of the House in both Houses.

Members' Pay and Conditions

Members of Parliament lead busy lives. The size of the postbag which Members' secretaries collect daily from the post room off the Members' Lobby is enough to make even those of a strong constitution feel just a little queasy. The fact that a large number of Members do not have their own office from which to deal with this vast amount of correspondence would make many give up in despair. Conditions are of course much improved in recent years with the addition of new office space in 1 Parliament Street and 7 Millbank. However, there are many secretaries and researchers struggling with just a desk in the corner of a room somewhere in the bowels of the Palace of Westminster. Occasionally they surface from their subterranean existence and emerge blinking into the sunlight to gain sustenance in the Strangers' Cafeteria or 'Plods'[3] as it is affectionately known. The situation in the House of Lords is, if anything, even worse. There, peers and their staff (where they can afford them) are lucky to find a desk, let alone an office. However, life is not all Dickensian toil and there are mercifully few Gradgrinds amongst

[3] A cafeteria off Westminster Hall much beloved of the policemen on duty in the Palace of Westminster.

Members, who do the best they can for staff out of what is not an overly generous office allowance. Most Members of Parliament maintain an office in their constituencies as well as at Westminster and much of an MP's day to day work is concerned with constituency problems. Even Ministers have to attend to constituency concerns; it is not a side of parliamentary life which even the most elevated can afford to ignore. Most MPs hold regular constituency 'surgeries', where constituents can come with complaints, problems, etc. The sort of case-work with which an MP has to deal varies according to the type of constituency. The sort of problems with which a Member for a deprived inner-city area has to contend with are a world apart from those encountered by one representing the leafy lanes of Surrey. This is not to say that the problems of the latter are less important than the former, just that they are usually of a very different nature.

Members' Pay

Whilst the levels of Ministers' pay is set out in the Ministerial and other Salaries Act 1975 as amended by the Ministerial and other Salaries Act 1997 and can be increased by Orders in Council, Members' pay is set out, not in statute, but in a resolution of the House of Commons. In 1996 the previous Conservative Government agreed to refer the matter of MPs pay to the Senior Salaries Review Body. Their report (Cm 3330) was accepted by the House on 10 July 1996. The resolution agreed by the House set MPs pay at £43,000, to be uprated yearly in line with the percentage increase awarded to the mid-point of the Senior Civil Service pay bands. At the time of writing an MP's yearly salary was £45,066. Ministers now receive the full parliamentary salary as well as a ministerial salary. Ministerial salaries are uprated in line with the same formula as the one used for ordinary parliamentary salaries. This formula was set out in the Ministerial Salaries Act 1997, which inserted a new section into the Ministerial and other Salaries Act 1975. The actual amounts of ministerial salaries are set out in the 1975 Act but these amounts can, and are, varied by Orders in Council. For example, on 31 March 1999 the Government announced by way of an answer to a Written Question in the House of Lords (HL Col: 92) that the Review Body on Senior Salaries had recommended increases in the salaries paid to junior (non-Cabinet level) Ministers in the House of Lords and in addition the Leader of the Opposition and the Opposition Chief Whip (in the House of Lords). The £8,500 increase was given effect by a draft order, considered by both Houses (for more information on draft orders and delegated legislation, see chapter nine). Schedule 1 of the Act states that the Prime Minister shall be paid a salary of £20,000. It will not surprise readers to learn that the actual amount of the Prime Minister's salary from 1 April 1999 is £107,179, although Rt Hon Tony Blair MP does not draw this amount, having settled for £42,000 less. It should be remembered that this is only his ministerial salary – he also takes an ordinary MP's salary, of £47,008. At the time of writing his fellow Cabinet members received, in addition to their parliamentary salaries, £49,807 – this is £14,500 less than their full ministerial salary, which is £64,307.

The highest paid member of the Government is not the Prime Minister, but the Lord Chancellor, who currently receives £151,002. This is a reflection of his rank – after the Royal Family[4] and the Archbishop of Canterbury, the Lord Chancellor is the most

[4] This means the Queen and her immediate family. For more information on precedence and rank please see DOD's Parliamentary Companion.

important person in the realm. He is sandwiched between two Archbishops – being followed by the Archibishop of York. The Prime Minister is next, followed by the Lord President of the Council (usually the Leader of the House of Commons). The Speaker is next in line, hotly pursued by the Lord Privy Seal (usually the Leader in the House of Lords).

The House of Commons Library produces a very useful Research Paper on parliamentary pay, also to be found on the Parliament website. The Paper also sets out the rates of MPs' Office Costs Allowance, which at the time of writing was £49,232, plus £4,923 for staff pension contributions. The House agreed on 10 July 1996 to uprate the Office Costs Allowance yearly in line with inflation. Members with constituencies in London can claim a yearly allowance of £1,406 and Members with constituencies outside London can claim £12,717 to reimburse them for the additional costs incurred in having to maintain a home in London.[5] There is also a mileage allowance and a bicycle allowance. These are uprated yearly in line with inflation. There is also a 'winding-up' allowance of £16,411 (one third of the Office Costs Allowance) paid in the event of a Member's death or resignation, which enables staff to be paid whilst constituency and parliamentary business is properly concluded. Members who fail to retain their seats in a General Election, or who retire at the dissolution of the previous Parliament and do not stand for election to the next, are entitled to a resettlement grant, based on age and length of service in the House (HC Col: 1033, 22 May 1991). For example, a Member aged 52 who had been in the House for 12 years, would be entitled to 63% of his or her yearly salary. The table is set out below.

	NUMBER OF YEARS IN HOUSE OF COMMONS						
AGE	*Under 10*	*10*	*11*	*12*	*13*	*14*	*15 or more*
under 50	50	50	50	50	50	50	50
50	50	50	52	54	56	58	60
51	50	52	55	58	62	65	68
52	50	54	58	63	67	72	76
53	50	56	62	67	73	78	84
54	50	58	65	72	78	85	92
55-64	50	60	68	76	84	92	100
65	50	58	65	72	78	85	92
66	50	56	62	67	73	78	84
67	50	54	58	63	67	72	76
68	50	52	55	58	62	65	68
69	50	50	52	54	56	58	60
70 and over	50	50	50	50	50	50	50

[5] A resolution passed in the House on 27 June 1997 (HC Col: 1130) listed the following as London constituencies for the purposes of the allowance: Battersea; Bethnal Green and Bow; Camberwell and Peckham; Cities of London and Westminster; Dulwich and West Norwood; Eltham; Greenwich and Woolwich; Hackney North and Stoke Newington; Hackney South and Shoreditch; Hammersmith and Fulham; Hampstead and Highgate; Holborn and St Pancras; Islington North; Islington South and Finsbury; Kensington and Chelsea; Lewisham Deptford; Lewisham East; Lewisham West; Southwark North and Bermondsey; Poplar and Canning Town; Putney; Regent's Park and Kensington North; Streatham; Tooting; and, Vauxhall.

Ministers also receive a payment equivalent to three months ministerial salary if they cease to hold office under the age of 65 and do not hold office again within three weeks. MPs also receive pensions as set out in regulations brought in under the Parliamentary and Other Pensions Act 1987.[6] MPs are paid by the Fees Office which is part of the Department of Finance and Administration. The Fees Office is responsible for the salaries, pensions, allowances, etc. of both Members of Parliament and their staff. The Department of Finance also includes a Finance Office, dealing with accounts and an Establishments Office, which deals with personnel matters such as staff pay and conditions.

Peers' Allowances

Peers can claim a daily allowance of £35.50 and an overnight allowance of £80.50 for each day the House sits, providing they 'make their mark' (turn up in the Chamber). Ministers in the House of Lords are in receipt of a ministerial salary and are therefore not entitled to this allowance; however, they can claim an allowance of £17,710 to help defray the costs of maintaining a second home in London. Peers can also claim a mileage or bicycle allowance and may receive £34.50 a day to assist with secretarial or other office assistance.

Broadcasting

Radio broadcasts of both the House of Commons and House of Lords began on 3 April 1978. The House of Lords was first televised on 23 January 1985 and the Commons on 21 November 1989. In the House of Commons, the Broadcasting Committee, a sub-committee of the Finance and Services Committee oversees broadcasting of the proceedings of the House and in the House of Lords, the Administration and Works Sub-Committee of the Offices Committee takes on this responsibility. The Parliamentary Broadcasting Unit Ltd, or 'Parbul' for short, was established in 1991 and is funded by the broadcasting companies, who also sit on its Board of Directors as shareholders, along with Members of both Houses. Parbul contracts an independent company to record the proceedings in both Houses (including Select Committee proceedings) and the broadcasting companies are then entitled to use those recordings. Continuous coverage of Parliament used to be provided by the Parliamentary Channel, created in 1992 and owned by Cable & Wireless Communications, NTL/Comcast UK, General Cable and

---

[6] Members contribute at a rate of 6% of salary and may also make Additional Voluntary Contributions under the Parliamentary Pensions (Additional Voluntary Contributions Scheme) Regulations 1993 (SI 3252). Details of pensions are set out in the Parliamentary Pensions (Consolidation and Amendment) Regulations 1993 (SI 3253).

Telewest and managed by Flextech plc. The BBC recently bought the Parliamentary Channel and it is now known as BBC Parliament. The BBC Parliament Channel is now available as a free-to-air service on Skydigital.

CHAPTER FIVE – ORGANISING PARLIAMENT - DEBATES, DECISIONS, DIVISIONS, ETC

THE PARLIAMENTARY YEAR

NOVEMBER*	State opening of Parliament, Queen's Speech and Debate on the Address, term continues until ....
LATE DECEMBER	Christmas recess, usually lasting about 2 weeks, Parliament returns in early January and term continues until mid February 'half term holiday', then continues until ...
SPRING	Easter recess, usually Bank Holiday plus one week, Parliament returns and term continues until .... Whitsun recess, usually lasting one week, House returns until ..
SUMMER	Summer recess, usually from late July to early October
AUTUMN	Parliament returns for 'spill over' period (the House of Lords usually returns one week before the House of Commons) lasting for approximately one week to 10 days – existing business held over from before the Summer recess is concluded

** in a General Election year, the State Opening is not necessarily in November; for example, in 1997, the new Parliament began in May – as a result the 1997/98 Session of Parliament was much longer than the average Session.*

A Parliament

A 'Parliament' is the period between the opening of a Parliament after one General Election and its dissolution before the next; for example, '1987 - 1992', 1992 – 1997'. Under the Septennial Act 1715, as amended by Section 7 of the Parliament Act 1911, a Parliament automatically terminates exactly five years after the date of its first meeting. However, the Parliaments of 1911 and 1935 were extended to 1919 and 1945 respectively in the exceptional circumstances of war. The agreement of both Houses is needed to extend the life of a Parliament, as any bill with this effect is not subject to the Parliament Acts; i.e., it cannot automatically be sent for Royal Assent if voted down by the House of Lords after being reintroduced in a subsequent Session.

A proclamation dissolves the existing Parliament and orders the issue of writs for the election of a new one as well as setting out the dates of its meeting. The Queen dissolves Parliament, but this prerogative power is not derived from any statute, it is a common law right which has never been codified. There is no exact date on which a new Parliament must meet following a General Election, except that it must meet within three years, as set out in the Meeting of Parliament Act 1694. The date for the meeting of a new Parliament is decided by the Prime Minister and is set out in the Royal Proclamation which dissolves Parliament and calls the General Election. It can be delayed by up to fourteen days by a further proclamation under the Prorogation Act 1867.

A Session

A Parliament consists of a number of 'Sessions'; for example, there were five Sessions in the 1992-97 Parliament; 1992/3, 1993/4, 1994/5, 1995/6, 1996/7. A new Session begins with the Queen's Speech at the State Opening of Parliament and ends with the formal closure of the Session, known as 'Prorogation'. An announcement of the 'Queen's command to prorogue Parliament' is made in the House of Lords, with Members of the House of Commons in attendance. The last time this was carried out by the monarch in person was in 1854.

Nowadays, prorogation is carried out by Royal Commission. A Royal Commission is basically a group of peers charged with carrying out certain procedures on the Queen's behalf. Members of a Royal Commission are known as Lords Commissioners and have been appointed as such by Letters Patent. They are also Privy Councillors and a Royal Commission must consist of at least three of them, including the Lord Chancellor. However, in general, when reference is made to a Royal Commission, it is to a committee set up to consider a particular issue; for example the Royal Commission established under the Chairmanship of Lord Wakeham, to consider the future of the House of Lords.

When prorogation takes place by Royal Commission, the Gentleman Usher of the Black Rod is commanded by the Lord Chancellor to 'Let the Commons know that the Lords Commissioners desire their immediate attendance in this House to hear the Commission read'. In the Commons, Black Rod says, 'Madam Speaker, the Lords who are authorised by virtue of her Majesty's Commission to declare Her royal Assent to Acts and Measures passed by both Houses, and also to declare the prorogation of Parliament, desire the presence of this honourable House in the House of Peers to hear the Commission read'. The Commons may only proceed as far as the Bar of the House of Lords, and, as always in the House of Lords, this is accompanied by some bowing and doffing of hats, although curiously, in the words of the Companion to the Standing Orders and Guide to the Proceedings of the House of Lords, 'Women Commissioners remain covered'. The procedures followed on prorogation are set out below (taken from House of Lords Hansard for 19 November 1998).

Royal Commission

The Lord Chancellor (Lord Irvine of Lairg): My Lords, it not being convenient for Her Majesty to be personally present here this day, she has been pleased to cause a Commission under the Great Seal to be prepared for proroguing this present Parliament.[1]

---

[1] When Parliament is prorogued without Royal Assent being given to various Bills at the same time, a different form of words is used. 'My Lords and Members of the House of Commons, Her Majesty, not thinking fit to be personally present here at this time, has been pleased to cause a Commission to be issued under the Great Seal to be prepared for proroguing this present Parliament; and we are commanded to deliver to you her Majesty's Speech in Her Majesty's own words'. After the Speech and Commision have been read, the Lord Chancellor says: 'My Lords and Members of the House of Commons, By virtue of Her Majesty's Commission under the Great Seal to us and other Lords directed and now read, we do in Her Majesty's Name, and in obedience to Her Majesty's Commands, prorogue this Parliament to ... the ... day of ... to be then here holden, and this Parliament is accordingly prorogued to ... the ... day of ...'.

Then, the Lords Commissioners (being the Lord Chancellor, the Viscount Cranborne, the Lord Rodgers of Quarry Bank, the Baroness Jay of Paddington, and the Lord Chalfont) being present and the Commons being at the Bar, the Lord Chancellor said: My Lords and Members of the House of Commons, Her Majesty, not thinking fit to be personally present here at this time, has been pleased to cause a Commission to be issued under the Great Seal, and thereby given Her Royal Assent to divers Acts which have been agreed upon by both Houses of Parliament, the Titles whereof are particularly mentioned, and by the said Commission has commanded us to declare and notify Her Royal Assent to the said several Acts, in the presence of you the Lords and Commons assembled for that purpose; and has also assigned to us and other Lords directed full power and authority in Her Majesty's name to prorogue this present Parliament. Which Commission you will now hear read.
A Commission for Royal Assent and Prorogation was read.
The Lord Chancellor: My Lords, in obedience to Her Majesty's Commands, and by virtue of the Commission which has been now read, We do declare and notify to you, the Lords Spiritual and Temporal and Commons in Parliament assembled, that Her Majesty has given Her Royal Assent to the several Acts in the Commission mentioned; and the Clerks are required to pass the same in the usual Form and Words.

Prorogation: Her Majesty's Speech

Her Majesty's most gracious Speech was then delivered to both Houses of Parliament by the Lord Chancellor (in pursuance of Her Majesty's Command) as follows:

"My Lords and Members of the House of Commons,
"The Duke of Edinburgh and I were pleased to receive the State Visits of his Excellency the President of Brazil in December 1997 and of Their Majesties the Emperor and Empress of Japan in May this year. We remember with great pleasure our visit to Canada in June and our State Visits to Pakistan and India in October 1997 and to Brunei and Malaysia in September of this year............

After which the Lord Chancellor said:

My Lords and Members of the House of Commons, by virtue of Her Majesty's Commission which has been now read We do, in Her Majesty's name, and in obedience to Her Majesty's Commands, prorogue this Parliament to the 24th day of this instant November, to be then here holden, and this Parliament is accordingly prorogued to Tuesday, the 24th day of this instant November.

Parliament was prorogued at eighteen minutes past four o'clock.

With the unintentional humour of which only Parliament is capable, the Companion to the Standing Orders states that after prorogation, 'The Commissioners leave the Chamber by the door on the spiritual side near the Throne, and disrobe'.

In the House of Commons, matters are far more sedate. Having returned from hearing the Royal Commission read, the following took place:

Message to attend the Lords Commissioners:
The House went;--and, having returned:

Royal Assent

Madam Speaker: I have to acquaint the House that the House has been to the House of Peers, where a Commission under the Great Seal was read, authorising the Royal Assent to the following Acts:
Statute Law Repeals Act 1998
Waste Minimisation Act 1998
Regional Development Agencies Act 1998
Scotland Act 1998
Northern Ireland Act 1998
Registration of Political Parties Act 1998

Prorogation

Her Majesty's Most Gracious Speech

Madam Speaker: I have further to acquaint the House that the Lord High Chancellor, one of the Lord Commissioners, delivered Her Majesty's Most Gracious Speech to both Houses of Parliament, in pursuance of Her Majesty's Command. For greater accuracy, I have obtained a copy and also directed that the terms of the speech be printed in the Journal of the House. Copies are being made available in the Vote Office.

The Gracious Speech was as follows: ....

Prorogation is a prerogative act of the Crown and technically, Parliament cannot continue without the consent of the monarch. However, in reality, it is the Government of the day which decides when a Session should begin and end, and hence the dates of both the State Opening and Prorogation. Prorogation automatically causes all pending parliamentary proceedings to fall and as a result, all Public Bills must receive Royal Assent before the end of the Session in order to be enacted. If a bill fails to complete all its stages, it has to be reintroduced in the next Session as a new bill. It cannot simply pick up again in the new Session where it left off in the last. The House of Commons has now made provision for 'carry-over motions', which would permit a Public Bill to be exempt from this rule, but at the time of writing, no such motions had yet been made. On 4 June 1998, the House of Commons agreed to the Third Report from the Select Committee on Modernisation of the House of Commons (HC 543 97/98) which recommended that certain bills could be carried over from one Session to another. However, the Committee specifically recommended that the procedure should only be used for bills which had not left the House in which they originated. A Public bill must therefore be renewed after a prorogation as if it were being introduced for the first time. Private and Hybrid bills are exempt from this rule and can be carried over from one Session to the next, often ad-nauseam.

A Session does not end with the Summer Recess as is sometimes thought. There is generally a 'spill-over' period when both Houses return in October, which usually lasts for about a week and which allows bills to complete any remaining stages before prorogation. The House of Lords usually returns a week earlier than the House of Commons for the spill-over period, simply because they are more likely than the Commons to have outstanding business to complete before prorogation. This is because the majority of Government bills are introduced in the House of Commons and as a result often only begin their House of Lords' stages late in the Session. It would be possible for Parliament to be recalled earlier than the date set out in the Royal Proclamation which prorogued Parliament if an emergency were to arise.

Terms and Recesses

The period between the end of one Session (Prorogation) and the State Opening of another is technically known as a 'Recess', whilst the period between, for example, Parliament adjourning for the summer break and returning for the 'spill-over' period is technically called an 'Adjournment'; however, it is known colloquially as a 'Recess'.

A Session is divided into 'terms'. The House sits from mid-October until Christmas when the House rises for the Christmas Recess (more properly known as an 'adjournment'). It then reassembles in the new year and – with the exception of the new February half-term break - sits until Easter when it is interrupted for an adjournment of about a week. The summer term is interrupted for a Whitsun Recess of about a week and then reassembles, sitting until late July when the House rises for the summer Recess which usually lasts until early October when the House returns for the 'spill-over' period. The First Report of the Committee on the Modernisation of the House of Commons (HC 60, 1998/99) proposed a week's adjournment in February to coincide with schools' half-term holidays. The report was accepted by the House on 16 December 1998 and in fact the House rose on Tuesday, 16 February for a 'half term holiday', returning on Monday 22 February.

Each House exercises its right to adjourn itself independently of the Crown and the other House and this is why the House of Lords often returns after an adjournnment a day or two earlier than the House of Commons. When the Government has decided on the dates for an adjournment, a motion is tabled and appears on the Order of Business.

To be decided without debate (Standing Order No. 52(1)(a)).

+ **3** ADJOURNMENT ***[No debate]*** Margaret Beckett
That this House, at its rising on Thursday 17th December, do adjourn till Monday 11th January 1999.

On the day the House rises, the following motion is taken after the half-hour Daily Adjournment Debate:

The motion having been made after Ten o'clock, and the debate having continued for half an hour, Mr. Deputy Speaker *adjourned the House without Question put, till Monday 11 January, pursuant to Resolution[8 December].*

Adjourned at seventeen minutes to Eleven o'clock.

A motion of this nature has to be put forthwith but can be put at any hour even if opposed (SO 25).

Under Standing Order 13, the House of Commons may return at an earlier date than the one set out in the Motion for the Adjournment to discuss urgent business (SO 14 has the same effect in the House of Lords). Parliament could also be recalled by a Royal Proclamation. Under the Meeting of Parliament Act 1799 as amended by the Meeting of

Parliament Act 1870, when Parliament is adjourned for more than 14 days, the Queen may issue a proclamation recalling both Houses six or more days later. The House of Commons was recalled on 24 September 1992 for two days during the summer adjournment to debate the economic crisis and the worsening situations in the former Yugoslavia, Somalia and Iraq. Parliament was also recalled during the summer adjournment in 1990 to consider the crisis in the Gulf and again in 1998 to discuss the response to the bombing in Omagh. The House also sat on a Saturday during the Falklands War. The House adjourns on the death of a member of the Royal Family and does not usually sit on occasions such as Royal Weddings.

THE STATE OPENING OF PARLIAMENT

Election of a Speaker

The opening of a new Parliament differs from the State Opening of Parliament at the beginning of a new parliamentary Session for two main reasons: firstly, a Speaker must be elected by the House of Commons and secondly all Members must take the oath. The election of a Speaker is usually preceded by inter-party consultations to agree on a suitable candidate. Since 1940, until the 1992 Parliament, Speakers have usually been members of the Governing Party. Traditionally, they are Back-benchers as opposed to Ministers.

On the first afternoon of a new Parliament, Members of both Houses assemble in their respective Chambers. In the House of Lords, the Lord Chancellor states: 'that it not being convenient for Her Majesty to be personally present here this day, She has been pleased to cause a Commission under the great seal prepared, in order to the holding of this Parliament'. The five Lords Commissioners command Black Rod to let the Commons know that their attendance is requested to hear the Commission read.

On receiving the message the Clerk and the Members of the House of Commons progress to the House of Lords where the Lord Chancellor informs them that 'We are commanded by Her Majesty to let you know that, it not being convenient for Her to be present here this day in Her Royal Person, she has thought fit by Letters Patent under the Great Seal to empower several Lords therein named to do all things in Her Majesty's name which are to be done on her Majesty's Part in this Parliament, as by the Letters Patent will more fully appear'. The Lord Chancellor then instructs the Commons that, 'We have it in command from Her Majesty to let you know that, as soon as the Members of both Houses shall be sworn, the causes of Her Majesty calling this Parliament will be declared to you: and, it being necessary that a Speaker of the House of Commons should be first chosen, it is Her Majesty's Pleasure that you, members of the House of Commons, repair to the place where you are to sit, and there proceed to the choice of some proper person to be your Speaker, and that you present such person whom you shall so choose here for her Majesty's Royal Approbation'. In the House of Lords, peers then take the oath. Although the following extract is taken from the House of Commons Hansard for 7 May 1997, the procedure followed is the similar to the procedure followed when the Speaker is first elected.

House of Commons

Wednesday 7 May 1997

The House being met; and it being the first day of the meeting of this Parliament, pursuant to Proclamation, DONALD WILLIAM LIMON, ESQUIRE, CB, *Clerk of the House of Commons,* WILLIAM ROBERT McKAY, ESQUIRE, CB, *Clerk Assistant, and* GEORGE CUBIE, ESQUIRE, *Principal Clerk of the Table Office, attending in the House, and the other Clerks attending, according to their duty,* SIR THOMAS STUART LEGG, KCB, QC, *Clerk of the Crown in Chancery in Great Britain, delivered to the said* DONALD WILLIAM LIMON *a book containing a list of the names of the Members returned to serve in this Parliament.*

Several of the Members repaired to their seats.

THE RIGHT HON. SIR EDWARD HEATH *took the Chair, pursuant to Standing Order No. 1 (Election of the Speaker).*

Message to attend the Lords Commissioners.

The House went; and a Commission having been read for opening and holding the Parliament, the Lords Commissioners directed the House to proceed to the Election of a Speaker, and to present the Speaker-Elect *tomorrow, in the House of Peers, for the Royal Approbation.*

And the House having returned:--

On their return to the Commons, the Chair (at the Table, not the Speaker's Chair) is taken by 'the Father of the House', a Member who is not a Government Minister and who has served for the longest continuous period in the House of Commons. In 1992, Rt. Hon Sir Edward Heath KB MBE MP presided over the election of Rt Hon Betty Boothroyd MP as the new Speaker. The Father of the House calls on two Back-benchers to move and second another Member as Speaker. The question that the person concerned, 'do take the Chair of this House as Speaker' is then proposed. The Member who has been proposed then makes a speech in which he or she 'submits' him/herself to the House. If another candidate is put forward an amendment is proposed to the original motion and then, similarly, the alternative candidate submits him/herself to the House. The House then divides on the amendment. If the amendment is carried, no further amendments can be moved and the question on the main motion is put. In 1992 the amendment proposed Rt Hon Betty Boothroyd MP as Speaker and was carried by the House (the main motion had proposed Rt Hon Peter Brooke CH MP). She therefore became the first woman Speaker of the House of Commons. The Member who has been chosen then addresses the House before being escorted by his/her proposer and seconder to the chair. Traditionally, he or she is meant to struggle, to signify an unwillingness to be Speaker. This dates from a time when the Speaker's job was such a dangerous and unenviable one that volunteers for the position were hard to find. Watching some of the more heated exchanges in the House of Commons one could be forgiven for concluding that the job has changed little.

Once the Speaker-elect has taken his or her place in the Speaker's Chair, the Mace is laid on the Table, where it must always be placed when the House is presided over by the Speaker (it is placed under the Table when the Chairman or one of the Deputy Chairman of Ways and Means is in the Chair). After speeches congratulating the new incumbent the House is adjourned until the following day.

A similar procedure is followed even when a Speaker continues in office after a General Election as can be seen from the following extract from the House of Commons Hansard for 7 May 1997.

Question put and agreed to.
Resolved,
That Miss Betty Boothroyd do take the Chair of this House as Speaker.
Whereupon Sir Edward Heath *left the Chair, and* Miss Betty Boothroyd *was taken out of her place and conducted to the Chair by* Mr. John MacGregor *and* Mrs. Gwyneth Dunwoody.

After speeches extolling the virtues of the Speaker, the House is adjourned:

Motion made, and Question proposed, That this House do now adjourn.--*[Mr. McAvoy.]*
Madam Speaker-Elect *thereupon put the Question, which being agreed to, the House adjourned accordingly until tomorrow, and* Madam Speaker-Elect *went away without the Mace before her.*
Adjourned accordingly at twenty-eight minutes to Four o'clock.

On the next day the Speaker-elect takes the Chair. In the House of Lords, the Lords Commissioners instruct Black Rod to summon the Commons, which he duly does. The Speaker-elect and the Commons proceed to the Bar of the House of Lords. The Speaker-elect stands at the Bar of the House and states that, 'I have to acquaint your Lordships that in obedience to the Royal Command, Her Majesty's most faithful Commons have, in the exercise of their undoubted rights and privileges, proceeded to the election of a Speaker, and that their choice has fallen upon myself. I now present myself at your Lordships' Bar, and submit myself with all humility for Her Majesty's gracious Approbation'. After some brief words from the Lord Chancellor, the Speaker-elect says the following: 'I submit myself with all humility and gratitude to Her Majesty's gracious Commands. It is now my duty in the name and on behalf of the Commons of the United Kingdom, to lay claim, by humble petition to Her Majesty, to all their ancient and undoubted rights and privileges, especially to freedom of speech in debate, to freedom from arrest, and to free access to Her Majesty whenever occasion shall require, and that the most favourable construction shall be put upon all their proceedings. With regard to myself I pray that, if in the discharge of my duties I shall inadvertently fall into any error, it may be imputed to myself alone and not to Her Majesty's most faithful Commons'. The Lord Chancellor then conveys Her Majesty's agreement to these rights and privileges, after which the Speaker and Commons then return to the House of Commons, where the Speaker makes the following statement.

Madam Speaker: I have to report to the House that, in the House of Peers, Her Majesty, by Her Royal Commissioners, has been pleased to approve the choice made of myself for the Office of Speaker, and that I have, in your name and on your behalf, made claim by humble petition to Her Majesty to all your ancient and undoubted rights and privileges, particularly to freedom of speech in debate, freedom from arrest and freedom of access to Her Majesty whenever occasion may require, and that the most favourable construction may be placed upon all your proceedings. All these Her Majesty, by Her Commissioners, has been pleased to confirm in as ample a manner as they have ever been granted or confirmed by herself or by any of Her Royal Predecessors. My first duty to the House is to report my respectful acknowledgments and my grateful thanks for the great honour you have conferred upon me in placing me in the Chair.

Once approved, the Speaker continues in office during the whole Parliament.[2]

Taking the Oath

At the beginning of a new Parliament, the Clerk of the Crown in Chancery delivers a 'Return Book' to the Clerk Assistant 'below the Bar' of the House. This lists all the Members returned at the General Election and is proof of election. The Speaker is the first to take the oath. On 7 May 1997 the Speaker made the following statement about the order in which Members would be called to take the oath:

It may be for the convenience of the House if I indicate my intentions with regard to the taking of the Oath by right hon and hon. Members. I propose to call, first, the Father of the House; then the Cabinet; then the shadow Cabinet; then all the Privy Counsellors not included in those two groups, wherever they may be sitting, and then other Ministers. Thereafter I shall call other hon. Members according to seniority determined by the basis of seniority, that is by the Parliament of first entry or, for those with broken service, that of most recent entry.
The first batch will be those elected in or before 1974. Thereafter I shall proceed by successive Parliaments. I hope that by late this afternoon to have made sufficient progress to enable all Members to swear in who wish to do so up to and including those elected to the 1992 Parliament. The House will sit again tomorrow at 9.30, when I shall call those Members first elected to the current Parliament as well as Members elected to earlier Parliaments who were not able to take the Oath today.
Finally, the House will meet again next Tuesday at 2.30 to enable Members to take the Oath who have not done so this week.
I hope that this announcement will be helpful to Members in planning their programmes. Progress will depend, of course, on the number of Members wishing to take the Oath at any particular time. I advise Members to watch the annunciators to establish progress and to speak to their Whips. I hope also that Members will come forward in an orderly manner. Let us now begin.

All Members elected to the House of Commons must take the oath or affirmation. On 14 May 1997 the Speaker made the following statement concerning Members not taking their seats.

---

[2] If a new Speaker has to be elected during the course of a Session two procedures are followed depending on whether the Speaker has died in office or is retiring. If the latter is the case, then the Speaker would normally preside over the election of a successor, if the former, the Father of the House would preside over the election and the procedure would be the same as for the election of a Speaker at the beginning of a new Parliament. In either case, a Government Minister informs the House that Her Majesty 'gives leave to the House to proceed forthwith to the choice of a new Speaker' and once the Speaker has been chosen, the same Minister instructs the Speaker to attend the House of Lords the following day to receive the 'Royal approbation'. The procedure in the House of Lords is as for the election of a Speaker, except for the omission by the Speaker of the claim of various ancient privileges.

Madam Speaker's Statement

Madam Speaker: I wish to make a statement about the availability of services in the House for those who do not take their seats after being returned here as Members.

This House has traditionally accommodated great extremes of opinion. I am sure therefore that the House would not wish to put any unnecessary obstacle in the way of Members wishing to fulfil their democratic mandate by attending, speaking and voting in this House. Equally, I feel certain that those who choose not to take their seats should not have access to the many benefits and facilities that are now available in the House without also taking up their responsibilities as Members.

The present position is that under the terms of the Parliamentary Oaths Act 1866, any Member who fails to take the oath or to make the affirmation that is required by law and who then votes or sits during any debate after the election of the Speaker is subject to a penalty of £500 on each occasion and his or her seat is automatically vacated. In 1924, one of my predecessors ruled that any such Member could not receive a salary, and this regulation also applies to allowances.

In the interests of the House, and making use of the power vested in the office of the Speaker to control the accommodation and services in the Commons parts of the Palace of Westminster and the precincts, I have decided to extend these restrictions. As from the date of the end of the debate on the Queen's Speech, the services that are available to all other Members from the six Departments of the House and beyond will not be open for use by Members who have not taken their seats by swearing or by affirmation.

For the avoidance of doubt, a schedule listing these various services will be appended to this statement in the *Official Report*. One of the purposes of this will, of course, be to enable officers and servants of the House and others to administer these new regulations with clarity and precision.

Of course, I accept that there may be occasional cases where an elected Member, for reasons of health or for other good reasons, cannot attend to take his or her seat immediately after election, but, nevertheless, desires to do so at the earliest possible moment. Provided such a Member sends me a letter informing me of his or her inability to attend and signifying his or her intention to attend to swear or affirm at the earliest possible time, I will give instructions that these new regulations should not be applied. This should be done not later than the date of the end of the debate on the Queen's Speech or, in the case of a by-election, after 10 sitting days.

The House will have noted that the date which I have set for the introduction of these regulations is the end of the debate on the Queen's Speech. That is not an ideal date, but the House needs notice of these changes. In a future Parliament, the effective date both for the cessation of services and for the deadline for the sending of the letter requesting excusal will be the date of the Queen's Speech itself.

The services to which the new regulations apply include:

Legal services
Procedural services, including the tabling of questions, motions and amendments, and public petitions
Broadcasting services
Vote Office services
Services available from the Parliamentary Office of Science and Technology
The provision of passes, special permits and car parking facilities
Access to those areas within the parliamentary precincts which are open only to pass holders

The booking of Committee Rooms, conference rooms and interview rooms
Office accommodation services for Members and their staff
Computer services, except those available to the public
The allocation of Gallery tickets
The sponsoring of exhibitions in the Upper Waiting Hall
Members' medical services
Library and research services, except for those services of the Public Information Office generally available to the public
Services provided by the Official Report
Payroll and other financial services provided to Members and their staff
Insurance services
Catering services provided for Members and their staff, including the sponsoring of banqueting services
Police and security advice available within the precincts
Services in the Members' post offices
Travel services

The form of the Oath is set out in the Promissory Oaths Act 1868 and the Oaths Act 1978. This is set out below:

"I .... do swear by Almighty God that I will be faithful and bear true Allegiance to Her Majesty Queen Elizabeth, Her Heirs and Successors, according to law. So help me God."

Under the Oaths Act 1978, those who object to taking of an oath can affirm using the following words:

"I ... do solemnly, sincerely, and truly declare and affirm that I will be faithful and bear true Allegiance to Her Majesty Queen Elizabeth, Her Heirs and Successors, according to law."

Peers also take the oath in the House of Lords using the same form of words. Peers who attempt to vote or sit in the House of Lords without having taken the oath are subject to a fine of £500. Similarly in the House of Commons if a Member attempted to sit or vote after the Speaker had been chosen, without having taken the oath, not only would they be subject to the same fine, but their seat would be vacated. Once an MP or peer has taken the oath, he or she signs the 'Test Roll', a book which has the oath or affirmation at the top of each page and which is kept by the Clerk of the House. The Member is then introduced to the Speaker. In the Lords, peers shake hands with the Lord Chancellor.

After the majority of Members have taken the oath the Commons proceeds to the Lords to hear the Queen's Speech.

The Queen's Speech

At the beginning of a new Session of Parliament, as opposed to the beginning of a new Parliament, the Session is opened by the Queen's Speech, rather than the election of a Speaker and swearing in of Members. No words can really describe the theatricality and hilarity of the State Opening of Parliament. There are heralds[3] with peculiar names such as Rouge Dragon Pursuivant, there are men with funny hats, hostages kept at Buckingham Palace in case the Queen should not return and other seemingly nonsensical practices. The peers sit in the Chamber in all their finery to listen to the Queen read a speech written by somebody else. However, it is all good clean fun so let us hope that the Government's reforms of the House of Lords do not extend to replacing the royal procession with a group of Armani-suited officials, swaggering into the Chamber to the strains of 'things can only get better'.

Included in the royal procession to Westminster are two Government Whips, the Deputy Chief Whip who is also the Treasurer of the Household and the Comptroller of the Household. There are three Government Whips who are also members of Her Majesty's Household. The third, the Vice-Chamberlain, is kept prisoner during the State Opening. He or she has to remain at Buckingham Palace as a hostage for the Queen's safe return. So should a group of militant anti-monarchists manage to abseil down from the public galleries during the Queen's Speech and snatch Her Majesty from under their Lordships' noses, the hapless Vice-Chamberlain would find him or herself indefinitely detained; although one images that incarceration at the Palace might not be quite as distressing as a spell in the Scrubs.

When the Queen has arrived at the House of Lords (by convention this is in the morning) she is met at the Sovereign's Entrance by the Lord Chancellor (who has the Queen's Speech in his purse.)[4], the Lord Great Chamberlain and the Earl Marshal. She puts on the ceremonial robes in the Robing Room and the royal Procession then moves through the Royal Gallery and the Prince's Chamber into the House of Lords. She takes her seat on the Throne and the Lord Chancellor stands at the steps and to the right of the Throne. The Queen then commands the Gentleman Usher of the Black Rod to summon the Members of the Commons to hear the Queen's Speech. The door to the Chamber of the House of Commons is shut and Black Rod knocks three times before being admitted. He makes three bows to the Chair, advances towards the Table and says: 'Mr Speaker, the Queen commands this Honourable House to attend Her Majesty immediately in the House of Peers '. The Speaker and the Members then progress to the House of Lords to

[3] There are 13 Heralds, all of whom have peculiar titles such as Bluemantle and Portcullis. The aforementioned are technically Pursuivants as opposed to Heralds. You can tell a Herald from a Pursuivant by his tabard, which is satin rather than damasked silk. Their home is the College of Arms (the HQ of the Order of the Garter) where, when they are not wearing tabards and doing strange things in Parliament, they undertake genealogical research. Black Rod is an officer of the Order of the Garter.

[4] The Purse is usually carried by the Purse Bearer in front of the Lord Chancellor on ceremonial occasions. Theoretically, the Purse contains the Great Seal (not an aquatic mammal) but a large chunk of silver from which Royal seals can be made, which are then attached to certain official documents. These documents have no effect until sealed in this way. In fact, the Purse is usually empty, the exception being the State Opening of Parliament, when it contains the Queen's Speech. When the time comes for Her Majesty to read the Speech, the Lord Chancellor extracts a copy from the Purse hands it to her and then walks backwards down the steps of the throne; always a slightly tense moment. The Lord Chancellor is Keeper of the Great Seal and the Purse serves as a symbol of his holding this office. When the House of Lords is sitting, the Purse, the Lord Chancellor's tri-corn hat and one of the Maces (the House of Lords has two, the Commons only one) must be placed behind him on the Woolsack.

hear the Queen's Speech. The Queen's Speech is read out by the Queen, having of course been written by the Government. The Queen does not have to be present for Parliament to be opened, although it would not be a 'State Opening' as such, but would take place by 'Royal Commission' . The form of words used would be:

'We are commanded by Her Majesty to let you know that, it not being convenient for Her to be present here this day in Her Royal Person, she has thought fit by Letters Patent under the Great Seal to empower several Lords therein named to do all things in her Majesty's name which are to be done on her Majesty's Part in this Parliament, as by the Letters Patent will more fully appear'.

The Queen's speech would be read out by the Lord Chancellor or another of the Lords Commissioners.

After the Speech has been read, the Speaker and Members return to the Commons. The sitting is adjourned until the afternoon, when the 'Debate on the Address' (the Queen's Speech) begins.

The Debate on the Address

The House of Commons reassembles at 2.30pm and the House of Lords at 3.30pm and the Queen's Speech is reported to the House, in the Commons by the Speaker and in the Lords by the Lord Chancellor. In both Houses, certain other parliamentary business is taken before the Debate on the Address, one item of which is the First Reading of a Bill. In the Commons, the Outlawries Bill[5] is read for the first time and in the Lords, the Select Vestries Bill. Neither bill is ever printed and neither is intended to make any progress whatsoever; their only function is to demonstrate the right of both Houses to debate a matter of their choosing before turning to any other business.

In the House of Lords, after the Select Vestries Bill has been read, the Debate on the Address is usually opened by a peer who is neither a member of the Government nor an Opposition Spokesman. For example, on 24 November 1998, Lord Clinton-Davis moved the 'Humble Address':

> "Most Gracious Sovereign--We, Your Majesty's most dutiful and loyal subjects, the Lords Spiritual and Temporal in Parliament assembled, beg leave to thank Your Majesty for the most gracious Speech which Your Majesty has addressed to both Houses of Parliament."

The Leader of the Opposition, the Leader of the Liberal Democrats and the Leader in the Lords usually follow and after the Chairman and Deputy Chairman of Committees have been appointed, the Sessional Orders read and the two Appeals and two Appellate Committees appointed, the debate is then adjourned until the following day. If there is no opposition to the appointments, the motion is agreed to, 'nemine dissentiente'.

---

[5] The Outlawries Bill is designed to prevent 'Clandestine Outlawries in Personal Actions' – whatever they are.

Chairman of Committees

Baroness Jay of Paddington: My Lords, I beg to move that the noble Lord, Lord Boston of Faversham, be appointed to take the Chair in all Committees of the House for this Session.
Moved accordingly, and, on Question, Motion agreed to nemine dissentiente.

Principal Deputy Chairman of Committees

Baroness Jay of Paddington: My Lords, I beg to move that the noble Lord, Lord Tordoff, be appointed Principal Deputy Chairman of Committees for this Session.
Moved accordingly, and, on Question, Motion agreed to nemine dissentiente.

Stoppages in the Streets--Ordered, That the Commissioner of the Police of the Metropolis do take care that during the Session of Parliament the passages through the streets leading to this House be kept free and open; and that no obstruction be permitted to hinder the passage of the Lords to and from this House; and that no disorder be allowed in Westminster Hall, or in the passages leading to this House, during sitting of Parliament; and that there be no annoyance therein or thereabouts; and that the Gentleman Usher of the Black Rod attending this House do communicate this order to the Commissioner aforesaid.

Appeal Committees--Two Appeal Committees were appointed pursuant to Standing Order.
Appellate Committees--Two Appellate Committees were appointed pursuant to Standing Order.

The Debate on the Address usually lasts for six days. If no amendments have been moved to the motion that a Humble Address be presented then the motion is 'agreed to nemine dissentiente' and the Address is 'presented to Her Majesty by the Lords with White Staves'. At this point anyone might be forgiven for wondering just who are these Lords with White Staves, and moreover, what do they do with them? Although the 'Lords with White Staves' sounds suspiciously like a jazz band, the aforementioned Lords are those, who, by virtue of their office, may present various 'Addresses' to Her Majesty; for example, the Humble Address in answer to the Queen's Speech. The White Staves are basically a symbol of office. The Lords with White Staves include the Lord Chamberlain and the Lord Steward. Confusingly, the Master of the Horse may present an Address to Her Majesty, despite having no White Staff as a symbol of office.

In the House of Commons, matters are much more mundane and sadly there are no MPs with White Staves, or indeed Staves of any colour. In the Commons, the Sessional Orders are read, which state that the House will deal severely with anyone who has been elected as a Member of the House as a result of bribery or 'other corrupt practices' and that the 'streets leading to the House be kept free and open and that no obstruction be permitted to hinder the passage of Members to and from this House, and that no disorder be allowed in Westminster Hall'. Orders are also read which permit the printing of the Votes and Proceedings and the Journal of the House. No Private Notice Questions or SO 24 applications are allowed on the first day of the Session.

SESSIONAL ORDERS

Elections

Ordered,

That all Members who are returned for two or more places in any part of the United Kingdom do make their Election for which of the places they will serve, within one week after it shall appear that there is no question upon the Return for that place; and if anything shall come in question touching the Return or Election of any Member, he is to withdraw during the time the matter is in debate; and that all Members returned upon double Returns do withdraw till their Returns are determined.

Resolved,

That no Peer of the Realm, except a Peer of Ireland, hath any right to give his vote in the Election of any Member to serve in Parliament.

Resolved,

That if it shall appear that any person hath been elected or returned a Member of this House, or endeavoured so to be, by Bribery or any other corrupt practices, this House will proceed with the utmost severity against all such persons as shall have been wilfully concerned in such Bribery or other corrupt practices.

Witnesses

Resolved,

That if it shall appear that any person hath been tampering with any Witness, in respect of his evidence to be given to this House, or any Committee thereof, or directly or indirectly hath endeavoured to deter or hinder any person from appearing or giving evidence the same is declared to be a high crime and misdemeanour; and this House will proceed with the utmost severity against such offender.

Resolved,

That if it shall appear that any person hath given false evidence in any case before this House, or any Committee thereof, this House will proceed with the utmost severity against such offender.

Metropolitan Police

Ordered,

That the Commissioner of Police of the Metropolis do take care that during the Session of Parliament the passages through the streets leading to the House be kept free and open and that no obstruction be permitted to hinder the passage of Members to and from this House, and that no disorder be allowed in Westminster Hall, or in the passages leading to this House, during the Sitting of Parliament, and that there be no annoyance therein or thereabouts; and that the Serjeant at Arms attending this House do communicate this Order to the Commissioner aforesaid.

Votes and Proceedings

Ordered,

That the Votes and Proceedings of this House be printed, being first perused by Madam Speaker; and that she do appoint the printing thereof; and that no person but such as she shall appoint do presume to print the same.

Outlawries

Bill for the more effectual preventing Clandestine Outlawries; *read the First time; to be read a Second time.*

Journal

Ordered,

That the Journal of this House, from the end of the last Session to the end of the present Session, with an index thereto, be printed.

Ordered,

That the said Journal and Index be printed by the appointment and under the direction of Donald William Limon, Esq, CB, the Clerk of this House.

Ordered,

That the said Journal and Index be printed by such person as shall be licensed by Madam Speaker, and that no other person do presume to print the same.

The answer to the Queen's Speech is in the form of a resolution which thanks Her Majesty for 'the gracious speech'. The motion is proposed by two Back-benchers chosen by the Government and the speeches are usually fairly light-hearted. The late Ian Gow gave one of the funniest of such speeches, opening the Debate on the Address in 1989 - the year that the Commons was first televised. He had the House in stitches when he regaled them with excerpts from a letter he and other Members had received from some image consultants offering to improve their appearance. Apparently the letter had asserted that only 7% of a speaker's impact was dependent on what they were actually saying. This, Mr Gow felt, might be of some comfort to the Opposition.

The Debate on the Address usually continues for six days and the Official Opposition chooses the subjects for debate. For example, in 1998 the subjects for debate were on the second day, trade and industry, education and employment; on the third day, health and welfare, on the fourth, foreign affairs and defence, on the penultimate day, the constitution and Parliament and finally, the economy.

On the first day, the debate is opened by two Back-benchers, chosen by the Government, followed by the Leader of the Opposition, the Prime Minister and the Leader of the Liberal Democrats. For example, in 1998, Joe Ashton MP and Dr Lynda Clark MP were called to propose and second the Address. On the final two days the Opposition opens the debate. Question time takes place as usual on the second and subsequent days of the Debate on the Address. The Speaker usually selects the amendment tabled by the Official Opposition and this is actually moved and debated by the House. The Speaker will usually call a second amendment, normally one tabled by the Liberal Democrats, at the conclusion of the debate on the last day, but this is not debated (SO 33). There are therefore, three Divisions beginning at 10.00pm – on the amendment by the Official Opposition, the amendment in the name of the Liberal Democrats and the motion itself.

When the resolution has been agreed to it is ordered to be presented to Her Majesty by Members of the Privy Council.

SITTINGS OF THE HOUSE

The hours in which the House of Commons sits are governed by Standing Orders, which have recently been amended to accommodate an earlier start to proceedings on Thursdays. The First Report from the Select Committee on Modernisation of the House of Commons (HC 60, 1998/99) was accepted by the House on 16 December 1998 and as a result, for the current 1998/99 Session at least, the House will sit from 11.30am on Thursdays. The House therefore sits as follows.

- Mondays, Tuesdays and Wednesdays from 2.30pm
- Thursdays from 11.30am
- Fridays from 9.30am (there are 10 non-sitting Fridays each Session)

In exceptional circumstances the House sits at the weekend. This is effected by the House agreeing to a resolution.

If for some reason the House sits all night, into the following morning and then beyond the start of the next day's sitting, the next day's sitting does not take place. This could mean that if the House sat through Monday night and Tuesday morning and beyond 2.30pm on Tuesday afternoon, though it might be Tuesday in the outside world, in the House of Commons it would still be Monday. Erskine May records the longest sitting as one which took place on 31 January 1881 on the Coercion Bill, when the House sat for an astonishing total of 41 and a half-hours (Erskine May, 22nd Edition, page 251).

The House of Lords meets on the following days:

- Mondays, Tuesdays and Wednesdays, from 2.30pm
- Thursdays from 3.00pm (Judicial business is heard at 2.00pm)
- Fridays from 11.00am *(the House of Lords does not sit every Friday)*[6]

[6] The House of Lords usually sits at 11.00am on the day the House adjourns for a recess.

PARLIAMENTARY SESSIONS – DATES OF TERMS AND RECESSES OF THE HOUSE OF COMMONS1987/88 TO 1997/98 **(In a General Election year the date of State Opening is a few days after the House returns for Members to take the oath)**

Session *denotes General Election year	State Opening	Christmas Recess	House returned	Easter Recess	House returned	Whitsun Recess	House returned	Summer Recess	Spill Over	Prorogation
1987-88	25 June 1987[1]	18 December 1987	11 January 1988	31 March 1988	12 April 1988	27 May 1988	7 June 1988	29 July 1988	19 October 1988	5 November 1988
1988-89	22 November 1988	22 December 1988	10 January 1989	23 March 1989	4 April 1989	26 May 1989	6 June 1989	28 July 1989	17 October 1989	16 November 1989
1989-90	21 November 1989	21 December 1989	8 January 1990	5 April 1990	18 April 1990	24 May 1990	5 June 1990	26 July 1990[2]	15 October 1990	1 November 1990
1990-91	7 November 1990	20 December 1990	14 January 1991	28 March 1991	15 April 1991	23 May 1991	3 June 1991	25 July 1991	14 October 1991	22 October 1991
1991-92	31 October 1991	20 December 1991	13 January 1992	16 March 1992						
*1992-93	6 May 1992[3]	17 December 1992	11 January 1993	2 April 1993	30 April 1993	27 May 1993	7 June 1993	27 July 1993	18 October 1993	5 November 1993

[1] House rose for 1987 Summer Recess on 24 July 1987 and returned on 21 October

[2] House returned to debate situation in Gulf on 6/7 September

[3] House rose on 22 May and returned on 2 June and sat until 16 July, returning on 24/25 September to debate the UK's removal from the ERM. It returned on 19 October

Session *denotes General Election year	State Opening	Christmas Recess	House returned	Easter Recess	House returned	Whitsun Recess	House returned	Summer Recess	Spill Over	Prorogation
1993-94	18 November 1993	17 December 1993	11 January 1994	31 March 1994	12 April 1994	27 May 1994	13 June 1994	21 July 1994	17 October 1994	3 November 1994
1994-95	16 November 1994	20 December 1994	10 January 1995	5 April 1995	18 April 1995	25 May 1995	6 June 1995	19 July 1995	16 October 1995	8 November 1995
1995-96	15 November 1995	20 December 1995	9 January 1996	3 April 1996	16 April 1996	3 May 1996	22 May 1996	24 July 1996	14 October 1996	17 October 1996
1996-97	23 October 1996	18 December 1996	13 January 1997	21 March 1997						
1997-98	14 May 1997[4]	22 December 1997	12 January 1998	8 April 1998	20 April 1998	21 May 1998	1 June 1998	31 July 1998[5]	19 October 1998	19 November 1998

[4] The House rose for the Summer Recess on 1 August and returned on 27 October 1997.
[5] The House was recalled to debate the Criminal Justice (Terrorism and Conspiracy) Bill on 2/3 September.

THE PARLIAMENTARY DAY IN THE HOUSE OF COMMONS

The following is an example of the where in the day certain types of business occur in the House of Commons. Proceedings can, of course, be interrupted to deal with urgent matters which require the immediate attention of the House.

The Speaker's procession leaves the Speaker's office at 2.25pm and moves through the Central Lobby preceded by the Serjeant-at-Arms carrying the Mace. Once the Speaker is in the Chair, the Division bells are rung once. They are then rung a further time at the conclusion of Prayers. No 'strangers' (members of the public) are admitted into the public galleries during Prayers. Members stand with their backs to the Table of the House, facing the benches, for prayers, which are usually taken by the Speaker's Chaplain. The main prayer is extremely appropriate, referring to the Commons as 'thine unworthy servants' and beseeching the Almighty for 'Heavenly Wisdom from above, to direct and guide us in all our consultations'. Some would argue that this prayer has clearly never been answered. The prayer goes on to call, perhaps a little optimistically, for, 'the uniting and knitting together of the hearts of all persons and estates within the same, in true Christian love and Charity one towards another'.

Backbench MPs must be present at Prayers if they wish to have a seat in the Chamber until the rising of the House. In order to reserve a place for a particularly popular debate, Members may put a card with their name on it, in a space in the back of the bench where they usually sit. Prayer cards may be obtained personally by Members from an attendant who is on duty from 8.00am in the morning (or after the rising of the House whichever is the later) until the House meets. A Member may only obtain a card for him or herself, not for another Member. Members of Select Committees may retain places without attending prayers, by fixing a pink card to the bench. A similar privilege is usually given to Members of Standing Committees which are meeting early that afternoon.

After Prayers (or at 2.30pm on Wednesdays)

Reports of Queen's Answers to Addresses

When an address has been presented to Her Majesty, for example the Address in reply to the Queen's Speech, the answer is reported to the House by a member of her Household. This is usually the Vice Chamberlain, who, having survived being taken hostage during the State Opening, has resumed his or her role as a Government Whip. Addresses can be presented to Her Majesty by either House on a variety of foreign and domestic issues and can be debated and amended. The motion which is put before the House usually states, 'That an humble Address be presented to Her Majesty ...' An amendment to remove the word 'humble' would not be in order.

Messages from Crown to Parliament usually fall into one of three categories: 'Queen's pleasure', 'Queen's recommendation' or 'Queen's consent'. These messages are nearly always written as opposed to verbal messages.

- 'Queen's Pleasure' is the form employed for communicating the Queen's wishes with regard to formal matters connected with parliamentary procedure; e.g., the election of a Speaker at the beginning of a Parliament and the Prorogation of Parliament at the end of a Parliamentary Session.

- 'Queen's recommendation' is a technical form of message, used in financial procedures. The Queen's recommendation is given to motions which involve any public expenditure or a grant of money not included in the annual estimates (now communicated in writing). For example, the Queen's recommendation has to be given to all money resolutions (these are discussed more fully in chapter seven on Legislation and chapter 13 on Financial Procedures). What the Queen's Recommendation signifies is that only the Crown (in reality the Government of the day) may initiate financial expenditure. The receipt of the Queen's Recommendation is noted in the Order of Business, thus: FIREWORKS BILL [MONEY]: Queen's Recommendation signified.

- The 'Queen's consent' is required to all bills affecting the prerogative, hereditary revenues, personal property or interests of the Crown, the Duchy of Lancaster or the Duchy of Cornwall (in which case the consent of the Prince of Wales is also required). Again, this is set out on the Order of Business, thus: DATA PROTECTION BILL [*LORDS*]: As amended in the Standing Committee, to be considered. (*Queen's and Prince of Wales's Consent to be signified on Third Reading.*) [*Until any hour*]. Consent is usually left until the latest possible stage in the Bill's progress through the House, so that any amendments passed at a late stage can be taken into account. Sometimes, if the interests of the Crown form the main purpose of the Bill, Queen's consent is signified at Second Reading or even before the bill is introduced. If amendments are made to a bill in Committee which require the Queen's consent, this has to be signified later. If the Queen's consent is not obtained, a bill which requires it cannot proceed. The Government could recommend to the Queen that Her consent should not be given to a particular bill; however, in practice, even if it disapproved of a bill it would recommend consent on the basis that the bill should at least be debated. Technically, a bill which affected the prerogative interests of the Crown could receive Queen's consent, but still be refused Royal Assent at the end of its progress through both Houses.

Formal Communications by the Speaker

Formal communications are basically announcements made by the Speaker on any number of different matters, the most common type being the announcement of the death of an MP.

Motions for New Writs

The death or resignation of an MP gives rise to a vacancy; technically, an MP cannot resign, he or she must apply to be appointed to a 'nominal office of profit under the Crown' which disqualifies him/her from membership of the House of Commons. The two offices used are the stewardships of the Chiltern Hundreds and the Manor of Northstead. There are no duties involved - 'taking the Chiltern Hundreds' is a mere technicality.

Traditionally, when a seat becomes vacant, the Chief Whip of the Party of the Member who has died or resigned 'moves the writ' for the by-election. Technically, any MP can move such a motion. The moving of writs is technically a 'matter of privilege', which means it can be moved 'without notice' and has precedence over all other business. When a writ is opposed the Speaker usually rules that debate be deferred until the conclusion of question time. On 29 March 1999, the Conservative Opposition moved the writ for the Newark by-election, after Labour MP, Fiona Jones was found guilty of a false declaration of election expenses. The motion, 'That Madam Speaker do issue her warrant to the Clerk of the Crown to make out a new writ for the electing of a Member to serve in this present Parliament for the county constituency of Newark in the room of Fiona Elizabeth Ann Jones', was taken at 4.30pm (HC Col: 748) and debated until 5.00pm. A Government amendment to the motion, that, 'this House do pass to the Orders of the Day' was carried by 260 to 97 and consequently the writ was not moved. Until quite recently, moving a writ was one of the methods used to delay proceedings in the House. On one occasion, Dennis Skinner MP moved a writ and spoke for almost an entire morning in an attempt to delay debate on Ann Widdecombe MP's Private Member's Motion on abortion. Now, if a writ is moved and opposed on a day when Private Members' business has precedence, proceedings on that motion lapse and the writ has to be moved on another day. The convention is that a by-election is held within three months of a vacancy arising and the by-election takes place on the third Thursday after the motion to issue the writ has been agreed.

Private Business

Private business is dealt with in the following order.

- Consideration of Lords Amendments
- Third Readings
- Consideration (Report Stage)
- Second Readings
- Notices of Motions relating to private business, other than stages of bills
- Stages of bills for confirming orders under the Private Legislation Procedure (Scotland) Act 1936 (arranged in the same order as Private Bills)

Private business has to end by 2.45pm and any outstanding business is held over until the next sitting. If, when an item of Private Business is announced, it is objected to by just a single Member, it becomes 'Opposed Private Business' and consideration is deferred until a future day. The time for taking Opposed Private Business is 7.00pm – usually on a Monday. The Chairman of Ways and Means has responsibility for allocating such business.

Presentation of Public Petitions (only on Fridays at this time)

(see later for details of petitions)

Motions for Unopposed Returns

This is basically a request for certain documents to be produced. It is rarely used nowadays because most information is readily available from Government departments by asking parliamentary questions or is provided in the form of Command Papers.

However, some 'annual returns' are presented in this way by custom; for example, the Financial Statement and Budget Report' – colloquially known as the 'Red Book'.

Questions

Questions for Oral Answer

These begin no later than 2.45pm on Mondays, Tuesdays and Wednesdays and no later than 11.45am on Thursdays. Question time is concluded at 3.30pm Mondays to Wednesdays and at 12.30pm on Thursdays. There is no question time on Fridays. The Prime Minister now answers questions on a Wednesday at 3.00pm for half an hour as opposed to twice-weekly on a Tuesday and Thursday at 3.15pm for 15 minutes. Questions are looked at in detail in the next chapter.

Private Notice Questions (PNQs)

These are questions of an urgent nature which are taken at 3.30pm (12.30pm on a Thursday and 11.00am on a Friday), provided they have been submitted to the Speaker before 12.00pm that day (10.30am on a Thursday and 10.00am on a Friday). There can only be one Private Notice Question (PNQ) each day and the Speaker may turn down applications if the question is one which is not sufficiently topical. PNQs are discussed more fully in the next chapter.

After Questions

Ministerial Statements (12.30pm on Thursdays, 11.00am on Fridays)

Statements are made fairly frequently by Government Ministers and subjects range from crises in the NHS, scandals involving local authorities, the use of UK forces abroad – in short, almost anything. The Government Whips' Office usually informs the Opposition Whips' Offices at around 12.00 noon if there are to be any Government statements. Those wishing to speak give their names to the Speaker's Office.

Although the Speaker's Office is informed of statements, neither the Speaker, nor the House itself has to grant permission for a Government Minister to make a statement. The Minister will usually speak for about 10-15 minutes during which time copies of the Statement are handed to members of the Press in the Press Gallery. Once the Minister has sat down copies of his/her statement and any accompanying documents are made available in the Vote Office. The relevant Opposition Spokesman will then reply to the statement (he or she will have been provided with a copy of the Statement before the Minister gets up to speak, but sometimes only minutes before. Opposition Spokesmen often have a difficult task in responding to Statements, as their occurrence is not always possible to predict. The Statement and reply from the Opposition is then followed by a question and answer session which provides Back-benchers with an opportunity to contribute to the debate.

There has been increasing concern amongst some Members that the Government is seeking to announce new policies, initiatives, etc. outside the House before making a Statement to the House. However, this criticism was also levelled at the previous

Government and there is little the Speaker can do to prevent announcements being made at times and in ways which suit the deadlines of the press rather better than the House of Commons. Statements can cover a wide range of subjects – from the situation in Kosovo to an announcement of a Government White Paper or the outcome of a European Council meeting. It is the practice of the Government of the day to make a Statement to the House after each European Council meeting. Exceptionally, Statements are made at other times during the sitting.

Introduction of New Members

After a by-election, the new Member, with two MPs as sponsors, approaches the Table of the House, bows and then is greeted by a Clerk at the Government Despatch Box where he or she takes either the Oath or Affirmation and signs the Test Roll.

Applications for Emergency Debates (Proposals to move the Adjournment of the House under Standing Order 24 (not on Fridays)

Any Member who wishes to apply for an emergency debate on an urgent matter must inform the Speaker of his intention to do so before midday. The MP moving such a motion rises in his place after questions and before public business and asks leave to move the adjournment of the House. He can speak for three minutes. It is up to the Speaker to decide whether or not to allow an 'SO 24' application. Most are disallowed, but if an application is accepted the Speaker must ask if the Member concerned has the 'leave' (permission) of the House. If this is not unanimously given, members supporting the motion are asked to rise in their places. If 40 or more Members rise the debate goes ahead. If there are less than 40, but more than 10 Members supporting the motion, the matter is decided by a Division.

A debate on an emergency motion usually takes place the following day at the beginning of public business (at 3.30pm or 12.30pm on a Thursday, but if the matter is particularly pressing, the Speaker may allow the debate to take place that day at 7.00pm until 10.00pm at the latest. In this case, the moment of interruption is delayed after 10.00pm by a period equivalent to the period spent on the emergency debate.

Ceremonial Speeches

This gives the House an opportunity to eulogise one of its former inmates; e.g., a previous speaker of the House of Commons or an illustrious Member of one sort or another who has recently passed away.

Personal Statements

Personal Statements are usually made when an MP or Minister resigns and some infamous examples have included the resignation speeches of Sir Geoffrey Howe, Nigel Lawson, Norman Lamont and more recently, Ron Davies and Frank Field. On 29 July 1998, the latter used the power of understatement to great effect, by saying, that: 'If the past 15 months have taught me anything, it is not only that the biggest of all reforms requires an executive position for a person with convictions about welfare reform, but that the entire Cabinet, especially the Chancellor, shares beliefs about that common endeavour.' (HC Col: 374). The Chamber is usually full for Personal Statements, as Members enjoy nothing better than watching one of their number slip a stiletto between the shoulder blades of a former colleague.

Consideration of Lords Amendments or Messages

Lords messages are taken at this point in the day's proceedings. Usually, Lords messages relate to Lords Amendments to bills and their consideration is usually set down for debate on a future day (on that day they would be set down as an 'order of the day' - see below); however, they can be dealt with on the day on which they are received. For example, in the case of the European Parliamentary Elections Bill 1997/98, Lords Amendments were received on 18 November, the penultimate day of the Session. The Commons insisted on its disagreement with the Lords Amendments and the bill returned to the Lords. The Lords were equally stubborn and the bill then returned the same evening to the House of Commons where the Home Secretary had to announce that the bill had been lost for the Session.

Matters of Privilege

Matters relating to breaches of privilege can be raised at this point. However, matters relating to the privilege of the House or alleged contempts of the House are now raised by Members writing to the Speaker in advance as opposed to raising them directly on the floor of the House at this point in the day's proceedings. Moving a writ for a by-election is an example of the House exercising the ancient privilege of deciding upon its own composition, but when writ is moved it is now moved at the beginning of the sitting. However, if the moving of the writ is opposed, it is taken at this point in the days' sitting (for more information on privilege see chapter 10).

At the Commencement of Public Business

Public business commences when the Speaker calls the first Member who has given notice to present a Bill, motion, etc. After the commencement of public business no Backbencher can move a motion for the House to be adjourned and no one can call for an emergency debate under SO 24. Before the Orders of the Day are read, four items may be taken.

Presentation of Public bills (SO 57)

Any Member can gain a First Reading for a bill by ensuring that its Long and Short Titles appear on the Order of Business. Having gained First Reading in this way, the bill can then be printed and set down for Second Reading. No such bill can be presented to the House until after the fifth Wednesday in a Session (for more information on SO 57 ('Ordinary Presentation Bills') see chapter seven on Legislation).

Government Motions Relating to Committees

Government motions to refer certain matters to standing committees are made at this point; for example, a motion to send a Negative Statutory Instrument to a Standing Committee on Delegated Legislation would be moved at this time.

Government Motions Regulating the Business of the House

Motions attempting to regulate the business of the House do not have precedence unless moved by a Government Minister; they are usually moved by the Leader of the House.

There are two kinds of business motion: those which are referred to in Standing Order 15 and relate to 'exempted business' (business which can be taken after 10.00pm) and those which are not covered by Standing Orders.

The former are moved at the 'interruption of business' (10.00pm) and usually state that, for example, the 'Chinese Noodles (No. 2) Bill can be 'proceeded with, although opposed, until any hour'. The latter are usually announcements relating to the times of emergency weekend sittings or notification that precedence is to be given to Government business on a particular day.

Motions under Standing Order 23 (Ten Minute Rule Bills, motions to nominate Select Committee Members)

'Ten Minute Rule Bills', as they are known, can be set down by Backbenchers for debate on Tuesdays and Wednesdays after the fifth Wednesday of the Session. Motions under this Standing Order can be set down by the Government for debate on any day except Friday, but in practice SO 23 is only used by Backbenchers. Motions for the discharge of members from, or addition of members to, a Select Committee can be taken at this point, but motions relating to the membership of Select Committees are now usually taken at 10.00pm.

Privilege Motions Requiring Notice

Matters relating to parliamentary privilege, of which notice has been given are raised at this point (see chapter 10 for more information on parliamentary privilege).

Order of the Day and Notices of Motions (Public Business)

Orders of the day are basically those items of public business to be discussed that day; rather like the items on an Agenda for a committee meeting. For example, an 'Order' might be the Second Reading or Report Stage of a Government Bill. When the Orders of the day are reached, the Clerk at the Table reads them out and they are then taken in the order in which they 'stand upon the Notice Paper'. When an Order of the Day is reached it must be proceeded with, appointed for a future day or discharged; it cannot be postponed until after another Order has been taken, except as the result of a Motion moved by a Minister at the commencement of public business. When the Orders of the day are being read out, no one may interrupt, except a Member of the Government and only then if the interruption is necessary to adjourn the House urgently or to ensure that a particular matter not already on the Order of Business is discussed. An Order of the day which is a stage of a bill, can be 'discharged' and the bill withdrawn if the Member in charge of the bill proposes this when the Order is read out by the Clerk.

'Notices of Motions which stand upon the Order Paper' basically means motions of which there has been prior notice: i.e., they have appeared on the Order of Business. If an Order of the day is a motion as opposed to a bill, it must be moved by the Member 'in whose name the notice stands'. However, there are two exceptions: motions moved by members of the Government and motions moved by the Committee of Selection relating to Select Committee membership. These can be moved in the first case by another Minister and in the second by another member of the Committee.

At the Moment of Interruption all the remaining Orders of the day which have not been reached are read out. If the Order concerned is a bill, the Member in charge may call out 'Now' when the title is read out. This secures the passing of that particular stage of the bill - for example, its Committee Stage - provided no other Member shouts 'object'. If another Member objects, the Member in charge names another day on which that stage of the bill's proceedings can be taken. If the Member is not present and no other Member names another day on which the deferred proceedings may take place, the bill becomes what is known as a 'dropped order'. Theoretically, once an Order has been set down for debate on a particular day, it cannot be debated any sooner than this; however, the Government has in the past allowed its own time to be used to debate Private Members' Bills which it wished to see passed before the end of a Session. In these cases, a motion can be tabled by the Government to bring forward debate to an earlier day.

Opposed Private Business

The day's business can be interrupted at 7.00pm for Opposed Private Business, which has been set down for discussion on that day.

The Moment of Interruption, Business Motions and Exempted Business

Moment of Interruption

Technically, the end of the parliamentary day is at 10.00pm (7.00pm on a Thursday, 2.30pm on a Friday). This is known as the 'Moment of Interruption'. Certain business is 'exempt' from the Moment of Interruption and can be debated after this time. If, at the Moment of Interruption (10.00pm), an 'order of the day' has not been reached it is read out by one of the Clerks and the Member in charge can say 'now' to ensure that it passes. He or she then names a day to which the business concerned is to be deferred. Unfortunately, for the Member concerned, if a single Member shouts 'object' or tries to continue the debate, the business in hand becomes 'opposed' business and cannot be proceeded with. If an amendment to a motion appears on the Order Paper, this effectively means that the Order is opposed and cannot be taken after the Moment of Interruption. The Moment of Interruption prevents the business of the House from proceeding indefinitely. If the Moment of Interruption did not exist, opponents of a particular measure could simply 'talk it out'.

Business Motions

The Government can move a motion at 10.00pm (or 2.30pm on a Friday or 7.00pm on a Thursday) under Standing Order 15 to exempt certain business from the provisions of

Standing Order 9 and allow it to be proceeded with 'until any hour' or until a specified hour, or until a specified period has elapsed. This motion must appear on the Order Paper and usually takes the following form; for example, the 'Abolition of Lobbyists Bill may proceed, though opposed, until any hour'. If a Division is being called at 10.00pm, 7.00pm or 2.30pm, it is concluded and any questions dependent on that division are also put; i.e. a closure motion and the motion itself. Any such motion is put 'forthwith'.

Exempted Business

There are certain types of business which are exempt from the moment of interruption and these include Ways and Means Resolutions, motions on statutory instruments and EC Documents, motions on deregulation orders, and money resolutions. Exempted business is explained more fully later in this chapter.

Presentation of Public Petitions

The first recorded petitions date from the reign of Richard II. The practice of presenting petitions to Parliament became ever more popular and since such petitions were always presented at the start of the day's proceedings they began to take up more and more of the time of the House of Commons. They were used as a means of raising subjects for debate without having to set them down on the Order Paper. In 1842 the House agreed to a Standing Order preventing any discussion of a petition on its presentation. Under SO 155, it is possible to discuss petitions relating to an urgent and 'personal grievance' (if discussed they would constitute exempted business). Petitions are usually presented to the House of Commons. Petitions are also used to seek the permission of the House for an MP to give evidence in court relating to proceedings of the House

On Mondays, Tuesdays, Wednesdays and Thursdays, petitions are presented just before the daily Adjournment Motion. On Fridays, they are presented at the beginning of the day's proceedings, between any Unopposed Private Business and any presentation of unopposed returns. Any petitions which have not been presented by 10.00am on a Friday have to stand over until the end of the day's business. This reform was introduced in response to Members attempting to use the presentation of petitions as a means of delaying debate on controversial Private Members' Bills. No petitions can be presented on the first day of a Session. Any Member wishing to present a petition must make sure their name is on the Public Petitions list in the Table Office by 12.00pm on the day on which it is to be presented (or before the House rises on Thursday in the case of petitions presented on a Friday). When a Member presents a petition he or she simply reads out the names of the person or persons in whose name or names the petition is made, the number of signatories, the 'prayer' and the main subject of the petition. The petition is then put in the bag behind the Speaker's chair (hence the expression 'it's in the bag'). Petitions can be presented at any time simply by placing them in the aforementioned bag whilst the House is sitting. Petitions are recorded as having been deposited in the Votes and Proceedings of the House. Petitions are sent to the relevant Government Minister and any 'observations' made in response are printed with the Vote.

Anyone wishing to present a petition must consult the Clerk of Public Petitions to ensure that the form of wording used is correct. The first page of a petition must be handwritten and all continuation sheets must be headed with the 'Prayer' (the object) of the petition. All signatures to a petition must be accompanied by an address. Petitions must not refer to what has acutally been said in debate in the House, although they can mention the debates themselves. As Erskine May makes clear (22nd Edition, page 812), this is to 'protect individual Members from petitions calling into question their speeches in the House'.

MPs usually present all petitions from their constituents, however preposterous and however much they might disagree with their contents. For some obscure reason, the Corporation of London may present petitions in person at the Bar of the House. A Sheriff of London is accompanied to the Bar by the Serjeant-at-Arms and is asked by the Speaker, 'Mr Sheriff, what have you got there?' Readers will be relieved to know that this is not a common occurrence in the House of Commons.

In the House of Lords, petitions must be presented and signed by a peer and either given to the Clerk of Parliaments or put on the Table of the House during a sitting. When the peer concerned presents the petition, just the Prayer and number of signatures is read out. Petitions are only printed if a motion is put down to debate the petition on a certain day. The presentation of petitions is noted in the Lords Minutes.

Daily Adjournment Motion

The day's sitting always ends with a half-hour daily Adjournment Debate. These are balloted and MPs usually raise issues which are of interest to their constituents. Frequently, there are only two members remaining in the Chamber by this stage, the Member concerned and the Minister whose job it is to reply to the debate. These debates are explained more fully in chapter eight.

THE PARLIAMENTARY DAY IN THE HOUSE OF LORDS

Judicial Business

The House of Lords meets at 2.00pm on a Thursday, albeit not every Thursday, for judicial business. This is basically to hear judgments. After judgments have been heard, the House adjourns until the beginning of public business. For more information on the judicial work of the House of Lords please see chapter three. The House of Lords can meet during a recess to deliver judgments and to hear appeals. Appeals can also be heard during a dissolution of Parliament, in which case the House would meet at 10.30am, with the sitting ending at 4.00pm.

Government business does not have precedence in the House of Lords and business is taken in the order set cut below according to Standing Order 38. If a bill or statutory instrument is to be taken earlier in the day than usual, because no debate is expected, the following sign - ¶ - appears on the Order Paper (this is not permitted on a Wednesday). Public bills, affirmative statutory instruments and Select Committee reports take precedence over other business, except questions, private business and Business of the House motions, on every day except Wednesday. However, this can be varied (but not on a Wednesday) with agreement of the Lord concerned, if notice is given on the Order Paper. If an item of business is to be moved to an earlier day, this requires a

'Business of the House Motion' to be agreed to by the House (such a motion would suspend SO 38 (HL)).

Business taken before Questions

Prayers

These are read at the beginning of the day's proceedings. When judicial business is to be heard, prayers are read before that and not again before the start of public business. No members of the public are allowed into the public galleries until after prayers.

Introductions

The Ceremony of Introduction for newly created peers in the House of Lords has recently been amended to reduce the amount of bowing, bobbing, kneeling and doffing of hats, etc. The House debated the report of the Select Committee on the Ceremony of Introduction (HL 78) on 30 April 1998 and agreed with one amendment to the Motion in the name of the then Leader of the House and Lord Privy Seal, Lord Richard that the recommendations of the Committee be implemented. Newly created life and hereditary peers no longer have to kneel before the Lord Chancellor or bow three times, doffing their hats on each occasion. It is the so-called 'placing' of peers which has been abolished. Prior to the reforms, the Garter King of Arms 'placed' the new peer by conducting him or her along replete with supporters, to the bench 'appropriate to their degree in the peerage'. They were then required to sit, put on their hats, rise, doff their hats and bow to the Lord Chancellor, three times. They would then leave the Chamber, the new peer shaking hands with the Lord Chancellor on the way out. It was felt by the Select Committee that this part of the ceremony had become outdated simply because peers now sit in the House of Lords on the relevant party's benches or on the Cross Benches and not according to rank. However, there was a general feeling in the House that the Garter King of Arms should still take part in the ceremony, on the basis that he represents the monarch, who does, after all, actually confer the peerage with the permission of the Government.

The ceremony has been shortened so that a newly created peer, accompanied by two 'supporters' (other peers), all of whom wear the correct parliamentary robes, proceeds to the Bar of the House, preceded by the Gentleman Usher of the Black Rod, Garter King of Arms carrying the Letters Patent (the document which effectively creates the peerage) and bows three times. The new peer then proceeds to the Table of the House where the Letters Patent[1] are read and the Oath is taken (the Writ of Summons is no longer read

[1] When a new peerage is granted, the document which actually creates the peerage is the Letters Patent. A new peer receives both a Writ of Summons and Letters Patent. However, all peers receive a Writ of Summons at the beginning of a new Parliament as do those who are ennobled during the course of a Parliament. 'Hereditary Peers of the First Creation' (newly created hereditary peers) receive Letters Patent, but 'peers by descent' (those inheriting titles) do not – this is because the title and the peerage in question has already been created, it is simply being handed on to the next generation. The Letters Patent are sealed using the Great Seal (*see above*).

out).[2] The Ceremonies of Introduction for a new Lord Chancellor, a member of the Royal Family and for the introduction of certain other peers differ from the above. The recommendations of the Select Committee adopted by the House related only to the introduction of newly created peers and Lords Spiritual (the bishops).

Peers who have simply inherited a title are not introduced – the ceremony being reserved for the following:

- newly created hereditary and life peers;
- peers 'advanced to a higher degree' (this has nothing to do with getting a PhD, but means a peer who has inherited another, higher, title);
- eldest sons of peers 'called up' whilst their father is alive by means of a 'writ in acceleration' (if a peer has more than one hereditary title, the Crown can accelerate the descent of one of them, so that it passes during the lifetime of the holder to his eldest son and heir apparent, entitling him to a seat in the House of Lords.
- newly appointed Lords of Appeal (Law Lords);
- an archbishop or bishop (either newly created or 'translated to another see' (i.e., if the Bishop of Bath was appointed the Bishop of London).

For more information on the composition of the House of Lords in general and titles in particular, please see chapter three.

Oaths

Peers must take the Oath of allegiance before they can sit in the House of Lords. They take the Oath when they first take their seat and then again at the beginning of each new Parliament. Oaths are usually taken at this point in the day's proceedings but may also be taken at the end of business. Peers can either take the Oath or make a 'solemn affirmation'.

Leave of Absence

Under SO 20(HL) a peer can apply for Leave of Absence if they feel they will be unable to attend any of the sittings of the House. This can be done at any time during a Parliament. Peers are expected to give one month's notice if they wish to attend sittings of the House during a period for which they have Leave of Absence. The House has to grant permission for a peer to be absent in this way.

Messages from the Crown (*also taken at any convenient time during the sitting*)

[2] A Writ of Summons is sent to any peer entitled to sit in the House of Lords prior to the start of each Parliament and to anyone on whom a peerage has been conferred or who has succeeded to a peerage during the course of a Parliament.

Messages from the Crown are usually in response to an Address from the House; for example, the Address in reponse to the Queen's Speech at the opening of Parliament.

Royal Assent (*also taken at any convenient time during the sitting*)

Royal Assent has to be given to all bills before they are enacted. Royal Assent is described in detail in chapter seven on the passage of legislation.

Addresses to the Crown

Addresses to the Crown are ordered to be presented at this point; for example the Address in reply to the Queen's Speech.

Tributes

Tributes to members of the House of Lords who have died would be made at this point in the day's proceedings.

Personal Statements

Personal Statements are sometimes made by peers in order to explain or perhaps apologise for a particular comment or course of action.

Sometimes, apologies can actually serve to compound the original offence. In 1988 Lord Monkswell obtained passes for four women to watch the debate on Clause 28 of the Local Government Bill which aimed to ban the 'promotion of homosexuality' by local authorities. Unfortunately for Lord Monkswell the women in question proceeded to abseil from the galleries, causing havoc in the Chamber. His 'apology' only served to further anger their Lordships as he criticised the Government for doing to homosexuals 'what the Germans did to the Jews'.

Questions

Starred Questions

Starred Questions are taken on every day except Friday. There are a maximum of four each day. The last question on a Wednesday and Thursday is a ballotted question on a topical issue. Starred Questions are described in more detail in chapter six.

Private Notice Questions

A Private Notice Question (PNQ) is a question on an urgent matter of which there has been no prior notice. Any Lord wishing to ask a PNQ has to apply in writing to the Leader of the House before 12.00 noon. PNQs are considered in more detail in chapter six. A PNQ asked in the House of Commons can be repeated in the House of Lords in the form of a statement.

Business Taken after Questions

Public Petitions

Under SO 70 petitions may be presented to the House of Lords provided they have been signed by a peer. Petitions may be handed in to the Clerk of Parliaments or handed into the Table of the House – they do not have to be presented to the whole House. If they are presented at this point in the proceedings, the peer in question simply reads out the Prayer of the petition and the number of signatories. Unless the peer in question tables a motion for the petition to be debated of a future day, it is not printed.

Privilege

Matters relating to parliamentary privilege can be raised at this point.

Business Statements

There are statements announcing that business will be interrupted for a dinner break and certain items of business (often an Unstarred Question) taken at that time.

Ministerial Statements *(may occasionally be taken at other times during the sitting)*

Statements made in the House of Commons by Government Ministers are usually repeated in the House of Lords at a convenient time after 3.30pm, if the Opposition Parties so wish. If the Minister concerned sits in the House of Lords the statement is made after questions. After the Minister has made the statement, the Opposition Parties' Spokesmen reply and this is followed by a response from the Minister. This is followed by a general discussion, lasting up to 20 minutes to which all Lords can contribute.

Introduction of Public bills *(may be taken at the end of business)*

An introduction of a bill is its First Reading. This is a purely formal procedure– there is no debate.

Messages from the House of Commons *(also taken at any convenient time during the sitting)*

Messages include those from the House of Commons to say that the latter has passed a bill (i.e., it has completed all its stages there) in which case the bill immediately has its first reading.

Private Bills

Formal proceedings on Private Bills (i.e., where there is no debate) are taken before public business, but if there is likely to be debate they are taken at this point in the day's proceedings.

Business of the House motions

Business of the House motions are made by the Leader of the House and enable Standing Orders 38 and 44 to be suspended so that business can be rearranged or that more than one stage of a bill can be taken on the same day. For example, on 30 April 1998 (HL Col: 388), the then Lord Privy Seal and Leader of the House, Lord Richard, moved the following motion:

'That Standing Order 38(5) (Arrangement of the Order Paper) be dispensed with on Wednesday, 6th May to allow the Second Reading of the Northern Ireland (Elections) Bill to be taken before the Motion in the name of the Lord Geddes; and that Standing Order 44 (No two stages of a Bill to be taken on one day) be dispensed with on Thursday, 7th May to allow the Bill to be taken through its remaining stages that day'.

Motions to amend Standing Orders

An example, from 18 November 1998 is set out below (HL Col: 1275).

Standing Orders (Public Business)

The Chairman of Committees: My Lords, I beg to move the second Motion standing in my name on the Order Paper.

Moved, That the Standing Orders relating to public business be amended as follows-
Standing Order 15
At end insert--
"(2) In order better to discharge his duties as a Minister of the Crown, the Lord Chancellor may, if he thinks fit, leave the Woolsack and sit in such other part of the House as he may find convenient; and in such circumstances his place on the Woolsack shall be taken by a Deputy Speaker or Deputy Chairman.";
Standing Order 16
At end insert "or such other part of the House as he may find convenient".--(The Chairman of Committees.)
On Question, Motion agreed to.

Motions Relating to Committees

These might be motions to appoint members of a particular Select Committee.

Public bills, delegated legislation and Select Committee Reports

This might include a Second Reading or Committee Stage of a bill or a motion on an affirmative instrument.

Motions

Motions taken at this point include Motions for Papers, Motions for Resolutions and Motions 'to take note'. These are explained more fully later in this chapter.

Unstarred Questions

There may only be one Unstarred Question each day and this may be taken during the dinner adjournment rather than at the end of the sitting. Unstarred Questions are discussed more fully in chapter six.

In the House of Lords there is no equivalent of the House of Commons' 'Moment of Interruption' and therefore no time is set for the adjournment of proceedings. A Government Whip usually moves: 'That the House do now adjourn' at the end of business.

CONTROL OF THE PARLIAMENTARY TIMETABLE

There are three main types of parliamentary business: public, private and Private Members' business. Private Bills are discussed in chapter 12 and Private Members' business in chapter eight. Public business comprises all Government business and the 20 days in each Session on which Opposition business has precedence. In addition there are certain 'Opposition-led' debates which take place in Government time; for example, the Debate on the Address and the Budget debate. The main item of Government business is legislation, and this is discussed fully in chapter seven. This chapter deals with certain other debates taken in Government time and Opposition Day debates and also looks at the way debates and motions are structured in the House of Commons. The 'forms of address' which are used in debate are considered, along with Divisions and procedures for ending debates. The chapter also looks at the types of motions and debates which take place in the House of Lords.

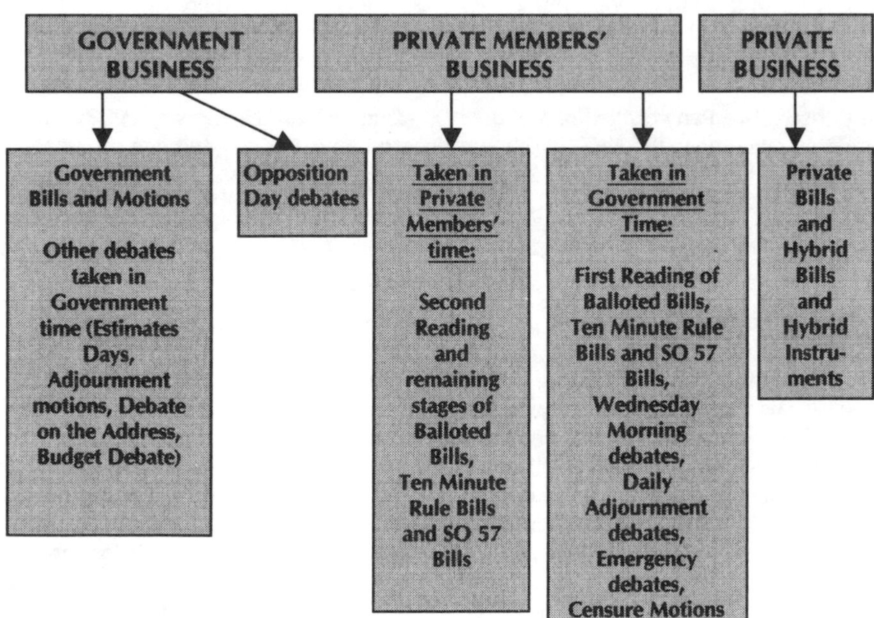

Standing Order 14(1) of the Standing Order of the House of Commons (Public Business) states that, 'government business shall have precedence at every sitting'. However, under section 2 of the Order, 20 days each session are allocated to the Opposition and on these days Opposition rather than Government business takes precedence. 17 of these days are 'at the disposal' of the Official Opposition (currently the Conservative Party) and the remaining three at the disposal of the Leader of the second largest Opposition Party. Under section 4 of the Order, on 13 Fridays in each Session, Private Members' business takes precedence (the number can be increased or decreased by the House agreeing to an amendment of the Order). Private Members' time is discussed more fully in chapter eight.

OPPOSITION DAY DEBATES

As stated above, SO 14(2) states that 20 days per session shall be days on which Opposition business takes precedence over Government business. The Order goes on to state that two Friday sittings equal one sitting on any other day (i.e., Monday to Thursday). 17 of the 20 days are 'at the disposal' of the Leader of the Official Opposition and two of those days may be divided into four half-days, provided they are not taken on a Friday. Three of the 20 days are 'at the disposal' of the Leader of the second largest Party (the Liberal Democrats) and one of those days may be taken as two half-days (again, not on a Friday). The Liberal Democrats usually make one of their Opposition Days available to the Nationalist Parties: Plaid Cymru and the SNP – who split the day between them. Where an Opposition Day is divided in two in this way, the first debate must be concluded by 7.00pm and the second must begin at 7.00pm. However, if Opposed Private Business has been set down for debate at 7.00pm, this takes precedence over an Opposition Day Debate. Similarly, if an Emergency Motion under SO 24 is to be taken at 7.00pm, the Opposition Day debate will held over until that debate has been concluded and will then be debated for up to three hours.

The Conservative Party divided one of their Opposition Days (18 January 1998) tabling a motion on rationing in the NHS, which was debated until 7.00pm and one on divided tax credits which was debated after 7.00pm. This is set out below. The debate began at 4.23pm (HC Col: 580 – 629).

NHS (Rationing)

Madam Speaker: I have selected the amendment in the name of the Prime Minister.

Miss Ann Widdecombe (Maidstone and The Weald): I beg to move,

That this House recognises that rationing has always been a part of how the Health Service manages health care resources; expresses its dismay at the comments of the Right honourable Member for Dulwich and West Norwood denying the obvious fact that rationing exists in the Health Service; expresses grave concern at the proposed changes to be effected by Her Majesty's Government, which through bureaucratic bodies such as a National Institute for Clinical Excellence and a Commission for Health Improvement will force clinicians to carry the burden on rationing decisions; recognises that the availability of modern drugs for conditions such as schizophrenia and MS makes clear the reality of rationing in today's Health Service; recognises the fact that

> waiting lists are a hidden form of rationing; notes that excessive political concentration upon waiting lists has been largely responsible for the continuing winter crisis in the Health Service, over which Her Majesty's Government appears wholly complacent and unconcerned; and urges Her Majesty's Government to acknowledge the concerns of professional bodies such as the BMA over rationing and embark upon a mature debate on the future of the Health Service.

After the speech by Shadow Health Secretary, Rt Hon Ann Widdecombe MP, the Secretary of State for Health, Rt Hon Frank Dobson MP moved an amendment to the motion on behalf of the Government.

The Secretary of State for Health (Mr. Frank Dobson): I beg to move, To leave out from "House" to the end of the Question, and to add instead thereof:

> "reaffirms the historic principles of the NHS, that if people are ill or injured there will be a national health service there to help, and access to it will be based on need and need alone, not on ability to pay or who their general practitioner happens to be or on where they live; welcomes the measures the Government has taken, is taking and will take that will ensure that comparable, top quality treatment and care are available in every part of the country through the introduction of new arrangements for spreading best practice, including the ending of the Conservative competition of the internal market, the introduction of local Health Improvement Programmes and Primary Care Groups to put local doctors, nurses and other health professionals in the driving seat in shaping local health care, the introduction of a new Commission for Health Improvement and National Institute for Clinical Excellence, and the creation of new legal duties of partnership and quality to ensure that all parts of the NHS and social services work together to deliver top quality services to all; welcomes the record £21 billion investment to be made in the NHS, including £18 billion for the NHS in England, over the next three years, notes the record 150,000 fall in NHS waiting lists since April 1998 and the 17 per cent increase in the number of new nurse trainees in the period since Labour came to power; and further welcomes the measures that the Government intends to take over the coming year to continue to build a modern and dependable NHS, including the extension of NHS Direct to cover 19 million people, the creation of 26 Health Action Zones covering 13 million people to target areas with particularly high levels of ill health--including cancer and heart disease--and reduce health inequalities, and the targeted investment of £30 million to modernise accident and emergency departments."

At the end of the debate the motion was voted on:

Question put, That the original words stand part of the Question:--
The House divided: Ayes 169, Noes 336.

Then, the Government's amendment was passed without a Division.

Question, That the proposed words be there added, *put forthwith, pursuant to Standing Order No. 31 (Questions on amendments), and agreed to.*
Mr. Deputy Speaker *forthwith declared the main Question, as amended, to be agreed to.*

Resolved, (in Hansard the text of the amendment follows)
The House then moved on to the second half of the Opposition Day – a debate on dividend tax credits.

Dividend Tax Credits

7.15 pm

Mr. David Heathcoat-Amory (Wells): I beg to move,

> That this House notes that from April 1999, 300,000 non-taxpaying pensioners and 330,000 other non-taxpayers will lose an average of £75 each because of the Government's decision to abolish the dividend tax credit; further notes that 80,000 of the pensioners affected will lose over £100 per year; considers that it is unacceptable that basic rate taxpayers and higher rate taxpayers are unaffected directly by this decision which only affects non-taxpayers, half of them poor pensioners, who by definition must be poorer than taxpayers; calls on the Government to act on the promise made to the House of 30th June when the then Paymaster General stated 'I am aware of the growing anxiety among poorer non-taxpayers who have been hit by the measure so I know that we need to make our position utterly clear as quickly as possible' (Official Report, 30th June, column 175); calls upon the Government to honour now this pledge by announcing that non-taxpayers will be able to continue to reclaim a 10 per cent. tax credit from April 1999 in the same way as taxpayers who hold PEPs or ISAs will be able to do so; and further notes that this is still a 50 per cent. cut from the current 20 per cent. dividend tax credit.

After David Heathcoat-Amory MP's speech, the Paymaster General moved the amendment for the Government.

The Paymaster General (Dawn Primarolo): I beg to move, To leave out from "House" to the end of the Question, and to add instead thereof:

> "notes that the fundamental reform of company taxation carried out by the Government has removed major company taxation distortions from the system and put in place a sound base for better quality investment and growth that will lead to greater prosperity for everyone in the UK, including pensioners; that the Government has taken significant steps to help pensioners, including a guaranteed minimum income for the poorest pensioners through an increase in Income Support from this April worth over £236 extra per year for single pensioners and over £377 extra for couples, a minimum guarantee on tax so that pensioners have no income tax to pay unless their income rises above a certain level, £20 of winter fuel payments for every pensioner household, the introduction of free eye tests for pensioners from this April, new travel concessions on public transport and an extra £21 billion invested in the National Health Service; and further notes that this contrasts sharply with the record of the previous Government which introduced VAT on fuel at 8% and tried to increase it to 17.5%, which introduced charges on eye tests for pensioners, which presided over the mis-selling of pensions which severely damaged the financial security of many pensioners, which ran down the National Health Service on which many pensioners rely, and which was

responsible for boom and bust economics which eroded the real value of pensioners' savings through inflation exceeding 10%.'.

At the end of the debate the Opposition motion was divided on.

Question put, That the original words stand part of the Question:--

The House divided: Ayes 166, Noes 336.

This was followed by a Division on the Government's amendment.

Question, That the proposed words be there added, *put forthwith, pursuant to Standing Order No. 31 (Questions on amendments):--*

The House divided: Ayes 332, Noes 155.

Mr. Deputy Speaker *forthwith declared the main Question, as amended, to be agreed to.*

The votes on an Opposition Day motion are taken in the reverse order to a Reasoned Amendment to a Second Reading. At Second Reading, a vote would be taken on the Reasoned Amendment and then the motion for Second Reading. On an Opposition Day motion, a vote is taken on the original motion and then the Government amendment. This is to give the Government the last word - as the final vote is on the motion as amended by the Government.

ADJOURNMENT DEBATES

There are three types of Adjournment Debate.

- Daily half-hour adjournment debates
- Wednesday morning adjournment debates
- Adjournment debates on general issues

The half-hour daily adjournment debates and Wednesday morning adjournment debates are discussed in chapter eight, as they are essentially opportunities for Back-benchers to initiate debate. The third type of Adjournment Debate, or Adjournment Motion as it should perhaps be more properly titled, is dealt with below.

Adjournment Motions

A Motion for the Adjournment can only be moved by a Government Minister, the only exception being an Emergency debate under SO 24 (see chapter eight).

The Government will sometimes use an Adjournment Motion as a means of holding a general debate on a particular subject. They are often held on a Friday and take place on the Motion: 'That this House do now adjourn'. The motion itself is usually withdrawn at the end of the debate, although if the matter is a contentious one, there may be a Division. The vote itself is not on the substance of the debate but simply on the motion that the House 'do now adjourn'. Members wishing to vote against the Government would vote for the motion; i.e. in favour of the House adjourning and subsequent business falling – the Government on the other hand vote against the motion; i.e., against the House adjourning. The situation is reversed however, when such a debate takes place during a parliamentary recess. Occasionally, the House is recalled during a recess to discuss a particularly important and urgent matter. In such a case, any Members opposing the Government must vote against the motion; i.e., they must vote to keep the House sitting during the recess. The Government, on the other hand, vote in favour of the motion that the House 'do now adjourn'; i.e. to end the sitting and continue with the recess. For example, the Debate on the Gulf War on 7 August 1990, was on a motion that, 'this House do now adjourn'. Those supporting the Government voted 'Aye' - in favour of adjourning the House, whilst those opposed to action in the Gulf, voted 'No', to oppose the Motion that 'this House do now adjourn'.

Amendments cannot be tabled to Adjournment Motions, so potential rebels must either vote against the motion or abstain.

Substantive and Subsidiary Motions

Erskine May describes the essentials of making decisions in the House of Commons as being: 'the moving of a motion; the proposing of a question by the Chair; and the putting of the question and collection of voices by the Chair' (page 328, 22nd edition). A substantive motion is one which in the words of Erskine May is 'self-contained', whereas a subsidiary motion is dependent on another; for example, an amendment to a motion.

Dilatory Motions

A dilatory motion is a motion 'That this House do now adjourn' or 'That the debate be now adjourned'. This is slightly different from a substantive Adjournment Motion, which can only be tabled by a member of the Government. The latter includes the adjournment debates often tabled by the Government on a Friday as a vehicle for a general debate, daily Adjournment Debates and Wednesday morning Adjournment debates (Private Members' debates). A motion to adjourn a debate is a dilatory motion which can be moved by any Member, interrupts debate and if successful leads to the House adjourning the matter under discussion before moving immediately to the next item of business. In the same way that she can refuse a closure, the Speaker can refuse to accept a dilatory motion. A motion 'That the House do now adjourn', if carried, means just what it says.

Discharging

An 'order' can be discharged; for example, the 'order' for the Second Reading of a Bill, can be 'discharged' if the mover of the bill decides it should be withdrawn. An order for a writ for a by-election could be discharged if a General Election was called, as the latter would supersede the former.

Censure Motions

Censure motions also take place in Government time. These are tabled by the Opposition and are basically an expression of 'no confidence' in the Government. It is by convention, rather than under a Standing Order of the House, that the Government always accedes to an Opposition request for discussion of a censure motion. One of the most famous (or infamous) was the motion of no confidence of 28 March 1979 on which the then Labour Government was defeated.

EARLY DAY MOTIONS

Early Day Motions (EDMs), in their current form, were first established in the 1940s. EDMs are tabled by backbench MPs and are technically motions tabled for debate on 'as early a day as possible'. In fact, they are never debated and are merely used as a means of expressing an opinion on a wide variety of subjects, ranging from the economic situation of the pig industry to the theft of rare birds eggs.

They are usually written on special forms available from the Table Office and should not be more than one sentence long and consist of no more than 250 words in total.

EDMs can be signed by other Members and amended. Prayers against negative SIs appear as EDMs. All EDMs fall at the end of the Session. Amendments to EDMs are printed in the Notice Paper – 'the blues', along with the main motion the following day. Members may withdraw a signature from an EDM at any time and the MP whose name appeared first when the motion was tabled may withdraw it at any time, without consulting the other signatories.

EDMs are printed in the Order Paper the day after they are tabled. For the rest of the week in which they were tabled and the week after that, they are only reprinted if more MPs add their signatures to them or if amendments are submitted. After those two weeks, they are only reprinted on a Thursday, and then, only if new signatures or amendments have been tabled. When EDMs are reprinted only the first six names and any names added subsequently are shown. By convention, Ministers do not sign or promote EDMs.

The subject matter of EDMs varies enormously, from the sublime to the ridiculous. An example of the sort of EDM (as it would appear in the Order Paper) which makes this author despair is set out below.

SWANSEA CITY FOOTBALL CLUB 14.01.99

Williams/Alan 11 signatures

Anderson/Donald	Caton/Martin	Edwards/Huw
Evans/Nigel	Gapes/Mike	Godman/Norman A
Jones/Barry	Lawrence/Jackie	Lewis/Julian
Thomas/Gareth R		

That this House congratulates Third Division Swansea City Football Club on its 'giant-killing' victory over Premier League West Ham United; congratulates both teams on providing fans with two exciting matches in the best traditions of the FA Cup, is delighted that both sets of fans at the Vetch supported their teams with full commitment but in a sporting spirit; and wishes Swansea City well in Cup and League.

Hundreds and sometimes thousands of EDMs are tabled each Session. In the 1992/3 Session, 2,574 EDMs were tabled. EDMs cost a great deal of public money to print and readers can be forgiven for thinking that, given that they are never debated (except perhaps, Prayers against negative SIs) there may be better uses for public funds. One possibility would be to print only Prayers against negative SIs and censure motions using public money. Members wishing to table any other kind of EDM would have to pay for it themselves and those wishing to congratulate football teams would have to pay a special premium.

The most effective way to track down an EDM is by using the EDM Database compiled by the House of Commons Information Office. This can be accessed through the Parliament website (http://www.parliament.uk).

AMENDMENTS

Amendments to bills are discussed fully in chapter seven, and are mentioned here only briefly in order to outline when different amendments are taken.

- Reasoned amendments to Second Readings of bills are taken before the decision on the Second Reading itself – hence there are frequently two Divisions after a Second Reading debate. The first is on the Reasoned Amendment tabled by the Opposition and the second is on the Second Reading of the Bill.
- Amendments tabled by the Government to Opposition Day motions are taken in the reverse order from the above. The first question is on the original motion (tabled by the Opposition) and is put in the form, 'That the original words stand part of the question'. If this is carried there is no further decision to be made; however, if as is likely, given that most Governments possess a majority, this motion is defeated, the question 'That the proposed words be there inserted' is put to the House.
- Amendments to delay the Second or Third Reading of a bill by removing the word 'now' and substituting, for example, 'this day six months', are put to the House by the Speaker asking, 'That the word, 'now' stand part of the question'.

MOTIONS IN THE HOUSE OF LORDS

Short Debates

In the period from the opening of the Session until the Whitsun Recess, one Wednesday each month is set aside for two short debates (technically these are 'motions for papers' – see below). Each debate can last for up to two and a half hours. These debates are balloted and only Backbenchers and Crossbenchers may take part. No peer may have more than one short debate per Session. Other debates, which are not balloted, also take place on other Wednesdays in the Session (usually on 'motions for papers'). The allocation of these debates is decided by the 'usual channels' (Party Whips). These are similar to the Opposition Day Debates in the House of Commons, although the motions themselves are not divided upon.

Motions to Take Note

These motions enable the House to discuss a matter without having to take a decision. It is usually used in order to 'take note' of a report of a Select Committee. For example, the Report of the Select Committee on the Ceremony of Introduction (HL 78) was debated in the House on 30 April 1998 on a Motion to 'take note'. The Motion to take note was agreed to without a Division – the motion which implemented the Committee's recommendations and on which the House divided was a motion: 'That this House agrees with the recommendations of the Select Committee'.

Motions for Papers

Any Lord can table a motion 'to move for papers'. Such a motion is really just a means of providing an opportunity for a general debate on a particular subject. Adding these words to the terms of a motion for debate gives the mover of the motion a right to reply. These motions are always withdrawn at the end of the debate, amendments are not moved and no Division takes place.

Motions for Resolutions

A Motion for a Resolution is the opposite of a Motion for Papers, in that it is specifically used where the Lord tabling the motion wants the House to reach a decision on the matter. Amendments can be made to such motions.

In the House of Lords, a Motion may only be withdrawn with 'leave' (permission) of the House. If one Lord objects the motion cannot be withdrawn; however, such objections are rare.

No Day Named

This is the nearest the House of Lords has to an Early Day Motion. It is rather more aptly named than its counterpart in the other place. There is a section entitled 'No Day Named' in each day's Lords Minutes. This is divided into three parts: Motions and Unstarred Questions; Motions for Short Debate and Select Committee Reports.

NO DAY NAMED

PART I

The Lord Simon of Glaisdale—To move to resolve, That the prolixity of the Statute Book has increased, is increasing and ought to be diminished.
The Lord Moynihan—To ask Her Majesty's Government what progress has been made on the institutional and financing reforms, including the re-weighting of votes in the Council of Ministers, necessary for European Union enlargement.
The Lord Hayhoe—To call attention to the case for establishing an Independent Statutory Commission responsible for the conduct of referendums, their organisation and administration; and to move for papers.
The Lord Campbell of Croy—To ask Her Majesty's Government whether they will give advice to police authorities on the circumstances in which police vehicles may exceed speed

limits, ignore traffic lights and in other ways disregard the regulations governing traffic on public roads ....

PART II

MOTIONS FOR SHORT DEBATE

[Ballot on 3rd February for debate on 17th February]

The Lord Campbell of Croy—To call attention to the amount of crime in the United Kingdom involving theft of road vehicles or breaking into them to steal the contents; and to move for papers.

The Lord Dean of Beswick—To call attention to the case for an accelerated public sector house building programme for houses to rent; and to move for papers..........................

PART III

SELECT COMMITTEE REPORTS

[The date in brackets is that on which the Report was published]

The Lord Geddes—To move, That this House take note of the Report of the European Communities Committee on Airline Competition (32nd Report, Session 1997-98, HL Paper 156). [*11th December*]

SPEAKING IN DEBATES IN THE HOUSE OF COMMONS

Red Lines, Swords and Despatch Boxes

If you have ever watched a debate from the Strangers Gallery you will probably have noticed two red lines on the floor of the Chamber of the House of Commons. These two lines run just in front of the respective Front Benches and when speaking, Members are not supposed to step over them. They are in fact, two sword-lengths apart. The tradition dates from a time when Members were a little more vigorous in their disagreements with one another than they are now and the lines on the floor were there to keep opposing Members apart. To this day, in the Members' cloakroom, each Member has a loop of pink tape on which to hang his sword. Apparently, these come in very handy for hanging up an umbrella, or perhaps even a shooting stick.

Members of the Cabinet sit on the Government Front Bench (known as the Treasury Bench after the fact that the Prime Minister is the First Lord of the Treasury) to the right of the Speaker (as do senior Government Ministers) and address the House from the Despatch Box. Opposition Front Bench Spokesman sit, not surprisingly, on the Front Bench Opposite, again, addressing the House from the Despatch Box. What do the Despatch Boxes contain? A cup of tea and a snack to keep a Minister going through a tedious debate? Unfortunately not; munching, chomping, chewing and guzzling are not allowed in the Chamber, although a Member who is speaking may be permitted an occasional sip of water and of course the Chancellor is allowed a tipple when presenting his Budget, although one feels it may sometimes be the taxpayer, rather than the Chancellor, who is more in need of a stiff drink on this occasion. The Despatch Box on the Government side contains copies of the Bibles on which most MPs swear the oath at the beginning of each new Parliament and the Box on the Opposition side contains a battered copy of the Authorised Version.

Members may not bring briefcases into the Chamber and they are not supposed to read any material other than that pertaining to the matter under discussion. However, this rule is lightly enforced, provided Members are not seen to be indulging in the latest Ken Follett or Jeffrey Archer.

A Member who has left one Party to join another; for example, Peter Temple-Morris MP, is said to have 'crossed the floor of the House'.

Members may only speak if they are called by the Speaker. In order to 'catch her eye', Members rise in their places – hence all the unseemly bobbing up and down at question time and when another Member has finished speaking in a debate. The Speaker usually calls a member from the Government side followed by a Member from the opposite side of the House, or where applicable, from those proposing and opposing the motion.

Members are not supposed to speak more than once on a particular question; i.e., a motion or an amendment. This rule is not strictly applied in the case of Ministers seeking to speak more than once and is not applied at all in a Committee of the Whole House or during the Wednesday morning Adjournment Debates. The rule is also not applied at Report Stage to the Member in charge of the bill or the mover of an amendment or New Clause or Schedule. In other cases the Member concerned requires the leave of the House in order to speak twice. Sometimes a Member may move a motion formally in order to be able to speak later in the debate.

Unparliamentary Language and Behaviour

Interventions

In the House of Commons, Members frequently intervene in one another's speeches, often to good effect. Some Members are better than others at turning an intervention to their advantage and some do not like to take interventions at all. To be fair, this is often because time is limited, particuarly where a Minister is making a winding-up speech at the end of a popular debate. Members who intervene are supposed to stand in their places to do so, and interventions from 'a sedentary position' are frowned upon by the House. The former Prime Minister, Margaret Thatcher used an intervention to good effect in her valedictory address to the House of Commons, during a debate on the Opposition's Motion of No Confidence (22 November 1990). When Alan Beith (LibDem, Berwick-upon-Tweed) asked if she would continue her opposition to the European Central Bank after her resignation as Leader, Dennis Skinner MP (Lab, Bolsover) intervened (albeit from a sedentary position) to suggest that she was going to be the Governor. After a slight pause, the former Member for Finchley replied, 'What a good idea'. It nearly brought the House down.

Unparliamentary Terms

The contrast between debates in the House of Commons and House of Lords couldn't be greater. The House of Lords is generally rather civilised and urbane - where else could one debate the joys of shooting widgeon by moonlight[3] – and peers are usually very well behaved; the Commons on the other hand is a rather more lively place and Members are not very good at concealing their feelings about fellow inmates. The groan which always accompanied Paddy Ashdown as he rose in his place at Prime Minister's Questions is a case in point. Some Members persist in treating all Members of minority parties with a mixture of bewilderment and disdain, under the mistaken impression that it gives them an air of superiority. There is, of course, a fine dividing line between robust debate and downright abuse and anything 'unparliamentary' will not be allowed by the Speaker. Terms which have been ruled out of order in the past include the monstrous 'cheeky young pup', 'blackguard' and even, 'swine'. Clearly, the Commons is no place for the faint-hearted. Muttering, sotto voce, can also lead to reprimands from the Speaker as the Member for Bognor Regis and Littlehampton, Nick Gibb, discovered when he was heard to observe that the Paymaster General was a 'stupid woman'. The Speaker, who was sure he had said 'stupid *women*' reacted furiously by asking him to withdraw the accusation, which he did. (HC Col: 466, 28 January 1999).

Disloyal, seditious, treasonable or just disrespectful language about Her Majesty is not permitted and any Member indulging in this sort of thing could find themselves being sent to the Tower; nor may Members cast 'opprobrious reflections' in debate upon the Heads of State of Commonwealth countries. Members are also forbidden from using language, 'calculated to degrade the legislature in the public estimation' (Erskine May, 22nd Edition, page 382). Members are also prohibited from referring to matters which are *sub judice*. In criminal cases, this means from the time when the charge is made and in a civil court, from the time the case is set down for trial. However, reference can be made to civil cases relating to ministerial decisions. Ministers are not supposed to read directly from Government documents, unless they are prepared to lay them on the Table.

Members are also advised not to hiss, clap, chant or boo. After the 1997 General Election this was too much restraint for Members who instinctively applauded the Prime Minister. Erskine May records that on one occasion in 1872, 'notice was taken of the crowing of cocks, and other disorderly noises, proceeding from Members' which were roundly condemned by the Speaker as 'gross violations of the orders of the House' (Erskine May, 22nd Edition, page 391).

The Speaker also has the power under SO 42, to deal with Members deemed guilty of 'irrelevance or tedious repetition' and some readers may be surprised that this power has not been more frequently used.

Grave Disorder

Under SO 46, the Speaker can suspend the sitting in the event of 'grave disorder' breaking out in the Chamber.

[3] Lord Massereene and Ferrard did just this on 27 January 1981 – apparently, it's a very manly sport, which takes place by moonlight on the mudflats.

Filibustering

Filibustering comes naturally to Members of Parliament. A 'filibuster' is 'one who engages in unauthorized warfare against a foreign state', 'a piratical adventurer pillaging Spanish West Indian colonies in the 17th Century', or 'an obstructionist in a legislative assembly'. It is the last definition which concerns us here, for filibustering is indeed a determined attempt to obstruct or delay parliamentary business. It is frequently encountered on Private Members' Fridays, when opponents of a bill will attempt to filibuster and therefore 'talk out' the Bill, causing debate on it to be adjourned to another day. Continuous filibustering may not always be to the advantage of the filibuster, resulting, as it often does, in the imposition of a guillotine by the Government.

Correct Forms of Address

During debates, Members must address their remarks to the Speaker not to the House in general[4] and must refer to other Members by their constituencies or by their position and not by their names. 'As Tony was saying just a moment ago' is not acceptable parliamentary parlance; 'the Right Honourable Gentleman, the Prime Minister' is the correct form of address. Given the near impossibility of remembering which of the 659 constituencies a Member represents, to avoid the embarrassment of referring to Mr Bloggs as the Member for Upper Warlingham when he is in fact, the Member for Whyteleafe South, Members often resort to 'my Honourable Friend' or the 'Honourable Member opposite'. If a Member is a Privy Councillor, he or she is the 'Right Honourable Member. The correct forms of address are set out below:

A fellow Backbencher	**My Honourable Friend**
A Backbencher from another Party	**The Honourable Member (for ....)**
A fellow Backbencher who happens to be a senior barrister	**My Honourable and Learned Friend**
A Backbencher from another Party who happens to be a senior barrister	**The Honourable and Learned Member (for ...)**
A Member who is the son of a duke, earl, etc	**The Noble Lord, the Member for ...**
A Member who has been a commissioned officer in the forces	**The Honourable and Gallant Member (for ...)**
A Minister	**Minister, or one of the above**
A Secretary of State	**Secretary of State, or one of the above**

[4] This does not mean that Members have to face the Speaker when addressing the House, simply that remarks must be addressed 'through' her.

Members are not supposed to read out pre-prepared speeches but reference to notes is permitted. This rule is not strictly adhered to, but occasionally, Members will call out 'reading' if they feel a speaker is simply reading out a pre-prepared text.

Presence in the Chamber

Following the Fourth Report of the Select Committee on Modernisation of the House of Commons on 'Conduct in the Chamber', which was approved by the House on 4 June 1998, Members will no longer receive priority in being called to speak in future debates if they do not observe the 'usual courtesies' of debate. This means that they should endeavour to be present for opening speeches, stay after they have spoken and return for any winding-up speeches.

Members are supposed to bow to the Speaker when leaving the Chamber and should not walk between a Member who is speaking and the Chair – this can mean taking a circuitous route through the Chamber in order to get out.

Precedence in Speaking

Until recently, precedence in debate was always given to Privy Councillors, but following the Fourth Report of the Select Committee on Modernisation of the House of Commons on 'Conduct in the Chamber', which was approved by the House on 4 June 1998, the Speaker is no longer obliged to call Privy Councillors before other Members.

Short Speeches

Under SO 47 the Speaker can impose a time limit on contributions of no less than 8 minutes. The limit was recently altered from 10 minutes following amendments to SO 47 stemming from the Fourth Report of the Select Committee on Modernisation of the House of Commons on 'Conduct in the Chamber', which was approved by the House on 4 June 1998. SO 47 was also amended to ensure that in calculating this period, the Speaker could disregard the time taken by interventions.

Quotations

Following the acceptance by the House of the Fourth Report of the Select Committee on Modernisation of the House of Commons on 'Conduct in the Chamber' on 4 June 1998, Members may quote directly from speeches made in the House of Lords in the current Session of Parliament. The House of Lords is usually referred to by the Commons as 'the other place' or 'another place' and similarly in the House of Lords, the Commons is referred to in this way. The ban on using direct quotations in supplementary questions has also been removed.

Maiden Speeches

A maiden speech is a Member's first speech as an MP and, unusually for the House of Commons, is heard in silence. It is supposed to be lucky to rub the left foot of the statue of Sir Winston Churchill, which stands in the Members' Lobby, before entering the

Chamber to make one's maiden speech. Sir Winston is said to have commented on the maiden speech of A P Herbert, 'That was no maiden, that was a brazen hussy of a speech'. The 1997/98 Session of Parliament saw a greater than usual number of maiden speeches, owing to Labour's huge majority in the General Election and hence the large number of new Labour Members. It is customary in a maiden speech to devote at least part of it to a few complimentary remarks about one's predecessor, whatever one really thought of him or her. This is usually followed by a description of the delights of one's new constituency, including the general good nature of the inhabitants, one's lifelong connections with the area, the immense honour felt at representing so illustrious a town/city, etc., etc. In his maiden speech, after winning the Barnsley by-election, Jeff Ennis MP was honest enough to admit that one of the reasons for his election was probably the fact that a large number of his constituents were actually related to him.

'My grandmother was the youngest of 22 children. My dad was the oldest of 10. My wife, Margaret, also comes from a big family, so the House will probably see why I have been elected to represent Barnsley--because I am related to almost everyone in my area. I think that hon. Members will see that it is not just the aristocracy of this country who come from large families.' (HC Col:183 - 14 January 1997).

Members speaking after a maiden speech has been delivered, are supposed to make some reasonably agreeable or good natured comment about its maker. New Members would be well advised to make the most of this, as it does not last for long.

'I Spy Strangers'

In their Fourth Report of the 1997/98 Session (HC 600 – 4 March 1998), the Select Committee on Modernisation of the House of Commons, considered Conduct in the Chamber. The report was approved by the House on 4 June 1998. Most of the report's recommendations could be implemented without the need to amend Standing Orders; there were however, some changes which required amendment and these related to short speeches, the suspension of Members and the motion 'I spy strangers'.

This peculiar motion was really a hangover from the days when the House did not allow strangers (members of the public to be present when the House was sitting). SO 163 enabled a Member to draw the attention of the House to the fact that there were strangers present, thereby requiring the Speaker to put the question, 'That strangers do withdraw'. However, the motion became a device used either by aggrieved Members wanting to disrupt business or as a means of calling a Division in an attempt to reveal that the House was inquorate. Under SO 41, if fewer than 40 Members are present in a Division (this means 35 MPs actually voting as the Speaker and four tellers do not vote) the House is inquorate and the business being voted upon is adjourned until the next sitting. This cunning little device was often resorted to during Private Members' Bills as the lack of a quorum in a Division would adjourn the bill in question until the next available Private Members' Friday, in many cases killing it off completely. If the Division on the question 'That strangers do withdraw' was actually successful, then the public would have to leave, along with the press, broadcasters and Hansard writers. The Committee recommended that the Commons introduce a procedure akin to that used in the House of Lords to move to the next item of business on the agenda – namely, a motion 'That the house do proceed to the next business'. This could be used as a vehicle for calling a Division and testing a quorum. In the House of Lords this motion is debatable, but the Committee recommended that in the Commons it should be put forthwith. It would only be possible to move the motion once in any sitting. However, this was not acceptable, as the then Leader of the House, Rt Hon Ann Taylor MP, pointed out in the debate on the report on 4 June 1998 because it could not be used during a debate on the Adjournment, because on those occasions there would be no next business. As a result, SO 163 was amended so that instead of shouting, ' I spy strangers' , the Member wishing to move the motion will simply propose, 'That the House sit in private'. This would be put forthwith and could not be moved more than once in a sitting.

Points of Order

Any Member can raise a point of order and these are usually taken after questions, PNQs, statements, have been dealt with, unless the matter is really urgent. Points of order are not supposed to be used either as a means of extending question time or as a way of intervening in a debate when a Speaker has said he or she will not accept interventions.

One of the recommendations of the Fourth Report of the Select Committee on Modernisation of the House of Commons (HC 600 – 4 March 1998) was to end the practice of Members having to be 'seated and covered' when moving a point of order during a Division. Two collapsible top hats were kept in the Chamber for this very purpose. Sadly, this harmless bit of buffoonery, which provided members of the public with a much needed chuckle or two, has now been dispensed with. The report recommended and the House accepted (on 4 June 1998) that in future any Member wishing to raise a point of order during a Division should do so from the second Bench, as near to the Chair as possible. This reform did not require the amendment of Standing Orders as the provisions which it replaced were based on a rule of the House and not on a Standing Order.

Naming and Shaming

Accusing a Member of lying is one of the worst possible insults and the Speaker will invariably ask the Member concerned to retract the statement.

Under SO 43, she has the power to deal with any 'grossly disorderly conduct'. Usually, a number of warnings are given to a Member guilty of such conduct, but if he or she persists, the Speaker can order them to 'withdraw immediately' from the House for the remainder of the sitting, or she can 'name' them. The procedure for naming a Member is set out in SO 44 and SO 45. The Speaker will say, 'I name Mr Fred Smith' and a senior Government Minister will move that, 'Mr Fred Smith be suspended from the service of the House'. There is sometimes a Division on the matter. If a Member refuses to go quietly, he or she can be removed by force if necessary and will be suspended for the rest of the Session. Where a Member has been named and has left the Chamber, in the first instance, he or she is suspended from the House for five days; if the offence is repeated, the suspension is for 20 days and if repeated again, suspension is for a period to be decided upon by the House.

In their Fourth Report of the 1997/98 Session (HC 600 – 4 March 1998), the Select Committee on Modernisation of the House of Commons, considered Conduct in the Chamber. As has been stated previously, the report was approved by the House on 4 June 1998. A new Standing Order was made which has the effect of temporarily removing the salary of any Member who has been suspended from the House under SO 45 for the period of their suspension. A Member who has been named and suspended can still sit as a member of a committee considering a Private Bill.

Rule of Anticipation

This rule is embodied in the House of Commons in Standing Order 28. In the House of Lords there is no such Standing Order and no formal rule exists against anticipation. In the House of Commons, SO 28 a motion will be ruled out of order if it 'anticipates' a motion or bill already set down for future debate 'within a reasonable time'. In the Lords, peers are advised not to table questions or motions which have already been tabled as 'No Day Named' motions unless the peer who has tabled the latter has been consulted.

SPEAKING IN DEBATES IN THE HOUSE OF LORDS

General Arrangements

In the House of Lords any peer may speak on any motion, debate, question, etc. However, there are some exceptions to the rule. Under SO 28 (HL), 'No Lord is to speak more than once to any Motion', except:

- when moving the motion concerned, in which case he or she may reply to the debate;
- when the House is in Committee;
- when the House has 'given leave' (permission) for him or her to explain a particular point made in his or her speech;
- during a debate on an Unstarred Question, where the House has given leave to explain a point made in his or her speech (the peer who has tabled the question does not have an automatic right of reply).

There are certain categories of peer who may speak more than once, provided leave of the House has been given and these include:

- the Chairman, or Deputy Chairman of Committees;
- the Chairman of a Select Committee during a debate on a report from that Committee;
- a Government Minister.

After a peer has exercised his right of reply, no one else may speak, except when debating a bill in Committee. Peers take interventions in much the same manner as MPs in the House of Commons.

Maiden Speeches

In the House of Lords, maiden speeches are usually brief and all other peers in the Chamber are expected to remain there to hear them and to hear any congratulations proffered by ensuing speakers. Newly created peers usually make their maiden speeches in those debates where speakers' lists have been drawn up as this gives other peers some notice of the fact.

Chairing and Calling

In the House of Lords, whilst the Lord Speaker puts the questions on motions, amendments, etc., he or she does not 'chair' the debate in the way that the Speaker does in the House of Commons. For example, he or she does not 'call' peers to speak in the way that the Speaker does in the Commons, nor does the Lord Speaker have responsibility for selecting amendments. This can be problematic, particularly when two peers rise to speak at the same time. If either one refuses to give way a Division has to be called to decide who should speak first. Mercifully, their Lordships being a good deal more civilised than their counterparts in the Commons, are courteous enough not to let this happen.

Lists of Speakers

For some debates a list of peers who wish to speak, is compiled by the Government Whips Office in consultation with the Opposition Parties' Whips. Peers must put their names on the list by 12.00 noon on the day of the debate (or 6.00pm the previous sitting day if the debate is in the morning). The list is not binding and it is possible for a peer who has not been able to put his name on the list to speak, usually just before the debate is wound-up; however, a limit of four minutes is usually applied to speeches made in this way. There are no speakers lists for the following:

- stages of bills other than Second Reading;
- debates on affirmative statutory instruments;*
- Private Bills.**

* *a list might be compiled if a large number of peers wished to speak*
** *lists are sometimes used for Private Bills*

Seating Arrangements

In the House of Lords the Government sits on what is technically known as the 'spiritual' side of the House. This does not mean that Government peers are of a generally more lofty and religious disposition, simply that they sit on the same side of the Chamber as the bishops. However, 'temporal' Lords (peers who are not bishops) may not under any circumstances speak from either of the two bishops' benches. This is a heinous crime and a temporal Lord caught trying to speak from one of these benches or impersonate a bishop in order to sit there, would be severely reprimanded by the House.

The Lord Chancellor sits on the Woolsack, but as this is technically outside the Chamber, when the Lord Chancellor speaks other than in his role as Lord Speaker, he has to move to the left of the Woolsack in order to do so. During a Committee of the Whole House he can speak from the Government despatch box. Standing Orders were recently amended to allow the Lord Chancellor to sit in another part of the Chamber. A Deputy Speaker or Deputy Chairman would then take his place on the Woolsack (18 November 1998 - HL Col: 1275).

Do's and Don'ts

Unless it is one made by a Government Minister, speeches made in the House of Commons may be referred to, but not quoted directly.

Criticism of Members of the House of Commons, the Speaker's rulings or the proceedings in the Commons is not permitted.

Lords may not refer to matters which are sub judice (matters awaiting, or under, proceedings in court). Exceptions can be made in cases of national importance.

Peers are expected to be present for the opening speeches in a debate if they wish to contribute, or if this is not possible, the speeches immediately before and after their own. Anyone leaving the Chamber when someone is speaking should not walk between the Woolsack and the Table of the House, nor between the Woolsack and the person speaking.

Forms of Address

The proper ways of referring to speakers in debate are:

Prince of Wales	**The noble Prince (the Prince of Wales)**
Archbishop	**The most reverend Primate (the Archbishop of ...)**
Bishop	**The right reverend Prelate (the Bishop of ...)**
Duke	**The noble Duke (the Duke of ...)**
Marquess	**The noble Marquess (Lord ...)**
Earl	**The noble Earl (Lord ...)**
Countess	**The noble Countess (Lady ...)**
Viscount	**The noble Viscount (Lord ...)**
Baron	**The noble Lord (Lord ...)**

Baroness *or* Lady	**The noble Baroness (Lady ...) *or* the noble Lady (Lady ...)**
Admiral of the Fleet, Field Marshal or Marshal of the Royal Air Force, or holders of the Victoria or George Cross	**noble and gallant**
Lord Chancellor, Lords of Appeal in Ordinary and Lords who are Law Officers of the Crown or Judges of the superior courts of the United Kingdom (or former holders of these offices)	**noble and learned**
Former Archbishops or Bishops who are subsequently created Lords	**The noble and right reverend Lord**
Fellow peer (member of same Party)	**My noble friend**
A relative	**My noble kinsman or my noble relative**

If a peer has more than one title but is known in the House by the title which is the lower in rank, he or she is referred to in Hansard, etc., by the Higher title. When he or she takes the Oath, all titles are recorded.

That the Noble Lord be no longer heard

There is really little one can do in the House of Lords to silence a colleague; however, if a speaker really seems to be digressing, any peer can move 'That the noble Lord be no longer heard'. Peers consider moving such a motion to be really rather bad mannered and it is used only rarely. The motion is debatable and although effective in silencing a garrulous Lord in the short term, he or she can still pipe-up again on any further motion or question to be debated that day.

Asperity of Speech

Under SO 30, agreed to by the House on 13 June 1626, 'asperity of speech' is to be avoided. This is designed to prevent peers making offensive speeches about one another. As a result, 'all personal, sharp, or taxing speeches' should, according to the Standing Order, 'be forborn'. As the Companion to Standing Orders so tactfully puts it: 'When heat is engendered in debate, it is open to any Lord to move that the Standing Order on Asperity of Speech be read by the Clerk' (page 453). If one Lord were to indulge in offensive remarks about another (this is hard to imagine in the House of Lords, where calling a Speaker 'ill-informed' is considered an insult) then any peer could move that SO 30 be read out by the Clerk. The Order calls upon the peer accused of using offensive language to, 'make a fair exposition or clear denial of the words that might bear any ill construction'.

On 10 March 1998, during the Third Reading debate on the Teaching and Higher Education Bill, Lord Whitty forgot himself completely and went so far as to accuse the Opposition of 'posing to be the students' friends' (HL Col: 167). Outraged by the accusation of 'posing', Earl Russell, notable historian and Liberal Democrat, leapt to their Lordships defence and asked Lord Whitty to withdraw the charge. The latter then compounded the matter by accusing the noble Lords of 'hypocrisy'. This was too much and Earl Russell moved that the Standing Order on Asperity of Speech be read. The motion to read this Standing Order is debatable and the Order can only be read if the House has so agreed. As a result their Lordships divided on Earl Russell's motion to move that the Standing Order be read. The House agreed, by 168 (Contents) to 99 (Not-contents) and the said Standing Order was duly read out. This was too much for some peers, who are just not used to this level of excitement. Readers may be reassured to learn that events in the House of Lords are rarely this stimulating.

Time Limits

In debates which are not time-limited, there are guidelines for length of speeches, which Lords are encouraged to follow: these are 20 minutes for opening and winding-up speeches and up to 15 minutes for others. Time limits can be applied to debates as a whole following agreement by the House to a Business of the House Motion. Where such a motion is agreed, time limits may be imposed on speeches as follows:

Length of Debate	Opening Speech	Reply by Opposition	Reply by Minister
Up to 2 hours	12 minutes	8 minutes	15 minutes
2-3½ hours	15 minutes	10 minutes	20 minutes
More than 3½ hours	20 minutes	12 minutes	25 minutes

INTERRUPTING DEBATES IN THE HOUSE OF COMMONS

There are a number of ways in which a debate or other proceedings in the House of Commons may be interrupted and these include:

- Disorder in the House
- Suspension of an MP or MPs
- a message from the Queen
- a message from the Lords Commissioners to 'attend' the House of Lords
- presentation of an answer from the Queen to an Address to Her Majesty made by the Commons

- a report from the Committee which has 'drawn up' the House of Commons reasons for disagreeing with certain Lords Amendments (see chapter seven on the progress of legislation for an explanation of Commons Reasons)

ENDING DEBATES IN THE HOUSE OF COMMONS

Debates in the House of Commons can be concluded in a number of ways, the most obvious of which is the absence of any more Members wishing to contribute to the debate. However, in order to avoid debate continuing indefinitely, the House has a number of devices at its disposal to bring proceedings to a conclusion; these are:

- lack of Speakers;
- the Moment of Interruption;
- moving the Closure;
- an Allocation of Time Order (the 'Guillotine');
- a Programme Motion;
- lack of quorum during a Division;
- suspension of sitting.

The Moment of Interruption

The Moment of Interruption is the point at which business in the House of Commons must be concluded. Under SO 9(3) as amended by the Resolution agreed by the House on 16 December 1998, business must end on Mondays, Tuesdays and Wednesdays at 10.00pm, on Thursdays at 7.00pm (as a trial measure for the 1998/99 Session) and on Fridays at 2.30pm. After the Moment of Interruption, only unopposed business or what is known as 'exempted business' may be taken. After the Moment of Interruption an Adjournment Motion must be made in order to allow the House to rise and this is why a half-hour daily Adjournment Debate is the last business of the day in the House of Commons. If, at the Moment of Interruption, no day is named for future consideration of the business under consideration at that time, it becomes a 'dropped order'. Readers may often have seen the word 'dropped' printed alongside one of the stages of a bill in the Weekly Information Bulletin. Business can be taken after 10.00pm, 7.00pm or 2.30pm, but only if unopposed. If a single Member shouts 'object', the business in question becomes opposed business and cannot proceed. This is why so many Private Members' Bills fall by the wayside. They are objected to at 2.30pm on a Friday and any further consideration is therefore postponed until the next day on which Private Members' Bills have precedence. At the Moment of Interruption, formal questions which are essential to the completion of business before the House can be put and if a Division is in process this is allowed to continue. Any subsequent questions necessary to dispose of business which is said to be 'contingent' upon a question which has already been decided upon by the House may also be put. Divisions on Reasoned Amendments and on Second Readings frequently continue well past 10.00pm.

Exempted Business

Certain parliamentary business is exempt from the Moment of Interruption under SO 15, 16 and 17. Exempted business includes:

1. Proceedings on bills founded on Ways and Means Resolutions.
2. Proceedings subject to a motion which has been tabled by the Government to allow opposed business to continue beyond the Moment of Interruption. Such motions are taken forthwith (without debate) at the Moment of Interruption and can propose that business continue for a specified period, until a specified hour or until any hour.
3. Motions for nominating or discharging members of departmental Select Committees, which have been opposed on a previous day. Such proceedings may last no longer than an hour and must end by 11.00pm, whichever is the later.
4. Debates on European documents and delegated legislation (affirmative orders) can proceed past the Moment of Interruption for one and a half hours. Debates on delegated legislation are limited to a period of one and a half hours, at whatever time of day they are taken.
5. Debates on negative Statutory Instruments are also limited to one and a half hours' debate and may also proceed beyond the Moment of Interruption, but not beyond 11.30pm. The Speaker can postpone such a debate if she feels there has been insufficient time; for example, if the debate followed other business and only began at 11.00pm. In such cases, any further debate on the postponed SI may not begin after 11.00pm and may not continue after 11.30pm.
6. Deregulation orders can be proceeded with after the Moment of Interruption.
7. Business which was interrupted at 7.00pm by an emergency motion under SO 24 (7) can be resumed and exempted from the Moment of Interruption for a period of time equal to the duration of the time spent earlier that evening debating the emergency motion. The Government may also put down a motion to allow the House to debate any business which has been postponed in this way, for a further specified period of time.
8. Under SO 52, Money Resolutions are taken 'forthwith' if put immediately after Second Reading, but if not, they may be debated for up to three quarters of an hour after the Moment of Interruption (or, indeed, at any other time during a sitting).
9. Reports from the Business Committee under SO 82 (see below under Allocation of Time Orders).

Closure Motions

A Closure Motion is most commonly used during the Second Reading of a Private Member's Bill on a Friday afternoon, but can be used at other times to bring forward the decision on a matter under discussion at the time. It is sometimes described as a vote on whether or not to vote. The Closure can be moved by any Member, who must stand in his place to move the motion. Under SO 36 and 37, the Member must use the words, 'I beg to move that the question be now put'. It is up to the Speaker (or the Chairman of Ways and Means or one of the Deputy Chairmen, during a Committee of the Whole House) to decide whether or not to allow the Closure. For example, let us imagine that Jo Smith, the newly elected Member for Biggin Hill West, who has come fourth in the ballot for Private Members' Bills, knows that his Beetroot (Compulsory Consumption) Bill is likely to excite both interest and opposition in equal measure. He is therefore prepared for the fact that a number of Conservative Members are likely to try and 'talk it out'. This means that they will endeavour to keep the debate going until 2.30pm – the 'Moment of Interruption', at which point the business under discussion will be adjourned until another day. After this time, no opposed business can be taken. Jo Smith has therefore spent a great deal of the past few weeks assiduously courting support from fellow Backbenchers – buying them cups of tea in the Strangers Cafeteria, even going so far as to slip in the odd rich tea biscuit and on one occasion recklessly splashing out on a whole packet of custard creams for the All Party Root Vegetable Group. He hopes that his efforts will be rewarded in the form of 100 Members turning up to support the Closure Motion, which he intends to move, either at 2.30pm or just before. He hopes to win, not just the Closure, but also the vote on Second Reading, allowing his bill to go forward to be debated in Standing Committee C.

In reality, things are not quite this simple. The Speaker has the power to decide whether or not to allow the Closure and may decide to disallow it on the grounds that there has been insufficient debate on the matter in hand. If she does allow the Closure, the motion that 'the question be now put' is put before the House. The wish of the majority may be obvious from the response, but where the 'Ayes' and 'Noes' appear to be equally balanced, a Division is called. This is where the crunch comes for many a Private Member's Bill, as, under SO 37, the proposer of the motion requires not just a majority voting in favour of the Closure, but, in addition, 100 Members voting in its favour (the two tellers for the Ayes are not included in the total). If the Closure is agreed to, the House immediately proceeds to a vote on the question which is before it– in the case of a Second Reading of a bill, 'that the bill be now read a second time' (SO 36(2)). This second part of SO 36 is particularly useful if the Closure is moved at 2.30pm on a Friday at the Moment of Interruption, as it allows not just a vote on the Closure, but on Second Reading as well.

The example below is from the Second Reading debate on the Wild Mammals (Hunting with Dogs) Bill on 28 November 1997. Here, Edward Garnier QC MP attempted to raise a point of order during the Division, the result being that the question on the Closure Motion was put again and decided without recourse to a Division. This was then followed by a Division on Second Reading.

Mr. David Hinchliffe (Wakefield) *rose in his place and claimed to move,* That the Question be now put.

Question put, That the Question be now put:--
The House proceeded to a Division—
Mr. Garnier (seated and covered): On a point of order, Mr. Deputy Speaker. The closure motion is wholly unnecessary. There are 20 minutes left until a Division needs to be called.
Mr. Deputy Speaker: The hon. and learned Gentleman knows that that is a matter of discretion for the Chair. I have used my discretion.
Mr. Garnier: I am appealing to your discretion, Mr. Deputy Speaker. There was no question of the Bill being talked out. I invite--
Mr. Deputy Speaker: Order. That is the hon. and learned Gentleman's opinion. There is now a Division. Perhaps the hon. and learned Gentleman may wish to take part in that Division. It is up to him. I shall now put the Question again.

Question agreed to.

Question put accordingly, That the Bill be now read a Second time:--

The House divided: Ayes 411, Noes 151.

So, why is the closure not used more frequently and why, for example, is it not used to end a debate on the Second Reading of a Government Bill? The reason is that there would be little point in the Opposition moving the Closure and effectively curtailing debate on the Second Reading of a Bill, as this would be to deny their own Members an opportunity to speak on the Bill. Equally, there would be little point in attempting to 'talk out' Second Reading, because any Government with a reasonable majority could simply move and win a Closure Motion. Debate on Second Reading and on many other matters ends, simply because there are no more Members wishing to speak. Debate on the Second Reading of a Government bill usually ends conveniently at 10.00pm simply because whoever is 'winding up' the debate for the Government finishes in time for the question on Second Reading to be put and, where necessary, a Division begun, before the Moment of Interruption.

When an Opposition Day is split into two debates with one ending at 7.00pm, the motion 'That the original words stand part of the question' is really a closure motion as under SO 14 (2)(c)(I) proceedings on the motion would simply lapse at 7.00pm, unless 'previously concluded'.

Quorum

The quorum of the House is 40 Members. SO 41(2) provides that: 'The House shall not be counted at any time'. However, if there are found to be fewer than 40 Members (minus the Speaker, or whoever is in the Chair and the four tellers) taking part in a Division, the business on which the House is attempting to vote, 'stands over' until the next sitting and the House moves on to the next item of business on the day's agenda.[5]

Suspension of Sitting

Sittings are sometimes suspended, rather than adjourned. For example, on Wednesdays, after the conclusion of the morning's Private Members' debates, the sitting is suspended at 2.00pm, resuming again at 2.30pm.

The Speaker may also suspend a sitting under SO 46 if 'grave disorder' breaks out. An Order which is under discussion when the sitting is suspended becomes a 'dropped order'. It can be replaced on the Order of Business if a motion is taken at the start or after the end of public business. Such a motion is usually just entered in the Votes and Proceedings without even being read out.[6] If it is a Government Order it is taken on the

[5] The quorum of the House of Lords is three.

[6] There are certain other items of parliamentary business which are usually entered in the Votes and Proceedings without actually being read out and these include the First Readings of Bills which have come from the House of Lords, Lords Amendments to be debated on a future day, a motion to postpone or discharge an Order and a motion to 'revive' a 'dropped' Order.

day following the suspension of the sitting and a motion to this effect is set down on that day's Order Paper at the start of public business. Any Orders not reached because of the suspension of a sitting are put down after the Orders of the day on the Order of Business for the next sitting day.

The Speaker may also suspend a sitting in cases where the business of the day has been concluded but where a message from the House of Lords is expected; for example, where the Commons needs to consider any Lords Amendments to a Bill. The House is always suspended on the first day of a new Session, after hearing the Queen's Speech and before resuming for the Debate on the Address.

Previous Question

A motion 'That the question be not now put' is rarely used, but can be moved in an attempt to prevent the House deciding on a particular question or motion. A Member proposes 'That the question be not now put'. If the motion is agreed to, the matter under discussion at the time cannot be decided and is effectively adjourned; if the motion is not agreed to, the original matter under discussion has to be taken forthwith. Putting the 'previous question' cannot be used to prevent a vote on an amendment and cannot be moved when a Member of the House is speaking, nor can it be moved during the Committee Stage of a Bill.

Using the Guillotine

This has nothing to do with Madame Defarges or the tumbrils, but is the means by which Governments curtail debate on legislation. Allocation of Time Orders, or Guillotine Motions as they are colloquially known, are used by Governments in order to curtail debate on bills which would otherwise take up a great deal of parliamentary time. They are not much liked by the Opposition, but are sometimes essential if the Government of the day is to make headway with its legislative programme. The use of such motions is usually avoided where bills of a constitutional nature are concerned. Under SO 83, Allocation of Time Orders may only be debated for up to three hours. Where such an order allots a certain number of days to a bill, the detailed Division of the bill is decided by the Business Committee, as set out under SO 82. The Business Committee consists of the Chairman of Ways and Means and no more than eight MPs nominated by the Speaker. The quorum of the Committee is four. The Committee is charged with dividing up the bill and its final Division of the bill is presented to the House and voted on forthwith. When a bill is guillotined in this way, a specified amount of time is often allocated to a particular number of clauses – this means that as amendments are debated, when the guillotine falls on that particular section, the Speaker (or Chairman of Ways and Means or Deputy Chairman in the case of a Committee of the Whole House) must put the question on the matter being debated at that time; for example, an amendment. The only other matters which can then be taken are Government amendments and New Clauses falling within that section of the Bill. The question that 'the Clause stand part of the Bill' can of course be put. Where there are amended Clauses or New Clauses to be disposed of, instead of the usual practice of putting first the question on the amended or New Clause followed by the question that the amended or New Clause be added to the Bill, only the latter motion is put before the House, in order to save time.

Supplemental Orders may also be tabled by the Government and these are limited to a debate of up to one hour. These are usually reserved for timetabling the debate on Lords Amendments.

It is usual when bills have been rejected by the House of Lords and reintroduced in the following Session in the House of Commons for the Committee Stage of the bill to be dispensed with and the Third Reading to be taken forthwith. The European Parliamentary Elections Bill was reintroduced in the 1998/99 Session after being defeated in the House of Lords in the previous Session and was the subject of an Allocation of Time Order which was debated in the House on 2 December 1998. The order, accompanied by an explanation, is set out below:

Table 23 – GUILLOTINE MOTION

What the Motion Says	What the Motion Means
Timetable 1. Proceedings on Second Reading, in Committee, on Consideration and on Third Reading shall be completed at the sitting this day and shall be brought to a conclusion, if not previously concluded, four hours after the commencement of proceedings on this Motion.	***All the stages of the bill – Second Reading, Committee, Report and Third Reading – will all take place today. The entire proceedings, including the three hours during which the Guillotine Motion itself may be debated, may not last for longer than four hours; i.e., the Guillotine Motion will be debated for three hours and all the stages of the bill for just one hour.***
Questions to be put 2. When the bill has been read a second time - (a) it shall, not withstanding Standing Order No. 63 (Committal of bills), stand committed to a Committee of the whole House without any Question being put (b) proceedings on the bill shall stand postponed while the Question is put, in accordance with Standing Order No.52(1) (Money resolutions and ways and means resolutions in connection with bills), on any financial resolution relating to the Bill (c) on the conclusion of proceedings on any financial resolution relating to the Bill, proceedings on the bill shall be resumed and the Speaker shall leave the Chair whether or not notice of an instruction has been given.	***Immediately after Second Reading, a Money Resolution will be voted on 'forthwith' (without debate). After this the bill will proceed to its committee stage – on the floor of the House (the Chair will be taken by the Chairman of Ways and Means or a Deputy).***
3. On the conclusion of proceedings in Committee the Chairman shall report the bill to the House without putting any question	***After Committee of the Whole House, Report Stage will follow immediately.***

and, if he reports the bill with amendments, the House shall proceed to consider the bill as amended without any Question being put.	
4. For the purpose of bringing any proceedings to a conclusion in accordance with paragraph 1 the Speaker or Chairman shall forthwith put the following Questions (but no others) – (a) any Question already proposed from the Chair; (b) any Question necessary to bring to a decision a Question so proposed; (c) the Question on any amendment moved or Motion made by a Minister of the Crown; (d) any other Question necessary for the disposal of the business to be concluded. 5. On a Motion made for a new Clause or new Schedule, the Chairman or Speaker shall put only the Question that the Clause or Schedule be added to the bill.	***At the end of the time allocated to proceedings on the bill (after four hours) if, for example, a particular amendment or Clause is under discussion, the House will be able to vote on it, if necessary. If it is an amendment to a Clause or a new Clause, the House will also be able to vote on the motion that the Clause be added to the bill. All other amendments, etc., will fall, unless they have been tabled by the Government.***
Miscellaneous	
6. Standing Order 15(1) (Exempted Business) shall apply to proceedings on the bill at the sitting this day; and the proceedings shall not be interrupted under any Standing Order relating to sittings of the House.	***The Guillotine Motion itself may be debated after 10.00pm (the Moment of Interruption) if necessary.***
7. The proceedings on any Motion made by a Minister of the Crown for varying of supplementing the provisions of this order shall, if not previously concluded, be brought to a conclusion one hour after commencement; and the Standing Order No. 15(1) shall apply to those proceedings.	***As the Allocation of Time Order has not been referred to a Business Committee, SO 82 will not apply. Any Supplemental Allocation of Time Order that might be necessary, may only be debated for an hour.***
8. Standing Order No. 82 (Business Committee) shall not apply in relation to proceedings on the bill.	
9. No Motion shall be made to alter the order in which any proceedings on the bill are taken.	***The order in which the various stages of the bill are to be taken may not be altered.***

10. No dilatory Motion shall be made in relation to the bill except by a Minister of the Crown. 11. If at the sitting this day a Motion for the Adjournment of the House under Standing Order No. 24 stands over to seven o'clock and proceedings on this Motion have begun before that time, the Motion for the Adjournment shall stand over until the conclusion of proceedings on the bill. 12. If the House is adjourned at the sitting this day, or the sitting is suspended, before the conclusion of proceedings on the Bill, no notice shall be required, of a Motion made at the next sitting by a Minister of the Crown for varying or supplementing the provisions of this order.	***Only the Government may move a motion to adjourn the House.*** ***If the Speaker has accepted an application for a debate on an emergency motion under SO 24 to be held at 7.00pm and the debate on this Guillotine Order has already begun before 7.00pm, the debate on the SO 24 motion will be deferred until after the debate on this Guillotine Motion.*** ***If, for whatever reason, the debate on this Guillotine Motion has to be adjourned or suspended, then the Government may vary the Order accordingly before the next Sitting.***
The Speaker will put the Question not more than three hours after proceedings begin (Standing Order No. 83)	***The debate on this Guillotine Motion may not last longer than three hours.***

Programme Motions

In its First Report of the 1997/98 Session, 'The Legislative Process' (HC 190), the Select Committee on Modernisation of the House of Commons made a number of suggestions for improving the way in which legislation was currently considered by the House. One of those recommendations was for the introduction of 'Programme Motions' as an alternative to Allocation of Time Orders, a recommendation duly accepted by the House on 13 November 1997. In the words of the Committee, Programme Motions would be 'more formal than the usual channels but more flexible than the guillotine'.

The Programme Motion, which can be debated for up to 45 minutes and which can be amended, stipulates the date by which the Standing Committee or Committee of the Whole House must complete its consideration of the bill. The Committee is left to decide how to divide up the time allocated to it. In the case of a Standing Committee, a Programming Sub-Committee is appointed by the Committee of Selection and is chaired by the Chairman of the Standing Committee in question. A 'Committee Programming Motion', which is also amendable, is then moved at the beginning of the first Standing Committee sitting and is debated for up to an hour. If a particular stage of a bill's proceedings is subject to a Programme Motion it cannot also be subject to an Allocation of Time Order.

Programme Motions were used to timetable debate on a number of Government bills in the 1997/98 Session, but as no amendments of, or additions to, the Standing Orders have yet been made, these motions are still only being used on an experimental basis. They were used in the 1997/98 Session in relation to the Crime and Disorder Bill, the Government of Wales Bill, the Human Rights Bill (three times), the Northern Ireland Bill (twice) and the Northern Ireland (Elections) Bill, the Northern Ireland (Sentences) Bill, the

Regional Development Agencies Bill (twice), the Scotland Bill (twice), and the Teaching and Higher Education Bill. An example of a Programme Motion is set out below.

Table 23 – PROGRAMME MOTION

What the Motion Says	What the Motion Means
Regional Development Agencies Bill (Programme) (No debate after 2.30pm) Mrs Ann Taylor, Mrs Gillian Shephard, Mr Paul Tyler (27 March 1998)	Unlike Allocation of Time Orders, Programme Motions are agreed between Government, Opposition and the second largest Opposition Party.
That the following provisions shall apply to the remaining proceedings on the Regional Development Agencies Bill:	
1. The proceedings on consideration shall, if not previously concluded, be brought to a conclusion at half-past Ten o'clock on Wednesday 1st April and proceedings on Third Reading shall, if not previously concluded, be brought to a conclusion at midnight on that day; and paragraph (1) of Standing Order No. 15 (Exempted business) shall apply to proceedings on the bill for two hours after Ten o'clock.	***The debate on Report Stage of the bill may last until 10.30pm and will be followed by the debate on Third Reading, which must end at midnight (both these will be exempt from the Moment of Interruption).***
2. Standing Order No. 82 (Business Committee) shall apply to proceedings on the bill.	***The Business Committee (as set out in SO 82) will agree on the detailed division of the bill; i.e., how long is to be devoted to debate on a particular section of the bill.***

3. For the purpose of concluding any proceedings which are to be brought to a conclusion at a time appointed by or under this Order – (1) The Speaker shall put forthwith the following Questions (but no others) – (b) any Question necessary to bring to a decision a Question so proposed (including in the case of a new Clause of Schedule which has been read a second time, the Question that the Clause of Schedule be added to the Bill); (c) the Question that any remaining new Clauses or new Schedules standing in the name of a member of the Government be added to the Bill; (d) the Question that all remaining amendments standing in the name of a member of the Government be made; and (e) any other Question necessary for the disposal of the business to be concluded. (2) Proceedings under sub-paragraph (1) shall not be interrupted under any Standing Order relating to sittings of the House and may be decided, though opposed, at any hour.	***When the time expires for debate on a specific section of the bill as identified by the Business Committee, the question under consideration at that time; e.g., on a particular New Clause or amendment, will be put as well as any 'contingent' questions; i.e, 'that the Clause (as amended) be added to the bill). After that, only Government New Clauses, New Schedules or amendments may be taken.***
If opposed, this item cannot be taken after 2.30pm.	***The Programme Motion itself is not exempted business and therefore if any Member opposes it, it cannot be taken after 2.30pm – the Moment of Interruption (27th March 1998 was a Friday).***
Regional Development Agencies Bill (Programme) (1 April 1998)	

<table>
<tr>
<td colspan="2">Motion made, and Question put forthwith, pursuant to Standing Order No. 82 (Business Committee),
That the Report (31st March) from the Business Committee be now considered (Mr. Clelland)
Question agreed to.
Report considered accordingly.
Resolved,
That this House doth agree with the Committee in its Resolution – (Mr. Clelland).
Following is the report of the Business Committee (31 March):
That it had come to a Resolution (31st March) in respect of the Regional Development Agencies Bill, which it had directed him to report to the House:

That each part of the Proceedings on Consideration shall, if not previously brought to a conclusion, be brought to a conclusion (in accordance with the Programme Order of 27th March) at the time specified in the following Table:</td>
<td>This Programme Motion is the result of the deliberations of the Business Committee which was set up under the auspices of the Programme Motion passed by the House on 27 March. The Business Committee proposed the detailed allocation of time to particular sections of the bill.

The Resolution of the Business Committee specified that particular New Clauses and amendments should be debated within the time limits set out in the table below left.</td>
</tr>
<tr>
<th>Proceedings</th>
<th>Time for conclusion of proceedings</th>
<td rowspan="7">Debates on these New Clauses and amendments must end at the appointed times. At 10.30pm any remaining amendments will be taken and deliberations on Report Stage will be completed. Third Reading will then take place from 10.30pm until midnight at the latest.</td>
</tr>
<tr><td>New Clause 2 and New Clause 1</td><td>5.30pm</td></tr>
<tr><td>New Clause 3</td><td>7.15pm</td></tr>
<tr><td>Remaining New Clauses and Amendments to Clauses 1 to 19</td><td>8.00pm</td></tr>
<tr><td>Amendments to Clauses 20 to 23</td><td>9.00pm</td></tr>
<tr><td>Remaining Amendments</td><td>10.30pm</td></tr>
<tr><td>Report to lie upon the Table</td><td></td></tr>
</table>

The timetable was followed, as the following extract from Hansard for 1 April 1998 demonstrates.

New clause 1

Activities of agencies in rural areas

'(1) The Secretary of State shall cause an annual assessment to be made of the effect of the activities of each regional development agency upon the rural parts of its area (if any).
(2) The Secretary of State shall lay before both Houses of Parliament a report containing the assessments made under subsection (1) and his proposals (if any) to deal with any matters identified in the assessments.

(3) Any report made under subsection (2) shall also contain a statement in the respect of each regional development agency as to whether, in the opinion of the Secretary of State, it has fulfilled its purposes under section 4(2).'.--[Mr. Yeo.]

Brought up, and read the First time.

Mr. Yeo: I beg to move, That the clause be read a Second time.

Madam Speaker: With this, it will be convenient to discuss amendment No. 1, in clause 7, page 3, line 39, at end insert

'and

(d) the needs of the rural areas within any region.'.

As the time for dispensing with New Clauses 2 and 1, New Clause 2 had already been voted on, so New Clause 1 was the subject under discussion as the following extract from Hansard shows.

It being half-past Five o'clock, Mr. Deputy Speaker, pursuant to the Order [27 March] and the Resolution [this day], put forthwith the Question already proposed from the Chair.

Question put, That the clause be read a Second time:--

The House divided: Ayes 166, Noes 295.

ENDING DEBATES IN THE HOUSE OF LORDS

Closure

A closure motion is rarely used in the House of Lords and if a peer does attempt to move the closure, a statement is read out which reminds the House that it is 'a most exceptional procedure'. If the Lord moving the closure insists, the motion, 'That the question be now put' is taken forthwith. This is rather different from the procedure in the House of Commons where the Speaker may decide whether or not there has been sufficient debate before agreeing to the closure.

Next Business Motion

If, for whatever reason, a peer does not wish the House to reach a decision on the motion which it is debating, he or she can move 'That the House do proceed to the next business'. A next business motion cannot be moved during the Committee Stage of a bill or during debate on an amendment. This is not the same as a closure motion.

As has been stated before, a basic rule of parliamentary procedure is that a matter which has been decided upon once, cannot be brought before the House again in the same Session. The rule of 1604 states, 'That a question, being once made and carried in the affirmative or negative, cannot be questioned again, but must stand as a judgment of the

House'. No resolution can be rescinded in the same sitting. The power to rescind a decision of the House is rarely used and previous resolutions are usually overriden by new ones.

It is a rule of the House that a matter which has been 'decided upon' cannot be reintroduced again in the same Session. For example; a bill which has been defeated cannot be reintroduced later in the Session. This is why amendments are often withdrawn in Committee and tabled again at a later stage in a bill's proceedings. If they have not been divided on, they avoid the rule that a motion or amendment which has been decided upon by the House cannot be introduced again in the same form in the same Session.

DIVISIONS IN THE HOUSE OF COMMONS

When the Speaker puts a question on a motion, amendment, bill, etc., to the House she does so by saying: 'The question is, That ....', followed by, 'As many as are of that opinion say, "aye" (those Members in favour shout 'aye' at this point) and, 'As many as are of the contrary opinion say, "no".' The Speaker will then 'collect the voices'; i.e., she will decide from general decibel level of the ayes and noes which side is in the majority. She will then say, 'I think the "ayes" (or "noes" as the case may be) have it'. If the House agrees with her decision there need be no further action; if, however, the minority disagree, they shout "aye" or "no" (whichever is in the minority) again. In this case the Speaker shouts, 'Clear the lobby' and a Division begins. A vote is called a 'Division' because the House does indeed divide – with the 'ayes' going to the right and the 'noes' to the left.[7] At this point the Division bells are rung.

When the Division bells sound, members of the public must leave the Members' Lobby. The bells sound, not just in the Palace of Westminster, but within the 'Division bell area', which extends some way from the Palace itself. Many MPs homes, restaurants and even lobbying companies, within striking distance of the Palace, have Division bells fitted, enabling busy Members to speed from dinner to Division within the requisite eight minutes.

In the House of Commons, Members have eight minutes in which to vote. Once the Speaker has called for the lobby to be cleared, the tellers' doors in both the 'aye' and 'no' lobbies are locked. After two minutes the Speaker puts the same question again and as before, the 'ayes' and 'noes' must shout for all they are worth. The Speaker must again declare either that the 'ayes' or 'noes' have it. If the Speaker's decision is not challenged the Division is called off. If her decision is challenged again, she directs the 'ayes to the right' and the 'noes to the left'. Tellers are then appointed, two for the ayes and two for the noes. One teller for the ayes and one for the noes proceed to each

[7] The procedure of the House physically dividing when voting probably grew up in the sixteenth century, when the Commons sat in St Stephen's Chapel. The ante-chamber was probably used as a 'lobby' for Members when voting. The current system of divisions dates from the Report of the Select Committee on Divisions (HC 66, 1835) (amended in 1906). Its recommendations were adopted and put into practice after the Palace of Westminster was rebuilt following the great fire of 1834.

lobby. If tellers cannot be found the Division cannot take place. If there are no tellers for the ayes then the noes have it, and vice versa.

Once the Division bells are rung, the Whips are on hand to direct MPs on how to vote and point them in the right direction. Members could not possibly be expected to have an intimate knowledge of the subject of each Division – during the report stage of a bill, there are often 10 or more Divisions in a sitting, often on complex amendments – so the Whips are there to ensure that Members vote according to the 'Party line'. Members do, of course, vote against their own Party on issues about which they feel strongly; for example, Europe. There are also what are known as 'free votes' where no Party whip is imposed and where Members are free to vote according to their conscience.

Once the tellers have been appointed, they proceed to the lobbies, the doors are unlocked and counting begins. Clerks are stationed at three desks at the end of each of the lobbies and as Members pass by, their names are marked off on a list of Members. The tellers count the numbers going out from the lobbies. As readers will see from the diagram overleaf, Members file through the lobbies in different directions, leaving and entering the Chamber at different ends. This is to avoid the scrum, and possible injuries, which would inevitably result from large numbers of MPs attempting to leave and re-enter the Chamber by the same route.

If Members are too ill to pass through the lobbies, they may vote by being within the precincts of the House and by giving their names to both clerks and tellers. There are now three clerks' desks in each lobby, the third having been added after the May 1997 Election in order to accommodate the large numbers of new Labour MPs all trying to vote in the same lobby at the same time.

After eight minutes have elapsed since the Speaker called for the lobby to be cleared, she directs the doors leading from the Members' Lobby to the Division lobbies to be locked. This period can be increased at the discretion of the Speaker and the actual time taken up by a Division is usually around 11 or 12 minutes, depending on the numbers voting. The doors remain locked until the numbers voting in each lobby are announced. When the tellers have finished counting, they inform the Clerk at the Table of the House. They then stand in front of the Table (with the winners on the right), bow to the Chair, take one step forward and bow again. One of the tellers for the winning side then reads out the result of the Division. This is then reiterated by the Speaker. If fewer than 35 MPs vote in a Division it is considered invalid; SO 41 states that if fewer than 40 Members take part in a Division, the matter being voted must be adjourned, but this number includes the Speaker and four tellers, who do not vote, so the actual number who must vote for a Division to be valid is 35. If any major 'irregularities' are found to have taken place whilst a Division is taking place, the Division has to be interrupted and begun again. The following are examples of major irregularities:

- where one of the tellers was absent;
- where one of the tellers voted;
- where tellers miscounted;

- where there was a disagreement between tellers;
- where the Division bells were not rung;
- where Members entered the lobby after the order had been given to lock the doors;
- where Members were confused as to whether they were voting on the Closure or the main question;
- where Members were prevented from voting.

If a mistake is made in the number of those voting in a Division, this is corrected in the Journal of the House of Commons, unless the sitting is still in progress in which case the Speaker reads out the correct numbers of 'ayes' and 'noes'. If a Member alleges, after a Division has taken place, that the tellers had left the lobby doors before he or she was able to vote, the Speaker usually asks for an explanation from the tellers and where appropriate, adds the names of the Members concerned to the Division lists and then reads out the corrected numbers.

If a Member votes in the wrong lobby he is bound by that vote, however, he can rectify his mistake by voting in the other lobby as well. Members who have voted in both lobbies must explain themselves on the following day, stating in which lobby they really intended to vote. There have been occasions in the past, most notably in the 18th century, where 'Strangers' (members of the public) mistakenly voted in Divisions. The author does not recommend that readers try this, as security is rather more extensive now than in the past. A Division, or another decision of the House, could be declared null and void if an irregularity was later discovered. For example, if a Money Resolution should have been passed after Second Reading and wasn't, later proceedings on the bill could be declared null and void; alternatively, the bill could be recommitted, if Third Reading had not been taken.

The Speaker's Casting Vote

The Speaker and her three deputies do not vote in the House of Commons; however, if the numbers voting in a Division are equal the Speaker has a casting vote. When casting that vote, she must bear three precedents in mind:

1. that the Speaker should always vote for more rather than less discussion;[8]
2. that decisions should be taken by a majority;[9]

[8] This is based on Mr Speaker Addington's decision of 1796, when he had the casting vote and voted with the 'ayes' that the Bill be read a third time tomorrow, on the basis that the Speaker should always vote for further discussion. More details and further precedents can be found in Erskine May (page 358/9).

[9] This is based on Mr Speaker Denison's decision of 1867, who when there were equal numbers voting on the Church Rates Abolition Bill, cast his vote with the 'noes' on the grounds that he felt a

3. that a bill should be left in its existing form.[10]

Pairing

'Pairing' is an arrangement whereby a Member of one Party agrees with a Member of an opposing Party that both should be absent for a particular vote, thereby cancelling out each other's votes. This enables both parties to the agreement to have a night off without in any way affecting the outcome of the Division. This is not an officially recognised practice and is arranged through the Parties' Whips Offices. When pairing was in use, the practice was for it to be used only on less important votes and not in cases where a three-line whip had been imposed (for more details of the functions of the Whips' Offices, see chapter four). Pairing has really fallen into abeyance since the 1997 General Election, simply because of the Labour Government's huge majority, but as a result, 'Bisques' have come to the fore. Apparently the term is taken from the game of Croquet. A Bisque is usually arranged on a alphabetical basis, so that, for example, on a Monday, Labour Members whose surnames begin with the letters A to C may be absent, etc.

Proposals for Reform

Since the 1997 General Election, the House of Commons Select Committee on the Modernisation of the House of Commons has looked at a number of possible reforms of the way in which votes are taken in the House. Their Fifth Report of the 1997/98 Session (HC 699 – 22 April 1998) was a consultation paper on voting methods and put forward a number of alternatives to the current system for Members to consider and comment upon. A number of electronic alternatives to the current system were looked at by the Committee; for example, the use of smart cards or touch screens. However, the response to the questionnaires sent out by the Committee revealed that the present system of Divisions was 'acceptable' to 70% of MPs. One reason for this may be that by forcibly herding Members together in a confined space, it provides a rare opportunity for an ordinary Backbencher to rub shoulders with and even lobby a Minister and possibly even a Secretary of State. If electronic voting were to be added to televised coverage, the disincentives to turning up in the Chamber might be so strong that Members might never see each other at all. Electronic voting might indeed be more expeditious and efficient but it just wouldn't be as much fun. However, as the Modernisation Committee pointed out in their Sixth Report (HC 779 – 3 June 1998) Members had some suggestions to make on other aspects of voting; for example, the impossibility at present of actually recording an abstention. A majority were in favour of devising some mechanism for this. Another suggestion, which the Committee said it would consider further was the possibility of grouping Divisions together rather than holding them immediately after the debate to which they related.

---

majority was actually opposed to the measure and that the decision should be left for the House to take in the future. More details are available in Erskine May, 22nd Edition, page 358.

[10] This is based on another decision by Mr Speaker Denison in 1860 when on a vote on an amendment to a bill, he cast his vote against the amendment on the grounds that the bill should be left in its original form. (For further details see Erskine May, 22nd Edition, page 360).

The Chamber of the House of Commons

Ayes

Those voting 'Aye' leave the Chamber this way

Noes

SPEAKER'S CHAIR

Aye Lobby

Government

Opposition

No Lobby

Those voting 'No' leave the Chamber this way

Ayes

Noes

The House of Lords divides in a similar way, with Contents leaving the Chamber on the spiritual side to the left of the Throne with the Not-contents leaving the Chamber on the temporal side by the Bar of the House.

DIVISIONS IN THE HOUSE OF LORDS

In the House of Lords, peers vote either 'Content' or 'Not-content'. At the end of a debate on a motion the Lord Speaker puts the question; for example, 'The question is, That the Motion .... be agreed to'. He then 'collects the voices' by saying, 'As many as are of that opinion will say 'Content'. The contrary, 'Not-content' . It may be obvious from the response whether the 'Contents' or Not-contents' are in the majority and if this is the case, the Lord Speaker will say, 'I think the Contents (or Not-contents) have it'. If his view is challenged, a Division will take place and he says, 'Clear the bar' (this is not a parliamentary version of 'last orders', but a reference to the bar of the House and a signal that the House will be dividing). Some divisions in the House of Lords are the occasion for what is known as an 'ambush'. This term is used to describe an example of guerilla warfare often deployed to good effect by their Lordships. Opposition peers secrete themselves away in remote corners of the House of Lords, safe from patrolling whips, ready to mount an attack when a Division is called. The absence of peers from the Chamber is designed to lull the enemy into a false sense of security and the success of an ambush depends on taking the Government by surprise in the Division lobbies.

The Division lobbies in the House of Lords are basically the corridors either side of the Chamber. Once the order to 'Clear the Bar' has been given, two 'tellers' for the 'Contents' and two for the Not-contents' must be appointed within three minutes. If one side cannot find any tellers or only one the Division is called off and the vote is taken as being in favour of the side which appointed two tellers. If neither side can find any tellers, the vote is decided in the same was as when there are equal numbers voting on both sides (see below for more details on 'equality of votes'). If both sides are successful in appointing two tellers, the Lord Speaker puts the question to the House again. If one side fails to respond, the Division is called off and the question decided in favour of the other side. If both sides respond the Division continues and another three minute period begins (this can be longer at the discretion of the Lord Speaker or Lord Chairman). One teller from the 'Contents' and one from the 'Not-contents' stands in each lobby along with two Clerks, who record the number of peers voting.

To denote their office, the senior tellers have ivory wands, which they wiggle about, in what seems a rather aimless fashion, as peers pass through the lobbies. At the end of the second three minute period the doors of the Chamber are locked and only those peers already in the lobbies can vote. After a report from the House of Lords Procedure Committee was agreed by the House on 22 March 1999, their Lordships now have eight minutes within which to vote – previously they only had six, which given the age and constitution of some peers always seemed rather inadequate.[11]

Once the wiggling of wands and counting of votes has been completed, the tellers return to the Table of the House. The numbers of those voting in the respective lobbies, plus the votes of the tellers themselves and the votes of the Lord Speaker or Lord Chairman (who vote in the Chamber rather than the lobbies) are added together and written down and handed by one of the tellers to the Lord Speaker or Lord Chairman. The result is then read out; for example, 'So the Contents have it'. If a Lord is found to have voted in both lobbies, his vote is disregarded. If, however, a Lord realises that he has inadvertently voted in the wrong lobby, he can inform the tellers and then state at the Table of the House which way he actually intended to vote. The quorum of the House of Lords is three and under SO 55(HL), If fewer than 30 peers appear to have voted in a Division on a bill or piece of delegated legislation, Division is adjourned until another sitting. If the numbers of Contents and Not-contents are equal in a Division on an amendment to a bill or a motion to reject a statutory instrument, the Division is decided

[11] House of Lords Procedure Committee (HL 33, 1999/2000) - agreed to by the House on 22 March 1999.

in favour of the Not-contents; i.e., the amendment or motion to reject the instrument is defeated. As far as all other motions are concerned, if the Contents and Not-contents are equal then the motion would be negatived.

CHAPTER SIX - QUESTIONS

QUESTIONS IN THE HOUSE OF COMMONS

Oral Questions

The first recorded parliamentary question was asked by Earl Cowper in the House of Lords on 9 February 1721 and was on the subject of the 'South Sea Bubble' financial disaster. In 1783 the Speaker declared that any MP had a right to question any Minister but that the Minister concerned was not bound to answer. By 1900 more than 5,000 questions were being asked each session and on one day took until 6.00pm to complete. As a result, from 1902, the time available for questions was limited to the period between 2.15 to 2.55pm (the timing was designed to meet press deadlines) eventually moving to its current place on the parliamentary timetable - between 2.30pm and 3.30pm Monday to Wednesday and, for the 1998/99 Session at least, between 11.30am and 12.30pm on a Thursday. A huge number of oral and written questions are answered each Session as can be seen from the extract from the Sessional Information Digest, set out below.

Questions appearing on the Order Paper –1997/98 Session*

Appearing on the Order Paper for Oral Answer	8,113(1)
Put down for priority Written Answer	25,532
Put down for non-priority Written Answer	29,120
Total	60,765

(1) 3,382 received an oral answer in the House on one of the 71 days on which such answers were given.

*Source: *Sessional Information Digest 1997/98*

The Digest also shows that in the 1997/98 Session, 190 hours were devoted to oral questions.

The first business of the day in the House of Commons, after Prayers of course, is any unopposed private business (see chapter 12 on Private Bills for more information) and oral questions therefore begin after any such business has been disposed of. This is usually at about 2.35pm. Under SO 20, unopposed private business may not continue after 2.45pm (11.45am on a Thursday), so this is the latest time at which oral questions can commence. Under SO 21, question time cannot continue after 3.30pm (12.30pm on a Thursday) On Thursdays (for the 1998/99 Session at least) oral questions begin at about 11.35am and continue until 12.30pm. There is no question time at all on a Friday.

The Prime Minister now answers questions for half an hour on a Wednesday from 3.00pm. This is in place of the former twice-weekly sessions, which used to last from 3.15pm to 3.30pm on a Tuesday and Thursday. The new timing was initiated by the Labour Government at the beginning of the 1997/98 Session. The timetable for oral questions is entirely a matter for the Government (although consultation through the 'usual channels' may take place) so no amendments to the Standing Orders of the House were required in order to move 'PMs questions' to Wednesday.

Parliamentary questions are answered on a rota basis; for example, Social Security questions might be answered on Monday 11 January, but would not be answered again until Monday 8 February – one month later. All Departments work on a rota basis in this way (see Table 22 below). The rota is set out in an Order of Questions, which is available from either the Vote Office in the House of Commons or from the Parliamentary Bookshop. Under Standing Order 21(2) a Minister can defer answering an oral question until 3.30pm and may also answer orally at that time, a written question set down for answer that day. This occasion might arise if a Statement to the House would have been necessary had the question not been tabled.

Table 24 - ORDER OF QUESTIONS

Monday 11 January	**Tuesday 12 January**	**Wednesday 13 January**	**Thursday 14 January**
Social Security	Department of Environment, Transport and the Regions	Cabinet Office Prime Minister (3.00pm)	Department for Education and Employment
Monday 18 January	**Tuesday 19 January**	**Wednesday 20 January**	**Thursday 21 January**
Home Office	Foreign and Commonwealth	Northern Ireland Prime Minister (3.00pm)	DTI (Millennium Experience at 12.20pm)
Monday 25 January	**Tuesday 26 January**	**Wednesday 27 January**	**Thursday 28 January**
Defence Church Commissioners/ Public Accounts Commission (3.20pm)	Scotland Lord Chancellor (3.15pm)	Wales Prime Minister (3.00pm)	Treasury

Monday 1 February	Tuesday 2 February	Wednesday 3 February	Thursday 4 February
Culture, Media and Sport President of the Council/House of Commons Commission/ Finance and Services (3.15pm)	Health	International Development Prime Minister (3.00pm)	Agriculture Attorney General (3.15pm)

Tabling Oral Questions

Under SO 22(5), oral questions must be tabled no earlier than 10 days before they are due to be answered. In practice, MPs table oral questions exactly 10 days before they are due to be answered, so that they are entered into the daily ballot. Using the above table as an example, questions to the Secretary of State for Defence, scheduled for Monday 25 January would have been tabled on Monday 11 January. If the House is to adjourn for up to four days, any day, (except for Saturday and Sunday) during that period, is counted as a sitting day for the purposes of calculating the earliest day on which questions can be tabled. Members may now only table one oral question at any one time to any one department, up to a maximum of two a day. These must be handed in personally to the Table Office. An MP can table a question on behalf of one other Member, subject to the same limit of one per department per day, up to a maximum of two departments.

Members table questions on a Monday, Tuesday and Wednesday between 10.00am and 5.00pm and on a Thursday between 9.00am and 5.00pm. All questions received each day before 5.00pm are 'shuffled' . This is known as the 'Five O'clock Shuffle' – in reality the names are entered into a computer in the Table Office and randomly ordered. Only a certain number of questions are actually printed on the Notice Paper the next day – in the case of departments which answer questions until 3.30pm – for example, Treasury questions – only the first 40 questions are printed. For those departments answering questions from 3.10pm (or 3.15pm) to 3.30pm, the quota is 30 and for the smaller departments, 20. Only the first 20 questions to the Prime Minister are printed. Questions lower down list than the quota are effectively dropped and a Member still wishing to ask the question would need to table it again.

The numbering of oral and written questions in the Order of Business, the 'blues' and the Order Book can appear rather confusing at first. The number in brackets after the question is a unique number given to that particular question which enables it to be tracked by departments and Members alike. It is worth making a note of this number if you think you may need to call a department to find out when a question is likely to be answered. The number to the immediate left of an oral question is the number of that question in the previous day's ballot. For example, on Tuesday 12 January questions were tabled to the Secretary of State for Scotland and the Lord Chancellor. As you will see from the example below, question 4 appears to be missing; this is because question

4 in the ballot was actually to the Lord Chancellor, so although Gordon Prentice MP was fourth in the ballot, he had the first question to the Lord Chancellor.

TUESDAY 26th JANUARY

Questions for Oral Answer

At 2.35p.m.

Oral Questions to the Secretary of State for Scotland

*1 **Rosemary McKenna** (Cumbernauld and Kilsyth): What steps are being taken to deal with the problems faced by owner occupiers in housing regeneration and improvement schemes

(65825)

*2 **Mr Tony Worthington** (Clydebank and Milngavie): If he will make a statement about the supply of nurses in Scotland.

(65826)

*3 **Mr Robert Maclennan** (Caithness, Sutherland and Easter Ross): If he will make a statement on the Government's policy towards the maintenance, repair and protection of Scottish war memorials.

(65827)

At 3.15p.m.
Oral Questions to the Minister of State, Lord Chancellor's Department

*4 **Mr Gordon Prentice** (Pendle): What steps he is taking to ensure that judges declare any relevant interests before hearing a case.

(65855)

Members must declare any relevant interests when tabling questions; for example, a Member whose family firm makes a type of nut used in the tail fin of a new missile, which the MoD is considering purchasing in large numbers, would be well advised to declare an interest when tabling a question to the Secretary of State for Defence. The letter [R] would then be printed after the member's name on the Notice Paper, Order Book and in the Order of Business.

Before an adjournment of the House, the Speaker sets out the dates for tabling questions for the first 10 days after the House returns.

Where a question has been incorrectly addressed to the wrong department, it is 'transferred' to the department which does have responsibility for that particular subject area. Members are not entitled to protest about a decision to transfer a question – it is entirely a matter for the Government. The Government has collective responsibility for answering questions and it is up to Ministers to decide amongst themselves who should respond to which questions. For more information on parliamentary papers, please see chapter 14.

Prime Minister's Questions

The first Prime Minister's Question Time - in the sense of a specific period of time set aside each week for grilling the PM - took place in 1961, during Harold Macmillan's period in office. It had been the practice for the PM to answer all questions after question No. 40 on Tuesdays and Thursdays, but since these were often not reached, the PM rarely came to the Despatch Box. As Christopher Jones recounts in 'The Great Palace', 'in the late 60s, the Labour Opposition decided not to turn up for the first three dozen questions. Mr Macmillan ... was forced to face the House for nearly an hour'. As a result, a twice-weekly Prime Minister's Question Time was introduced (now consolidated into one session per week). Questions to the Prime Minister are invariably of the type asking the Prime Minister to list his/her engagements for the day. This is to avoid the question being transferred to another department on the grounds that it falls within their remit rather than the Prime Minister's and also to avoid giving the Prime Minister any prior notice of questions. The aim of an Opposition Member in asking such a question is to come up with a really devious and awkward 'supplementary' which will catch the Prime Minister unawares and improve the standing of the Member concerned in the eyes of his colleagues. The aim of a loyal Backbencher in asking the question is to thoroughly ingratiate himself by asking something along the lines of 'does the Prime Minister not agree with me that he is doing a wonderful job and should be congratulated by one and all'. His or her aim is invariably rapid promotion.

At 3.00 p.m.

Oral Questions to the Prime Minister

*Q1 **Mr Ben Chapman** (Wirral South): If he will list his official engagements for Wednesday 16th December.

(62722)

*Q2 **Mr John Bercow** (Buckingham): If he will list his official engagements for Wednesday 16th December.

(62723)

Occasionally, there are variations, as shown below.

*Q3 **Mr Anthony Steen** (Totnes): If he will visit Brixham in order to take a sea voyage on a beam trawler.

(62724)

During Prime Minister's Question Time, the Leader of the Opposition is always called by the Speaker to put what is technically a supplementary question and is usually called to put four or five supplementary questions after his initial question. The Speaker will also call the Leader of the next largest Opposition Party – at present, the Leader of the Liberal Democrats, Paddy Ashdown – to ask a couple of supplementary questions.

The following exchange took place on Wednesday 13 January 1998 (HC Col:299):

Mr. William Hague (Richmond, Yorks): Does the Prime Minister now regret that the Health Secretary said, just two months ago, that the national health service can look forward to the winter with confidence?
The Prime Minister: As a result of the money that we have put in--money opposed by the previous Government--we have managed to get through this winter in far better shape than we otherwise would.
Mr. Hague: There was no answer to the question there. In the past few weeks we have seen intensive care bed availability at its lowest ever level, doctors and nurses under even more pressure than before, pregnant women told not to give birth, refrigerated lorries used as temporary morgues, and people on trollies in hospitals. All those people were told they could look forward to the winter with confidence. Have not this Government's decisions made the NHS's winter difficulties worse than they should have been?
The Prime Minister: It is this Government who have put in £2.5 billion extra over the spending plans that we inherited from the Conservative Government. I visited one accident and emergency department last night, and I shall tell the House exactly what it said the problems were: a shortage of nurses; a lack of proper co-ordination between hospitals and social services; and a lack of long-term investment in the health service--all problems left to us by the Conservative Government, and all dealt with by the incoming Labour Government.
Mr. Hague: For the Prime Minister, there is always someone else to blame. The NHS is in crisis, and he says that the Government are innocent. Whatever happens in this Government, everybody always says that they are innocent. The Trade Secretary resigns, and he is innocent; the Paymaster General resigns--now we know why he was called the Paymaster General--and he is meant to be innocent; the Chancellor's press secretary resigns, or intends to resign, as we have just been informed, and he is innocent; the NHS is in crisis, and the Prime Minister is innocent. St. Tony, the angel of Islington, is always innocent. The Government announced in November money that could have been announced in September. They cut the number of trainee nurses that we had announced and distorted clinical priorities by their targets. Why do not they take responsibility for something for a change?
The Prime Minister: It did not take the right hon. Gentleman long to try to get off the subject of the health service. His allegation that we have cut the number of nursing trainees is absolutely false. I will tell him why we have the problem with nursing shortages in the national health service today. The Tories cut by 4,000 the number of places between 1992 and 1994--while he was in government. There are 2,500 more trainee nurses today than there were when we came to office. Furthermore, if the Tories had matched our commitment to training, there would be 14,000 extra nurses on the wards.

It takes three years to train a nurse. We are putting in more resources, training more nurses and will see that nurses are properly rewarded and that there is recruitment and retention in the health service. In other words, we will deal with the appalling mess that we inherited from the Government of whom the right hon. Gentleman, who said nothing about the health service, was a member.
Mr. Hague: And of course the right hon. Gentleman says nothing about an increase in trainee nurses that would have been 14 per cent., but that this Government have achieved 11 per cent. The reason that they have not been able to handle matters this winter is that they have been too busy attacking each other. The Prime Minister has been too busy: first, trying to protect the right hon. Member for Hartlepool (Mr. Mandelson), and then trying to rehabilitate him. What is the Prime Minister doing treating the right hon. Gentleman as the come-back kid, when he is actually the kick-back kid? Why does he not recognise that? Have not the past few weeks been a disgrace? Is it not time he buried the spin-doctoring

politics of new Labour along with the self-serving, high-living career of the politician who invented it?

The Prime Minister: Perhaps we can return to the health service for a moment. The right hon. Gentleman made a specific allegation that it was our decision to cut planned new nurse training places by 3 per cent. I have looked into that allegation. That cut was actually made in January 1997, when his Government were still in office. In fact, far from cutting back, we achieved about 1,500 new nurses in training--more than were due that year.

Mr. Hague: What about some answers on the money announced in November that could have been announced in September, and the complete distortion of clinical priorities? While the NHS has been in crisis, personal feuds have taken the place--*[Interruption.]*

Madam Speaker: Order. This House will come to order. Members will be heard--*[Interruption.]* Order.

Mr. Hague: The Prime Minister refuses to take responsibility for the Government's decisions. While the NHS has been in crisis, personal feuds have taken the place of political principle, personal loans have taken the place of political priorities. Does he not realise that, on that basis, no matter how often he relaunches the Government, a Government who believe in everything and in nothing cannot succeed?

The Prime Minister: One thing in which we do believe is the national health service. As a result of this Government's proposals, we have put in an extra £2.5 billion above the Conservative's published spending plans. We know what the Conservatives would have done, and we have exceeded it by £2.5 billion. From April, a further £21 billion is going into the NHS--what the right hon. Gentleman's shadow Chancellor calls "reckless and irresponsible spending". So the idea that the right hon. Gentleman is in a position to make any criticisms of the health service is absurd. As for all the personal feuds, I will tell the House what would worry me about any Cabinet Minister, past or present. It would worry me if I ever caught any of them being filmed making train journeys across Spain.

Later, Paddy Ashdown was called to put a supplementary question: (HC Col: 302).

Madam Speaker: Mr. Ashdown.

Hon. Members: Oh!

Mr. Paddy Ashdown (Yeovil): And a happy new year to you too.

Earlier today, the Prime Minister expressed the hope that his Government would be judged not on the basis of scandals, but on the basis of their record on crime, health and education. On which of these three would he like to be judged? Would he like to be judged on the basis of falling police numbers, longer NHS waiting times or the worst crisis in teacher recruitment for more than a decade?

The Prime Minister: There are problems in schools and hospitals; but let us analyse for a moment some of the problems that people no longer raise in the way that they used to. NHS waiting lists have fallen by more than 100,000 in the past few months. That does not mean that problems do not still exist in the health service, but we are tackling them.

There are 100,000 five, six and seven-year-olds who started school in September in classes of fewer than 30 who would otherwise not have done so, and there is a £2.5 billion investment programme for schools. Over the next two or three years, every school will be linked to the internet and given the computer equipment that it needs. Yes, teacher recruitment is a problem--which is why we are presenting proposals to transform teacher recruitment, teacher training, teacher performance and teachers' pay over the next few years.

The right hon. Gentleman asks on what we would like to be judged. We would like to be judged on the basis of the progress that we are making--and, at the next election, we shall have fulfilled each of our manifesto pledges.
Mr. Ashdown: But that is a promise. The truth is that the Government are travelling in the wrong direction. Does the Prime Minister dispute any of these three facts? There are now 780 fewer police officers than there were when he was elected; there are 10,000 vacancies for teachers in our schools; and there are 8,000 fewer nurses than the NHS needs. Does the Prime Minister not understand that the people did not vote to kick out the Tories in order to make public services worse?

Let me put this to the Prime Minister. If he were a Labour voter, lying on a trolley outside a ward that had been shut because the nurses could not be found to staff it, would he be more interested in what the Government had promised, or in why the Government had not delivered?
Mr. Dennis Skinner (Bolsover): Sack him!
The Prime Minister: I do not think that we will put that one to the vote. I think that the right hon. Gentleman will recognise, if he reflects and is reasonable about it--I am sure he will be--that, of course, there are still huge problems in the health service. We do not put right 20 years of neglect in schools and health in 20 months, but there are things happening in the health service. We have got rid of the Tory internal market that cost so much and did so much damage. We are introducing, for example, proper nursery education for four-year-olds. There are the extra kids in class sizes under 30. Waiting lists are coming down. Yes, we have to deal with waiting times too. We have to deal with nursing shortages, and we are. There are 2,500 more trainee nurses today than there were when we took office.

Therefore, I do not dispute that, to people who are facing difficulty today, it comes as cold comfort to be told that the Government are going to do it--but we are going to do it. [Hon. Members: "When?"] In our 20 months in office, we have done more already for the health service than that lot ever did, but we will do more. At the next election, people will see that the promises that we made on schools and health are exactly what we have delivered.

Procedure for Oral Questions

When questions begin the Speaker calls the Member whose question appears first on the Order Paper. He or she stands and replies: 'No. 1, Madam Speaker' (there is no need to read out the text of the question, as this available to other Members on the printed Order of Business). The Minister answers the question; frequently, even if a question has been tabled to the Secretary of State for the relevant department, a junior Minister will reply, if that question lies within his or her particular area of responsbility. As he or she sits down, other MPs wishing to ask questions rise in their seats in an attempt to 'catch the Speaker's eye'. The MP who tabled the question concerned is then called to ask a 'supplementary' question. The Speaker usually allows a few supplementary questions from other MPs on the same subject. MPs have been caught out by attempting to ask supplementaries on completely unrelated areas. For example, it would be inappropriate to ask a supplementary question on genetically modified tomatoes, if the original question had been on EC fishing quotas. The Speaker will decide how many supplementary questions to call and when she feels that enough time has been devoted to question 1 on the Order Paper, she will move to question 2. However, questions are not always taken in the order that they appear on the Order Paper; this is because questions 1, 3 and 7 may all relate to pelican crossings in Scotland whilst questions 2 and 8 relate to proposals to establish a new White Fish Authority. Questions 1, 3 and 7 would probably be answered together and the Members responsible for tabling them would be called in succession to ask their supplementary questions.

The practice of taking supplementary questions not just from Members who have tabled oral questions, but from those who have not, means that only about half the tabled questions will be reached during question time. Any oral questions not reached by 3.30pm are answered as written questions and appear at the back of the next day's Hansard, along with the other written questions.

The procedure for Prime Minister's Questions has now been altered so that the Speaker calls the Member whose question appears first on the Order Paper, but, as the questions are invariably the same – asking the Prime Minister to list his/her engagements for the day - only the Member with the first question says 'No. 1, Madam Speaker', all others simply ask their supplementary question immediately.

The following extract is from the Order Paper of 7 December 1998. Where a Member is not present, or his or her question is not reached, it is answered by way of a written question, which appears in Hansard.

At 2.30 p.m. **Prayers**

Afterwards

Oral Questions to the Secretary of State for Defence

*1 **Mr Nicholas Soames** (Mid Sussex): What changes are planned to public duties following the Strategic Defence Review.

(61337)

*2 **Mr Nick St. Aubyn** (Guildford): If he will make a statement about the development of the Eurofighter Typhoon.

(61338)

*3 **Mr Tony McWalter** (Hemel Hempstead): What plans he has to ensure that cadet-only units of the TA have access to senior and trained personnel from the regular forces and from other TA units; and if he will make a statement.

(61339)

*4 **Mr John Heppell** (Nottingham East): What proposals his Department has to assist ex-servicemen and women return to civilian life.

(61340)

The following extract from Hansard for 7 December 1998, shows how the questions above, were actually answered:

Eurofighter Typhoon

2. **Mr. Nick St. Aubyn (Guildford):** If he will make a statement about the development of the Eurofighter Typhoon. [61338]

The Parliamentary Under-Secretary of State for Defence (Mr. John Spellar): The development of Eurofighter in conjunction with our partners from Germany, Italy and Spain is continuing to meet the planned delivery of the first production aircraft to the Royal Air Force in mid-2002. Seven development aircraft are flying and have completed more than 620 sorties. A number of notable milestones have been achieved, including supersonic flight, care-free handling, air-to-air refuelling and missile firings.

Mr. St. Aubyn: Given the changes in policy and personality since the last election, what guarantee can the Minister give the House that the export prospects of the Eurofighter have been unharmed and undiminished as a result of the actions of his Government and some of his colleagues?

Mr. Spellar: What an extraordinary question, not least because it was this Government who took the most important step to ensure that Eurofighter was a viable project--getting the agreement signed and by negotiating and discussing that with the previous German Government. We are involved in discussions--at ministerial level and at the level of officials and defence export sales organisations--with a number of other countries for the future prospects of this extremely good aircraft.

Mr. Menzies Campbell (North-East Fife): Is not the importance of Eurofighter not simply that it gives the Royal Air Force an outstanding aircraft, but that it illustrates eloquently the advantages of European co-operation in defence procurement? In view of the success of co-operation in defence procurement, is it not now logical to consider co-operation across defence as a whole? May we hear from the Minister a little more about the Government's proposals for greater co-operation in European defence?

Mr. Spellar: The hon. and learned Gentleman will have noted that there have been discussions and an initiative by the Government to try to ensure that Europe plays a greater role in NATO's defence. We must ensure that we are getting a better return across Europe for the expenditure that is being made, by ensuring a greater degree of interoperability and the ability of NATO European forces to act in operations in which the United States is not involved.

Those discussions are taking place, and we welcome the hon. and learned Gentleman's support for them. They run in parallel with a greater degree of involvement in the harmonisation of defence procurement through OCCAR and also with initiatives such as those taken by the leaders of the main industrial countries in order to rationalise the European defence industry so that it can compete more effectively with the United States and co-operate more effectively with the new US defence giants.

Mr. Keith Simpson (Mid-Norfolk): The House will be pleased to hear from the Minister how well the Eurofighter Typhoon programme is coming on the initial hard work having been done, of course, by the previous Government. I am sure that hon. Members will want to know, as will our friends in British industry, whether the Eurofighter will be delivered on time, given the shortfall and overspend in the air equipment budget for the long-term costing in excess of £1 billion. Can the Minister confirm that there is such a shortfall? What impact is it likely to have on the delivery of the Eurofighter?

Mr. Spellar: The hon. Gentleman says that the previous Government put in hard work; they certainly made heavy weather of it, given the time that they took to get to the position that they reached. It was this Government who ordered Eurofighter. It is on schedule to be delivered in mid-2002. We do not anticipate any slippage in that programme.

Territorial Army

3. **Mr. Tony McWalter (Hemel Hempstead):** What plans he has to ensure that cadet-only units of the TA have access to senior and trained personnel from the regular forces and from other TA units; and if he will make a statement. [61339]

The Minister for the Armed Forces (Mr. Doug Henderson): All cadet units will continue to be affiliated to either a Regular or a TA unit, which will provide the cadets with both equipment and access to senior and trained personnel.

Mr. McWalter: My hon. Friend is aware that in my constituency the TA has been reduced to a cadet-only force. I am concerned about the consequences of that diminution in status for access to trained personnel, especially as it seems that the 29 officers in my local TA are being pensioned off. Will my hon. Friend confirm that it is possible that cadet-only units might be upgraded to full TA units, especially in cases where the nearest units have been closed down?

Mr. Henderson: I can assure my hon. Friend that every facility for personnel and equipment support that his unit used to have will continue to be provided at that location using officers and equipment from other locations.

On the future of cadet-only units, the Secretary of State announced to the House the future plans for the Territorial Army for the period ahead of us. These matters are subject to review over the long term. I have no doubt that any future Government will want to return to the issue of TA locations, as all such matters will be subject to review.

Miss Anne McIntosh (Vale of York): As a result of the changes announced by the Government, the nearest TA unit to the vale of York will be in Scarborough, which will pose enormous problems of access to trained personnel and to training in general. The settlement announced last week for North Yorkshire does not allow enough money for the police force to police the millennium celebrations effectively within the present budget. If it is envisaged that it will have to have recourse to the TA--as has been considered north of the border--what provisions will be made for the TA to be given special training for this capability before the millennium?

Mr. Henderson: The hon. Lady will be aware that those who wish to serve in the TA - we want them to serve - will be able to do so at a number of other locations. The police will have responsibility for policing at the time of the millennium celebrations. Any requirement for reinforcements would be considered in the usual way, but that is a prime function of our Regular Army. I emphasise that the main responsibility for policing the millennium celebrations will lie with the police, and they should be able to carry it out.

Mr. Lindsay Hoyle (Chorley): Will the Minister confirm whether the cadet force at Chorley has a future under the review? Has he reconsidered the nonsensical removal to north Wales of the 101 Battalion headquarters?

Mr. Henderson: I have discussed this matter with my hon. Friend on several occasions, and my hon. Friend the Under-Secretary responded to an Adjournment debate on it last week. I assure the House that, when there is a change in the location of a cadet force, we will guarantee that at least an equivalent level of service support, equipment and buildings are made available. Land Command will discuss with the Territorial, Auxiliary and Volunteer Reserve Association how that can best be achieved in Chorley.

Mr. Mike Hancock (Portsmouth, South): I am grateful for the Minister's comments about protection for the cadet force. Will he carefully consider the cadet force currently located at the Connaught drill hall in Portsmouth, which is due to be disposed of by the Ministry of Defence? Will he also reconsider the relocation of the TA units that are staying in the Portsmouth area from the Perone road depot to the Connaught drill hall? That would kill two

birds with one stone. It would keep the cadets where they are currently located, and it would keep this much-cherished building in public ownership. It would also allow the MOD to dispose of two buildings that would be easier to dispose of than the Connaught drill hall.
Mr. Henderson: As the hon. Gentleman will know, I shall be visiting Portsmouth tomorrow. I shall be happy to receive representations from him or his colleagues at an appropriate point in my itinerary. The decision on future locations of TA facilities within Portsmouth will be made by Land Command in consultation with TAVRA and others.

Questions 1 and 4 were not asked and were answered by means of written answers, which appeared in the same volume of Hansard, for 7 December 1998.

1. **Mr. Soames:** To ask the Secretary of State for Defence what changes are planned to public duties following the strategic defence review. [61337]
Mr. George Robertson: Armed Forces personnel will continue to play an important role in State Ceremonial occasions and a range of Public Duties. The Strategic Defence Review has had no effect on our commitment to these duties. (Col:56 (W))

4. **Mr. Heppell:** To ask the Secretary of State for Defence what proposals his Department has to assist ex-service men and women return to civilian life. [61340]
Mr. Doug Henderson: We provide a wide range of support to help Service personnel return to civilian life. On 5 October, I opened a veterans Advice Unit to help guide ex-Service personnel around the maze of help available to them. Details of the Unit are in a booklet, copies of which have been placed in the Library and Vote Office. (Col:53 (W))

Written Questions

Written questions are handed in to the Table Office and must be signed either by the MP or someone acting on his or her behalf. There is no limit to the number of written questions which a Member may table on any one day. These may be 'priority' or 'non-priority'.

Priority questions must be answered on a certain day and appear in the Notice Paper and Order Book marked 'N' ('named day'). The period of notice required is the same as for oral questions; i.e., no earlier than 10 sitting days before the question is to be answered and with sufficient notice to ensure that the question appears on the Notice Paper at least two sitting days before the day on which it is to be answered. So a priority written question to be answered on a Thursday, would need to appear on Tuesday's Notice Paper, hence it would have to have been tabled the day before – Monday. Non-Priority questions (where the Member tabling the question has given no indication of the day on which he or she wishes the question to be answered) are theoretically for answer two sitting days after tabling, but in reality are unlikely to be answered so speedily. The Government endeavours to answer such questions within a week of their first appearance on the Order Paper and frequently a holding answer is given. Holding answers are not printed in Hansard, but the date on which the holding answer was given is printed next to the full answer when this appears in Hansard. A Member may specify that he or she wishes a written question to be answered on the following day. These are known as 'planted questions' and have usually been set down by a Member on behalf of the Government in order to give a Minister the opportunity to make a statement without actually appearing before the House. This practice has come in for some criticism in the past as it allows Ministers to make unpopular statements without having to face direct questions from Members on the floor of the House. Planted questions are indicated in the Order Paper, thus:

Written Questions tabled on Friday 15th January for answer today ‡

1 **Mr David Drew** (Stroud): To ask the President of the Board of Trade, what arrangements are being made to return to Japan nuclear materials recovered from reprocessing Japanese spent nuclear fuel at BNFL's Sellafield plant. (66647)

Written questions tabled the day before the day on which they are to be answered can be found in the daily Order of Business. Other written questions tabled for answer on that day but tabled earlier than the previous day are to be found in Part I of the Order Book. Questions tabled on days prior to the previous day for answer on future days are to be found in Part II of the Order Book.

The following is taken from Part 1 of the Order Book for Wednesday 13 January 1998.

Here you can browse the Written Questions for answer on Wednesday 13 January of which previous notice has been given in the Notices of Questions paper. They are arranged in alphabetical order of answering Department.
For other Written Questions for answer on Wednesday 13 January, of which no previous notice has been given, see the Order of Business.
For Written and Oral Questions for answer from Thursday 14 January, see Part 2 of this Paper.

Notes:
* *Indicates a Question for Oral Answer.*
+ *Indicates a Question not included in the random selection process but accepted because the quota for that day had not been filled.*
[N] *Indicates a Question for Written Answer on a named day, i.e. the Member has indicated under S.O. No. 22(4) the day on which he wishes the Question to be answered.*
[R] *Indicates that a relevant interest has been declared.*

WEDNESDAY 13th JANUARY

1 **Mr Bill Rammell** (Harlow): To ask the Chairman of the Administration Committee, how much was spent on prepaid envelopes for honourable and Right honourable Members in each financial year since 1980. (65640)

2 **Mr Desmond Swayne** (New Forest West): To ask the Minister of Agriculture, Fisheries and Food, what assessment his Department has made of (a) the potential side effects on consumers of milk and (b) the effect on milk output and price, of the use of bovine somatotrophin. (65658)

3 **Mrs Virginia Bottomley** (South West Surrey): To ask the Secretary of State for Culture, Media and Sport, what plans he has to meet the chairman of the Royal Society of Literature. (65574)

4 **Mr Crispin Blunt** (Reigate): To ask the Secretary of State for Defence, what is his

estimate of the number of civilian casualties caused by the bombing of Iraq during December 1998.

(65480)

5 **N Mr Tam Dalyell** (Linlithgow): To ask the Secretary of State for Defence, what were the circumstances in which missiles landed on the Hail Adel residential district of Baghdad during the recent raids on Iraq.

(65382)

Part 2 of the Order Book lists questions tabled for answer on future days; an example is set out below.

MONDAY 25th JANUARY

Questions for Written Answer

Notices given on Monday 11th January

1 **N Mr Tam Dalyell** (Linlithgow): To ask the Secretary of State for International Development, what action the Government has taken since his oral statement in the adjournment debate on 1st July to protect coral reefs.

(65477)

Notices given on Tuesday 12th January

1 **N Dr Brian Iddon** (Bolton South East): To ask the Secretary of State for Defence, if United Kingdom production levels of highly enriched uranium are adequate to meet current demand.

(65526)

Notices given on Wednesday 13th January

1 **N Mr Keith Simpson** (Mid Norfolk): To ask the Secretary of State for Trade and Industry, if he will refer the proposed merger of BAE and GEC Marconi to the Monopolies and Mergers Commission.

(65749)

2 **N Mr Lindsay Hoyle** (Chorley): To ask the Secretary of State for Trade and Industry, if he will make a statement on the Government's progress in achieving 10 per cent. of the country's energy from renewable sources.

(66076)

3 **N Mr Harry Cohen** (Leyton and Wanstead): To ask the Minister of State, Lord Chancellor's Department, what plans he has for the public registration of judges' interests; and if he will make a statement.

(65866)

4 **Dr Vincent Cable** (Twickenham): To ask the Minister of Agriculture, Fisheries and Food, if he will set out the number of incidents of harassment of Ministry abattoir inspectors by abattoir staff for each year over the last five years.

(66386)

5 **Paul Flynn** (Newport West): To ask the Minister of Agriculture, Fisheries and Food, what rules or guidance his Department has to govern the (a) formal and (b) informal interaction between his civil servants and commercial lobbyists.

(66203)

6 **Mr Christopher Gill** (Ludlow): To ask the Minister of Agriculture, Fisheries and Food, what assessment he has made of the prospects for decentralising the control of fisheries to zonal management committees within EU member states.

Written answers to questions are delivered to MPs with copies also being sent to the Library, the Table Office, the Official Report and the Press Gallery after 3.30pm Monday to Thursday and after noon on Fridays. They are printed within the next few days in Hansard, along with oral questions which were not reached. Sometimes, Ministers will make written statements by attaching them to previous written questions which they have already answered, describing the new information as being 'pursuant' to the earlier question.

A written question may be withdrawn at any time up until 3.30pm on the day on which it appears on the Order of Business (or before 12.00 noon on a Friday). If it is withdrawn before it appears on the Order of Business, a notice to that effect appears in the next day's issue of the 'blues'. An MP can convert an oral question to a written one and this is signified in the Order of Business or in the 'blues'.

What type of oral or written question may be asked?

The Speaker has ultimate control over the content of questions and may refuse to allow a question to be put, even though it has been printed on the Order Paper.

Members may not table the following questions:

- Oral or written questions to the Speaker – this is not to say that Members may not ask the Speaker questions, only that they must be addressed privately to her office, as opposed to being 'tabled'. Any questions relating to parliamentary privilege have to be raised as points of order on the floor of the House.
- Questions not applicable to the Minister concerned - questions must relate to a Minister's departmental responsibility. Questions which are not relevant will be transferred to the correct department. This is not a matter for the Speaker, but for the Ministers concerned and the Speaker does not seek to intervene. Members may not ask a Minister the reason for transferring such a question.
- Questions to Backbenchers, although there are exceptions, as follows:
  - the Member answering on behalf of the Church Commissioners (e.g., at present, Stuart Bell MP, Second Church Estates Commissioner);
  - the Chairman of the Public Accounts Commission (not to be confused with the Public Accounts Committee)
  - a Member of the House of Commons Commission, answering on behalf of the Commission;
  - the Chairman of the Finance and Services Committee;
  - the Chairmen of the various House of Commons domestic committees; e.g., Accommodation and Works, Catering, etc.

(the above all have allocated times on the rota for oral questions, with the exception of the Chairmen of the domestic committees)

- Questions which are excessively lengthy or which are really speeches masquerading as questions.
- Questions which attempt to put forward arguments or seek opinions – according to Erskine May, 'Questions which seek an expression of an opinion, or which contain arguments, expressions of opinion, inferences or imputations, unnecessary epithets, or rhetorical, controversial, ironical or offensive expressions, are not in order' (Erskine May, 22nd Edition, page 297).
- Questions which are simply extracts from speeches, books, newspapers, etc.
- Questions referring to the conduct of a Member not related to his or her public duties (i.e., questions about Ministers' extra-marital affairs are therefore out of bounds).
- Questions which attack Heads of State of foreign countries with which the UK enjoys 'friendly' relations are definitely out of order (so, rude remarks about the President of the United States are not acceptable, but attacks on Saddam Hussein are generally welcomed).
- Questions about members of the Royal Family, although questions can be asked about such matters as the future of the Royal Yacht, the upkeep of Royal Palaces, etc.
- Certain questions relating to the royal prerogative; for example, questions relating the granting of honours, ecclesiastical appointments, the appointment of Privy Councillors, etc. (some questions relating to some of the Crown's public duties can be asked).
- Questions relating to the internal affairs of bodies for which the Government does not have responsibility; e.g. BP or Scottish Gas – this does not mean that questions which relate to private companies or other bodies, cannot be tabled, merely that they must relate in some way to the Minister's area of responsibility.
- Questions which fall within the jurisdiction of a Chairman of a Select Committee and questions relating to evidence given to a Select Committee which has not yet been published in one of its reports.
- Questions which suggest possible amendments to a bill (unless the question relates to an amendment which cannot be tabled because a Minister has not tabled the necessary Money Resolution or Ways and Means Resolution).
- Questions relating to an opposition party's policies.
- Questions about the business of the House, unless asked as a supplementary at the weekly business questions on a Thursday (business questions on a Thursday technically arise on a Private Notice Question asked by the Shadow Leader of the House, to which the Leader of the House replies with a statement of the following week's business and the provisional business for a further week).
- Questions which have already been answered.
- Questions which a Minister has previously refused to answer (these questions may be tabled again after an interval of three months).

- Questions which include criticisms of decisions of either House.
- Questions which refer to debates or questions of the current session, unless they are seeking to clarify a previous answer.
- Questions relating to matters which are before the UK courts (some questions relating to civil proceedings may be allowed where there is no danger of the question being prejudicial to those proceedings). Where a question already tabled becomes sub-judice, the Member is asked to withdraw it or the Speaker may simply order that it be removed from the Notice Paper. If it is already on the Order of Business she may refuse to allow the question to be asked.

Private Notice Questions

Private Notice Questions (PNQs) are questions of an urgent nature which are taken at 3.30pm on a Monday, Tuesday and Wednesday, at 12.30pm on a Thursday and 11.00am on a Friday, provided they have been submitted to the Speaker before 12.00pm, or 10.30am on a Thursday, or 10.00am on a Friday. Only one PNQ is allowed each day and the Speaker frequently turns down applications. In the 1997/98 Session of Parliament, a total of 12 hours and 52 minutes was devoted to PNQs. PNQs are usually tabled by an Opposition Front Bench Spokesman and replied to by the relevant Minister. As was previously mentioned, the weekly business question is in fact a response by the Leader of the House to a PNQ tabled by the Shadow Leader of the House.

PNQs are very similar in nature to Government statements and follow the same format: the question is answered by the relevant Minister, who is followed by the relevant Opposition Spokesman. The Speaker will then call other Members wishing to ask questions and participate in what is really a general debate lasting, on average, 30 minutes. When a PNQ is allowed the title appears on the annunciators around the House.

The subject matter of PNQs varies enormously, from the extremely serious to the downright hilarious. In a scene which could have been from a Ealing Comedy, on 5 December 1991, the Labour Opposition asked a Private Notice Question concerning the discovery of some Canadian diplomatic bags at Wandsworth Prison. Mark Lennox Boyd MP, was the Foreign Office Minister whose onerous task it was to inform the House that some Canadian bags had inadvertently been included in a consignment of other diplomatic bags sent by the Government to Wandsworth prison to be laundered. Mr Lennox Boyd's attempts to take the matter seriously, the revelation that the Government routinely sent material for laundering to a prison and the fact that the diplomatic bags appeared to have passed through the relevant security checks with their contents intact, all combined to convulse both sides of the House. Tongue-in-cheek, Rt Hon Gerald Kaufman MP demanded that the 'Government come clean' on the matter. Some Members looked as though the general merriment might be too much for them – leading to a fit or seizure of some kind. Others, who had never previously been known to smile, let alone actually laugh out loud, looked fit to burst. The Speaker seemed concerned that such jocundity might actually be dangerous, saying at one point that he wondered if he should have granted the question in the first place. Unfortunately, PNQs are not usually the occasion for such ribald humour. In the 1997/98 Session, there were 28 PNQs in total.

QUESTIONS IN THE HOUSE OF LORDS

Starred Questions

Starred questions (marked '*' on the House of Lords Order Paper are the House of Lords' equivalent of oral questions in the House of Commons and are the first item of business after Prayers and introductions. Up to four 'Starred Questions' may be taken on any sitting day, except Friday. On a Wednesday and Thursday, the final Starred Question is a balloted question on a topical issue. Peers are not allowed more than two of these 'topical Starred Questions' per session. The ballot takes place at 2.00pm on the previous Monday for Wednesday's topical Starred Question and on Tuesday for Thursday's question. A peer may only table one Starred Question per day and may not have more than one Starred Questions on the Order Paper at any one time (unless successful in the ballot for a topical question). Starred Questions are really requests for information and are addressed to the Government as a whole as opposed to a specific Minister. Questions can also be directed to the Leader of the House or the Chairman of Committees. Starred Questions may not be tabled more than one month (a calendar month) in advance of the day for answer.[1] They may also not be tabled less than 24 hours before they are due to be answered.

Starred Questions are not the subject of general debate but supplementary questions can be asked by peers, although these supplementaries must be short, not seek to raise more than two points, not put forward opinions, and be confined to the subject of the original Starred Question. The peer who asked the Starred Question puts the first supplementary question but has no automatic right to ask a final question. Starred Questions usually last between 20 minutes and half an hour each. If the peer who has tabled the Starred Question cannot be present in the Chamber, he can ask a fellow peer to put the question on his or her behalf, provided he has notified one of the Clerks at the Table of the House in advance.

The subject matter of Starred Questions varies enormously, from the alleged problems of organophosphates to the plight of the pelicans in St. James's Park. On Wednesday, 16 December 1987, Rt Hon Lord Stodart of Leaston asked the Government, 'how many pelicans there are in St. James's Park; and of this number now many are males and how many females'. The exchange which followed, which their Lordships greatly enjoyed, is worth reproducing in full:

Lord Hesketh: My Lords, there are five pelicans in St. James's Park. Your Lordships may be as surprised as I was to learn that it is particularly difficult for humans to determine the sex of pelicans, and so I fear we do not know the sexes of the pelicans in the park.

---

[1] In the House of Lords, no motions or questions other than those relating to bills or subordinate legislation, may be accepted by the Table Office for a day more than one month in advance. This period does not include times when the House is in recess, except where Starred Questions are concerned.

Lord Stodart of Leaston: My Lords, may I thank my noble friend for that explicit answer. I hope that the investigations that he has had to undertake have not proved excessively laborious or too indelicate. Does it not give him satisfaction in these days, when there is considerable concern about the invasion of privacy that, if I may paraphrase his reply correctly, the only person who knows the sex of a pelican is another pelican? Just in case a happy event were to take place during the coming spring, even if it were very unexpected, will he agree to pay a visit to the park to see whether anything is going on?

Lord Hesketh: My Lords, I am grateful for my noble friend's supplementary question. I am more than happy to agree to take a pleasant lakeside walk in St. James's Park in the spring. The only thing I am certain of is that, since we believe that pelicans first arrived under the reign of James I and there has been no productive activity since that date, it may be a wasted walk.

Lord McIntosh of Haringey: My Lords, would it not be more seemly for the noble Lord to start at the other end of the pelican? Is it not the case that:

> "A wonderful bird is the pelican,
> His bill will hold more than his belican.
> He can take in his beak,
> Food enough for a week,
> But I'm damned if I see how the helican"?

Lord Hesketh: My Lords, the noble Lord is entirely correct. I am told that if you look closely at the knobs at the base of the top mandible of a pelican, as they approach the breeding season there is a change of colour to those who have particularly sharp eyes.

Lord Cledwyn of Penrhos: My Lords, if these pelicans have not laid an egg since the time of James I, where do they come from? If they were Celtic pelicans they would reproduce and if there were Anglo-Saxon pelicans I am sure they would do well. But the noble Lord should explain to the House whether it is the baleful influence of Whitehall?

Lord Hesketh: My Lords, we are in a sense dependent on diplomatic charity with regard to the pelicans. We have had them from Louisiana and from Texas, and we have even been grateful to receive them from His Highness the Amir of Bahawalpur. At the moment, of the pelicans we have, four come from Ravensden Zoo in Northamptonshire - and no finer county could they come from - and the fifth bird was donated by the state of Louisiana in 1982.

Baroness Strange: My Lords, is my noble friend aware of what the pelicans think themselves?

"Ploffskin, Pluffskin, Pelican Jee!
We think no birds so happy as we!
Plumpskin, Ploshkin, Pelican Jill!
We thought so them, and we think so still!".

Lord Hesketh: My Lords, they looked very happy the last time I saw them as I walked through the park.

Lord Scarman: My Lords, is not the truth that the pelicans are in St. James's Park as a symbol of political life? The beak holds more than the belly can.

Lord Hesketh: My Lords, I am grateful to the noble and learned Lord, Lord Scarman, for his observation.

Lord Kilbracken: My Lords, is it not a well known fact that male pelicans are bigger than female pelicans?

Lord Hesketh: My Lords, I fear that that may not be quite the case. If I refer to the matter of the knobs on the base of the top of the mandible, which appears to be the only certain form of detection, there is a slight difference in colour. The male knob of the pelican is a lemon-yellow and the female's a rich orange, but unfortunately the colours are variable and not a certain guide to the sex.

Lord Stodart of Leaston: My Lords, is it not a possibility that a stork may visit the pelican house and then one would get a new connotation of the expression "pelican crossing"?

Lord Hesketh: My Lords, I am sure that that would be the case. Whether or not a productive result would be the outcome is another matter.

The House of Lords is far less prescriptive in its approach to questions than the House of Commons and more or less anything is in order provided it does not cast aspersions on the Royal Family, deal with matters which are the responsibility of the Church of England, matters which are sub judice and questions which are in any way offensive. Their Lordships are quite fearless and will tackle the most unpromising of subjects: on 14 January 1998 Lord Soulsby of Swaffham Prior asked what action the Government was taking 'to regulate the qualification of people practising equine dentistry'; Lord Campbell of Croy asked about the contribution of UK monitors in Kosovo; the Lord Bishop of Oxford asked about action being taken to encourage the contribution of poetry to national culture and Lord Mackay of Ardbrecknish asked about the impact of unemployment in Renfrewshire given the closure of the Royal Ordnance Factory at Bishopton.

Unstarred Questions

Unstarred Questions may be put down on the Order Paper for any sitting day and give rise to general debates. The peer asking the question has ten minutes in which to speak, followed by 12 minutes for the Minister replying to the question. The peer moving the question has no right of reply. Unstarred Questions are usually taken at the end of the day's business or during the dinner adjournment (this fact is denoted on the Order Paper, although Unstarred Questions always appear as the final business on the Order Paper, even when it is intended to take them in the dinner adjournment). When an Unstarred Question is taken during the dinner adjournment, the debate may not last for longer than one hour, whereas Unstarred Questions taken at the end of the day's business can be debated for up to one and a half-hours. For example, the Lords Notices and Orders of the day for Monday 18 January denoted that Lord Phillips of Sudbury's Unstarred Question on the Crick Advisory Group would be taken during the dinner adjournment. This is set out below:

NOTICES AND ORDERS OF THE DAY

Items marked † are new or have been altered.

Items marked ‡ are expected to be taken during the dinner adjournment

MONDAY 18TH JANUARY

At half-past two o'clock

***The Lord Pilkington of Oxenford** – To ask Her Majesty's Government whether they intend to extend the policy of allowing parents to vote on the future of grammar schools to other education issues.

***Lord Dean of Beswick** – To ask Her Majesty's Government what action they propose to take following the publication of the Cervical Screening Programme Review 1998.

***The Lord Avebury** – To ask Her Majesty's Government what was discussed by the Prime Minister at his meeting with the Prime Minister of Bahrain in the Seychelles.

***The Baroness Ludford** – To ask Her Majesty's Government what steps are being taken to ensure that European banks charge minimal commission for euro-zone currency conversions by individual travellers.

Youth Justice and Criminal Evidence Bill [HL] – Committee [The Lord Williams of Mostyn]

‡ **The Lord Phillips of Sudbury** – To ask Her Majesty's Government what plans they have to implement the recommendations of the final report of the Crick Advisory Group on *Education for Citizenship and the Teaching of Democracy in Schools*

A second Unstarred Question may sometimes be taken in exceptional circumstances.

Private Notice Questions

PNQs are taken after Starred Questions in the House of Lords. Any peer who wishes to ask a Private Notice Question must apply in writing to the Leader of the House by 12.00 noon on the day in question (by 10.00am on any day when the House is to sit before 1.00pm). It is up to the Leader of the House to decide whether or not to accept the PNQ, but if he/she decides not to accept such a question, the peer concerned may challenge this decision, provided he/she gives notice to this effect to the Leader of the House. PNQs are treated in the same way as Starred Questions. Sometimes, a PNQ which has been asked in the Commons will be repeated in the Lords by means of a Government statement and sometimes a statement being made by the Government in the House of Commons will be made in the House of Lords by means of a Private Notice Question tabled in that House.

For example, on 25 February 1998, Baroness Hayman repeated the statement being made in the House of Commons by Rt Hon Michael Meacher MP concerning the publication of the Government's consultation document 'Access to the Countryside' by means of an answer to a Private Notice Question. Such PNQs are taken at a convenient time in the day's proceedings – there is no specific time at which PNQs and statements are taken as there is in the House of Commons. On 8 June 1998, Lord Clinton-Davis repeated, by means of a Statement, a Private Notice Question made that day in the House of Commons on the Dounreay Nuclear Reprocessing Plant.

Written Questions

Written Questions in the House of Lords are usually answered within two weeks of being tabled. They appear in the House of Lords Minutes the day after they are tabled and answers appear in Hansard. The House of Lords Procedure Committee recently recommended that all unanswered Written Questions should be republished once a week in the Mintues and that all questions not anwered after 21 days should be republished in the minutes each day until answered (HL 144, 1997/98).

CHAPTER SEVEN - HOW A BILL BECOMES AN ACT

THE POLICY MAKING PROCESS

The Manifesto

Any Party's General Election Manifesto has usually been developed in some detail long before an Election is called, particularly if that Party is in opposition. However, the Manifesto itself is a public declaration of intent and contains a broad outline of the Party's plans for its first term in office. This does not of course mean that a Party's Manifesto commitments will be carried out – only that they *are* commitments and they *may* be carried out. Labour's 1997 Manifesto stated that: 'We are committed to a referendum on the voting system for the House of Commons'. It is beginning to look as though this particular commitment may have to wait until Labour's second term in office.

Not all Government policies are set out in black and white in an Election Manifesto; they are often merely hinted at or buried deep within the recesses of an obscure Think-Tank Pamphlet published long before the Election itself. Such was the case with the present Government's granting of independence to the Bank of England so soon after the Election. Whilst this had not been explicitly set out in the Manifesto, it had been put forward as a possibility in a number of Speeches and publications by the then Shadow Treasury Team. A careful reading of the collected pre-election works of messrs. Brown and Balls would have alerted a more vigilant press to this particular policy objective. An Opposition Party will usually have developed its policies in the run up to the Election with a number of influential supporters but, more significantly, may well have had confidential discussions with key civil servants on how its objectives could be implemented should it win the forthcoming Election. As Hugh Pym and Nick Kochan make clear in their biography of Gordon Brown, 'Gordon Brown – the first year in power' *(Bloomsbury, 1998)* Ed Balls, the Chancellor's adviser, began a series of meetings with Sir Terence Burns, Permanent Secretary to the Treasury, in 1996. They also point out that: 'During the election campaign Balls was also having meetings with groups of civil servants about Labour's budgetary principles'.

After an Election

By the time the Labour Party won the General Election in 1997, the civil servants awaiting their arrival in Whitehall probably had a better grasp of their policies than they did themselves. As Gerald Kaufman points out in 'How to be a Minister' *(Faber and Faber, 1997)*: 'When you enter your department after your election victory, your officials will know at least as much about your policies as you do. They will have studied all your party's policy pronouncements, read all its pamphlets. More than that, they will have spent the months leading up to the election preparing actively for your arrival, just in case you win'. Whilst some Ministers may have a very clear idea of exactly what they want to do and how to go about doing it, others may be less well prepared. Some may have a general idea that they would like to clean up the environment or contribute to the general well-being of mankind, but have little or no idea of how to go about it. The time-honoured response to this is to establish either a Royal Commission or an independent enquiry headed by a respected member of the House of Lords (the recent Jenkins' enquiry into electoral reform and Lord Marshall's study of energy taxes are good examples of this). This allows the Secretary of State responsible for the enquiry to say that full consideration will of course be given to the results of this very useful study, but that the matter must now be thrown open for a wide-ranging public debate.

Implementing Policy

Labour's 1997 General Election Manifesto did not specifically commit the Party to the introduction of energy taxes, but talked generally of discouraging environmental pollution through the tax system. Nor did the Manifesto specifically state that there would be a review of the North Sea Fiscal Regime. However, policies often emerge in Government in response to that most pressing of exigencies, the need to raise money. In this case, whilst the Treasury may take the lead, other Departments will inevitably become involved. The possibility of reforming a particular tax or group of taxes may be discussed at departmental level and also at one or more of the various Cabinet Committees; for example, the Sub-Committee on Energy Policy or the Economic Affairs Committee, before being discussed at a full meeting of the Cabinet itself. The No. 10 Policy Unit will almost certainly have formed a view, based in part on any discussions its officers have had with those in commerce and industry. If the matter is a financial one, the announcement of some form of review may be included in the Green Budget or the Budget itself. This may not necessarily form part of the Chancellor's speech but may be confined to a passing reference in the Financial Statement and Budget Report (Red Book) or in one of the many departmental press releases.

The establishment of an inter-departmental review provides outside bodies and interest groups with an opportunity to put forward their views and concerns on the matter. Whilst the review may be headed by a junior Minister, the real work is carried out by the civil servants whose job it is to service the committee. These are the people with a really detailed knowledge of the matter in hand; they are also the people with whom pressure group, trade associations, etc., are most likely to meet and who act as a filter between their Ministers and the wider world outside Whitehall. Civil servants do not have to be directors of departments or permanent secretaries to be influential.

Pressure Groups

It is this review process which really provides outside organisations, business groups, individual companies, trade associations, sectional groups, charities, voluntary organisations, etc., with an opportunity to put forward their views directly to civil servants and Ministers. Often, the process is a genuinely consultative one, particularly where ministers are keen to avoid the pitfalls of badly-drafted and ill-thought-out legislation. The system is a mutually beneficial one; after all, ministers and their civil servants cannot be experts in all matters which require their attention. They need the information and expertise provided by outside organisations, just as much as the latter need their voices to be heard.

Depending on the nature of the review process or consultation period, the findings may be published as a Green or White Paper, or if the matter is a financial one, incorporated into the next Budget and ensuing Finance Bill.

The Role of Parliament

There are some who would argue that such is the influence of the single-issue group, the trade association or industry body, Parliament is now a redundant part of the policy-making process. This is only partly true; Parliament has a more formal part to play in the legislative process, but its role is essential. Parliament too is changing to ensure greater consultation during the passage of a bill through both Houses. The use of special select committees and pre-legislative scrutiny is being encouraged and the Pension-Sharing Bill, published on 9 June 1998 was the first Government bill of the current Session to undergo this process.

The Manifesto
Party in Opposition develops policies which are incorporated into General Election Manifesto

Discussions in Opposition
Party discusses possible methods of implementing policies; discussions may include civil servants

Cabinet Discussions
Discussions in Cabinet, Cabinet Committees and with No. 10 Policy Unit Advisers, Special Advisers and key civil servants

Setting up an Enquiry
Once in Office, Government Department announces review of policy area, Green Paper may be published – groups invited to submit responses in consultation period

Results of Review
Results published – possibly in a White Paper or draft bill – may be further consultation

Bill Presented to Parliament
First Reading of bill in either House – new pre-legislative committee may be used

WHAT IS A BILL?

A bill sets out in detail, proposed new laws and/or amendments to existing ones. As our legal system is based both on common law precedent and the interpretation of statutes by the courts, it is essential that bills are drafted in such a way as to avoid multiple interpretations. This is not always the case and often Government bills will be amended during their passage through Parliament, not just by the Opposition but by Ministers as well. Some bills are Government bills, some are promoted by Backbenchers – known as 'Private Members' Bills' - whilst others are promoted by organisations established under Statute – known as 'Private Bills'. Hybrid Bills are a cross between Public and Private Bills and combine elements of both.

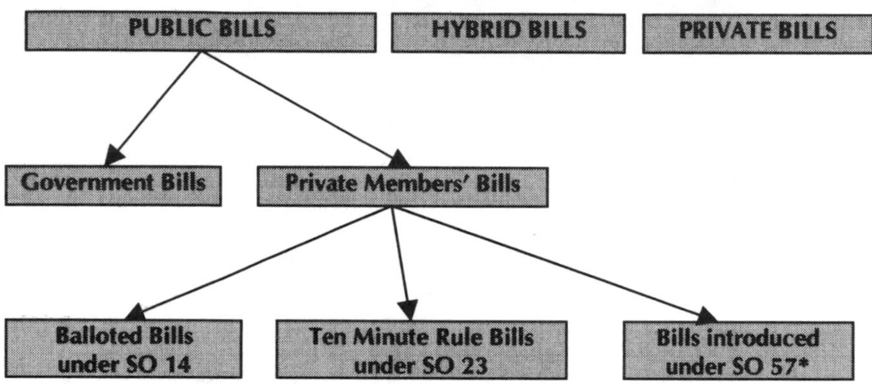

* Government bills may also be brought in under SO 57

In this chapter, every attempt has been made to explain what may appear to be rather arcane and outmoded language. For example, to anyone with any common sense, a 'Standing Committee that sits' seems to be a contradiction in terms. The phrase refers to a Committee which has been constituted solely to consider a particular piece of legislation and which is not a permanent committee of the House, and which 'sits' (meets) for as long as is necessary to debate a bill, clause by clause. Attempts have been made throughout the chapter to explain terms such as the 'bill is committed' or the House meets for 'consideration on report'. Whilst those who follow parliamentary matters on a regular basis will be familiar with such terminology, many will not. These two terms mean, respectively, that a bill is either sent to a Standing Committee or has its Committee Stage on the floor of the House (i.e., in the Chamber, where all Members may participate) and that once a bill has been debated in Committee it is 'reported' to the House for its 'consideration'. This 'consideration' is what is commonly referred to as 'Report Stage'. Thoroughly confused? Read on.

EXPLANATORY NOTES

The structure of bills has been altered during the last Session of Parliament, after implementation of the Second Report of the Select Committee on Modernisation of the House of Commons (HC 389, 1997/98). This is part of the drive by the new Labour Government to update, reform and clarify the procedures of the House, and in particular, the language of Government.

Prior to the current 1998/99 of Parliament, Government bills were printed with an Explanatory and Financial Memorandum, with Notes on Clauses (explanations of the bill's Clauses) printed as a separate document. These two have now been merged into one set of notes, called 'Explanatory Notes' which appear at the beginning of all new Government bills. Using the European Parliamentary Elections Bill as an example, the bill as first issued in the 1997/98 Session, before the above reforms were implemented, began with an 'Explanatory and Financial Memorandum', whereas the same Bill, reintroduced in the current Session (1998/99), began with 'Explanatory Notes'. Every bill now contains a declaration by the Government Minister in charge of the bill, that the bill complies with the provisions of the new Human Rights Act 1998. This forms part of the new Explanatory Notes.

The Explanatory Notes are followed by a list of all the Clauses and Schedules of a Bill.

THE LONG TITLE

The Long Title of a bill defines its general purposes. This is very important because the provisions of the bill may not exceed the Long Title, so all the bill's Clauses must fall within the scope of the Long Title. However, the Long Title may itself be amended if certain amendments to the bill render this necessary.

An example of a Long Title, from the European Parliamentary Elections Bill, is set out below:

> **An Act to amend the European Parliamentary Elections Act 1978 so as to alter the method used in Great Britain for electing Members to the European Parliament; to make other amendments of enactments relating to the election of Members of the European Parliament; and for connected purposes.**

The Long Title used to be followed by a Preamble, setting out the reasons for and the intended effects of the bill in question, but these are rarely used nowadays, the exception being Private Bills.

ENACTING FORMULA

The enacting formula is a form of words, which has been used since the Fifteenth Century, which states that under our unwritten constitution, bills must pass both Commons and Lords before receiving Royal Assent.

> **Be it enacted by the Queen's most Excellent Majesty, by and with the advice and consent of the Lords Spiritual and Temporal, and Commons, in this present Parliament assembled, and by the authority of the same, as follows: -**

The wording used for the Finance Bill and Consolidated Fund bills is slightly different. For example, the Finance Bill uses the formula:

> **Most Gracious Sovereign, We Your Majesty's most dutiful and loyal subjects, the Commons of the United Kingdom in Parliament assembled towards raising**

> **the necessary supplies to defray Your Majesty's public expenses, and making an addition to the public revenue, have freely and voluntarily resolved to give and grant unto Your Majesty the several duties hereinafter mentioned and do therefore most humbly beseech Your Majesty that it may be enacted, and be it enacted by the Queen's most Excellent Majesty, by and with the advice and consent of the Lords Spiritual and Temporal, and Commons, in this present Parliament assembled, and by the authority of the same, as follows: -**

In the case of a Consolidated Fund Bill the wording is slightly different again.

> **Most Gracious Sovereign, We Your Majesty's most dutiful and loyal subjects, the Commons of the United Kingdom in Parliament assembled towards making good the supply which we have cheerfully granted to Your Majesty in this Session of Parliament, have resolved to grant unto Your Majesty the sum hereinafter mentioned and do therefore most humbly beseech Your Majesty that it may be enacted, and be it enacted by the Queen's most Excellent Majesty, by and with the advice and consent of the Lords Spiritual and Temporal, and Commons, in this present Parliament assembled, and by the authority of the same, as follows: -**

CLAUSES

A bill is divided into Clauses, a longer bill is usually divided into Parts, chapters and Clauses. These clauses are numbered and subdivided; i.e., 2(2). The lines in a bill are numbered to ease identification when amendments are considered (unfortunately, these are not provided on some internet versions of bills). There are certain standard Clauses, which you will find in most Government bills, which state, for example, how the bill is to be interpreted or what sort of delegated legislation can be brought in under the Bill, once it has been enacted. For example, Schedule 1, paragraph 4, (1) (b) of the European Parliamentary Elections Bill states that the Secretary of State shall 'make by order such amendments of column (3) of the table as he considers necessary to ensure that result'. There are usually some interpretation Clauses; for example, Clauses which state that 'in this section, Secretary of State means Home Secretary'.

There may also be Commencement Clauses saying how and when a bill, or particular parts of it, will actually take effect. 'Enactment' and 'Commencement' are two different things, the former is when the bill receives Royal Assent and the latter is when the provisions of the bill actually take effect. In the case of the European Parliamentary Elections Bill, Clause 5 states that the bill will come into force on such a 'day as the Secretary of State may appoint by Order'. The last Clause is what is known as the 'citation and short title' and is the name by which the Act will be known; for example, 'This Act may be cited as the European Parliamentary Elections Act 1998'.

SCHEDULES

The Schedules of a bill contain the finer details of a bill – they are dependent on the preceding Clauses of the Bill. For example, Clause 2 of a bill might simply state that a new Advisory Board was to be established, leaving the details of its membership, their methods of appointment, etc. to be set out in a Schedule to the Bill. Schedules are divided into 'parts' and 'paragraphs' rather than Clauses and Sub-clauses. Frequently, Schedules to a bill are used to add new Schedules to existing Acts. This means that when the bill is passed, it will effectively amend an existing Act of Parliament, by inserting a new Schedule. This can make life very confusing indeed when reading a Bill, as it may be necessary to refer to a previous Act of Parliament, simply to make sense of the bill itself. For example, Schedule 1 of the European Parliamentary Elections Bill adds a new Schedule 2 to the European Parliamentary Elections Act 1978 and Schedule 2 of the bill amends Schedule 1 of the 1978 Act.

The final Schedule of a bill usually sets out the 'repeals and revocations' which result from the provisions of the bill; i.e., which existing Acts are to be either repealed in their entirety or partially amended by the bill.

USEFUL TIPS FOR FOLLOWING BILLS

If, for whatever reason, you need to follow a bill through all its stages in both Houses, there are a few items which you should have beside you at all times in your legislative journey. First and foremost, it's always a good idea to have a copy of the bill in question; this may seem so obvious as to be hardly worth stating, but for 'copy' read 'the latest edition of the Bill'. Bills are reprinted after their various stages, so make sure you have the latest copy to hand. For example, amendments at Report Stage refer to the bill as reprinted after Committee Stage, not to the bill as first printed. If no amendments at all have been made to the bill in Committee then the bill will remain unchanged, but most bills are amended in some way, even if the only alteration has been to remove 'it' and insert 'to' in line three. It is particularly important to keep a copy of the bill as first printed in the House of Lords. DO NOT UNDER ANY CIRCUMSTANCES THROW THIS AWAY under the mistaken impression that you will not need it after the bill has returned to the House of Commons (if it began life in that House). As you will see later in this chapter, you will need it again.

It is always a good idea to have a copy of the House of Commons Standing Orders relating to Public Business and the House of Lords' counterpart. These are available on the Parliament Website or can be obtained from The Stationery Office. The House of Lords Companion to the Standing Orders and Guide to the Proceedings of the House of Lords is also immensely useful. For those with a strong constitution, there is always Erskine May's Parliamentary Practice, published by Butterworths and now in its 22nd Edition. It is the 'Bible' of parliamentary procedure, but definitely not for the faint-hearted. Unfortunately, many of the procedures employed by both Houses are not enshrined in Standing Orders but are based on precedent, on previous rulings by former Speakers of the House of Commons, on long-standing resolutions first passed by the House in the 17th century or on long forgotten reports from the Select Committee on Procedure. These are gathered together in Erskine May, so for the serious Parliament watcher, it's advisable to have a copy fairly close to hand.

FIRST READING

Bills can be introduced in either the House of Commons or the House of Lords. In the 1997/98 Session of Parliament, of the Public Bills which received Royal Assent, 42 began their legislative passage in the House of Commons and 20 in the House of Lords. Of the 42 which began in the Commons, 8 were Private Members' Bills. 140 Public Bills failed to gain Royal Assent and of those which began life in the Commons, all but one were Private Members' Bills; of those which were introduced in the Lords (12 in total) all were Private Members' Bills. In order to become an Act, a bill must progress through all its stages (as set out below) in both Houses, before it can receive Royal Assent. It is usual, for major Government bills, particularly those which impinge upon the Constitution, to begin life in the House of Commons. For example, in the 1997/98 Session of Parliament, the Government of Wales Bill, the Scotland Bill and the European Parliamentary Elections Bill all began life in the House of Commons.

What are known as 'bills of aids and supplies' must originate in the House of Commons. The main examples are the Finance Bill and the Consolidated Fund Bill. The House of Commons has the exclusive right to 'grant supply' and 'impose charges'; i.e. spend and raise money. For this reason the House of Lords may not amend such bills. If they did, it would be regarded as an 'intolerable breach' of Commons' privilege, as set out in the resolution of the House of 3 July 1678, which states, 'That all aids and supplies, and aids to his Majesty in Parliament, are the sole gift of the Commons; and all bills for the granting of any such aids and supplies ought to begin with the Commons; and that it is the undoubted and sole right of the Commons to direct, limit and appoint in such bills the ends, purposes, considerations, conditions, limitations and qualifications of such grants, which ought not to be changed or altered by the House of Lords'. It is for this reason that the House of Lords does not amend the Finance Bill and in fact, proceedings on the bill in the House of Lords are limited to a Second Reading debate.

Under SO 50 a bill which has the imposition of a charge as its main purpose can be introduced in the House of Lords, if taken forward in the House of Commons by a Government Minister. When a bill originates in the House of Lords it has the letters [HL] after the title and when it is proceeds to the House of Commons it has the word [Lords] after the title. A bill which originates in the House of Commons has no similar suffix.

The First Reading of the European Parliamentary Elections Bill took place on 29 October 1997. The First Reading of a bill is merely a formal introduction of a bill – so the following brief statement was all that appeared in the Order Paper:

Formal first reading: no debate or decision

*EUROPEAN PARLIAMENTARY ELECTIONS **[No debate]***

Mr Secretary Straw

Bill to amend the European Parliamentary Elections Act 1978 so as to alter the method used in Great Britain for electing Members of the European Parliament; to make other amendments of enactments relating to the election of Members of the European Parliament; and for connected purposes.

In Hansard, the following was all that was recorded:

European Parliamentary Elections

Mr. Secretary Straw, supported by the Prime Minister, Mr. Secretary Prescott, Mr. Secretary Cook, Mr. Secretary Dewar, Secretary Majorie Mowlam, Mr. Secretary Davies, and Mr. George Howarth, presented a Bill to amend the European Parliamentary Elections Act 1978 so as to alter the method used in Great Britain for electing Members of the European Parliament; to make other amendments of enactments relating to the election of members of the European Parliament; and for connected purposes: And the same was read the First time; and ordered to be read the Second time tomorrow, and to be printed [Bill 69].

This does not actually mean that the bill had its Second Reading on the following day, merely that it was added to what are known as the 'remaining orders of the day' (see chapter on Parliamentary Papers) for Second Reading at some future date.

There are a number of ways of 'bringing in a bill' in the House of Commons and they are permitted under certain Standing Orders - the rules governing procedures in the House of Commons. New procedures usually require some amendments of existing Standing Orders, and any such amendments must be agreed by the House.

SO 49 & 50

The basic premise underlying the introduction of any bill is that 'financial initiative lies with the Crown' – i.e., only the 'Queen's Ministers' (the Government) may introduce bills whose primary purpose is financial. Under SO 49 and 50 a bill whose main aim is to spend money may only be 'brought in' (introduced) by a Minister of the Crown. SO 50 allows a Minister to introduce a bill before the relevant 'financial resolution' i.e., a Ways and Means or Supply Resolution (these are explained in chapter 13) has been brought before the House, or to take charge of a bill which has come from the House of Lords (which was introduced in the House of Lords). Prior to the passing of the SO 50, all bills had to be brought in upon such resolutions.

Any Government bill which involves spending public money has to be followed at Second Reading by a Money Resolution. These are taken 'forthwith' (without debate) if moved directly after Second Reading, or if taken at any other time, may be debated for up to 45 minutes.

SOs 49 and 50 do not prevent backbenchers from introducing bills where an incidental purpose of the bill may be to spend public money, but it cannot be its primary purpose.

Standing Orders 57, 23 and 14(6)

SO 57 allows a backbench MP to introduce a bill at any time 'without leave'. SO 57 can be used by a backbench MP to take up a Private Member's Bill from the House of Lords, but in this case the First Reading is the day on which the MP informs the Public Bill Office of his or her intention to take up the bill. It is then set down for Second Reading, but not before the fifth Wednesday of the Session (SO 14). SO 57 Bills are presented at the beginning of public business in the House of Commons and are not debated. They should not be confused with Ten Minute Rule Bills, where 'leave' has been given to bring in a bill under SO 23. Where a bill is being presented under SO 57, the words used on the Order Paper are: 'Notice of Presentation of Bill' . All the MP presenting the bill has to do is to give the long and short title of the bill to the Public Bill Office before the rising of the House the day before he intends to present the Bill.

The words, 'Notice of Motion for Leave to Bring in a Bill', denote a Ten Minute Rule Bill. Ten Minute Rule Bills can only be presented after the 5th Wednesday of the Session. They are not permitted on the Tuesday of the Budget and a Ten Minute Rule Bill which would have been presented on that day is held over to the following Monday. No Ten Minute Rule Bills can be tabled more than 15 sitting days before they are to be presented, so MPs often queue up all night to ensure that they are first through the door of the Public Bill Office at 10.00am, on the Tuesday or Wednesday, 15 sittings days before the day of presentation. MPs give the long and short title to the Public Bill Office – the title can be changed up to five sitting days before the bill is due to have its First Reading. Another difference between SO 57 bills and SO 23 (Ten Minute Rule Bills) is that when the latter are presented, the Member in charge can make a 10 minute speech, followed by a 10 minute speech from a Member who opposes the Bill. When SO 57 Bills are presented a dummy copy of the bill is put on the table and is presented by the 'Member in charge' (the MP proposing the Bill).

SO 23 may also be used to nominate Select Committee members, but such a motion can only be proposed by a member of the Committee of Selection and Select Committee members are now usually nominated under SO 121 & 152 (see chapter 11 on Committees for more details).

The balloted Private Members' Bills are brought in under SO 14(6) and their First Reading is on the fifth Wednesday of the Session (for more information on the procedures relating to Private Members' Bills see chapter Eight).

A bill's sponsors are listed on the back of the bill – no bill may have more than 12 sponsors.

After First Reading, the bill is sent for printing and is given a serial number. Immediately prior to its printing, it is checked by the Public Bill Office to make sure it conforms to all the relevant Standing Orders and should not have been brought in upon a ways and means resolution and to ensure that it is not a Hybrid Bill. A Hybrid Bill is one which has elements of both a Public and a Private Bill. If a bill is found to be hybrid, the Standing Orders relating to private business apply and the bill is sent to the Examiners (see chapter on Private Bills).

A bill must be printed in order to have a Second Reading, if it is not printed it will become a 'lapsed' order. You will often see the following words in brackets after a bill's entry in the Weekly Information Bulletin: '(not printed) (Order for 2nd Reading lapsed)'.

Bills are reprinted after subsequent stages and a bill will be given a new serial number after reprinting. After it has completed its stages in the House of Commons, it will be printed for the first time in the House of Lords and given a House of Lords number. It is then reprinted after subsequent stages in the House of Lords. When the bill returns to the House of Commons for Consideration of Lords Amendments, the amendments refer to the bill as first printed in the House of Lords, so, if you are following a bill, you will need to keep a copy of this edition of the bill.

According to a rule agreed by the House on 1 June 1610, 'no bill of the same substance should be brought in in the same Session'. This has been modified to the extent that if one bill has had its Second Reading another with very similar provisions may not be proceeded with. There are some exceptions to this rule; for example, if a bill is withdrawn, another with very similar contents may be introduced.

INTERVALS BETWEEN STAGES OF A PUBLIC BILL

In the House of Lords

The time required for the various stages of a bill is regulated by Standing Order 44, which provides that no two stages be taken in one day. There are also conventions as to minimum recommended intervals between stages of a bill. These are:

(a) two week-ends between the introduction of a bill and the debate on Second Reading;
(b) fourteen days between Second Reading and the start of the Committee Stage;
(c) on all bills of some length and complexity, 14 days between the end of the Committee Stage and the start of the Report Stage;
(d) three sitting days between the end of the report stage and Third Reading

Sometimes Standing Order 44 (Lords) is suspended, allowing bills to pass through a number of stages in one day. Even if SO 44 has not been suspended there may be occasions when the conventions set out above are not adhered to, in which case it is marked on the order paper with the following symbol: '§'. If a bill has to pass through all stages in both Houses in a day (as a result of a national emergency, for example) both SO 44 and 84[1] are suspended in the House of Lords.

In the House of Commons

There are no rules in the House of Commons which forbid taking several or all stages of a bill at one sitting. However, bills introduced on Ways and Means Resolutions are not supposed to pass through more than one stage on the same day, but this practice is often waived.

SECOND READING

A Second Reading debate is centred on the main principles of the bill in question and certain amendments can be moved, not to the bill itself, but to the question that the bill be read a second time. Second Reading debates usually begin at about 3.30pm after

[1] Under SO 84 notice of the intention to move that SO 44 be suspended is required. If there is no time to give any advance warning of the intention to suspend SO 44, SO 84 can be suspended as well.

oral questions, but if there are any Statements or Private Notice Questions (PNQs), the debate may not begin until 4.30pm or 5.00pm. The debate is usually opened by the 'Member in charge of the Bill'; i.e., the relevant Secretary of State, or Minister who will be responsible for piloting the bill through Parliament. He or she uses the words, 'I beg to move that the bill be now read a Second Time'. In the case of the European Parliamentary Elections Bill, this was the Home Secretary, Rt Hon Jack Straw MP. The relevant Official Opposition Front Bench Spokesman then replies to the Government's opening speech. Members who wish to speak in the debate write to the Speaker (this may be done on behalf of the MP by the respective Party Whips' office) saying that they hope the Speaker will call them 'should (they) attempt to catch her eye'. There is sometimes a limit on the length of speeches and under SO 47 the Speaker can impose a time limit on contributions of no less than 8 minutes.

Speakers in any debate in the House of Commons are frequently interrupted; however, some of these interruptions are more properly called 'interventions' and it is up to the Member who is speaking to decide whether or not to respond. Sometimes a Member will say that he or she is not willing to 'take interventions'. There is nothing the Speaker can do to force a Member to respond to an intervention. Refusing to take interventions often makes the Member concerned look as though he or she has something to hide, is incapable of thinking on his or her feet, or is unable to answer difficult questions for which answers could not have been prepared in advance. In his opening speech on the Second Reading debate on the European Parliamentary Elections Bill on 25 November 1997, Rt Hon Jack Straw MP, the Home Secretary, took interventions from Gwyneth Dunwoody, Sir Peter Tapsell, Alan Beith, Douglas Hogg, Llew Smith, William Cash, Dr Tony Wright, Christopher Gill, Richard Shepherd, Dale Campbell-Savours and Margaret Ewing . Interventions from a 'sedentary position' are roundly condemned by the House as being extremely indecorous and evidence of a general lack of breeding on the part of the Member concerned, so MPs wishing to intervene are expected to be on their feet at the time.

Consolidation bills (those which consolidate existing Acts of Parliament) are no longer debated at Second Reading and are taken 'forthwith'. There may be discussion at Committee Stage, although a Minister may table a motion that the 'bill be not committed', in which case it can go through all its stages in a day. An example from the 1997/98 Session is the Statute Law Repeals [HL] Bill which completed all its stages on 9 November 1998. The bill had been sent to the Joint Committee after Second Reading in the House of Lords.

Amendments at Second Reading

Three or Six Month Amendments

These seek to amend the motion that the bill 'be now read a second time' to read, 'upon this day 3 or 6 months'. This basically constitutes rejection of the bill because, if the Session lasted for longer than three or six months, the order for Second Reading would not be renewed on the Order Paper. The question actually put by the Speaker in the case of such amendments, is 'that the word now stand part of the question' (SO 31(1). If this is carried the question on Second Reading is taken forthwith.

Reasoned Amendments

These are quite common and are used to declare opposition to the bill in question. When a Reasoned Amendment has been tabled and selected by the Speaker, the two questions put by the Speaker at the end of the debate are firstly, 'that the amendment be made' and secondly (if, as usually happens, the Reasoned Amendment is defeated) 'that the bill be now read a Second time'. An example from the House of Commons Hansard of 11 June 1997, is set out below:

Firearms (Amendment) Bill

Order for Second Reading read.

Madam Speaker: I have selected the amendment in the name of the Leader of the Opposition.............

The Secretary of State for the Home Department (Mr. Jack Straw): I beg to move, That the Bill be now read a Second time.

(the Home Secretary then made his opening speech) ....

Mr. Michael Howard (Folkestone and Hythe): I beg to move, To leave out from 'That' to the end of the Question, and to add instead thereof:

'this House declines to give a Second Reading to the Firearms (Amendment) Bill since the Firearms (Amendment) Act 1997 has dealt comprehensively with the problems identified by Lord Cullen; believes that there is no justification for a total ban on all handguns including those of .22 calibre which would eliminate all legitimate target shooting; and calls on the Government to delay this intemperate Bill until the Firearms (Amendment) Act has been fully implemented and a proper assessment made of its impact'.

(the debate then continued until 10.00pm) .....

Question put, That the amendment be made: -

The House divided: Ayes 173, Noes 384

(this was then followed by) ....

Question put, That the bill be now read a Second time: -

The House divided: Ayes 384, Noes 181.

If a reasoned amendment is carried a bill proceeds no further, although the Second Reading could be moved on another occasion. The Speaker selects the amendments to be debated and usually selects the amendment tabled in the name of the Leader of the Official Opposition. Only one amendment can be selected for obvious reasons. If two were selected and one was carried, the other would fall by default.

Amendments under SO 63(2)

A reasoned amendment could commit a bill to a Select Committee although this is more usually done under SO 63(2). Motions under this Standing Order can commit a bill to a Committee of the Whole House (as in the case of the European Parliamentary Elections Bill), to a Select Committee, a Joint Committee or a Special Standing Committee. These motions are taken forthwith after Second Reading. SO 63 does not apply to Consolidated Fund bills, Appropriation bills or Provisional Order (Confirmation) bills. An example of the motion made after the Second Reading of the European Parliamentary Elections Bill on 25 November 1997 is set out below:

Bill accordingly read a Second time.

Motion made, and Question put forthwith, pursuant to Standing Order No. 63 (Committal of Bills)

That the Bill be committed to a Committee of the whole House. – [*Mr. George Howarth.*]

Question agreed to.

Committee tomorrow.

This does not mean that the Committee Stage of the bill actually took place on the following day, just that it was added to the 'remaining orders of the day'; i.e., the list of those Government measures waiting to be scheduled for debate at some point in the future.

Second Reading Committees

Bills are automatically committed to a Standing Committee after Second Reading but under SO 90 a Minister can propose that a bill be referred to a Second Reading Committee. 10 days' notice must be given and if 20 Members object the motion is defeated. Private Members' bills can be dealt with in this way under SO 90, but only if 10 days' notice has been given and only on a day on, or after, the 8th Friday on which Private Members' Bills have precedence. If a single MP objects, the motion falls. Only one Private Member's Bill has been proceeded with in this way – David Amess MP's Raoul Wallenberg Memorial Bill (1989/90), which proceeded no further than a Second Reading Committee.

A Second Reading Committee is basically a Standing Committee which considers whether or not the bill should have a Second Reading. When it reports to the House, the motion is put forthwith. If the motion is that the bill should receive a Second Reading, the Second Reading is set down for a future day, but on the appointed day there is no debate on the motion for Second Reading and it is taken forthwith. A bill which has been considered by a Second Reading Committee may be considered on Report by a Committee (have its Report Stage in a Standing Committee), in which case it will have been debated entirely off the floor of the House (SO 92). In its First Report of the 1997/98 Session (HC 190), the Select Committee on Modernisation of the House of

Commons recommended greater use of Second Reading Committees for non-controversial bills.

Jellicoe Procedure

Under the so-called 'Jellicoe Procedure', bills which give effect to Law Commission proposals are automatically sent to Second Reading Committees. The name derives from the fact that Earl Jellicoe chaired the Committee which first recommended the procedure (HL Paper 35 – I, 10 February 1992). Bills are automatically referred to a Second Reading Committee unless a Minister puts down a motion not to refer the bill in this way. There is no debate and the motion is taken forthwith. The same procedure is used in the House of Lords, the only difference being that the bill is sent to a Special Public Bill Committee. The procedure was first used with the Law of Property (Miscellaneous Provisions) Bill in the 1993/94 Session.

Tax Simplification Bills

A new Standing Order – SO 60, was agreed by the House in March 1997 on the recommendation of the Procedure Committee. Under this Order, 'Tax Simplification bills' – bills which result from the deliberations of the Tax Law Review Committee follow a different procedure from most bills. The Committee was set up by the Institute for Fiscal Studies in 1994. Lord Howe of Aberavon was the Committee's President, and its Chair, Graham Aaronson QC. Other members included Rt Hon Francis Maude MP and Quentin Davies MP. The new procedure was recommended by the Procedure Committee after reading the special report of the Tax Law Review Committee (Parliamentary Procedures of the Enactment of Tax Law) which was published in November 1996. This recommended that tax law should be simplified and rewritten in plain English. Under SO 60, a Minister certifies that a bill is a Tax Simplification bill and tables a motion that it should be proceeded with as such. This is taken forthwith and the bill is automatically referred to a Second Reading Committee unless a Minister specifically tables a motion not to refer it to such a Committee. If the Committee decides that the bill should receive a Second Reading, the Second Reading is set down for a future day, but on the appointed day there is no debate on the motion for Second Reading and it is taken forthwith. The bill is then re-committed to a Committee of the Whole House unless a Minister moves a motion 'that the House be discharged from considering the Bill', immediately after the Order of the day has been read for the House to resolve itself into a Committee of the Whole House. The motion does not require notice and is decided upon forthwith. If the motion is passed the bill immediately has its Third Reading. The motion can be moved at any hour and is exempt from the Moment of Interruption.

Scottish Grand Committee

Under SO 97 if the Speaker certifies that a bill relates exclusively to Scotland, the Minister in charge of the bill may put down a motion at Second Reading, which is taken forthwith, that the bill be referred to a Scottish Grand Committee.

The Scottish Grand Committee then debates the motion for two hours and reports to the House that the bill 'be read' (or 'not read') a second time. This is a way of taking the debate off the floor of the House whilst still retaining a formal vote on the Second

Reading of the bill in the Chamber. When the formal 'order for Second Reading' is taken, the Minister in charge of the bill can move that the bill 'be committed to a Scottish Standing Committee' or a 'Special Standing Committee' and this motion is taken forthwith (without debate). A Scottish Standing Committee must include at least 16 MPs representing Scottish constituencies. The First Scottish Standing Committee considers Government bills and the Second, Private Members' Bills. For example, the Licensing (Amendment) (Scotland) Bill (1995/96 Session) was debated at Second Reading in the Scottish Grand Committee on 18 December 1995, and was returned to the House for a formal Second Reading on 9 January 1996 before being sent to a Special Scottish Standing Committee for its Committee Stage. Bills which have been considered by a Second Reading Committee or a Scottish Grand Committee may, after their Committee Stage, be referred for consideration on report (SO 92) to a Standing Committee of no fewer than 20 and no more than 80 members or to the Scottish Grand Committee. The motion to do this is moved by a Minister forthwith and if 20 MPs object the motion is negatived. The last time this procedure was used was during the 1967/68 Session with the Water Resources Bill. After Report Stage, a bill which has been considered in a Scottish Grand Committee may be sent back to the Grand Committee for Third Reading. After a one and a half hour debate it is then returned to the House for a formal vote on Third Reading.

Welsh Grand Committee

Under SO 106 a bill which relates exclusively to Wales can be referred to the Welsh Grand Committee for its Second Reading. 10 days' notice of such a motion must be given but if 20 Members object, the bill proceeds in the normal way. Under SO 92 a bill relating exclusively to Wales which has been considered at Second Reading by a Second Reading Committee may be sent to a Standing Committee for its Report Stage. The Committee would consist of all MPs representing Welsh Constituencies.

Northern Ireland Grand Committee

Under SO 113, a bill which relates exclusively to Northern Ireland can be referred to the Northern Ireland Grand Committee for its Second Reading. Debate is limited to two and a half hours. When the bill returns to the House, Second Reading is taken forthwith. Such bills can also be sent to the Northern Ireland Grand Committee for a one and a half hour Third Reading debate. Third Reading in the House would then be taken forthwith.

Special Standing Committees

Under SO 91 bills can be referred to Special Standing Committees which sit initially for a month, taking evidence in a similar way to Select Committees. They can hold three, three-hour public evidence-taking sessions, and one, three-hour private session where possible amendments are discussed. The rest of the sittings then proceed in the same way as other Standing Committees.

Select and Joint Committees

Bills can also be referred to Joint Committees with equal numbers of members from both Houses. These are usually only used for Private and Hybrid Bills .

COMMITTEE STAGE

Bills are automatically referred to a Standing Committee under SO 63(1) except in the case of Consolidation bills, Provisional Order Confirmation bills, Tax Simplification bills and Law Commission bills or if the House otherwise orders. Bills relating to constitutional measures are committed to a Committee of the Whole House. Consolidated Fund bills and Appropriation bills do not usually have a Committee Stage.

Any Member can put down a motion to be taken immediately after Second Reading to commit a bill to a Committee of the Whole House, a Special Standing Committee or a Select or Joint Committee, but under SO 32(4) the Speaker selects such motions and she would be most unlikely to select anything other than a motion tabled by a member of the Government. Such a motion, if made immediately after the bill has been read a second time, does not require notice and must be decided forthwith. If passed, the Member in charge of the bill may move that the Committee Stage should be taken there and then; however, if there is any objection, the MP concerned must move that, 'This House will immediately resolve itself into the said Committee' – this is opposed business and therefore cannot be decided after the Moment of Interruption. If any Member objects the Committee Stage has to be taken on a future day.

A Backbench MP could put down a similar motion at a later date, but such a motion could only be taken during the time when Private Members' business takes precedence – i.e., a Friday. It would then run the risk of being talked out.

In the case of the Finance Bill, some Clauses are debated in a Standing Committee and some in a Committee of the Whole House. Under SO 63(3) a motion to consider a bill in this way can only be moved by the Member in charge of the bill – usually a Government Minister. The motion is moved after Second Reading without notice and can be debated after 10.00pm (7.00pm on a Thursday and 2.30pm on a Friday). If such a motion is opposed, the Member in charge of the bill may make a brief statement explaining why he or she proposes to split the bill in this way, followed by a speech from a Member opposing such a move.

Instructions to Committees

Before a Standing Committee begins its consideration of a Bill, an 'instruction' may be given to it, either to allow it to do something which it could not otherwise do, or to set out a particular course of action for it to follow. The first type is 'permissive' and the second 'mandatory'. Mandatory instructions may only be given to Select Committees or Private bill Committees. Some instructions may be considered 'inadmissible'. Instructions can be taken at any time during a bill's progress after Second Reading.

An instruction to a Committee of the Whole House is usually moved when the Order of the Day for the first sitting of the Committee has been read and before the Speaker has left the Chair, or in the case of a Standing Committee as soon as the bill has been committed. Instructions can be debated at Second Reading. Under SO 65, Committees of the Whole House or Standing Committees have the freedom to make more or less any type of amendment to a bill under consideration provided 'they be relevant to the subject matter of the Bill'. The Standing Order goes on to add that if any amendment is not within the Long Title of the Bill, it should be 'amended accordingly'. Given the wide scope for amendments, you might think the scope for instructions to Committees, dictating how a bill should be considered would be rather limited and indeed this is the case. They are best known for the infrequency with which they are tabled.

For aficionados of instructions, examples of 'admissible instructions' are given in Erskine May's 'Parliamentary Practice' (22nd edition) 1997 on pages 515 to 517. They include the following:

Admissible Instructions

❖ ***Extending the provisions of a Bill***

An instruction is necessary to authorise the introduction of amendments which extend the provisions of the bill beyond its original scope.

❖ ***Extending the Bill's geographical scope***

An instruction would be needed to extend the scope of a bill in terms of its geographical area; e.g., from being applicable to London to being applicable to the UK (this only applies if a bill is deliberately restricted to a particular geographical area by its Long Title).

❖ ***Dividing a Bill***

An instruction would be necessary to enable a Committee to divide a bill into two or more bills (this would only be permitted if a bill obviously fell into two distinct halves).

❖ ***Consolidating a Bill***

An instruction is required to consolidate two bills into one.

❖ ***Prioritising a Bill***

An instruction is required in order to give priority to consideration of one portion of a bill rather than another.

❖ ***Calling witnesses***

Instructions can be given, via a petition, to a Committee of the Whole House to empower it to hear Counsel and examine witnesses.

❖ ***Considering amendments***

A Mandatory Instruction can be given to a Select Committee to consider certain amendments.

❖ ***Inserting a Clause Similar to one previously rejected by the Committee***

If a bill is recommitted to a former Standing Committee, a Permissive Instruction can be given to the Committee allowing it to insert in the Bill, a Clause similar to one which it has previously rejected.

Inadmissible Instructions

There are certain instructions which are not allowed; for example, any which are inconsistent with the decision of the House at Second Reading, or which attempt to introduce matters which should really form a distinct bill or measure in their own right; or, those which would involve imposing a 'charge' (i.e., a tax or levy of some sort). An instruction is regarded as 'superfluous' if it seeks to give a Committee the power to do something, which it already has. Instructions which attempt to divide a bill in an impractical way, to delete part of a bill or which are generally 'incoherent', are not permitted.

The Speaker has the power to select instructions to Committees in the same way as she does amendments. Members may also table amendments to instructions. MPs are limited to tabling one instruction per bill (although this is based on precedent and is not set out in Standing Orders).

Membership of Standing Committees

Several Standing Committees are set up each Session – A, B, C, etc. C is always set aside for Private Members' Bills. Membership of Standing Committees is decided by the Committee of Selection (comprising Party Whips) and is based on Party proportions in the House itself and the 'qualifications' of Members; for example, whether they contributed to the Second Reading debate, their general interest or expertise in a particular subject, their seniority in the House, etc. The size of Standing Committees varies, depending on the bill in question, but must be between 15 and 60 MPs (SO 86). The Committee of Selection is itself a Select Committee and meets every Wednesday. If, for example, you were interested in discovering who had been selected to serve on the Standing Committee on a particular bill, which had received its Second Reading on Monday, you would look in the Votes and Proceedings on Thursday (the day after the Committee's meeting) to see who had been appointed.

The Chairmen of Standing Committees are appointed from a panel of not less than 10 Members nominated by the Speaker at the beginning of every Session to act as temporary chairmen of Committees of the Whole House when so requested by the Chairman of Ways and Means. The Chairman's Panel may also consider certain procedural matters and occasionally produce reports, such as their response to the first report of the Select Committee on Modernisation of the House of Commons of the 1997/98 Session (HC 190) on reforming the legislative process.

Only those MPs nominated to a Standing Committee may participate in its proceedings or sit on the Committee, although non-members may table amendments. The exceptions to this rule are the law officers (the Attorney General, the Solicitor General, the Lord Advocate and the Solicitor General for Scotland[2]) who may participate in any Standing Committee but may not move amendments or vote.

Times of Standing Committee Sittings

A Standing Committee meets in one of the many rooms off the Committee Corridor. The room is set out rather differently from a Select Committee with Government and Opposition facing each other as they would do in the Chamber. Traditionally, Standing Committees begin their proceedings on Tuesdays and Thursdays at 10.30am and, under Standing Order 88, may continue until 1.00pm the following day, except that they may not sit between 1.00pm and 3.30pm (this ensures that Members can be present for oral questions in the House). In fact afternoon sittings usually begin at 4.30pm. The Chairman may prolong a morning sitting until 1.15pm in order to complete any urgent matters. SO 88 has recently been amended after the First Report from the Select Committee on Modernisation of the House of Commons (HC 60, 1998/99) was accepted by the House on 16 December 1998. For the remainder of the 1998/99 Session, the House of Commons will meet at 11.30am on a Thursday. This means that Standing Committees will not be permitted to sit between 11.30am and 12.30pm on Thursdays, although a sitting may be extended to 11.45am if necessary. Most Standing Committees now begin their deliberations at 2.30pm on Thursdays, although they may sit at 9.00am and 2.00pm; for example in the 1998/99 Session, the Greater London Authority Bill Standing Committee met at 2.30pm on Thursdays, but the Health Bill met at 9.00am and 2.00pm. Standing Committee C, which considers Private Members' Bills is not affected, as it meets on a Wednesday.

The number of times a Standing Committee meets depends on the bill in question. Sometimes, if a bill is fairly uncontroversial, a Committee need only meet two or three times in order to complete its consideration; on other occasions, a Committee may meet twice a week, morning and evening for several weeks. For example, in the 1997/98 Session, Standing Committee D sat between 13 January and 17 Februrary 1998 to discuss the National Minimum Wage Bill, whereas the same Standing Committee (with different Members) met only between 24 and 26 February 1998 to discuss the Fossil Fuel Levy Bill.

Suspension and Adjournment of Proceedings

The quorum of a Standing Committee is 17 or one third of its membership, whichever is less (excluding the chair). The chair must suspend the sitting if it becomes inquorate. If no quorum is reached within 20 minutes the Committee is adjourned until its next scheduled meeting. For a closure motion to be agreed by the committee, the number of those supporting the closure must be at least equal to the quorum of the committee and

[2] The current Solicitor General for Scotland is not a Member of either House. Now that the Scottish Parliament is up and running, the Lord Advocate and the Solicitor General for Scotland (they need not be MSPs) have ceased to be members of the UK Government and a new law officer, the Advocate General for Scotland has been appointed to advise the UK Government on Scottish Law.

constitute a majority. Standing Committee proceedings must also be suspended if there is a Division in the House; for example, Committees are often interrupted to allow Members to vote in the afternoon and evenings during the Report Stage of a Bill. The Chairman of a Committee has no power to adjourn a Committee except at the end of a sitting or if the meeting becomes inquorate. Only the MP in charge of the bill or a Government Whip can propose a motion to adjourn the committee. He or she would move that 'further consideration of the bill be now adjourned', or, during a debate on a particular question, 'that the debate be now adjourned'. A sitting can be suspended informally and this usually happens in the evenings to enable Members to partake of the mouth-watering delicacies on offer in the Members' Dining Room. Morning and afternoon sittings are treated as separate sittings.

Guillotining Standing Committees

A Standing Committee's proceedings can be guillotined. If a bill is before a Standing Committee when an Allocation of Time Motion is made, Standing Order 120 applies and a detailed timetable is recommended to the Standing Committee by a Sub-Committee known as the Business Sub-Committee, consisting of the Chairman (or one of the two Chairmen) of the Standing Committee in question and seven other Members nominated by the Speaker. It has a quorum of four.

The Allocation of Time Order gives general instructions to the Standing Committee and fixes a date on or before which the bill must be reported to the House. A draft recommendation is submitted to the Sub-Committee by the Member in charge of the Bill. This recommendation consists of a detailed timetable showing the number of sittings to be allotted to the consideration of the Bill, the business to be taken at each sitting and the hour at which proceedings must be concluded. This is considered by the Sub-Committee and can be amended. No minutes of the meeting are available. The recommendation is then printed and the Standing Committee itself makes a decision on the resolution, without any amendment or debate.

If the resolution is agreed to by the Standing Committee it operates as if it had formed part of the Allocation of Time Order made by the House. If it is disagreed to, it has to be recommitted to the Business Sub-Committee. Further meetings of the Business Sub-Committee may be called at the discretion of the Chairman where necessary; for example, to amend the original timetable.

Divisions in Standing Committees

Standing Committees divide on amendments just as a Committee of the Whole House might do. When a Division is called in a Standing Committee, Members usually have two minutes within which to reach the Committee Room. The Chair has the casting vote. If a Division is called when the Committee is inquorate, the Chairman must suspend the proceedings until a quorum is present, or, if this is not possible, proceedings are adjourned until the afternoon sitting or to a further day. In a Standing Committee an MP's 'vote must agree with his voice'. When the Chairman puts the question on a particular Clause or amendment, a Member cannot shout 'Aye' and then proceed to vote the opposite way in an ensuing Division.

Standing Committees and Money Resolutions

Standing Committees cannot consider a Clause in a bill which imposes a charge (for example, some form of tax or levy on the public) unless the House has agreed to a resolution authorising such a charge. The Committee usually proceeds to consider the bill in the hope that the House will pass such a motion in the near future.

Printing Standing Committee Proceedings

Standing Committee proceedings are printed the following day in a supplement to the Votes and Proceedings. These proceedings simply list the decisions taken by the Committee, they are not verbatim reports of who said what and when. Standing Committee Hansards are produced and are usually available the day after the sitting in question.

How a Bill is considered in Committee

Procedure in Standing Committees is governed by Standing Orders and is similar to proceedings in a Committee of the Whole House. The rules which govern the admissibility of amendments in a Committee of the Whole House apply to proceedings in Standing Committees.

When the House becomes a Committee of the Whole House, the Speaker leaves the Chair and the mace is then placed under the Table and the Chairman of Ways and Means, or one of his deputies, takes his seat at the Table (not in the Speaker's Chair). The Speaker has three deputies, the Chairman of Ways and Means and two Deputy Chairmen of Ways and Means. At present they are:

The Speaker	*- Rt Hon Betty Boothroyd MP (Lab)*
The Chairman of Ways and Means	*- Sir Alan Haselhurst MP (Con)*
First Deputy Chairman of Ways and Means	*- Michael J Martin MP (Lab)*
Second Deputy Chairman of Ways and Means	*- Michael Lord MP (Con)*

The tradition of the Chairman of Ways and Means taking the Chair in a Committee of the Whole House derives from the practice of the House excluding the Speaker whenever it wanted to meet in private. In both a Standing Committee and a Committee of the Whole House, a bill is considered in the following order:

1.) Clauses
2.) New Clauses
3.) Schedules
4.) New Schedules
5.) Preamble (if any)
6.) Title (if an amendment is proposed)

A motion known as an 'Order of Consideration' is often moved to consider the bill in a different order. This enables the schedules to be considered after the clauses to which they relate. The Chairman will usually only select such a motion if tabled by the Member in charge of the bill. Such motions can be moved at any time in the bill's proceedings, but are usually the first item on the agenda at a Committee's first sitting, particularly when a bill is considered in Standing Committee. At its first meeting, the Standing Committee will usually consider a sittings motion, setting out when the Committee will meet, followed by an Order of Consideration motion setting out the order in which clauses and schedules are to be debated.

How Clauses, Schedules and Amendments are Considered in Committee

Manuscript and Starred Amendments

It is usual, though not obligatory, to give notice of an amendment to a bill in Committee. The Chairman of a Committee will usually be unwilling to take 'manuscript' amendments (amendments of which there has been no advance warning) or those tabled on the day before the Committee is due to meet (these are known as 'starred amendments' because they are marked with a star on the notice paper) – so in practice, two sitting days' notice needs to be given of any amendment.

Amendments Printed in 'The Blues'

Amendments appear on the Order Paper the day after they have been tabled in what are colloquially known as 'the blues' (the section of the Order Paper devoted to forthcoming business, which is printed on blue paper – white paper denotes that particular day's business) in the order in which they were tabled.

Marshalled Lists

On the day before amendments are to be considered in Committee, they are 'marshalled' on the Order Paper in the order in which the bill is to be considered, or if they relate to the same point in the bill, the order in which they were handed in. This is known as the 'marshalled blue list'. A marshalled list is produced in the 'whites' on the day the Committee sits. Amendments retain the number given them when first tabled so the numbering can often appear quite arbitrary. After the first appearance of an amendment on the Notice Paper, the names of Members attached to it are limited to six and the names of Members who subsequently support it are printed to the bottom right hand side on one occasion only.

Amendments by the Member in charge of the bill take precedence over all others relating to the same place in a clause. Where several amendments are offered at the same place in a clause, an amendment to leave out certain words in order and insert others takes precedence over an amendment which simply omits certain words. An example of Notices of Amendments is set out below:

NOTICES OF AMENDMENTS

given up to and including

Thursday 10th December 1998

New Amendments handed in are marked thus*

STANDING COMMITTEE B

ROAD TRAFFIC (NHS CHARGES) BILL

1 Mr Simon Hughes
Dr Evan Harris
Sir Robert Smith

Clause 1, page 1, line 8, after first 'a', insert 'direct'.

Tabling Amendments

Amendments cannot usually be tabled until after Second Reading; however, exceptions are made when a bill is due to go through all its stages in a day, in which case a motion allowing amendments to be tabled before Second Reading has to be passed by the House.

When the House is sitting, amendments may be tabled at any time before the rising of the House. On non-sitting Fridays, they may be tabled between 11.00am and 3.00pm and on other non-sitting days, before 4.30pm. Amendments may not be tabled at weekends, or on bank holidays or public holidays.

The Chairman of the Committee selects the amendments and produces a grouping of amendments in advance of the sitting. 'Groups' of amendments are listed with the first to occur in the bill appearing first. These groupings of amendments are available at the Committee.

Procedure for Debating Clauses and Amendments

The Chairman calls the first Clause. This means that the Clause can be considered by the Committee; however, it does not mean that a Member of the Committee can talk generally about the Clause, as there is nothing for the Committee to debate until an amendment to the Clause is moved or until the question, 'That the clause stand part of the Bill' is actually proposed. If no one has tabled an amendment to that particular Clause, or if the Chairman has decided not to select an amendment, the question that the Clause stand part of the bill is proposed. If, however, an amendment has been selected, the Chairman calls the Member who has tabled the amendment to move it. After there has been a debate on the amendment, the Chairman reads it, stating the page and line in the bill which it seeks to alter and then puts the question that the amendment be made. An amendment can only be withdrawn at the request of the member moving it provided the Committee Members agree unanimously. The Chairman may also decide that an amendment is being offered at the wrong place in the Bill.

For the sake of convenience, the Chairman can permit debate to range over several amendments at once, provided they relate in some way, to different aspects of the proposals in the actual amendment under consideration. The lead amendment is either withdrawn, negatived or voted upon. At the Chairman's discretion one or more of the amendments grouped for discussion with the selected amendment may be voted on as well as the 'lead' amendment. There can be no further discussion on other amendments in the group once a decision has been taken on the first amendment. If the lead amendment is passed then some of the others in the group will have to be agreed to formally.

An example of the above, taken from a sitting of Standing Committee B on the Road Traffic (NHS Charges) Bill on Tuesday 15 December 1998 (morning sitting) is set out below:

Dr. Harris: I beg to move amendment No. 2, in page 1, line 14, leave out, 'the appropriate' and insert 'a fixed proportion of the'

The Chairman: With this, it will be convenient to discuss the following amendments: No. 3, in page 1, line 14, after 'charges' insert

'specified in regulations under this section'.

No. 4, in page 2, leave out lines 19 to 23.

No. 5, in page 2, lines 19, leave out 'appropriate'.

(a discussion on the amendments followed)

Question put, 'That the amendment be made: -

The Committee divided: Ayes 2, Noes 13.

The Chairman of the Committee then invoked SO 68, which allows the question, 'That the Clause Stand Part of the Bill' to be put by the Chair, if there has been adequate discussion. Alan Duncan MP argued that a particular aspect of Clause 1 had not been fully debated; however, the Chairman felt there had been sufficient debate and proceeded to invoke the above Standing Order as follows:

Question proposed, that the clause stand part of the Bill.

The Committee divided: Ayes 9, Noes 6.

......

Question accordingly agreed to.
Clause 2 ordered to stand part of the Bill.

Inadmissible Amendments

There are certain amendments which are likely to be ruled out of order by the Chairman. These are set out more fully on pages 525-527 of Erskine May.

- Those which are not relevant to the subject matter.
- Those which are beyond the scope of the Bill.
- Those beyond the scope of the Clause in question.
- Amendments dependent upon those which have already been voted against.
- Amendments inconsistent with the bill as so far agreed to by the Committee.
- Amendments which are unintelligible without reference to subsequent amendments of which no notice has been given.
- Amendments which are incomplete.
- Amendments which would reverse the principle of the bill as agreed to at Second Reading.
- Amendments to leave out clauses (the correct procedure is to vote against 'Clause Stand Part', although such amendments appear on the notice paper just to give an indication that an MP wishes to oppose the Clause)
- Amendments which remove the only effective words in a Clause.
- Amendments which should really be New Clauses.
- Amendments which make a Clause unintelligible or ungrammatical, incoherent or inconsistent with the rest of the Bill.
- Amendments which are too 'vague'.
- Amendments which are offered at the wrong place in the Bill.
- Amendments seeking to delay the coming into effect of a bill in England until a similar measure has been passed in Scotland.
- Amendments or new clauses creating public charges if no money resolution has been passed or if the amendment is not covered by the terms of the resolution.
- When a clause contains two or more subsections which are not mutually dependent, an amendment to leave out a subsection is in order. It is not in order when the two subsections are mutually dependent, as the amendment would wreck the clause.
- A clause imposing a charge is either printed in italics or authorised by an expenses clause. Neither can be considered by a Committee unless the House has agreed to a money resolution authorising them.

Postponing and Dividing Clauses

The Committee has power to divide one clause into two. It may also transfer one clause from one part of the bill to another. A debate on a clause may be postponed provided that no amendment has been made to it, or has been proposed and defeated and provided that the question on 'clause stand part' has not been proposed. If an amendment has been proposed and withdrawn the clause may be postponed. A clause cannot be postponed until after debate on some of its sub-clauses. Part of a clause cannot be postponed. Postponed clauses are usually considered after all other clauses have been debated and considered and before any New Clauses.

New Clauses

New Clauses are usually considered after the bill's existing clauses have been debated. They are considered in the order in which they are handed in but New Clauses tabled by the Member in charge of the bill are considered first and may be taken in the order he or she wishes. The principle of a New Clause is debated followed by any amendments which have been tabled to it. After the New Clause is called (this is technically its First Reading) the Member proposing the New Clause says at the beginning of his or her speech, 'I beg to move, That the clause be read a Second time'. The Chairman may then ask that certain other New Clauses or amendments be considered at the same time. If pushed to a vote, the Second Reading of the New Clause would be voted on and would be immediately followed by a vote to add the New Clause to the Bill. It is not unknown for Members to vote on the question that the New Clause be read a Second time, only to forget that they need to vote again, to add the clause to the Bill. Vital amendments have been lost in this way. If any amendments have been tabled to a New Clause, the New Clause would be read a Second time, voted upon and if passed, votes on amendments would follow. If any were agreed to by the House, the last vote would be that the New Clause, as amended be added to the bill.

The rules which apply to the inadmissability of amendments also applies to New Clauses and therefore the following are deemed to be out of order:

- New Clauses which are beyond the scope of the bill.
- New Clauses which are inconsistent with clauses already agreed to by the Committee.
- New Clauses which are substantially the same as a clause previously voted against by the Committee.
- New Clauses which are really just a redrafting of clauses already in the bill.
- New Clauses which should really be moved as an amendment to an existing clause.
- New Clauses which really require an instruction to the Committee to be tabled before they can be considered.

A New Clause may be withdrawn even after its Second Reading if it has not been voted on or agreed to at that stage. It can be postponed if it has not had a Second Reading, but if its Second Reading has been agreed to, it cannot be postponed. It is not up to the Committee to decide where a New Clause, if passed, should be inserted into the bill – it is a matter for the Government, on the advice of the Public Bill Office.

REPORT STAGE

If a bill has been 'reported' from a Committee of the Whole House without amendment, it is ordered either to be read the third time forthwith (immediately without debate) or on a future day as appointed. If amendments have been made to the bill the Member in charge names a day on which the bill is to be considered; i.e., to have its Report Stage.

If there is some degree of urgency, Report Stage can be taken on the same day. A House of Commons' bill reported from a Select or Joint Committee is normally recommitted to a Committee of the Whole House. If a bill is amended in Committee it is reprinted.

If a bill is reported from a Standing Committee, whether amended or not, it must be 'considered on Report' by the House.

Report stage is taken on the floor of the House and provides another opportunity to table amendments. Any Member may table amendments, which are selected by the Speaker. The Speaker's selection of amendments is made available at midday and is placed in the No Lobby. In response to a question from Ivor Caplin MP during the adjourned Report Stage of the Wild Mammals (Hunting With Dogs) Bill on 13 March 1998 (HC Col: 851), the Speaker defined her power to select amendments in the following way:

'The power of selection exists to prevent repetition and to secure reasonable opportunities for the expression of all varieties of opinion in an orderly manner. Exercising the power in this instance was something to which I have given much anxious thought over the past 24 hours. Many hon. Members would have been disappointed whatever decision I reached on the selection of new clause 35, but I have tried to act in the best interests of this debate, and, of course, in the very best interests of the House of Commons'.

Amendments withdrawn in Committee may be tabled again.

At Report Stage, a bill is considered in the following order:

1.) New Clauses
2.) Amendments to the Bill
3.) New Schedules
4.) Amendments to Schedules

There is no debate on 'Clause Stand Part', so amendments to leave out Clauses are in order.

New Clauses

No New Clause may be debated unless notice has been given. No Member may move a Clause unless he has put his name to it. New Clauses are considered in the order in which they 'stand upon the paper', that is, the order in which they have been handed in, except that priority is given to Clauses offered by the Member in charge of the Bill, who may arrange such Clauses in any order he wishes. When called by the Speaker, the Member in charge of the New Clause proposes it and speaks in its favour (this constitutes the first reading of the Clause). The Speaker then proposes that the 'Clause be read a second time'. The New Clause may then be opposed. When the New Clause has been read a second time, amendments can be made.

The Speaker finally proposes that the New Clause or New Clause as amended be added to the Bill. New Clauses can be withdrawn but they cannot be postponed.

When all the New Clauses have been taken, amendments are debated. New Schedules are considered after amendments to Clauses and may be proposed and amended in the same way as New Clauses. When all the New Clauses, amendments, new Schedules and Schedules have been disposed of, the title of the bill is amended, if required.

RECOMMITTAL

If any irregularities have occurred in Committee, the bill is usually recommitted. A bill may be recommitted to a Committee of the Whole House, a Standing Committee or a Select Committee The motion for recommittal may relate to the whole bill or only to specific Clauses. Any Member may move a recommittal motion but priority is given to the Member in charge of the Bill. Recommittal is usually made in order to enable a New Clause to be added or to enable the Committee to take advantage of an instruction from the House to make amendments which would otherwise be outside the scope of the bill or to enable the Committee to reconsider amendments.

Under SO 74, if a motion for recommittal of the bill as a whole is opposed, a brief statement of the reasons for and against are given by the Members moving and opposing the motion. The question is then put without further debate. If the motion is for partial recommittal there is no limit on speakers, but debate is restricted to those parts of the bill which are to be recommitted. Members can move amendments to the motion. If a bill is recommitted in respect of specified amendments to a Clause, only those amendments and amendments relevant to them may be moved. A bill may be recommitted as often as the House sees fit.

On Friday, 30 March 1990, a motion was moved for the recommittal of clause 12 of the Consumer Guarantees Bill, a Private Members' Bill, because of the failure of the House to pass a Money Resolution. The need for a money resolution was only realised after the bill had completed its Committee Stage. The bill was recommitted to a Committee of the Whole House in respect of Clause 12. If a bill has been partially recommitted, the only amendments which can be moved on Report are those relating to the Clauses which have been recommitted. If all the bill has been recommitted then Report follows the same format as any normal Report Stage.

THIRD READING

When a bill is reported from a Committee of the Whole House without amendment or when consideration of a bill, as amended, is concluded, the Member in charge may move the Third Reading of the bill forthwith or name a future day for that stage. Third Reading is usually a three-hour debate following Report Stage. No amendments can be tabled to a bill at Third Reading in the House of Commons; however, it is possible to move a Reasoned Amendment to the Order for Third Reading.

Once a bill has completed all its stages in the House of Commons, the Clerk of the House adds the words (in Norman French) 'Soit baillé aux Seigneurs' to the bill (if it is a bill which originated in the House of Commons). It is then sent to the House of Lords where it undergoes a similar process. If the House of Commons passes a bill which originated in the House of Lords without amendment, the words ' A ceste Bille les Communes sont assentus' are written on the Bill. If the bill has been amended, the words are, 'A ceste Bille avecque des Amendemens (or avecque une Amendement) les Communes sont assentus'.

LEGISLATIVE STAGES IN THE HOUSE OF LORDS

INTRODUCTION AND FIRST READING

As chapter six of the House of Lords Companion to the Standing Orders and Guide to the Proceedings of the House of Lords states, 'It is the privilege of any Lord to present a bill without notice and without moving for leave to bring it in'. However, the current practice is for any peer wishing to introduce a bill to inform the Public Bill Office at least a day before he or she intends to introduce it.

Any peer wishing to do so rises in his place at the beginning of Public Business, after Starred Questions and before Notices and Orders of the day are called on, or at the end of Public Business immediately before the adjournment of the House and reads the long title of the Bill. This is the Bill's formal First Reading. The Peer presenting the bill 'rises in his place' (this refers to the fact that he or she must be standing up and not to some bizarre form of parliamentary levitation) and says: 'My Lords, I beg to introduce a bill to (he then reads out the Long Title of the Bill) ... I beg to move that this bill be now read a first time'. As soon as the question, 'That this bill be now read a first time', has been put he or she hands a draft of the bill to one of the Clerks at the Table. Unlike the House of Commons, there is no distinction between Government time and Private Members' time, therefore, Government bills do not have precedence over Private Members' Bills.

A debate may then take place, not on the merits of the bill, as the bill is printed only after First Reading, but on the question of whether or not legislation in this area is desirable. Only on four occasions has a First Reading of a bill been opposed: The Local Government (England and Wales) Act 1988; the Parliament (Reform) Bill 1933; the Statute of Westminster Bill 1931 and the Parliament (No.6) Bill 1968/9. The last of these had a majority of 150 in the House of Commons on Second Reading and would have established a two-tier House of Lords, with voting and non-voting Peers.

After a bill has received its First Reading it is examined by the Public Bill Office to ascertain whether it might affect any private interests. If this is found to be the case the bill is then referred to the Examiners. The Second Reading cannot proceed until they have reported. If they find that the bill does affect private interests then the bill is treated as a Hybrid Bill.

When a bill has completed its stages in the House of Commons it is brought to the House of Lords by the Clerk of the House of Commons with a message that the Commons has passed the bill. The message is read at the Table and the First Reading of the bill is moved forthwith, usually by the Chief Whip. An Order is made for the bill to be printed and the peer who is to take charge of the bill in the House of Lords may give notice of a date for Second Reading. The bill may be printed before First Reading if there is to be an early Second Reading. If a bill reaches the House of Lords and has to wait 12 days for a peer to notify the House of a date for Second Reading, it can only be proceeded with after eight days.

A bill which has originated in the House of Lords may be withdrawn at any time after First Reading by the peer who presented the bill. This is done at the beginning or end of public business. All bills are now considered by the Delegated Powers and Deregulation Select Committee (this does not apply to Supply or Consolidation bills) which reports on any delegated powers contained in the bill.

SECOND READING

This is a debate on the general principles of a bill. A bill may be opposed at Second Reading in three ways:

Opposing the Second Reading

This is achieved by challenging a vote on the motion for the Second Reading. If the motion for Second Reading is defeated the bill is technically only negatived for that day but in practice is removed from the list of bills in progress.

Delaying Amendment

This attempts to delay the Second Reading until the end of the Session by moving to leave out the word 'now' in the question that the bill be now read a second time and inserting the words 'this day six months'. Notice is generally given in the Order Paper. The mover of such an amendment usually speaks after the peer moving the Second Reading has spoken. The Lord Chancellor or Chairman puts the question in the following way: 'The original motion was that this bill be now read a second time, since when an amendment has been moved to leave out ('now') and at end to insert ('this day six months'). The Question I now therefore have to put is: that this amendment be agreed to.' If the amendment is carried the bill is deemed to be rejected. A recent example is from the debate on the Second Reading of the Sexual Offences (Amendment) Bill, which aimed to reduce the age of consent for homosexuals to 16 (13 April 1999 HL: Col 758)

The Chairman of Committees (Lord Boston of Faversham): My Lords, the original Question was that this Bill be now read a second time, since when an amendment has been moved, to leave out "now" and at end to insert "this day six months". The Question is that the amendment be agreed to.

On Question, Whether the said amendment shall be agreed to?

Their Lordships divided: Contents, 222; Not-Contents, 146.

Baroness Young, who had moved the amendment then said (HL Col: 756):

"I accept what the Minister said: that the Government will invoke the Parliament Act. Of course, that is their right. In your Lordships' House we can do only what we are constitutionally allowed to do. Our powers are limited. I accept all that. But because they are limited, it does not mean that they should not be used. I think that noble Lords are perfectly entitled to say what they think on this important matter of social policy. That is the answer to that question".

Reasoned Amendment

Notice is always required for this type of amendment. The amendment sets out the reasons why the House declines to give a Second Reading to the bill and the question is put in the same way as for a delaying amendment.

When several amendments are moved to the Second Reading of a bill, they are dealt with in the order in which they relate to the motion, or if they all relate to the same place in the motion, then the order in which they were tabled. In this case, it is usual for the whole debate to take place on the first amendment, but the peers who have tabled other amendments contribute to the debate. At the end of the debate, the question is put on each amendment or on as many as possible until one is carried. It is possible to move a motion for Rejection of a Bill, but this procedure is now virtually obsolete. On a motion for Second Reading, if there are equal numbers of Contents and Not Contents the motion is agreed to; however, on a vote on an amendment to such a motion, if the Contents and Not Contents are equal, the amendment is defeated.

There are other motions which can be moved to Second Reading; e.g., a 'friendly' amendment which does not seek rejection of a bill but which simply seeks to record a particular point of view. For example, such an amendment was divided on at Second Reading of the House of Lords Bill on 30 March 1999 (HL Col: 427)

The Chairman of Committees (Lord Boston of Faversham): My Lords, the original Question was that this Bill be now read a second time since when an amendment has been moved, at end to insert "but this House regrets that the Bill radically alters the historic composition of the House of Lords for party political advantage, without consultation or consensus on the successor House's role and composition and without making it more democratic". The Question is that the amendment be agreed to.

On Question, Whether the said amendment shall be agreed to?
Their Lordships divided: Contents, 192; Not-Contents, 126.

A motion can be tabled to adjourn Second Reading (this does not prevent Second Reading from being taken on another day). A resolution can be tabled opposing certain aspects of a bill on the day that Second Reading is taken but it should be sufficiently differently worded to avoid breaking the rule that a question which is more or less the same as one on which a decision has already been taken cannot be tabled again.

The Salisbury Convention

The Salisbury Convention, as it is known, is the convention by which the House of Lords does not reject a Commons' bill at Second Reading, particularly if it honours a manifesto commitment. However, the convention has been ignored in recent years; for example the last Conservative Government's defeat on the War Crimes Bill on 30 April 1991 (the second successive Session in which the bill was introduced) and the rejection of the present Government's European Parliamentary Elections Bill at Second Reading in the 1998/99 Session (the second time the bill was introduced). Both bills were enacted under the Parliament Acts. The title of the convention stems from the agreement reached between the Leader of the Conservative Opposition in the House of Lords, the Marquis of Salisbury and the Labour Prime Minister, Clement Attlee, MP, in the period of the 1945-51 Labour Government.

Instructions to Committee

There are two kinds of instructions: permissive and mandatory.

Permissive Instructions

The object of a permissive instruction is to confer authority on the Committee to carry out something, which, without the instruction they would be unable to do. Examples include: dividing a bill into two bills; consolidating two bills into one, or extending the scope of the bill. The Committee's use of the power conferred on them in this way is discretionary.

Mandatory Instructions

The object of these is to define the course which the Committee must follow. The most common instruction to the Committee is to consider the schedules to the bill immediately after the related clause, or in an order other than that in the bill.

COMMITTEE STAGE

Committee Stage in the House of Lords, usually takes place over three or four days, but may be more or less depending on the size of the bill in question. Any peer may table an amendment, which will be debated unless withdrawn by its mover. The motion, 'that the House do now resolve itself into a Committee upon the Bill' may be opposed by reasoned amendment or by an amendment to postpone the Committee Stage. In the House of Lords, the Committee Stage is usually taken on the floor of the House; however, there are alternatives.

Public Bill Committees

Some technical and non-controversial bills are sent to a Public Bill Committee for their Committee Stage in the House of Lords rather than having a Committee on the Floor of the Whole House. This procedure was introduced in 1968 for public bills of a technical and non-controversial nature. Although the Committee consists of, usually between 12 – 14 peers, all other peers are free to speak, if not to vote. After Committee Stage the bill has its Report Stage.

Special Public Bill Committees

Law Commission Bills are now sent to Special Public Bill Committees for their Committee Stages. These committees take evidence over a 28 day period. There are usually nine or ten members, chosen by the Committee of Selection (the House of Lords has its own Committee of Selection). Proceedings are in public except for a brief private meeting where possible amendments to the bill are decided on. The following proceedings are then the same as a Public Bill Committee. After Committee Stage the bill has its Report Stage.

Grand Committee (Committee of the Whole House Off the Floor)

When a bill is committed to a Grand Committee, debate takes place away from the main Chamber, but any peer can take part. A recent example is the Public Processions etc. (Northern Ireland) Bill (HL) (1997/98). All peers can attend such a Committee and amendments can be debated, but not voted on, so only those amendments passed without any dissent are permitted. Bills debated in this way then return to the House for Report Stage.

Select or Joint Committee

A bill may be committed to either a Select or Joint Committee at any stage between Second or Third Reading if a more detailed investigation of the bill is called for. This enables evidence to be heard. Rather than proceeding directly to Report Stage, the bill is then recommitted (returns to the House) to a Committee of the Whole House, unless the Committee has recommended that the bill should not proceed, in which case a note to this effect appears in the list of bills in progress until the end of the Session. However, a peer can move a motion that such a bill be recommitted to a Committee of the Whole House. Consolidation bills for example, are sent to the Joint Committee on Consolidation bills. After Committee Stage, they are then recommitted to a Committee of the Whole House. The 'Order for Commitment' is usually 'discharged', enabling the bill to proceed straight to Third Reading (this is denoted by the letters 'OCD' in the Weekly Information Bulletin) (see below).

Scottish Select Committee

Bills can also be sent to a Scottish Select Committee at Committee Stage. Such a Committee consists of between 9 and 11 peers and has 28 days in which to take evidence. It cannot amend bills. After Committee, the bill in question is then committed back to the house to Committee of the Whole house.

Recommittal

Particular clauses of a bill can be recommitted at any time to a Committee of the Whole House or a Grand Committee at any time before Third Reading; for example, if a bill had to be substantially redrafted for any reason. A motion to recommit a bill may be debated in the same way as a motion to commit a bill to a Committee.

Financial Bills

Bills of aids and supplies cannot be, and Money bills generally are not, amended by the House of Lords, so there is no Committee Stage at all in the Upper Chamber. The best known example is the Finance Bill, which simply has a Second Reading debate in the House of Lords. In this case the words 'That this bill be not committed' are put and if passed the Committee is said to be 'negatived'.

Committee of the Whole House

OCD

Under SO 45 (HL) if no one wishes to speak at Committee Stage, or where no amendments have been tabled, the peer' in charge of the bill' may move that 'the order of commitment be discharged'. You will often see the letters OCD after a bill in the Weekly Information Bulletin. Notice of such a motion must be given. If the motion is agreed to the bill will then be set down for Third Reading. It is possible to take the Third Reading on the same day if SO 44 (HL) has been suspended. This Standing Order stipulates that no two stages of a bill may be taken on the same day. It there has been no notice of a motion to discharge the Committee, but no amendments have been tabled and no one wishes to speak against the Bill, the Chairman of Committees will say:

"My Lords, I understand that no amendments have been set down to the bill. With the agreement of the Committee, I will now put the Question that I report the bill to the House without amendment".

Amendments

Amendments may be handed in at any time after Second Reading and are published the next working day. Amendments appear as they are published on separate papers, numbered a,b,c,d, etc. However, on the first Committee day, amendments will be numbered and printed in the order in which they relate to the bill, in what is known as the 'marshalled list'. If the Committee Stage takes more than one day, marshalled lists will appear on each day of Committee. As an experiment (at least until the summer Recess, 1999) marshalled lists are to appear the day before Committee Stage, to enable the Government to group amendments by 2.30pm on the day before Committee Stage rather than on the day itself. This means that peers must table amendments which they wish to appear on the marshalled list, before 5.00pm at least two days before the relevant day of the Committee Stage. Amendments handed in after this time will be published on a revised marshalled list or supplementary list. New or altered amendments are marked with an asterisk *. The experiment is being confined to Committee Stage.

Again, for an experimental period, amendments must be handed in by 5.00pm (5.30pm for a marshalled list) or 4.00pm on a Friday.[3]

When more than one amendment is handed in relating to the same place in the bill, precedence is given to the peer in charge of the bill - thereafter, amendments are debated in the order in which they were received. Amendments may appear in the names of up to four peers, or five, if the peer in charge of the bill wishes to add his name. An amendment may be withdrawn after it has been tabled and can be moved by any peer.

Amendments must not be inconsistent with a previous decision of the Committee. Only the House itself can rule an amendment out of order, the officers of the House may only draw the House's attention to amendments which they feel are inadmissible. For an experimental period, until the summer Recess 1999, the House has agreed that an amendment which is identical to one pushed to a vote by the mover and defeated in Committee should not be retabled at Report Stage. In addition, it will not be possible to reverse at Report Stage an amendment agreed to on division in Committee except with the unanimous agreement of the House.[4]

An amendment to leave out words takes precedence over an amendment to leave out the same words and insert others. Amendments to proposed New Clauses are considered before the Clause itself. An amendment to insert a new clause is considered at the place in the bill where the new clause is to be inserted. Once an amendment has been moved it can only be withdrawn by leave of the Committee, which must be unanimous.

Amendments to leave out clauses are not really amendments; they are intentions to oppose the question that the 'clause stand part' of the bill. Any peer wishing to oppose a particular clause, does not table an amendment to leave out that clause, but simply opposes the motion that the clause stand part of the bill. Notice is usually given and such notices are printed in italics in the marshalled list. Unlike the practice at Committee Stage in the House of Commons, New Clauses are taken as amendments rather than being debated after the bill's existing clauses. An amendment to take out a clause and substitute a New Clause or an amendment simply to insert a New Clause, is taken as amendment when the relevant part of the bill is reached. Amendments to New Clauses are taken after the New Clause has been moved for the first time, but would be voted upon before the New Clause itself.

Manuscript amendments are those of which no notice has been given. They may be moved in Committee but are not encouraged on the basis that their Lordships will not have had an opportunity to consider them in advance.

Frequently, peers table what are known as 'probing' amendments. These seek to elicit some form of commitment from the Government that it will return at a later stage in the bill's proceedings with their own amendment on this subject in question. If such a

[3] These alterations were brought in on an experimental basis as a result of a report from the House of Lords Procedure Committee (HL 33, 1999/2000) agreed to by the House on 22 March 1999.
[4] *ibid*

commitment is made, the peer who has tabled the amendment will usually withdraw it. A 'wrecking' amendment is one which really goes against the spirit of the bill in question and would if passed, wreck an essential part of it.

An example of the order in which amendments are marshalled and voted upon at Committee Stage is reproduced below:

Clause 2

Page 2, line 2, leave out subsection (2)

Page 2, line 2, leave out subsection (2) and insert "(2) the import of all foreign root vegetables shall be prohibited"

Page 2, line 3, leave out "turnip"

Page 2, line 3, leave out "turnip" and insert "parsnip"

Page2, line 3, after "turnip" insert "or parsnip"

Leave out Clause 2 and insert the following new Clause "2 The consumption of swedes may be curtailed under an order laid before both Houses by the Secretary of State"

Baroness Awford of Rochester Row gives notice of her intention to oppose the question that Clause 2 stand part of the Bill.

Transpose Clause 2 to after Clause 99

When amendments are tabled to the same place in a bill, any tabled by the Lord in charge of the bill take precedence. If, for example, the House were to vote on the following amendments:

1. page 2, line 2, leave out "turnip" and insert "parsnip"

2. page 2, line 2, leave out "turnip" and insert "swede"

3. page 2, line 2, leave out "turnip" and insert "beetroot"

they would be taken in the following way: if amendment 1 was carried the word parsnip would be inserted into the bill; as a result, amendment 2 would become, 'leave out "parsnip" and insert "swede" '– if amendment 2 was carried, amendment 3 would become, 'leave out "swede" and insert "beetroot".

Committee Proceedings

Immediately before the House 'resolves itself into a Committee', the peer in charge of the bill moves, 'That the House do now resolve itself into a Committee upon a Bill'. The Lord Chancellor actually puts the question and the motion may be opposed by a Reasoned Amendment or by a motion to postpone Committee Stage, or to send the bill to a Select Committee. If it is agreed to, the Lord Chancellor leaves the Woolsack and the Lord Chairman or Deputy Chairman takes his place at the Table.

The first question is that the title of the bill be postponed and then, where appropriate, that the preamble be postponed. They are therefore considered after all the bill's clauses and schedules have been debated. The clauses of the bill are then considered in order. In the House of Lords there is no selection of amendments and unless an amendment is withdrawn, with 'leave' (agreement) of the House, it must be moved. It does not have to be moved by the peer who tabled it – another peer can move it if necessary.

The Lord Chairman (who does not have a casting vote as the Speaker does in the House of Commons) first calls any amendments to a clause and then when these have been disposed of, he puts the question that the clause itself, or the clause as amended, 'stand part of the bill'.

Amendments are usually grouped together by the Government Whips' Office and the 'groupings' are made available to Party Whips' Offices on the morning of the relevant Committee day. Peers who have tabled amendments are advised in the Companion to Standing Orders to 'consult the Government Whips' Office between 11.00am and 1.30pm on the day on which the amendments are to be debated, in order to discuss possible groupings'. However, these groupings are informal and can be challenged. A peer may speak to a group of amendments when the first amendment in the group is called and debate will take place on the first amendment even if this is minor or technical.

However, the question must be put separately on each amendment in the group when the amendment is called according to its place in the marshalled list. Proceedings on later amendments in a group are often formal but further debate may take place. Amendments may also be moved en bloc provided that: they appear consecutively on the marshalled list; all relate to the same clause or schedule; are consequential on an amendment already agreed to and that no peer objects. If there is objection each amendment must be put separately. A Division can take place on amendments en bloc, but is described in the Companion to the Standing Orders as being 'undesirable'. If an amendment to which others are linked has been disagreed to, the other amendments are not usually voted on. Amendments cannot be withdrawn en bloc, this must be done separately.

Where there are several consecutive clauses to which no amendment has been set down, it is the practice to put the question on all, or groups of them, together 'en bloc'. Clauses or even parts of bills may be postponed if they have not been amended, on a motion of which notice has been given. A clause may be divided by an amendment - this is taken after the clause has become part of the bill. A clause may also be transposed to another part of the bill, again, after it has become part of the bill.

Schedules are considered in order after Clauses and may also be postponed, divided or transposed. A peer cannot table an amendment to leave out a schedule but can oppose a motion that, 'this be Schedule ... to the Bill'. The questions on the preamble and title of the bill are put after all clauses and schedules have been disposed of and amendments may be tabled.

An example of how amendments are taken is set out below:

"Amendment No. 1 – Baroness Francis of Vauxhall"

Baroness Francis would then speak to her amendment, which is to Clause 2 of the bill and which aims to encourage greater use of turnips in the House of Lords Dining Room. When she has finished speaking, the Chairman of Committees says:

"Amendment proposed, page 2, line 5, leave out "parsnips" and insert "turnips of the highest quality"

There then follows a heated debate on the subject, to which several peers contribute. At the end of the debate, Baroness Francis may withdraw the amendment – she would 'beg leave to withdraw the amendment', in which case the Chairman of Committees would say:

"Is it your Lordships' pleasure that this amendment be withdrawn? Amendment, by leave, withdrawn."

If this is not agreed to unanimously, the following question is put:

"That this amendment be agreed to."

The same question is put to the House if Baroness Francis does not wish to withdraw her amendment.

If there are no further amendments, the Chairman would put the question:

'That Clause 2(or Clause 2, as amended) stand part of the Bill'.

There may be a general debate on this question and it is at this point that any peer who wishes to leave out the clause would speak. A peer who has not put down an amendment to this effect (which appears on the Marshalled List in italics) is supposed to warn the Chairman of Committees that he intends to oppose 'clause stand part'. The question put on the various Schedules to the bill is:

'That this be the first schedule to the bill',

or, where the Schedule has been amended,

'That this schedule as amended by the first schedule to the bill'.

The Committee Stage of a bill in the House of Lords is often interrupted in the evening. The House of Lords, being the more civilised of the two Houses, has a specific break in proceedings for dinner, allowing their Lordships to indulge in a lamb chop or a sticky pudding. Other business is usually taken in the dinner break – for example, an Unstarred Question. Where it is intended to 'interpose' other business in this way, the question put to the House is 'That the House be resumed' (meaning the full House as opposed to just a Committee of the House).

At the end of Committee Stage, the Chairman will put the question:

"That I report this bill to the House with amendments (or 'with an amendment' or 'without amendment')".

The Chairman then puts the question 'That the House be resumed' and if this is agreed to the Lord Chancellor or other Deputy Speaker or Chairman goes to the Woolsack and the Chairman of Committees goes from the Chair to the Despatch Box on the 'spiritual side' of the House (the side on which both the Government and the Bishops sit) and 'reports' the bill. If no one is waiting to take the Woolsack the Chairman of Committees does just that and reports the bill to the House from the side of the Woolsack. He uses the following words:

"My Lords, The Committee of the Whole House, to whom the Turnip Promotion Bill was committed, have gone through the same and have directed me to report it to your Lordships with amendments (or 'with an amendment' or 'without amendment')".

PROCEEDINGS AT REPORT STAGE

If a bill has been amended it is reprinted before Report Stage. If no amendments have been made the peer in charge of the bill moves that 'the report be now received' and the next stage is Third Reading. Since 1957, Report Stage can be taken at a later date even when there have been no amendments at Committee Stage. The motion that the 'report be now received' may be opposed and divided on and an amendment may be tabled to postpone the Report Stage.

Amendments

These are circulated and printed in the same manner as amendments at Committee Stage. The bill is not discussed clause by clause but amendments are called as they have been marshalled, thus an amendment to leave out a clause or schedule is a true amendment, whereas at Committee it appeared as a peer's intention to speak against a clause when the question is put. Amendments tabled at Report Stage should not be substantially the same as those on which a decision was taken at Committee Stage.

A peer may speak only once on an amendment at Report Stage unless he/she is the mover of the amendment (except Government Ministers or where leave has been granted to a peer to explain a point). Only the mover should speak after the Minister has replied. If amendments are made at Report Stage the bill is reprinted before Third Reading.

THIRD READING

The question, 'That this bill be now read a third time' is put formally and not debated. If agreed to, amendments may then be moved, provided notice has been given (manuscript amendments are not allowed). The principal aim of amendments at this stage is to clarify any uncertainties and to enable the Government to fulfil any undertakings (which may have been given at either Committee or Report Stage) to come back at a later stage with new amendments. These are usually in response to amendments tabled earlier in the bill's proceedings which, whilst they may have not been successful in a Division, or were withdrawn, have alerted the Government to the House's concern on a particular matter. Amendments which seek to reopen matters which have been fully debated and decided upon at an earlier stage are discouraged.

If a bill begins in the Lords, a privilege amendment is inserted before the bill returns to the Commons. The House of Lords may not infringe the 'privilege' of the House of Commons where public money is concerned. The House of Lords may not initiate any financial proposals; however, to enable major Government bills which may involve such measures to begin their parliamentary life in the House of Lords, their Lordships insert a privilege amendment after all other amendments have been dealt with at Third Reading. The amendment states that, ' Nothing in this Act shall impose any charge on the people or on public funds, or vary the amount or incidence of or otherwise alter any such charge in any manner, or affect the assessment, levying, administration or application of any money raised by any such charge'. The motion that 'the privilege amendment be agreed to' is put forthwith. When the bill is printed in the Commons these words are printed in bold and then deleted by a Government amendment. Lords Amendments infringing financial privilege can be allowed if a Money Resolution is passed. If not, they must be disagreed to.

When a bill has completed all its stages in the House of Lords, the question that 'the bill do now pass' is put. The House of Lords agreed on 22 March 1999 that this motion should normally be moved formally and should not usually be debated, but that Ministers could if necessary reply to points made by other peers.[5] It then returns to the Commons for Consideration of Lords Amendments. Where a bill has originated in the House of Lords the Clerk of Parliaments writes 'Soit baillé aux Communes' on the bill. Where the bill originated in the House of Commons, he writes, either 'A ceste Bille Les Seigneurs sont assentus' (where no amendments have been made) or 'A ceste Bille avecque des amendements Les Seigneurs sont assentus' (where there have been amendments) on the bill.

LORDS AMENDMENTS

Any Lords Amendments are amendments to the bill as first presented in the Lords (which is why it is a good idea to keep a copy of the bill as first printed in the Lords). Their Lordships' amendments are printed separately as are any proposed amendments to the Lords Amendments. Lords Amendments may be agreed to by the Commons or, alternatively, disagreed to or amended. A motion is made that: 'This House doth agree (or disagree) with the Lords in the said amendment'. When considering Lords Amendments it is essential to have copies of the bill as first printed in the Lords, the Lords Amendments themselves and any Commons' amendments to the Lords Amendments.

[5] This proposal was contained in a report from the House of Lords Procedure Committee (HL 33, 1999/2000) agreed to by the House on 22 March 1999.

Notice may be given of motions to disagree with Lords Amendments. Notice of motions to disagree with, or amendments to, Lords Amendments are printed in advance of the debate.

The Speaker selects the amendments to Lords Amendments and amendments in lieu of Lords Amendments in the same way as she selects the amendments for debate at Report Stage.

The House of Commons may do the following:

agree to the Lords amendment;

disagree to the Lords Amendment;

amend the Lords Amendment;

agree to an amendment in lieu of the Lords Amendment.

If a Lords Amendment is disagreed to or amended it must return to the House of Lords for 'Consideration of Commons Reasons'.

Where the House has agreed to the Lords Amendments, the words, 'A ces amendemens Les Communes sont assentus' are added to the bill before it returns to the House of Lords;

Where the House has disagreed to the Lords Amendments the words, 'ceste Bille est remise aux Seigneurs avecque des raisons' are added to the bill.

If no other words are offered in place of those disagreed to, a Committee is appointed to 'draw up reasons' – this is a Select Committee which chooses its own Chairman and Members are nominated in the usual way. It usually meets immediately after the debate on Lords Amendments and reports to the same sitting before communicating 'Commons Reasons' to the House of Lords.

CONSIDERATION OF COMMONS REASONS

When a bill originates in the House of Lords, Consideration of Commons Reasons is really the House of Lords equivalent of the Consideration of Lords Amendments in the House of Commons. However, the examples below relate to Consideration of Commons Reasons as if a bill originating in the House of Commons has been amended by the House of Lords, returned to the House of Commons for Consideration of Lords Amendments and then returned to the House of Lords for Consideration of Commons Reasons.

When the bill returns to the House of Lords, their Lordships can do one of the following:

1. Accept the Commons Reason for disagreeing to its amendment
2. Reject the Commons Reason for disagreeing to its amendment and insist on its original amendment
3. Not insist on their original amendment but offer an alternative amendment 'in lieu'

4. Where the Commons has amended their original amendment, they may agree to the amendment
5. Where the Commons has amended their original amendment, they may disagree to the amendment
6. Where the Commons has amended their original amendment, they may further amend the Commons amendment or offer an alternative amendment in lieu
7. Where the Commons has put forward an amendment in lieu of the original Lords amendment, the Lords may agree to this amendment
8. Where the Commons has put forward an amendment in lieu of the original Lords amendment, the Lords may disagree to the amendment in lieu
9. Where the Commons has put forward an amendment in lieu of the original Lords amendment, the Lords may disagree to the amendment in lieu but offer their own alternative amendment in lieu, or amend the Commons amendment in lieu

If you are confused at this point, you are not alone.

If the Lords disagree with the Commons Reasons, the words "Ceste Bille est remise aux Communes avecque des Raisons" (or 'une Raison') are added to the bill before it is returned to the House of Commons. The House of Commons is told:

1.) The Lords Reason for insisting upon their amendment;
2.) The Lords' Reason for disagreeing to the Commons amendment to or in lieu of the original Lords Amendment;
3.) The Lords Amendment to the Commons amendment to or in lieu of the original Lords Amendment;
4.) The Lords Amendment made in lieu of their original amendment disagreed to by the Commons.

Lords Reason for Insisting upon their Amendment

The Commons considers the Lords Reason for insisting upon their amendment. If they refuse to accept it and insist on their disagreement to the Lords Amendment the bill is usually lost unless the Commons offers an alternative amendment to the Lords Amendment which is acceptable to both Houses.

Lords Reason for Disagreeing to Commons Amendment to or in Lieu of the Original Lords Amendment

In this case the Commons may insist on their amendment to the Lords Amendment or may amend the bill in lieu of their amendment to the Lords Amendment. Again the bill will usually fall through lack of parliamentary time unless one or other House agrees to compromise.

Lords Amendment to Commons Amendment to or in Lieu of the Lords Amendment

The Commons may further amend the Lords Amendment to the Commons' amendment to or in lieu of the Lords Amendment or may disagree with the Lords Amendment in lieu of their amendment to the original Lords Amendment. Again, unless either House is prepared to compromise or give way, the bill is likely to fall.

Lords Amendment to the Bill in Lieu of Lords Amendment Disagreed to by the Commons

The Commons may amend the Lords Amendment made in lieu of the Commons disagreement to the Lords' original amendment, or they may disagree to it.

Essentially, if one House insists on an amendment that the other House has rejected and the other House insists on its rejection and no alternatives are offered the bill is lost. If communications between the two Houses are continuing at the end of a Session, the bill is lost. As Erskine May points out: 'In order to secure agreement and save the bill, every effort at compromise is usually made' (page 553). However, the interchange of amendments can be taken even further. Usually, the proceedings do not go beyond the above stage and one House will waive its disagreements. Erskine May points out that, 'there is no binding rule or order which governs these proceedings in either House, and, if there is a desire to save a bill, some variation in the proceedings may be devised in order to effect this object.' (page 553).

The best way to understand these comings and goings is to look at some recent examples. The first is the Criminal Justice Bill of the 1991/92 Session and the other, which is considered in some detail, is the European Parliamentary Elections Bill of the 1997/98 Session.

A recent example of a bill returning to the Commons after Lords disagreement with Commons Reasons was the Criminal Justice Bill 1991/92 which received Royal Assent just before the 1992 General Election. The House of Lords considered Commons Reasons for disagreeing with the Lords Amendments and Commons' amendments in lieu of Lords Amendments and the bill had to return to the House of Commons. The original Lords Amendment on Mandatory Life Sentences was defeated by the Commons, but the Government amendment in lieu of the Lords Amendment which introduced 'discretionary life sentences' was passed by the Commons but subsequently amended by the Lords. The Government then opposed the amendment when the bill returned to the Commons.

THE EUROPEAN PARLIAMENTARY ELECTIONS BILL 1997/98 AND 1998/99

The Government first introduced the European Parliamentary Elections Bill in the 1997/98 Session of Parliament.

Controversy centred on its replacement of the current First Past the Post system of elections with a 'closed list' system of PR under which electors vote for a political party rather than a specific candidate (this is explained more fully in chapter two). In the House of Lords, an amendment was tabled at Third Reading on 20 October 1998, by Lord Mackay of Ardbrecknish (Conservative) to permit electors to vote, not just for a political party but for a named candidate. The amendment was passed by 165 (Contents) to 140 (Not-Contents).

Consideration of Lords Amendments took place in the House of Commons on 27 October. The Lords Amendments were printed separately as set out below:

LORDS AMENDMENTS TO THE EUROPEAN PARLIAMENARY ELECTIONS BILL

[*The page and line refer to HL Bill 88 as first printed for the Lords*]

Amendment
No.

Clause 1

1 Page 2, line 1, leave out ("a registered party, or")*

**(Three other amendments were grouped with this one in the Lords and were printed underneath this first amendment)*

The question, 'That this House does disagree with the Lords in the said amendment' was passed by the House of Commons by 338 votes to 131.

The bill then returned to the House of Lords for Consideration of Commons Reasons. The Reasons were printed separately as follows:

European Parliamentary Elections Bill

COMMONS REASONS

[*The page and line refer to HL Bill 88 as first printed for the Lords*]

Amendment
No.

Clause 1

LORDS AMENDMENT

1 Page 2, line 1, leave out ("a registered party, or")*

1A *The Commons disagree to this Amendment for the following reason – Because it would result in a voting system which is undesirable.*

**(The other Lords Amendments to which the Commons disagreed were printed after this one)*

Consideration of Commons Reasons took place on 4 November. Lord Mackay of Ardbrecknish moved, 'That this House do insist on their Amendment No. 1, to which the Commons have disagreed for their reason numbered 1A'. This motion was divided on and was won by 221 (Contents) to 124 (Not-Contents).

The bill then returned to the House of Commons. The Lords Reasons were printed separately as follows:

LORDS REASONS FOR INSISTING ON THEIR AMENDMENTS
TO WHICH THE COMMONS HAVE DISAGREED
TO THE
EUROPEAN PARLIAMENTARY ELECTIONS BILL

[*The page and line refer to HL Bill 88 as first printed for the Lords*]

Clause 1

LORDS AMENDMENT

Page 2, line 1, leave out ("a registered party, or")

The Lords insist on their Amendment to which the Commons have disagreed, for the following Reason –

Because electors should be able to vote for the individual party candidate of their choice.

(the other Lords Amendment to which the Commons disagreed and on which the Lords insisted were printed under this one)

The House of Commons debated the Lords Reasons for insisting on their amendments, to which they had disagreed on 10 November. At this point, the Government proposed its own amendment in lieu of the Lords Amendment. They proposed this amendment because not to have offered an alternative amendment would have meant that the bill was lost (if one House insists on an amendment that the other House has rejected and the other House insists on its rejection and no alternatives are offered the bill is lost). The amendment offered by the Government was for a review of the new electoral system after six months. This amendment in lieu was passed by the House of Commons and the bill returned again to the House of Lords.

The following was printed separately:

European Parliamentary Elections Bill

MOTION TO BE MOVED ON CONSIDERATION OF A COMMONS
AMENDMENT IN LIEU OF LORDS AMENDMENTS

[*The page and line refer to HL Bill 88 as first printed for the Lords*]

Amendment
No.

Clause 1

LORDS AMENDMENTS

1 Page 2, line 1, leave out ("a registered party, or")

(the other Lords Amendments were then printed and followed by the following):

COMMONS AMENDMENT IN LIEU

The Commons insist on their disagreement with the Lords in their Amendments 1 to 4 but propose the following Amendment to the Bill in lieu thereof –

(the Commons amendment in lieu was then printed).

The House of Lords considered the Commons amendment on 12 November. Lord Mackay of Ardbrecknish moved, 'that the House do insist on their amendments to which the Commons have disagreed and do disagree with the Commons in their amendment in lieu thereof'. The House divided on this as follows: Contents, 237 and Not-Contents, 194. The bill then returned to the House of Commons, where the following was printed:

LORDS REASON FOR INSISTING ON THEIR AMENDMENTS
TO WHICH THE COMMONS HAVE DISAGREED
AND FOR DISAGREEING TO THE
COMMONS AMENDMENTS IN LIEU TO THE
EUROPEAN PARLIAMENTARY ELECTIONS BILL

[*The page and line refer to HL Bill 88 as first printed for the Lords*]

Amendment
No.

Clause 1

LORDS AMENDMENTS

1 Page 2, line 1, leave out ("a registered party, or")

(the other Lords amendment to which the Commons disagreed and on which the Lords insisted were printed under this one)

COMMONS AMENDMENT IN LIEU

After Clause 2

(the Commons amendment in lieu was printed here)

The Lords insist on their Amendments to which the Commons have disagreed and disagree with the Commons in their Amendment in lieu thereof, for the following Reason –

Because electors should be able to vote for the individual party candidate of their choice, and this should not be conditional on the outcome of a review.

The House of Commons met on 16 November to discuss the Lords Reasons for insisting on their amendments to which the Commons had disagreed and for disagreeing to the Commons amendment to the bill in lieu. The Home Secretary moved, 'That this House insists on its disagreement with the Lords in their amendments, but does not insist on its amendment in lieu'. The House divided on the motion which was passed by 309 votes to 122. The Commons had again refused to accept the Lords Amendments, but had decided not to insist on the amendment which they had previously offered in lieu, offering instead another similar amendment which would have ensured that the proposed review of the new electoral system took into account, 'how the ability of electors to vote for particular persons on a party's list of candidates might affect the results of an election'. The further amendment in lieu was passed by the House.

The bill then returned to the House of Lords where it was debated on 17 November. It was by now almost the end of the Session and unless either House decided to give way, or an agreement could be reached, the bill would be lost. Lord Mackay of Ardbrecknish moved the following motion: 'My Lords, I beg to move that this House do insist on their Amendments Nos. 1 to 4 to which the Commons have disagreed and do disagree with the Commons in their Amendment No. 4C in lieu thereof'. The motion was divided on and the result was as follows: Contents, 261; Not-Contents, 198.

The bill therefore returned to the House of Commons on 18 November, the penultimate day of the Session. The Home Secretary moved the following motion, 'That this House insists on its disagreement with the Lords in their Amendments but does not insist on its Amendment in lieu.'

The motion was divided upon and won by 326 votes to 133. The Government proposed another amendment in lieu which was passed by the House.

The bill then returned the same day to the House of Lords where Lord Mackay of Ardbrecknish moved 'that this House do insist on their Amendments Nos. 1 to 4 to which the Commons have disagreed and do disagree with the Commons in their Amendment No. 4L in lieu thereof'. The motion was divided on and won by 212 (Contents) to 183 (Not-Contents).

The bill then returned the same evening to the House of Commons where at 10.00pm the Home Secretary announced that, 'The European Parliamentary Elections Bill has, therefore, been lost for this Session. It will be reintroduced in the next Session under the procedures of the Parliament Acts'.

This is indeed what happened. The bill was introduced in the House of Commons on 27 November 1998, was subject to an Allocation of time Order and passed through all its subsequent stages in the House of Commons on 2 December 1998. It was introduced in the House of Lords on 3 December 1998 and received its Second Reading on 15 December 1998. Lord Mackay of Ardbrecknish moved a reasoned amendment declining to give the bill a Second Reading 'on the grounds that it includes an undemocratic 'closed list' system'. The bill was defeated by 167 votes (Contents) to 73 (Not-Contents). Under the Parliament Acts, unless the House of Commons directs to the contrary, such a bill, having been defeated at Second Reading, goes for Royal Assent without the agreement of the House of Lords.

PROCEEDINGS ON ROYAL ASSENT

There are a number of ways in which Royal Assent can be given, the first is the most common, but at the end of a Session the third variant is used.

1.) *Royal Assent Notified to each House separately*

Royal Assent is notified to each House, sitting separately, at a time convenient to each House during the course of the day's business by the Speaker of that House. The Speaker uses the following words: 'I have to notify the House, in accordance with the Royal Assent Act 1967 that the Queen has signified her Royal Assent to the following Acts and Measures...'

2.) *Royal Assent given by the Sovereign in Person*

This was last done on 12 August 1854. Royal Assent was last refused by Queen Anne in 1707. The words used would be 'La Reyne se avisera'.

3.) *Royal Assent Pronounced by Commission*

Three or more of the Lords Commissioners command the Usher of the Black Rod to signify to the Commons that their attendance is desired in the House of Peers to hear the commission read. When this message has been delivered, the Commons, with the Speaker, immediately come to the Bar of the Lords. The Clerk of Parliaments reads out the following in Norman French after the title of the bill to which assent has been given:

in the case of a Public or Private Bill: 'La Reyne le veult';

in the case of a Supply Bill: 'La Reyne remercie ses bons sujets, accepte leur benevolence, et ainsi le veult';

in the case of a Personal Bill: 'Soit fait comme il est desire'.

AFTER ROYAL ASSENT

After a bill receives Royal Assent, it becomes an Act of Parliament and is printed and numbered (the number is referred to as the chapter number). There are four series of Acts: Public General Acts, Provisional Order Confirmation Acts and Local Acts, Personal Acts and General Synod Measures.

THE PARLIAMENT ACTS

The gradual practice of the House of Commons of embodying all taxation changes in a single bill, the Finance Bill, meant that the House of Lords could reject the entire bill and hence all the Government's revenue raising plans. The rejection by the House of Lords of the Liberal Government's so-called 'People's Budget' (the Finance Bill of 1909) resulted in the passing of the 1911 Parliament Act.

The Government introduced the Act to restrain the powers of the House of Lords. In order to ensure the bill's passage through the House of Lords, they threatened to create 1000 Liberal peers. The King refused to consent unless a General Election was called, which the Liberals subsequently won. The Parliament Act was finally enacted in 1911.

Money Bills

Under the Parliament Act 1911, if a bill is certified as a 'Money Bill' and is sent up to the House of Lords (having already been passed by the House of Commons) one month before the end of the Session, it will immediately be presented for Royal Assent, even if it has not been passed by the Lords without amendment, one month after being received. Amendments can be made by the their Lordships if this is done within one month of receiving the bill, but the House of Commons is at liberty to disregard such amendments.

Other Public bills

The Act also provided that any other Public Bill, except one for extending the life of a Parliament, could become an Act of Parliament without the consent of the House of Lords if it had been passed by the House of Commons in three successive Sessions - two years having elapsed since its first Second Reading in the House of Commons and its final passing in that House, provided it had been sent up to the House of Lords at least one month before the end of each of the three Sessions. The Act also reduced the maximum duration of a Parliament from seven to five years. The Parliament Act 1949 reduced the number of sessions (which need not necessarily be two sessions of the same Parliament) in which a bill must be passed by the House of Commons from three to two and reduced the period between the first Second Reading and the final passing of the bill from two years to one.

The effect of the two Parliament Acts is therefore, that when a bill which originated in the House of Commons is passed in two successive Sessions, one year having elapsed between the first Second Reading and the final passing of the bill in the House of Commons, it will receive Royal Assent, even if disagreed to by the House of Lords, provided it was sent from the House of Commons to the House of Lords one month before the end of each Session.

Exceptions to the Parliament Acts

The Parliament Acts do not apply to the following: bills originating in the House of Lords, bills to extend the life of a Parliament beyond five years, Provisional Order Confirmation bills, Private Bills and delegated legislation. When a bill, other than a Money Bill, is presented to the Queen for Royal Assent, it must be endorsed with the signed certificate of the Speaker that the provisions of section 2 of the Parliament Act 1911 have been complied with.

CARRY OVER MOTIONS

On 4 June 1998 the House of Commons agreed to the Third Report from the Select Committee on Modernisation of the House of Commons (HC 543 97/98) which recommended that certain bills could be carried over from one Session to another. At present only Private and Hybrid bills can be carried over from one Session to the next. However, the Committee specifically recommended that the procedure should only be used for bills which had not left the House in which they originated. As yet, no carry-over motions have been tabled, but they may be used on an ad hoc basis and if successful embodied in amendments to Standing Orders. The House of Lords Procedure Committee accepted the principle of carrying over Public Bills in its third report (HL 106, 1997/98).

PRE-LEGISLATIVE COMMITTEES

The First Report of the Select Committee on Modernisation of the House of Commons (HC 190) of the 1997/98 Session was agreed to by the House on 13 November 1997. It suggested the use of pre-legislative committees to discuss draft legislation in the Session prior to the proposed bill's introduction. The draft Pension Sharing Bill was the first bill to be considered in this way in the last Session (1997/98) by the House of Commons Social Security Select Committee. The draft Food Standards Agency Bill was debated not in a departmental Select Committee but in a committee constituted specifically to consider the bill. The following motion, establishing the Committee, was agreed to by the House on 8 February 1999.

Food Standards

Motion made, and Question proposed,

That a select committee of thirteen Members be appointed to report on the draft bill on the Food Standards Agency (Cm. 4249);

That Ms Diana Organ, Ms Sally Keeble, Audrey Wise, Dr. Howard Stoate, Dr. Lewis Moonie, Mr. Martyn Jones, Mr. Kevin Barron, Dr. Stephen Ladyman, Mr. Owen Paterson, Mr. David Curry, Mr. Robert Walter, Dr. Peter Brand and the Reverend Martin Smyth be members of the Committee;

That the Committee have power

(a) to send for persons, papers and records;

(b) to sit notwithstanding any adjournment of the House;

(c) to adjourn from place to place within the United Kingdom;

(d) to appoint specialist advisers; and

(e) to communicate to any select committee of either House their evidence and any other documents relating to matters of common interest; and

That the Committee shall report by 31st March 1999.--[*Mr. Mike Hall.*]

At the time of writing, no amendments had been made to Standing Orders to enable such committees to be a permanent feature of the House of Commons.

CHAPTER EIGHT - PRIVATE MEMBERS' BILLS AND DEBATES

OPPORTUNITIES FOR BACKBENCHERS

The opportunities for Backbenchers to bring forward bills of their own choosing and to initiate debate are limited in the House of Commons by the fact that the majority of the parliamentary timetable is controlled by the Government. However, opportunities for Backbenchers do exist, on those days when Private Members' Bills 'have precedence' over Government business and on certain 'Motions for the Adjournment', which, whilst technically taken in Government time, are traditionally given over to Backbenchers. Under Standing Order (SO) 14, balloted Private Members' Bills are taken on those Fridays on which Private Members' business has precedence. Whilst the so-called 'Ten Minute Rule Bills' and bills brought in under SO 57 are presented in Government time, any further proceedings on these bills must take place on the aforementioned Private Members' Fridays. SO 24 debates (emergency debates), Wednesday morning adjournment debates and the half-hour daily adjournment debates all take place in Government time.

The opportunities for Backbenchers are therefore as follows:

Private Members' Bills

Balloted Bills brought in under SO 14

Ten Minute Rule Bills brought in under SO 23

Bills presented under SO 57

Private Members' Debates

Half-hour daily adjournment debates under SO 9

Wednesday morning adjournment debates under SO 10

Emergency debates under SO 24

BALLOTTED BILLS

Standing Order 14 (4) states that 'Private Members' Bills shall have precedence over government business on 13 Fridays in each session to be appointed by the House.' This Standing Order can be varied by the House if fewer or more than 13 days are to be given over to Private Members' Bills, for example:

Standing Order No. 14 (Arrangement of Public Business) shall have effect for this Session with the following modifications, namely: In Paragraph (4) the word 'fourteen' shall be substituted for the word 'thirteen'; in paragraph (5) the word 'ninth' shall be substituted for the word 'eighth'

In the 1997/98 Session of Parliament, SO 14 was not amended and the following appeared on the Order Paper on 19 May 1997.

1 *BUSINESS OF THE HOUSE*
Mrs Ann Taylor

That Private Members' Bills shall have precedence over Government business on 28th November, 12th December 1997 and 16th, 23rd and 30th January, 6th and 13th February, 6th, 13th, 20th and 27th March, 24th April and 3rd July 1998.

2 *SITTINGS OF THE HOUSE*
Mrs Ann Taylor

That the House shall not sit on the following Fridays: 13th June, 4th July (this later became a sitting Friday) 31st October 1997 and 20th February, 3rd April, 1st and 15th May, 12th and 26th June and 10th July 1998.

*The Speaker will put the question forthwith, pursuant to Standing Order No. 12**

* SO 12(1) specifies that the 'House shall not sit on ten Fridays in each session to be appointed by the House.'

The ballot for Private Members' Bills takes place at 12.00 noon on the second Thursday of each Session, Members having had the opportunity to sign the ballot paper which is placed in the 'No' Lobby for two days prior to the ballot. Only the top 20 names are drawn. Titles of bills are made known on the fifth Wednesday of the Session. At the commencement of Public Business on this day, each bill is presented by the Member concerned, or by another Member whose name has been given to the Clerk at the Table. The texts of the bills may not appear for some time after this. One should not assume from the fact that a Private Member's Bill is presented by a Backbencher, that he or she has in fact written the bill – this is most unlikely. A Member who has been successful in the ballot will usually find him or herself at the receiving end of a stream of requests from organisations interested in promoting legislation of one form or another. Charities, voluntary organisations, pressure group, etc., will usually have bills already drafted which they will try and persuade a successful MP to adopt. For the MPs who have been successful in the ballot, the difficulty lies in deciding which bill, out of several worthy causes, to promote. There are those who prefer to promote a controversial bill which, although it stands little chance of ever reaching the statute book, will secure a great deal of attention from press and public alike and those who prefer to promote a bill which perhaps makes only minor changes to existing law, but is supported by the Government and which has a greater chance of achieving Royal Assent.

In the 1997/98 Session, the following Members came top in the Ballot (the ten Members placed highest in the ballot may claim £200 to assist in the process of drafting their bills).

Michael Foster MP *(Worcester)*
Dr Julian Lewis MP
Teresa Gorman MP
Sir George Young Bt MP
Cynog Dafis MP
John Burnett MP
Chris Pond MP
Nigel Evans MP
Linda Perham MP
Richard Shepherd MP
Mike Hall MP
Roger Berry MP
Michael Trend MP
Marsha Singh MP
Oona King MP
Piers Merchant MP
Ben Bradshaw MP
Clive Efford MP
Linda Gilroy MP
Dennis Turner MP

The following bills were duly presented on 18 June 1997 after question time and before the Orders of the Day. It is at this point that Members must decide on which of the available Fridays they wish their Second Reading to take place.

BILLS PRESENTED

Wild Mammals (Hunting with Dogs)

Mr. Michael Foster, supported by Mr. Roger Gale, Mr. Kevin McNamara, Mr. Simon Hughes, Angela Smith, Sir Teddy Taylor, Mr. Ivor Caplin, Mrs. Jackie Ballard, Ms Jackie Lawrence, Mr. Nigel Jones, Mrs. Margaret Ewing and Mr. Ian Cawsey, presented a bill to make provision for the protection of wild mammals from being pursued, killed or injured by the use of dogs; and for connected purposes: And the same was read the First time; and ordered to be read a Second time upon Friday 28 November, and to be printed [Bill 7].

Mental Health (Amendment)

Dr. Julian Lewis, supported by Mrs. Gillian Shephard, Mr. Simon Hughes, Mr. Kevin McNamara, Mrs. Angela Browning, Mr. Charles Kennedy, Mr. Donald Anderson, Mr. Nicholas Winterton, Mr. David Marshall, Mr. Iain Duncan Smith, Mr. Chris Mullin and Mr. John Bercow, presented a Bill to amend the Mental Health Act 1983 to provide greater access to hospital accommodation for mentally ill people; and for connected purposes: And the same was read the First time; and ordered to be read a Second time upon Friday 12 December, and to be printed [Bill 8].

Referendum (English Parliament)

Mrs. Teresa Gorman, supported by Mr. Christopher Gill, Mr. Richard Shepherd, Mr. David Amess, Mrs. Ann Winterton, Mr. Nicholas Winterton, Mr. John Hayes and Mr. Peter Luff, presented a Bill to make provision for the holding of a referendum in England on the establishment and tax-varying powers of an English Parliament: And the same was read the First time; and ordered to be read a Second time upon Friday 16 January, and to be printed [Bill 9].

Private Hire Vehicles (London)

Sir George Young, supported by Sir Sydney Chapman, Mr. Alan Clark, Ms Margaret Hodge, Miss Kate Hoey, Mr. Simon Hughes, Mr. Piers Merchant, Mr. Richard Ottaway, Mr. Clive Soley and Dr. Jenny Tonge, presented a Bill to provide for the licensing and regulation of private hire vehicles, and drivers and operators of such vehicles, within the Metropolitan Police District and the City of London; and for connected purposes: And the same was read the First time; and ordered to be read a Second time upon Friday 23 January, and to be printed [Bill 10].

Road Traffic Reduction (United Kingdom Targets)

Mr. Cynog Dafis, supported by Ms Joan Walley, Mr. Peter Bottomley, Sir Richard Body, Mr. Alan Simpson, Mr. Don Foster, Mr. Dafydd Wigley, Mr. Jim Cousins, Ms Julia Drown, Mr. Stephen Pound and Mr. Andrew Robathan, presented a Bill to make further provision for road traffic reduction targets; and for related purposes: And the same was read the First time; and ordered to be read a Second time upon Friday 30 January, and to be printed [Bill 11].

Energy Efficiency

Mr. John Burnett, supported by Mr. Richard Allan, Mr. John Austin, Mr. Tim Boswell, Mr. Michael Colvin, Mr. Cynog Dafis, Ms Julia Drown, Mrs. Linda Gilroy, Mr. Alan Simpson, Mr. Matthew Taylor, Ms Joan Walley and Mr. Tim Yeo, presented a Bill to make further provision for energy efficiency: And the same was read the First time; and ordered to be read a Second time upon Friday 6 February, and to be printed [Bill 12].

Employment of Children

Mr. Chris Pond, supported by Mrs. Ann Clwyd, Mr. Jeremy Corbyn, Mrs. Llin Golding, Ms Margaret Hodge, Miss Oona King, Mr. Archy Kirkwood, Mrs. Alice Mahon, Mr. Andrew Rowe, Mr. Richard Shepherd, Angela Smith and Mr. Peter Temple-Morris, presented a Bill to make further provision for the protection of persons in employment under the upper limit of school age, by restricting hours of employment, especially on Sundays, and by other means: And the same was read the First time; and ordered to be read a Second time upon Friday 13 February, and to be printed [Bill 13].

Cold Weather Payments (Wind Chill Factor)

Mr. Nigel Evans, supported by Audrey Wise, Mr. David Atkinson, Mr. David Ruffley, Mr. Edward Garnier, Mr. Nick Hawkins, Mr. Stephen Day, Mr. Brian Sedgemore, Mr. Jamie Cann, Mr. Donald Anderson, Mrs. Margaret Ewing and Mr. Menzies Campbell, presented a Bill to provide that wind chill factor is taken into account in the calculation of cold weather payments; and for connected purposes: And the same was read the First time; and ordered to be read a Second time upon Friday 23 January, and to be printed [Bill 14].

Employment (Age Discrimination in Advertisements)

Ms Linda Perham, supported by Mr. David Winnick, Mr. Roger Berry, Ms Yvette Cooper, Mrs. Linda Gilroy, Angela Smith, Mr. Don Foster, Mr. Ieuan Wyn Jones, Mrs. Margaret Ewing, Mr. David Atkinson, Mr. Andrew Rowe and Mr. Quentin Davies, presented a Bill to prohibit discrimination on the basis of age in the advertising of employment vacancies: And the same was read the First time; and ordered to be read a Second time upon Friday 6 February, and to be printed [Bill 15].

Public Interest Disclosure

Mr. Richard Shepherd, supported by Mr. Malcolm Bruce, Mr. Dale Campbell-Savours, Mr. Ross Cranston, Sir Patrick Cormack, Mr. Cynog Dafis, Mr. Iain Duncan Smith, Mr. John Healey, Mr. Giles Radice, Mr. Andrew Rowe, Mr. Don Touhig and Dr. Tony Wright, presented a Bill to protect individuals who make certain disclosures of information in the public interest; to allow such individuals to bring action in respect of victimisation; and for connected purposes: And the same was read the First time; and ordered to be read a Second time upon Friday 12 December, and to be printed [Bill 16].

Breeding and Sale of Dogs

Mr. Mike Hall, supported by Mr. Nick Ainger, Ms Helen Southworth, Mr. Tim Loughton, Angela Smith, Mr. Matthew Taylor, Helen Jones, Mr. Colin Pickthall, Laura Moffatt, Mr. Andrew Miller, Mr. Terry Lewis and Mr. John Heppell, presented a Bill to amend and extend certain enactments regulating the breeding and sale of dogs; to regulate the welfare of dogs kept in breeding establishments; to extend powers of inspection; to establish records of dogs kept at such establishments; and for connected purposes: And the same was read the First time; and ordered to be read a Second time upon Friday 30 January, and to be printed [Bill 17].

Disability Rights Commission

Mr. Roger Berry, supported by Mr. Harry Barnes, Miss Anne Begg, Mr. Peter Bottomley, Mr. Paul Burstow, Mr. Robin Corbett, Valerie Davey, Mrs. Margaret Ewing, Lorna Fitzsimons, Mr. Tom Levitt, Rev. Martin Smyth and Mr. Dafydd Wigley, presented a Bill to establish a Disability Rights Commission to make recommendations on legislation to achieve comprehensive and enforceable civil rights for disabled people; and for connected purposes: And the same was read the First time; and ordered to be read a Second time upon Friday 16 January, and to be printed [Bill 18].

Chamber of Commerce (Protection of Title)

Mr. Michael Trend, supported by Mr. Andrew Lansley, Mr. Graham Brady, Mr. Robin Corbett, Mr. Nick Harvey, Mr. Richard Page, Mr. James Paice, Mr. Nick St. Aubyn, Mrs. Caroline Spelman and Mrs. Gisela Stuart, presented a Bill to control the use of the title "Chamber of Commerce" and related titles; and for connected purposes: And the same was read the First time; and ordered to be read a Second time upon Friday 23 January, and to be printed [Bill 19].

Community Care (Residential Accommodation)

Mr. Marsha Singh, supported by Mr. Andrew King, Mr. Tony Clarke, Mr. Bob Laxton, Ms Kali Mountford, Mr. Paul Burstow, Mr. David Borrow, Mr. Bernard Jenkin, Mr. Roy Beggs, Mr. Ieuan Wyn Jones, Mr. John Austin and Mr. Christopher Leslie, presented a Bill to restrict the amount of a person's capital which may be taken into account by a local authority in determining whether he should be provided with residential accommodation that would be, or would be treated as, provided under Part III of the National Assistance Act 1948: And the same was read the First time; and ordered to be read a Second time upon Friday 28 November, and to be printed [Bill 20].

Local Authority Tenders

Miss Oona King, supported by Mr. Chris Pond, Mrs. Ann Keen, Mr. Keith Vaz, Mr. Ben Bradshaw, Mr. Jim Fitzpatrick, Mr. Andrew Love, Mr. Martin Bell, Mrs. Diana Organ, Ms Caroline Flint and Mr. David Lock, presented a Bill to amend the law in respect of non-commercial matters to which local authorities may have regard in awarding contracts; and for connected purposes: And the same was read the First time; and ordered to be read a Second time upon Friday 16 January, and to be printed [Bill 21].

Waste Prevention

Mr. Piers Merchant, supported by Sir Teddy Taylor, Angela Smith, Mrs. Margaret Ewing, Mr. Matthew Taylor, Mr. Nigel Evans and Mr. Cynog Dafis, presented a Bill to enable certain local authorities to make arrangements to minimise the generation of waste in their areas: And the same was read the First time; and ordered to be read a Second time upon Friday 12 December, and to be printed [Bill 22].

Pesticides

Mr. Ben Bradshaw, supported by Ms Candy Atherton, Mrs. Linda Gilroy, Fiona Mactaggart, Miss Oona King, Mrs. Gisela Stuart, Ms Tessa Kingham, Mr. Matthew Taylor and Mr. Simon Hughes, presented a Bill to amend the Food and Environment Protection Act 1985 in respect of the power to make regulations concerning pesticides and in respect of the enforcement of provisions relating to the control of pesticides: And the same was read the First time; and ordered to be read a Second time upon Friday 28 November, and to be printed [Bill 23].

Energy Conservation (Housing)

Mr. Clive Efford, supported by Mr. John Austin, Mr. Matthew Taylor, Mr. Clive Soley, Ms Joan Walley, Mr. Cynog Dafis and Mr. Alan Simpson, presented a Bill to make further provision for energy conservation related to housing; and for connected purposes: And the same was read the First time; and ordered to be read a Second time upon Friday 6 February, and to be printed [Bill 24].

Fireworks

Mrs. Linda Gilroy, supported by Mr. Richard Burden, Mr. Ian Davidson, Mr. Patrick Hall, Ms Barbara Follett, Mr. Andy Love, Mr. Piers Merchant, Mr. Barry Sheerman, Angela Smith, Ms Kali Mountford, Mr. Matthew Taylor and Mr. James Wallace, presented a Bill to make further provision about fireworks and other explosives: And the same was read the First time; and ordered to be read a Second time upon Friday 28 November, and to be printed [Bill 25].

Weights and Measures (Beer and Cider)

Mr. Dennis Turner, supported by Ms Jenny Jones, Mr. Ken Purchase, Mr. John Cummings, Mr. Ronnie Campbell, Mr. Mike Hall, Mr. Nigel Jones, Mr. Colin Pickthall, Mr. George Stevenson, Mr. Stephen Day, Mr. Gerald Bermingham and Mr. Robin Corbett, presented a Bill to amend the law of weights and measures in relation to measures of beer and cider; and for connected purposes: And the same was read the First time; and ordered to be read a Second time upon Friday 12 December, and to be printed [Bill 26].

Order of Debate

On, and after the first eight Fridays allocated to Private Members' Bills (variable by an amendment of SO 14), Second Readings take precedence. After the eighth Friday bills are arranged in the following order:

Consideration of Lords Amendments
Third Readings
Consideration of Report not already entered upon (new Report Stages)
Adjourned proceedings on Consideration (adjourned Report Stages)
Bills in progress in Committee of the Whole House
Bills appointed for Committee of the Whole House
Second Readings

(For more information on these terms and on the various legislative stages, please see the preceding chapter, chapter seven)

This means that on any Friday after the eighth Friday where Private Members' Bills have precedence, Private Members' Bills returning from the House of Lords for Consideration of Lords Amendments take precedence, followed by those awaiting Third Readings, those awaiting Report, those whose Report Stage has been adjourned, those already in Committee of the Whole House whose proceedings have been adjourned, those awaiting their Committee Stage in a Committee of the Whole House and finally Second Readings. It is for this reason that those Members in the top seven of the ballot stand the best chance of gaining a Second Reading for their bill and for the same reason that other Members, lower down in the ballot often choose one of the first seven Private Members' Fridays for their Second Readings, even though they may be behind one or even two other Private Members' Bills.

Members may nominate a day for Second Reading in accordance with the results of the ballot. It is obviously to the advantage of the Member drawn first in the ballot to nominate the first available Friday. Debates frequently last from approximately 9.30am to 2.30pm on Fridays and consequently not even all the balloted bills set down for debate on that day will necessarily be debated.

For example, a Member who has come ninth in the ballot and who has put his bill down for Second Reading on the first available Friday may find that the bill which is to be debated first (usually the bill of the Member who came first in the ballot) is not particularly controversial and that time is left to debate his own Bill. If this is not the case then the Member concerned may still be able to receive a Second Reading for his bill at 2.30pm, without debate. However, if a single Member shouts 'object', the Bill's Second Reading is adjourned and the Member 'in charge of the Bill' must nominate another Friday for the debate. For example, in the 1997/98 Session, Nigel Evans MP (eighth in the ballot) chose Friday 23 January (the fourth Private Member's Friday) for his Second Reading, rather than the eighth available Friday.

A bill which is read a second time 'on the nod' on a Friday will usually be committed to a Standing Committee, but, if the Member so wishes, the bill may go to a Committee of the Whole House. The Speaker, or Deputy Speaker will put the question 'That the bill be committed to a Committee of the whole House'. At this point the Speaker will ask, 'Committee what day?'. If the Member in charge replies, 'Now, Sir', (or Madam, depending who is in the Chair) the House proceeds to a lightening Committee Stage, providing no Member shouts 'object'. The Speaker leaves the Chair and the Mace is put under the Table. The author of the bill will then beg leave to report that the Committee has considered the bill and made no amendment.[1] The Mace is then replaced, the Speaker takes the Chair and the Report and Third Reading are taken together. If, however there is an objection to the motion that the Committee Stage be taken on that day, the MP concerned must move that, 'This House will immediately resolve itself into the said Committee'; however, this is opposed business and therefore cannot be decided after the Moment of Interruption. If any Member objects the Committee Stage has to be taken on a future day.

The Member in charge of a Private Members' Bill, whether introduced under the ballot, the 10 Minute Rule, or Standing Order 57, can move that the bill be referred to a Second Reading Committee. This can only be done after the eighth Private Members' Bill Friday, providing 10 days notice has been given.

The Use of the Closure

On the floor of the House, if opponents of a Private Member's bill are still speaking at 2.30pm, the bill's sponsor, or a colleague, must seek to move 'that the question be now put' (known as the 'Closure') otherwise the debate will be adjourned at the Moment of Interruption. Business under consideration at this time is adjourned and the only business which can be taken after this time is unopposed or exempted business (see chapter five). One hundred Members voting in its favour as well as a majority are needed to secure the Closure. The Chair will not allow a Closure if there has been insufficient debate. The Closure has sometimes been described as a vote on whether or not to vote.

The Closure can be moved by any Member, who must stand in his or her place to move the motion. Under SO 36 and 37, the Member must use the words 'I beg to move that the question be now put'. It is up to the speaker (or thc Chairman of Ways and Means or one of the Deputy Chairmen, during a Committee of the Whole House) to decide whether or not to allow the Closure. For example, if certain Members are opposed to a particular Private Member's Bill, they will attempt to 'talk it out'. This means that they will endeavour to keep the debate going until 2.30pm – the 'Moment of Interruption', at which point the business under discussion will be adjourned until another day. After this time, no opposed business can be taken.

A Member who knows that his bill is likely to be opposed will try and ensure that 100 Members turn up to support the Closure Motion, which he will move, either at, or just before, 2.30pm. He will hope to win, not just the Closure, but also the vote on Second Reading, allowing his bill to go forward to be debated in Standing Committee C. In reality, things are not quite this simple. The Speaker has the power to decide whether or not to allow the Closure and may decide to disallow it on the grounds that there has been insufficient debate on the matter in hand. If the Speaker does allow the Closure, the motion that 'the question be now put' is put before the House. The wish of the majority may be obvious from the response, but where the 'Ayes' and 'Noes' appear to be equally balanced, a Division is called. This is where many Backbenchers lose their

[1] It is possible to move amendments to a bill at this point, but any attempt to debate them is taken as being an objection and therefore constitutes 'opposed business' and cannot be taken after the Moment of Interruption at 2.30pm. Unless an amendment was passed 'on the nod' without debate the Committee Stage would be adjourned as being opposed business.

bills for whilst they are able to gain a majority in a Division on the Closure motion, they fail to gain the requisite 100 votes as well. If the Closure is agreed to, the House immediately proceeds to a vote on the question which is before it – in the case of a Second Reading of a Bill, 'that the bill be now read a second time' (SO 36(2)). This second part of SO 36 is particularly useful if the Closure is moved on a Friday at 2.30pm (the Moment of Interruption), as it allows not just a vote on the Closure, but on Second Reading as well.

The example below (which was cited in chapter five) is from the Second Reading debate on the Wild Mammals (Hunting with Dogs) bill on 28 November 1997.

Mr. David Hinchliffe (Wakefield) *rose in his place and claimed to move,* That the Question be now put.

Question put, That the Question be now put:-
The House proceeded to a Division—

Mr. Garnier (seated and covered): On a point of order, Mr. Deputy Speaker. The closure motion is wholly unnecessary. There are 20 minutes left until a Division needs to be called.
Mr. Deputy Speaker: The hon. and learned Gentleman knows that that is a matter of discretion for the Chair. I have used my discretion.
Mr. Garnier: I am appealing to your discretion, Mr. Deputy Speaker. There was no question of the Bill being talked out. I invite--
Mr. Deputy Speaker: Order. That is the hon. and learned Gentleman's opinion. There is now a Division. Perhaps the hon. and learned Gentleman may wish to take part in that Division. It is up to him. I shall now put the Question again.
Question agreed to.

Question put accordingly, That the Bill be now read a Second time:-

The House divided: Ayes 411, Noes 151.

Most Private Members' Bills are unlikely ever to reach the statute book unless they receive Government support. This is because of the limited parliamentary time available for debate on Private Members' Bills and the relative ease with which a bill can be 'talked out' by its opponents. Whilst neither the Government nor the Opposition officially imposes a whip on Private Members' Bills, a certain amount of unofficial whipping is carried out.

If the Government objects to a Private Member's Bill it may either oppose it outright at Second Reading; as it did, for example, in the case of Rosie Barnes MP's, 'National Health Service (Compensation) Bill', 1990/91 (which sought to establish a system of no-fault compensation for the victims of medical accidents) or it may decide to let the bill run out of parliamentary time. If the Government supports a Private Member's Bill its chances of gaining Royal Assent are good. In the case of the aforementioned Member's 'Stillbirth (Definition) Bill', 1991/2, the Government supported the bill and it passed all its Commons' stages in one day. All Private Members' bills must pass through all stages in both Houses in the same way as any other Public Bill, so even a Private Member's bill which has completed all its Commons' stages, may find it runs out of time in the House of Lords.

Balloted Bills in Standing Committee

Most Private Members' Bills are committed to Standing Committee 'C' (see chapter seven). Sometimes the Members of Committee C, who are discussing a previous bill, will filibuster (talk endlessly and in a long-winded manner) in order to delay the passage of a controversial Private Members' Bill. It will then be held up in a queue awaiting debate in Committee. For example, a Member whose bill was third in the ballot may find that not only does he have the two bills who came first and second in the ballot ahead of him in the queue for Standing Committee C, but also those bills lower down in the ballot, whose Second Readings were taken after the first two bills. For example, in the 1991/92 Session, Ray Powell, who came third in the ballot, found that his 'Shops (Amendment) Bill' was behind four other bills, those which came first, second, eighth and ninth in the Ballot.

This is set out below:

Local Government (Overseas Assistance) Bill (first in ballot)
Second Reading, 11 December 1992, Committee Stage, 20 and 27 January 1993

Osteopaths Bill (second in ballot)
Second Reading, 15 January 1992, Committee Stage, 3 February 1993

Road Traffic (Driving Instruction by Disabled Persons) Bill (eighth in ballot)
Second Reading, 11 December 1992, Committee Stage, 3 February 1993

Medicines Information Bill (third in ballot)
Second Reading, 15 January 1993, Committee Stage, 17 and 24 February 1993

Bills are considered by the Committee in the order of their allocation, unless the Member in charge of a bill agrees to give precedence in Committee to a bill behind him in the queue. By arrangement with the Ministers in charge of Government bills, Private Members' Bills occasionally take precedence over Government bills in other Standing Committees.

The Committee Members are chosen by the Committee of Selection as they would be for any Public Bill. Where there has been a free vote at Second Reading, the membership roughly corresponds to the proportions voting for and against the bill at Second Reading. At least one member of the Committee must be a Government Minister. The Member in charge of the bill will usually suggest names to the Committee as will the Party Whips. Often MPs will write to the Chairman of the Committee of Selection asking to be considered for the Committee, particularly if they have been unable to speak or attend the Second Reading debate. The number of Members on the Committee really depends on the interest expressed in the Bill. The size of Standing Committee C may therefore vary.

Occasionally, the Government decides to provide some of its own time for the discussion of a Private Member's Bill; for example, the Government may provide time for the discussion of Lords Amendments to Private Members' Bills received at a late stage of the Session. In all cases the bill in question is treated as a Government order of the Day. The 1967 Abortion Act began life as a Private Member's Bill, promoted by David Steel, MP, then a humble Backbencher (now Lord Steel of Aikwood). The Labour Government of the day, and the then Home Secretary, Roy Jenkins, now Lord Jenkins of Hillhead, supported the principles of the bill and gave time for its passage through the House.

In the last Session of Parliament (1997/98) the Private Hire Vehicles (London) Bill and the Road Traffic Reduction (National Targets) Bill were considered in Standing Committees usually reserved for Government bills - Standing Committees D and E respectively, rather than the usual Standing Committee C. The Breeding and Sale of Dogs Bill and the Fireworks Bill were both sent to Standing Committee A, but ran out of Parliamentary time. The Energy Conservation (Housing) Bill and the Public Interest Disclosure bills were sent to Standing Committee D – the former ran out of time, but the latter gained Royal Assent.

Progress of Balloted Bills in Standing Committee C in 1997/98 Session

Bill	Position in Ballot	Position/ Entering Standing Committee C	Date Entering Standing Committee C	Date Leaving Standing Committee C
Wild Mammals (Hunting with Dogs)	1	1	17.12.97	25.2.98
Mental Health (Amendment)	2	NA – no cttee. stage		
Referendum (English Parliament)	3	NA – no cttee. stage		
Private Hire Vehicles (London)	4	NA - sent to SC D		
Road Traffic Reduction (National Targets)	5	NA – sent to SC E		
Energy Efficiency	6	5	25.3.98	25.3.98
Employment of Children	7	NA – no cttee. stage		
Cold Weather Payments (Wind Chill Factor)	8	NA – no cttee. stage		
Employment (Age Discrimination in Advertisements)	9	NA – no cttee. stage		
Public Interest Disclosure	10	NA – sent to SC D		
Breeding and Sale of Dogs	11	NA – sent to SC A		
Disability Rights	12	NA – no		

Bill	Position in Ballot	Position/ Entering Standing Committee C	Date Entering Standing Committee C	Date Leaving Standing Committee C
Commission		cttee. stage		
Company and Business names (Chamber of Commerce, etc)	13	6	10.6.98	10.6.98
Community Care (Residential Accommodation)	14	NA – Committee of Whole House		
Local Authority Tenders	15	4	18.3.98	18.3.98
Waste Prevention	16	NA – no cttee. stage		
Pesticides	17	2	4.3.98	4.3.98
Energy Conservation (Housing)	18	NA – sent to SC D		
Fireworks	19	NA – SC A		
Weights and Measures (Beer and Cider)	20	3	11.3.98	11.3.98

NA = not applicable

THE FATE OF SELECTED BALLOTED PRIVATE MEMBERS' BILLS IN THE 1997/98 SESSION

The Wild Mammals (Hunting with Dogs) Bill 1997/98

Michael Foster MP, the new Labour Member for Worcester came first in the Private Members' Ballot in the 1997/98 Session. His decision to introduce a bill to ban fox hunting caused controversy from the start and, quite literally, got the countryside on the march. Despite a ban on fox hunting being Labour Party policy, ultimately the Government was not prepared to allocate any Government time to the bill and it was eventually withdrawn.

The proceedings on the bill serve as a useful reminder of just how difficult it is to get a Private Member's Bill onto the Statute Book.

The Second Reading of the bill was on 28 November 1997, the first available Private Members' Friday. Soon after 2.00pm, David Hinchliffe MP moved the Closure (HC, Col: 1267).

Mr. David Hinchliffe (Wakefield) *rose in his place and claimed to move,* That the Question be now put.

Question put, That the Question be now put:--

The House proceeded to a Division—

Mr. Garnier (seated and covered): On a point of order, Mr. Deputy Speaker. The closure motion is wholly unnecessary. There are 20 minutes left until a Division needs to be called.

Mr. Deputy Speaker: The hon. and learned Gentleman knows that that is a matter of discretion for the Chair. I have used my discretion.

Mr. Garnier: I am appealing to your discretion, Mr. Deputy Speaker. There was no question of the Bill being talked out. I invite—

Mr. Deputy Speaker: Order. That is the hon. and learned Gentleman's opinion. There is now a Division. Perhaps the hon. and learned Gentleman may wish to take part in that Division. It is up to him. I shall now put the Question again.

Question agreed to.

Question put accordingly, That the Bill be now read a Second time:--

The House divided: Ayes 411, Noes 151.

Having received its Second Reading, the bill was committed to Standing Committee C. The Committee had 10 sittings, during which time the bill was effectively rewritten. As Tony Baldry MP pointed out during Report Stage: 'For many weeks the Committee did not progress further than line 1 of clause 1. We were then confronted with the extraordinary situation whereby the bill was effectively rewritten. The bill before the House today consists almost entirely of new clauses, which were not before the House on Second Reading, so it is not unreasonable that we should turn our attention to these issues'.

Report Stage took place on 6 March 1998. The first Clause to be considered was New Clause 1 – Fox control in national parks. Several other New Clauses were grouped with new Clause 1 – New Clauses 3,6,7,19 and 25. The usual practice with New Clauses which have been grouped is for a Division to take place on the first New Clause in the group. It is up to the Speaker to decide whether or not to put any of the remaining New Clauses in the group to a vote. If they are divided on, the Division occurs at the relevant place in the bill and not necessarily immediately after the first New Clause in the group. This is shown in the selections from the debate at Report Stage, set out below.

Wild Mammals (Hunting with Dogs) Bill
As amended (in the Standing Committee), considered.

New clause 1

Fox control in national parks

(text of New Clause)

Brought up, and read the First time.

9.36 am

Mr. Dale Campbell-Savours (Workington): I beg to move, That the clause be read a Second time.

Madam Speaker: With this, it will be convenient to discuss the following:
New clause 3--*Mink*--

(text of New Clause)

New clause 6--*Gun Packs*--

(text of New Clause)

New clause 7--*Control of foxes in national parks*--

(text of New Clause)

New clause 19--*Circumstances in which shooting is unsafe or impractical*--

(text of New Clause)
New clause 25--*Licensing of terrier work*--

(text of New Clause)

Mr. Campbell-Savours *rose—*

Mr. Peter Atkinson (Hexham): On a point of order, Madam Speaker. Before we start the debate on this wide-ranging group of new clauses, may I seek your guidance on a question of procedure? At some stage, no doubt, we shall have a Division on new clause 1. There are those of us who would, for example, disagree with new clause 1 but agree with new clauses 3 and 6. Will we have an opportunity to have separate Divisions on new clauses 3 and 6 and, for all I know, on other new clauses in the group?

Madam Speaker: At this early stage of the debate, I am not prepared to commit the Chair. I need to hear the debate. I am aware that there are distinctions between the new clauses. I shall consider separate Divisions when we reach that stage. I understand the point of order that has been raised by the hon. Gentleman.

- the debate continued ... until:

Mr. Baldry: In that case, I shall speak to new clause 19, which stands in my name. I am not sure why hon. Members on the Government Benches are so restive. Some of us sat for many weeks in the Standing Committee that considered the Bill, and for many weeks the Committee did not progress further than line 1 of clause 1. We were then confronted with the extraordinary situation whereby the Bill was effectively rewritten. The Bill before the

House today consists almost entirely of new clauses, which were not before the House on Second Reading, so it is not unreasonable that we should turn our attention to these issues.

Mr. Tom King (Bridgwater): May I be clear about this, as it is alleged that filibustering might occur today? My hon. Friend said that in Committee it took many weeks to reach the second line of the Bill, but is it not true that the filibustering that took place in Committee was by the Bill's supporters, not its opponents?
Mr. Baldry: My right hon. Friend is correct. The House and the country can draw its own inferences from the fact that those of us who were opposed to the Bill played an intelligent and constructive part in the Committee's proceedings, because, if passed, the Bill will be part of the criminal law of this country, so it is important that Parliament should get it right. It was a frustrating role, because for many weeks it was clear that the supporters of the Bill did not wish to make progress, simply because they wanted to hog the Committee's time.
Mr. Garnier: Does my hon. Friend recall that not only did the hon. Member for Worcester (Mr. Foster) encourage filibustering tactics throughout the first five sittings of the Committee, during which we discussed only the first two lines of the Bill, but he then tabled amendments and voted against them?

Mr. Baldry: Absolutely. If ever there were evidence of the tactics that the hon. Gentleman adopted, it is that he tabled and voted against his own amendments, which was pretty bizarre.

After interventions from Rt Hon Douglas Hogg QC MP and Rt Hon Michael Heseltine CH MP, Tony Baldry MP continued ....

Mr. Baldry: The 14 new clauses that now form part of the Bill were not before the House on Second Reading, so we are considering an entirely new Bill today. The Committee having spent so many weeks considering just line 1, the Home Office panicked and had to rewrite the Bill entirely.

Mr. Nicholas Winterton (Macclesfield): On a point of order, Mr. Deputy Speaker. I am concerned by what my hon. Friend has just said. I was under the impression that this was a private Member's Bill, yet we hear that the Home Office is responsible for a massive redraft. I hope that, in what has so far been an excellent speech, my hon. Friend the Member for Banbury (Mr. Baldry) will explain precisely what has happened for the benefit of the House, which is very interested in private Members' bills. He says that much of what we are now debating did not exist on Second Reading or in Committee. The House has a role to play in scrutinising not only what has happened, but the detail of the new clauses.

Mr. Deputy Speaker: Hon. Members may refer to those matters, but only in so far as they are relevant to the new clauses before us.

Mr. Baldry: The clauses before us are all new and, as I am sitting next to my hon. Friend the Member for Macclesfield (Mr. Winterton), who chairs the Procedure Committee, I should tell him that although the Government claim to be neutral on the Bill, when they saw that the way in which it was drafted by the hon. Member for Worcester was such a complete and utter shambles--a dog's breakfast--they felt beholden at least to put some order into it and redraft it. I suspect that it is for the Procedure Committee or some other Committee of the House to decide whether it is appropriate for the Government to profess to be neutral, while helping hon. Members by drafting their Bills.

Mr. Michael Colvin (Romsey): My hon. Friend would be the first to acknowledge that there are such things as private Members' Bills in the form of Government handouts. I took through the House a private Member's Bill that was essentially a Government Bill and assisted the Government in getting their business on the statute book, when there was not enough parliamentary time for them to do so themselves. Does my hon. Friend suggest that the Bill, in its present form, is effectively a Government handout?

Mr. Baldry: I can report only that the Bill consists almost entirely of new clauses written by parliamentary draftsmen on behalf of the Home Office. Conservative Members who, at some time, had the opportunity of serving in the previous Government, know that when Ministers introduce new clauses, they have the benefit of notes on clauses. A Committee usually has the benefit of notes on clauses, too, because, as a courtesy, Ministers make them available to members of the Committee. This situation is truly bizarre, because the Minister concerned wanted to remain neutral and did not even give the notes on clauses to the promoter of the Bill. Thus parliamentary draftsmen handed to the Minister new clauses that he did not understand, and the Minister handed the new clauses to the hon. Member for Worcester, who understood them even less, so neither was in a position to explain them to the Committee. They were totally unable to explain to the Committee the meaning of simple English legal words such as "permit" or "allow".

The debate continued and at noon Andrew Bennett MP attempted to move the Closure, but this was not permitted by the Speaker.

Mr. Bennett *rose in his place and claimed to move,* That the Question be now put, *but* Mr. Deputy Speaker *withheld his assent, and declined then to put that Question.*

Mr. Bennett: On a point of order, Mr. Deputy Speaker. I should not want in any way to challenge your ruling, but I ask you to reconsider, before one of my colleagues moves the same Question. The minority has every right to filibuster, but the majority has the right to put the Question after the debate has continued for a reasonable time. I hope that you will agree that that point is rapidly approaching.

The debate continued, but, later, Kevin McNamara MP attempted to move the Closure, to no avail.

Mr. Kevin McNamara (Hull, North) *rose in his place and claimed to move,* That the Question be now put, *but* Mr. Deputy Speaker *withheld his assent, and declined then to put that Question.*

The debate continued and eventually, Andrew Bennett MP was successful and the Closure was granted on New Clause 1 at about 12.15pm.

Mr. Bennett *rose in his place and claimed to move,* That the Question be now put.
Question put, That the Question be now put:--

The House proceeded to a Division—
Sir Peter Emery (East Devon) *(seated and covered):* On a point of order, Mr. Deputy Speaker. May I ask you to cast your eye over Standing Order No. 36(1) which clearly states that if a closure is granted, it must not infringe the rights of the minority? Five new clauses are being debated, each with an entirely different subject. That means that each subject has been granted slightly under 35 minutes, which certainly does not seem to be fair or proper. The new clauses were taken together for the convenience of the House, but that should not mean that the rights of the minority are infringed. Might I suggest, therefore, Mr. Deputy Speaker, that we call off the Division and allow the minority a little more than 35 minutes' debate on each new clause?

Mr. Deputy Speaker: The Standing Order gives the Chair the discretion to decide on these matters, and I have decided that I will accept the closure motion.

The House having divided: Ayes 186, Noes 60.

The Closure having been won, the House then voted on the Second Reading of New Clause 1.

Question put accordingly, That the clause be read a Second time:--

The House proceeded to a Division—

The House having divided: Ayes 64, Noes 187.

The Deputy Speaker was then asked if a vote would be taken on other New Clauses, which had been grouped with New Clause 1, on which they had just divided. The Deputy Speaker informed the House that a Division on any of the remaining New Clauses in the group would have to be taken after the next group of amendments.

Mr. Deputy Speaker: Order. This is turning into a debate. There is a simple point of order to be determined. It is in the Chair's discretion to decide at the appropriate time whether a separate Division is to be taken on a new clause or amendment that was part of a group. That will fall to be determined, in the case of new clause 3, after we have dealt with the next group of amendments.

The House then turned to New Clause 2.

New clause 2

Power to amend

(text of New Clause)
Brought up, and read the First time.

Mr. Luff: I beg to move, That the clause be read a Second time.

Mr. Deputy Speaker: With this, it will be convenient to discuss the following: New clause 20--*Power to amend section 1--*

(text of New Clause and Amendments 54 and 54)

Andrew Bennett MP tried to move the Closure just before 2.30pm, but the Deputy Speaker, 'withheld his assent' and as a result, the New Clause was under discussion at the Moment of Interruption at 2.30pm – the bill was therefore 'talked out' and the debate adjourned until 13 March.

Having considered new clause 2—

It being half-past Two o'clock, the debate stood adjourned.

Debate to be resumed on Friday 13 March.

The debate on New Clause 2 resumed on Friday 13 March as follows:

Orders of the Day

Wild Mammals (Hunting with Dogs) Bill

[Madam Speaker in the Chair]

As amended, further considered.

New clause 2

(text of New Clause)

Brought up, and read the First time.

Question proposed [6 March], That the clause be read a Second time.

Question again proposed.

Madam Speaker: I remind the House that we are considering new clause 2 and that this is a resumed debate. With this, it will be convenient to discuss the following: new clause 20 (text of New Clause and Amendment Nos. 53 and 54)

Mr. Edward Garnier had the Floor—

Mr. Ivor Caplin (Hove): On a point of order, Madam Speaker. I was looking at the list of selected amendments, and wondered whether you could explain to me, as a new Member, the procedure that led to new clause 35, tabled by my hon. Friend the Member for Worcester (Mr. Foster), not being selected for debate today.

Madam Speaker: I appreciate that, as a new Member, the hon. Gentleman may not understand that the Speaker does not give reasons for non-selection or selection. The Standing Order gives the Speaker complete discretion over the selection of amendments. However, following the tabling of amendments, including new clause 35, on Wednesday evening, I am prepared to tell the House the general principles that I take into account in coming to a decision. The power of selection exists to prevent repetition and to secure reasonable opportunities for the expression of all varieties of opinion in an orderly manner. Exercising the power in this instance was something to which I have given much anxious thought over the past 24 hours. Many hon. Members would have been disappointed whatever decision I reached on the selection of new clause 35, but I have tried to act in the best interests of this debate, and, of course, in the very best interests of the House of Commons.

Later in the debate, Andrew Bennett MP moved the Closure.

Mr. Andrew F. Bennett (Denton and Reddish) *rose in his place and claimed to move,* That the Question be now put.

Mr. Nick Hawkins (Surrey Heath): On a point of order, Mr. Deputy Speaker. Several of my hon. Friends and myself have sat throughout the whole debate on the clauses—

Mr. Deputy Speaker (Sir Alan Haselhurst): Order. Accepting or refusing a motion on closure is entirely a matter for the Chair, and is not a matter of argument.

Question put, That the Question be now put:--

The House proceeded to a Division—

Mr. Denis MacShane (Rotherham) (*seated and covered*): On a point of order, Mr. Deputy Speaker. I am making this point of order, wearing this ludicrous hat, so as not to take up debating time. Can you give me guidance? In the light of last week's filibustering, and the unspeakable behaviour of the Tories, who pursued indefensible tactics against the will of the people and of Parliament, do you have power under the procedures laid down in *Erskine May* to ensure that debate on the Bill is completed by 2.30 pm, and that it passes to the House of Lords?

Mr. Deputy Speaker: The hon. Gentleman knows that he is expecting far too much of the powers of the Chair. The Chair presides over the orderly conduct of debate, according to well accepted rules. We shall make such progress as is possible, according to how many hon. Members seek to catch my eye, and the manner in which they pursue the discussion of the content of the groups of amendments that are before us. We shall proceed through the amendments in an orderly manner--there is no short cut that the Chair can impose.

The House having divided: Ayes 132, Noes 42.

Question put accordingly, That the clause be read a Second time:--

The House divided: Ayes 44, Noes 136.

At this point the House divided on New Clause 3, which had been grouped with New Clause 1, in the first group of amendments to be considered.

New Clause 3

Mink
(text of New Clause)

Brought up, and read the First time.

Motion made, and Question put, That the clause be read a Second time:--

The House proceeded to a Division—

The House having divided: Ayes 42, Noes 139.

New Clause 6

(text of New Clause)

Brought up, and read the First time.

Motion made, and Question put, That the clause be read a Second time:--

The House divided: Ayes 43, Noes 138.

The debate then continued with the next group of New Clauses, lead by New Clause 18.

New Clause 18

(text of New Clause)

Brought up, and read the First time.

Mr. Ken Maginnis (Fermanagh and South Tyrone): I beg to move, That the clause be read a Second time.
Mr. Deputy Speaker: With this, it will be convenient to discuss the following: New clause 32--*Incidental hunting in Northern Ireland—*

Mr. Michael J. Foster: Having considered new clause 18, on this occasion I am perfectly willing to accept it.

Mr. Maginnis: I am heartened that common sense is to prevail, but for the benefit—

Mr. Gray: The hon. Member for Worcester (Mr. Foster) may be prepared to accept new clause 18 but I am not, and I shall happily try to speak to that effect shortly.

Mr. Maginnis: I shall try to proceed at least to the stage where I have read the new clause.

The debate continued until Andrew Bennett MP attempted to move the Closure at 12.15pm.

Mr. Bennett: On a point of order, Mr. Deputy Speaker. I beg to move, That the Question be now put.

Mr. Deputy Speaker: I am afraid that I cannot take a closure at this point.

At 12.45 pm Kevin McNamara MP moved the Closure.

Mr. McNamara *rose in his place and claimed to move,* That the Question be now put, *but* Mr. Deputy Speaker *withheld his assent, and declined then to put that Question.*

A little later, the Speaker allowed the Closure (moved by Andrew Bennett MP).

Mr. Bennett *rose in his place and claimed to move,* That the Question be now put.
Question put, That the Question be now put:--

The House divided: Ayes 150, Noes 40.

Question put accordingly, That the clause be read a Second time:--

The House divided: Ayes 31, Noes 154.

The House then proceeded to Divisions on others of the New Clauses grouped with New Clause 1.

New Clause 19

(text of New Clause)

Brought up, and read the First time.
Motion made, and Question put, That the clause be read a Second time:--

The House divided: Ayes 42, Noes 128.

Mr. Kenneth Clarke (Rushcliffe): On a point of order, Mr. Deputy Speaker. While the Minister is reflecting on that, may I ask whether you would allow a vote on new clause 20 if it were now to be moved formally? It was selected for debate by Madam Speaker and formed part of the subject matter of our longest debate so far today. I know that we have already had a debate on new clause 2, but the substance of new clause 20 is different, as the former would have allowed the activities defined in the Bill to be reduced by an order of the Secretary of State, whereas the latter would simply allow the definitions to be changed if they proved inaccurate. On that basis, I think that the opinion of the House should be tested, and I wonder whether you will allow a vote.

Mr. Hawkins *rose—*

Mr. Deputy Speaker: Order.

Mr. Hawkins: It is further to the point of order, Mr. Deputy Speaker.

Mr. Deputy Speaker: Order. Let me answer the point of order. It is for the Chair to decide whether to allow a vote, and I have decided that we will not have a vote on the matter. We must move on to the next new clause.

The debate then moved on to the next group of New Clauses, headed by New Clause 21.

New Clause 21

Local Referendums
(text of New Clause)

Brought up, and read the First time.

Mr. Öpik: I beg to move, That the clause be read a Second time.

Mr. Deputy Speaker: With this, it will be convenient to discuss amendment No. 97, in clause 14, page 5, line 34, leave out from 'force' to end of line 35 and insert 'upon the making of an order by the Secretary of State which shall be made by statutory instrument and shall not be made unless a draft has been approved by each House of Parliament.

Debate continued until 2.30pm and was effectively 'talked out'. The debate was therefore adjourned.

It being half-past Two o'clock, the debate stood adjourned.

Debate to be resumed on Friday 20 March.

In fact, debate was not resumed on 20 March and the bill was later withdrawn.

Mental Health (Amendment) Bill 1997/98

The Mental Health (Amendment) Bill was scheduled for Second Reading on 12 December 1997. The bill was talked out and debate adjourned until 16 January 1998. The Order for Second Reading was read out at 2.30pm, but Members objected and the Second Reading was therefore adjourned until 23 January. On 23 January Members again objected and the Second Reading was again adjourned, this time until 30 January. On this occasion the Second Reading was not moved and the bill therefore became a 'dropped order'.

Energy Efficiency Bill 1997/98

The Energy Efficiency Bill was debated in Standing Committee C on 25 March 1998. It was set down for consideration (Report Stage) on 24 April, but Eric Forth MP objected to the Order for consideration, which was read out at 2.30pm, and as a result, this stage of the bill's proceedings was adjourned until 3 July – the last Private Members' Friday of the 1997/98 Session.

ENERGY EFFICIENCY BILL

Order read for consideration (as amended in the Standing Committee).
Hon. Members: Object.
Mr. Colin Breed (South-East Cornwall): On a point of order, Mr. Deputy Speaker. Is it in order for the right hon. Member for Bromley and Chislehurst (Mr. Forth) to object to the Bill and impose his will on the House, when the Bill has the support of his Front Bench and of the Government?
Mr. Deputy Speaker (Mr. Michael Lord): It is quite in order for the right hon. Gentleman to object in that way.
To be considered on Friday 3 July.

On 3 July, the bill was objected to again.

ENERGY EFFICIENCY BILL

Order read for consideration (as amended in the Standing Committee).
Hon. Members: Object.
To be considered upon Monday 6 July 1998.
Whilst consideration was set down for another day (6 July) the bill had effectively run out of time as 6 July was not a day on which Private Members' Bills had precedence.

Private Hire Vehicles (London) Bill 1997/98

The Private Hire Vehicles (London) Bill had its Second Reading on 23 January 1998 and was originally set down for a Committee of the Whole House on 6 February 1998, but this had to be deferred until 20 March to allow a Money Resolution and a Ways and Means Resolution to be passed by the House. These are necessary where a bill intends to impose charges or requires public spending of some sort. These resolutions were passed on 16 March 1998 and Committee Stage was scheduled for 20 March. Eric Forth objected to the Order for Consideration and Consideration was therefore adjourned until the next available Private Members' Friday, 27 March. However, Eric Forth objected once again and the bill was once again adjourned – until 24 April. Eric Forth again objected to the Order for Consideration, which was therefore adjourned until 3 July. However, this was the last Private Members' Friday and there were concerns that should the bill be objected to again, it would be lost for the Session. As this was a measure that the Government supported, it agreed to allocate the bill to Standing Committee D, which met on 23 June 1998. The bill was given a formal Third Reading on 3 July and was sent to the House of Lords, eventually receiving Royal Assent on 28 July 1998.

TEN MINUTE RULE BILLS

The words, 'Notice of Motion for Leave to Bring in a Bill', denote a Ten Minute Rule bill on the Order Paper. These bills are brought in under SO 23 and the House has to 'give leave' – agree - to their First Reading. Bills introduced under this order are not, in general, serious attempts at legislation. The procedure allows an MP to introduce a bill after questions at 3.30pm (this may in fact be later if there has been a previous Private Notice Question (PNQ) or statement) on a Tuesday or Wednesday after the fifth Wednesday of the Session. This is designed to give the balloted bills a head start. They are set down for Second Readings before any Ten Minute Rule Bills or SO 57 bills.

SO 23 allows the Member presenting the bill a ten minute speech in which to extoll the virtues of the bill; this is followed by a short speech from a Member who opposes it. Ten Minute Rule Bills are sometimes divided on. For example, Joe Ashton MP attempted to introduce a bill under SO 23 on 10 December 1997 which would have permitted euthanasia under certain circumstances. The 'motion for leave' was defeated on a Division. If a Member is not 'given leave' to bring in a Ten Minute Rule bill it is treated as having been rejected and the same bill cannot be introduced again in the same Session.

Doctor Assisted Dying

4.14 pm

Mr. Joe Ashton (Bassetlaw): I beg to move,

> That leave be given to bring in a Bill to enable a person who is suffering distress as a result of his terminal illness or incurable physical condition to obtain assistance from a doctor to end his life; and for connected purposes.

After Joe Ashton had proposed his measure, Kevin McNamara opposed the motion to bring in the bill and the House divided:

Question put, pursuant to Standing Order No. 23 (Motions for leave to bring in Bills and nomination of Select Committees at commencement of public business):--

The House divided: Ayes 89, Noes 234.

A Motion for Leave to Bring in a bill must be placed in the Public Bill Office by the Member concerned, or another MP acting on his behalf, by 10.00am on a Tuesday or Wednesday for a Tuesday or Wednesday between the fifth and the fifteenth sitting day after that day. In practice what this means is that MPs table Ten Minute Rule Bills (technically they table a 'Motion for Leave to Bring in a Bill') on Tuesdays and Wednesdays for those days three weeks later. There would be no point in trying to table a Ten Minute Rule bill for the following Tuesday as this slot would already have been filled two weeks previously by another Member. There is great competition for Ten Minute Rule Bills and Members often queue up all night in order to be the first through the door of the Public Bill Office on a Tuesday or Wednesday morning. There can only be one Ten Minute Rule bill on each of the relevant Tuesdays and Wednesdays. Under Standing Order 23(3) no Ten Minute Rule Bills are allowed on Budget Day. If a bill is tabled for this day, it is transferred to the first Monday on which the House sits after the Budget debate is opened.

When the Order of Leave to Bring in a Bill has been granted it is presented to the House by one of the Members acting as sponsor. The Speaker asks: 'who will prepare and bring in the Bill?'. The Member in charge reads the names of the Members, concluding with his own. A dummy bill is obtained from the Public Bill Office and on his name being called by the Speaker, the Member proceeds to the Table, bowing three times before handing the bill to the Clerk of the House who reads the Short Title aloud. This constitutes the First Reading of the Bill.

Ten Minute Rule Bills are only printed after they have received a First Reading, and then only if the Member promoting the bill feels it to be worthwhile. Once a Ten Minute Rule Bill has been presented and had its First Reading, it joins the back of the queue for Private Members' Bills on one of the Fridays. On that Friday, it is unlikely to be reached until 2.30pm and its Second Reading will be adjourned until a future Friday, etc. until it eventually runs out of parliamentary time.

BILLS INTRODUCED UNDER SO 57

SO 57 allows a backbench MP to introduce a bill at any time 'without leave'; i.e. unlike Ten Minute Rule Bills, First Reading does not require the agreement of the House. Bills introduced in this way are not high up on the list on Second Reading Fridays and there is little practical likelihood of their being debated. SO 57 can be used by a backbench MP to take up a Private Member's Bill from the House of Lords, but in this case the First Reading is the day on which the MP informs the Public Bill Office of his or her intention to take up the bill. It is then set down for Second Reading, but not before the 5th Wednesday of the Session (SO 14). SO 57 Bills are presented at the beginning of public business in the House of Commons and are not debated. They should not be confused with Ten Minute Rule Bills, where 'leave' has been given to bring in a bill under SO 23. Where a bill is being presented under SO 57, the words used on the Order Paper are: 'Notice of Presentation of Bill'. All the MP presenting the bill has to do is to give the long and short title of the bill to the Public Bill Office before the rising of the House the day before he intends to present the bill. They are sometimes referred to as 'Ordinary Presentation Bills'.

PRIVATE MEMBERS' DEBATES

Wednesday Mornings

The House sits on Wednesdays from 9.30am until 2.00pm,[2] at which point the House is then adjourned until 2.30pm. These Wednesday morning debates are technically taken in Government time and are proceeded with on a 'Motion for the adjournment of the House made by Minister of the Crown (SO 10(1)). Subjects for debate on Wednesday mornings are decided by a ballot held on the preceding Wednesday.

Members must ensure that their applications are with the Speaker's Office on the day before (Tuesday) by 10.00pm or the rising of the House (whichever is earlier). Members successful in the ballot in one week cannot enter the following week's ballot. Members can enter both the ballot for the Wednesday Adjournment debates and the ballot for Daily Adjournment debates; however, if they succeed in one ballot, they cannot be successful in the other.

The times of the debates are set out in SO 10 (5) and are as follows:

9.30am until 11.00am
11.00am until 12.30pm
12.30pm until 1.00pm

---

[2] New procedures for sittings for the House were introduced on an experimental basis by Sessional Order at the beginning of the 1994/5 Session of Parliament (HC: Col 1456 to 1509 - 19 December 1994). These were then confirmed by way of amendments to Standing Orders at the beginning of the 1995/6 Session (HC: Col 405 to 450 - 2 November 1995). Balloted Private Members' motions were dispensed with. Under the old system, ballots were held roughly two weeks before the relevant dates for Private Members' motions, which were set down in a resolution put before the House early in the Session. There used to be ten Fridays (on average) each Session and two half days (Mondays) set aside for Private Members' Motions. Members wishing to participate had to sign a ballot paper placed in the No Lobby. These motions have now been superseded by Wednesday morning debates. Adjournment Debates following Consolidated Fund Bills, Adjournment Debates fixing dates of recesses and Adjournment Debates on the last day before each recess were dispensed with and in exchange, alternative time was given to Private Members' debates on Wednesday mornings. As Private Members' motions on Fridays were dispensed with, those Fridays instead became 'constituency' or 'non sitting' Fridays. There are 10 such Fridays each Session as set out in SO 12.

1.00pm until 1.30pm
1.30pm until 2.00pm

By convention, other Members can only intervene in the Wednesday morning half-hour debates with the agreement of the Member initating the debate and the Minister responding (the same principles applies to Daily Adjourment Debates) but other Members may participate in the one and a half hour debates.

So 10(5) provides that on three Wednesdays in each Session, the period between 9.30pm and 12.30pm should be given over to debate on reports from Select Committees as chosen by the Liaison Committee (a Select Committee consisting of all the Chairmen of the Departmental Select Committees). On the final Wednesday before a holiday adjournment, the period from 9.30am until 12.30pm is set aside for debate on 'matters to be raised before the forthcoming adjournment' (this is basically a general debate).

An example of the variety of subjects debated on Wednesday mornings is set out below, from Wednesday, 13 January 1998. A Motion for the Adjournment of the House (on which these Private Members' Debates arise) can only be moved by a Government Minister, hence the motion at the beginning of the morning's proceedings:

Motion made, and Question proposed, That this House do now adjourn.--[*Mr. Mike Hall.*]

The following subjects were debated:

9.33am	**Nurses, Midwives and Health Visitors** - Simon Hughes MP (LibDem - Southwark, North and Bermondsey)
11.00am	**Select Committee Reform** - Andrew Mackinlay MP (Lab – Thurrock)
12.30pm	**Post Office** - Richard Page MP (Con – Hertfordshire South-West)
1.00pm	**Visitors' Visas** - Keith Vaz MP (Lab – Leicester East)
1.30pm	**George Atkinson** - Desmond Swayne MP (Con– New Forest West)

Daily Adjournment Debates

In the dim and distant past, any MP could move a motion at any time 'that the House should adjourn'. Irish MPs made a habit of using this to obstruct Government business. In 1882 a Standing Order was passed to restrict this practice and by 1945 the present system was in place. Under SO 9(7) the House can only be adjourned by a resolution proposed by a Government Minister, or by the Speaker under SO 46. However, SO 9(7) stipulates that when such a resolution is proposed at or after 10.00pm (or 2.30pm on a Friday, or 7.00pm on a Thursday) debate may take place for up to half an hour, after which time the House is automatically adjourned. The subjects of these Daily Adjournment debates are chosen by ballot, except for Thursdays when the Speaker chooses the subject for debate. In their Second Report of the 1998/99 Session, the Select Committee on Modernisation of the House of Commons alludes to evidence from the Speaker's Officer that there are five applications for each daily adjournment debate (seven for each Wednesday morning half-hour debate and ten for each Wednesday morning one and a half hour debate). Names of successful Members usually appear on the Order Paper on Friday. The ballot is held on Thursday and applications must be handed in writing to the Speaker's Office by 10.00pm on the preceding Wednesday, or the rising of the House if earlier. If a member is successful in the ballot he or she may not enter next week's ballot. If a member wishes to change the subject of his or her Adjournment debate, 48 hours notice is required. If he or she no longer wishes to discuss the subject originally chosen and cannot give 48 hours notice of a change of subject matter, his or her right to have the Adjournment debate lapses. The subject matter of the debate on a Thursday cannot be altered without the Speaker's consent. Members may not swop Adjournment dates. When Members enter the ballot for Daily Adjournment debates they have to declare any relevant interest.

Daily Adjournment debates provide a useful opportunity for a Member to raise a matter which otherwise might not receive a hearing in the House and, additionally, to receive a response from a Government Minister. As these debates are the last item of business at each sitting, frequently the only Members present are the Member whose debate it is and the Minister replying on behalf of the Government. In fact, the Speaker will usually only allow other Members to intervene if both the Member whose debate it is and the Minister replying agree to it. If all the business for that day is concluded before the Moment of Interruption, the Adjournment Motion is moved by a Member of the Government and the Daily Adjournment debate scheduled for 10.00pm (or 2.30pm or 7.00pm) begins immediately. It then continues until the Moment of Interruption at which point the Adjournment motion lapses and another Adjournment Motion is moved (which can be debated for half an hour). Debate continues on the same subject which was under discussion at the Moment of Interruption. For example, if the day's business ended at 9.00pm, an Adjournment Motion would be moved by a Government Minister. The subject debated on this motion would be the subject of that day's balloted Daily Adjournment motion; for example, Primary Education in Croydon. The debate would continue until 10.00pm at which point another Adjournment motion would be moved. The subject debated would be the same; i.e. Primary Education in Croydon.

If a Ministerial Statement is to be made after business has been completed it has the effect of supplanting the Adjournment Debate. If all the business of the day is concluded early a Government Minister will immediately move the Adjournment.

An example of a typical Daily Adjournment debate is set out below:

At the end of the sitting:

5ADJOURNMENT
Proposed subject: ***Telecommunication installations in residential areas*** *(Mr Phil Willis).*
Debate may continue until 10.30 p.m. or for half an hour, whichever is later (Standing Order No. 9).

There are certain rules which apply to all types of Adjournment Motion and these are:

- Adjournment Motions may not be on subjects already set down as Orders or Notices; for example, if a Member already has a motion down on the Notice Paper to discuss the extinction of the Rusty Numbat, another Member could not raise the matter on an Adjournment Motion, however important he or she felt it to be. Nor could a Member use a Wednesday morning Adjournment Debate to oppose a Government Bill whose Second Reading was to take place that afternoon. He or she would also be prevented from using such a debate as an opportunity to promote a colleague's Private Member's Bill, due for Second Reading the following Friday.
- Adjournment Motions should not be on matters which require legislation, but the possibility of legislation can be mentioned during the debate on such a motion. The distinction to be made is between an Adjournment Debate whose prime purpose is to call for legislative action and one which mentions legislation only incidentally.
- Adjournment Motions must be on matters for which the Government has responsibility.
- Adjournment Motions must not be on matters which can only be debated on a 'substantive motion' which allows the House to make a decision.
- Adjournment Motions must not be on subjects which have already been debated that day.

Emergency Debates (SO 24)

This form of Adjournment Motion enables a Member to propose the discussion of an urgent and important matter. These motions are proposed at the beginning of public business (Mondays to Thursdays) and the Member proposing the Motion is allowed three minutes to make his case. If the Speaker agrees that the matter should be discussed the Member can either obtain the leave of the House or, if this is refused, the agreement of 40 Members rising in their places to support the Motion. If there are fewer than 40 but more than 10 MPs, a Division is called. If the Speaker considers the matter urgent enough it may be debated at 7.00pm the same day, if not, it is held over until the commencement of public business on the following day and is debated for three hours. An application for a SO 24 debate must be given to the Speaker's Office by 12 noon, but if a particularly dramatic event occurs after that hour, applications should be made to the Speaker as soon as is practicable. The Speaker can defer a decision until a suitable break in that day's proceedings. The Speaker does not have to give her/his reasons for refusing an application under SO 24 .

PROGRESS OF PRIVATE MEMBERS' BILLS IN THE 1996/97 AND 1997/98 SESSIONS

Progress of Balloted Private Members' Bills in the 1996/97 Session

First Reading means that the bill was given a First Reading in the House but then failed to progress any further - the bill was either not printed, in which case the Order for Second Reading lapses, or no day was named for Second Reading – it was 'dropped', or it ran out of time, in which case it is also said to have been 'dropped'.

Bill	***Introduced by***	***Place in Ballot***	***Stage Reached***
Knives	Jimmy Wray MP	1	Royal Assent
Public Entertainments Licences (Drug Misuse)	Barry Legg MP	2	Royal Assent
Confiscation of Alcohol (Young Persons)	Dr Robert Spink MP	3	Royal Assent
Jurisdiction (Conspiracy and Incitement)	Nigel Waterson MP	4	Third Reading (abandoned through lack of quorum)
Cold Weather Payments (Wind Chill Factor)	Audrey Wise MP	5	Second Reading (debate adjourned)
Prisons (Alcohol Testing)	John Ward MP	6	Royal Assent
Road Traffic (Reduction)	Don Foster MP	7	Royal Assent
Criminal Evidence (Amendment)	Nigel Evans MP	8	Royal Assent
Telecommunications (Fraud)	Ian Bruce MP	9	Royal Assent
United Nations Personnel	John Marshall MP	10	Royal Assent
General Teaching Council (England and Wales)	Sir Malcolm Thornton MP	11	First Reading
Local Government (Gaelic Names) (Scotland)	Tommy Graham MP	12	Royal Assent
Human Fertilisation and Embryology (Consents)	Anne Campbell MP	13	Bill withdrawn after First Reading
Witness Protection	Irene Adams MP	14	Second Reading (debate adjourned)
Police (Health and Safety)	Sir Ray Whitney MP	15	Royal Assent
Sexual Offences (Protected Material)	Robert G Hughes MP	16	Royal Assent
Breeding and Sale of Dogs	Diana Maddock MP	17	First Reading
Policyholders Protection	John Butterfill MP	18	Royal Assent
Police (Property)	David Evennett MP	19	Royal Assent
Pharmacists (Fitness to Practise)	Sir Michael Shersby MP	20	Royal Assent

14 out of the 20 balloted Private Member's Bills received Royal Assent.

Progress of Ten Minute Rule Bills in the 1996/97 Session

First Reading means that the bill was given a First Reading in the House but then failed to progress any further - the bill was either not printed, in which case the Order for Second Reading lapses, or no day was named for Second Reading – it was 'dropped', or it ran out of time, in which case it is also said to have been 'dropped'.

Bill	***Introduced by***	***Stage Reached***
Abortion (Amendment)	David Amess MP	First Reading
Adoptive Mothers (Maternity Leave)	Margaret Hodge MP	First Reading
Age Discrimination	Quentin Davies MP	First Reading
Airports and Aerodromes (Noise)	Jim Cunningham MP	First Reading
Building Societies (Distributions)	Douglas French MP	Royal Assent
Bull Bars (Prohibition)	Paul Flynn MP	First Reading
Civil Actions (Limit on Proceedings)	Andrew Robathan MP	First Reading
Companies (Millennium Computer Compliance)	David Atkinson MP	Report Stage (debate adjourned)
Constitutional Change	Bill Walker MP	First Reading
Fire Safety	John Heppell MP	First Reading
Holocaust Denial	Mike Gapes MP	Committee
House Numbering and Home Delivery	Tim Devlin MP	First Reading
Licensing (Reform)	Paddy Tipping MP	First Reading
Local Authorities (Youth Expenditure)	Andrew Rowe MP	Bill withdrawn after First Reading
Local Government (Conduct of Officers)	Chris Davies MP	First Reading
National Lottery (Regionalisation)	Ian Pearson MP	First Reading
Overseas Development and Co-operation	Hugh Bayley MP	First Reading
Partial-Birth Abortion	Elizabeth Peacock MP	First Reading
Political Fundraising	David Winnick MP	First Reading
Rights at Work and in Retirement	Andrew Mackinlay MP	First Reading
School Intruders (Criminal Offence)	Peter Butler MP	First Reading
Statute Law Balancing (Limit on Maximum Quantity)	Anthony Steen MP	First Reading
UK Membership of European Union (Research)	Hartley Booth MP	First Reading
UK Membership of the EU (Referendum)	Teresa Gorman MP	First Reading
Victims of Crime	Walter Sweeney MP	First Reading
Warm Homes and Energy Conservation (15 Year Programme)	Alan Simpson MP	First Reading

One Ten Minute Rule Bill received Royal Assent.

Progress of SO 57 Bills in the 1996/97 Session

First Reading means that the bill was given a First Reading in the House but then failed to progress any further - the bill was either not printed, in which case the Order for Second Reading lapses, or no day was named for Second Reading – it was 'dropped', or it ran out of time, in which case it is also said to have been 'dropped'.

Bill	*Introduced by*	*Stage Reached*
Abolition of Pharmaceutical Monopolies in Rural Areas	William Cash MP	First Reading
Access to the Countryside	Paddy Tipping MP	First Reading
Dartford-Thurrock Crossing (Amendment)	Andrew Mackinlay MP	Referred to Examiners
Disabled Persons and Carers (Short-Term Breaks)	Rt Hon Alf Morris MP	First Reading
Dogs (Electric Shock Collars)	David Rendel MP	First Reading
European Communities (Amendment) (No. 2)	Rt Hon Tony Benn MP	First Reading
Government Communications Headquarters (Restoration of Trade Union Rights)	David Winnick MP	First Reading
Government of Wales	Dr John Marek MP	First Reading
Great Apes (Prohibition of Experiments)	Tony Banks MP	First Reading
Human Tissue (Amendment)	John Marshall MP	Second Reading (debate adjourned)
Mental Health (Joint Commissioning Consortia)	Peter Thurnham MP	First Reading
Parking Penalty Charge	Piers Merchant MP	Second Reading (debate adjourned)
Pensioner Trustees	Brian Jenkins MP	First Reading
Regulation of Diet Industry	Alice Mahon MP	First Reading
Representation of the People (Amendment)	Paul Flynn MP	First Reading
Residential Homes	David Congdon MP	First Reading
Right to Work	Sir Ralph Howell MP	First Reading
Road Traffic Speed Limit Reduction	Chris Davies MP	First Reading
Sale of Medicines (Young People)	Paul Flynn MP	First Reading
Single Homeless Persons (Scotland)	Andrew Welsh MP	First Reading
Town Centres (Insurance and Restoration)	Rt Hon Dafydd Wigley MP	First Reading
War Widows and Pensioners (Equal Treatment)	Simon Hughes MP	First Reading
Waste Prevention	Gary Waller MP	Committee Stage

No SO 57 Bill received Royal Assent.

Progress of Balloted Private Members' Bills in the 1997/98 Session

First Reading means that the bill was given a First Reading in the House but then failed to progress any further - the bill was either not printed, in which case the Order for Second Reading lapses, or no day was named for Second Reading – it was 'dropped', or it ran out of time, in which case it is also said to have been 'dropped'.

Bill	***Introduced by***	***Place in Ballot***	***Stage Reached***
Wild Mammals (Hunting with Dogs)	Michael Foster MP	1	Report Stage (debate adjourned)
Mental Health (Amendment)	Dr Julian Lewis MP	2	Second Reading (debate adjourned)
Referendum (English Parliament)	Teresa Gorman MP	3	Second Reading (debate adjourned)
Private Hire Vehicles (London)	Rt Hon Sir George Young Bt MP	4	Royal Assent
Road Traffic Reduction (National Targets)	Cynog Dafis MP	5	Royal Assent
Energy Efficiency	John Burnett MP	6	Standing Committee
Employment of Children	Chris Pond MP	7	Bill withdrawn at end of Second Reading debate
Cold Weather Payments (Wind Chill Factor)	Nigel Evans MP	8	Second Reading (debate adjourned)
Employment (Age Discrimination in Advertisements)	Linda Perham MP	9	Second Reading (debate adjourned)
Public Interest Disclosure	Richard Shepherd	10	Royal Assent
Breeding and Sale of Dogs	Mike Hall MP	11	Standing Committee
Disability Rights Commission	Roger Berry MP	12	First Reading
Company and Business names (Chamber of Commerce, etc)	Michael Trend MP	13	Report Stage
Community Care (Residential Accommodation)	Marsha Singh MP	14	Royal Assent
Local Authority Tenders	Oona King MP	15	Report Stage (debate adjourned)
Waste Prevention	Piers Merchant MP	16	First Reading
Pesticides	Ben Bradshaw MP	17	Royal Assent
Energy Conservation (Housing)	Clive Efford MP	18	Report Stage
Fireworks	Linda Gilroy MP	19	Lords Amendments (debate adjourned)
Weights and Measures (Beer and Cider)	Dennis Turner MP	20	Standing Committee

Five of the 20 balloted bills received Royal Assent.

Progress of Ten Minute Rule Bills in the 1997/98 Session

First Reading means that the bill was given a First Reading in the House but then failed to progress any further - the bill was either not printed, in which case the Order for Second Reading lapses, or no day was named for Second Reading – it was 'dropped', or it ran out of time, in which case it is also said to have been 'dropped'.

Bill	***Introduced by***	***Stage Reached***
Access to the Countryside	Paddy Tipping MP	First Reading
Acquisition and Possession of Air Weapons (Restriction)	Dr Nick Palmer MP	First Reading
Adoption and Fostering	Julian Brazier MP	First Reading
Adoption (League Tables)	Julian Brazier MP	First Reading
Animal Health (Amendment)	Paul Flynn MP	Royal Assent
British Museum (Lindisfarne Gospels)	Fraser Kemp MP	First Reading
Building Societies (Joint Account Holders)	John Healey MP	First Reading
Children's Nurseries (Safety)	Lindsay Hoyle MP	First Reading
Cities (Process and Criteria for Designation)	Jane Griffiths MP	First Reading
Community Reinvestment Disclosure	Tony Colman MP	First Reading
Companies (Millennium Computer Compliance)	David Atkinson MP	First Reading
Companies (Political Funds)	Roger Godsiff MP	First Reading
Concessionary Television Licence (Amendment)	John Swinney MP	First Reading
Conduct of Referendums	Eleanor Laing MP	First Reading
Countryside Protection (Landfill and Opencast Mining)	David Taylor MP	First Reading
Crown Estate (Amendment)	James Wallace MP	First Reading
Deregulation of Racecourses	Laurence Robertson MP	First Reading
Disability Discrimination (Provision of Voting Facilities)	John Heppell MP	First Reading
Disabled Persons and Carers (Short-Term Breaks)	Huw Edwards MP	First Reading
Disposal and Re-use of White Goods	Dr Alan Whitehead MP	First Reading
Doctor Assisted Dying Bill	Joe Ashton MP	Motion for Leave to Bring in Bill defeated
Doors Supervisors (Registration)	Dr Phyllis Starkey MP	First Reading
Drinks Containers (Redemption)	Christopher Leslie MP	First Reading
Education (School Parenting Role)	Michael Fabricant MP	First Reading
Electricity (Maintenance of Supplies)	Rt Hon Dafydd Wigley MP	First Reading
Electro-Convulsive Therapy (Restrictions on Use)	John Gunnell MP	First Reading
Empty Homes (Value Added Tax)	Jonathan Shaw MP	First Reading
Energy Efficiency (Information)	Julia Drown MP	First Reading
Film Classification Accountability and Openness	Julian Brazier MP	First Reading
Flood Warnings (Vulnerable Properties)	Sally Keeble MP	First Reading
Football Sponsorship Levy	Gillian Merron MP	First Reading
Freedom of Information	Andrew Mackinlay MP	First Reading

Bill	*Introduced by*	*Stage Reached*
Hairdressers Registration (Amendment)	Austin Mitchell MP	First Reading
Hare Coursing	Colin Pickthall MP	First Reading
Home Zones	Helen Brinton MP	First Reading
Housing (Home Repossessions)	Adrian Sanders MP	First Reading
Housing Service Charges (Amendment)	Barry Gardiner MP	First Reading
International Bribery and Corruption	Hugh Bayley MP	First Reading
Labelling of Products	Vernon Coaker MP	First Reading
Lead in Paint (Health and Safety)	Melanie Johnson MP	First Reading
Legal Aid (Reform)	John Bercow MP	First Reading
Legal Reform	Austin Mitchell MP	First Reading
Local Exchange Trading Schemes	Linda Gilroy MP	First Reading
Local Government Boundary Changes (Referendum)	Ronnie Fearn MP	First Reading
Local Government (Consultation with Young People)	Dr Ashok Kumar MP	First Reading
Millennium Conformity	David Atkinson MP	First Reading
Motor Accident Injury Compensation	Dr Desmond Turner MP	First Reading
National Health Service (Equity of Funding)	Andrew George MP	First Reading
National Transport Safety	Gwyneth Dunwoody MP	First Reading
Organ Donation	Dr Evan Harris MP	First Reading
Parliamentary Boundary Commissions (Amendment)	Richard Page MP	First Reading
Parliamentary Currency Commission	Michael Fabricant MP	First Reading
Ports of Entry (Special Status) (No.2)	Gwyn Prosser	First Reading
Press Complaints Commission	Antony Steen MP	First Reading
Prevention of Delay in Trials	Anne McIntosh MP	First Reading
Prohibition of Bull Bars	Richard Spring MP	First Reading
Prostitutes' Advertisements (Public Telephone Boxes)	Karen Buck MP	First Reading
Protection of Animals (Amendment)	Dr Nick Palmer MP	First Reading
Reform of Quarantine Regulations	David Amess MP	First Reading
Registration of Dogs	Richard Allan MP	First Reading
Registration of Nannies	Keith Vaz MP	First Reading
Regulation of Wet Bikes	Gareth Thomas MP	First Reading
Religious Discrimination and Remedies	John Austin MP	First Reading
Remission of Third World Debt (Jubilee 2000)	William Cash MP	First Reading
Representation of the People (Amendment)	Harry Barnes MP	First Reading
Restoration of Damage to Sites of Special Scientific Interest	Candy Atherton MP	First Reading
Road Traffic Reduction (National Targets) (Amendment)	Tom Brake MP	First Reading
Rural and Community Hospitals	David Prior MP	First Reading
Sale of Alcohol to Young Persons (Prohibition)	Paul Truswell MP	First Reading

Bill	***Introduced by***	***Stage Reached***
School Absenteeism	Harry Cohen MP	First Reading
School Buses (Safety)	Malcolm Bruce MP	First Reading
School Children's Clothing and Footwear (Value Added Tax)	Tim Loughton MP	First Reading
School Transport	Dr George Turner MP	First Reading
Stakeholder Pension	Frank Field MP	First Reading
Television Licence Payments (Age Exemption)	Howard Flight MP	First Reading
Temporary Classrooms	David Heath MP	First Reading
Town and Country Planning (Amendment)	Elfyn Llwyd MP	First Reading
United Kingdom Passports	Howard Flight MP	First Reading
Unsolicited Facsimile Messages	Christopher Fraser MP	First Reading
Voluntary Personal Security Cards	David Amess MP	First Reading
War Memorials Preservation	David Maclean MP	First Reading
War Widows and Pensioners (Equal Treatment)	Andrew Mackinlay MP	First Reading
Water Charges (Amendment)	Colin Breed MP	First Reading
Water Industry (Amendment)	David Kidney MP	First Reading
Welfare of Broiler Chickens	Bill Etherington MP	First Reading
Welfare of Pigs	Chris Mullin MP	First Reading
Youth Parliament	Andrew Rowe MP	First Reading

One Ten Minute Rule Bill received Royal Assent.

Progress of SO 57 Bills in the 1997/98 Session

First Reading means that the bill was given a First Reading in the House but then failed to progress any further - the bill was either not printed, in which case the Order for Second Reading lapses, or no day was named for Second Reading – it was 'dropped', or it ran out of time, in which case it is also said to have been 'dropped'.

Bill	***Introduced by***	***Stage Reached***
Elections (Visually Impaired Voters)	Paul Burstow MP	First Reading
Farming of Animals for Fur (Prohibition)	Norman Baker MP	First Reading
Financial Services (Ethical Considerations)	Tony Colman MP	First Reading
Housing Service Charges (Amendment) (No.2)	Barry Gardiner MP	First Reading
Internet (Dissemination of Child Pornography)	Ann Winterton MP	First Reading
Licensing (Amendment)	Paul Truswell MP	Standing Committee
Mobile Telephones (Prohibition of use in Designated Places)	Michael Fabricant MP	First Reading
North America Free Trade Area (Parliamentary Commission)	Michael Fabricant MP	First Reading
Parliamentary Currency Commission	Michael Fabricant MP	First Reading
Parliamentary Declaration	Rt Hon Tony Benn MP	First Reading
Parliamentary Oaths Proposed Bill	Kevin McNamara MP	Motion for Leave to Bring in Bill defeated
Parliamentary Reform	Rt Hon Tony Benn MP	First Reading
Participants in Sporting Events (Assaults, Etc.)	Paul Flynn MP	First Reading
Pet Ownership (Residential and Sheltered Accommodation)	Paul Burstow MP	First Reading
Police	Andrew Mackinlay MP	Second Reading (debate adjourned)
Ports of Entry (Special Status)	Gwyn Prosser MP	First Reading
Preventative Health Care and Home Insulation	Simon Hughes MP	First Reading
Public House Names	Nicholas Winterton MP	First Reading
Public Records (Amendment)	Norman Baker MP	Second Reading (debate adjourned)
Recycled Content of Newsprint	David Chaytor MP	First Reading
Registered Establishments (Scotland) Bill	Dr Lynda Clark MP	Royal Assent
Religious Discrimination	John Austin MP	First Reading
Representation of Dependencies at Westminster	Andrew Mackinlay MP	First Reading
Representation of Gibraltar at Westminster and in the European Union	Andrew Mackinlay MP	First Reading
Residential Care Homes and Nursing Homes (Medical Records)	Paul Flynn MP	First Reading
Warm Homes and Energy Conservation (Fifteen Year Programme)	Linda Gilroy MP	First Reading

Bill	*Introduced by*	*Stage Reached*
Waste Minimisation	Angela Smith MP	Royal Assent
Widening of the M25 Motorway	Andrew Mackinlay MP	First Reading
Wildlife	David Lepper MP	First Reading

Two SO 57 bills received Royal Assent.

The House of Commons Information Office has produced, in conjunction with the Members' Library, a fascinating paper on the success of Private Members' Bills in the Post-war period. This is available on the Parliament website (www.parliament.uk) or from the Public Information Office. In the 1948/49 Session, five of the balloted Private Members' Bills were successful, including Sir Dymoke White's Docking and Nicking of Horses Bill (16th in the ballot) and in the 1950/51 Session, Parliament found time to pass Sir Walter Monslow's Bill on Fraudulent Mediums. Over the years, Members seem to have been unduly preoccupied with salmon, harbours and piers, deer, pets of one sort or another and dangerous drugs. What is interesting is the variation in the number of Private Members' Bills reaching the Statute Book in each session; for example, in the 1963/64 Session, 34 such bills were successful, but in the 1988/89 Session only nine received Royal Assent. The years with the lowest totals are usually General Election years, when the session in question would have been curtailed, leaving less time available for Private Members' Bills.

CHAPTER NINE - BIVALVE MOLLUSCS – HAVING FUN WITH DELEGATED LEGISLATION

WHAT IS DELEGATED LEGISLATION?

Delegated legislation is legislation brought in under existing Acts of Parliament. An Act of Parliament is an example of 'primary' legislation and delegated legislation is an example of 'secondary' legislation. Delegated legislation is often referred to as 'secondary' or 'subordinate' legislation. An Act of Parliament under which delegated legislation is made is referred to as the 'parent' Act. You will often see the terms delegated legislation, statutory instruments, orders and regulations used interchangeably, but this is not quite accurate. Delegated legislation is a type of legislation – a statutory instrument is an example of that type. Statutory instruments are sometimes called orders and sometimes regulations; for example, 'The Food Protection (Emergency Prohibitions) (Paralytic Shellfish Poisoning) (No. 2) Order 1998', but 'The Spreadable Fats (Marketing Standards) (Amendment) (No. 2) Regulations 1998.

There are SIs governing every imaginable subject, from 'The Potatoes Originating in Egypt (Amendment) Regulations 1998 (No. 3167)' to the 'Penrhos Point Mussel Fishery Order 1998 (No. 1466)'. As you will gather from the titles of these Statutory Instruments ('SIs' for short) there are many hours of fun to be had perusing delegated legislation. So what are the advantages of SIs? Most Acts of Parliament could not possibly contain all the detail required to bring them into effect, so many establish a framework under which more detailed legislation can be made by the relevant Secretary of State, at a later date. This detailed delegated legislation is not subject to the same rigorous parliamentary scrutiny as primary legislation and is unamendable. Some SIs do not even have to come before Parliament and many are never debated at all. Whilst this might seem at first to be a gross abuse of the democratic process, Government would simply grind to a halt under the weight of its own legislative programme if all delegated legislation had to be considered as thoroughly as primary legislation. The remit of Government is wide ranging and there are few aspects of our daily lives not regulated in some way by legislation. Even the humble mollusc cannot escape, subject as he is to the Food Safety (Live Bivalve Molluscs and other Shellfish) Regulations 1992, amongst others. Road humps in Scotland are subject to the Road Humps (Scotland) Regulations 1998 and the much-loved English apple must not fall foul of the Apple and Pear Orchard Grubbing Up Regulations 1998.

Occasionally a clause in a bill will permit an existing Act of Parliament to be amended by 'order' (by an SI). Such clauses are known as Henry VIII Clauses and are strongly deprecated by the House. However since the passing of the Deregulation and Contracting Out Act 1994, a new class of delegated legislation, called the Deregulation Order, has been established specifically to amend Acts of Parliament enacted before 1994. Deregulation Orders are discussed in more detail later in this chapter.

The name Statutory Instrument was first used after the passing of the Statutory Instruments Act 1946. Practically all delegated legislation made under parent statutes enacted after this date can be correctly referred to as Statutory Instruments. The Act also provided that 'rules' made under Statutes enacted before this date could also be referred to in the same way.

WHEN IS AN SI NOT AN SI?

There are some documents which whilst not technically SIs must, by virtue of their parent Acts, be laid before Parliament; examples include Immigration Rules, draft Codes of Practice on Industrial Relations and Recommendations for the Welfare of Livestock. An example is the occasional, but always eagerly awaited debate in the House of Lords on the Welfare of Ducks and Rabbits. Rabbits have a habit of popping up from time to time in Parliament. On 20 March 1997, Paul Flynn MP asked the then Minister, Nicholas Soames, 'under what circumstances domestic rabbits are used in Royal Marines training?' Apparently, some 200 rabbits are killed each year in the course of teaching necessary military survival techniques. Presumably this has more to do with teaching raw recruits how to catch, skin and eat the unfortunate creatures than now to tackle a group of insurgent bunnies armed with Kalashnikovs.

There are also certain bye-laws, usually made by local authorities under the powers delegated to them by Statute, which whilst requiring the approval of Ministers, do not have to be laid before Parliament. Some delegated legislation made under parent Acts not subject to the Statutory Instruments Act 1946 undergoes a different form of parliamentary scrutiny again.

COMMENCEMENT ORDERS

Often it is impossible for an Act of Parliament to be brought into force on the day on which it receives Royal Assent. The Enactment and Commencement of an Act are not one and the same – a bill is enacted the day it receives Royal Assent and commences when either the provisions of the Act itself or orders made under it so specify. Commencement Orders are a form of SI designed to bring into force all or part of an Act.

CLASSIFICATION AND PUBLICATION

Statutory Instruments must be printed, numbered and published and must, if they are 'general' instruments, be available for sale to the public. Notice of publication appears on the Stationery Office Daily List and notice of SIs which have been laid before the House of Commons and House of Lords appears in the Votes and Proceedings of the House of Commons and in the House of Lords Minutes, respectively. The Daily List is available on the Stationery Office website. All SIs must be classified as either 'local' or 'general' according to their subject matter. 'General' instruments are those whose Parent Acts are public and general Acts. Local instruments (made under private or personal Acts) are not printed unless the Minister so directs.

STATUTORY INSTRUMENTS WHICH COME INTO EFFECT BEFORE PUBLICATION

An SI may have legal effect before it is published. Under Section 3(2) of the Statutory Instruments Act (1946), proof that an SI had not been issued at the date when it was contravened is a defence in any criminal proceedings. However, the prosecution has a case if it can prove that reasonable steps were taken to ensure that the intention and scope of the instrument were brought to the notice of the public, or persons likely to be affected, or the person charged with contravening the SI. Failure to publish does not necessarily make an instrument invalid, although failure to lay it before Parliament could render it inoperative. However, departments try to follow a general rule that negative instruments should not come into force until 21 days after being laid before Parliament. It is worth bearing in mind that some SIs do not have to be laid before Parliament at all.

INSTRUMENTS COMING INTO FORCE BEFORE BEING LAID

Some SIs have effect before they are laid before Parliament. For example, the Food Protection (Emergency Prohibitions) (Paralytic Shellfish Poisoning) Order 1998 Partial Revocation (No. 2) Order 1998 was made on 19 August 1998, laid before Parliament on 21 August 1998, but came into force at '18.00 hours on 19th August 1998'. This was one of a category of Statutory Instruments which are laid before Parliament even though they are not subject to any parliamentary proceedings.

INSTRUMENTS WHICH REQUIRE NO PARLIAMENTARY PROCEEDINGS

There are some SIs which are not subject to any parliamentary proceedings at all. For example, under the Metropolitan Public Carriage Act 1869 and the London Cab and Stage Carriage Act 1907, the Secretary of State for the Environment may make Orders relating to the provision of taxis in London; for example, the London Cab Order 1998 (SI 1998, No. 1043). This was made on 4 April 1998 and came into force on 25 April 1998. In its reports, the Joint Committee on Statutory Instruments lists those instruments to which it 'does not draw the special attention of both Houses'. There is usually a section for 'Instruments not subject to parliamentary proceedings not laid before Parliament'. For example, in its 31st Report of the 1997/98 Session (HL 97 HC 33-xxxi), the Pelican and Puffin Pedestrian Crossings General (Amendment) Directions 1998 (SI 1998, No. 901) is listed as just such an SI. On the front of the SI itself you would have seen that it was made on 25 March and came into force on 1 April 1998.

WHAT CONSTITUTES 'LAYING' AN SI?

What constitutes 'laying' an SI is set out in the Standing Orders of the House of Commons and House of Lords. Under SO 159 of the Standing Orders of the House of Commons (Public Business) 'laying' an SI before the House means placing a copy in the Vote Office of the House of Commons at any time except during a dissolution (when, of course, there is no Parliament). However, this Standing Order does not apply to Special Procedure Orders (dealt with in a later chapter on Private Bills) or to affirmative SIs (discussed later in this chapter). Affirmative SIs can only be laid when the House is sitting. Traditionally, negative SIs are not laid at weekends, bank holidays, Good Friday, Christmas Day or after 3.30pm on Fridays (unless for some reason the House is still sitting). References to SIs having been laid on the Table of the House actually refer to their having been sent to the Vote Office and placed in the House of Commons Library.

Under SO 68 (HL) the House of Lords directs that laying an SI means the receipt of a copy by the Clerk of the Parliaments, between 11.00am and 5.00pm at any time, except during a dissolution. Again, SIs are not laid at weekends or bank holidays or on Christmas Day or Good Friday. Again, Special Procedure Orders and affirmative SIs must be laid when the House is sitting. Notification of laying appears in the House of Lords Minutes and in the House of Commons Votes and Proceedings (which forms part of the Vote Bundle).

SIs are available in Parliament from the House of Lords' Printed Paper Office and from the House of Commons' Vote Office and to the general public from The Stationery Office. SIs are listed in The Stationery Office Daily List the day after their publication. SIs are now available on the internet, via the Parliament website, 15 days after being laid. A list detailing the number of 'praying days' - days left for an annulment/approval of SIs is issued each week by the Journal Office in the House of Commons. You can access this list via the Parliament website. The list is divided into four parts:

- PART I - NEGATIVE SIs
    - Negative SIs with dates when laid before the House and number of remaining praying days (see below)

SI Number	Title of Instrument	Laid before the House	Number of days unexpired on date of issue
3168	Potatoes Originating in The Netherlands (Amendment) Regulations 1998	17 Dec	7

- Negative SIs which have not appeared in previous editions
- Other Rules; e.g. Rules brought in under Northern Ireland Orders in Council (see below)

Title of Instrument	Statutory Period	Number of days unexpired on date of issue
Construction Contracts Exclusion Order (Northern Ireland) 1999 (SR (NI) 1999, No. 32)	40 days beginning 9 Feb	37

- PART II - SPECIAL PROCEDURE ORDERS
- PART III – AFFIRMATIVE SIs
    - Affirmative SIs approved by the House of Commons since the last list
    - Affirmative SIs subject to approval within a specific time
    - Affirmative Sis subject to approval within a specific time, passed since the last edition of the list
    - Church of England Measures and other miscellaneous delights

- PART IV – SIs NOT SUBJECT TO ANY PARLIAMENTARY PROCEDURE and laid since the last edition of the list.

Under section 4 of the 1946 Act all SIs which have to be laid before Parliament, must state the date on which they will come into force and the date on which they either have been, or will be laid. Most SIs also state the date on which they were made. Where an SI comes into force before copies have been laid, the Lord Chancellor and the Speaker are notified and sent an explanation of why the SI has become operational before laying. Under SO 160 and SO 69 (HL) this explanation is laid on the Table of both Houses.

ULTRA VIRES

Subordinate legislation is invalid if it is 'ultra vires' (goes beyond its legitimate scope). There are two forms - 'substantive' and 'procedural'. 'Substantive' means the instrument has gone beyond the scope of its parent Act, and 'procedural' means that the correct procedure for laying the instrument has not been followed.

AFFIRMATIVE AND NEGATIVE STATUTORY INSTRUMENTS

SIs are usually subject to either the 'affirmative' or 'negative' procedure, as specified in the Parent Act. Unfortunately, SIs do not proclaim their parentage by stating that they are either 'negative' or 'affirmative'. The relevant section of the Parent Act under which they have been made states the type of parliamentary scrutiny to which they will be subject. In most cases it is possible to determine to which procedure an SI will be subject by considering its wording, but this is by no means foolproof. The wording of an SI which is laid but not subject to any parliamentary proceedings may be the same as the wording used by an affirmative SI which has immediate effect. The wording of an SI which is laid before Parliament despite not being subject to any proceedings there, may be the same as a draft affirmative instrument.

Affirmative Procedure

The affirmative procedure is usually reserved for the most important SIs. An affirmative instrument has no effect, or its effect does not continue, until Parliament has expressly approved it. Depending on the formula of the enabling Act, there are three types of affirmative SI.

1. An SI which has immediate effect, but whose effect will not continue after a certain period of time (usually 28 or 40 days) unless one or both Houses agrees within that time to resolutions approving it. For example, the Food Protection (Emergency Prohibitions) (Paralytic Shellfish Poisoning) (No. 2) Order 1998 (SI 1998, No. 1582), which was made on 29 June 1998, laid before Parliament on 1 July 1998, but which had immediate effect at 10.00pm on 29 June 1998.

STATUTORY INSTRUMENTS

1998 No. 1582

PUBLIC HEALTH, ENGLAND AND WALES

PUBLIC HEALTH, SCOTLAND

PUBLIC HEALTH, NORTHERN IRELAND

CONTAMINATION OF FOOD

The Food Protection (Emergency Prohibitions)
(Paralytic Shellfish Poisoning) (No. 2) Order 1998

Made	*29th June 1998*
Laid before Parliament	*1st July 1998*
*Coming into force in accordance with article 1(1)**	

*article 1(1) states that the Order shall come into force at 22.00 hours on 29th June 1998.

2. A draft SI which is laid in 'draft' form before either one or both Houses and which does not have effect unless either one or both Houses agrees to a resolution approving the draft SI. This procedure also applies to Orders in Council, in which case either one or both Houses, presents an 'Address to the Crown, praying for an Order to be made. An example of part of a draft SI is set out below.

Draft Regulations laid before Parliament under section 101(3A) Transport Act 1968 for approval by each House of Parliament

DRAFT STATUTORY INSTRUMENTS

1999 No.

ROAD TRAFFIC

The Community Drivers' Hours and Recording Equipment (Amendment) Regulations 1998

Made	*1998*
Coming into force	*1998*

Once approved by both Houses the SI was reprinted as follows:

STATUTORY INSTRUMENTS

1999 No. 2006

ROAD TRAFFIC

The Community Drivers' Hours and Recording Equipment (Amendment) Regulations 1998

Made	*10th August 1998*
Coming into force	*24th August 1998*

3. An SI which is laid before Parliament but which has no effect unless, and until, a resolution has been passed approving it. These SIs are not very common. An example is the Urban Development Corporations in England (Area and Constitution) Order 1998. The wording on the face of the Order was as follows: 'Order made by the Secretary of State for the Environment and laid before Parliament under sections 134, 135 and 141 of the Local Government, Planning and Land Act 1980 for approval by resolution of each House of Parliament'. Such instruments are classified as Draft Statutory Instruments until they have been passed by both Houses. This particular Order was made on 19 January 1998, laid before Parliament on 27 January and came into force on 3 April. Once the instrument had been passed by both Houses it was reprinted and given a number – The Urban Development Corporations in England (Area and Constitution) Order 1998 (SI 1998, No. 769). Excerpts from both are set out below:

Order made by the Secretary of State for the Environment and laid before Parliament under sections 134,135 and 141 of the Local Government, Planning and Land Act 1980 for approval by resolution of each House of Parliament.

STATUTORY INSTRUMENTS

1998 No.

URBAN DEVELOPMENT

The Urban Development Corporations in England (Area and Constitution) Order 1998

Made	*19th January 1998*
Laid before Parliament	*27th January 1998*
Coming into force	*3rd April 1998*

The Order as passed by both Houses was reprinted as follows:

STATUTORY INSTRUMENTS

1998 No. 769

URBAN DEVELOPMENT

The Urban Development Corporations in England
(Area and Constitution) Order 1998

Approved by Parliament

Made	*19th January 1998*
Laid before Parliament	*27th January 1998*
Coming into force	*3rd April 1998*

Negative Procedure

There are two types of negative procedure.

1. An SI is laid before the House but ceases to have effect if either House annuls it within a certain time. ***This does not mean that an SI will not come into effect if either House passes a resolution to annul it - it means that the SI will come into effect on an appointed day, but will cease to have effect if after a certain time, either House annuls it.*** The wording used in the parent Act is that the order, 'shall be subject to annulment in pursuance of a resolution of either House of Parliament'.

STATUTORY INSTRUMENTS

1998 No. 1448 (S.74)

ROADS AND BRIDGES, SCOTLAND

The Road Humps (Scotland) Regulations 1998

Made	*7th June 1998*
Laid before Parliament	*25th June 1998*
Coming into force	*16th July 1998*

A motion to annul an SI is known colloquially as a 'prayer'. A Member or peer may move a prayer to annul an instrument within 40 days of its being laid before the House (this includes weekends but does not include dissolutions, prorogation or adjournments of 4 days or more). A 'Prayer' is a motion stating why a particular order should be annulled –

it appears in the Order Paper amongst the Early Day Motions ('EDMs'). An example is set out below:

EDM 154

HALLMARK (S.I., 1998, No. 2978)

17.12.98
Hague/William
Arbuthnot/James
Boswell/Tim
Chope/Christopher
Redwood/John
Lilley/Peter

That an humble Address be presented to Her Majesty, praying that the Hallmarking (Hallmarking Act Amendment) Regulations 1998 (S.I., 1998, No. 2978), dated 3rd December 1998, a copy of which was laid before this House on 4th December, be annulled.[1]

2. A draft SI is laid before Parliament and if, within a certain period of time (usually 40 days) either House resolves that the SI 'be not made' (or in the case of a draft Order in Council that the draft 'be not submitted to Her Majesty') then the SI proceeds no further. An example of the form of words used on the face of the Order is set out below (taken from the Charities (Seamen's Hospital Society) Order 1998).

'Draft Order laid before Parliament under section 17(2) of the Charities Act 1993, on 22nd October 1998; draft to lie for forty days, pursuant to section 6(1) of the Statutory Instruments Act 1946, during which period either House of Parliament may resolve that the Order be not made.'

DRAFT STATUTORY INSTRUMENTS

1998 No.

CHARITIES

Charities (Seamen's Hospital Society) Order 1998

Made *1998*

Coming into force *1998*

[1] Consultation on the above Regulations was undertaken by the DTI, ending on 30 October 1998. On 14 December 1998, in response to a written question from Rosie Winterton MP, the then Secretary of State, Rt Hon Peter Mandelson MP stated that both the Hallmarking (Hallmarking Act Amendment) Regulations and the Hallmarking (Hallmarking Act Amendment) Order 1998 had been laid in Parliament on Friday 4 December 1998 (HC, Col: 367, written). The aim of the Regulations and Order is to align UK law with EU single market. They will amend Section 2 of the Act so as to recognise certain hallmarks from other European countries as "approved hallmarks".

Negative SIs have to be laid before Parliament under the terms of the 1946 Act. The 40 day period begins for each House when a copy of the instrument is laid before it. When the document is a draft and is laid in each House on a different day, the period begins with the later of the two days. Departments also try to adhere to the so-called '21 day rule' (first proposed by the Joint Committee on Statutory Instruments in its First Report of 1972/73 (HC76/HL 184)) that wherever possible, an instrument subject to the negative procedure will be laid at least 21 days before it is to come into effect. For example, the Road Humps (Scotland) Regulations 1998 (set out above) were laid before Parliament on 25 June and came into force 21 days later on 16 July.

ORDERS IN COUNCIL

Orders in Council are made after a draft Order has been approved by one or both Houses of Parliament. Such draft Orders can be subject to either the affirmative or negative procedure.

An interesting example is provided by the House of Commons (Disqualification) Act 1975, which may be amended by Order in Council after a resolution has been passed by the House of Commons. In the debate on the draft Order in the House of Commons on 13 February 1997, Jeff Rooker MP made the point that, 'It is interesting to note that we are not dealing with a statutory instrument or with delegated legislation, but are being asked to amend a Schedule to an Act of Parliament on the say-so of a motion on the Order Paper' (HC Col: 493). As the draft Order was in the form of a resolution of the House, it was possible to amend it and in fact the Speaker selected the amendment tabled by Nigel Spearing MP. His amendment would have disqualified Recorders and Assistant Recorders from being Members of the House on the grounds that it was anomalous that temporary judges in Scotland and lay members of Industrial Tribunals should be barred from sitting as MPs, when part-time judges (Recorders) were not (at the time, three MPs were Recorders). Part of the Order is attached.

STATUTORY INSTRUMENTS

1997 No. 861

PARLIAMENT

The House of Commons Disqualification Order 1997

Made — *19th March 1997*

Coming into force — *19th March 1997*

At the Court at Buckingham Palace, the 19th day of March 1997

Present,

The Queen's Most Excellent Majesty in Council

Whereas section 5 of the House of Commons (Disqualification) Act 1975(a) enables Her Majesty by Order in Council to amend Schedule 1 to that Act in accordance with a resolution of the House of Commons:

And whereas on 13th February 1997 it was resolved by the House of Commons that Schedule 1 to the Act of 1975 be amended:

Now, therefore, Her Majesty, in pursuance of the said section 5 and in accordance with the said resolution, is pleased, by and with the advice of Her Privy Council, to order, and it is hereby ordered, as follows:-

1. This Order may be cited as the House of Commons Disqualification Order 1997.

EMERGENCY POWERS ACT 1920

Regulations may be made under the Emergency Powers Act 1920. They have to be presented to Parliament as soon as they are made but do not continue in force after seven days from being laid. However, Parliament can pass a resolution allowing them to continue, but not for more than one month.

AMENDMENTS

Most SIs are unamendable; however, there are some draft SIs which can be amended. For example, a draft Order in Council seeking to amend the House of Commons (Disqualification) Act 1975, can be amended by the House of Commons.

DEBATING DELEGATED LEGISLATION IN THE HOUSE OF COMMONS

Most SIs are now debated, not on the floor of the House, but in Standing Committees on Delegated Legislation, members of which are appointed by the Committee of Selection and usually consist of between 16 and 19 members. These are called, unsurprisingly, the First Standing Committee on Delegated Legislation, the Second Committee, etc., etc. The membership of each Committee is reconstituted for each instrument.

Affirmative SIs

Under SO 118, all affirmative SIs are now automatically referred for consideration to one of the Standing Committees on Delegated Legislation, unless a member of the Government tables a motion to de-refer the SI in question. A Standing Committee on Delegated Legislation can debate the SI for up to one and a half hours (two and a half in the case of Northern Ireland Orders). However, debate is on a motion that, 'the Committee has considered the instrument'. It can 'negative' (vote against) this motion. Once the Committee has debated the SI, it 'reports' this fact to the House and the question on the SI is put forthwith (without debate). For example, the draft Financing of Maintained Schools Regulation 1998 was debated in the First Standing Committee on Delegated Legislation on 15 December 1998. The Committee divided on the motion,

'That the Committee has considered the draft Financing of Maintained Schools Regulations 1998', with three Conservative Members voting against. However, the motion that was put before the House of Commons, the following day, 16 December was, 'That the draft Financing of Maintained Schools Regulations 1998, which were laid before this House on 3rd December, be approved' (HC Col:1062).[2] Even if the Standing Committee which considered the instrument had voted against the motion 'that the Committee has considered the instrument', it would have made no difference – the motion put before the House would still have been only a motion to approve the instrument. Affirmative instruments must be approved by a resolution of either one or both Houses, not a resolution of a Committee. Although sending SIs to Standing Committees for debate might seem a futile exercise, given that they have no effective veto over the instruments they consider, it does at least afford some opportunity for debate in what is always a crowded parliamentary timetable.

Negative SIs

Under SO 118(4), where a Member has 'prayed against' a negative SI, the Government may refer the SI to a Standing Committee. A Minister would propose a motion at the start of public business, 'that the instrument be referred to the (first) Standing Committee on Delegated Legislation'. If 20 or more Members object the motion is defeated. The Committee does not debate the prayer against the instrument, but the motion that 'the Committee has considered the instrument'. There is no compulsion to refer a negative SI which has been prayed against, to a Committee. Even if it is debated in such a Committee, given that the motion on which the Committee can divide is only a motion 'that the Committee has considered the instrument', it has no effect. The presumption with a negative instrument is that it will continue to have effect unless one or both Houses agrees to a motion annulling it. Only the House, and not a Committee, can agree to a prayer to annul an instrument. A negative instrument could only be annulled by a prayer being passed on the floor of the House. Theoretically, under SO 118(6), once a Committee has reported its deliberations on a negative instrument, the Member who prayed against it, could move the prayer on the floor of the House and it would be taken forthwith. However, given the size of the Government's majority and the rather prosaic nature of most SIs, the Opposition never takes advantage of SO 118(6).

Where a prayer is debated on the floor of the House, as was the case on 10 November 1998 with the Personal Equity Plan (Amendment) regulations 1998 (SI, 1998, No. 1869), the form of words used to move the motion is as follows:

Mr. Nick Gibb (Bognor Regis and Littlehampton): I beg to move,
That an humble address be presented to Her Majesty, praying that the Personal Equity Plan (Amendment) Regulations 1998 (S.I., 1998, No. 1869), dated 31st July 1998, a copy of which was laid before this House on 31st July, be annulled'.

The motion was defeated by 293 (Noes) to 116 (Ayes).

[2] Where the instrument concerned is an Order in Council the motion is that an 'humble address be presented to Her Majesty praying that the ... Order be made in the form of the draft laid before the House on ...'

Exempted Business

Debates on the floor of the House on both negative and affirmative SIs are classified as 'exempted' business; i.e., debate can take place on the floor of the House after the Moment of Interruption (10.00pm Monday to Wednesday, 7.00pm on Thursday and 2.30pm on Friday). Debates on affirmative SIs can proceed past the Moment of Interruption for one and a half hours (debates on affirmative and negative SIs are limited to a period of one and a half hours, at whatever time of day they are taken).

Debates on negative Statutory Instruments are also limited to one and a half hours' debate and may also proceed beyond the Moment of Interruption, but not beyond 11.30pm. The Speaker can postpone such a debate if there has been insufficient time for a full discussion; for example, if the debate followed other business and did not begin until 11.00pm. In such cases, any further debate on the postponed SI may not begin after 11.00pm and may not continue after 11.30pm.

DEBATING DELEGATED LEGISLATION IN THE HOUSE OF LORDS

Time is always found to debate prayers against negative SIs in the House of Lords, but few are tabled. Although delegated legislation is not subject to the Parliament Acts, the House of Lords rarely opposes negative or affirmative instruments. As SIs are unamendable, if the House of Lords rejected an instrument, the result would probably be its wholesale rejection. This is not to say that there are no Divisions on SIs in the House of Lords.

The Conservative opposition divided the House against the Southern Rhodesia (United Nations Sanctions) Order 1968 and defeated the Government. This was the last time an affirmative order was defeated. The House has never agreed to a prayer against a negative SI. Affirmative and negative SIs can be debated 'en bloc' in the House of Lords, but only with the unanimous agreement of the House. A motion to take SIs en bloc must appear in at least two issues of the Order Paper before the day in question. Peers can oppose a motion to approve an affirmative SI, seek to amend that motion or table a motion criticising the SI. For example, on 23 July 1998, the House of Lords debated the draft Conditional Fee Agreements Order 1998. Lord Ackner tabled an amendment calling on the Government to withdraw the Order and re-lay it in 'amended form'. The amendment was voted down, 55 (Not-Contents) to 24 (Contents). Peers can oppose negative SIs by praying against them or, indirectly, by tabling a motion critical of the instrument.

In 1984, an Order was laid under the Local Government (Interim Provisions) Bill to cancel the GLC elections. The bill had stipulated that cancellation could only take place after the principle of abolition of the authorities concerned had been approved by Parliament. The Opposition in the House of Lords did not oppose the Order, but tabled a motion stating that the House saw cancellation of the elections as prejudicial to peers' consideration of the Local Government Bill (still before the Commons). This motion was defeated. Had it been carried the motion would not have defeated the SI, merely expressed the view of the House. Occasionally, such tactics have caused the Government to withdraw and amend an order.

Most SIs are debated at the end of the day's proceedings in the House of Lords; for example, the draft Financing of Maintained Schools Regulations 1998, which was debated in a Standing Committee on Delegated Legislation in the House of Lords, was debated on the floor of the House of Lords on 14 January 1998 from 7.14pm until about 8.00pm on a motion 'that the draft regulations laid before the House on 3rd December be approved' [2nd Report from the Joint Committee]. The motion was agreed to by the House without Division. After the debate on these regulations, there was a brief debate on the Industrial Training Levy (Engineering Construction Board) Order 1999 which was debated together with the Industrial Training Levy (Construction Board) Order 1999 – as a result the second Order was simply moved formally by the Minister, Lord Hunt of Kings Heath.

Hybrid Instruments

Hybrid instruments are considered in the House of Lords but not in the House of Commons. The procedures are set out in Standing Orders 216 and 216A (HL) (Private Business). Where the Chairman of Committees considers that an affirmative instrument should really be the subject of a Private or Hybrid Bill, he or she reports the fact to the Minister in charge of the instrument. It then becomes known as a Hybrid Instrument and can be petitioned against for a period of 14 days after the Chairman of Committees has submitted his or her report. If a petition is received, both it and the instrument are referred to the Hybrid Instruments Committee, the Chair of which is the Chairman of Committees. The Committee can take evidence from any petitioner, or his or her counsel or agents, before deciding whether or not the petitioner concerned has a 'locus standi' (the necessary grounds on which to petition). If the Committee agrees that the petition does have such grounds, it can recommend that the instrument should be sent to a Select Committee of five peers (nominated by the Committee of Selection), for a further enquiry. The Select Committee can recommend that the instrument should proceed as an opposed Private Bill. There is also an 'expedited hybrid instrument' procedure which shortens the petitioning period to 10 days and where any further enquiry is conducted by the Hybrid Instrument Committee rather than a Select Committee.

THE SCRUTINY OF STATUTORY INSTRUMENTS

The Joint Committee on Statutory Instruments

The Joint Committee on Statutory Instruments is sometimes known as the 'Scrutiny Committee' and membership is drawn from both the House of Commons and the House of Lords. Its remit is set out in the Standing Orders of both Houses (Standing Order 151 and Standing Order 70A (HL)). The Chairman is usually an Opposition MP and there are six other Commons' members and seven Lords' members. It is not responsible for considering the merits of secondary legislation, but considers important technical matters. For example, the Committee would consider whether or not the SI was 'ultra vires' or whether its drafting was defective. It does not consider Northern Ireland Orders in Council, Deregulation Orders or Church of England Measures. Proceedings are conducted in private. Even if the Committee discovers a fault in an instrument, it cannot prevent the Government from furthering its progress in the House. In the Lords, an affirmative SI cannot be approved until the Joint Committee has reported (the exceptions are SIs under the Emergency Powers Act 1920, Church of England Measures, Northern Ireland Orders in Council and draft orders under section 1 of the Deregulation and Contracting out Act 1994) but an adverse report can be ignored. In addition, SO 70 can be dispensed with by agreement of the House in exceptional circumstances; for example, on 29 July 1998 SO 70 was suspended to enable the draft Northern Ireland (Sentences) Act 1998 (Specified Organisations) Order 1998 to be debated before the Joint Committee had reported. In the Commons, SIs are frequently debated before the Joint Committee has had time to consider them properly and a note in italics to this effect appears in the Order of Business.

The Committee may draw the attention of the House to SIs on the following grounds.

1. If there is a likelihood of the imposition of a tax on the public.

2. If the SI attempts to exclude the jurisdiction of the courts.

3. If the SI is retrospective.

4. If the SI's publication has been delayed.

5. If the SI has come into operation before being laid before Parliament and the Lord Chancellor and the Speaker have not been informed.

6. If the SI is of doubtful vires.

7. If the SI needs 'elucidating'.

8. If the SI's drafting is defective.

Before drawing Parliament's attention to an SI, the Committee must give the department concerned time to offer an explanation either orally or in writing. These responses appear in Appendices to the Joint Committee's reports. For example, the Third Report of the Joint Committee (HL 10, HC 50-iii, 1998/99) drew the attention of both Houses to the Education (School Government) (Transition to New Framework) Regulations 1998 (SI 1998/2763) on the grounds that 'they are defectively drafted'. The memorandum which the Committee had received from the Department of Education and Employment was attached as Appendix IV.

Sometimes the Government meets the points made by the Committee; for example, in the aforementioned Joint Committee report, Appendix 1 was a Memorandum from the Privy Council Office relating to the General Osteopathic Council (Conditional Registration) (Amendment) Rules Order of Council (SI 1998/2695). The Committee had been concerned that copies of the Order had not been made available free of charge to those affected by the rules. The Memorandum from the Privy Council Office thanked the Committee for drawing the matter to its attention and stated that this had not been done earlier owing to an administrative oversight.

SIs are occasionally withdrawn by the Government after a hostile report, but they are usually reintroduced at a later stage in a modified form. For example, the Police Act 1997 (Provisions in relation to the NCIS Service Authority) (No. 2) Order 1997 (SI 1997, No. 2391) was withdrawn after a report from the Joint Committee and a new order issued – the Police Act 1997 (Provisions in relation to the NCIS Service Authority) Order 1998. Instruments to which the Joint Committee does not draw the attention of either House are usually set out in the Annex to the Committee's report.

SIs awaiting consideration by the Joint Committee are listed in the daily Lords Minutes. For example, on 13 January 1998 you would have seen under the following heading: Affirmative Instruments in Progress, the words, 'Waiting for consideration by the Joint Committee'. These instruments included, the 'Draft European Communities (Definition of Treaties) (North-East Atlantic Fisheries Commission) Order 1999' and the 'Draft European Communities (Immunities and Privileges of the North-East Atlantic Fisheries Commission) Order 1999'.

The Select Committee on Statutory Instruments

The Select Committee on Statutory Instruments consists merely of the House of Commons members' of the Joint Committee. The Committee considers delegated legislation which the parent Act stipulates is only to come before the House of Commons; for example, delegated legislation concerning financial matters. Financial privilege belongs to the House of Commons and the House of Lords rarely considers financial matters; for example, consideration of the Finance Bill is limited to a Second Reading debate in the House of Commons.

THE STATUTORY INSTRUMENTS REFERENCE COMMITTEE

The Statutory Instruments Reference Committee considers questions of numbering, classification and printing of SIs. Members are nominated by the Lord Chancellor and the Speaker and the Committee consists of the Lord Chairman of Committees, the Chairman of Ways and Means and six senior officers of both Houses.

NORTHERN IRELAND LEGISLATION

Since the suspension of the Northern Ireland Assembly in 1974 and the imposition of direct rule[3], Northern Ireland legislation has been implemented by the Queen, by Order in Council, providing such Orders have been approved by resolutions of both Houses of Parliament, within 40 days. Orders may be made before parliamentary consent has been given, but to remain valid both Houses must approve them within 40 days (this does not include dissolutions, periods when the House is prorogued or adjournments of four days or more). Northern Ireland Orders in Council are effectively primary legislation and are

[3] Direct rule actually dates from 1972 when the Northern Ireland Parliament was prorogued under the Northern Ireland (Temporary Provisions) Act 1972. Section One of this Act provided for Northern Ireland legislation to be made by means of Orders in Council (which would be subject to the affirmative procedure as per draft SIs). However, these provisions were later superseded by the establishment of a Northern Ireland Assembly. This attempt at devolution failed and in 1974 direct rule was resumed under the Northern Ireland Act 1974.

therefore exempt from the terms of reference of the Joint Committee on Statutory Instruments.

Orders in Council or draft Orders may be debated on the floor of the House for up to one and a half hours. They are exempted business and may therefore proceed after the Moment of Interruption. They may also be sent to a Standing Committee under SO 118, where they may be debated for two and a half hours (although this can be extended to three hours if the Order in question is sent to the Northern Ireland Grand Committee under SO 109). An example of a draft Order in Council and the Order as reprinted after approval by both Houses is set out below:

DRAFT STATUTORY INSTRUMENTS

1998 No. (N.I.)

NORTHERN IRELAND
Criminal Justice (Children) (Northern Ireland) Order 1998

Made *1998*

Coming into operation on days to be appointed under Article 1(2)

At the Court at ,the day of 1998

Present,

The Queen's Most Excellent Majesty in Council

Whereas a draft of this Order has been approved by a resolution of each House of Parliament:

Now, therefore, Her Majesty, in exercise of the powers conferred by paragraph 1 of Schedule 1 to the Northern Ireland Act 1974 and of all other powers enabling Her in that behalf, is pleased, by and with the advice of Her Privy Council, to order, and it is hereby ordered, as follows:-

The Order as reprinted after being passed by both Houses was as follows:

STATUTORY INSTRUMENTS

1998 No. 1504 (N.I.9)

NORTHERN IRELAND

Criminal Justice (Children) (Northern Ireland) Order 1998

Made *14th June 1998*

Coming into operation on days to be appointed under Article 1(2)

At the Court at Buckingham Palace, the 24th day of June 1998

Present,

The Queen's Most Excellent Majesty in Council

Whereas a draft of this Order has been approved by a resolution of each House of Parliament:

Now, therefore, Her Majesty, in exercise of the powers conferred by paragraph 1 of Schedule 1 to the Northern Ireland Act 1974 and of all other powers enabling Her in that behalf, is pleased, by and with the advice of Her Privy Council, to order, and it is hereby ordered, as follows:-

Some Northern Ireland legislation is subject to the negative procedure. This is usually where an Act which relates to Great Britain contains a clause stipulating the equivalent measures for Northern Ireland be brought in by means of an Order in Council under the 1974 Act, but subject to the negative rather than the more usual affirmative procedure. The draft Order would be presented to Her Majesty unless a motion was passed that 'the Order be not made'.

Delegated legislation for Northern Ireland is made by Statutory Rules; for example, 'The Imported Food (Bivalve Molluscs and Marine Gastropods from Japan) Regulations (Northern Ireland) 1992 Statutory Rule 1992: No. 333'. Statutory Rules, where they must be laid before the House under the terms of the parent Order, are subject to the negative procedure. They are scrutinised by the Joint Committee on Statutory Instruments and in the House of Commons may be referred to a Standing Committee on Delegated Legislation under SO 118. They may also be sent to the Northern Ireland Grand Committee under SO 109.

A new Northern Ireland Assembly has recently been established under the Northern Ireland Act 1998. There are 108 seats in the Assembly and the first elections were held on 25 June 1998. Section 5(6) of the 1998 Act specifically states that: 'This section does not affect the power of the Parliament of the United Kingdom to make laws for Northern Ireland'.

CHURCH OF ENGLAND LEGISLATION

The fact that the Church of England cannot make its own rules without securing parliamentary approval seems to many people to be a complete anachronism. The Church of England is the 'State' Church and as it has not yet been disestablished, its rules, or 'Measures' as they are known, must be approved by resolutions passed by both Houses of Parliament and given Royal Assent. Church of England delegated legislation is governed by the Church of England (Assembly) Powers Act 1919 (amended by the Synodical Government Measure 1969).

The 1919 Act states that 'Measures' should have effect as Acts of Parliament. After the General Synod has agreed to a particular Measure, it is considered by the Ecclesiastical Committee consisting of 15 Members from each House, nominated by the Lord Chancellor and the Speaker. The Ecclesiastical Committee is not really a parliamentary committee at all as it was set up by Statute - the 1919 Act in fact. However, its procedures are similar to those of a Joint Committee of both Houses. It is appointed at the beginning of each Parliament and its sessions are held in private, except for those meetings which are joint meetings with the Legislative Committee of the General Synod. It may not amend Measures, but once it has considered a particular Measure it sends a report to the Legislative Committee. The Legislative Committee decides whether or not the report and the Measure itself should be presented to both Houses. The Measure is then laid before Parliament by the Lord Chairman of Committees in the House of Lords and the Chairman of Ways and Means in the House of Commons. Motions are tabled in both Houses, but cannot be amended. In the House of Commons such motions are exempted business and may therefore take place after the Moment of Interruption. They may be debated for up to an hour and a half. They may also be referred to a Standing Committee under SO 118(4)(b), unless 20 Members object. Measures can be carried over from one Session to the next

A recent example of a Church of England Measure was the National Institutions Measure, debated in the House of Lords on 29 June 1998 and in the House of Commons on 18 June 1998. In the House of Lords the motion was introduced by the Lord Bishop of Blackburn with the following words: 'That this House do direct that, in accordance with the Church of England Assembly (Powers) Act 1919, the Measure be presented to Her Majesty for the Royal Assent'. In the House of Commons the form of words used is slightly different and there, Stuart Bell MP, Second Church Estates Commissioner, moved: 'that the National Institutions Measure, passed by the General Synod of the Church of England, be presented to Her Majesty for Royal Assent in the form in which the said Measure was laid before Parliament'.

Delegated legislation can be made under Measures in the same way that SIs can be made under parent Acts. Most 'schemes' as they are sometimes called, brought in under Measures are not subject to parliamentary scrutiny, but some Measures provide that schemes brought in under them should be subject to the negative procedure.

DEREGULATION ORDERS

The Deregulation and Contracting Out Act 1994 gave the Government power to amend existing legislation by laying regulations rather than by promoting new primary legislation. Section one of the Act is effectively what is known as a 'Henry VIII' clause. It enables the Secretary of State to amend existing enactments by laying unamendable statutory instruments. Section one of the Act enables a Minister to amend or repeal previous Acts of Parliament by order where: the effect of the relevant part of the Act imposes a burden 'affecting any person in the carrying on of any trade, business or profession', and where amending or repealing that part would remove or reduce that burden, without removing any 'necessary protection'. An order laid before Parliament under this section cannot impose any burdens on industry more onerous than those imposed by the Act which it seeks to amend.

Under Section 1(5)(c) of the Act, deregulation orders cannot be used to amend legislation passed in Sessions following the Session in which the Deregulation and Contracting Out Act was passed; i.e., only Acts passed before or during the 1993/94 Session can be amended by Deregulation Orders.

Both the House of Commons and House of Lords have established committees to deal specifically with Deregulation Orders: the Deregulation Select Committee in the House of Commons and the Delegated Powers and Deregulation Select Committee in the House of Lords.

Section three of the Deregulation and Contracting Out Act 1994 establishes a consultation procedure to be followed by a Minister before making a Deregulation Order under section one of the Act. He must consult those organisations 'as appear to him' to represent interests likely to be affected by his proposals. If he decides to proceed, the Minister must lay a proposal for a draft Order before Parliament, together with details of the burden on industry which the order seeks to remove, how 'necessary protection' is to be continued, etc. Orders laid under section one of the Act are subject to affirmative resolution.

The Deregulation Committees have 60 days to scrutinise a proposed Order (this does not include time when the House is dissolved or prorogued or when adjourned for more than four days). They must consider whether the proposed Order removes an unnecessary burden 'affecting any person in the carrying on of any trade, business or profession' and whether it would do so without removing any 'necessary protection'. They must also consider whether consultation has been adequate.

Proceedings in the House of Commons

When a proposal for a draft order is laid before the House, the Deregulation Committee considers the proposal and reports to the House one of the following:

- that an Order similar to the proposal should be laid before the House;
- that the proposal should be amended before a draft Order is laid before the House;
- or, that an Order should not be made.

The Committee also considers whether the proposals appear to be an appropriate use of delegated legislation.

At the end of the 60-day period the Minister concerned may come forward with a draft Order which is laid before the House, along with a report setting out conclusions of the reports made by the Committees in both Houses as well as any other representations which have been received. The report should also state any changes which have been made to the proposed Order as a result of the above Committees' recommendations. The draft Order is then referred again to the Deregulation Committee. At this stage they cannot recommend any changes to the draft Order. Under SO 141(15) the Deregulation Committee has 15 sitting days within which to report to the House. There is no time limit on the deliberations of the Delegated Powers and Deregulation Select Committee in the House of Lords. There are three possible outcomes:

1. The Committee reports that the draft Order should be approved, having reached that decision without a Division, and a motion is then put before the House and taken forthwith.

2. The Committee reports that the draft Order should be approved, but having divided on the matter, a debate of up to an hour and a half takes place on the floor of the House.

3. The Committee reports that the draft Order should not proceed. A debate of up to three hours takes place on a motion to disagree with the Committee's report and no motion to approve the draft Order can be moved unless the House has approved a motion to disagree with the Committee. If the House agrees with the Committee - the draft order is withdrawn. The above debates are all exempted business and may proceed after the Moment of Interruption.

Proceedings in the House of Lords

In the House of Lords, Deregulation Orders are considered by the Delegated Powers and Deregulation Committee, set up in 1992 to consider the powers delegated by primary legislation. In addition to its role in considering draft Orders under the Deregulation and Contracting Out Act 1994, the Committee has the power to report on the delegated powers contained in bills coming before the House, excluding any Supply bills or Consolidation bills. It considers, amongst other things, whether the proposed delegated powers contained in a bill will be subject to sufficient parliamentary scrutiny; for example, whether the proposed delegated legislation will be subject to the affirmative or negative procedure. In particular, the Committee scrutinises any 'Henry VIII' Clauses (Clauses which allow primary legislation to be subsequently amended by delegated legislation). The Committee's terms of reference with regard to deregulation orders were agreed by the House on 1 December 1994.

The Committee currently has ten members, including the Chairman and when considering bills receives written evidence from the relevant Government Department. The Committee can also hear oral evidence. The Committee's role is purely advisory – it has no power to amend bills or proposals for draft Orders. There is an informal understanding in the House that when the Committee has approved the delegated powers in a particular bill, those powers should not then become the subject of debate during the Bill's passage through the House. Frequently, the Government will respond to the Committee's recommendations and amend its own Bill's accordingly.

The Committee can appoint sub-committees and specialist advisers and has the same powers as other House of Lords' Select Committees.

The Committee has 60 days within which to scrutinise any proposal for a Deregulation Order. Its report may be debated in the House within this period of time. Under SO 70, if, after the 60-day period, the Government decides to lay a draft Order, no motion for its approval can be put before the House until the Committee has reported. During its deliberations on the Order the Committee performs the functions of the Joint Committee on Statutory Instruments. Any Peer may table a motion relating to a report on a draft Order and such a motion would be taken immediately before the motion to approve the draft Order. Amendments could be made to the motion.

As the Fourth Report of the Select Committee on the Scrutiny of Delegated Powers (Special Report on Deregulation Orders - Session 1994/5, HL 48) stated: 'the House will be able to vote on any such motion or amendment, allowing a decision to be reached on a final draft Order without breaching the convention that the House does not vote on affirmative instruments directly'. If the House votes in favour of a motion stating that the Order should not be approved, the motion to approve the Order is not moved.

Deregulation Orders in Practice

Greyhounds

The first Deregulation Order to progress through the House was the Deregulation (Greyhound Racing) Order 1995. A proposed draft Order and an explanatory memorandum were laid before both Houses on 5 April 1995.

In their first report of the 1994/95 Session (HC 409 – 4 May 1995) the House of Commons Deregulation Committee reported that the Home Office had not fulfilled the conditions set out in Section 3(3) and (4) of the Deregulation and Contracting Out Act 1994 in that, when a Minister lays proposals for a Deregulation Order before Parliament, he is, at the same time, supposed to lay before the House details of any consultation undertaken as required by the Act. Such a report was not provided by the Home Office. Rather than requiring that the proposed Order be withdrawn and laid again, the Committee requested that the details of the consultation be set out in a supplementary paper. The Committee was also concerned about the unavailability of an amended version of the Betting, Gaming and Lotteries Act 1963 (which the Greyhound Racing Order sought to amend). The 1963 Act has been amended on a number of occasions and the Committee was concerned that no amended version of the Act was provided by the Home Office.

The proposed draft Deregulation (Greyhound Racing) Order 1995 was considered by the Deregulation Committee, which took both oral and written evidence from a number of sources, including the British Greyhound Racing Board and National Greyhound Racing Club. It reported on the proposed draft Order in its Second Report of the 1994/95 Session (HC 535 - 20 June 1995). It concluded that 'the proposals for the Deregulation (Greyhound Racing) Order 1995 should be amended before a draft Order is laid before the House'.

The proposed draft Order was duly amended by the Home Office before being laid before the House on 16 October 1995 as an affirmative instrument with explanatory memorandum. The instrument was due to come into force 28 days after the day on which it was made.

In its Sixth Report of the 1994/95 Session (HC 817 - 31 October 1995), the Deregulation Committee stated that: 'We note with pleasure that the Home Office has accepted all our recommendations', adding that, 'We recommend unanimously that the draft Order should be approved'.

In the House of Lords, the Delegated Powers and Deregulation Committee reported on the proposed Deregulation (Greyhound Racing) Order 1995 in its Ninth Report of the 1994/95 Session (HL 67 - 25 May 1995). It recommended approval of the order, provided one amendment was made.

In its 17th Report (HL 108 - 1 November 1995) the Committee reported that the Government had taken its views into account and that there was now, 'no difference outstanding between the two Committees and the Government'. It also reported that there was nothing in the draft Order which the Joint Committee on Statutory Instruments would have drawn to the special attention of each House. The draft Order, which was laid before the House of 16 October, was approved by the House of Lords on 28 November 1995.

Pipes

The Government laid a proposal for a draft Deregulation (Pipe-lines) Order before Parliament on 15 June 1998. The Deregulation Select Committee in the House of Commons and the Delegated Powers and Deregulation Committee in the House of Lords had 60 days within which to consider the proposed Order. The Pipe-lines Act 1962 regulates the laying of certain onshore pipelines (not those of the major utilities). Those exceeding ten miles in length (known as 'cross-country pipelines') require authorisation from the Secretary of State in the form of a Pipe-line Construction Authorisation (PCA). Pipes under ten miles in length are 'local' pipelines and require planning permission. The Secretary of State must be notified of any proposals for local pipelines.

The proposed draft Order would have amended the Act in four ways:

1. by introducing a system of written objections to PCA applications;

2. by removing the requirement for applicants for local pipelines to notify the Secretary of State 16 weeks prior to construction;

3. by repealing section 7 of the 1962 Act (which requires a PCA where two existing pipelines are to be connected or where one is to be added to another in order to create a pipeline with a total length of more than ten miles);

4. by repealing section 3 of the 1962 Act which requires a 'pipeline diversion authorisation' if a cross-country pipeline is diverted from the course set out in the PCA or where a local pipeline is diverted so that its length becomes more than 10 miles.

The House of Commons Deregulation Committee published a report on the proposed order on 31 July 1998 (HC 939 Ninth Report of the House of Commons Select Committee on Deregulation, 1997/98). It concluded that, 'the proposal for the Deregulation (Pipe-lines) Order 1998 should be amended as set out in paragraphs 71 and 85 above before a draft Order is laid before the House'. Paragraph 71 recommended that an applicant for a PCA should be allowed to object to the use of the proposed written representations procedure on the basis that there might be occasions when an applicant would wish to embark on a public inquiry instead. The Committee also recommended that the proposed draft Order be amended so that where a cross-country pipeline had not been constructed the Secretary of State should retain authority for a diversion. In its Thirtieth Report of the 1997/98 Session (HL 141), published on 30 July 1998, the Select Committee on Delegated Powers and Deregulation in the House of Lords recommended that 'the proposal for the Draft Deregulation (Pipe-lines) Order

1998 meets the requirements of the Deregulation and Contracting Out Act 1994 and is appropriate to be made under it, without amendment'.

After consideration of the reports of both Committees, the Government laid a draft Deregulation (Pipe-lines) Order 1999 before Parliament on 30 November 1998. The draft Order had been amended to take account of the two amendments proposed by the House of Commons Deregulation Select Committee and as a result when that Committee considered the draft Order it recommended unanimously that the draft Order be approved (HC 79, First Report of the House of Commons Select Committee on Deregulation, 1998/99). In its Second Report of the 1998/99 Session (HL 8), published on 9 December 1998, the House of Lords Delegated Powers and Deregulation Committee reported that, 'the draft order is in a form satisfactory to be submitted to the House for affirmative resolution', adding that, 'there is nothing in the draft order which the Joint Committee would have needed to draw to the attention of each House'.

The Order was considered in the Commons on 19 January 1999 and in the Lords on 24 February 1999. In the Commons the motion to approve the Order was taken forthwith – in the Lords there was a debate, lasting approximately three minutes.

DEREGULATION

Motion made, and Question put forthwith, pursuant to Standing Order No. 18(1)(a) (Consideration of draft deregulation orders),

Pipe-Lines

That the draft Deregulation (Pipe-Lines) Order 1999, which was laid before this House on 30th November 1998, be approved.--*[Mr. Dowd.]*

Question agreed to.

Deregulation (Pipe-lines) Order 1999

10.51 p.m.

Lord McIntosh of Haringey rose to move, That the draft order laid before the House on 30th November 1998 be approved [2nd Report from the Delegated Powers and Deregulation Committee].

You can track the progress of Deregulation Orders in the Weekly Information Bulletin, published each Saturday. For example, the Weekly Information Bulletin of 19 December 1998 showed the following:

DEREGULATION AND CONTRACTING OUT ACT 1994 SECTION 3(3) ORDERS PROCEEDINGS AS AT 12 DECEMBER 1998

......Committee recommendation

a) a draft order in the same terms as the proposal should be laid before the House

b) proposal should be amended before a draft order is laid before the House
c) the order-making power should not be used in respect of the proposals
d) draft order should be approved (*indicates Committee's recommendation was agreed after a Division)
e) draft order should not be approved

Draft Proposals

Date	Laid	Lords Committee Report and Recommendation	Commons Committee Report and Recommendation
16.6.98	Pipe-lines	HL 141, 97/98 (a)	HC 939, 97/98 (b)
30.11.98	Pipe-lines	HL 8, 98/99 (d)	HC 79, 98/99 (d)

REMEDIAL ORDERS UNDER THE HUMAN RIGHTS ACT 1998

The Human Rights Bill received Royal Assent on 9 November 1998. Under section 4 of the Act, if any of the higher courts (the House of Lords, the Judicial Committee of the Privy Council, the High Court, the Courts-Martial Appeal Court, the Court of Appeal or the High Court of Justiciary) find that a provision of an Act of Parliament or delegated legislation is incompatible with the Convention rights as set out in the Human Rights Act 1998, they can make a declaration of incompatibility. Under section 6 of the Act it will also be unlawful for a public authority to act in a way which is incompatible with the Convention rights; however, 'public authority' does not include Parliament. A public authority will not be deemed to have acted unlawfully, if as the result of primary legislation it could not have acted differently.

The courts will not have the right to strike down legislation and necessary amendments to existing legislation will be a matter for Parliament under section 10 of the Act. Where delegated legislation is concerned, if the court determines that the primary Act under which it was brought does not prevent its revocation, it may be quashed, but where the primary Act does prevent its removal, the court may still make a declaration of its incompatibility with the Convention rights as set out in the Human Rights Act 1998. Under section 10, a Minister will be able to amend the offending piece of primary legislation by order. Schedule 2 of the Act specifies that these orders will be draft orders, to be approved by both Houses after a period of 60 days. If the Minister wishes to change the order, as a result of any representations which have been made during the 60-day period, he or she can do so, provided notification is given of these changes. However, in urgent cases, an order can be made without being first laid in draft. However, it is still laid before the House and representations may be made within a 60 day period. If, as a result of any of the representations, the Minister wishes to replace the original remedial order with a new one, he/she can do so, but this will cease to have effect unless confirmed by both Houses within another 60 days (120 days after the original order was made).

TRACKING DOWN AN ELUSIVE SI

You have seen the following headline in the Guardian: 'World Stunned as UK bans import of marine gastropods'. Is this a vicious rumour, alarmist scare-mongering or the result of a devious piece of delegated legislation? You aim to find out, but where to begin? You decide to call the Ministry of Agriculture, Fisheries and Food and you are eventually put through to the Office of Marine Organisms, an Executive Agency based in Hull. Unfortunately, they are undergoing a thorough reorganisation and have lost the key to the filing cabinet in which copies of the SI in question are kept. However, they are able to inform you that the SI in question is being brought in under the Ocean-going Gastropods (Miscellaneous Provisions) (No. 2) Act 1971. They agree to read you the relevant section over the 'phone. This states that: 'the Minister has the power under this section to introduce regulations restricting the import of marine gastropods and such regulations shall be subject to annulment in pursuance of a resolution of either House of Parliament'. This tells you that you are looking for a negative statutory instrument.

Although they do not have copies to hand, the Office of Marine Organisms is able to point you in the right direction by telling you that SIs are listed on the Stationery Office Daily List the day after publication. You telephone the Stationery Office, who are able to tell you when the SI was published. You now know that the SI was published three weeks ago, but you want to know if it has been laid before Parliament. Unfortunately, you do not have access to the internet (which would have saved you a great deal of time and effort) so you catch the No. 7 bus to your local reference library, which to your amazement is actually open. You locate the Votes and Proceedings of the House of Commons and the House of Lords' Minutes.

The Votes and Proceedings reveals that the SI has in fact been laid. You wonder if anyone has bothered to 'pray against' the SI. After a trawl through several Notice Papers you find an Early Day Motion tabled by Sir Mowbray Wiffin QC MP, which is in fact a prayer against the SI in question. Rejoicing at Sir Mowbray's good sense, you wonder if the SI will be debated in a Committee? You decide to look at all the copies of the House of Commons Hansard subsequent to the day on which Sir Mowbray's EDM first appeared in the Order Paper. To your delight you find that at the start of public business only a few days' later, the Government proposed that the 'Gastropods (Import Restriction) Order 1998 be referred to the Ninth Standing Committee on Delegation Legislation'. As there was no objection to this, the Order has been so referred. You now need to find out when the Committee intends to meet to discuss the Order. You turn to the Weekly Information Bulletin and in the most recent edition find that the Ninth Standing Committee is scheduled to meet the following week to discuss the Order.

You resolve; firstly, to write to each Member of the Committee, urging them to speak out against this heinous Order; and, secondly, to buy a modem for your computer so that you can track down future elusive SIs in the comfort of your own home.

CHAPTER TEN – PRIVILEGES, RIGHTS & STANDARDS

PARLIAMENTARY PRIVILEGE

At the beginning of each Parliament, the Speaker, on behalf of the House of Commons, lays claim to the 'ancient and undoubted rights and privileges' of the House of Commons. Erskine May describes parliamentary privilege as 'the sum of the peculiar rights enjoyed by each House collectively as a constituent part of the High Court of Parliament, and by Members individually, without which they could not discharge their functions, and which exceed those possessed by other bodies or individuals.'[1] Some privileges reside in the *'lex et consuetudo parliamentii'* - the law and custom of Parliament, while some are actually set out in statute. At the beginning of each Parliament, the Speaker states: 'It is now my duty in the name and on behalf of the Commons of the United Kingdom, to lay claim, by humble petition to Her Majesty, to all their ancient and undoubted rights and privileges, especially to freedom of speech in debate, to freedom from arrest, and to free access to Her Majesty whenever occasion shall require, and that the most favourable construction shall be put upon all their proceedings.'

As Erskine May points out, 'After some three and a half centuries, the boundary between the competence of the law courts and the jurisdiction of either House in matters of privilege is still not entirely determined'.[2]

An extremely useful and concise guide to parliamentary privilege can be found in the Memorandum submitted by the Clerk of the House of Commons, Sir Donald Limon KCB, to the Joint Committee on Parliamentary Privilege (HL 50 i and HC 401 i, 1997/98). The conclusion is particularly interesting and suggests that whilst, 'For very many years it has been successfully argued that it was inappropriate to codify privilege in a statute. The Committee might wish to reconsider whether this principle still remains valid, or at least as valid as it was. Circumstances may have altered the balance of advantage'.

Freedom of Speech

Whilst freedom of speech is always referred to as an 'ancient right', it is not possible to date its origin with any degree of accuracy. Erskine May states that by the late 15th Century, freedom of speech in debate was an acknowledged right. Statutory recognition came in the form of Article 9 of the Bill of Rights of 1689, which states, ***'That the freedom of speech and debates or proceedings in Parliament ought not be be impeached or questioned in any court or place out of parliament'.*** After the Civil War, the monarchy was restored in the shape of Charles II. He was succeeded by James II, a Catholic. James went a great deal further than simply attempting to allow Catholics to hold office and it was feared that he would attempt to impose Catholicism on the nation as a whole. William of Orange, James II's son-in-law, a Dutch Protestant, was sent for by a group of eminent politicians and when he landed, James II left – for France. The Parliament which was summoned in 1689 issued a 'Declaration of Rights' (later enshrined in the Bill of Rights) setting out the ancient privileges and rights of Parliament.

[1] Erskine May (22nd Edition) page 65
[2] Erskine May (22nd Edition) page 153

Article 9 still has as much force today as it did at the time of the Glorious Revolution, as those who have recently attempted to evade its strictures in court, have discovered.

The exact meaning of Article 9 is disputed. One possible interpretation is that the Article simply affords protection to Members against actions for libel based on comments made during parliamentary proceedings; e.g. during the course of debate. Another, rather wider interpretation, is that the Article prevents any questioning of parliamentary proceedings in court; i.e., referring to what a Member said in debate in order to prove that he meant 'x' and not 'y'. Two legal cases in particular led to an examination of Article 9 in relation to the law of defamation.

In the case of *Allason v Haines*[3] and *Hamilton and another v The Guardian* the judge relied on the decision in *Prebble v Television New Zealand Ltd*[4]. In this case, which was referred to the Judicial Committee of the Privy Council, a New Zealand MP, Hon Richard Prebble had brought an action for libel against a broadcaster. The defence needed to rely on statements made by the the MP during the course of a parliamentary debate. The question for the Judicial Committee was whether or not this was contrary to Article 9 of the Bill of Rights, which has force in New Zealand law. The Judicial Committee concurred with the decision of the New Zealand Court of Appeal that it would indeed be contrary to Article 9.

It was largely in response to this judicial impasse that an amendment was tabled to the Defamation Bill – this later became section 13 of the Defamation Act 1996. The section allows an MP to waive his or her right to parliamentary privilege under Article 9 of the Bill of Rights, if he or she is concerned in an action for defamation. The right is not extended to any other type of action nor does it affect the immunity which the Member concerned enjoys from actions for libel for anything said during a proceeding in Parliament. It simply allows parliamentary statements, questions, etc., made by the Member concerned to be used as evidence in a libel action. His joint action against the Guardian having collapsed, Neil Hamilton then began a separate action against Mohamed Al Fayed, which the High Court concluded should be allowed to proceed. However, Al Fayed was granted leave to appeal against the decision on the grounds that to allow the case to continue would be contrary to Article 9 of the Bill of Rights. The defence argued that as the Parliamentary Commissioner for Standards and the Committee for Standards and Privileges had reported on the 'cash for questions' affair, questioning these reports in court would be tantamount to questioning 'proceedings' in Parliament - contrary to Article 9. George Carman QC for the defence argued in addition, that the application of the European Convention on Human Rights was limited by Parliament's right to investigate the conduct of its own Members. In an interesting article in the Independent on Sunday (14 March 1999) Alan Watkins argued that, 'plaintiffs and defendants alike should be able to refer freely to proceedings in Parliament irrespective of whether they are member or engaged in defamation proceedings ... the ancient confusion between freedom of speech in the House and the right of Parliament alone to regulate its own proceedings should at last be cleared away'. Interestingly, the Court of Appeal ruled that although the Committee of Standards and Privileges report was a 'proceeding in Parliament', its consideration by a court in a libel action should be permitted provided it did not

[3] *Allason v Haines* (1995) NLJR 1576
[4] *Prebble v Television New Zealand Ltd* (1995) 1 AC 321 (1994) 3 All ER 407

constitute an 'impermssible collateral attack' on Parliament. Another interesting feature of the case was the involvement of the House authorities in the form of the Solicitor General, acting on behalf of the Speaker. This illustrates the dual role of the Law Officers, as legal advisers both to the Government and to the House of Commons. Giving evidence to the Joint Committee on Parliamentary Privilege (HC 405 – v, 1997/98), the Attorney General, Rt Hon John Morris QC MP referred to the fact that 'the Attorney may intervene in court proceedings to assert the privileges of either House'.[5]

A Member is entitled to protection for what may be a slanderous statement, when it forms part of a 'proceeding' of the House. What exactly is a proceeding? A proceeding is usually taken to mean the formal transaction of business with the Speaker in the Chair or in a properly constituted committee. A Member will not be subject to the jurisdiction of the ordinary courts for anything said in debate, however criminal its nature. He or she may, however, be subject to the disciplinary procedures of the House.

For example, if Member A walked into the Chamber and shot Member B, he could be arrested and prosecuted. If, however, Member A simply stated that he thought Member B was a fool and ought to be shot (however unjustified his view might be) he would be protected from any subsequent action by the parliamentary privilege of freedom of speech afforded by Article 9 of the Bill of Rights. He might, however, be asked to withdraw an unparliamentary term and on refusal could be 'named' and suspended from the House. If Member A accused Member B of having shot another, Member A would again be protected by Article 9 and could not be prosecuted for libel. However, if Member A repeated the accusation outside Parliament, he or she could be sued for libel.

As a rule, criminal acts in the House are not beyond the bounds of criminal justice, but there is some dispute as to whether this rule extends to acts which can be considered as part of a proceeding in Parliament. In one case, the Deputy Serjeant at Arms was held to be justified in committing an assault as he was pursuing an order of the House, namely, to exclude a Member from the precincts of Parliament.[6] It would be difficult to argue that a serious assault by one Member on another was part of a 'proceeding' in Parliament, even if it took place in the Chamber itself, during a debate. As Erskine May points out, 'Apart from *Eliot's case* over 350 years ago, no charge against a Member in respect of an allegedly criminal act in Parliament has been brought before the courts' .[7] In this case, Sir John Eliot, along with two other Members, was arrested for 'seditious words' used in a debate in the House of Commons and for attacking the Speaker.[8]

Freedom from Arrest

Erskine May dates the earliest claim to freedom from arrest as being 1340 when a Member was released from prison in order to take his seat in the House. It was recognised in a resolution of the House in 1675 that this right did not extend to criminal matters, so an MP accused of a criminal offence could not claim sanctuary by locking

---

[5] For an interesting discussion of the role of the Law Officers, see Chapter VI, 'Legal advice and representation for Parliament', by Barry Winetrobe in 'Law and Parliament' (Butterworths, 1998).

[6] *Bradlaugh v Gosset* (1883-4) 12 QBD 271

[7] Erskine May (22nd Edition) page 99

[8] *R v Eliot, Holles and Valentine* 3 State Tr 293-336

himself in the Members' Tea Room and refusing to come out. The resolution stated that, 'by the laws and usage of Parliament, privilege of Parliament belongs to every Member of the House of Commons, in all cases except treason, felony and breach of the peace'. Members of Parliament can claim freedom from arrest in civil cases, although since the Judgments Act 1838 and subsequent legislation, imprisonment in civil cases has, to all intents and purposes, been abolished.

As Erskine May makes clear, 'The privilege of freedom from arrest has never been allowed to interfere with the administration of criminal justice or emergency legislation'.[9] However, attempting to arrest a Member within the precincts of Parliament, whilst the House was sitting, without obtaining leave of the House, would be a breach of privilege and a contempt. A Member can claim freedom from arrest for 40 days after every prorogation or dissolution and 40 days before the next appointed meeting of Parliament.

In the House of Lords, freedom from arrest is governed by SO 79 (HL) which states that, 'when Parliament is sitting, or within the usual times of privilege of Parliament, no Lord of Parliament is to be imprisoned or restrained without sentence of order of the House, unless upon a criminal charge or for refusing to give security for the peace. Notification of any order whatsoever for the imprisonment or restraint of a Lord of Parliament should be given to the House by the Court or authority ordering such restraint or imprisonment.' MPs may be detained under section 141 of the Mental Health Act 1983, but the law relating to deranged or disturbed peers is not at all clear. The introduction of legislation on this matter was proposed as long ago as 1983 by the House of Lords Committee for Privileges in their report on 'Parliamentary Privilege and the Mental Health Legislation' (HL 254, 1983-84) but has yet to surface. Some have unkindly suggested that this may be due to the difficulty of ascertaining any noticeable difference between those to whom the legislation might apply and the remainder of the inmates in the Upper Chamber.

Freedom of Access

The claim of freedom of access to Her Majesty is medieval in origin. The right is a corporate privilege of the House and is exercised through the Speaker. It is now confined to the presence of the Commons in the House of Lords to hear the Queen's Speech and to the presentation of Addresses. The right is a collective one, which means that a Backbencher cannot pop round to the Palace for a cup of tea and a quick chat about his or her latest Ten Minute Rule Bill. Peers, on the other hand, do have an individual right of access to the monarch and whilst she would be prevented from attending the House of Commons, there is nothing to prevent the Queen turning up to listen to a debate in the House of Lords.

Favourable Construction

This claim is now a mere formality and asks that the most favourable construction be placed upon all Parliament's proceedings. This dates from the days when the Speaker of the House of Commons needed to be assured that the monarch would not misinterpret the actions of the House.

[9] Erskine May (22nd Edition) page 100

Constitution of the House

It is a longstanding privilege of the House of Commons to decide on its own constitution; i.e., who should or should not be entitled to be a Member of the House. This is now set out in statute, particularly the House of Commons Disqulification Act 1975.

'Exclusive Cognisance'

Both Houses of Parliament have always claimed to have 'exclusive cognisance' of their own proceedings, what Erskine May describes as the 'right to be the sole judge of the lawfulness of their own proceedings, and to settle – or depart from – their own codes of procedure'. What this meant in practice, in a court of law, was that Acts of Parliament could only be interpreted by reference to the wording of the Acts themselves – it was not permissible to refer for clarification to any debates which there might have been in either House. Hansard was effectively out of bounds. For example, in the case of *Wellesley v Duke of Beaufort*[10] Lord Chief Justice Brougham said that, 'a court knows nothing judicially of what takes place in Parliament till what is done there becomes an Act of the legislature'. However, as a result of the ruling of the House of Lords in *Pepper v Hart* in 1992[11], Hansard may be referred to by a court when the wording of an Act is 'ambiguous or obscure'. It was the case of *Stockdale v Hansard* (in fact the former brought four actions against Hansard) which led to statutory protection being given to papers produced and published by Parliament. In the first case (1836)[12] Stockdale brought an action against Hansard for libel contained in a report which they had printed and which had been 'laid on the Table'. Hansard succeeded, but the House felt concerned enough to appoint a Committee to look into the matter. As a result a resolution was passed by the House of Commons to the effect that only Parliament and not the courts, could decide what was and was not a privilege. Stockdale then began another action against Hansard.[13] The latter's defence was that printing a report was a privilege of Parliament. Lord Chief Justice Denman accepted that Parliament had the sole right to determine its own internal procedures, but that the courts had a right to decide whether or not a matter could be regarded as an internal matter over which only Parliament had jurisdiction. Parliament did not have the right to claim that a particular procedure was a matter of privilege just because it declared it to be so. After a third and then a fourth action were brought by Stockdale, Parliament resorted to legislation and under the Parliamentary Papers Act 1840, statutory protection is now given to all papers published by order of either the House of Commons or the House of Lords. In the case of *Dingle v Associated Newspapers Ltd* (1960) 2 QB, it was stated that a newspaper which reprinted part of a report from a Select Committee was protected by the above Act.

CONTEMPTS

Erskine May describes a contempt as 'any act or omission which obstructs or impedes either House of Parliament in the performance of its functions, or which obstructs or impedes any Member or officer of such House in the discharge of his duty, or which has

[10] *Wellesley v Duke of Beaufort* (1831) 36 ER 554
[11] *Pepper v Hart* (1993) AC 593; (1993) 1 All ER 42
[12] *Stockdale v Hansard* (1836-37) 173 ER
[13] *Stockdale v Hansard* (1839) 112 ER

a tendency, directly or indirectly, to produce such results'.[14] In characteristically anachronistic language it goes on to warn that, 'Any disorderly, contumacious or disrespectful conduct in the presence of either House or a committee will constitute a contempt, which may be committed by strangers, parties or witnesses'. As far as visitors to the House are concerned, disturbances in the Strangers' Gallery or in a Committee are usually dealt with under SO 161. It was not until the 1993/94 Session that members of the public were allowed to take notes in the Strangers' Gallery. This practice is no longer punishable.

Both Houses still retain the power to imprison offenders for contempt. This extends to all contempts, whether committed by Members or Strangers, whether committed within the confines of the Palace of Westminster, or outside. Theoretically, the House of Commons may imprison an offender until the end of the Session, the House of Lords may detain them for even longer. The House of Lords may also impose fines. However, no one has actually been imprisoned by the House of Commons since 1880. Charles Bradlaugh, the Member for Northampton, was imprisoned in the Clock Tower for refusing to take the oath. Both Houses may also suspend or even expel Members. In the House of Commons, Members are usually suspended under the provisions of SO 44, although the House may still suspend a Member without recourse to Standing Orders (for example, the suspension of Graham Riddick MP and David Tredinnick MP after the report of the Committee of Privileges in 1994/95 (HC 351). Ultimately, a Member can be expelled from the House; however, he or she could stand for re-election (for example, at a by-election) in the same Parliament in which he or she was expelled.

If a Member feels that there has been an alleged breach of privilege or contempt, he or she informs the Speaker in writing. The latter must then decide whether or not the matter should take precedence over other parliamentary business. The Speaker will then make an announcement to the House. The MP who raised the matter then tables a motion for debate the following day, proposing that the issue be referred to the Committee of Standards and Privileges. If the Speaker considers the matter sufficiently urgent it can be dealt with immediately.

If the Committee of Standards and Privileges finds that a serious breach of privilege has occurred, the Member alleged to have committed the offence, is usually ordered to attend the debate on the Committee's report and will use the debate as an opportunity to explain his or her actions to the House. Members can be suspended or even expelled from the House. The latter constitutes disqualification and therefore, the seat of the Member concerned becomes vacant. Members can be expelled for contempt, libel and other offences against the House. In the House of Lords, a report from the Committee of Privileges would usually take precedence over other business.

The following, according to Erskine May, are contempts:

- refusal to attend either the House or a committee when summoned;
- prematurely publishing a Committee report;

[14] Erskine May (22nd Edition) page 108

- 'frivolously, vexatiously or maliciously submitting a petition which contains false, scandalous or groundless allegations against any person';

- deliberately misleading the House, or accepting bribes designed to influence conduct in the House (Members may not accept fees for professional services connected with proceedings in Parliament - a Member may not, therefore, practice as counsel before the House or any Committee or advice as counsel on any Private Bill);

- bribing an MP;

- bringing the House and its proceedings into disrepute either by writing or the spoken word, or by 'publication of false or perverted reports of debates and premature publication or disclosure of committee proceedings';

- obstructing Members of either House - for example, it would be a contempt to try and prevent an MP from entering the House unless he or she agreed to vote in a particular way;

- assaults and insulting and abusive behaviour against officers of either House;

- attempting to prevent witnesses from giving evidence according to the resolution of 8 March 1688 which states, 'That it is the undoubted right of this House that all witnesses summoned to attend this House, or any committee appointed by it, have the privilege of this House in coming, staying and returning'; [15]

- attempting to obstruct anyone 'having business before either House'; for example it is a contempt to obstruct someone petitioning the House or to bring an action for libel relating to material contained in a petition;

- claiming to be a Parliamentary Agent whilst unqualified (see chapter 12 for more information on Parliamentary Agents and Private Bills);

- using the symbol of the House of Commons, the portcullis, on a non-parliamentary publication (in addition, Members are not supposed to use House of Commons stationary for party political purposes);

[15] Under the Witnesses (Public Inquiries) Protection Act 1892, anyone who 'injures' a witness may be fined or imprisoned. See also the Sessional Orders agreed to by the House at the beginning of each Parliament, which state, 'That if it shall appear that any person hath been tampering with any Witness, in respect of his evidence to be given to this House, or any Committee thereof, or directly or indirectly hath endeavoured to deter or hinder any person from appearing or giving evidence the same is declared to be a high crime and misdemeanour; and this House will proceed with the utmost severity against such offenders.'

Bribery

Recent events have led to a general reappraisal of the way in which the acceptance of 'bribes' – a contempt of the House - is treated by the House. This has long been a problem for the House. In 1976 a Royal Commission on Standards of Conduct in Public Life (the 'Salmon' Commission) (CM 6524) recommended that bribery and corruption of MPs should be brought within the remit of the criminal law as in its view, MPs were not public officers for the purposes of the common law offence of corruption.[16] However, views on whether or not MPs can be subject to the common law offence of bribery appear to differ. The Nolan Committee (Committee on Standards in Public Life), set up by the Conservative Government in 1994 argued in its first report (Cm 2850) that MPs accused of taking bribes could be tried in a court for a common law offence. In 1994, the acceptance of payments by Graham Riddick MP and David Tredinnick MP to table questions led to an enquiry by the then Committee of Privileges. In their First Report (HC 351 – 1994/95) they said, not that the two Members were guilty of having accepted bribes, but that their conduct, 'fell short of the actions the House was entitled to expect'.

Given the recommendations of both the Nolan Committee and the Select Committee on Standards in Public Life that the law relating to bribery should be clarified and reviewed and the allegations of sleaze which beset the previous Conservative Government, the Labour Government issued a further statement and Consultation Paper on 9 June 1997 – 'The Prevention of Corruption: Consultation and Amendment of the Prevention of Corruption Acts 1889-1916' . The consultation period ended on 31 August 1997. In addition, on 9 June 1997, the Leader of the House announced the establishment of a Joint Committee on Parliamentary Privilege to review the existing rules of both Houses relating to privilege. The Joint Committee published their report on Parliamentary Privilege on 9 April 1999 (HL 43 - I, II, III / HC 214 - I, II, III). In addition, the Law Commission published a Consultation Paper on 18 March 1997, 'Legislating the Criminal Code: Corruption' (No.145). Its full report was published on 3 March 1998 (No. 248). It concluded that the present law, as contained in the Prevention of Corruption Acts 1889 to 1916 and the common law were, 'outmoded, uncertain and inconsistent' and should be replaced by a single new offence of corruption covering both the public and private sectors. However, neither of these documents dealt with the particular problems of Members of Parliament accused of bribery.

In addition, the Neill Committee (Committee on Standards in Public Life) published its own brief Consultation Document, 'Misuse of Public Office' in July 1997. This dealt with offences other than bribery and corruption. It seems likely that the Government will bring forward proposals for a single offence of corruption covering both public and private sectors and for extending existing statutes to cover the misuse of public office now that the Joint Committee on Parliamentary Privilege has reported.

---

[16] Bribery of a Member of either House or the acceptance of such a bribe, is not an offence under the Prevention of corruption Act 1889-1916. Neither House is considered a 'public body' as defined by the Public Bodies Corrupt Practices Act 1889 and a Member of either House is not deemed to be an 'agent' under the Prevention of Corruption Act 1906.

In its first discussion paper, 'Clarification of the Law Relating to the Bribery of Members of Parliament' (December 1996) the Home Office suggested that there were four possible ways in which to deal with allegations of bribery:

- by the continued use of parliamentary procedures for dealing with contempts of Parliament;
- by subjecting Members accused of bribery to the law on corruption which applies to others in public service;
- by allowing Parliament to deal with some allegations of bribery and the courts, others;
- by making any criminal proceedings subject to approval by Parliament.

There is an excellent discussion of the problems which each of these four options would pose in Patricia M Leopold's contribution to The Law and Parliament – 'The application of the civil and criminal law to members of Parliament and parliamentary proceedings'(see *Further Reading*). As Patricia Leopold points out, 'If Parliament decides to apply the statute law on corruption to members and to allow investigation and prosecution to be determined in the normal way, it will have to decide what to do about the use of parliamentary proceedings as evidence in such a case'. The Joint Committee has recommended that Members of both Houses should be brought within the ambit of the criminal law. Evidence relating to parliamentary proceedings would be admissible, 'notwithstanding Article 9'.

THE JOINT COMMITTEE ON PARLIAMENTARY PRIVILEGE

As previously mentioned, on 9 June 1997, the Leader of the House announced the establishment of a Joint Committee on Parliamentary Privilege to review the existing rules of both Houses relating to privilege. The Joint Committee published their report on Parliamentary Privilege on 9 April 1999 (HL 43 - I, II, III / HC 214 - I, II, III) and made the following recommendations:

- There should be three exceptions to the general principle set out in Article 9 of the Bill of Rights, which should be set out in a new Parliamentary Privileges Act. The rule established in *Pepper v Hart* should be enshrined in law (this allows a court to examine 'proceedings in Parliament' where they relate to the interpretation of a particular Act of Parliament or subordinate legislation. It should also be possible to refer to parliamentary proceedings in cases of judicial review and finally, courts should be able to refer to parliamentary proceedings 'where there is no suggestion that anything forming part of those proceedings was inspired by improper motives or was untrue or misleading and there is no question of legal liability'. This, of course, would rule out references to parliamentary proceedings in court where an MP was alleged to have accepted 'cash for questions'.
- Section 13 of the Defamation Act 1996 should be replaced by a section allowing the House of Commons as a whole to waive Article 9 where appropriate (this would not necessarily be an action for defamation). However, the House would not be able to do this in cases where it would 'expose the Member or other person concerned to any risk of legal liability'.

- The term 'proceeding in Parliament' would include a letter of complaint to the Parliamentary Commissioner for Standards only if taken up by the Commissioner for investigation.
- Members of both Houses should be included within the scope of any new legislation on corruption and Article 9 should be set aside in any criminal proceedings for bribery and the consent of a Law Officer would be required before a prosecution could take place.
- The privilege of each House to manage its own affairs should be set out in statute, but this should be confined to activities directly and closely related to proceedings in Parliament.
- Parliament's powers to imprison those guilty of contempts should be abolished.
- Failure to attend a Select Committee, if called as a witness, should be made a criminal offence, punishable by a fine of an unlimited amount or three months' imprisonment.
- Members' freedom from arrest in civil cases should be abolished.
- Peers suffering from a mental illness should not be able to sit and vote in Parliament if detained under mental health legislation.

REGISTERING OUTSIDE INTERESTS

In the House of Commons

Background to the Code of Conduct

The 'Nolan Committee' (the Committee on Standards in Public Life) was established by the then Prime Minister, Rt Hon John Major MP, on 25 October, 1994, 'to examine current concerns about standards of conduct of all holders of public office, including arrangements relating to financial and commercial activities'. The Committee's remit did not include the investigation of specific allegations of misconduct. The Committee was to consider the current arrangements by which Members registered outside interests and the problems arising from Members links, financial or otherwise, with outside organisations; for example, lobbying companies. Its first report (Cm 2850) was published on 12 May 1995 and was debated in the House of Commons on 18 May 1995. In response to the report, the House established a new Select Committee on 6 June 1995, to consider its recommendations.

The Select Committee on Standards in Public Life, under the Chairmanship of Rt Hon Tony Newton, at that time the Leader of the House, reported on 6 July 1995. Its recommendations were debated on 19 July 1995 and a number of interim resolutions were passed by the House. The Committee's second report was published in October, and a further debate was held on 6 November 1995.

One of the resolutions passed by the House on 19 July 1995 called for the appointment of a Parliamentary Commissioner for Standards, as recommended by the Nolan Committee.

The Nolan Committee had recommended the establishment of an independent Parliamentary Commissioner, who would not be a career member of the House of Commons staff and who would take over the responsibility of maintaining the Register of Members' Interests and who would advise members on conduct, ethics, etc. The Commissioner would have similar powers to those of the Comptroller and Auditor General and the Parliamentary Commissioner for Administration. He or she would have the power to decide whether or not to investigate a complaint in the first instance and subsequently, whether or not to refer it to a Select Committee.

The Select Committee on Standards in Public Life accepted the need for such an independent Commissioner. In its report the Committee pointed out that the Comptroller and Auditor General (CAG) and the Parliamentary Commissioner for Administration (Ombudsman) were both appointed, not by the House, but by letters patent under the Crown. The Nolan report had recommended that the new Commissioner be supported by a Select Committee, primarily to avoid the necessity of introducing legislation to establish the new position (as was the case with the Parliamentary Commissioner for Administration (the Ombudsman) under the Parliamentary Commissioner Act 1967). The Select Committee report stated (para. 24) that, 'Without statutory authority, however, he (the Commissioner) can only operate, under the procedures of the House, through the Committee'. It went on to state that: 'All the Commissioner's findings and conclusions will have to be made to a Committee, and only a Committee will have the power to publish them'.

The Select Committee also recommended that the main duties of the Commissioner should be to maintain and monitor the Register of Members' Interests; to provide advice to MPs and the proposed Select Committee on Standards and Privileges; to receive and investigate complaints about the Conduct of Members and to report his findings to the Committee. The Select Committee report stated that: 'Any powers to compel the attendance of Members before the Commissioner will be exercisable only by the Committee acting on a request from the Commissioner'.

The Select Committee proposed that once the general resolution (set out above) had been passed by the House, the House of Commons Commission should begin a recruitment process, culminating in the House approving a further motion actually appointing a named individual - the aim being to have a Commissioner in place by November 1995. The Commissioner could only be removed from office by a substantive resolution of the House.

The Motion passed by the House on 6 November 1995, established, by way of a new Standing Order (now SO 150) the office of Parliamentary Commissioner for Standards. The duties of the new Commissioner are to maintain the Register of Members' Interests and any other registers set up by the House, to advise both individual Members and the Committee on Standards and Privileges on any matters concerning registration of interests or any Code of Conduct, to monitor the operation of the Register and Code and to receive complaints from both MPs and members of the public relating to the registration or declaration of interests and MPs conduct. The Commissioner reports to the Committee on Standards and Privileges but is, ultimately, answerable to and may be dismissed by, the House. Sir Gordon Downey, KCB was appointed as the first

Parliamentary Commissioner for Standards by resolution of the House on 6 November 1995. He was succeeded by Elizabeth Filkin on 17 November 1998.

The Nolan Committee recommended that the proposed Parliamentary Commissioner for Standards be supported by a Select Committee or rather a Sub-Committee of the Privileges Committee, consisting of seven Members. It suggested that the Members Interests' Select Committee could be dispensed with altogether. It also suggested that the Committee's hearings be in public and that Members who so wished could be accompanied by advisers.

The Select Committee on Standards in Public Life recommended in their report that both the Privileges Committee and the Select Committee on Members' Interests be abolished and replaced by a new Select Committee on Standards and Privileges. Proposed terms of reference for the Committee were set out in an Appendix to the Select Committee's report. The Resolution before the House on 19 July 1995, simply stated that such a Committee be established from the beginning of the 1996/97 Session.

The Resolution passed by the House on 6 November 1995 established, by way of a new Standing Order (now SO 149) the Select Committee on Standards and Privileges. This new Select Committee replaced both the Select Committee on Members' Interests and the Privileges Committee. The Committee's remit is to consider specific matters referred to it by the House, to oversee the work of the Parliamentary Commissioner for Standards, to oversee the arrangements for the compilation of the Register of Members' Interests, to consider matters relating to the conduct of Members, including any specific complaints relating to breaches of the Code of Conduct, to which the Commissioner has drawn their attention. The Law Officers can attend the Committee's proceedings, but cannot vote or move amendments.

The Nolan Committee recommended that a Code of Conduct be drawn up for Members of Parliament to include the following key principles:

- a Member should not promote any matter in the House in return for payment;
- a Member with a financial interest should declare it when speaking in the House or in Committee;
- a Member with a personal financial interest likely to give rise to a conflict with the public interest should either dispose of the former or take no part in any public business related to the personal financial interest.

The Select Committee felt that the House should make a decision in principle on a Code of Conduct before a specific code was drawn up. The Resolution before the House on 19 July 1995, 'instructed the appropriate Select Committee to prepare such a draft Code for approval as soon as possible, taking into account the suggestions of the Nolan Committee ... and whilst restating its commitment to the objectives of the Resolution of the House of 15 July 1947 relating to Privileges, accepts the need to review its wording in the context of the work to be undertaken on the draft Code'.

The 1947 Resolution stated that, 'it is inconsistent with the dignity of the House, with the duty of a Member to his constituency, and with the maintenance of the privilege of freedom of speech, for any Member of the House to enter into any contractual agreement with an outside body, controlling or limiting the Member's complete independence and freedom of action in Parliament or stipulating that he shall act in any way as the representative of such outside body in regard to any matters to be transacted in Parliament; the duty of a Member being to his constituency and to the country as a whole, rather than to any particular section thereof'.

The Nolan Committee recommended that the House should restate this motion, but the Select Committee felt that this might pre-empt any subsequent decisions by the House on establishing a Code of Conduct. The new Select Committee on Standards and Privileges compiled a Code of Conduct for Members and a guide to the rules on advocacy. The Code of Conduct was published on 12 July 1996 and approved by the House on 24 July 1996.

The Nolan report recommended that Members' interests should be declared by means of appropriate symbols appearing on the Order Paper. An existing Resolution of the House of 12 June 1975 stated that: 'Any interest declared in a copy of the register of Members' Interests shall be regarded as sufficient disclosure for the purpose of taking part in any Division of the House or in any of its Committees'. It went on to define 'proceedings' as not including the 'giving of any written notice, or the asking of a supplementary Question'.

The Select Committee on Standards in Public Life did not feel that a symbol should appear retrospectively beside division lists or that Members should have to declare an interest when asking supplementary questions. However, it felt that different considerations applied to oral and written questions, EDMs and amendments to bills, where interests should be registered.

The Resolution passed by the House on 19 July 1995 stated, 'That with effect from the beginning of the next Session, the Resolution of the House of 12th June 1975 relating to Members' Interests (Declaration) (No. 2) be amended by leaving out the words "the giving of any written notice or". As a result, Members tabling written and oral questions, amendments to bills, or who simply add their names to EDMs, must indicate any relevant interest. The letter ['R'] appears next to the question on the Order Paper and Notice Paper.

The Resolution before the House on 19 July 1995 called for further examination of the recommendations of the Nolan Committee concerning consultancies (including multi-client consultancies) and disclosures in the Register of Members' Interests and recommended that the Select Committee on Standards in Public Life bring forward proposals by the end of the current Session.

The Nolan Committee recommended that Members should be prohibited from providing services to those organisations providing Parliamentary services (lobbying and consultancy) to multiple clients and suggested that from the beginning of the 1995/96 Session, Members should deposit in full with the Registrar contracts relating to the provision of services in their capacity as Members and should declare in the Register annual remuneration in respect of such agreements. Remuneration would be declared in bands: under £1,000; £1,000 - £5,000; £5,000 - £10,000 and then in £5,000 bands. An estimate of the value of benefits in kind would also be made.

When the Select Committee considered the matter, the Labour Members of the Select Committee proposed a declaration of remuneration but were outvoted by the Conservative and Liberal Democrat Members of the Committee. When the matter was again debated for the second time, on 6 November 1995 the Government was defeated by 51 votes on the question of declaration of earnings. The Labour amendment passed by the House means that MPs must register earnings from extra-parliamentary work as advisers, in bands of up to £1,000, £1,000 to £5,000, £5,000 to £10,000 and in bands of £5,000 thereafter.

A resolution passed by the House on 6 November 1995 effectively bans paid advocacy (based on the 1947 resolution). The resolution states that 'It is inconsistent with the dignity of the House, with the duty of a Member to his constituents, and with the maintenance of the privilege of freedom of speech, for any member of this House to enter into any contractual agreement with an outside body, controlling or limiting the Member's complete independence and freedom of action in Parliament or stipulating that he shall act in any any way as the representative of such outside body in regard to any matters to be transacted in Parliament; the duty of a Member being to his constituents and the country as a whole, rather than to any particular section thereof; and that in particular no Members of the House shall, in consideration of any remuneration, fee, payment or reward or benefit in kind, direct or indirect, which the Member or any member of his or her family has received is receiving or expects to receive, i) advocate or initiate any cause or matter on behalf of any outside body or individual, or (ii) urge any other Member of either House of Parliament, including Ministers, to do so, by means of any speech, Question, Motion, introduction of a Bill or amendment to a Motion or Bill'.

The Code of Conduct & The Guide to the Rules Relating to the Conduct of Members

The Code of Conduct was published on 12 July 1996 and approved by the House on 24 July 1996. The Code itself is brief and restates the seven principles of public life identified by the Nolan Committee. These are:

- Selflessness (holders of public office should not take decisions in order to gain financial advantage)
- Integrity (holders of public office should not take on financial obligations to outside organisations which might influence their official duties)
- Objectivity (if a holder of public office makes any recommendations for appointment to public offices, these should be on merit)
- Accountability (holders of public office are accountable to the public)
- Openness (information should only be restricted by holders of public office 'when the wider public interest clearly demands' it)
- Honesty (holders of public office should declare any relevant private interests relating to public duties and where there is a conflict between a private and public interest it should be resolved in the interest of the latter)
- Leadership (holders of public office should set a good example)

The Code states that, 'The acceptance by a Member of a bribe to influence his or her conduct as a Member, including any fee, compensation or reward in connection with the promotion of, or opposition to, any Bill, Motion, or other matter submitted, or intended to be submitted to the House, or to any Committee of the House, is contrary to the law of Parliament'. The Code also states that, 'Members shall fulfil conscientiously the requirements of the House in respect of the registration of interests in the Register of Members' Interests and shall always draw attention to any relevant interest in any proceeding of the House or its Committees, or in any communications with Ministers, Government Departments or Executive Agencies.' The Code bans paid advocacy outright by stating that, 'No Member shall act as a paid advocate in any proceeding of the House'.

It is the Guide to the Rules Relating to the Conduct of Members which sets out in detail what is expected of Members under the Code

The Committee on Standards and Privileges, being the successor to the Committee on Members' Interests, inherited the previous resolutions of the House relating to the declarations which MPs must furnish to the Register of Members' Interests, in particular the resolutions of the House of 22 May 1974 and 12 June 1975, respectively. These resolutions state that Members must register outside interests and where those interests have been registered that is regarded as 'sufficient disclosure' for the purposes of voting in a division. The registration form itself has ten categories of interests and Members must return the form within three months of taking their seats. They must notify the Registrar of any new interests as they arise. The Register is published each year and is available on the Parliament website. It is updated in between publications and is available for inspection in the Committee Office in the House of Commons. The ten categories of registerable interests are:

1. Remunerated directorships
2. Remunerated employment (including membership of Lloyd's)
3. Provision of services dependent upon remunerated employment as set out in categories 1 and 2, which arise from a Member's position as MP. Clients to whom the services are provided must be listed; e.g. where an MP is an adviser to a firm of Parliamentary Consultants, he or she must list those of the Consultants' clients to whom he or she provides advice
4. Financial support exceeding 25% of election expenses paid prior to an election and any other financial or material sponsorship, involving personal payment (this does not include donations made directly to a constituency party, which is not linked to that particular Member's candidacy)
5. Gifts, benefits and hospitality received by the Member of his or her spouse of a value greater than £125, or a material benefit of a value greater than 0.5% of current parliamentary salary given by any person 'within the UK' which relates to the MP's membership of the House
6. Overseas visits, where the costs was not met by the MP or from public funds
7. Overseas benefits and gifts received by the Member of his or her spouse of a value greater than £125 or a material benefit of a value greater than 0.5% of current parliamentary salary which relates to the MP's membership of the House
8. Land and property apart from an MP's home which has a 'substantial' value or from which 'substantial' income is derived

9. Shares held by the Member, or with or on behalf of his or her spouse or children, in any public or private company which are greater than 1% of the issued share capital of the company or less than 1% of the issued share capital but more than £25,000 in nominal value (MPs are advised to register other shareholdings as well if they are likely to influence his or her actions in the House)
10. Any other matter likely to influence a Member in his or her duties as an MP, or which others might think could influence him or her, even where no financial benefit is gained

According to the resolution of the House of 6 November 1995, Members must register any 'agreement which involves the provision of services in his capacity as a Member of Parliament' (provided it is not an agreement to act as advocate for a particular cause as such agreeements are banned) and must provide a copy of the agreement including any fees payable, indicating in which band they fall:

up to £1,000
£1,000 - £5,000
£5,000 - £10,000

Members tabling written and oral questions, amendments to Bills, or who simply add their names to EDMs, must indicate any relevant interest. The letter ['R'] appears next to the question on the Order Paper and Notice Paper. Members requesting emergency debates under SO 24, or entering the ballot for daily or Wednesday morning adjournment debates, must notify the Speaker of any relevant interests

It is the application of the advocacy rule which is one of the most contentious elements of the Code of Conduct. When is an MP acting as an advocate? Basically, if he or she is required to register an interest, then it falls within the remit of the advocacy rule. If an MP is in receipt of any pecuniary benefit from a particular organisation, he or she may not *initiate* any parliamentary 'proceeding' relating directly to the interests of that particular organisation or any organisation or group whose interests are 'substantially' the same as those of the outside body concerned. A 'proceeding' includes:

- presenting a bill or petition
- tabling and asking a parliamentary question
- initiating a debate;
- tabling or moving a motion or an amendment to a bill;
- proposing a draft report or moving an amendment in a Select Committee;
- applying for an emergency or daily adjournment debate

A Member with a registered interest may *participate* in a debate provided he or she does not seek to promote *exclusively* the interests of the outside body or individual with whom he or she has a financial or other agreement. Participation in debate includes participation in Standing and Select Committee proceedings and the asking of supplementary questions in the House. Whilst visits to UK dependencies, paid for by the Government of the country in question, must be registered, they fall outside the scope of the advocacy rule. However, the Guide to the Rules states that, 'Members may not, for example, either initiate or advocate in debate increased United Kingdom financial assistance to a Government from which they have recently received hospitality. Nor may the member initiate any proceeding in Parliament which seeks to bring specific and direct benefit to the host Government. However, provided they had registered the hospitality, they could participate in a debate relating to the country concerned.

Members who have a 'direct pecuniary interest' in a matter which is to be voted on, should not take part in that Division; however, this only applies to interests which are 'immediate and personal' (Erskine May, (22nd Edition) page 361. This is derived from a decision by Mr Speaker Abbot (17 July 1811) and means that Members should not take part in Divisions on matters which affect them, financially in a direct rather than indirect way. For example, Erskine May (page 362) cites a decision of the Speaker in 1986 that members of Lloyds could vote on an amendment to bring Lloyds within the terms of the Financial Services Bill on the grounds that this was a matter of public policy. The same rule holds good for Private Bills and any Member with a personal interest in a Private bill would not be able to serve as a member of an Opposed Private Bill Committee.

The Register of Members' Interests is published each year and contains the details of MPs' paid consultancies and any gifts, donations, etc., which Members are expected to register under the rules of the House. The Register is published annually as a House of Commons Paper and is available on the Parliament website. Much illuminating information can be found therein. Sir Paul Beresford MP, when he is not in the House, is gainfully employed as a dental surgeon and, one imagines, likes nothing better than a molar extraction or some really challenging root canal work, before attending oral questions. Dr Peter Brand MP enjoys the generous gift of an Isle of Wight Council Car Parking Pass and Angela Browning MP records that on 5 June 1998 she 'was presented with a Honiton lace brooch in a silver case by Honiton Museum and the Honiton Lacemakers'. Ronnie Campbell MP was presented with a Penny Black stamp, and, improbable as it may sound, Dale Campbell-Savours MP was paid by the National Democratic Institute of Washington, to visit Katmandu, Nepal, to lecture on constitutional issues. James Clappison MP records 'unpaid research assistance provided by Mr. Howard Spratt, of Potters Bar, Hertfordshire'.

After a glance at the Register, one is drawn inescapably to the conclusion that those things which ought to be recorded are not, and those which are, ought not to be.

In addition to the Register of Members' Interests, there are three other Registers: the Register of Parliamentary Journalists (those journalists who hold a parliamentary pass which admits them to the Press Gallery and Lobby); the Register of Members' Staff and the Register of All Party and Parliamentary Groups (see chapter 11). These Registers may now be inspected by the public. Journalists must register the employment which entitles them to the pass and also any other paid occupation or employment which may be relevant. Similarly, Members' Secretaries and Research Assistants must register 'other' employment.

On several occasions the House has considered whether or not there should be a Register of Lobbyists or some form of statutory regulation of lobbying companies. The problem with either approach is that is might actually hinder access for those who did not wish to employ the services of a lobbying company. It would also make a false distinction between companies who lobby on their own behalf and those who employ professional public affairs consultancies. At present there are two organisations representing lobbying companies: the Public Relations Consultants Association (PRCA) and the Association of Professional Political Consultants (APPC). They have their own registers and codes of conduct.

The Resolutions relating to Members' interests (as included in the Code of Conduct and Guide to the Rules Relating to the Conduct of Members) are set out below:

Resolutions of 22 May 1974 - Members' Interests (Declaration)

"In any debate or proceeding of the House or its Committees or transactions or communications which a Member may have with other Members or with Ministers or servants of the Crown, he shall disclose any relevant pecuniary interest or benefit of whatever nature, whether direct or indirect, that he may have had, may have or may be expecting to have."

"Every Member of the House of Commons shall furnish to a Registrar of Members' Interests such particulars of his registrable interests as shall be required, and shall notify to the Registrar any alterations which may occur therein, and the Registrar shall cause these particulars to be entered in a Register of Members' Interests which shall be available for inspection by the public."

Resolution of 12 June 1975, amended on 19th July 1995 - Members' Interests (Declaration)

"For the purposes of the Resolution of the House of 22nd May 1974 in relation to disclosure of interests in any proceeding of the House or its Committees,
(i) any interest disclosed in a copy of the Register of Members' Interests shall be regarded as sufficient disclosure for the purpose of taking part in any division in the House or in any of its Committees.
(ii) the term `proceeding' shall be deemed not to include the asking of a supplementary question."

Resolution of 12 June 1975 - Members' Interests (Declaration)

"Pursuant to the Resolutions of the House of 22nd May 1974, this House agrees with the recommendations made in the Report of the Select Committee on Members' Interests (Declaration) relative to the arrangements for the registration of Members' Interests, and with the recommendations contained in paragraphs 43 and 47 of that Report in relation to the declaring of such interests; and that a Register of such interests be established as soon as possible in accordance with the proposals made in that Report."

Paragraph 43 of the First Report from the Select Committee on Members' Interests (Declaration) (Session 1974-75) HC 102, reads:

"No difficulty should arise in any proceeding of the House or its Committees in which the Member has an opportunity to speak. Such proceedings, in addition to debates in the House, includes debates in Standing Committees, the presentation of a Public Petition, and meetings of Select Committees at which evidence is heard. On all such occasions the Member will declare his interest at the beginning of his remarks in exactly the same way as he has hitherto done by convention. It will be a matter for his judgement, if his interest is already recorded in the Register, whether he simply draws attention to this or makes a rather fuller disclosure."

Paragraph 47 of the same Report provides that declarations of interest made in Select Committees shall be recorded in their Minutes of Proceedings.

Resolution of 17 December 1985 - Register of Members' Interests

"This House ... emphasises that it is the personal responsibility of each Member to have regard to his public position and the good name of Parliament in any work he undertakes or any interests he acquires; confirms that the scope of the requirement to register remunerated trades, professions or vocations includes any remunerated activity in the fields of public relations and political and parliamentary advice and consultancy; in particular ... in regard to the registration and declaring of clients that the services which require such registration and, where appropriate, declaration, include, as well as any action connected with any proceedings in the House or its Committees, the sponsoring of functions in the Palace, making representations to Ministers, Civil Servants and other Members, accompanying delegations to Ministers and the like ..."
[Note: This Resolution should be read in conjunction with the Resolutions of 6th November 1995 on advocacy (Conduct of Members) and delegations (Standards in Public Life).]

Resolution of 6 November 1995 - Employment Agreements

"(1) With effect from Wednesday 15th November 1995, any Member proposing to enter into an agreement which involves the provision of services in his capacity as a Member of Parliament shall conclude such an agreement only if it conforms to the Resolution of the House of 6th November 1995 relating to Conduct of Members; and a full copy of any such agreement including the fees or benefits payable in bands of: up to £1,000, £1,000-£5,000, £5,000-£10,000, and thereafter in bands of £5,000, shall be deposited with the Parliamentary Commissioner for Standards at the same time as it is registered in the Register of Members' Interests and made available for inspection by the public;
(2) any Member who has an existing agreement involving the provision of services in his capacity as a Member of Parliament which conforms to the Resolution of the House of 6th November 1995 relating to Conduct of Members, but which is not in written form, shall take steps to put the agreement in written form; and no later than 31st March 1996 a full copy of any such agreement including the fees or benefits payable in bands of: up to £1,000, £1,000-£5,000, £5,000-£10,000, and thereafter in bands of £5,000 shall be deposited with the Parliamentary Commissioner for Standards and registered in the Register of Members' Interests and made available for inspection by the public;"

Resolution of 13 July 1992 - Members' Interests (Interests of Chairmen and members of Select Committees)

"This House takes note of the First Report from the Select Committee on Members' Interests, Session 1990-91 (House of Commons Paper No. 108), relating to the interests of Chairmen and members of Select Committees, and approves the recommendations of the Committee relating to declaration of interest in Select Committees (paragraphs 8 to 16), withdrawal from Committee proceedings (paragraph 24) and procedures prior to the election of a Chairman (paragraph 25)."

Resolution of 2 May 1695 - Against offering Bribes to Members

"The Offer of any Money, or other Advantage, to any Member of Parliament, for the promoting of any Matter whatsoever, depending, or to be transacted, in Parliament, is a high Crime and Misdemeanour, and tends to the Subversion of the Constitution."

Resolution of 22 June 1858 - Rewards to Members

"It is contrary to the usage and derogatory to the dignity of this House, that any of its Members should bring forward, promote or advocate, in this House, any proceeding or measure in which he may have acted or been concerned for or in consideration of any pecuniary fee or reward."

Resolution of 15 July 1947, amended 6 November 1995 - Conduct of Members

"It is inconsistent with the dignity of the House, with the duty of a Member to his constituents, and with the maintenance of the privilege of freedom of speech, for any Member of this House to enter into any contractual agreement with an outside body, controlling or limiting the Member's complete independence and freedom of action in Parliament or stipulating that he shall act in any way as the representative of such outside body in regard to any matters to be transacted in Parliament; the duty of a Member being to his constituents and to the country as a whole, rather than to any particular section thereof and that in particular no Member of the House shall, in consideration of any remuneration, fee, payment, reward or benefit in kind, direct or indirect, which the Member or any member of his or her family has received, is receiving, or expects to receive-

(i) advocate or initiate any cause or matter on behalf of any outside body or individual, or

(ii) urge any other Member of either House of Parliament, including Ministers, to do so, by means of any speech, Question, Motion, introduction of a Bill or amendment to a Motion or Bill."

Resolution of 6 November 1995 - Standards in Public Life

"This House agrees with the recommendations in the Second Report from the Select Committee on Standards in Public Life (House of Commons Paper No. 816) relating to the cessation of paid advocacy (paragraph 54); and further that a Member with a paid interest should not initiate or participate in, including attendance, a delegation where the problem affects only the body from which he has a paid interest."

Resolution of 19 July 1995 - Code of Conduct

"This House endorses the principle of a Code of Conduct, and instructs the appropriate Select Committee to prepare such a draft Code for approval as soon as possible, taking into account the suggestions of the Nolan Committee and any relevant overseas analogues; and whilst restating its commitment to the objectives of the Resolution of the House of 15th July 1947 relating to privileges, accepts the need to review its wording in the context of the work to be undertaken on the draft Code."

Resolution of 24 July 1996 - Code of Conduct

"This House approves the Third Report from the Committee on Standards and Privileges, House of Commons Paper No. 604, and in particular-

(a) approves the Code of Conduct prepared pursuant to the Resolution of the House of 19th July 1995,

(b) approves the Guide to the Rules relating to the Conduct of Members, the modifications to the rules of the House contained therein, and the guidelines to the application of the Resolution of the House of 6th November 1995, (Conduct of Members) contained in paragraph 58 of the Guide, and

(c) authorises the Committee on Standards and Privileges to make such minor amendments to the Guide to the Rules as appear to it to be justified by experience or necessarily reflect decisions of the House; and to report such amended versions of the Guide to the House."

The Work of the Committee on Standards and Privileges

The Committee on Standards and Privileges has 11 members (the quorum is five) appointed at the beginning of each Parliament. Under So 149, the Committee on Standards and Privileges has three functions:

- to deal with any questions relating to privilege, referred to it by the House itself (the Parliamentary Commissioner for Standards is not involved in these enquiries);

- to oversee the work of the Parliamentary Commissioner for Standards, including the Commissioner's arrangements for the 'compilation, maintenance and accessibility of the Register of Members' Interests' and to consider any complaints about failure to register referred to it by the Commissioner;

- to consider any questions about the conduct of a particular Member which has been referred to it by the Parliamentary Commissioner.

If, after a complaint has been made to the Parliamentary Commissioner for Standards, either by a Member of the House or a member of the public, the Commissioner decides that there is sufficient evidence to pursue the matter further, the Member of whom the complaint has been made will be asked to respond before conducting a preliminary enquiry. After investigation, the Commissioner reports to the Select Committee on Standards and Privileges, which then undertakes its own enquiry.

The decisions of the Commissioner are final as Mohamed Al Fayed discovered when the the former rejected Mohamed Al Fayed's allegations that a previous Home Secretary, Rt Hon Michael Howard MP had accepted payments from Tiny Rowland. Al Fayed sought judicial review. The case then went to the Court of Appeal (*R v Parliamentary Commissioner for Standards, ex parte Al Fayed* (1997) but the appeal was dismissed by the Master of the Rolls on the grounds that whilst the decisions of the Parliamentary Commissioner for Administration could be reviewed, because they dealt with administrative processes outside Parliament, the decisions of the Parliamentary Commissioner for Standards could not, because they were concerned with Parliament's regulation of its own procedures.

The new system is not without problems, not least of which is the absence of any mechanism by which a Member accused of misconduct can appeal against either the Commissioner's or the Committee's findings. However, the Committee recognised this omission and on 24 March 1998 issued a consultative document (HC 633, 13th Report, 1997/98) containing the views of various interested parties on possible reforms. There was a wide range of views and several of those who submitted evidence wanted the Committee to adopt judicial procedures in assessing appeals, with some calling for a full re-hearing of the evidence on appeal. There were others who wanted appeals to be heard by a sub-committee of the full Committee.

A number of those who gave evidence to the Committee were of the view that the Committee on Standards and Privileges is ***not*** a court of law and that therefore any suggestion of its introducing a more judicial style of proceedings is fundamentally misplaced. In his letter to the Clerk of the Committee, Sir Clifford Boulton GCB, former Clerk of the House, wrote that 'while I am a strong supporter of the rights (and duty) of the House to regulate its own discipline, I can see advantages in the House being able to hand over certain cases to the courts where allegations amounting to bribery or corruption are involved'. In his evidence to the Clerk, Anthony Bevins of the Independent, put the matter even more forcibly: 'Bribery is a crime, and it should not be tolerated in any part of society, let alone Parliament. The current situation is a public scandal, and the fact that your committee has still not addressed the issue is a disgrace'. He went on, 'Sir Gordon (at that time Parliamentary Commissioner for standards) is neither policeman nor public prosecutor; you are not a court. You should stop this pretence because it is foolish and risks bringing Parliament into contempt. Leave the serious offences to the criminal law, for investigation by the police, and prosecution in the courts of law. The proper appeal process is ready and available there'.

The Study of Parliament Group suggested in its evidence that, 'The transfer of such cases to the criminal courts, which we support in principle, would undoubtedly significantly lessen the need for complex hearings – both at original and appeal stages. This is a powerful reason for making such a transfer'. In a letter to the Guardian, reproduced as Appendix 19 of the report, Dale Campbell-Savours MP, said, 'I am neither judge, juror nor lawyer. I do not believe that a committee of Parliament stuffed with MPs is capable of conducting the investigative and cross-questioning aspects of an inquiry into members' conduct'. However, Mr Campbell-Savours does not favour handing the matter over the courts preferring to limit the role of the Select Committee itself to overseeing the Commissioner's investigations. Where the subject of the Commissioner's investigations sought to appeal against a report and where the Committee agreed that leave to appeal should be granted, a panel of judicial assessors would be appointed by the Committee, to hear the appeal. There were others who felt that Parliament should continue to regulate itself, rather than subject Members to the full rigours of the criminal law. In her evidence to the Committee, Rt Hon Gillian Shephard MP made it quite clear that in her view, 'the responsibility for investigating allegations of misconduct by Members of

Parliament should remain with the House of Commons. Successful self-regulation should enhance the standing of the House in the eyes of the public'.

A final report (HC 1191, 21st Report, 1997/98) was published on 19 November 1998. The Committee made the following recommendations:

- appointment of a legally qualified assessor to assist the Commssioner in his initial investigation
- where the Commissioner does not accept a Member's account of the facts, the Commissioner should inform the Member concerned of his findings of fact after he has completed his report. If the Member disagrees with those findings and wanted to appeal he or she would inform the Commissioner
- the Committee would receive the Commissioner's report and be informed of the Member's wish to appeal
- the Committee would be able to dismiss 'frivolous or unsubstantiated' appeals
- where an appeal related to procedural matters, the Committee itself would conduct a review, where the appeal required a re-hearing, the Committee could refer the matter to an ad hoc tribunal for a report before proceeding with its own report to the House
- the tribunal would consist of three independent people (not MPs) appointed by the Committee and would report solely on the facts of the case
- the tribunal could examine and cross-examine witnesses (the Commissioner would not play a part in the proceedings)
- the Committee would then consider both the Commissioner's report and the tribunal's assessment

These proposals would require amendments to SO 149.

In the House of Lords

In the House of Lords, the Third Report from the Procedure Committee (1994/95) was agreed to on 7 November 1995 and the House resolved that peers must 'always act on their personal honour' and should not accept 'financial inducement as an incentive or reward for exercising Parliamentary influence'. Where a peer does have a financial interest in a particular matter, or where he or she may have an financial arrangement, for example, with a lobbying company, he or she should not take part in or vote on a matter directly related to that financial interest or arrangement. However, the decision on whether or not to speak and vote rests with peers themselves, but where they do take part in debates in which they have an interest, they are supposed to declare an interest before speaking. The House of Lords also has a Register of Lords' Interests. There are three parts: consultancies for which peers accept payment or some other 'reward' for providing advice; financial interests in lobbying companies; any other matters. Any agreements falling into the first two sections, should be registered within a month; those in section three are voluntary.

The Register is published annually (it is available on the Parliament website) and is updated regularly. The updated edition is available for inspection in the Record Office. The Committee on Lords Interests (a sub-committee of the Committee for Privileges) can investigate any allegations of non-compliance with rules relating to registration and can also offer advice to Lords on the application of the guidelines. Three Law Lords must be present when the Committee conducts such an enquiry.

THE MINISTERIAL CODE

Ministers not only have to abide by the same Codes and Resolutions as other MPs and peers, but must also abide by the Code of Conduct and Guidance on Procedures for Ministers. The essential elements are set out below (the full Code and Guidance can be found on the Cabinet Office website – http://www.cabinet-office.gov.uk/).

- Ministers must uphold the principle of collective responsibility
- Ministers are accountable to Parliament
- Ministers must not knowingly mislead Parliament
- Ministers should only keep information from Parliament where disclosure would not be in the public interest
- There should be no conflict between Ministers' public duties and private interests
- Ministers should avoid accepting gifts or hospitality which 'might, or might reasonably appear to, compromise their judgement or place them under an improper obligation'
- The roles of Minister and constituency MP must be kept separate
- Departmental resources must not be used for party political purposes

Paragraph 114 of the guidance to ministers states that they must 'scrupulously avoid any danger of an actual or apparent conflict of interest between their Ministerial position and their private financial interests. Paragraph 119 advises ministers to 'consider placing all investments (including derivatives) into a bare trust, i.e. one in which the Minister is not informed of changes in investments or of the state of the portfolio, but is still fully entitled to both the capital and income generated'. This was course of action followed by Lord Sainsbury of Turville on becoming a Minister in 1998. As far as the acceptance of gifts are concerned, they should be reported to the Permanent Secretary, and whilst those valued at less than £140 may be retained, those whose value is higher can either be handed over to the Department or repurchased (minus £140). Gifts may also be retained in the Department for five years, if disposing of them would cause offence. So, if consigning that leather-bound first edition of the collected speeches of President X to the departmental dustbin is likely to be the cause of a major diplomatic incident, it may be displayed prominently in the departmental canteen.

FURTHER READING

The Law and Parliament, Edited by Dawn Oliver and Gavin Drewry (Butterworths, 1998)
Representation: Theory and Practice in Britain, David Judge (Routledge, 1999)
So You Want to be a Lobbyist? The Inside Story of the Political Lobbying Industry, Corinne Souza (Politico's Publishing, 1998)
One Man's Word:The Untold Story of the Cash-for-Questions Affair, Ian Greer (Andre Deutsch, 1997)
Sleaze: The Corruption of Parliament, David Leigh and Ed Vulliamy (Fourth Estate, 1997)
Trial by Conspiracy: The Lies, Cover-Ups and Injustices Behind the Neil Hamilton Affair, Jonathan Boyd Hunt (GreeNZone Publishing, 1998)
Prime Ministers and the Rule Book, Amy Baker (Politico's Publishing, 1999)
The Justice Game, Geoffrey Robertson (Vintage, 1999)

CHAPTER ELEVEN - COMMITTEES

SELECT COMMITTEES IN THE HOUSE OF COMMONS

Departmental Select Committees

In 1979, the then Leader of the House, Rt Hon Norman St John Stevas MP, now Lord St John of Fawsley, proposed the reform of the existing Select Committees of the House of Commons, based on a report of the Select Committee on Procedure. This led to the establishment of Departmental Select Committees whose function is to 'shadow' Government Departments. There were already a number of non-departmental 'Select Committees' or 'Sessional Committees' in existence; for example, those dealing with Procedure, Privilege and Statutory Instruments.

Membership

The number or Members of each departmental Select Committee (in most cases this is 11, including a Chairman, elected by the Committee) is set out in SO 152 and SO 152(A).

Departmental Select Committees

Committee	No. of Members	Quorum*
Agriculture	11	3
Culture, Media & Sport	11	3
Defence	11	3
Education & Employment (the work of the Committee is carried out by two sub-committees - Education and Employment)	17	5
Environment, Transport and Regional Affairs (the work of the Committee is carried out by two sub-committees -Transport and Environment)	17	5
Environmental Audit (this Committee's remit covers all Government Departments)	16	4
Foreign Affairs (may appoint one sub-committee)	12	3
Health	11	3
Home Affairs (may appoint one sub-committee) (also considers matters relating to the Lord Chancellor's Department, the Law Officers' Departments, the Treasury Solicitor's Department, the Crown Prosecution Service and Serious Fraud Office	11	3
International Development	11	3
Northern Ireland Affairs	13	4
Science and Technology	11	3

Committee	No. of Members	Quorum*
Scottish Affairs	11	3
Social Security	11	3
Trade and Industry	11	3
Treasury (can appoint one sub-committee)	12	3
Welsh Affairs	11	3
* Chairman is counted as part of quorum		

Members of the Government and Opposition Front Bench Spokesmen are excluded from membership of Select Committees (although this is a convention rather than a rule of the House and is not specified in Standing Orders). Members serve for the lifetime of a Parliament unless they become a Minister or Front Bench Spokesman, or resign, in which case they are replaced by a Member nominated by the Committee of Selection and approved by the House. You will often see motions on the Order Paper to replace Member A with Member B on a particular Select Committee. This is usually because Member A has been elevated to a ministerial position. Members of Select Committees cannot resign unless the House agrees to a motion discharging them from membership of a particular committee. Under SO 121, no motion may be made for the nomination of members of the Departmental Select Committees (or the Domestic Committees) unless two sitting days' notice of the motion has been given and unless the motion is tabled in the name of the Chairman of the Committee of Selection or another member of that Committee. However, there is a provision for Back Benchers to nominate members of Select Committees. Under So 23 Back Benchers may also put forward amendments to the Committee of Selection's Motion, proposing different Members to those nominated.

Traditionally, the Chairmen of the Public Accounts Committee (PAC), the Joint/Select Committee on Statutory Instruments and the European Scrutiny are members of one of the opposition parties. When a Select Committee meets for the first time in a new Parliament, it elects a Chairman. More than one Member of the Committee may be proposed, in which case a vote is taken on each nomination. According to the Resolution of the House of 13 July 1992, before a Chairman can be elected, all Committee members must send details of 'pecuniary interests' to the Committee Clerk. Members must not take part in Committee proceedings where they have relevant interests and once the Chairman has been elected he or she must ask each member to declare any relevant interests. Members must also declare relevant interests when asking questions of witnesses.

Under SO 152, departmental Select Committees may appoint specialist advisers to assist them. Each Select Committee has one, or in some cases, two Clerks assigned to it. The title 'Clerk' is, in some ways, a rather unfortunate one; being associated in most people's minds with the words, 'filing' and 'junior'. Select Committee Clerks are far from junior and have more onerous tasks to undertake than filing. They are responsible for administering the work of the Committee and overseeing the publication of its reports. The role of the specialist advisers is of great importance. Many of the subjects tackled by the Select Committees are extremely complex and Members could not possibly be expected to be experts on all matters likely to be discussed by the Committee in the course of an enquiry.

The scope of a Select Committee's deliberations is defined by its 'order of reference' (the order by which the Committee is appointed). For example, under SO 152A, the Environmental Audit Committee is empowered to 'consider to what extent the policies and programmes of government departments and non-departmental public bodies contribute to environmental protection and sustainable development, to audit their performance against such targets as may be set for them by Her Majesty's Ministers; and to report thereon to the House'. Select Committees divide on issues in the same way as the Whole House, most frequently when trying to agree a report. The Chairman of a Select Committee has similar powers to the Chairman of a Committee of the Whole House. He or she cannot vote, but does have a casting vote if there are equal numbers in a division. When a Select Committee votes, a roll call is taken and any MP not present to hear the question being divided on, cannot vote. The results are recorded in the Select Committee's minutes.

Select Committee Meetings

Under SO 152 and 152(A) all the departmental Select Committees can 'send for persons, papers and records'. They are also able to hold their meetings away from Westminster, enabling them, in some cases, to undertake extensive visits abroad. In the 1997/98 Session of Parliament the Foreign Affairs Select Committee visited Luxembourg, Estonia, Paris and Brussels, New York and Washington, Hong Kong, Geneva, Thailand and the Philippines, Qatar, Kuwait and Israel, Kenya and Uganda, Vienna, Poland, the Czech Republic and Hungary, Cyprus and Slovenia and, last but not least, the Chinese Embassy in London. This is all rather arduous of course, and the members of the Environment Sub-Committee contented themselves with a visit to Fulham Palace Meadows Allotments and Redgate Mill in Eastbourne, along with a few other modest UK outings. When Select Committees visit foreign countries they cannot call witnesses or request papers, etc., they are essentially restricted to 'fact-finding' and 'evidence-gathering'.

All Select Committees, except the Public Accounts Committee and Standing Orders Committee can meet when the House is adjourned.

The Select Committees can call witnesses to give either written or oral evidence and can ask for certain publications to be made available to them. A departmental Select Committee will usually undertake two or three major enquiries each Session. The announcement of a new enquiry is usually made by means of a press release, setting out the terms of the enquiry and inviting interested parties to submit evidence. For example:

Home Affairs Committee Press Notice No. 1 of Session 1998-99 dated 27 November 1998

COMMITTEE ANNOUNCES INQUIRY INTO DRUGS AND PRISONS

The Home Affairs Committee's next major inquiry (on completion of its inquiry into Police Training and Recruitment) will be into ***Drugs and Prisons***. The scope of the inquiry will be broad, but will include the following matters:

- the extent of drug use amongst those entering prisons, and the degree to which drug use has been a cause of their criminal behaviour
- sentencing issues and the appropriateness of custodial sentences for drug related crime (including the new Drug Treatment and Testing Orders)

- the introduction of the Prison Service's new (May 1998) drug strategy *Tackling drugs in prison* and its place within the national strategy *Tackling drugs to build a better Britain*
- the extent of drug use amongst prisoners (and prison staff)
- the methods by which drugs enter prisons and means of reducing the supply
- the operation of the Mandatory Drug Testing Programme (including its effect on the relative use of cannabis and opiates)
- the use of drug-free wings, voluntary drug testing, incentives, and other initiatives relating to affecting drug users' behaviour within prisons
- the provision and effectiveness of detoxification and rehabilitation programmes and throughcare arrangements
- the release of drug users and former drug users from prison back into the community
- any distinct points relating to the above issues as they apply specifically to women prisoners and those in Young Offender Institutions.

The Committee is likely to begin hearing oral evidence for the inquiry in late February. It would therefore be helpful if any written submissions could be received by Monday 1st February. Announcements about the precise timing of oral evidence sessions will be made in due course.

Select Committee press notices can be found on the Parliament website.

Select Committee meetings are divided into two types: those at which witnesses are called to give evidence and which are usually held in public and those held in private when the Committee considers, for example, what should be included in its final report. Often, a Select Committee meets in private for about 10 to 15 minutes before a public evidence-giving session. Many Select Committee meetings are now broadcast both on radio and television, so if you are thinking of attending a Select Committee you may want to place yourself strategically out of range of the cameras. Detailed discussions of the Common Agricultural Policy or proposed bus routes in Manchester, have been known to induce feelings of weariness in some and you will not impress your family and friends if caught napping on the BBC's Parliamentary Channel. It has been suggested that Members of Committees should be allowed refreshments to keep them going during lengthy meetings. This author feels a supply of caffeinated beverages should be made available not just to Committee members, but to the press and public who have to cover their meetings as well. It is a contempt of the House to behave in a 'disorderly' manner in a Committee, so if you feel impelled to cry out 'down with fiscal neutrality' or 'save the Pound', during a meeting of the Treasury Select Committee, you are likely to be peremptorily removed. Those who fear they may find the temptation overwhelming are advised not to attend at all. Some may find the subject matter of the Committee's deliberations a little too stimulating, and those of an excitable disposition may wish to avoid discussions of the Maastricht Convergence Criteria altogether.

Some Select Committee meetings are more popular than others and you may have difficulty in finding a seat on some occasions. Everyone enjoys seeing a Minister or two grilled, or even roasted; so if the Foreign Secretary is on the menu for the Foreign Affairs Select Committee, you may find yourself in competition with most of Fleet Street for a place in the queue (a euphemism for an unregulated huddle in the Committee Corridor).

Even Ministers reluctantly recognise the influence of Select Committees. Paddy Tipping, speaking during a Wednesday morning adjournment debate initiated by Andrew Mackinlay MP, said 'Like many other hon. Members, I listen regularly to the "Today" programme and I have reached the conclusion that the Chairman of the Foreign Affairs Committee is in residence there. He is there almost every day because he pursues the Select Committee's line. His status arises from the Select Committee's achievements.' (HC Col: 264, 13 January 1999)

Select Committee Reports

Select Committees print 'evidence' after a sitting for the use of the Members of the Committee, but these are often not published until many weeks after the meeting in question, so if the evidence of a particular witness is important to you, you would be well advised to attend the meeting, rather than rely on reports in the press or wait for the Minutes of Evidence to be published. You can find out which Minutes of Evidence have been published by looking in the Weekly Information Bulletin which is published each Saturday.

A report must be accepted by a majority of the Committee before publication, but decisions do not have to be unanimous. If a Committee cannot agree to a report it makes a special report to that effect. When a Committee meets to finalise and agree its report, Members of the Committee may put forward alternative 'draft' reports. A motion to consider the report in the name of the Chairman of the Committee will be moved and it is open to another Member of the Committee to move an amendment to this motion, that an alternative report be considered. If the amendment is accepted, the alternative report is the one which is then considered paragraph by paragraph. If, as is more likely, such an amendment is defeated, the Chairman's report will form the basis of the Committee's discussion and will be considered paragraph by paragraph. Amendments can be moved to individual paragraphs.

It is a contempt of the House to publish or disclose a Select Committee report, before it has been published by that Committee. Until 1980, it was also a contempt of the House to publish evidence taken before a Select Committee until that Committee had reported. Now, under SO 135 and 136 the press are free to report what was said at a public Select Committee meeting, but the premature publication of a Select Committee report is still a contempt of the House. It was for this reason that Ernie Ross MP resigned from the House of Commons Foreign Affairs Select Committee in February 1999. He admitted he had leaked the Committee's report on the Sandline 'arms to Sierra Leone' affair to the Foreign Secretary before its publication by the Committee. The former Committee of Privileges recommended in their Second Report (HC 555, 1984/85) a new procedure for dealing with leaked reports. The Committee concerned investigates the matter and reports to the Select Committee on Standards and Privileges.

You can find Select Committee reports on the Parliament website, or obtain them from the Parliamentary Bookshop or The Stationery Office.

The Government Department to whom the Select Committee's report relates usually comments on the Committee's findings and recommendations – and these comments are usually published in the form of a 'Command Paper' or Memorandum to the

Committee. Departments try to respond to Committee reports within two months of their publication. In the case of the Public Accounts Committee, a Treasury Minute is laid before the House early each session embodying the Government's views on Committee reports of the previous session (this co-ordinates all the replies of the different Government Departments). Occasionally, Government replies are given in the form of written answers to parliamentary questions. There are usually debates on the floor of the House on the most important Select Committee reports.

As far as matters deemed to be' sub judice' are concerned, the principle that matters pending decision in a court of law should be not be raised in the House, extends to Select Committees, although this is not explicitly stated. However, such matters may be raised by a Select Committee in private session.

Witnesses

Select Committees have the right, under Standing Orders to call witnesses to come and give evidence. If a witness refuses to comply, the Committee can 'formally' request them to attend[1]. Failure to attend after a formal request is actually a 'contempt' of the House. The House, rather than the Committee would then take action and could order the Serjeant at Arms to serve a Speaker's Warrant on the witness concerned. If the witness still refused to attend, they could, theoretically, be called to the bar of the House to explain themselves. It is also a contempt to prevent a witness from attending a Committee. A warrant was issued in 1992 to secure the attendance of Kevin and Ian Maxwell at a meeting of the Social Security Select Committee.

As the Committee discovered, Select Committees are not courts of law and whilst they may have theoretical powers to compel witnesses to attend they cannot force them to give evidence. When Kevin and Ian Maxwell were called to give evidence to the Committee, they attended but refused to give evidence on the grounds that it might have prejudiced any subsequent prosecution in the courts (HC 353, First Special Report, 1991/92).

Theoretically, both Kevin and Ian Maxwell could have been summoned to the Bar of the House. As Erskine May states (21st Edition): 'Should the attendance of a witness be required, to be examined at the bar by the House of Commons, or by a Committee of the Whole House, he is simply ordered to attend at a stated time; and the order, signed by the Clerk of the House, is served upon him personally, if he is in or near London; but if he is at a distance, it is forwarded to him by the Serjeant at Arms, either by post, or, in special cases, by a messenger. If the witness does not obey the order for his attendance he may be ordered to be sent for in custody of the Serjeant at Arms, and Mr. Speaker may be ordered to issue his warrant accordingly; or he may be declared guilty of a breach of privilege, and ordered to be taken into the custody of the Serjeant at Arms.'

[1] As far as the summoning of Members is concerned, Erskine May (21st Edition) points out: 'When a select committee has the power to send for persons, that power is unqualified, except to the extent that it conflicts with the privileges of the Crown and of Members of the House of Lords, or with the rights of Members of the House of Commons.' Select Committees cannot therefore formally request other MPs to give evidence (the exception is the Committee on Standards and Privileges) and peers cannot be forced to attend and give evidence to Commons' Select Committees.

Erskine May states that a witness, 'is bound to answer all questions which the committee sees fit to put to him, and cannot excuse himself, for example, on the ground that he may thereby subject himself to a civil action'.

However, in the Maxwells' case, criminal proceedings were concerned and in March 1993 the Serious Fraud Office prevented the House of Commons Social Security Select Committee from questioning former Maxwell associates in public session on the grounds that this might prejudice the trial of Kevin and Ian Maxwell. In a progress report, issued on 1 March, 1993, the House of Commons Social Security Committee requested the Procedure Committee to look at the legal position of the inquiry and whether it was possible to frame enquiries in such as way as to avoid a clash with the judicial system.

According to Erskine May (22nd Edition, page 653) witnesses who give false evidence or present forged or falsified documents to a Committee, or, 'who are guilty of disrespectful conduct to the committee in a state of intoxication may be reported to the House to be dealt with as may be determined.' Under section 1 of the Perjury Act, 1911, where evidence is given upon oath[2], the giving of false evidence is punishable. The House may punish the giving of false evidence and imprison witnesses 'upon its own authority' and if it appears likely that a conviction can be obtained, the House can direct the Attorney General to prosecute the offending witnesses for perjury. Where evidence is not given on oath, false evidence is punishable only as contempt.

Witnesses are protected by parliamentary privilege in as much as legal proceedings brought against a witness arising from evidence given to a Committee would be considered as a contempt. According to the resolution of the House of 26 May 1818, 'all witnesses ... are entitled to the protection of this House in respect of anything that may be said by them in their evidence'. Tampering with witnesses is prohibited under the Sessional Orders agreed to by the House at the beginning of each Session of Parliament.

> 'That if it shall appear that any person hath been tampering with any Witness, in respect of his evidence to be given to this House, or any Committee thereof, or directly or indirectly hath endeavoured to deter or hinder any person from appearing or giving evidence the same is declared to be a high crime and misdemeanour; and this House will proceed with the utmost severity against such offender.'

Civil servants are frequently requested to give evidence to Select Committees. It is the usual practice for Select Committees to leave the choice of which individual civil servants should give evidence, to the Department or Minister concerned, although they can request that a particular, named individual be called before the Committee. Special guidance to civil servants summoned to give evidence is provided in what are known as the 'Osmotherly Rules', which set out the sorts of questions they may be expected to answer. However, these have never been agreed by any parliamentary motion and are therefore, purely advisory.

There is no general restriction on a Select Committee's power to request the production of papers by private bodies or individuals, provided that such papers are relevant to the

---

[2] Witnesses can be requested to give evidence on oath under the Parliamentary Witnesses Oaths Act 1871.

Committee's work as set out in its Order of Reference. A Select Committee cannot, however, order a Secretary of State to produce papers.

Witnesses cannot be summoned from overseas to give evidence, but foreign or Commonwealth nationals are often invited to attend to give evidence before Committees. EC officials, irrespective of nationality have given evidence in recent years. It would be unusual for foreign or commonwealth nationals resident, either temporarily or permanently, in the UK, to be summoned.

There is a very useful guide for witnesses published on the Parliament website. which gives advice on the form and content of both written and oral evidence and contains the invaluable advice to witnesses to 'speak up' when giving evidence. Unfortunately, most witnesses appear not to have read this invaluable document and continue to mutter inaudibly.

Sessional Select Committees

The Committee of Selection

The Committee of Selection has an extremely important role to play in the life of the House. It has the responsibility for nominating members of Select Committees and for selecting members of Standing Committees. By a curious anomaly, the Committee of Selection itself, is actually established under one of the .Standing Orders relating to private business (SO 109). There are nine members (three constitutes a quorum) and there are usually five party whips at least on the Committee (two Labour, two Conservative and one Liberal Democrat).

The Liaison Committee

The Liaison Committee oversees the work of all the Select Committees and its members consist of their Chairmen. It considers applications from Committees wishing to arrange overseas visits. The House of Commons Commission fixes a limit on the amount which can be incurred each year on such visits, but the decision as to which visits to permit is left to the Liaison Committee. The Committee is also responsible for deciding which Select Committee reports should be debated on the three Wednesdays in each Session, (the period between 9.30pm and 12.30pm) given over to such debates. It also decides which Select Committee reports should be debated on the three Estimates Days (one may be divided into two half days) which, since 1982, have been set aside as 'Select Committee Days'.

The Select Committee on Public Administration

The Select Committee on Public Administration considers the reports of the Parliamentary Commissioners (ombudsmen); i.e. the Parliamentary Commissioner for Administration, who is also the Health Service Commissioner and the Northern Ireland Parliamentary Commissioner. These 'ombudsmen' deal with complaints made by members of the Public and referred to them by Members of Parliament about maladministration by Government Departments or the Health Service. The Committee also considers issues relating to the Civil Service generally (this used to be the remit of the Treasury Select Committee).

The Procedure Committee

The Procedure Committee is established under SO 147 and consists of 17 members (the quorum is five) and exists to examine the procedures and practices of the House. Its role has been somewhat superseded by the advent of the Select Committee on the Modernisation of the House of Commons, set up by the House in the aftermath of the 1997 General Election. However, at the time of writing, the Procedure Committee was undertaking a follow-up enquiry to its Interim First Report of the 1998/99 Session on the consequences of devolution for Scotland, Wales and Northern Ireland, on the procedures of the House of Commons.

The Public Accounts Committee

The Public Accounts Committee (PAC) is set up under SO 148 and has 16 members (4 of whom form a quorum). Traditionally, the Chairman is a member of the main opposition party. The PAC examines National Audit Office (NAO) reports. The NAO, under the auspices of the Comptroller and Auditor General (CAG), is responsible to Parliament and has the task of auditing the Government's accounts. It also undertakes value-for-money studies of various Departments and it is often these which are the focus of the PAC's attention. The Committee meets in public and takes evidence from Ministers, civil servants and others in much the same way as other Select Committees. It produces a number of reports each Session; for example, between 24 December 1998 and 26 February 1999 alone, the PAC produced six reports including one on the sale of British Energy (Fifth Report, HC 242, 25 February 1999) and one on the flotation of the National Grid (Third Report, HC 651, 31 December 1998) The Government replies to PAC reports in the form of a Treasury Minute, a compilation of the responses from all the Departments on which the PAC's reports have commented. These Minutes are published at least one each Session and usually from the basis of one day's debate in the House.

The Committee on Standards and Privileges *(see chapter 10)*

The Deregulation Committee *(see chapter nine)*

The Select Committee on Modernisation of the House of Commons

This Committee was established on 4 June 1997, for the duration of the 1997 Parliament at least. It has 15 members (the quorum is five) and its remit is to consider ways in which the practices and procedures of the House of Commons can be modernised. It produced eight reports in the 1997/98 Session alone and most of the recommendations contained in those reports were accepted and put into practice by the House. For example, its proposals for pre-legislative committees have proved successful and at the time this book was being written, two draft Government bills had, or were being considered by pre-legislative Select Committees. Recently, the Committee has been considering proposals for a 'Main Committee' – a parallel Chamber to the House of Commons which would be able to consider uncontroversial matters for which there was no time, or insufficient time, in the Chamber. The Committee produced an interim report on the matter (HC 60, First Report, 1998/99 Session) and has just published its final report on the matter – 'Sittings of the House in Westminster Hall' (HC 194, Second Report, 1998/99 Session). The title 'Main Committee' takes its name from the body which exists in the Australian House of Representatives to debate non-controversial legislation and some committee reports. All decisions have to be taken unanimously and where unanimity cannot be reached, the matter has to be referred to the Chamber. Even unanimous decisions have to be ratified by the Chamber.

In their First Report on the subject the Committee suggested that, 'successive Governments have complained that there is simply not enough time in the legislative programme for a number of worthy, essentially non party-political and basically uncontroversial, measures, which are thereby condemned to languish on departmental shelves ... there are many other cases where legislation is desirable if only time could be found'. To an outsider, it does seem slightly peverse to be reducing the hours in which the House sits whilst at the same time lamenting the fact that there is insufficient time in which to consider important issues. MPs cannot be in two places at once; if they are in the Main Committee they will not be in the Chamber and vice versa. If all decisions in the Main Committee had to be reached unanimously and if all such decisions had to be ratified by the Chamber anyway, what on earth would be the point in its creation? One cannot help but feel that there are certain people who will not be satisifed until the House of Commons has been replaced by some soporific horseshoe-shaped affair full of dull-grey Members nodding sagely in agreement with one another. By the time this happens the House will probably be run by a firm of Management Consultants who will have rationalised and downsized it out of all recognition. Alarmingly, in their Second Report, the Modernisation Committee argues for the Main Committee to sit in the Grand Committee Room, off Westminster Hall – in a 'hemicycle'. This all sounds dangerously continental. 'Westminster Hall' – as it will be known, will be a parallel chamber chaired by the Deputy Speakers and the four longest-serving members of the Chairman's Panel and would sit at the following times to debate the following matters:

Times of Sittings	Debates
Tuesdays – 10.00am to 1.00pm	Private Members' Debates
Wednesdays – 9.30am to 2.00pm	Private Members' Debates currently held in the Chamber
Thursdays – 2.30pm to 5.30pm	Business agreed through 'usual channels'; for example, debates on Select Committee reports, etc.

The Committee argues that the Tuesday and Wednesday sittings 'will not coincide with sittings in the Chamber and do not therefore run the risk of being interrupted by divisions' – so have them in the Chamber. What on earth is the point of transferring Wednesday morning Private Members' debates to a parallel Chamber, leaving the Chamber of the House of Commons empty? Why not leave them where they are?

Domestic Committees

The Finance and Services Committee

The Finance and Services Committee is set up under SO 144 and its members are usually the Chairmen of the four Domestic Committees, the Chairman of the Broadcasting Committee, the Government and Opposition Deputy Chief Whips and the Liberal Democrat Chief Whip. The Committee advises the House of Commons Commission and its Chairman is a member of the Commission. The Finance and Services Committee, along with the four Domestic Committees and the Broadcasting Committee, whilst having the power to call witnesses, rarely takes oral evidence but meets to consider administrative matters relating to the running of the House itself.

The Four Domestic Committees

There are four Domestic Committees appointed under SO 142 and these are:

- Accommodation and Works
- Administration
- Catering
- Information

The Accommodation and Works Committee had the task of considering all matters pertaining to the office accommodation of Members and staff. Its has recently been considering the redevelopment of buildings in Bridge Street, opposite Big Ben and adjacent to Westminster Underground Station (which had to be developed for the new Jubilee Line Extension). The new building, 'Portcullis House', will be used primarily as office space for the 200 Members who currently do not have their own office and the aim is for work to be completed in 2001. The Administration Committee has a wide remit and considers matters relating to the day to day administration and running of the House of Commons. The Catering Committee, as one would imagine, deals with all matters relating to the provision of catering facilities in the House of Commons. The Information Committee considers matters relating to the House of Commons Library and to information services generally. For example, its first report of the 1998/99 Session was entitled "The Supply of Members' Information Technology Equipment, Software and Associated Services" (HC 76, 1998-99) and was published on 18 December 1998.

Each Committee has nine members (the quorum is three) and is assisted by the relevant officers of the House. The Committees reports are usually considered by the Finance and Services Committee, particularly if they concern requests for expenditure.

The Broadcasting Committee

The Broadcasting Committee is set up under SO 139 and consists of 11 members. It reports to the Finance and Services Committee and it has the responsibility of overseeing the provisions relating to the televising of Parliament. It should not be confused with PARBUL – a private company consisting of directors from both Houses and from the Broadcasters themselves, which oversees the company which actually records Parliament.

Pre-Legislative Committees *(see chapter seven)*

EUROPEAN SCRUTINY COMMITTEE AND EUROPEAN STANDING COMMITTEES

Both the House of Commons and House of Lords have important roles to play in the scrutiny of European legislation. The three European Communities (European Coal and Steel Community, European Atomic Energy Community and the European Economic Community) comprise the 'First Pillar' of the European Union and legislation is enacted under this Pillar. However, the Second and Third Pillars (Common Foreign and Security Policy and Co-operation on Justice and Home Affairs, respectively) of the European Union, introduced in the Maastricht Treaty are equally important and until recently, the Standing Orders relating to the scrutiny of European legislation in the House of Commons did not cover documents brought in under these two Pillars. It was for this reason that SO 143 was recently amended to allow documents under all three Pillars to be subject to scrutiny by the House.

The Scrutiny Reserve

In 1990, the House of Commons agreed to a Resolution preventing Ministers from agreeing to a legislative proposal in the Council of Ministers if it was still under consideration by the House of Commons Select Committee on European Legislation or was awaiting consideration by the House. The resolution was recently replaced by à new Resolution following the seventh report of the Select Committee on Modernisation of the House of Commons (HC 791, 1997/98). The majority of the Committee's recommendations were accepted by the House on 17 November 1998 and the requisite amendments made to Standing Orders (HC Col: 778 – 782).

The effect of the Resolution agreed on 17 November 1998 is that:

- a Minister may not agree to a proposal for EC legislation or to a common position or joint action under Title V (Second Pillar) or a joint position, joint action or convention under Title VI (Third Pillar), if the European Scrutiny Committee *(formerly called the House of Commons Select Committee on European Legislation)* has not completed its scrutiny of the proposal or if the proposal has been sent for consideration to one of the three European Standing Committees and the House has not yet reached a decision on it
- a proposal is defined as being: a programme, plan or recommendation for EC legislation, a political agreement, agreement to a common position or to a joint text or to confirmation of the common position (with or without amendments from the European Parliament)
- a Minister may agree to a proposal which is still subject to scrutiny, if the proposal is 'confidential, routine or trivial or is substantially the same as a proposal on which scrutiny has been completed' or where the Scrutiny Committee has said that agreement can be given even though it has not completed its own scrutiny process

- a Minister can also agree to a proposal still subject to scrutiny where he or she feels that there are 'special reasons' for so doing

The Resolution provided for its own amendment after the Treaty of Amsterdam comes into force.

Explanatory, Un-numbered and Supplementary Memoranda

EC documents must be deposited in Parliament within two days of their receipt in London[3] and the Government must provide what is known as an 'Explanatory Memorandum' ten days after that. This Memorandum is really a note explaining the content of the document, the proposed timetable for consideration in the EU and its likely impact on the UK, particularly in terms of its effect on existing legislation. Often the Government will also provide a 'compliance cost assessment' as well. Sometimes a Memorandum will be referred to as an 'Un-numbered Explanatory Memorandum', which means that the actual EC document to which it relates was unavailable at the time the Memorandum was writen. Occasionally, the Government will submit a Supplementary Explanatory Memorandum as well if there have been amendments to the original EC document.

Weird and Wonderful Numbers

If you have ever had the misfortune to be tasked with tracking down an obscure EC document on the evidence of a peculiar number and an even more peculiar title, do not despair: consider the following.

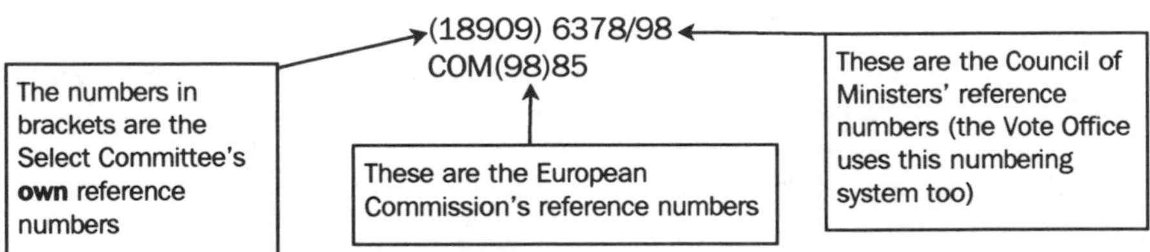

This particular set of numbers relates to the European Commission's proposed Draft Directive amending Directive 90/220/EEC (yet more numbers) on the deliberate release into the environment of genetically modified organisms – the subject of a recent report by the House of Lords European Communities Committee (see below). Their numbering system is slightly different again and the above proposal had the following number in the House of Lords: 6378/98/98 (Com(98) 85). Members can obtain European documents from the Vote Office in the House of Commons (by using the yellow form issued for the purpose) and the Printed Paper Office in the House of Lords. Members of the public can

[3] For some reason, European Community Documents are not laid on the Table of the House, but are made available in the Vote Office, so there is no record in the Journal of their having been laid before Parliament.

obtain European documents from The Stationery Office, but four pages will set you back £5.10.

The New European Scrutiny Committee

Standing Order 143 was amended by the House on 17 November 1998 and as a result the old House of Commons Select Committee on European Legislation is now called the European Scrutiny Committee. The Committee consists of 16 members and can appoint sub-committees and specialist advisers. It can also take evidence from Ministers and call other witnesses where necessary. The Committee can also host joint meetings with the House of Lords European Communities Committee or one of its Sub-Committees, the Select Committee on Public Administration, the Public Accounts Committee, the Environmental Audit Committee and any departmental Select Committee. The Committee can consider any of the following documents:

- proposals under the Community Treaties for legislation by the Council of Ministers or the Council acting together with the European Parliament
- documents submitted to the European Council, the Council of Ministers or the European Central Bank
- proposals to define a common position or proposals for joint action under Title V (Second Pillar) of the TEU which is to be submitted to the Council
- proposals for a joint position, joint action or convention under Title VI (Third Pillar) of the TEU which is to be submitted to the Council
- other documents published by one EU institution for submission to another, which do not relate exclusively to a proposal for legislation
- other documents relating to EU affairs, deposited by a Minister in the House

The Committee is a busy one, publishing eight reports between 7 December 1998 and 18 February 1999 alone. The Committee usually divides the documents which it considers in its reports into the following sections.

- ♦ Politically (and/or Legally) Important: for debate

The Committee will make this recommendation when it feels that the document should be considered by one of the European Standing Committees. For example, in its Third Report (1998/99, HC 34 iii) the Committee recommended that the proposals for a draft Directive amending Directive 90/220/EEC on the deliberate release into the environment of genetically modified organisms should be debated in Standing Committee A.

- ♦ Politically (and/or Legally) Important: not cleared

The Committee will make this recommendation where it still has some concerns – to the extent that it cannot 'clear the proposal', but where either debate is not warranted or where the European timetable is such that there would be no time for Standing Committee consideration before, for example, adoption by the Council of Ministers.

- ♦ Politically (and/or Legally) Important: cleared

The Committee may 'clear' a document, despite designating it as being politically or legally important, or both.

- Documents not raising questions of legal or political importance

The Committee will list those documents which it does not feel raise any issues of significance.

Standing Committees

The Standing Orders relating to European Standing Committees were amended by the House on 17 November 1998 and as a result there are now three such Committees, A, B and C, each with 13 members. The European Scrutiny Committee can refer any of the documents referred to in SO 143 to one of the Standing Committees. If the European Scrutiny Committee feels that a particular document warrants debate on the floor of the House, it will automatically refer that document to one of the European Standing Committees. This is because it does not have the authority to table a debate on the floor of the House – only the Government can do this. Such a document will be referred to one of the European Standing Committees, unless a Government Minister tables a motion to de-refer it under SO 119(2), thereby ensuring a debate on the floor of the House. Such a motion is taken at the beginning of public business and is voted on forthwith. The debate on the document itself would be limited to 1½ hours under SO 16, but constitutes exempted business and could therefore continue after the Moment of Interruption.

Each of the Committees deals with a different area of EU policy.

A	Agriculture, Fisheries and Food; Environment, Transport and the Regions; Forestry Commission
B	HM Treasury (inc. Customs and Excise); Social Security; Foreign and Commonwealth Office; International Development; Home Office; Lord Chancellor's Department;
C	Trade and Industry; Employment and Education; Culture, Media and Sport; Health

The European Standing Committees are very different from Standing Committees on Bills in that their membership remains the same. Ministers usually attend the meetings of European Standing Committees and can answer questions on a particular document for up to one and a half hours. The Committee can then debate the motion for a further two and a half hours. Amendments may be tabled to the motion in front of the Committee and once the Committee has reached a decision on the document, this is reported to the House.

For example, the Select Committee on European Legislation (as it was previously called) considered proposals relating to the Agrimonetary Scheme after the introduction of the Euro on 28 October 1998 and recommended the following (taken from its 38th Report, HC 155,13 November 1998)

The Select Committee on European Legislation has made further progress in the matter referred to it and has agreed to the following Report:—

AGRIMONETARY ARRANGEMENTS FOLLOWING THE INTRODUCTION OF THE EURO

(19219) 9597/98 COM(98)367	**(a) Draft Council Regulation establishing agrimonetary arrangements for the euro.** **(b) Draft Council Regulation on transitional measures to be applied under the Common Agricultural Policy with a view to the introduction of the euro.**
Legal base:	Articles 42 and 43; qualified majority voting
Department:	Agriculture, Fisheries and Food
Basis of consideration:	SEM of 12 October 1998
Previous consideration:	HC 155-xxxiii (1997-98), paragraph 3 (8 July 1998)
Committee's assessment:	Politically important
Committee's decision:	Recommended for debate in European Standing Committee A

European Standing Committee A considered the matter on 18 November 1998 and reported the following resolution to the House. The following appeared in the Votes and Proceedings for 18 November 1998.

European Standing Committee A,—Mr Peter Atkinson reported from European Standing Committee A the following Resolution:

> That the Committee takes note of European Community Document No. 9597/98, two draft Council Regulations establishing agrimonetary arrangements and the transitional arrangements to be applied under the Common Agricultural Policy with a view to the introduction of the euro; and supports the Government's intention to support the proposals which simplify the current agrimonetary arrangements by moving to a system which more closely reflects market realities, reducing the costs to taxpayers, consumers and businesses, and also the scope for distortions of competition whilst respecting UK international obligations without discriminating against those Member States not participating in the euro.
>
> Report, together with Resolution, to lie upon the Table.

When the House votes on the Committee's resolution, the decision is taken forthwith, although amendments can be tabled and may be put after the Moment of Interruption. For example, the following extract is taken from Hansard of 1 December 1998.

Agrimonetary Arrangements Following the Introduction of the Euro,—A Motion was made, and the Question being put forthwith, pursuant to Standing Order No. 119 (European Standing Committees), That this House takes note of European Community Document No. 9597/98, two draft Council Regulations establishing agrimonetary arrangements and the transitional arrangements to be applied under the Common Agricultural Policy with a view to the introduction of the euro; and supports the Government's intention to support the proposals which simplify the current agrimonetary arrangements by moving to a system which more closely reflects market realities, reducing the cost to taxpayers, consumers and businesses, and also the scope for distortions of competition whilst respecting UK international obligations without discriminating against those Member States not participating in the euro.—(*Mr Greg Pope*):—It was agreed to.

GRAND COMMITTEES

The role of the Grand Committees and the Select Committees on Scotland, Wales and Northern Ireland after the full establishment of the devolved Parliament and Assemblies, is one which the Government and the House itself will need to consider carefully in the months ahead. Presumably, once the devolved assemblies are fully functioning, these Committees will restrict themselves to matters which are 'reserved' to the Westminster Parliament; i.e. those matters on which the devolved assemblies cannot legislate. In her Memorandum to the Procedure Committee's First Report (HC 148, 18 January 1999), the Leader of the House, Rt Hon Margaret Beckett MP, admitted that, 'some of the procedures currently in standing orders will either no longer be needed or will have to be adapted to changing circumstances'. However, she was keen to stress that there would still be business for the Grand Committees to discuss; for example, the block grants made each year to the various devolved assemblies. She added that 'A regular pattern of meetings could be established to debate reserved matters. The Government expects that, in the light of experience, there will be a need to adjust the procedures of the grand committees, but it would prefer not to make any changes at this stage'.

Scottish Grand Committee

The Scottish Grand Committee is comprised of all MPs representing Scottish constituencies (the quorum of the Committee is 10).[4] Ministers may take part in the proceedings but cannot vote. Date and agendas for meetings (which may be in Westminster, or in Scotland) are set out in a Motion which must be agreed by the House. The Scottish Grand Committee has a 45 minute question time, similar to question time in the House of Commons, and questions are handed in to the Table Office 10 days before a sitting of the Committee in the same way that they would be for an ordinary question time. Statements may be made to the Grand Committee and it may also act as a Second Reading Committee and may also consider Bills at Report Stage and Third Reading (for more information on the role of the Grand Committees in debating legislation, please see chapter seven). The Committee may also consider delegation legislation in a similar way to a Standing Committee on Delegated Legislation. Eight days are set aside for debates on the Adjournment of the Committee (similar to the Adjournment debates used by the Government in the House itself to debate general

[4] The quorum during a half-hour adjournment debate at the end of the day's proceedings is three – this applies to all the Grand Committees.

matters); however, four of these are at the disposal of the Government, two are at the disposal of the largest opposition party in Scotland and two at the disposal of the next largest opposition party in Scotland.

Welsh Grand Committee

The Welsh Grand Committee consists of all Members representing Welsh constituencies, along with five other Members nominated by the Committee of Selection (the quorum is seven). Ministers may take part in debates but cannot vote. Dates and agendas of meetings are set out in Motions which must be passed by the House. The Committee has a half-hour question time and questions are tabled in the usual way, 10 days before a sitting. Bills may be debated at Second Reading in the Committee. Statements may be made to the Committee and there is provision for half-hour adjournment debates. Meetings may be held in Westminster or in Wales. The Welsh Grand Committee cannot consider delegated legislation or the Report Stage or Third Readings of Bills

Northern Ireland Grand Committee

The Northern Ireland Grand Committee consists of all MPs for Northern Ireland constituencies[5] and in addition, 25 other Member nominated by the Committee of Selection. The quorum of the Committee is 10. Dates and agendas for meetings must be set out in a Motion put before the House. The Committee has a half-hour oral question time and a half-hour adjournment debate and Ministers can make Statements to the Committee as they would to the House itself. The Committee can also consider bills at Second and Third Reading (see chapter seven for more information on the role of Grand Committees in the legislative process) as well as delegated legislation, usually in the form of draft Orders in Council (see chapter nine for more information on delegated legislation).

English Regions

Now that Scotland, Wales and Northern Ireland have their own devolved assemblies, there have been suggestions that an 'English Grand Committee' should be established at Westminster as a forum for Members representing English Constituencies. In fact, SO 117 already provides for a Standing Committee on Regional Affairs, consisting of all English Members. This last met in 1978. The Leader of the House, Rt Hon Margaret Beckett MP said, in reply to a question from John Wilkinson MP on 1 February 1999 (HC Col: 476) that she would be submitting a proposal to the Select Committee on the Modernisation of the House of Commons, to revive the Standing Committee. At the time of writing, there had been no further movement on this matter. In their Second Interim Report of the 1998/99 Session - 'Procedural Consequences of Devolution' (HC 376) the Procedure Committee suggested that the Select Committee on Modernisation of the House of Commons' proposed parallel debating Chamber - 'Westminster Hall' ('Sittings of the House in Westminster Hall' - HC 194, Second Report, 1998/99 Session) would provide an ideal forum for debating 'territorial matters'. 'If the experiment of sittings in Westminster Hall is successful, there may be no need for the Grand Committees to

[5] With the exception of Gerry Adams and Martin McGuinness, the two Sinn Fein Members for Belfast West and Mid Ulster, who have not taken their seats.

continue', they state. They argue that specifically Scottish or Welsh legislation could be sent to Second Reading Committees and that whilst the experiment with Westminster Hall sittings takes place (the Modernisation Committee suggests 1999/2000 for this) Grand Committees should be suspended.

BACKBENCH COMMITTEES

Both the Labour and Conservative Parties have a formal system of Back Bench Committees, although these are now called Departmental Committees in the case of the Labour Party and Party Committees in the case of the Conservative Party. In the latter case, this is because the membership has been broadened beyond MPs. Foremost of the Conservative Party Committees is the 1922 Committee, the membership is all Conservative Back Bench MPs when the Party is in Government and all MPs when the Party is in opposition. The Committee is an influential one and has an important role to play in the election of Leader of the Conservative Party. Other Committees shadow the main Government Departments, such as Defence and Trade and Industry. As well as Departmental Groups, the Labour Party has Regional Groups for all Members within a particular region; for example the East Midlands, London, the South West, etc. The above Committees are all set up and run by the Parties themselves; they are not House of Commons Committees and are therefore not subject to any rules and Standing Orders of the House.

SELECT COMMITTEES IN THE HOUSE OF LORDS

Select Committees in the House of Lords are either 'Sessional' Select Committees or 'ad hoc' committees. Sessional Select Committees are appointed at the beginning of each Parliament, but do not need to be reappointed at the beginning of each Session. Other Select Committees cease to exist at the end of the parliamentary Session. Ad hoc Committees can sit during a recess, but only Sessional Select Committees may sit during prorogation.

Ad Hoc Select Committees

Ad hoc Select Committees can only be appointed after the necessary motions have been agreed to by the House of Lords. For example in the 1998/99 Session an ad hoc Committee was established to enquire into the 'Monetary Policy Committee of the Bank of England'. William Keegan, writing in the Observer on 21 February 1999, was fulsome in his praise of this particular committee, saying that during its deliberations, 'one sees the Upper House at its best'. Although ad hoc Committees are usually expected to report by the end of the Session in which they were established, they can be re-established at the beginning of the following Session in order to complete an enquiry. The motion establishing the Committee and setting out its orders of reference was agreed to by the House on 30 November 1998. The Liaison Committee proposes the orders of reference, but the Leader of the House actually moves the relevant motion. The orders of reference set out the remit of the enquiry and the Committee may not consider any matters which do not fall within the terms of the motion; however, a motion extending the remit of a Committee's enquiry may always be agreed to by the House at a later date. The orders of reference of a sub-committee are determined by the main Committee. The motion setting out the membership of the Committee was agreed by the House on 7 December 1998. The Chairman or Deputy Chairman of Committees chairs all Select Committees unless the House agrees to a motion appointing another Lord as Chair of the Committee. The Committee of Selection nominates the members of a Committee, and the Chairman of Committees, in his role as Chairman of the Committee of Selection proposes the motion to the House. This motion also specifies the time of the Committee's first meeting and also gives permission for the Committee to 'have power to adjourn from place to place' and 'to appoint specialist advisers'.

The Public Service Committee

The Public Service Committee was appointed on 30 April 1996 to consider the 'present condition and future development of the Public Service in Great Britain'. This excluded local government, the NHS, educational establishments and the enquiry was really confined to the Civil Service, including executive agencies and certain other non-departmental public bodies. The Committee's first report on the 'The Government's Proposals for the Privatisation of Recruitment and Assessment Services (RAS)' was published on 16 July 1996 (HL 109, 1996/97) – its advice, against privatisation, was not heeded however, as RAS was sold to Capita Group soon after its publication. Its final report (HL 55, 1997/98) was published on 11 February 1998 and provides a fascinating overview of the current role and functions of the Civil Service. The report was debated by the House on 3 December 1998 and the Committee completed its work in January 1999.

Sessional Select Committees

Sessional Select Committees are appointed at the beginning of a Parliament and then re-appointed again at the beginning of each Session. The following Sessional Select Committees are all re-appointed under SO 62 at the beginning of each Session:

Consolidation Bills Committee (Joint Committee)
Delegated Powers and Deregulation Committee
European Communities Committee**
House of Lords' Offices Committee*
Hybrid Instruments Committee*
Personal Bills Committee*
Committee for Privileges
Procedure Committee*
Science and Technology Committee**
Standing Orders (Private Bills) Committee*
Statutory Instruments Committee (Joint Committee)

Rotating Peers

Although this sounds most alarming, it refers not to an unpleasant neurological condition forcing afflicted peers to whirl uncontrollably, but to a rule of the House that Members of Select Committees must not be members of those Committees indefinitely.

The Committees listed above and marked thus '*', are all subject to a system of rotation whereby members may not serve for more than three consecutive Sessions. After a gap of one Session they are again eligible for membership. Members of the Committee of Selection and the Liaison Committee are also subject to a system of rotation. Certain Lords are exempt from the rule: the Leaders and Chief Whips, the Convenor of the Cross Benches, the Lord Chancellor, the Chairman of Committees, the Principal Deputy Chairman of Committees, the Deputy Leader of the House and the Deputy Leader of the Opposition.

The Committees marked '**' - the European Communities Committee and the Science and Technology Committee and its Sub-Committees, operate a rotation rule which stipulates that Members must not serve for more than four consecutive Sessions – this applies both to full members and co-opted members. However, if a member leaves one Sub-Committee after four Sessions, he may immediately be appointed to another Sub-Committee. A peer who has been rotated (!) may return to a Sub-Committee after a gap of one Session. The Chairman of the Science and Technology Committee and the Chairmen of the Sub-Committees of both Committees are exempt from the rule for up to three Sessions.[6]

Sessional and ad hoc Committees have the power to co-opt members, without reference to the Committee of Selection. In general, meetings of the House of Lords Select Committees are held in public. Meetings are held in either the Committee Corridor or Upper Committee Corridor and are usually held in the lower-numbered Committee Rooms; e.g. 1, 2, 3, etc. These are to be found at the far end of the corridor, to the right of the desk in the Upper Waiting Hall. House of Lords Select Committees operate in a similar way to their counterparts in the House of Commons, although there is a less party-political atmosphere and, as one would expect, their Lordships are usually rather more courteous to their witnesses than some Commons' Committees. This, of course, is not to everyone's taste. If you are in search of high drama and passion, you will not find either in a meeting of Sub-Committee D of the House of Lords European Communities Committee. If political confrontation and emotional outbursts are what you crave, do not expect to find them in a meeting of the Hybrid Instruments Committee. However, should you require enlightened questioning and a little intellectual diversion, then a meeting of one of the Sub-Committees of the Science and Technology Committee has much to commend it.

Select Committees usually announce their intention of seeking oral and written evidence well in advance and requests for evidence are available on the Parliament website. Select Committee reports are also available on the website. When a Select Committee has concluded its enquiry a draft report is usually prepared. This is put to the Committee by the Chairman for its agreement. Other members of the Committee may put forward an alternative draft report if they are unhappy with the draft report submitted by the Chairman. Usually only one draft report is considered and each paragraph of the report has to be agreed to. If a peer objects to a particular paragraph, he or she can seek to move an amendment to it. Committees can issue special reports and ad-hoc Select Committees frequently issue special reports at the beginning of their enquiries, setting out their interpretation of the orders of reference. The Government endeavours to

[6] The Chairman of the European Communities Committee is always the Chairman of Committees.

respond to House of Lords Select Committee reports within six months, and in the case of the European Communities Select Committee, within two.

The roles of the various Sessional Select Committees is summarised below, except for the Joint Committees which are considered later in the chapter.

Delegated Powers and Deregulation Committee

The Delegated Powers and Deregulation Committee was established in 1992 to consider the delegated powers contained in all public bills (except supply and consolidation bills). Delegated legislation is discussed more fully in chapter eight. Bills frequently contain clauses which give Ministers the power to enact certain aspects of a bill by means of delegated legislation. Delegated legislation is not subject to the same level of scrutiny as primary legislation and for this reason their Lordships felt the need to establish a committee to keep an eye on the executive for any possible abuses of its powers. Unlike the House of Commons Deregulation Committee whose remit is only to consider deregulation orders, the Delegated Powers and Deregulation Committee in the House of Lords considers both deregulation orders and scrutinises all primary legislation for any abuse of delegated powers. It was the passage of the Education (Student Loans) Bill 1990, which was really the catalyst for the creation of the Committee. A brief four-clause bill, it left most of its provisions to be brought in by means of delegated legislation. Many saw the bill as nothing more than an extended 'Henry VIII clause'. The discussion of the proposals for delegated legislation in this Bill took up a great deal of time on the floor of the House and the Committee was set up partly to ensure that delegated powers in primary legislation could be discussed in committee, away from the Chamber itself.

The Committee currently has ten members, including the Chairman and during its consideration of a bill, it may hear oral evidence and receive written evidence from the relevant Government Department. The Committee issues separate reports on Bills and on deregulation orders (for more information on deregulation orders please see chapter nine).

The Committee pays particular attention to any 'Henry VIII clauses', which give Ministers extensive powers to amend primary legislation without commensurate parliamentary scrutiny. The Committee also considers whether the type of parliamentary scrutiny of any proposed delegated legislation is adequate; i.e. whether it should be subject to the affirmative rather than the negative procedure.

The Committee's role is purely advisory – it has no power to amend bills or proposals for draft Orders. However, peers may table amendments to bills in response to criticisms made by the Committee. There is an informal understanding in the House that when the Committee has approved the delegated powers in a particular bill, those powers should not then become the subject of debate during the bill's passage through the House. Frequently, the Government will respond to the Committee's recommendations and amend its own bills accordingly.

The Committee can appoint sub-committees and specialist advisers and has the same powers as other House of Lords' Select Committees.

The Committee has 60 days within which to scrutinise any proposal for a Deregulation Order. Its report may be debated in the House within this period of time. Under SO 70, if, after the 60-day period, the Government decides to lay a draft Order, no motion for its approval can be put before the House until the Committee has reported. During its deliberations on the Order the Committee performs the functions of the Joint Committee on Statutory Instruments. Any peer may table a motion relating to a report on a draft Order and such a motion would be taken immediately before the motion to approve the draft Order. Amendments could be made to the motion.

As the Fourth Report of the Select Committee on the Scrutiny of Delegated Powers (Special Report on Deregulation Orders - Session 1994/5, HL 48) stated: 'the House will be able to vote on any such motion or amendment, allowing a decision to be reached on a final draft Order without breaching the convention that the House does not vote on affirmative instruments directly'. If the House votes in favour of a motion stating that the Order should not be approved, the motion to approve the Order is not moved.

Science and Technology

The Science and Technology Committee was established in 1980 and at the time of writing consisted of 17 members. The Committee usually establishes at least two Sub-Committees each Session and these consist of members of the main Committee, along with some co-opted members. Given the composition of the House of Lords, many of the Committee's members are eminent scientists in their own right. At the time of writing the Chairman was Lord Winston, whose achievements in the fields of obstetrics, gynaecology and fertility are too numerous to mention. The Committee is free to enquire into almost any aspect of science and technology, although it tends to avoid overtly political issues or matters of only short-term interest. The length of Sub-Committee enquiries varies, but on average, they last about a year. In the last Session of Parliament (1997/98) the Committee established four Sub-Committees, on Cannabis, Digital Images as Evidence, Resistance to Antibiotics, the Management of Nuclear Waste (at the time of writing the latter had not reported). The former Sub-Committee was chaired by Lord Perry of Walton FRS a former Professor of Pharmacology and founding Vice-Chancellor of the Open University and other notable members included a former Nobel Prizewinner, Lord Porter of Luddenham, Lord Soulsby of Swaffham Prior, Emeritus Professor of Animal Pathology at Cambridge, Lord Walton of Detchant, a former Professor of Neurology and Lord Winston, the Chairman of the main Committee. The Committee recommended that doctors should be able to prescribe cannabis for medical uses such as pain relief. The Science and Technology Committee's reports are often very influential and in the past have acted as catalysts to important developments in the scientific arena. A report by the Committee in 1988 led to the establishment of a Director of Research and Development for the NHS.

European Communities Committee

The European Communities Committee was established in 1974, to consider and scrutinise European Community (now European Union) proposals. The Committee is chaired by the Principal Deputy Chairman of Committees – currently, Lord Tordoff. The members of the main Committee all sit on a different Sub-Committee along with a number of co-opted members. These are set out below.

Sub-Committee	Areas Covered
A	Economic and Financial Affairs, Trade and External Relations
B	Energy, Industry and Transport
C	Environment, Public Health and Consumer Protection
D	Agriculture, Fisheries and Food
E	Law and Institutions
F	Social Affairs, Education and Home Affairs

The role of the European Communities Committee involves both investigation and scrutiny.

'The Scrutiny Reserve' and 'The Chairman's Sift'

The Government must submit copies of all Commission proposals to both Houses of Parliament, within two days of their receipt. The relevant Department then prepares an explanatory memorandum setting out the financial, legal and political implications of the proposal. The Government has undertaken not to agree to any proposal in the Council of Ministers (except under exceptional circumstances) until it has been cleared by the Committee. This is known as the 'Scrutiny Reserve'. Whilst this affords the House of Lords an opportunity to influence the Government's position in the Council of Ministers, its advice is not mandatory. Being 'cleared from scrutiny' by the Committee is taken to mean one of the following

- when the Chairman of the Committee has sifted it and decided it requires no further attention;
- when a Sub-Committee has considered it and decided no further action is required;
- when, after a report has been made by the Committee, it has been debated by the House, or a response received from the Government;
- when, in the case of a document which has been the subject of correspondence with Ministers, that 'correspondence is closed'[7]

When any of these conditions apply, the 'Scrutiny Reserve' is said to have been 'lifted'.

The Chairman distinguishes between those EC proposals not requiring scrutiny - known as 'A' proposals and those requiring attention from the Committee or the House - known as 'B' proposals. The Chairman of the Committee (in reality the Clerk, the Legal Adviser and Legal Assistant) decide which proposals should be sent to the appropriate Sub-Committee for consideration. This process is known as the 'Chairman's sift'. A 'Progress of Scrutiny' document is then published, listing proposals sifted since the previous edition and including all proposals awaiting, or under, scrutiny by the various Sub-Committees. About a third of all proposals are referred to the Sub-Committees and frequently, the latter decide to give them no further consideration. Only a few proposals are the subject

[7] See Erskine May (22nd Edition, page 834).

of reports to the House. The Sub-Committee may write to Ministers where it feels that a full-scale enquiry would not be appropriate, but where there are still some legitimate concerns about a particular proposal. These letters, along with the relevant ministerial replies, are published every six months in reports entitled: 'Correspondence with Ministers' (these also contain the Government's response to Committee reports). The 11th Report of the European Communities Committee of the 1997/98 Session, published on 12 February 1998, was a compilation of such correspondence (HL 60). The report was divided into four parts: A - General policy questions; B - Cases where effective scrutiny had not been possible; C - Legal and procedural issues and D - Correspondence about Committee reports. For example, Part A included some correspondence relating to proposals for directives on motor vehicle emissions and fuel quality. The Parliamentary Under-Secretary of State at the Department of the Environment, Transport and the Regions, Glenda Jackson CBE MP, wrote to Lord Tordoff informing him that, 'it is our intention to signal to the Presidency our preparedness to support a further strengthening on the sulphur content of petrol ... We also propose to agree to the Presidency proposal for tightening on benzene.' Lord Tordoff replied on behalf of the Committee that he was still concerned about the proposals relating to leaded petrol. He therefore informed the Minister that, 'We shall maintain the scrutiny reserve for the time being'.

Part B of the document (relating to cases where effective scrutiny had not been possible) contained a letter from Baroness Hayman, Parliamentary Under-Secretary in the Department of the Environment, Transport and the Regions relating to the so called 'Auto-oil' Programme explaining why there had been a delay in supplying essential papers to the Committee (the delay in supplying the papers was the reason why the matter had been included in Part B of the Committee's report) and promising that these would soon be forwarded.

Debates on reports take place on the floor of the House on a motion by the Chairman of the Sub-Committee to 'take note' of the report.

The European Communities Committee produces numerous reports in each Session – 33 reports in total were agreed in the 1997/98 Session. The Committee's 19th Report was in response to the European Commission's proposal for a new chocolate directive. Under the 1973 directive, milk chocolate containing 25% cocoa and 14% milk is 'milk chocolate' and milk chocolate containing 20% cocoa and 20% milk is not 'milk chocolate' but 'milk chocolate with a high mik content' – a phrase which for some inexplicable reason is translated on the Continent as 'household milk chocolate'. The UK and Ireland have a derogation from the directive allowing them to sell 'household milk chocolate' as just – 'milk chocolate'. The European Commission, rather sensibly, decided to make no alteration to the current position. The European Parliament, however, in a fit of complete lunacy, decided that the UK and Ireland should no longer be allowed to continue with such anti-European practices and should be forced to sell 'milk chocolate' as 'milk chocolate with a high milk content'. Having taken evidence from the improbably named 'Seed Crushers' and Oil Processors' Association' and the 'Association Royale Belge des Industries du Biscuit, du Chocolat, de la Confiserie et de la Praline' House of Lords European Communities Sub-Committee D pronounced with their usual good common sense that 'In truth we see no good reason why there need to be two separate products, "milk chocolate" and "milk chocolate with a high milk content" ... and why both products cannot be allowed to trade under the description of "milk chocolate"' (para. 36 – 19th House of Lords European Communities Committee – Sub-Committee D, HL 85 – 17 March 1998 (1997/98)). The Report was debated in the House on 30 April 1998 on a motion 'to take note of the Report'. The debate was opened on behalf of Sub-Committee D, by Lord Reay, its Chairman, who, clearly a man of taste and discernment, admitted to being 'a life-long, confirmed chocaholic'. The motion to take note of the report was passed by the House.

The Three Pillars

The Maastricht Treaty (1993) established the three pillars of the European Union: European Community legislation; Common Foreign and Security Policy and Justice and Home Affairs. The second and third Pillars are effected by intergovernmental co-operation as opposed to legislation. The House of Lords European Communities Committee felt that agreements under these pillars should be subject to scrutiny if they were likely to require UK legislation. The Government agreed that draft documents should be provided to the Committee but did not agree that the Scrutiny Reserve should apply to them.

Enquiries

Whilst the basis of the Sub-Committees' work is the consideration of specific proposals, their enquiries are inevitably wider-ranging than this. They are often an invaluable source of much detailed and useful information. The recent report, resulting from the enquiry by Sub-Committee D, is a case in point. The report: 'EC Regulation of Genetic Modification in Agriculture' was published on 21 January 1999 (2nd Report, HL 11 - 1998/99). Whilst enquiries are carried out by the Sub-Committees, the reports are published by the main European Communities Committee. The basis of this particular report was the proposed modification of the existing directive 90/220/EEC on the deliberate release into the environment of genetically modified organisms. The Sub-Committee had as its scientific adviser, Dr Julian Kinderlerer, Assistant Director of the Sheffield Institute of Biotechnological Law and Ethics at Sheffield University and a member of ACRE the Government's Advisory Committee on Releases to the Environment. The importance of the role played by the specialist advisers to the various Sub-Committees, the Clerks and their assistants (who must service the Committees and physically produce their reports) cannot be overstated. Simply compiling the reports and transforming them into publishable documents is a monumental task in itself. In the case of the aforementioned report, they have done an excellent job. The Sub-Committee took evidence from a wide range of interested parties, ranging from Monsanto and Zeneca to Greenpeace UK and the Consumers' Association. The Committee members themselves had a wealth of experience between them, ranging from Lord Jopling, a former Minister of Agriculture and a farmer, to Baroness Young of Old Scone, the Chairman of English Nature, an organisation which favours a three-year moratorium on some genetically modified crops.

House of Lords Offices Committee

The House of Lords Offices Committee is the nearest the House of Lords has to the House of Commons Commission. It is chaired by the Chairman of Committees and the Clerk of the Parliaments is also a member. The Committee is responsible for staffing and accommodation and a wide range of other matters. Responsibility for accommodation is delegated to Black Rod as agent of the Administration and Works Sub-Committee. The Committee has a number of other Sub-Committees: Finance and Staff, Library and Computers, Refreshment and an Advisory Panel on Works of Arts which reports to the Administration and Works Sub-Committee.

The Hybrid Instruments Committee

The role of the Hybrid Instruments Committee is dealt with in more detail in both chapter nine on delegated legislation and in chapter 12 on Private Bills.

The Procedure Committee

The Procedure Committee considers proposals for amending the procedures of the House and in particular any suggested alterations to the Standing Orders of the House. In the last Session of Parliament (1997/98) the Committee produced four reports. The Fourth (HL 144, 1997/98) published on 22 October 1998 dealt with the delicate question of the Lord Chancellor's tights and breeches. The Lord Chancellor had requested that he be allowed to wear black trousers and forgo his tights and buckled shoes. Whilst some peers regarded such a request as a monstrous affront to the ceremonial dignity of the House, the Committee took a more sanguine view and recommended that the Lord Chancellor's request should be granted and that his ceremonial attire should be reserved for ceremonial occasions. The Committee also accepted that the Lord Chancellor should be able to speak from the Government Front Bench, when the House was not sitting as a Committee of the Whole House (his place on the Woolsack being taken by a Deputy Speaker).

The Standing Orders (Private Bills) Committee

The functions of this Committee are dealt with in chapter 12 on Private Bills. In brief, its role is to consider whether a Private Bill has complied with the relevant Standing Orders or whether, in some cases, the Standing Orders should be dispensed with.

Personal Bills Committee

The Personal Bills Committee examines petitions for Personal Bills as set out in SO 154 (HL Private) (these bills are discussed in chapter 12 on Private Bills).

Committee for Privileges

The Committee for Privileges is appointed under SO 74 and consists of 17 peers along with any four Lords of Appeal in Ordinary (Law Lords). The Committee considers any questions relating to the privilege of the House which are referred to it, any questions relating to claims of peerage, disputed peerages, precedence, etc. The Committee now has a Sub-Committee on Lords' Interests consisting of five peers, along with any two Lords of Appeal in Ordinary. The Clerk of the Committee for Privileges is also the Registrar of Lords' Interests.

The Committee of Selection

The Committee of Selection plays an extremely important role in the life of the House of Lords as it is responsible for nominating peers to sit on the various Select Committees. At the beginning of each Session the Committee produces a report proposing the members and chairmen of Committees to the House. The House itself must make the final decision by approving the motion to accept the report of the Committee. The members of the Committee of Selection itself, the members of both the Appeal and Appellate Committees, the members of the Ecclesiastical Committee, the members of the Private Bill Committees[8] and the Lords members of the Joint Committee on Consoldiation Bills are not proposed by the Committee of Selection. The members of the Committee of Selection are chosen at the beginning of each Session by the House itself. The Chairman is the Chairman of Committees and other members include the Leaders and Chief Whips of the various parties and the Convenor of the Cross Benches.

The Liaison Committee

Like the Committee of Selection, the Liaison Committee is not a Sessional Committee, but is appointed anew at the beginning of each Session. It is however, subject to the rule of rotation. It is a fairly recent creation, having been first established in 1993. The Committee's role is to review the work of all the Select Committee and to consider requests for new ad hoc committees. The Committee consists of the Leader of the House of Lords, the Leaders of the two other main parties, the Convenor of the Cross Benches and, at present, six other peers. The current chairman is the Chairman of Committees.

JOINT COMMITTEES

Joint Committees can be established to consider bills and other matters, which require the attention of both Houses: for example, parliamentary privilege (see below). The number of Members from both Houses do not have to be equal.

The Joint Committee on Statutory Instruments

The role of the Joint Committee on Statutory Instruments is considered in chapter nine on Delegated Legislation.

The Joint Committee on Parliamentary Privilege

The Joint Committee on Parliamentary Privilege was established on 30 July 1997 to review the existing rules of parliamentary privilege. The Committee consists of six MPs

[8] Members of the following committees are not appointed by the Committee of Selection unless either the Chairman of Committees feels they should be or if two or more of the members of the following committees themselves request they should be. Select Committees on Private Bills, Select Committees on Opposed Personal Bills, Select Committees on Opposed Provisional Order Confirmation Bills, Joint Committees under the Private Legislation Procedure (Scotland) Act 1936 (Lords members) and Joint Committees under the Standing Order (Special Procedure) Act 1945 (Lords members).

and six Peers (its quorum is three) and because it is not a Sessional Select Committee, it has to be reappointed at the beginning of each new parliamentary Session. For more information on parliamentary privilege please see chapter 10.

The Joint Committee on Consolidation Bills

The Joint Committee on Consolidation Bills is established at the beginning of each Parliament under SO 140 in the House of Commons and SO 49(HL). As the name suggests, it considers 'consolidation' bills, which are referred to it after their Second Reading in the House of Lords (where consolidation bills are introduced). These bills do not seek to enact new legislation, but simply to consolidate existing legislation. Whilst some consolidation bills simply revise or consolidate existing statutes; e.g. Statute Law Revision Bills and bills brought in under the Consolidation of Enactments (Procedure) Act 1949, others consolidate law by the repeal of existing statutes. About 5,000 Acts have been repealed by Statute Law (Repeals) Acts since 1965. These are based on the recommendations of the Law Commission.[9] The Committee considers the bill in question and may make amendments. In the House of Lords, it then returns to a Committee Stage on the floor of the House, followed by Report and Third Reading. In the House of Commons, such bills are usually given a formal Second and Third Reading. If no amendments have been tabled (these may be tabled before Second Reading), a Government Minister may propose that the Committee Stage be dispensed with.

The Joint Committee on Human Rights

The Leader of the House of Commons announced on 14 December 1998 that a Joint Committee on Human Rights would soon be set up by the House to conduct enquiries into human rights issues in the UK and to consider the question of whether there should be a human rights commission to monitor the Human Rights Act 1998. At the time of writing this Committee had not yet been established.

ALL-PARTY PARLIAMENTARY GROUPS

All-Party Groups are open to Members of all political persuasions from both Houses of Parliament and from the European Parliament. There are two types of All-Party Group: Registered All-Party Groups, whose membership consists solely of MPs and Peers and Registered Parliamentary Groups, who permit non-parliamentarians to join. Within both these categories there are 'subject' groups and 'country' groups; for example, there is an All-Party Azerbaijan Group and an All-Party Tanzania Group. The subject groups are many and varied, ranging from the All-Party Beer Club and the All-Party Diabetes Group to the All-Party Sustainable Waste Group and the All Party Scottish Sports Group. There is even an All Party Plumbing Group.

[9] The Law Commission for England and Wales and the Law Commission for Scotland were set up by Act of Parliament in 1965 to review and suggest proposals for the reform of common law and statute law. Since 1968 it has been engaged in a project to codify the criminal law and in 1989 produced a Draft Code. The aim is to produce a series of draft bills, which, if enacted, will form the country's 'criminal code'. The Law Commission also revises and consolidates statutes. The Statute Law (Repeals) Act 1998 will enable a number of obsolete statutes to be repealed together.

All the All-Party Groups and Parliamentary Groups must ensure they have an entry in the Register of All Party and Parliamentary Groups. They must register the names of office holders and any benefits, whether financial or 'in kind' which have been given to the Group. This includes the 'loan' of staff to the group by outside organisations, in which case, the occupation of such staff would need to be registered. All-Party Groups hit the headlines in November 1998, when on 10 November 1998, the Independent's lead item read: 'Lobbyists pay for MP's junkets'. The authors, Fran Abrams and Andrew Mullins claimed that 'Dozens of parliamentary groups of MPs, operating inside the Commons, are being run by outside commercial interest groups ... no fewer than 14 are based in the offices of lobbying companies'. It is certainly true that a number of All-Party Groups and Parliamentary Groups receive generous funding and support from outside organisations, but in some cases, without it, worthy Groups would not be able to function at all.

It is not just the obviously commercial groups which benefit from outside assistance – in some cases voluntary organisations assist All-Party Groups by seconding staff to give unpaid assistance to such groups and in other cases they actually provide funding and office space. What is of legitimate concern is the implication of the Independent's article that some Groups are not registering this assistance, financial or otherwise. Complaining that it is unfair that one group receives greater funding than another is rather like complaining that a small local charity receives less from the public than Oxfam or Save the Children. Surely, the only legitimate concern about All-Party Groups is whether or not the links between industry, commerce, lobbying companies and All Party Groups are made explicit and the levels of funding registered. Provided parliamentarians and the public know that Lobbying Company A provides secretarial assistance to the All-Party Mollusc Group is there any harm in it? The fact that the British Greyhound Racing Board sponsors a dog on behalf of the All-Party Greyhound Group would hardly seem to be evidence of corruption on a grand scale. Apparently, winnings are given to Retired Greyhound Trust, so presumably the arrangement has made some old dog extremely happy.

On 29 July 1998, the House of Commons agreed to amend a Resolution of 17 December 1985, which permitted inspection of the Register by Members only, to allow it to be inspected by members of the public.

OTHER GROUPS

British-Irish Inter-Parliamentary Body

The British-Irish Inter-Parliamentary-Union was established in 1990 to promote co-operation and understanding between the two legislatures. It consists of 25 members from each Parliament.

Commonwealth Parliamentary Association

The Commonwealth Parliamentary Association (CPA) is a charity which promotes the interests of good parliamentary government. Its predecessor was the Empire Parliamentary Association. There are 140 branches and the Committee of the CPA has

32 members, drawn from throughout the Commonwealth. The Secretariat is based in London as is the secretariat of the UK branch, in offices just off Westminster Hall.

The Council of Europe

The Council of Europe was established in 1949 and 40 countries are now members. The Council's aims are to promote human rights and social and economic development within the member nations. It has a Committee of Ministers (Foreign Ministers from the member countries) and a Parliamentary Assembly. The members of the Assembly are elected or appointed by the Parliaments of the 40 countries. In the UK, members are appointed by the Prime Minister. There are currently 36 members (including substitute members) reflecting the balance of the political parties in both Houses.

The Inter-Parliamentary Union

The Inter-Parliamentary Union (IPU) was set up in 1892 with the laudable aim of promoting peace, co-operation amongst nations and the development of representative institutions. The members of the IPU are groups representing their national parliaments. The Council of the IPU consists of two Members of Parliament from each Member State. The Council meets twice a year in different member Parliaments. The Secretariat is based in Geneva. The British Group of the IPU has an Executive Committee comprising Members of both Houses.

The North Atlantic Assembly

The North Atlantic Asssembly was established in 1955 and aims to provide a link between NATO authorities and the national Parliaments of its members. There are 188 members of the Assembly and the UK delegation is appointed by Ministers from Members of both Houses.

Organisation for Security and Co-operation in Europe

The Parliamentary Assembly of the Organisation for Security and Co-operation in Europe (OSCE) first met in 1992. It was set up under the auspices of the Conference on Security and Co-operation in Europe which met in November 1990. There are 317 delegates drawn from the 54 member States. The UK delegation has 13 members and some substitute members appointed by Ministers.

Western European Union

The Western European Union was established in 1954 and has ten Member States (who are also Members of the European Union). The organisation deals with defence matters. A declaration relating to the WEU was attached to the Treaty on European Union whereby the Members States of the WEU agreed to develop it as the defence component of the EU. The WEU has a Council of Ministers and a Parliamentary Assembly, which consists of the same members as the Parliamentary Assembly of the Council of Europe (see *above*).

CHAPTER TWELVE – BRIDGES, BARRAGES & BYPASSES – A BRIEF GUIDE TO PRIVATE BILLS

INTRODUCTION

Whereas Public Bills - either Government bills or Private Members' Bills – have what is known as a 'general application', Private Bills apply specifically to a particular group. Private Bills are 'promoted', not by the Government or by a Backbencher, but by a particular group or organisation; for example, a corporation, local authority, academic institution, etc. A Public Act, for example, the Human Rights Act 1998, applies generally to the nation as a whole, whereas the Croydon Tramlink Act 1994 applies solely to one part of the country. A Private Bill is not promoted by an individual MP, although it does require a parliamentary sponsor, but is deposited by the parties interested in promoting it and is 'founded' on a petition. Some bills are neither wholly Public or Private Bills, but contain elements of both, in which case they are said to be 'hybrid'.

Private Bills have their roots in the petitions traditionally presented to Parliament for the redress of private wrongs. Where grievances could not be dealt with by the common law, they gradually came to be rectified by promoting Private Bills. From the beginning of the 18th Century, a large number of Private Bills were designed to effect the construction of canals, railways, etc. Some measures which used to require Private Bills can now be given the necessary legislative effect by orders made under the Transport and Works Act 1992. The Act was an attempt to release the parliamentary timetable from the growing burden of Private Bills. They are dealt with more fully later in this chapter.

Parliamentary Agents, such as Rees and Freres or Dyson, Bell, Martin are employed by those wishing to promote Private Bills, to help them steer a course through the minefield of parliamentary procedure in this area. They deal with the legal and technical aspects of a Bill's progress. There are two types of Parliamentary Agent, those who both promote and oppose Private Bills and those who only oppose them. The former are included in the Permanent Register (Roll A) of Parliamentary Agents to the Speaker, whilst the latter sign Roll B in the Private Bill Office. This latter registration lasts for only one parliamentary session. Private Bills cannot be purchased from the Parliamentary Bookshop or Stationery Office, but must be obtained instead, either from the agents promoting the bill in question or from the Vote Office. The Weekly Information Bulletin shows both the progress of Private Bills and the Parliamentary Agents dealing with them. The following example is taken from the Bulletin from 3 April 1999.

UNITED REFORMED CHURCH (Dyson Bell Martin)
Lords 1R: 14.1.99 2R: 18.2.99 UBC: 18.3.99
UNIVERSITY COLLEGE LONDON 98/99 (Rees and Freres)
Commons 1R: 25.1.99 2R: 2.2.99 BC: 25.2.99 UBC:16.3.99 BAC: 23.3.99 3R: 30.3.99
Lords 1R: 30.3.99

BC = Bill committed (as yet the type of Committee is not known)
UBC = Unopposed Bill Committee
BAC = Bill as amended by the Committee considered (Report stage) (House of Commons only)

PETITIONS, MEMORIALS, EXAMINERS AND THE STANDING ORDERS COMMITTEE

A Private Bill is introduced by means of a petition, which must be deposited by the promoters in the Private Bill Office of the House of Commons and the Office of the Clerk of the Parliaments in the House of Lords on or before 27 November, along with a printed copy of the proposed bill. A 'General List of Petitions for Private Bills' is then drawn up. This lists all the Private Bills which are to be 'heard by the Examiners'. There are two Examiners – one appointed by the Speaker and one appointed by the House of Lords. It is their role to ensure that the bill complies with the Standing Orders governing private business. Both Houses have a separate set of Standing Orders for private business, which set out, amongst other things, the conditions which petitioners must fulfil before depositing a bill.

If the Examiners feel that the Standing Orders of both Houses[1] have not been complied with, anyone who opposes the bill may put forward what is known as a 'memorial' (a complaint that the bill does not comply with the Standing Orders). Anyone depositing a petition (the petitioners) or a memorial (the memorialists) must pay a fee and two copies of either the petition or the memorial, must be deposited in the Private Bill Office of the House of Commons on or before 17 December, or the fourth day before the Examiners are to consider the petition, in the case of bills deposited after 27 November (or, if the House is not sitting, the day before the next sitting day).

Under Standing Order 107A (House of Commons), where the Examiners report that the Standing Orders have not been complied with, only those parties who have deposited memorials may appear before the Standing Orders Committee to argue that the Standing Orders should not be dispensed with. The passage of Private Bills is overseen by the Chairman of Committees in the House of Lords and the Chairman of Ways and Means in the House of Commons.

The Examiners begin their public sittings on 18 December (or the following Monday, when 18 December is a Saturday or Sunday). Each Examiner sits separately and considers roughly half the number of total petitions. The Examiners must give seven days notice of the day set down for the examination of each petition. The Parliamentary Agents promoting the bill appear before the Examiner with a 'statement of proofs', which must show that all the relevant Standing Orders have been adhered to by the promoters of the bill. The name of a witness who can prove the statement must be 'set down' against each 'proof'.

The 'agents' for the 'memorialists' (those opposing the bill because it fails to comply with Standing Orders) must 'enter their appearances'. An 'appearance' is a paper from the Private Bill Office certifying that the agent has 'entered' him or herself as agent for the memorialists. Nothing can be raised before the Examiners if it has not been specifically referred to in the memorial. Objections can be made to allegations set out in the memorial. The allegations themselves must be confined to breaches of Standing Orders and not to the merits or demerits of the bill itself. Under SO 70 (HC) [private business]

[1] SO 4 to 68 (HC) [private business] & SO 4 to 68 (HL) [private business].

and SO 72 (HL) [private business] the Examiner informs the House whether in his or her view the relevant Standing Orders have been complied with (this includes all Private Bills, irrespective of which House they are likely to originate). If, in the Examiner's view, Standing Orders have not been complied with, this is reported to both Houses and to the Standing Orders Committee. The Standing Orders Committee consists of the Chairman of Ways and Means (ex-officio Chairman), the Deputy Chairmen and eight other Members nominated by the Committee of Selection at the beginning of the parliamentary Session.

The Standing Orders Committee has to decide whether the Standing Orders have been complied with or whether or not they should be dispensed with and the bill allowed to proceed. The Standing Orders Committee receives written statements from the agents for the bill and the agents for the memorialists. These are deposited in the office of the Chairman of Ways and Means. If the Committee reports that Standing Orders should be dispensed with, the House has to give its consent (this is usually done formally). If the Committee feels that Standing Orders should not be dispensed with the House simply acknowledges the decision rather than passing any form of resolution; however, such a decision is usually fatal to the bill. Very occasionally the House has objected to a decision of the Standing Orders Committee and the matter has been referred back to them to reconsider. Erskine May cites two well-known and much loved cases in which bills were recommitted in this way: the Macclesfield and District Railless Traction and Electricity Supply Bill (Lords) 1911 and the Great Central Railway (Grimsby Fish Dock) Bill (Lords) 1912. In exceptional cases, the promoters might be given leave to deposit a petition for another bill.

On or before 8 January each year, the Chairman of Ways and Means in the House of Commons and the Chairman of Committees in the House of Lords decide which bills should begin in which House. Occasionally, they will allow a bill to go forward, even if a petition has not been deposited by 27 November – these are known as 'late bills'. Petitions for or against Private Bills may be deposited in the Private Bill Office by Members, parties or agents and copies can be obtained upon payment of a small fee. By convention, Government departments do not petition either in favour or against Private Bills, although they are not prohibited from so doing. Petitions against a Private Bill originating in the House of Commons, which has been judged by the Examiner to have complied with Standing Orders, must be presented before 30 January, or, when this is a Sunday, 29 January, or if 30 January is a non-sitting day, the next sitting day. Some petitions may be presented after this date; for example, petitions for or against 'additional provisions'. These petitions are referred to the Committee considering the bill. Where a petition is deposited later, the petitioners must present another petition, requesting the dispensation of Standing Orders in their case. In the House of Lords, the Committee on the Bill and in the House of Commons, the Court of Referees must decide on the 'locus standi' of those petitioning against the bill - they must decide whether they have the right to petition. A petitioner is generally considered to have the relevant 'locus standi' to petition against a bill if his or her 'property or interests' are specifically affected by the bill's provisions (a comprehensive list of the decisions relating to locus standi can be found in the 21st Edition of Erskine May). The necessary locus standi required to petition against a bill are set out in SOs 92-102 (HC) [private business]. SO 98 (2) (HC) [private], for example, states that: 'The council of any county .... alleging that its administrative area ... may be injuriously affected by the provisions of any bill proposing to authorise the construction ... of any tramway ... shall be entitled to be heard against the bill'.

THE COURT OF REFEREES

The Court of Referees consists of the Chairman of Ways and Means, the Deputy Chairmen and the Counsel to the Speaker along with seven others Member of the House of Commons, appointed by the Speaker, usually for the duration of a Parliament. Three 'Referees' constitutes a 'Court'. A petitioner may present his or her own case to the Court or use his or her counsel or agent.

If the promoters want to object to the right of a petitioner against the bill to be heard, they must give notice of their objection to the Clerk of the Court of Referees and the petitioners' agents, no later than the eighth day after the day on which the petition was deposited in the Private Bill Office. Occasionally, notice can be given after this time. The Court of Referees hears first from the petitioners against the bill, followed by the promoters. Some petitioners 'pray to be heard' against the premble of the bill, some to all the clauses and some only to particular clauses. The Court of Referees may, therefore, limit the locus standi of a petitioner to particular clauses in the bill, rather than the bill as a whole. This restricts the rights of the petitioner to object only to those clauses specified by the Court of Referees. The Court of Referees decides only on the locus standi of petitioners against a bill, the Committee on the bill itself decides on the locus standi of 'petitioners against alterations'. Petitions against alterations are petitions against amendments which the promoters intend to make to the bill in committee.

CONDUCT OF PRIVATE BUSINESS IN THE HOUSE OF COMMONS

Private business in the House of Commons is taken after prayers and before Questions on Mondays to Thursdays, but not on Fridays. Private business is set down in the Order Paper in the following order:

Consideration of Lords Amendments
Third Reading
Report Stage
Second Reading

Only unopposed private business may be taken at this time. If an item of private business is 'blocked'; i.e. by a Member shouting 'object', followed by the tabling of a 'blocking motion', it becomes opposed private business and the Chairman of Ways and Means may appoint it for consideration on a future day at 7.00pm (usually a Monday). Any unopposed private business still under discussion at 2.45pm (or 11.45am on a Thursday) stands adjourned until the next sitting. The Second Reading or any later stage of an opposed Private Bill is moved by a Member who has agreed to act on behalf of the promoters. The promoters of the bill must pay a fee of £3,500 at First and Third Reading (less for personal bills and bills concerning educational institutes, charities, etc) in addition to £20 on the deposit of a petition. The level of fees charged is set by the Speaker.

Private Bills must be printed and copies delivered to the Vote Office and Private Bill Office before 27 November. A Private Bill is presented to the House by being deposited in the Private Bill Office and by being laid upon the Table of the House on the next sitting day. Where the Examiner has reported that the Standing Orders have been complied with, the Bill must be presented to the House on 21 January or the first sitting day thereafter. The Examiner's report may be laid on the Table on 21 January, in which case the bill itself must be laid the day after. Where the Examiner has reported that Standing Orders have not been complied with, but the House, after considering a report from the Standing Orders Committee, decides that they ought to be dispensed with, the bill must be presented by the following day, or if the House is not sitting, the next available sitting day, or if the House reaches its decision before 21 January, on 21 January. A Private Bill is deemed to have had its First Reading when it is laid upon the Table of the House, when it has originated in the House of Lords, when it is received in the House of Commons. Bills which give certain powers to companies established by Act of Parliament are referred to the Examiners after First Reading to ensure that they comply with what are known as the 'Wharncliffe' Orders (SO 62-67 (HC) [private business] & SO 62-67 (HL) [private business]). These are named after Lord Wharncliffe who devised the first of these Orders in 1838. They are designed to ensure that companies promoting bills comply with certain conditions; for example, that the consent of the owner or directors has been obtained, etc.

There must be at least four and not more than eight days between the First and Second Reading of a Private Bill (unless the bill has come from the House of Lords). The agent for the bill must give three days' notice in writing to the Private Bill Office of the day proposed for the Second Reading . The Second Reading is a general debate on the bill, after which it is referred to the Committee of Selection.

After Second Reading, the House may give instructions to the Committee which is to consider the bill. The Committee considering a Private Bill may not allow any new provisions which would go beyond the scope of the bill as defined by the clauses and schedules annexed to the petition for the bill. This is to prevent the insertion of provisions which had they been included in the original bill might have been objected to by those whose interests were affected. The promoters of the bill can insert new provisions provided they have petitioned for their inclusion. Instructions can be either 'mandatory' or 'permissive'. Mandatory instructions include those directing the Committee to insert certain provisions in a bill, or to require certain safeguards to be made before passing the bill or those directing the Committee to omit certain provisions from the bill. Permissive instructions give the Committee the power to do something. Some instructions are deemed inadmissible; for example, instructions seeking to reverse the rejection by the House of a reasoned amendment at Second Reading; instructions which are too vague or those which impose unreasonable restrictions on the discretion of the Committee.

At least four days' notice must be given in the Private Bill Office of the first sitting of an Opposed Bill Committee. Copies of any amendments proposed by the promoters must be given to those petitioning against the bill one day before the Committee's first sitting. Where a bill affects a charity or educational institution, it cannot be considered by a committee until a report from the Attorney General has been presented to the House. A copy of every Private Bill must be deposited with the Treasury and other Government departments (depending on their content) on or before 4 December. This enables departments to assess whether they need report to the House on any aspect of the bill in question.

COMMITTEES

Unopposed Bills are referred by the Committee of Selection to the Committee on Unopposed Bills, which includes the Chairman of Ways and Means (who, although he is ex-officio Chairman does not attend the Committee), the Deputy Chairmen and four other Members, who are selected by the Chairman of Ways and Means from the 14 members of the Unopposed Bills Panel, appointed by the Committee of Selection at the beginning of each Session.

An Opposed Bill is one against which a petition has been presented. The Committee on an Opposed Private Bill consists of four Members who have no local or other interest in the bill. The Committee of Selection nominates one of the four Members as Chairman of the Committee. Each member of an Opposed Bill Committee must sign a declaration that neither he/she nor his/her constituents have any interest in the bill. There must be six days between a bill being sent to an Opposed Bill Committee and its first sitting and at least four days' notice must be given of the meeting (one day's notice for an Unopposed Bill Committee). Occasionally, Private Bills dealing with subjects which the House believes to be of particular importance are referred to either a Select Committee, nominated party by the House and partly by the Committee of Selection or a Joint Committee.

Two days before the first meeting of an Opposed Bill Committee (one in the case of an Unopposed Bill), the agents for the promoters must deposit a copy of the 'filled-up' bill in the Private Bill Office. This is the bill with any proposed amendments attached. The day before the Committee's first meeting the agents must send a copy of the amendments to any petitioners against the bill who request them and must send a copy of the bill to the Chairman of Ways and Means (two days before in the case of an opposed bill). An Opposed Bill Committee may not proceed if more than one member is absent and decisions are taken by a majority of those voting. At its first meeting, if none of the petitioners attends, the bill becomes an Unopposed Bill. When the Committee is hearing counsel or witnesses, it's proceedings are open to the public; however, it meets in private when deliberating on the bill in question. Counsel for the bill appears first, followed by counsel for those petitioning against the bill. Parties promoting or opposing a bill must 'enter appearances' on the day on which the bill is to be considered. The agent for a petition must have a certificate from the Private Bill Office that he has 'entered an appearance' upon the petition. This document is then delivered to the Committee Clerk on the first day on which the Committee considers the bill. If parties have not entered appearances at the correct time, they will not be entitled to be heard. If an 'appearance' has not been taken out on any petition, the opposition of the petitioners is said to have been abandoned and the bill becomes unopposed. Petitioners against alterations may also be heard.

The Preamble to a bill is usually considered first and may be opposed. Counsel for the bill addresses the Committee and witnesses may be called to give evidence and may be cross-examined by counsel for the petitioners against the bill. Counsel for the bill are followed by counsel for the petitioner, who in turn may call witnesses, etc. After counsel for both sides have been heard, the room is cleared and the question put that 'the Preamble is proved'.

If the Preamble is proved, the Committee goes on to consider the bill clause by clause. Clauses which are opposed on petition are heard first, followed by those which are the subject of reports from Government departments. Once all the clauses have been debated, new clauses may be put forward. If the Preamble is not proved, this is reported to the House. Occasionally, an attempt is made to have a bill recommitted in these circumstances so that the decision can be reversed. When the Preamble to the Crossrail Bill was not proved in the 1993/94 Session, an attempt was made to have the bill recommitted. However, this was objected to and the bill proceeded no further. Where the Committee finds the Preamble not proved and feels that one or more of the petitioners has been put to unnecessary expense it may award costs against the promoters of the bill. Conversely, if the Committee finds that petitioners against a bill have put the promoters to unnecessary expense, they may recover costs from the former.

After Committee stage, the Chairman reports the bill to the House. Copies of the reprinted bill as amended, must be made available in the Vote Office three days before the Bill's Report Stage and the agents for the bill must give at least one day's notice in writing to the Private Bill Office of the day proposed for Report Stage. If the bill's promoters wish to table further amendments to the bill, they have to give one day's notice to the Private Bill Office. Amendments may also be tabled by ordinary Members. No amendments can be moved at Report Stage if they could have been moved in Committee. Third Reading follows Report Stage. The bill then undergoes a similar procedure in the House of Lords, before returning to the Commons for Consideration of Lords' Amendments. Notice of such amendments must be given in the Private Bill Office, no less than one day before they are to be considered. The promoters may also table amendments to the Lords' Amendments. Private Bills may be suspended from one Session to the next and one Parliament to the next.

All petitions relating to Private Bills are presented in the House of Commons except petitions for 'late bills' and petitions for 'additional provision', where the bill in question originated in the House of Lords. When a bill originates in the House of Commons, on arrival in the House of Lords it is referred to the Examiners to ensure that it complies with any standing orders which were not considered in the House of Commons. Again, memorials may be submitted on the same basis as in the House of Commons and the Standing Orders Committee, whose chairman is the Chairman of Committees, must decide whether or not the bill complies with Standing Orders or, if not, whether they should be dispensed with. First Reading (which is purely formal) takes place no later than seven sittings days after the Committee has reached its decision. Petitions may be presented opposing the bill by 6 February (or in the case of late bills and bills from the Commons, 10 days after First Reading) and these are considered by the Select Committee to which the bill is sent after Second Reading, if opposed. There is usually no debate at Second Reading in the House of Lords. Unopposed bills are sent to an Unopposed Bill Committee. The Select Committee which considers the bill consists of five, or very occasionally seven, peers, chosen either by the Chairman of Committees or the Committee of Selection. The Select Committee considers petitions against bills and the Committee itself decides the locus standi of petitioners. Once the Select Committee has reported, any unopposed provisions in the bill are referred to an Unopposed Bill Committee. There is no Report Stage on a Private Bill in the House of Lords, but amendments can be moved at Third Reading.

THE PRIVATE LEGISLATION PROCEDURE (SCOTLAND) ACT 1936

In Scotland, the Private Legislation Procedure (Scotland) Act bears greater resemblance to delegated legislation than to Private Bill procedure. Under the Act, the Secretary of State issues a Provisional Order which has no validity until confirmed by Parliament. Organisations which in England and Wales would have been required to introduce a Private Bill, proceed in Scotland by this method. Petitions for the issue of a Provisional Order have to be deposited at the Scottish Office before 27 November or 27 March. Copies have to be sent to the Private Bill Offices in both Houses, the Treasury and certain other bodies. Petitions may be made against a proposed Provisional Order and these must be deposited not later than six weeks after 11 December or 11 April.

The Lord Chairman of Committees and the Chairman of Ways and Means report to the House and to the Secretary of State. If they report that the provisions relate to non-Scottish matters or raise questions of public policy then the promoters must resort to a Private Bill, called a 'substituted bill'. Provisional Orders must comply with 'General Orders', which are similar to the Standing Orders for Private Bills. The Private Bill Examiners go through every draft Order to ensure compliance and report to the Chairmen and Secretary of State. The Chairmen at their discretion may allow an Order to proceed even if it does not fully comply. The Secretary of State considers the application after the Chairmen and the Examiners report. He issues the actual Provisional Order. If the Order is opposed, or if the Secretary of State considers it necessary, an inquiry is instituted and opponents may Petition against the Order.

The Commissioners for these inquiries are drawn from three panels: 15 peers chosen by the Chairman of Committees; 25 MPs chosen by the Committee of Selection; 25 non-parliamentarians, qualified to act as commissioners and nominated by the Chairmen and the Secretary of State. The Commission of Inquiry (consisting of four members from the panels) sits in Scotland and meets daily if possible, acting as an Opposed Private Bill Committee. The Commissioners will either report that the Order should be issued with or without amendments or that it should be rejected completely. Petitions against proposals for the issue of Orders must be received by 23 January or 24 May. As soon as the Order has been issued the Government presents a Confirming Bill, usually to the House of Commons. These bills give effect to provisional orders. If no enquiry has been held the Order is considered to have passed all its stages up to and including Committee and it therefore proceeds straight to Report Stage and then Third Reading. The same procedure is then followed in the House of Lords. If there has been an inquiry there is, after First Reading, an additional opportunity for objection if a Member Petitions, within seven days, to commit the Bill to a Joint Committee of both Houses, comprising six Members, three from each House nominated by the Lord Chairman of Committees and the House of Commons Committee of Selection. They hear arguments from promoters and Petitioners and report to the House for confirmation with or without amendment. If the Committee recommends rejection the Government will withdraw the bill. If the Committee reports that the Order ought to be confirmed, the bill then proceeds to a

Report Stage, if it has been amended, or to Third Reading if there are no amendments. Where there has been no Joint Committee, the order has a Second Reading, report and then Third Reading. Procedure in the second House depends on whether or not a Joint Committee has been appointed in the first House. If a Joint Committee was appointed in the first House, then the bill receives a First and Second Reading and then progresses straight to a Third Reading. This means that where the House of Commons is the second House, no amendments may be made (Standing Order 75).

In cases where a Joint Committee was not appointed in the first House, procedure in the second House differs according to whether or not the second House is the House of Lords or the House of Commons. If the second House is the House of Commons, the bill has a first Reading and Second reading, is deemed to have had a Committee Stage and is followed by Report and Third Reading (taken consecutively, one after the other). If the second House is the House of Lords, after First Reading, the bill is considered to have had a Second Reading and Committee Stage, so proceeds to Report and third Reading.

Schedule 4, paragraph 1(2) of the Scotland Act 1998 states that the Private Legislation Procedure (Scotland) Act 1936 cannot be modified by an Act of the Scottish Parliament.

PROVISIONAL ORDER BILLS

These are now virtually obsolete. Provisional Orders are made under particular Acts, usually by local authorities and are confirmed by Ministers or Parliament. The Order is usually preceded by a local enquiry and followed by a confirming bill, which has to be presented to Parliament by 15 May and referred to the Examiners of Private Bills. The Examiners must consider whether or not Standing Orders[2] have been complied with. If they have, or are not applicable, the bill proceeds to Second Reading. If they are applicable, but have not been complied with, the bill is considered by the Standing Orders Committee. If the bill is opposed by a Member putting down a blocking motion, it has to be debated at 7.00pm. The bill then proceeds much in the same way as a Private Bill.

SPECIAL PROCEDURE ORDERS

Special Procedure Orders under the Statutory Orders (Special Procedure) Acts, 1945 and 1965 are made where an Act prescribes, 'special parliamentary procedures'. This involves the opportunity to object to the Order at a local inquiry and by Petition to Parliament. The Order may be amended as a result of a report by a joint committee of both Houses. These Orders are very rare and there have only been two Confirming Bills since 1945, the Mid-Northamptonshire Water Order Confirmation (Special Procedure) Bill of 1948/49 and the Okehampton By-Pass (Confirmation of Orders) Bill of 1985/86.

The first feature of the Special Procedure Order is the preliminary local enquiry. After this the Minister concerned must give not less than three days notice in the London Gazette of his intention to lay the Order before Parliament. The Order, when laid, must be accompanied by a certificate from the Minister stating that the necessary preliminary

[2] SO 4 to 68 (HC) [private business] & SO 4 to 68 (HL) [private business].

requirements have been complied with. Copies of the Order must be deposited in the Private Bill Office and the Vote Office, the Office of the Clerk of Parliaments and made available to the public on application to the Minister.

Petitions against the Order may be presented to each House within a period of 21 days beginning with the day on which the Order is laid before Parliament, or if the Order is laid on different days before the two Houses, from the later of the two days. There are two types of Petition: Petitions for Amendment, praying for particular amendments to be made to the Order (these must specify the amendments) and Petitions of General Objection. Both types must be deposited in the Private Bill Office of the House of Commons or in the Office of the Clerk of the Parliaments.

The day after the Petition has been deposited, a copy must placed in the appropriate office of the other House and with the Minister concerned. Copies must be sent to the applicant and made available to any member of the public on application to the Petitioner or agent.

Within a period of seven days beginning with the day on which the Petition is presented, the Minister concerned or the applicant for the Order may deposit a 'Memorial' addressed to the two Chairman (the Chairman of Committees and the Chairman of Ways and Means) objecting to the Petition, or if the Petition has been presented as one for amendment, the memorialist may object on the grounds that the Petition is in fact a Petition of General Objection.

After the end of the Petitioning period and the time allowed for Memorials objecting to Petitions, the two Chairmen are required by section 3(3) of the Act to take into consideration all Petitions referred to them, and if they are satisfied that the provisions of the Act and standing Orders have been complied with, they must certify that the Petition is 'proper to be received', and is either a Petition for Amendment or a Petition of General Objection. If a Memorial has been deposited, the Chairmen must give notice of the time and place at which the Petition and Memorial will be considered.

If the Chairmen decide that a Petition which has been presented as a Petition of Amendment is in fact a Petition of General Objection and would have the effect of nullifying the entire Order they must certify it as such, or must delete that part of the Petition which would have such an effect and certify the remainder of the Petition as a Petition for Amendment. The Chairmen must report to both Houses on Petitions against Special Procedure Orders. They must state whether Petitions have been received, whether they have been certified and into which category of Petition they fall.

Counter-Petitions may be presented to the Chairmen within 14 days of the Chairmen's report to both Houses. These take the form of complaints that amendments in a particular Petition would affect the interests of those presenting the Counter-Petition. They are presented to the House to which the original Petition was presented and must be deposited in either the Private Bill Office or the Office of the Clerk of the Parliaments in the Lords. Counter-Petitions must be prepared and signed in strict conformity with the rules and Orders of each House. Counter-Petitions are not referred to the two Chairmen for examination.

Any Member of either House may move that the Order be annulled. In the Commons, such motions are exempted business and can be considered, even if opposed, after the Moment of Interruption. If a motion for annulment is carried, the Order becomes void and no further proceedings may be taken. If neither House passes an annulment motion the next stages depend on whether or not there are Petitions against the Order. If there are and if neither House resolves that the Petitions 'be not referred to a Joint Committee', a committee stage will be required. If there are no Petitions, the Order will come into operation at the end of the 21-day period, or on such later date as may be specified in the Order. The only way of amending a Special Procedure Order is through the machinery of a Joint Committee.

The Joint Committee must consist of six members, three from each House, nominated by the Chairman of Committees in the Lords and the Committee of Selection in the Commons. The Committee considers Petitions for Amendment, Petitions of General Objection and all Counter-Petitions. Petitioners are heard by the Committee as is the Minister concerned and usually the applicant. The latter may be heard in lieu of the Minister if the Minister so decides. Counter-Petitioners do not have an automatic right to be heard, but the Committee may hear them if they feel that an amendment in a Petition affects the interests of the Counter-Petitioner. The minutes of evidence are reported to both Houses. The procedure of the Committee follows that of a Joint Committee on a Private Bill. The onus of proof lies on the Petitioners to prove their case. The Committee reports an Order either without amendment or with such amendments as it thinks fit. If they are satisfied that effect should be given to a Petition of General Objection, it may report the Order with amendments. It may report that the Order 'be not approved'. The Joint Committee's report is then laid before both Houses.

If there has been no Joint Committee and neither House has resolved that the Order be annulled, the Order comes into effect on the expiry of the resolution period or a later date if specified in the Order. Where an Order is reported by a Joint Committee without amendment, it comes into operation on the date on which the report of the Committee is laid before both Houses, or on such later date as may be specified in the Order.

Where an Order is reported from a Joint Committee with amendments, if the Minister concerned accepts the amendments, the Order is brought into operation on such date as the Minister may determine. If he does not accept the amendments he may withdraw the Order. Where an Order has been reported to the House with amendments which the Minister does not accept or where the Committee has reported that the Order be not approved, the Minister may still decide to press ahead with the Order in its original form. He may only do this by presenting a Confirming Bill to Parliament. If the Order was amended by the Committee the Minister will present it to the House in a Confirming Bill setting out the Order as amended in Committee. It is then treated as a Public Bill.

After presentation, however, there is no Second Reading or Committee Stage and the bill proceeds immediately to Report Stage where amendments may be moved; i.e. the Minister may move amendments to the bill which would have the effect of removing the offending amendments passed by the Joint Committee. It then has a Third Reading and proceeds to the House of Lords where a similar procedure is followed.

Where a Joint Committee reports that an Order be not approved, a bill may be presented for its confirmation setting out the Order as it was when originally referred to the Committee. The bill then proceeds as above, unless there are any outstanding Petitions for amendment. Where a duly certified Petition for amendment has not been dealt with by the Joint Committee, the bill has a Second Reading and is then referred to the original Joint Committee for consideration of the Petition. It is then considered on Report and read a Third Time. In the second House, it is deemed to have passed all stages up to and including Committee.

The following was taken from the House of Commons Weekly Information Bulletin for 22 May 1999 and demonstrates the relative rarity of Special Procedure Orders and the virtual demise of Provisional Orders.

Bill to confirm Orders for the purposes of the Statutory Orders (Special Procedure) Act 1945
None
Order Confirmation Bills under the Private Legislation Procedure (Scotland) Act 1936
None

There were, however, some Draft Provisional Orders.

Copies of Draft Provisional Orders deposited under the Private Legislation Procedure (Scotland) Act 1936
The Chairman of Committees (Lords) and Chairman of Ways and Means (Commons) have reported that these orders should be allowed to proceed:

Burrell Collection (Lending)	(Dyson Bell Martin)
City of Edinburgh Rapid Transit	(Dyson Bell Martin)
Lothian Regional Council	(Dyson Bell Martin)
Lothian Regional Council (Port Edgar)	(Dyson Bell Martin)
Strathclyde Crossrail	(Rees and Freres)
Strathclyde Tram	(Dyson Bell Martin)

HYBRID BILLS

A Hybrid Bill is one which has the characteristics of both a Private and a Public Bill, for example, the Channel Tunnel Bill 1987/88. This was essentially a measure affecting the general interest of all, but also the specific interests of particular, individuals. Erskine May gives two reasons why bills affecting private rights are properly introduced as Hybrid Bills: firstly, whilst they may in part be of a private nature, their main object is a public one; secondly, there may be no parties able and willing to present a petition. Occasionally, doubts arise as to whether a Public Bill should have been introduced as a Private Bill, or vice versa. The House will order the bill to be considered by the Examiners. If they find that certain of the Standing Orders relating to private business are applicable to the bill, it is treated as a Hybrid, and its passage through Parliament is governed by a special procedure. If the Standing Orders do not apply, then the bill proceeds as a Public Bill.

PROCEDURE ON HYBRID BILLS

After a Public Bill has had its first reading, a draft is sent to the Public Bill Office. If they feel that the Standing Orders relating to private business may be applicable to the bill, they must inform the Member in charge of the bill, who refers it to the Examiners. The order for Second Reading of the bill remains on the notice paper with a note 'to be reported on by the Examiners'.

The Second Reading cannot be moved until the report of the Examiners has been received. The Examiners must decide whether Standing Orders 4 to 68 of both the Standing Orders relating to private business of both House of Commons and House of Lords should apply to the bill.[3] These Standing Orders detail the measures promoters of Private Bills must take to comply with correct procedures. If the Examiners report that none of the Standing Orders are applicable to the bill, it proceeds as an ordinary Public Bill. If they report that the Standing Orders are applicable and have been complied with the note 'to be reported upon by the Examiners' is removed from the Order Paper and the Second Reading can be moved in the ordinary way. If they report that the Standing Orders applicable to the bill have not been complied with; i.e. the Government has put forward a Public Bill which is in fact Hybrid, the report is referred to the Standing Orders Committee.

The order of the day relating to Second Reading remains on the Order Paper with a note that the bill is to be reported on by the Standing Orders Committee. The Committee must decide whether the Standing Orders should or should not be dispensed with and whether in their opinion the parties should be permitted to proceed with the bill, or any portion of it, and upon what terms and conditions. If they report to the House that the Standing Orders should be dispensed with, the Second Reading follows in the normal way. They do not have to explain the grounds for their decision. If they report that Standing Orders should be dispensed with, the House may agree, thereby giving the parties leave to proceed. If they decide that Standing Orders cannot be dispensed with, the promoters will generally acquiesce in their decision. Sometimes the House takes exception to the Committee's verdict and refers the decision back to them for further consideration.

If the Committee reports that the Standing Orders ought not to be dispensed with, the order of the day for the Second Reading of the bill is read and discharged, after which the bill is usually withdrawn. When a bill has been rejected, or lost through disagreement, it cannot be reintroduced in the same Session. After being read a second time a Hybrid Bill is committed to a Select Committee nominated partly by the House and partly by the Committee of Selection or to a Joint Committee. The Channel Tunnel Bill 1987/88 and the Cardiff Bay Barrage Bill 1992/93 were both recently committed to Select Committees for consideration before being debated in Standing Committees. The House has in the past treated some bills on which the Examiners have reported that no Standing Orders are applicable (Dublin Barracks Bill 1892 and Osborne Estate Bill 1902) and even bills which have not been referred to the Examiners (Barge Owners, etc Liability Bill 1892, Merchant Shipping (Tonnage Deduction for Propelling Powers) Bill 1907) as Hybrid Bills. If there are no petitions against the bill, the Select Committee stage is

[3] A bill may be sent to the Examiners at other stages apart from Second Reading.

dispensed with and the bill proceeds to a Committee of the Whole House or to a Standing Committee.

The proceedings in a Select Committee on a Hybrid Bill are conducted in much the same way as an Opposed Bill Committee or a Select Committee on a Private Bill. Petitioners who have the relevant 'locus standi' are entitled to be heard. When the petitioners' cases have been heard, the Committee goes through the clauses of the bill and reports it with or without amendments. Amendments may be made in Committee which, if the bill were a Private Bill, would require a petition for additional provisions. In this case, when the bill is reported further reference must be made to the Examiners. A Hybrid Bill reported from a Select Committee or a Joint Committee is normally recommitted to a Standing Committee or sometimes to a Committee of the Whole House and thereafter proceedings are the same as other Public Bills. The bill will undergo a similar procedure in the House of Lords. Hybrid Bills can be suspended from Session to Session.

PERSONAL BILLS

Personal bills are those which deal with the 'estate, property, status or style' of a particular individual (SO 3 (HL) [private business]). Such bills, which for the most part are designed to authorise a particular marriage, all originate in the House of Lords. Since the passsage of the Marriage (Prohibited Degrees of Relationship) Act 1986, which removed the prohibition on certain marriages, they have become extremely rare. There have been two since 1987. The promoters of the bill must deposit a petition in the Office of the Clerk of the Parliaments, along with a copy of the bill itself. The Chairman of Committees must then decide whether or not the bill falls within the definition of a personal bill in SO 151 (HL). If it does, it is then referred to the Personal Bills Committee consisting of seven peers, including the Chairman of Committees and two Lords of Appeal in Ordinary. Under SO 166 (HL) [private business] all parties affected by the bill must agree to its contents – as a result, there is no such thing as an opposed personal bill. If the Personal Bills Committee approves the bill, it has its First Reading in the House of Lords. If the Committee does not approve it, it can proceed no further. After First Reading, a personal bill which is a marriage enabling bill (in the last 20 years, all personal bills have fallen into this category)[4] is given a formal Second Reading without debate and is then sent to a Select Committee comprising the Chairman of Committees, a bishop and two other peers. The promoters of the bill give evidence in private.

THE TRANSPORT AND WORKS ACT 1992

In recent years the number of Private Bills being introduced in each Session has grown, as has the time devoted to their debate. The increasing amount of parliamentary time taken up by Private Bills forced Parliament to re-evaluate their effectiveness. A Joint Committee on Private Bill Procedure was established in 1987, reporting in 1988 and concluding that most Private Bills could be replaced by Ministerial Orders. In June 1990 the Government issued a consultation paper setting out a possible replacement for Private Bill procedure; this was largely embodied in the Transport and Works Act 1992. Part One of the Act provides for a system of Ministerial Orders to authorise, 'the construction or operation of a transport system of any of the following kinds, so far as it

[4] Erskine May (22nd Edition) page 942

is in England and Wales - (a) railway; (b) a tramway; (c) trolley vehicle system; (d) system using a mode of guided transport'.

A Ministerial Order provides a successful applicant with the same authority as would previously have been provided by a Private Bill and in addition confers powers of compulsory acquisition as well as planning permission. Under the Transport and Works Act, all new railway, light railway and tram proposals can be authorised by Ministerial Order. Such an Order includes powers to repeal or amend provisions of earlier railway enactments and confers powers to dispense with statutory restrictions in former private legislation.

Under Part I of the Act, any public or private sector promoter in England and Wales applies to the Secretary of State for an Order to authorise a railway, light rail, rapid transit, guided passenger transport system or inland waterway system. The draft order contains the same particulars as those which used to be contained in a Private Bill. These can be submitted at any time unlike Private Bills which can only be deposited at one time in the Parliamentary year. Under Clause 8, the Secretary of State may prescribe 'model' clauses to be included in applications – they are not mandatory. Applicants will also have to supply an Environmental Statement unless they have obtained a waiver from the Secretary of State.

Immediately before a formal application, a promoter must publish his intention to apply for an Order in the local press and in the London Gazette. Copies of the notice are then served on those directly affected by the proposals (anyone whose land would be compulsorily purchased) and displayed at the site of the proposed works. Any objections are made within 42 days of the date of the application for an order. Copies of documents supporting the application are made available for public inspection during this period and are deposited with the relevant local authorities.

If there are no objections at the end of the 42 day period the Order can be made. If there are outstanding objections they will be considered in one of three ways: by written representations; a hearing or a public inquiry. Eligible objectors are set out in Clause 11 (4). On the basis of the evidence the Secretary of State will decide whether or not to make an Order to be approved by both Houses of Parliament.

Where schemes are of 'national significance' (dealt with by Section 9 of the Act itself), Parliament will have a role earlier on in the proceedings. The policy and principle of a scheme will be debated in advance of a public enquiry. If Parliament does not like the scheme in principle then neither promoters nor objectors will be put to the expense of a public enquiry.

The Act requires an interval of at least 56 days between the publication of the proposed scheme in the London Gazette and any parliamentary debate. Just as with other applications, responsibility for the final approval of schemes of national significance lies with the Secretary of State, who is not obliged to make an order, the principle of which Parliament has endorsed. If both Houses of Parliament approve the resolution endorsing a scheme of national significance, the application will then continue through the rest of the procedures in much the same way as any other application (probably by means of a public inquiry).

FURTHER READING

Blackstone's Guide to the Transport & Works Act, 1992, Joe Durkin, Peter Lane and Monica Peto (Blackstones, 1992)
Promoting New Transport Projects: Role of the Transport and Works Act 1992 (Chartered Institute of Transport in the UK, 1998)

CHAPTER THIRTEEN – MONEY, MONEY, MONEY – THE BUDGET AND THE ESTIMATES

When people think of the Budget, they invariably think of Red Boxes, the Chancellor's Budget tipple, purdah, income tax and cigarettes. Along with the Queen's Speech, the Budget is one of the great annual parliamentary occasions, and the attendant media circus provides much needed employment for an army of cash-strapped economists and newspaper columnists. Television studios burst at the seams with worthy commentators, city pundits and experts on everything from ISAs to OEICs. Increasingly bizarre computer graphics are designed to assist a bewildered public through the maze of personal allowances, tax thresholds, borrowing requirements and debt repayments. However, the Budget is only one of a number of financial matters dealt with throughout the year by the House of Commons. As well as agreeing to the Chancellor's Budget measures, the means by which the Government raises the money it needs, the House of Commons must also give its consent to the Estimates, the details of how that money is to be allocated amongst the various Government Departments.

THE GOLDEN RULES OF FINANCIAL MATTERS

There are two types of financial 'charges', 'charges upon the public revenue' and 'charges upon the people'. 'A charge upon the public revenue' or 'upon public funds' is an item of national expenditure whilst a 'charges upon the people' are taxes, customs, duties, etc.

There are four rules which govern financial proceedings in the House of Commons:

1. Charges on the people (taxes) and charges on the public revenue (expenditure) must be 'brought in' on the appropriate resolutions - Ways and Means and Supply and Money Resolutions respectively
2. Charges on the people and charges on the public revenue must be authorised by legislation (the Finance Bill and the Consolidated Fund Bill)
3. Only the Crown can demand taxes or expenditure. Standing Order 46 states: 'This House will receive no petition for any sum relating to public service or proceed upon any motion for a grant or charge upon the public revenue, whether payable out of the Consolidated Fund or the National Loans Fund or out of money to be provided by Parliament, or for releasing or compounding any sum of money owing to the Crown, unless recommended from the Crown.'
4. No more than one stage of a Bill founded upon resolutions can be taken on the same day (Consolidated Fund Bills have been exempted).

What do these rules mean in practice? Taking the third rule first; this does not mean that the Queen has a quiet chat with the Chancellor the night before the Budget in order to effect an increase in the Civil List, but simply that 'financial initiative' belongs to the Crown; i.e. the Queen's Ministers, the Government. Only the Government can initiate measures that require public spending or taxation. Only the Government can introduce the necessary Ways and Means resolutions on which the Budget or the Finance Bill is based, which gives legislative effect to its measures. A group of disgruntled Backbenchers could not, for example, decide to introduce their own alternative Budget by means of a Private Member's Bill. SO 48 clearly states that public spending is only acceptable where, 'recommended from the Crown'. Under SO 50, a bill which, whilst it does not have to be brought in on a Ways and Means Resolution, still has as its main purpose, expenditure, may only be introduced by a Government Minister. These rules prevent any Backbencher from introducing a Private Member's Bill whose primary purpose entails public expenditure. In some cases, where such expenditure is secondary to the main subject of the Private Member's Bill, the Government will agree to table the necessary Money Resolution, allowing it to proceed further.

The House of Commons provides the 'Ways and Means' by which the Government raises money, through its agreement to the Budget and authorises its 'Supply' (expenditure) by its consent to the Estimates, which are themselves given effect by legislation. Departmental spending is also set out in the Financial Statement and Budget Report and the various Departmental Reports, which are usually published in February/March each year. The National Audit Office (NAO), under the Comptroller and Auditor General, is responsible for auditing the accounts of the Government Departments and the House of Commons Public Accounts Committee is responsible for scrutinising the reports of the NAO.

The Comptroller and Auditor General's full title is 'Comptroller and Auditor General of the receipt and issue of Her Majesty's Exchequer and Auditor General of Public Accounts'. He has a staff of around 900 in the National Audit Office (NAO). He is responsible to Parliament, being appointed by the Crown after approval by the House of Commons (the motion is made by the Prime Minister with the agreement of the Chairman of the Public Accounts Committee). The Comptroller and Auditor General (CAG) works closely with the House of Commons Committee of Public Accounts. NAO reports are analysed and reported on by the Public Accounts Committee – a Select Committee of the House of Commons. All government departments and many other public sector bodies have their accounts certified by the Comptroller and Auditor General. He can also undertake value-for-money studies, similar to those conducted by the Audit Commission.

The Public Accounts Commission - not to be confused with the Public Accounts Committee - was established by the National Audit Act 1983 and comprises the Chairman of the Committee of Public Accounts, the Leader of the House of Commons and seven other Members of the House of Commons, who may not be Ministers. The Commission analyses the estimates of expenses of the National Audit Office and appoints the NAO's auditors. In a way, it is the watchdog's watchdog. The Public Accounts Commission should not be confused with the Public Accounts Committee, which is a House of Commons Select Committee. It makes occasional reports to Parliament, the last being its Ninth Report (6 July 1998).

The terms 'Ways and Means' and 'supply' are ancient ones. In the past, the House sat as a 'Committee of Ways and Means' when considering taxation and as a 'Committee of Supply' when considering expenditure. The terms are still used today and measures to impose taxes can only be pursued if the appropriate 'Ways and Means Resolution' has been passed by the House and bills which will entail new spending are dependent on the proper 'Money Resolution' being agreed to. SO 49 requires that any 'charge on the public revenue ... shall be authorised by a resolution of the House'. Both Ways and Means Resolutions and Money Resolutions can only be intitiated by a Government Minister.

Erskine May summarises the relationship between the Sovereign and Parliament, thus:

'The Crown demands money, the Commons grant it, and the Lords assent to the grant'.

Each financial year is treated as an entirely separate period and money voted for one year cannot be held over for use in a subsequent year. However, the financial year usually overlaps two parliamentary sessions.

You may also come across the terms, 'Consolidated Fund' and 'National Loans Fund'. Just as an individual has a bank account, so does the Government – and these are its two bank accounts. To refer again to SO 49, the Order states that, 'Any charge upon the public revenue whether payable out of the Consolidated Fund or the National Loans Fund or out of money to be provided by Parliament ... shall be authorised by a resolution of the House'. Taxes are paid into the Consolidated Fund. Payments from this account are made to the National Loans Fund to service the national debt.

ESTIMATES

Details of Government expenditure are presented to Parliament in:

- the Financial Statement and Budget Report (how the money will be raised)
- the Departmental Reports (how the money will be spent by the relevant Departments)
- the Supply Estimates (how the money is to be allocated amongst the Departments)

Supply Procedure

All Governments need to raise money; however, raising and spending money has to be sanctioned by Parliament and this is done by the Government presenting the 'Estimates' to the House of Commons at various times in the parliamentary calendar. Expenditure is known as 'supply' and 'supply' can only be incurred with parliamentary approval. The 'Estimates' set out in detail the 'Supply' that the Government will need during the financial year. An announcement that 'Estimates will be laid before the House of Commons' is contained in the Queen's Speech at the State Opening of Parliament. Estimates are presented 'by command' of Her Majesty' only to the House of Commons. There are other areas of public expenditure which are not covered by Supply Estimates; for example, payments to local authorities and the EU. Where a sum has been appropriated (allocated) in the Estimates to a particular service it cannot be spent on another and the sum appropriated is the maximum that can be spent. It can only be used in the financial year in which it was appropriated, so any money not spent by a Department in one financial year *cannot* be carried over to the next, but has to be paid into the Consolidated Fund.
There are four stages:

1.) The Government presents Supply Estimates which request money and explain how it is to be spent.

2.) The House of Commons votes on the Estimates (Estimates are presented only to the House of Commons).

3.) Parliament passes an Act authorising the Bank of England to make available the relevant amount of money.

4.) An audit takes place after the money has been spent.

Although Estimates cover one financial year, they are not voted at the beginning of the year.

Main Estimates (Ordinary Annual Estimates)

The Main Estimates are presented to the House in the Spring, in one volume, accompanied by a memorandum on all the Estimates by the Chief Secretary to the Treasury. They must be approved by 5 August.

Estimates are divided into 20 'classes', which broadly relate to the different Government departments. These are then sub-divided into 'votes' (theoretically, the House could make a decision on each of these separately) which are further sub-divided into 'subheads'. Each vote is divided into four parts:

- Part I of the vote specifies the services for which the estimate is presented and the net[1] amount of the grant demanded from Parliament – this is known as the 'ambit' (spending must fall within the ambit of the vote) - the total sum contained in part one of each Estimate is reproduced in the annual Appropriation Act
- Part II divides the vote into separate subheads - expenditure on subheads can be redistributed; for example, Class III, Vote I might be the vote to maintain the Office of Science and Technology and once statutory authority has been given by the Appropriation Act this total *cannot* be used for any other Department; however, the total under Vote I could be redistributed within different subheads – this is known as 'virement'
- Part III details receipts which are to be paid into the Consolidated Fund
- Part IV analyses the total in Part I of the vote by type of expenditure – distinguishing, for example, between current and capital expenditure

Revised Estimates for the current year may also be presented (these do not request more money but may change the ambit of previous votes).

In addition to the ordinary Main Estimates, there are also separate Defence Estimates, known as 'Votes A'. They must be agreed to by 18 March. The Queen may not maintain a Standing Army without the authorisation of Parliament, so these votes specify the maximum number of personnel which can be maintained in each of the Armed Forces.

---

[1] This is the difference between the total expenditure as set out in the subheads in Part II and any receipts which may be received; e.g., through payments of licences, fees, etc.

Supplementary Estimates

Supplementary Estimates are usually presented to the House at least three times a year in the spring, summer and winter. They are designed to cover both additional costs which have arisen in relation to existing services and new costs which have arisen since the Main Estimates were agreed. The summer Supplementary Estimates must be approved by 5 August. The Winter Supplementary Estimates are published in November and must be passed by 6 February. The Spring Supplementary Estimates are published in February and must be approved by 18 March.

Votes on Account

Votes on Account are used to tide the Government over in the period between the end of one financial year and the beginning of the next.

Excess Votes

These are required when a Department has spent more on an existing service than was granted in that financial year. They are presented about 11 months after the end of the financial year to which they relate. Excess Votes are usually voted on in March. They are subject to special parliamentary scrutiny by the Public Accounts Committee. The PAC bases its report to the House on the findings of the Comptroller and Auditor General.

Supply Timetable

Authorisation of Supply expenditure for one year lasts over a two and a half year period and during the course of a Session, Main Estimates, Supplementary Estimates, Votes on Account and Excess Votes all relating to three different financial years come before the House.

There are usually three occasions during a parliamentary Session when Estimates are voted upon (these are set out in Standing Order 53).

No later than 6 February and usually before Christmas	**No later than 18 March**	**No later than 5 August**
Votes on Account for the coming financial year Winter Supplementary Estimates for the current year *A Consolidated Fund Bill follows the Estimates.*	Votes A (defence votes) Spring Supplementary Estimates for the current year Excess Votes for the previous year (if the PAC has reported) *A Consolidated Fund Bill follows the Estimates*	Any outstanding Estimates (Main Estimates and Summer Supplementary Estimates) *A Consolidated Fund (Appropriation) Bill follows the Estimates and the Appropriation Act is passed into law just before the summer adjournment.*

Consideration of Estimates

Since 1982, three Estimates Days (one may be divided into two half days) have been set aside as 'Select Committee Days'; i.e. the Estimates discussed on these days are effectively chosen by a Committee consisting of Select Committee Chairmen (the Liaison Committee). The Liaison Committee must assess competing claims for debate from the various Select Committees.

Under SO 54 three days (not Fridays) before 5 August are set aside each Session 'for the consideration of Estimates set down under the provisions of paragraph (2) of Standing Order No 145' and one of these days may be taken as two half day debates. Under SO 145 it is the Liaison Committee which decides the Estimates to be debated. It may decide that all three days should be devoted to the Main Estimates, or that one at least should be devoted to the Supplementary Estimates. These 'Estimates days' are usually the days on which the other Estimates – those which are not being debated – are voted, but there is no rule which says that they must be taken on the same day. The votes on remaining Estimates are taken at 10.00pm. In fact the debate on these days centres on particular Select Committee reports, chosen by the Liaison Committee as being the most appropriate for debate, and not really on the Estimates at all. The Select Committee reports chosen usually relate to a particular Class and Vote in the Estimates, but the debate itself is centred on reports from one or more Select Committees.

For example, the first allotted Estimates Day of the 1998/99 Session was on 10 December 1998 (in fact this was two half day debates) and the Estimates under consideration were the Votes on Account 1999-2000, Class IV, Vote I and Class IV, Vote 2 (these related to the Third Report on prison sentences, from the House of Commons Home Affairs Select Committee (1997/98) (HC 486) and the Government's response (Cm 4174); Class 1, Vote 1, Class 1, Vote 3 and Class XII (relating to the Seventh Report from the House of Commons Education and Employment Select Committee (1997/98) on 'Pathways into Work for Lone Parents (HC 646) and the Government's response (HC 1122) and the Eighth Report from the House of Commons Education and Empoyment Select Committee (1997/98) on New Deal Pathfinders (HC 1059) and the Government's response (HC 1123) and the Department for Education and Employment's Departmental Report 'The Government's Expenditure Plans 1998-99 (Cm 3910). The remaining Estimates, on which votes were taken at 10.00pm were the 1998/99 Navy Vote A, the Supplementary Estimates for 1998/99 and the remaining Votes on Account 1999-2000.

The Following motion, relating to the first of the Estimates debates (until 7.00pm) appeared in the order paper for 10 December 1998:

Prison Sentences

[Relevant documents: Third Report from the Home Affairs Committee of Session 1997-98, on Alternatives to Prison Sentences, HC486, and the Government's response thereto, Cm 4174; and the Home Office Departmental Annual Report 1998, Cm 3908.]

Motion made, and Question proposed,

That a sum, not exceeding £2,299,414,000 be granted to Her Majesty out of the Consolidated Fund, on account, for or towards defraying the charge for the year ending

> on 31st March 2000 for expenditure by the Home Office on police; the Forensic Science Service; registration of forensic practitioners; emergency planning; fire services; the Fire Service College; criminal policy and programmes including offender programmes; the prevention of drug abuse; crime reduction and prevention; provision of services relating to the Crime and Disorder Act; criminal justice service research; criminal injuries compensation; organised and international crime; control of immigration and nationality; issue of passports; community and constitutional services; firearms compensation and related matters; and on administration (excluding the provision for prisons administration carried on Class IV, Vote 2).--*[Mr. Boateng.]*

The debate on prisons continued until 7.00pm and then, according to the provisions of SO 54 (3) and (4), the next debate, on the New Deal, began and the decision on the Votes relating to prisons (Votes on Account 1999-2000, Class IV, Vote I and Class IV, Vote 2) was deferred until 10.00pm.

At 10.00pm the following motion was put:

It being Ten o'clock, Mr. Deputy Speaker *proceeded to put forthwith the deferred Questions which he was directed by paragraphs (4) and (5) of Standing Order No. 54 (Consideration of estimates) to put at that hour.*

Once the House had reached a decision (there was no division) on the Votes on Account relating to prisons and the New Deal, votes were taken on the remaining Estimates.

Mr. Deputy Speaker *proceeded to put forthwith the Questions which he was directed to put by Standing Order No. 55 (Questions on voting of estimates, etc.).*

The Standing Order also stipulates that when a whole day is given over to the consideration of the Estimates, they must be considered before any other business and that other business may only be taken before 10.00pm if the consideration of Estimates has been concluded. However, when Estimates are taken on half days and private business or an SO 20 (emergency) debate is scheduled to take place at 7.00pm, debate on the Estimates is held over until after private business or the SO 20 debate has finished and may then be debated for up to three hours, and may continue after 10.00pm if necessary. The only type of amendment to a motion to accept an Estimate is one which attempts to reduce the amount voted. In recent years, no Backbench amendment to reduce an estimate has been accepted by the Speaker. Under SO 55, no amendments may be tabled to the remaining estimates which are voted on at 10.00pm.

Consolidated Fund Bills

The 'Consolidated Fund' is the Government's general bank account at the Bank of England. Taxes are paid into the Consolidated Fund by virtue of Section 10 of the Exchequer and Audit Departments Act, 1866. The Government can only issue money out of the Fund if it has statutory authority to do so. Once the relevant Estimates have been agreed they are followed by 'Consolidated Fund Bills'. Proceedings on these are purely formal (see SO 56) – there is no debate at Second Reading and the question on the Second Reading is taken forthwith – the bill then proceeds immediately to Third Reading, again this is put forthwith (these stages can be taken after the Moment of Interruption).

Consolidated Fund and Consolidated Fund (Appropriation) Bills are bills of Aids and Supplies and are always certified by the Speaker as Money Bills. Proceedings in the House of Lords are therefore purely formal. If Parliament were to be dissolved or prorogued before the necessary Appropriation Act had been passed, technically all the money which the Commons had voted it in the Estimates would be null and void. They would need to be voted again the in the next Session for them to be valid.

The final Consolidated Fund Bill of the Session is the Consolidated Fund (Appropriation) Bill which, once enacted, is called the Appropriation Act. The Appropriation Act, 'appropriates' (allocates) money to the particular services to which the individual Votes in the Estimates relate and which has been authorised both by the Act itself and by the two Consolidated Fund Acts which preceded it. An example is set out below:

Appropriation Act 1998 - Chapter 28

SCHEDULE (B) - Part 13

CLASS XI Schedule of Sums granted, and of the sums which may be applied as appropriations in aid in addition thereto, to defray the charges of the several Services herein particularly mentioned, which will come in course of payment during the year ending on 31st March 1999, viz -

	Sums not exceeding	
	Supply Grants	Appropriations in Aid
	£	£
1. For expenditure by the Department of Health on hospital, community health, family health and related services. (Including a supplementary sum of £6,600,000)	31,865,014,000	9,296,624,000

In the autumn, the Government's accounts – the Appropriation Accounts – are audited by the Comptroller and Auditor General (in reality the staff of the National Audit Office) and are presented to the House of Commons by the end of January the following year. These accounts are scrutinised by the Committee for Public Accounts.

If Parliament were to reject the Estimates as a whole or defeat the Second or Third Reading of a Consolidated Fund Bill the Government would effectively have been denied funds. If confidence in a Government had sunk this low, it would be unlikely to win a motion of no confidence and a dissolution would be imminent.

Theoretically, the House of Commons should vote for expenditure before it is incurred; however, there are three exceptions: Votes of Credit, exceptional grants and expenditure from the Contingencies Fund. The Government applies for Votes of Credit when faced with the need for immediate and unforseen expenditure, the limits of which cannot accurately be defined; exceptional grants can be made for 'expenditure of an unusal character'; and finally, the Treasury can permit spending from the Contingencies Fund to meet costs likely to arise before the Estimates are voted by the House. Spending from the Contingencies Fund is limited by law to 2% of the previous year's total authorised supply expenditure and any money drawn out of the Fund must be repaid.

In the 1997/98 Session of Parliament, the House of Commons Procedure Select Committee undertook an enquiry into the way in which the House currently scrutinises the Estimates (HC 848 – Financial Procedure). The Committee considered whether the Estimates should be referred automatically to the relevant Departmental Select Committees and whether there should be a new mechanism which would allow Members greater scope for amending the individual subheads set out in the Estimates. At the time of writing, a report had not been published.

MONEY RESOLUTIONS

Most Government spending is covered by the Estimates, but those Estimates cannot and do not cover 'new and distinct' expenditure; for example, spending which arises from new legislation. If new spending is needed, so is a Money Resolution. Just as taxation requires a Ways and Means Resolution, spending requires a Money Resolution. Where a Government bill entails the spending of public money, that bill will also require a Money Resolution in order to be brought into effect. For example, if a Bill establishes an advisory panel whose members are to be paid, a Money Resolution will be required to permit such payments to be made from public funds. Where the words to be paid for 'out of money to be provided by Parliament' are used in a Government Bill, a Money Resolution will be necessary.

Money resolutions are usually taken forthwith after the Second Reading of the Bill to which they relate, but they can be debated for up to 45 minutes if taken at any other time. Although Money Resolutions always appear in the name of the Financial Secretary to the Treasury, the relevant departmental minister is the person with actual responsibility for taking the Resolution through the House. A Money Resolution must be passed by the House before a Standing Committee considering a bill can consider any clauses which entail expenditure (such clauses are marked in italics)

The Queen's recommendation is necessary where any money is to be 'provided by Parliament' (as set out in SO 48) as all financial initiative resides with the Crown (in fact, the Government). As a result, the only type of amendment which could be moved to a Money Resolution would be one designed to reduce rather than increase expenditure. The following is an example of a Money Resolution (HC Col: 277, 10 March 1998).

Road Traffic Reduction (United Kingdom Targets) Bill [Money]

Queen's recommendation having been signified--
Motion made, and Question proposed,

That, for the purposes of any Act resulting from the Road Traffic Reduction (United Kingdom Targets) Bill, it is expedient to authorise the payment out of money provided by Parliament of any expenses of the Secretary of State which are attributable to the Act.--*[Mr. Jamieson.]*

WAYS AND MEANS RESOLUTIONS

Although a Ways and Means Resolution is not recommended by the Crown as is the practice with a Money Resolution, it can only be moved by a Government Minister. As Erskine May states, 'In the case of Ways and Means resolutions for imposing taxes, the exercise of the royal initiative, otherwise unexpressed, is taken to be implied through the principle that no more money should be raised by taxation than is deemed necessary by the Crown to cover the Supply already voted by, or at any rate requested from, the House of Commons'.[2]

The following must be initiated by ways and means resolutions:

- Taxation, including increases in rates of taxation or the extension in scope of taxation - new taxes or duties may not come into force immediately under the Provisional Collection of Taxes Act 1968 and new duties on separate items may not be included in the same Ways and Means Resolution

- The repeal or reduction of existing exemptions from tax; for example, the abolition of zero-rated VAT on childrens' clothes would require a Ways and Means Resolution

- The granting of borrowing powers to the Government in emergency situations

- Provision for payment into the Consolidated Fund or National Loans Fund of receipts not arising from taxation (for example, fees or licences under a particular Act)

The following charges - similar to charges upon the people, do not require Ways and Means Resolutions:

- Local receipts (taxes payable to local funds)

- The alleviation of taxation

- Levies on an industry for its own uses (examples include charges on employers to finance activities designed to benefit their particular industry)

- Charges for services provided by Government departments

- Provisions authorised by existing law

- Charges which will not come into effect unless further legislation is passed

Under SO 51, a Ways and Means Resolution may be put before the House without any prior notice (the Government usually does give prior indication of such a Resolution). Apart from the Budget resolutions, each Ways and Means Resolution is considered separately. Under SO 51(3), when a series of Ways and Means Resolutions is to be

---

[2] Erskine May (22nd Edition) page 738

taken, the votes on them are usually taken forthwith, except for the first. Bills brought in on Ways and Means Resolutions are exempt from the Moment of Interruption.

Local Authority Funding

Central Government financial support for local authorities is made by way of Revenue Support Grant as set out in the Local Government Finance Act 1988, the Abolition of Domestic Rates etc. (Scotland) Act 1987 and the Local Government Finance Act 1992.

THE BUDGET AND THE FINANCE BILL

The Chancellor begins his Budget Speech at approximately 3.30pm. By convention the Budget is on a Tuesday (although this is not always adhered to, for example, in 1997) and now takes place in March. Until 1993, the Budget dealt entirely with taxation, leaving public expenditure to be set out in what was known as the Autumn Statement. 1993 saw the first 'unified Budget', bringing together both revenue raising and departmental spending. From 1993 until Labour's victory in the 1997 General Election, the unified Budget took place in November. Labour decided after the Election to revert to holding the Budget in the spring. The present Chancellor, Gordon Brown's first Budget was in July 1997, but the next Budget was not until March 1998.

The Chancellor also decided to introduce a 'Green Budget', in the autumn preceding the Budget Statement. The Green Budget is an opportunity for the Chancellor to indicate some of the issues being considered for inclusion in next spring's Budget Statement and is really a consultation exercise, which many organisations have taken advantage of. In the first Green Budget in November 1997, the Chancellor indicated his intention to reform Corporation Taxes. As a result of the representations received, it was possible to fine-tune the proposals before, rather than after, implementation.

There is nothing to stop a Chancellor making more than one Budget Statement in a year – during his time in No. 11, Dennis Healey's predilection for mini-Budgets endeared him to the nation.

The Budget debate itself is chaired not by the Speaker, but by the Chairman of Ways and Means – this dates from the time when taxation was dealt with by the Committee of Ways and Means, of which the Deputy Speaker was Chairman.

On Budget day, after the Chancellor has finished speaking, the 'Red Book', whose proper title is the 'Financial Statement and Budget Report' is made available to MPs and members of the Public. In addition to the Red Book, there are often a number of other accompanying documents and an enormous quantity of departmental press releases, setting out the Chancellor's Budget measures in detail. Details of the next three year's public expenditure are contained in the Red Book, but more information is contained in the individual Departmental Reports, published in the Spring each year. In 1991, these replaced the old Public Expenditure White Paper, which used to be published at the time of the Autumn Statement.

After the Chancellor's speech, the Leader of the Opposition replies to the Budget – arguably one of the most difficult parliamentary tasks of the year. He or she has to respond immediately to the Chancellor's speech and it is not a challenge for the faint-hearted. An army of advisers works frantically outside the Chamber to provide their Leader with enough ammunition to make a creditable performance and teams of eager Backbenchers relay messages to and from the Front Bench. The task is made even more impossible when the Chancellor decides to implement policies which some members of the Opposition are actually on record as supporting. At least the Leader of the Liberal Democrats has a little longer in which to consider his or her response. Unfortunately, the slot after the Leader of the Opposition's speech, usually coincides with an unseemly rush for tea and toast on the part of the Backbenches and the hapless Leader can find him or herself addressing a Chamber which is less than overflowing.

The Budget debate actually lasts over four or five days. At the end of this period, the Commons is asked to vote on a number of Ways and Means resolutions, which form the basis of the taxation elements in the Finance Bill. Once they have been agreed to, the Finance Bill, which incorporates the Budget, is presented to the House.

The Finance Act gives final authority to the taxation proposals contained in the Budget but many of the proposals take effect within hours of the Chancellor's Statement; for example, duties on petrol and cigarettes. This is permitted by the 'Provisional Collection of Taxes Act', 1968, as amended by Section 1(5) of the Finance Act, 1972. The Provisional Collection of Taxes Act does not apply to new taxes. The Provisional Collection of Taxes Act 1913 was introduced as a result of the People's Budget of 1909. The statement was made in March but the Finance Bill was not passed by the House of Commons until November and was rejected by the House of Lords. The collection of taxes in that year was therefore not strictly legal. In 1912 a Conservative Back Bencher, Gibson Bowles, refused to pay some taxes on the grounds that the Finance Bill had not received Royal Assent. The Provisional Collection of Taxes Act 1913 was passed to allow the collection of taxes until 5 May of those taxes continued or amended in the Budget. Under section 5 of the Provisional Collection of Taxes Act, several different Budget resolutions may have immediate effect if a motion (set out below) is moved as soon as the Chancellor has delivered his Budget speech (HC Col: 191, 9 March 1999).

Provisional Collection of Taxes

Motion made, and Question,

That, pursuant to section 5 of the Provisional Collection of Taxes Act 1968, provisional statutory effect shall be given to the following motions:--

(a) Sparkling cider (rate of duty) (motion No. 2);

(b) Hydrocarbon oil duties (rates and rebates) (motion No. 3);

(c) Tobacco products duty (rates) (motion No. 5);

(d) Vehicle excise duty (increase in general rate) (motion No. 7);

(e) Vehicle excise duty (rates for goods vehicles etc.) (motion No. 9).--[*Mr. Gordon Brown.*]

put forthwith, pursuant to Standing Order No. 51 (Ways and Means Motions), and agreed to.

Any immediate changes announced in the Budget must be confirmed by the House agreeing within ten sitting days to the Ways and Means Resolutions on which they are based, the Second Reading of the Finance Bill being held within 30 sitting days after the day on which the Resolutions were agreed to and the passage into law of the Finance Bill within a period of four months after the Resolutions were passed (or the day on which they are to take effect if this is different).

Amendment of the Law

As soon as the Chancellor sits down a motion is moved which, if approved, allows debate on the Budget as a whole. This is known as the 'Amendment of the Law'. Although it is moved on the first day of the Budget, it is not usually voted on until the last day of the Budget debate. Under SO 50(3), when a series of Ways and Means Resolutions are put before the House, debate can only take place on the first Resolution and all the others must be taken forthwith. By moving a general motion to amend the fiscal law, debate can take place on the Budget as a whole rather than on just one of the Ways and Means Resolutions.

The Amendment of the Law motion provides for the 'general amendment of the fiscal law'. When a bill, such as the Finance Bill, is brought in on Ways and Means Resolutions, all its provisions, not just those which impose taxation, must be covered by those resolutions. The Amendment of the Law motion ensures that all the provisions of the Finance Bill not covered by specific Ways and Means Resolutions are covered. Without an Amendment of the Law motion, debate on the Finance Bill and the scope for amendments would be extremely limited.

Sometimes the 'Amendment of the Law' resolution is framed in such a way as to exclude or restrict the amendment of a particular tax. For example, the Amendment of the Law motion proposed at the beginning of the 1993 Budget debate, stated that, 'it is expedient to amend the law with respect to the National Debt and the public revenue and to make further provision in connection with finance; but this Resolution does not extend to the making of any amendment with respect to value added tax so as to provide - (a) for zero-rating or exempting any supply, acquisition or importation'.

Ways and Means resolutions are usually moved without notice and questions on all but the first in a series are put forthwith. As a result, amendments to such motions are rare. However, as Erskine May states: 'if an amendment is offered, it is compared with the terms of the resolution proposed from the Chair, and is ruled out of order if it in any way increases the amount or extends the area of incidence of the charge defined in those terms'.[3]

The Ways and Means Resolutions are often divided upon after the close of the Budget Debate; for example, on 22 March 1993 there were divisions on the Amendment of the Law, VAT on fuel and power and finally on Petroleum Revenue Tax. In 1994, the then Labour Opposition tabled an amendment to the motion on the Amendment of the Law, to try and ensure debate and future votes on the second stage of the imposition of VAT on fuel.

[3] Erskine May (22nd Edition) page 784

The motion and amendment appeared on the Order Paper (1 December 1994) thus:

WAYS AND MEANS: Adjourned Debate on Question (29th November)

A Motion was made, and the Question being proposed, That it is expedient to amend the law with respect to the National Debt and the public revenue and to make further provision in connection with finance; but this Resolution does not extend to the making of any amendment with respect to value added tax so as to provide –

(a) for zero-rating or exempting any supply, acquisition or importation;
(b) for refunding any amount of tax;
(c) for varying any rate at which that tax is any time chargeable; or
(d) for relief other than relief applying to goods of whatever description or services of whatever description

Labour's amendment read:

Line 4, after 'tax', insert 'other than in respect of value added tax on fuel and power for domestic or charity use'.

The alternative amendment tabled by the Liberal Democrats read:

Line 9, at end add 'unless that amendment relates solely to the rate of VAT levied on domestic fuel.

The House voted by 319 to 311 in favour of the Labour amendment. This would have enabled the tabling of amendments on VAT on fuel during the passage of the Finance Bill. However, the Government accepted defeat and introduced alternative measures to make good the shortfall in revenue, resulting from VAT on fuel remaining at 8% rather than rising to 17.5%.

The following example of an Amendment of the Law motion is taken from the first day of the 1999 Budget (HC Col: 191)

Mr. Deputy Speaker: I now call the Chancellor of the Exchequer to move the motion entitled "Amendment of the law". It is on that motion that the debate will take place today and on succeeding days. The remaining motions will not be put until the end of the Budget debate next week, and they will then be decided without debate.

Budget Resolutions and Economic Situation

AMENDMENT OF THE LAW

Motion made, and Question proposed,

That it is expedient to amend the law with respect to the National Debt and the public revenue and to make further provision in connection with finance; but this Resolution does not extend to the making of any amendment with respect to value added tax so as to provide--

(a) for zero-rating or exempting a supply, acquisition or importation;

(b) for refunding an amount of tax;

(c) for varying any rate at which that tax is at any time chargeable; or

(d) for any relief other than a relief which--

(i) so far as it is applicable to goods, applies to goods of every description, and

(ii) so far as it is applicable to services, applies to services of every description.--[*Mr. Gordon Brown.*]

Theoretically, a Finance Bill should not impose a tax which is not to be demanded until after the end of the current financial year; however, the Government tabled a motion in 1993, passed on the last day of the Budget debate (7 December 1993) to allow, 'any Finance Bill of the present Session' to 'contain the following provisions taking effect in a future year' (a list of provisions followed).

PROCEDURE ON THE FINANCE BILL

The Finance Bill has a Second Reading in the normal way, but its Committee Stage is split between a Standing Committee and a Committee of the Whole House. The more controversial clauses are usually dealt with on the floor of the House and this is generally agreed through the 'usual channels'. The Committee of the Whole House usually precedes the Standing Committee. Membership of the Standing Committee is decided as usual by the Committee of Selection which meets on a Wednesday and there are usually about 35 to 40 members – rather larger than the average Standing Committee. Two days are usually spent on Report and Third Reading.

Amendments to the Finance Bill may not 'exceed the scope, increase the amount, or extend the incidence of, any charge upon the people, defined by the terms of the Ways and Means Resolutions, by which the provisions proposed to be amended are authorised' (Erskine May). If a Member wishes to move a new clause or amendment which exceeds the terms of the relevant Ways and Means Resolutions, further resolutions must be voted, with instructions to the Committee on the Bill before such new clauses or amendments can be considered.

Erskine May states that, 'The House of Commons has long found it necessary to place restrictions on the moving of amendments in order to keep intact the principle of the financial initiative of the Crown'. No amendment may be tabled to a bill in Committee which would increase a 'charge' beyond the limits set out in the relevant Money Resolution or impose a new charge not covered by the Money Resolution. However, if the charge concerned is less than the upper limit set out in the money resolution, an amendment could be tabled to increase it up to that limit.

Amendments which try to increase one tax by reducing another are not usually accepted; however, difficulties have arisen in the past when an amendment which increases a charge forms part of a group of amendments which, taken together, have the effect of reducing a charge. In these circumstances it is usual to consider the effect of each amendment singly, on the basis that the House or Committee might reject other amendments forming part of the group, thus negating the general effect of reducing the charge in question. However, if the amendments which reduce the charge are agreed to first, the other amendments can be taken, provided the group of amendments as a whole reduces the charge.

In the House of Lords, debate on the Finance Bill is usually confined to a brief Second Reading debate for the reasons set out below.

FINANCIAL MATTERS AND THE HOUSE OF LORDS

The House of Lords may not initiate or amend financial measures. The financial privilege of the House of Commons is based on a resolution of 1671, which states that, 'in all aids given to the King by the Commons, the rate or tax ought not to be altered by the Lords'. A further resolution of 3 July 1678 states that, 'all aids and supplies, and aids to his Majesty in Parliament, are the sole gift of the Commons; and all bills for the granting of any such aids and supplies ought to begin with the Commons; and that it is the undoubted and sole right of the Commons to direct, limit, and appoint in such Bills the ends, purposes, considerations, conditions, limitations, and qualifications of such grants, which ought not to be changed or altered by the House of Lords'.

The financial privilege of the House of Commons is jealously guarded. For example, on 4 April 1990, during the debate on the Lords' Amendments to the Education (Student Loans) Bill, the Speaker ruled that, 'Lords amendment No. 8 imposes a charge on the public revenue not authorised by a resolution of the House, under paragraph 3 of Standing Order No. 76 (now SO 78)' and that therefore, 'the Lords amendment is deemed to be disagreed with'. The amendment had attempted to ensure that Regulations brought in under the Bill allowed special conditions to be set for the repayment of loans taken out by students and graduates with disabilities (HC Col: 1300, 4 April 1990).

Where the House of Lords has passed an amendment to a bill, the Commons can disagree to the amendment on the grounds that it infringes Commons' privilege – the reasons for disagreeing to the amendment are usually that it 'interferes with the public revenue', alters taxation, involves a charge on public funds. The Lords may table further amendments in place of those amendments which the House of Commons has rejected on the grounds of privilege (see chapter seven for more information on Lords' Amendments). The Commons may agree to 'waive privilege' in certain circumstances and accept Lords amendments which technically violate Commons privilege. Under SO 78 (3), the Commons may reject a Lords' Amendment, if it imposes a charge which ought to have been brought in on a Resolution of the House under SO 49 (a Supply or Money Resolution). The Commons may also reject a Lords Amendment which requires a Ways and Means Resolution.

Whilst the House of Lords may not, as a general rule, initiate or amend financial measures, the Commons does not have exclusive rights over bills which: impose charges on the property and revenues of the Church or deal with the land and property revenues of the Crown. Under Standing Order 79, the House of Commons agrees not to 'insist on its ancient and undoubted privileges' in the case of bills which impose 'pecuniary penalties', 'fees' or 'forfeitures', where the aim is to 'secure the execution of the Act, or the punishment or prevention of offences', or to pay for 'services rendered' under the Act. If the House of Lords cannot initiate or amend bills which contain provisions to levy both 'charges on the people' and 'charges on the public revenue', how is it possible that many public bills begin their passage through Parliament in the House of Lords?

Under SO 80, public bills may start life in the House of Lords and be taken up in the House of Commons if they do not contain any provisions to levy charges (except for those which fall under the remit of Standing Order 79); or, where a bill does impose or alter a 'charge', a Government Minister informs the Clerk at the Table of his 'intention to take charge' of the bill. Where a bill clearly does involve raising or spending money, the House of Lords avoids infringing Commons' privilege by inserting a subsection to the last clause of the bill in question at Third Reading. This is known as a 'Privilege Amendment' and it states that: 'Nothing in this Act shall impose any charge on the people or on public funds, or vary the amount or incidence of, or otherwise alter, any such charge in any manner, or affect the assessment, levying, administration or application of any money raised by any such charge.' The Privilege Amendment is subsequently removed at Committee Stage in the House of Commons.

Bills of Aids and Supplies

Whilst the Commons will accept some encroachment on their financial privilege by the House of Lords where ordinary public bills are concerned, amendments to bills of aids and supplies are another matter entirely. An amendment by their Lordships to one of these is regarded as an 'intolerable breach of prvilege' under the terms of the Resolutions of 1671 and 1678 and is considered completely beyond the pale. A bill of aids and supplies is one whose primary but not sole purpose is to levy taxes authorising expenditure, e.g. Consolidated Fund Bills and Finance Bills. The House of Lords never amends such bills. The Finance Bill is always a bill of aids and supplies but is not always a Money Bill; however, the House of Lords does not attempt to amend it. Proceedings on bills of aids and supplies are in the case of the Finance Bill, limited to a Second Reading debate and in the case of Consolidated Fund Bills, purely formal.

Occasionally bills are introduced which have some of the characteristics of bills of aids and supplies but which have been amended by the Lords. In these cases the House of Commons usually disagrees to the Lords Amendments on the grounds of infringement of Commons privilege, but does not necessarily argue that the bill cannot be amended at all.

It is important to note that whilst their Lordships cannot amend bills of aids and supplies, they can reject them completely. The Commons, with its usual deviousness, used to add all manner of unrelated clauses to bills of aids and supplies in the knowledge that the Lords would either have to accept or reject the entire bill. As a retaliatory measure, in 1702, their Lordships eventually passed SO 50 (HL) which states that annexing extraneous clauses in this way is 'unparliamentary and tends to the destruction of constitutional government'. Quite right too.

Money Bills

The gradual practice of the House of Commons of embodying all taxation changes in a single bill, the Finance Bill, meant that the House of Lords could reject the entire bill and hence all the Government's revenue raising plans. The rejection by the House of Lords of the so-called 'People's Budget' (the Finance Bill of 1909) resulted in the passing of the 1911 Parliament Act. Section 1(2) of the Act defines a 'Money Bill' as one which (in the opinion of the Speaker) contains 'only' provisions which deal with all or any of the following: 'the imposition, repeal, remission, alteration or regulation of taxation; the imposition, for the payment of debt or other financial purposes, of charges on the Consolidated Fund or National Loans Fund or on money provided by Parliament, or the variation or repeal of any such charges; supply; the appropriation, receipt, custody, issue or audit of accounts of public money; the raising or guarantee of any loan or repayment thereof, or subordinate matters incidental to those subjects or any of them'.

Procedure on Money Bills

If a Money Bill is passed by the House of Commons, sent one month before the end of the session to the House of Lords, and is not passed by the Lords without amendment within one month after having been received, it is immediately presented for Royal Assent. When a Money Bill is sent to the House of Lords or presented for Royal Assent, it must be endorsed as such by a Speaker's certificate. The decision by the Speaker to certify a bill as a Money Bill cannot be questioned in any court. When deciding whether or not to certify a bill as a Money Bill, the Speaker must consult the two members of the Chairman's Panel appointed specifically for this purpose at the beginning of the Session by the Committee of Selection.

A Money Bill is not the same as a bill of aids and supplies. The former contains only the provisions set out above whereas the latter may contain other non-financial matters. A Finance Bill is not necessarily a Money Bill, as it may well contain provisions other than those set out in the above definition of a Money Bill. Roughly half the Finance Bills sent to the House of Lords since the passing of the Parliament Act have not been certified as Money Bills. They are all, however, bills of aids and supplies. This means that theoretically, the House of Lords could amend a Finance Bill, but in practice they do not. There is nothing to prevent the House of Commons accepting Lords Amendments to a Money Bill. However, it cannot accept some amendments, reject others and then claim that the bill should receive Royal Assent under the provisions set out in section 1 of the Parliament Act 1911.

CHAPTER FOURTEEN - PARLIAMENTARY PAPERS

THE 'VOTE BUNDLE'

The Vote Bundle (it is usually just referred to as 'the Vote') is the name given to those House of Commons papers printed daily and circulated along with the Votes and Proceedings of the House (the note of all decisions taken in the House on the previous day). The Vote Bundle includes the following papers, all of which are usually included within one document. Items relating to the current day's business are printed on white paper and those relating to future business on blue paper. Readers may have heard parliamentarians talk about 'the blues'; this does not refer either to a general sense of hopelessness and despair amongst Members, or to a type of music favoured on the Back Benches, but to that section of the Vote more properly called the Notice Paper.

- The Summary Agenda and Order of Business (white)
- Amendments to public bills to be debated on that day (white)
- Proceedings in Standing Committees, which sat the day before (white)
- The Votes and Proceedings (white)
- The Notice Paper *(includes oral questions tabled on the previous day for answer on future days, written questions tabled on the previous day for answer on future days, Early Day Motions and amendments to public bills to be debated on future days (blue)*
- Private Business (blue)

The Summary Agenda and Order of Business

Soon after the General Election of 1997, the Labour Government reformed the style of the Order Paper to make it more user-friendly. As a result the Order Paper now consists of the Summary Agenda and Order of Business. It does not contain a complete list of all questions to be answered that day. Oral questions to be answered on that day are included in the Vote, ***but only those written questions tabled on the previous day are listed*** – the so-called, 'planted questions'. Written or oral questions tabled on the previous day for answer on future days are still included in the Vote. Written questions tabled on previous days for answer that day are now included in Part I of the Order Book and written and oral questions tabled on previous days for answer on future days are included in Part II of the Order Book (*see below*).

Summary Agenda

This is a brief summary of the day's proceedings in the House. The following example is taken from the Summary Agenda for 11 February 1999.

11.30am	Prayers
Afterwards	Oral Questions to the Secretary of State for Education and Employment
12.30pm	Private Notice Questions, Ministerial Statements (if any). (*The*

	Leader of the House is expected to announce future business and answer questions)
Afterwards	Local Government Finance (Wales) (Motions for approval) (*may continue until 4.00pm*)
	Local Government Finance (Scotland) and Housing (Scotland) (Motions for approval) (*for up to 1½ hours*)
	Constitutional Law (Motions for approval) (*may continue until 7.00pm*)
	Social Security Contributions (Transfer of Functions, etc) Bill [Lords] (Motion) (*no debate after 7.00pm*)
	Food Standards (Motion) (*no debate after 7.00pm)*
At the end of the sitting	Adjournment Debate: Criminal convictions review procedure: the case of NJ Hyam (Mr Peter Bottomley) (*until 7.30pm or for half an hour, whichever is later)*

The Order of Business

The Order of Business is really an Agenda of the days events in the Chamber. For obvious reasons, it does not contain the text of any Statements or Private Notice Questions (PNQs), as the decision to make a Statement or allow a PNQ is not taken until the day in question. Items appear on the Order of Business in the order that they would be taken during the day's sitting (see chapter five for more information on a typical day's sittting in the House of Commons). The following is taken from the Order of Business for 11 February 1999.

Oral Questions

This lists those questions which were successful in the ballot for oral questions – on 11 February, questions were to the Secretary of State for Education and Employment.
Preliminary Business

This consists of First Readings of Bills (which are not debated) and 'Ten Minute Rule Bills'. On 11 February there was no such business.

Main Business of the Day

This section of the Order of Business sets out the main items of Government business to be debated that day. On this occasion there were three motions relating to local government finance in Wales, all of which could be debated until 4.00pm.

LOCAL GOVERNMENT FINANCE (WALES) ***[Until 4.00 p.m.]***
Mr Secretary Michael

That the Local Government Finance Report (Wales) 1999-2000 (HC 203), which was laid before this House on 3rd February, be approved.

LOCAL GOVERNMENT FINANCE (WALES) ***[Until 4.00pm]***
Mr Secretary Michael

That the Local Government Finance (Amendment) Report (Wales) 1998-1999 (HC 204), which was laid before this House on 3rd February, be approved.

LOCAL GOVERNMENT FINANCE (WALES) ***[Until 4.00pm]***
Mr Secretary Michael

That the Special Grant Report (Wales) 1999 (HC 177), which was laid before this House on 28th January, be approved.

The Speaker will put the Questions on the above three Motions in the name of Mr Secretary Michael not later than 4.00pm (Order of 8th February).

Similar reports relating to central Government support for local authorities in England are debated each year. The above motions were followed by two similar motions on local government finance and housing support grant in Scotland, which could be debated for one and a half hours – until 5.30pm at the latest. Debate on the draft Scotland Act 1998 (Transitory and Transitional Provisions) (Finance) Order 1999 and the draft Scotland Act 1998 (Transitory and Transitional Provisions (Appropriations) Order 1999 could take place until 7.00pm (the Moment of Interruption on a Thursday – for the current, 1998/99 Session at least). Two other motions were set down on the Order of Business, which if opposed, could not be taken after the Moment of Interruption (7.00pm).

SOCIAL SECURITY CONTRIBUTIONS (TRANSFER OF FUNCTIONS, ETC.) BILL [LORDS] ***[No debate after 7.00pn]***
Margaret Beckett

That, during the proceedings on the Social Security Contrbutions (Transfer of Functions, etc.) Bill *[Lords], the Standing Committee on the Bill shall have leave to sit twice on the first day on which it shall meet.*[1]

If opposed, this item cannot be taken after 7.00pm

FOOD STANDARDS ***[No debate after 7.00pm]***
Margaret Beckett
Mr Nicholas Brown

That the quorum of the Committee appointed by Order [8th February] to report on the draft bill of the Food Standards Agency (Cm.4249) shall be five.

If opposed, this item cannot be taken after 7.00pm

[1] Standing Committees usually only meet once on the first day of consideration of a bill.

Adjournment Debate

On a Thursday, the Daily Adjournment Debate follows the close of the main business of the day, and may continue until 7.30pm or for up to half an hour, whichever is later.

List of the day's Committee meetings

This is a list of all the Standing and Select Committees sitting that day, with times and venues; for example

Standing Committee A	2.30pm	Room 11 (public)

Further to consider the Greater London Authority Bill (except Clauses 1 to 4 and Schedules 1 and 2)*

* these clauses were debated in a Committee of the Whole House.

Planted Questions – (Written Questions tabled yesterday for answer today)

Planted Questions are listed in this section of the Order of Business.

Standing Committee Notices

These are announcements of future meetings of Standing Committees.

Miscellaneous Memoranda

On 11 February the Memorandum section of the Order of Business consisted of a notice about Wednesday Morning Adjournment Debates on 24 February, reminding the House that there would one debate between 9.30am and 12.30pm – on two Select Committee reports.

Future Business

This is divided into three groups, A, B and C.

- A - business announced by the Leader of the House (usually for the next two weeks)
- B - remaining business set down 'formally' for that day, but which is unlikely to be reached
- C - future weeks' business (items of business already set down for debate on days after those in Part A; e.g. Private Members' Bills)

List of Available Papers

This lists the contents of the Order Paper and reminds readers that written questions for answer today but tabled before yesterday are now available in the Order Book.

Amendments

This section of the Vote includes amendments to bills to be debated on that day, either in Standing Committee or on the floor of the House, and is printed on white paper.

Standing Committee Proceedings

The section of the Vote Bundle, devoted to proceedings in Standing Committees is simply a record of any decisions taken by those Standing Committees sitting the previous day. The Proceedings should not be confused with Standing Committee Hansards which are a record of what was actually said in those Committees. The text of any amendments is set out, along with decisions reached; i.e. agreed to, negatived, withdrawn, not moved or divided on. Division lists are not included – so to find out how a particular member of the Committee voted, you will need to consult the Standing Committee Hansard.

Votes and Proceedings

The Votes and Proceedings sets out decisions taken by the House and is not a verbatim report of what was actually said in the Chamber. If an amendment was considered; for example, at Report Stage, it would only appear in full in the Votes and Proceedings if it had either been withdrawn or negatived. If an amendment is passed, its number is noted in the Vote. If a Division took place, the wording of the amendment is printed along with the number of 'ayes' and 'noes' voting. A full division list of those voting is not included in the Votes and Proceedings but can be found in Hansard.

The Vote has a number of appendices:

- Appendix I – this lists the statutory instruments and other papers 'laid on the table' on the previous day along with other miscellaneous reports; for example, on 11 February 1999 the report from the Law Commission (Scotland) on the 'Abolition of the Feudal System' was laid on the Table.
- Appendix II – this details various appointments to Standing Committees (if you are following a bill and want to find out who has been appointed to the relevant Standing Committee, you need to look at this section of the Votes and Proceedings on the Thursday after the bill's Second Reading. This is because the Committee of Selection, which nominates members of Standing Committees meets on a Wednesday and its reports appear in Appendix II the following day – Thursday.)
- Appendix III – this lists any Select Committee reports which have been received and are to be printed; for example, on the aforementioned day, the Third Special Report from the Culture, Media and Sport Committee was 'to be printed' (when there is no report from the Committee of Selection, Appendix III becomes Appendix II).

The Vote includes some items which are not recorded in Hansard; for example, the Votes and Proceedings for 11 February 1999 recorded the fact that the Sixth Standing Committee on Delegated Legislation had considered the draft Railways (Rateable Values) (Scotland) Order 1999.

The Supplement to the Votes and Proceedings contains petitions and any Government responses.

The Notice Paper

The Notice Paper is known colloquially as 'the blues' (as it is printed on blue paper) and contains future business; i.e. oral and written questions tabled on previous days for answer on future days Written questions marked 'N' are for answer on a 'named' day. The 'blues' also contains Early Day Motions (EDMs).

Amendments tabled on the previous day, to bills to be debated on future days, either in Standing Committee or on the floor of the House are included in the Notice Paper. Sometimes you will see the words 'For other Amendments see the following pages of Supplement to Votes: .....'. This means that you will find amendments tabled prior to the previous day in previous editions of the Vote Bundle. Amendments are available separately from the Vote Office, but not from the Parliamentary Bookshop or Stationery Office. You will need to either purchase the relevant copies of the Vote Bundle or access the amendments via the Parliament website.

Early Day Motions

EDMs are printed in the Notice Paper the day after they are tabled. For the rest of the week in which they were tabled and the week after that, they are only reprinted if more MPs add their signatures to them or if amendments are submitted. After those two weeks, they are only reprinted on a Thursday, and then, only if new signatures or amendments have been tabled. When EDMs are reprinted only the first six names and any names added subsequently are shown. By convention, Ministers do not sign or promote EDMs.

Public Bill List

The Public Bill List is a list of all public bills published during the Session with the date of the last stage reached. It is circulated with the Vote on a Monday and printed on white paper. A word of warning – at the beginning of a Session, the dates for Second Readings of Public Bills may not be the actual day on which Second Reading is taken. As was previously mentioned, when a bill has its First Reading, Second Reading is set down for 'tomorrow'. All this means is that the bill joins the list of public bills awaiting Second Reading on the next available sitting day. Following the progress of legislation in the Weekly Information Bulletin is probably advisable in order to avoid any confusion.

List of European Union Documents

The European Union documents list is published on a Saturday and circulated with the Vote on the following Monday and printed on white paper. It sets out the Standing

Committees to which EU documents have been referred, the dates on which they were so referred and any progress to date.

The Deregulation Proposals and Draft Orders List

The Deregulation Proposals and Draft Orders List is published every Wednesday on white paper. It sets out the progress made on deregulation proposals and draft orders (see chapter nine for more details of deregulation orders). You can also track the progress of deregulation orders in the Weekly Information Bulletin.

The Statutory Instruments List

This list details, amonst other things, the number of 'praying days' left for an annulment/approval of certain SIs and is issued each week by the Journal Office in the House of Commons. It is published (on white paper) each Monday BUT IS NOT PART OF THE VOTE. You can access this list via the Parliament website.

The list is divided into four parts:

- PART I - NEGATIVE SIs
    - Negative SIs with dates when laid before the House and number of remaining praying days (see below)

SI Number	Title of Instrument	Laid before the House	Number of days unexpired on date of issue
3168	Potatoes Originating in The Netherlands (Amendment) Regulations 1998	17 Dec	7

- Negative SIs which have not appeared in previous editions
- Other Rules; e.g. Rules brought in under Northern Ireland Orders in Council (see below)

Title of Instrument	Statutory Period	Number of days unexpired on date of issue
Construction Contracts Exclusion Order (Northern Ireland) 1999 (SR (NI) 1999, No. 32)	40 days beginning 9 Feb	37

- PART II - SPECIAL PROCEDURE ORDERS
- PART III – AFFIRMATIVE SIs

- Affirmative SIs approved by the House of Commons since the last list
- Affirmative SIs subject to approval within a specific time
- Affirmative Sis subject to approval within a specific time, passed since the last edition of the list
- Church of England Measures and other miscellaneous delights

- PART IV – SIs NOT SUBJECT TO ANY PARLIAMENTARY PROCEDURE and laid since the last edition of the list.

THE ORDER BOOK

The Order Book is divided into two parts. Part I contains Written Questions due for answer that day, tabled on previous days, and Part II, Oral and Written questions tabled on previous days for answer on future days. Oral Questions for answer that day and Written Questions tabled the day before (Planted Questions) are included in the Order of Business.

HOUSE OF LORDS MINUTES

The House of Lords Minutes is really the equivalent of the Vote Bundle in the House of Commons and contains both current and future business. It contains a record of the previous day's business, the current day's business, future business, future questions, details of that day's and future days' Select Committee meetings as well as written questions and 'No Day Named' motions.

The first part of the Lords Minutes is the 'Minutes of Proceedings', which looks as follows:

HOUSE OF LORDS

MINUTES OF PROCEEDINGS

Die Jovis 11° Februarii 1999

The house met at two o'clock

PRAYERS were read by the Lord Bishop of Carlisle

Judicial Business

1. Regina v. Secretary of State for the Home Department (Respondent) ex parte Salem (A.P.) (Appellant) ....

As the highest court in the land, the House of Lords has important judicial as well as parliamentary business to attend to. When the House hears judicial business on a Thursday, the House of Lords meets again at 3.00pm

The Minutes also lists any statutory instruments laid before the House that day as well as the public business transacted. Where a Report Stage of a Bill has taken place, the Minutes simply record that, 'amendments were agreed to; amendments were moved and (by leave of the House) withdrawn'. The Minutes also includes a Division List (Divisions are also listed in Hansard) for all Divisions which took place the previous day.

The next section of the Minutes is devoted to that day's business and begins with any judicial business; for example, a morning meeting of one of the Appellate Committees. This is followed by the Order Paper, which looks as follows:

NOTICES AND ORDERS OF THE DAY

Items marked † are new or have been altered.

Items marked ‡ are expected to be taken during the dinner adjournment.

MONDAY 15TH FEBRUARY

At half-past two o'clock

***The Lord Barnett** – To ask Her Majesty's Government what European Union tax harmonisation proposals they have agreed to propose to agree

***The Lord Bishop of Lincoln** – To ask her Majesty's Government what plans they have to ensure that by the year 2000 the prison system is less stretched and better able to rehabilitate prisoners.

***The Lord Razzall** – To ask her Majesty's Government when they anticipate that they will receive the Office of Fair Trading report on supermarket pricing.

***The Lord Dixon-Smith** – To ask Her Majesty's Government what is their latest estimate of the date on which the Dartford-Thurrock crossing of the River Thames will become toll-free.

Development Commission (Transfer of Functions and Miscellaneous Provisions) Order 1999 – The Lord Whitty to move, That the draft Order laid before the House on 27th January be approved *[7th Report from the Joint Committee]*

Scotland Act 1998 (Transitory and Transitional Provisions) (Finance) Order 1999 – The Lord Sewel to move, That the draft Order laid before the House on 4th February be approved. *[8th Report from the Joint Committee].*

Railways (Rateable Values) (Scotland) Order 1999 – The Lord Sewel to move, That the draft Order laid before the House on 21st January be approved. *[6th Report from the Joint Committee].*

The Minutes continue with future business, usually for the next three weeks or so.

The following section of the Minutes is devoted to 'No Day Named' motions. These are the nearest the House of Lords has to Early Day Motions. The section is divided into three parts: Motions and Unstarred Questions; Motions for Short Debate and Select Committee Reports. For example, in the Lords Minutes of Monday 15 February 1999, Part I of the No Day Named section began thus:

NO DAY NAMED

PART I

The Lord Simon of Glaisdale – To move to resolve, That the prolixity of the Statute Book has increased, is increasing and ought to be diminished.

Part II began thus:

PART II

MOTIONS FOR SHORT DEBATE

[Ballot on 17th March for debate on 31st March]

The Lord Campbell of Croy – To call attention to the amount of crime in the United Kingdom involving theft of road vehicles or breaking into them to steal the contents; and to move for papers.

Part III of the No Day Named section began with:

PART III

SELECT COMMITTEE REPORTS

[The date in brackets is that on which the Report was published]

The Lord Geddes – To move, That this House take note of the Report of the European Communities Committee on Airline Competition (32nd Report, Session 1997-98, HL Paper 156) *[11th December]*.

After the No Day Named section, Written Questions are listed. These take up several pages with subjects ranging from cryptography and the proposed Standing Orders for the Scottish Parliament, to VAT on postal services and proposed reforms of the Crown Prosecution Service.

The next section of the Lords Minutes lists 'Bills in Progress'; for example, all bills waiting for Second Reading, Committee of the Whole House, Report, Third Reading, and finally a list of bills which have completed all their legislative stages in the House of Lords and been sent to the Commons. This section also lists those Church of England Measures, Affirmative Instruments[2] and Deregulation Proposals in progress.

---

[2] Affirmative Instruments are divided into those awaiting consideration by the Joint Committee and those waiting for affirmative resolution.

Finally, the Lords Minutes lists the times of future Committee meetings.

HOUSE OF LORDS WEEKLY REPORT

The Weekly Report, which as you might expect is published each week (on a Friday) sets out the programme of future committee meetings in the House of Lords. Unlike the Lords Minutes, it lists the witnesses who have been called to give evidence to various enquiries. It also lists any forthcoming Select Committee enquiries and sets out any requests for both oral and written evidence. Unfortunately, this document is not available on the Parliament website; however, forthcoming Select Committee meetings are listed in the Weekly Information Bulletin.

HANSARD

Hansard is more properly known as the Official Report. Separate Hansards are printed for each House on a daily basis. Hansard is a verbatim report of proceedings in the Chamber, but also includes written answers. Weekly Hansards and bound copies consisting of two weeks' worth of daily Hansards, are also published. Hansard is now available from the Parliament website. The House of Lords Hansard is available from 9.00am the following day and the House of Commons Hansard from midday. If the House sits late, proceedings after 10.30pm are usually printed not in the following day's Hansard but in the Hansard for the day after that. Readers may find this worth bearing in mind when looking for written answers in the *printed* edition of Hansard. Occasionally, whilst the Hansard reference may be for column 83, 9 February 1999, the answer itself may actually be contained in the Hansard for 10 February 1999.

Standing Committee Hansards are also published and these are usually available the day after the Committee has sat (they are also available on the Parliament website). Select Committee proceedings on the other hand are usually not made available to the public until several weeks after the sitting in question. If the Select Committee in which you are interested is not likely to be broadcast, make sure you attend, or you will have to rely on reports (if any) in the following day's broadsheet newspapers. Unless the hearing was a particularly controversial or topical one, it is most unlikely to be mentioned at all.

It was not until 1771 that the reporting of parliamentary debates was even tolerated by Parliament. There had been some reporting of parliamentary affairs before this date, but theoretically it was a breach of privilege of the House. Edward Cave had begun his 'Gentlemen's Magazine' in 1729, employing as reporter, one, Dr Samuel Johnson. There have been other notable parliamentary scribes; Samuel Taylor Coleridge found the life most uncongenial and decided to forgo journalism for poetry, whilst Charles Dickens found inspiration for some of the characters in his novels. He was clearly not particularly impressed with what he saw, if his portrayal of Mr Gregsbury in Nicholas Nickleby is anything to go by. Current secretaries and researchers may find that Mr Gregsbury's definition of the duties of an assistant strike a familiar chord. 'My secretary would have to make himself master of the foreign policy of the world ... it would be necessary for him to make himself acquainted from day to day with newspaper paragraphs on passing events ... upon which I might found a question to the Secretary of State for the Home Department'. He goes on to add that 'You must always bear in mind, in such cases as this, where our interests are not affected ... to put it very strong about the people, because it comes out very well at election-time'. He ends by reminding Nicholas that 'This is a hasty outline of the chief things you'd have to do, except waiting in the lobby every night, in case I forgot anything'! Plus ca change.

After many altercations, reprimands at the Bar of the House and even confinements in the Tower, the Commons realised that they could not prevent reports of their deliberations from being published. In 1835 the press obtained a reserved portion of the public gallery in the House of Commons.

Hansard takes its name from Luke Hansard, printer to the House of Commons, whose son Thomas Curson began 'Hansard's Parliamentary Debates' in 1829. He bought the 'Political Register' from William Cobbett, who had established it in 1803, and renamed it. Hansard was eventually taken over by the Government in 1908 and debates in the Lords were printed separately from 1909. In that year it became known as the Official Report, but in 1943 the word Hansard was added in brackets.

It was not until 16 July 1971 that the House of Commons passed a resolution exempting those reporting parliamentary debates from being accused of a breach parliamentary privilege. The resolution stated that, 'notwithstanding the Resolution of the House of 3 March 1762 and other such Resolutions, this House will not entertain any complaint of contempt of the House or breach of privilege in respect of the publication of the debates or proceedings of the House or of its committees, except when any such debates or proceedings shall have been conducted with closed doors or in private, or when such publication shall have been expressly prohibited by the House'. Other resolutions passed at the same time gave the same freedom from contempt to publications of notices of questions and motions. A resolution of 31 October 1980 removed restrictions on reporting evidence given at Select Committee meetings.[3]

It is often assumed that Hansard reporters are the official shorthand reporters in Parliament, but that title is more properly bestowed on Gurney's (or W G Gurney & Co to give the company its full title). The firm was established by Joseph Gurney and his son was the first to be appointed official shorthand writer to Parliament in 1806. Gurney's provides shorthand reporters and stenographers for all the Select Committees and Private Bill Committees in Parliament. Gurney's also have the dubious honour of reporting the proceedings of anyone tried at the Bar of the House and one of the firm's shorthand writers must be present if an MP is tried in an Election Court.

Both Houses of Parliament has always claimed to have 'exclusive cognisance' of their own proceedings, what Erskine May describes as the 'right to be the sole judge of the lawfulness of their own proceedings, and to settle – or depart from – their own codes of procedure'. What this meant in practice, in a court of law, was that Acts of Parliament could only be interpreted by reference to the wording of the Acts themselves – it was not permissible to refer for clarification to any debates which there might have been in either House. Hansard was effectively out of bounds. For example, in the case of *Wellesley v*

[3] Broadcasters were not protected from actions for libel relating to the contents of parliamentary broadcasts until the passing of the Defamation Act in 1996.

Duke of Beaufort[4] Lord Chief Justice Brougham said that, 'a court knows nothing judicially of what takes place in Parliament till what is done there becomes an Act of the legislature'. However, as a result of the ruling of the House of Lords in *Pepper v Hart* in 1992[5], Hansard may be referred to by a court when the wording of an Act is 'ambiguous or obscure'. Under the Parliamentary Papers Act 1840, statutory protection is given to all papers published by order of either the House of Commons or the House of Lords.

THE WEEKLY INFORMATION BULLETIN

The Weekly Information Bulletin is published each Saturday when the House is sitting and is an extremely useful guide to forthcoming business in both Houses, including Select and Standing Committee proceedings, progress on bills, etc. The Bulletin contains the following:

- Forthcoming business in both Houses
- Full list of public bills with completed and forthcoming legislative stages
- Full list of private bills and completed and forthcoming legislative stages
- Full List of Transport and Works Act Orders
- Full List of Draft Provisional Orders and Order Confirmation Bills
- Full List of Northern Ireland Legislation
- Forthcoming Standing Committee meetings
- Forthcoming Select Committee meetings
- List of Select Committee publications received since the last Bulletin
- White and Green Papers received since the previous Bulletin
- EU Documents received since the previous Bulletin
- Early Day Motions tabled since the last Bulletin
- By-elections since the previous General Election
- State of the parties in the House of Commons

THE SESSIONAL INFORMATION DIGEST

This document is a must for all devotees of parliamentary facts and figures; it is awash with them. The Sessional Information Digest is produced at the end of each Session of Parliament and is really a Sessional version of the Weekly Information Bulletin. The Digest lists all public and private legislation of the Session in question, including dates of bills' legislative stages. It lists all Select Committee reports produced during the Session, Green and White Papers produced by the Government and a wealth of other useful information besides. It is now available on the Parliament website.

SESSIONAL RETURNS

Another useful document, packed full to the brim with exciting parliamentary facts and figures. The 1997/98 Sessional Returns are now available. They have been published by The Stationery Office, in their present form, since 1986/87. The main focus of the Returns is the activities of the various Select Committees and the information provided is

[4] Wellesley v Duke of Beaufort (1831) 36 ER 554
[5] Pepper v Hart (1993) AC 593; (1993) 1 All ER 42

fairly exhaustive. For example, all the instruments considered by the Joint Committee are listed as are all the visits made by the Agriculture Select Committee. If you need to find out what the Committee was up to on 24 February 1998, this is the place to look (they visited Tesco in Lincoln). The first part of the Returns consists of various statistics relating to the business of the House. It will impress your friends enormously if you can say with great authority that the total number of priority written questions appearing on the Order Paper in the 1997/98 Session, was 23,532. Alternatively, they may feel that you are a rather sad and lonely individual who has nothing better to do to while away the long winter evenings. However, the following facts may come in useful:

1997/98 Session – House of Commons

Number of Early Day Motions tabled in the 1997/98 Session	1,757 (300 of these were Prayers against negative SIs)
Total number of petitions presented	99
Total number of sitting days	241 (the House sat beyond midnight on 33 of those days)
Total number of hours in which the House sat	2117.36
Total number of hours in which the House sat beyond 10.00pm (2.30pm on a Friday)	228.24

HOUSE OF COMMONS AND HOUSE OF LORDS PAPERS

The letters HC or HL on a publication denote that it is a parliamentary paper as opposed to a Government publication. For example, House of Commons Select Committee reports are all given an HC number whilst their counterparts in the House of Lords have an HL number. It is useful to make a note of both the HC or HL number as well as the Session in which the report was published when ordering publications from either the Parliamentary Bookshop or the Stationery Office, as they will inevitably ask you for it. It also facilitates finding the document amongst the many hundreds published each Session.

COMMAND PAPERS

Command Papers are Government publications, and include everything from Green and White Papers to annual departmental reports and Government responses to Select Committee reports. They are not required by statute to be presented to Parliament. They are available to Members and their staff from either the Vote Office in the House of Commons or Printed Paper Office in the House of Lords. They are available to the public from the Parliamentary Bookshop or Stationery Office and some are now available on the internet, via the various departmental websites (http://www.open.gov.uk/). Together with Act Papers (papers required by statute to be presented to Parliament) they form a series of papers known as 'Parliamentary Papers'. If a paper is said to have been presented to the House of Lords, this means it has been given to the office of the Clerk of the Parliaments and if presented to the House of Commons, that it has been given to the Votes and Proceedings Office.

THE JOURNALS OF THE HOUSE OF LORDS

The House of Lords possesses copies of the Journals of the proceedings of the House of Lords, with some omissions, from 1510. The Journals are compiled from the daily Minutes and are a record of decisions taken and peers present in the Chamber.

THE HOUSE OF COMMONS JOURNAL

The Commons' Journal is the official record of the proceedings in the House of Commons and is published annually. There is a more or less complete set from 1547 onwards. There is very little difference between the Journal and the Votes and Proceedings.

HOUSE OF COMMONS LIBRARY RESEARCH NOTES

The Research Staff in the House of Commons Library produce a prodigious array of research notes on a wide range of subjects of topical interest to Members. The notes cover everything from the political situation in the Balkans to welfare reform, tax credits and immigration and asylum.

To the enormous benefit of those members of the public interested in current issues, these are now available on the Parliament website. It should be noted, however, that the authors are not able to discuss the contents with members of the public, only with Members of Parliament. These research notes are a tremendous public resource, particularly for anyone studying politics at either school or undergraduate level. If you do not have access to the internet, you can obtain copies of Library research notes, free of charge, from the House of Commons Information Office.

HOUSE OF COMMONS INFORMATION OFFICE FACTSHEETS

The House of Commons Information Office produces a series of useful factsheets on a wide range of parliamentary matters, from the role of the Speaker in the House of Commons to a summary of the legislative stages of a public bill. However, some of the factsheets have not been updated, in some cases, since June 1995, so it may not be advisable to rely on them exclusively.

COMPANION TO THE STANDING ORDERS

The Companion to the Standing Orders and Guide to the Proceedings of the House of Lords is a very useful document indeed and contains information on the practices and procedures of the House of Lords in general as well as the Standing Orders in particular. It is available from the Parliamentary Bookshop or from the Parliament website. Unfortunately, the equivalent document in the House of Commons, the Manual of Procedure in the Public Business, whilst still available, is now rather out of date, the 14th Edition having been published in 1987.

FURTHER INFORMATION

The best place to start looking for more information about Parliament is the Parliament website. This has been extended and expanded since its inception and now includes a wealth of information on almost everything you could wish to know about either the House of Commons or House of Lords. It is an invaluable public resource and it is worth getting yourself a modem and internet access just to use it. For example; is you wish to write to your MP but do not know who he or she is, or indeed, which parliamentary constituency you live in, then do not despair, you can simply look it up using the Constituency Locator on the UK Parliament website. You will find the locator listed in the index on the website and if you have your postcode to hand you should be able to find the information you require without any difficulty at all.

Hansard is now on the website; the previous day's proceedings from the House of Lords are available from 9.00am and the House of Commons' from 12.00 noon. You can also look at the Order of Business, track down obscure questions, find out what stage a bill has reached and much, much more besides.

The website contains complete information for the last two Sessions of Parliament, but if you require information from previous Sessions, Context Electronic Publishing (http://www.context.co.uk) provides a service called Justis Parliament, containing references to parliamentary information dating back to the 1979-83 Parliament. Justis is available to purchase either on CD-Rom or online. Justis is an excellent system, but it contains Hansard references not complete copies of Hansard. Chadwyck-Healey (http://www.chadwyck.co.uk) publishes Hansard on CD-Rom, but only from the 1988/89 Session onwards. For earlier copies of the printed edition of Hansard, you will need to contact your local reference library.

The Weekly Information Bulletin is available on the Parliament website. Published on a Saturday, it contains much extremely useful information about committees, legislation, etc. Select Committee press releases are available on the website, as are the House of Commons' Library Research Notes. These are so useful, it is impossible to sing their praises highly enough. They cover all manner of subjects ranging from analyses of various voting methods, to detailed papers on the workings of the new Scottish Parliament to in-depth studies of most of the current Government bills. House of Commons Factsheets are also available and for teachers and students alike, these are extremely informative and easy to read. They cover a vast range of subjects from the role of the Speaker to the Gunpowder Plot. So go and buy a modem now and start surfing.

The address of the Parliament website is: **http://www.parliament.uk.**

If you are not one of the lucky ones with internet access you can either telephone the House of Commons Information Office on 0171 219 4272 or write to them at the following address: The Public Information Office, House of Commons, 1 Derby Gate, London SW1A 2DG. They will send you factsheets, Library Research Notes, etc. The House of Lords Information Office can be contacted on the following number 0171 219 3107. Their address is: Information Office, House of Lords, London SW1A OPW. *Please note that the authors of the Research Notes are not able to answer questions directly from the public.*

If you wish to order Stationery Office publications online, you can do so by accessing the Stationery Office Virtual Bookshop at the following address: http://www.national-publishing.co.uk. By using the Search facility you can find out whether or not publications are still in print, their availability and cost.

If you wish to purchase a copy of a bill or green paper, or any other Government publication, Politico's stock a great many of them; alternatively, the Parliamentary Bookshop at 12 Bridge Street, London SW1A 2JX (opposite Big Ben on the corner of Parliament Square) has almost everything your heart could desire in the way of parliamentary and government information. The Bookshop can be contacted on the following number: 0171 219 3890 or faxed on the following number: 0171 219 3866. You can also purchase Government publications from various Stationery outlets, including the following. If you do not live anywhere near one of these, they should be able to give you the telephone number of a bookshop in your area which will be able to order publications for you.

Stationery Office Bookshops

London
123 Kingsway, London WC2B 6PQ
Tel: 0171-242 6393 Fax: 0171-242 6394

Edinburgh
71 Lothian Road, Edinburgh EH3 9AZ
Tel: 0131-228 4181 Fax: 0131-229 2734

Belfast
6 Arthur Street, Belfast BT1 4GD
Tel: 01232-238451 Fax: 01232-230782

Manchester
9-21 Princess Street, Albert Square, Manchester M60 8AS
Tel: 0161-834 7201 Fax: 0161-833 0634

Birmingham
68/69 Bull Street, Birmingham B4 6AD
Tel: 0121-236-9696 Fax: 0121-236-9699

Bristol
33 Wine Street, Bristol BS1 2BQ
Tel: 01179-264306 Fax: 01179-294515

Cardiff
The Stationery Office, Oriel Bookshop, The Friary, Cardiff CF1 4AA
Tel: 01222 395548 Fax: 01222 384347

The membership of Select Committees and other Committees of both the House of Commons and House of Lords have not been listed in this publication for the simple reason that the membership of such committees can and does change and would therefore soon be out of date. If you need to keep track of changes in membership of any committees PMS publish a very useful Update Bulletin on a weekly basis which lists all manner of useful information relating to Parliament. This complements their quarterly Parliamentary Companion, which is highly recommended. This lists all Government Ministers and their responsibilities and all Opposition Spokesmen as well as much other useful information. You can of course, obtain much of this information from the daily Order Paper and Hansard, but having a quarterly publication to hand, which is frequently updated is often a much easier way of keeping abreast of any changes in ministerial positions, Standing Committee membership, etc., etc., than ploughing through the relevant parliamentary publications on a daily basis.

Students of Parliament and of politics generally may be interested in the Hansard Society for Parliamentary Government which was established in 1944 to promote interest in parliamentary democracy. The Society publishes papers on a wide range of different subjects, from electoral reform to the Scott Report and the role of quangos. Parliamentary Affairs is the journal of the Hansard Society and includes articles by academic experts in parliamentary government. The Hansard Society can be contacted at St Philips Building North, Sheffield Street, London WC1A 2EX, Tel: 0171 955 7478, Fax: 0171 955 7492 – http://hansard-society.org.uk.

INDEX

A

B

C

D

E

F

G

H

I

J

L

M

N

O

P

Q

R

S

T

U

V

W